JEAN PIAGET

Consensus and Controversy

JEAN PIAGET

Consensus and Controversy

EDITED BY

Sohan Modgil, Ph.D.

Reader in Educational Research and Development
Brighton Polytechnic

AND

Celia Modgil, Ph.D.

Senior Lecturer in Educational Psychology
Goldsmiths College London University

FINALE

incorporating Jean Piaget's contemporary thinking

BY

Bärbel Inhelder

Geneva University

PRAEGER SPECIAL STUDIES • PRAEGER SCIENTIFIC

Published in 1982 by Praeger Publishers
CBS Educational and Professional Publishing
A Division of CBS, Inc.
521 Fifth Avenue, New York, New York 10175, USA

Copyright © 1982 Holt, Rinehart and Winston Ltd.
Copyright for the paper by Dr Susan Buck-Morss is held by
S. Karger AG, Medical and Scientific Publishers,
Switzerland. Copyright for the paper by Professor Robert
Ennis is held by the American Educational Research
Association, Washington DC.

ISBN 0-03-059936-9

Library of Congress Catalog Card Number 81-84205

Printed at The Lavenham Press Ltd, Lavenham, Suffolk, England.

Last digit is print number: 9 8 7 6 5 4 3 2 1

Contributors

Dr Magali Bovet, *Geneva University*
Dr Derek Boyle, *Aberdeen University*
Professor Susan Buck-Morss, *Cornell University*
Professor Margaret Donaldson, *Edinburgh University*
Dr Rosalind Driver, *Leeds University*
Dr Alison Elliot, *Edinburgh University*
Dr Colin Elliott, *Manchester University*
Professor Robert Ennis, *Illinois University*
Dr Frank Fincham, *Oxford University*
Dr Paul Ghuman, *The University College of Wales*
Professor Frederick Grant, *Dubuque University*
Dr Barbara Hodkin, *Wilfred Laurier University*
Professor Richard Hofmann, *Miami University*
Professor Bärbel Inhelder, *Geneva University*
Dr Wolfe Mays, *Manchester University*
Professor Thomas McFarland, *Dubuque University*
Dr Celia Modgil, *London University*
Dr Sohan Modgil, *Brighton Polytechnic*
Professor Joseph Novak, *Cornell University*
Professor Denis Phillips, *Stanford University*
Professor Linda Siegel, *McMaster University*
Professor Hermina Sinclair, *Geneva University*
Mrs Joan Tamburrini, *Froebel Institute*
Professor Carol Tomlinson-Keasey, *California University*
Professor J. Jacques Vonèche, *Geneva University*
Dr Helen Weinreich-Haste, *Bath University*
Professor Derek Wright, *Leicester University*

Acknowledgments

The undertaking of this ambitious enterprise was only possible in collaboration with the numerous distinguished contributors herein. We are greatly indebted to them for demonstrating their trust by accepting our invitation to join forces to provide statements of how Piaget's theory is seen in relation to particular disciplines.

The volume has been greatly enhanced by the recognition given to it by Bärbel Inhelder, who increased our confidence in the Project by kindly agreeing to write the concluding chapter. We thank Professor Inhelder for her very kind and generous support and for her edifying contribution to the content.

We are further grateful to Holt, Rinehart and Winston Ltd, Publishers, for the British edition and Praeger Special Studies for the American edition. We express our gratitude to Stephen White, Helen Mackay and the Production team.

Sohan and Celia Modgil
July 1981

Contents

To
Gita, Ramayana, Kush-Luv, Radha and Krishan Arjuan
With Love

Chapter 1

Jean Piaget 1896—1980: Consensus and Controversy

SOHAN AND CELIA MODGIL

Until a few years ago, criticisms of Jean Piaget's widely acknowledged theory were concerned mostly with his sampling techniques, lack of statistical treatment and minor details. Although Piaget continues to be frequently acknowledged as 'one of the giants in the history of psychology', in accordance with the evolutionary process of the development of understanding and attitude change, it now appears opportune for his theory to receive serious consideration. Piaget himself has modestly claimed that he has '. . . laid bare a more or less evident general skeleton which remains full of gaps so that when these gaps will be filled the articulations will have to be differentiated, but the general lines of the system will not be changed,' Sinclair de Zwart (1977, p. 1). That the theory will be open-ended and tentative and subject to revisions is, in part, a validation of it as a developmental theory which is developing.

THE MOMENTUM OF CRITICAL ANALYSES OF PIAGETIAN THEORY

Early in the 1970s, Peter Bryant of Oxford University promoted a fundamental challenge. His verification that very young children are capable of logical deductions, which Piaget considers improbable, was even reported in the popular press. Subsequently, the anti-Piaget movement has gained momentum. In the *Times Educational Supplement* (UK) of 18 March 1977, a section entitled 'Piaget in the Dock' elaborates that 'piercing questions are being asked about the Genevan educational psychologists'. The article highlights a symposium on Piaget published in the 1977 volume of the *British Journal of Educational Psychology*, in which, among others, Geoffrey Brown and Charles Desforges of Lancaster University 'go through some of the more recent anti-Piagetian findings'. They claim to have shown that the 'stage' theory is not only conceptually wrong but empirically untenable.

1

Existence of Stages of Development

Brown and Desforges elaborate that the search for a structure irrespective of content has led to generalities which cannot be sustained. It would seem more appropriate to attempt to locate cognitive structures within specific content domains and subsequently identify any generalities after sufficient taxonomies have been pursued. Brown and Desforges (1979) reiterate that the notion of 'stage' creates more conceptual problems than it solves. Brown and Desforges, in detail, and Boden (1979), in outline, provide a critique of stages of development, furnishing evidence from cross-cultural and individual differences together with methodological experimentation. In a critical analysis of the presupposition behind Piaget's characterization of mathematics, evolution and mental equilibrium, Rotman (1977) focuses on the conflict between Piaget's claims that his model of cognitive advance is an evolutionary one (with its fact that it is 'a branching tree-like affair of many possibilities as opposed to a linear progression') and his description of that advance as an inevitable linear progression through a fixed series of stages. Further, Rotman identifies, the description is static: 'it is more nearly a taxonomic, than an evolutionary one, since it does not refer to any principle of change'. Flavell (1977) concludes that the concept of stage will not figure importantly in future scientific work on cognitive growth, and Elkind (1976) appears to hold a similar view when he regards the concept of stage as simply 'to designate one mode of behaviour in a necessary sequence of behaviour that is related to, but not determined by, age'.

   More recently, it is evident that the Genevan School does not consider the concept of stage to be central to Piaget's theory: 'it is a descriptive tool and the hallmark of Piaget's anti-empiricism' (Gruber and Vonèche, 1977; Vonèche, 1980).

Cognitive Bias

Smedslund, another contributor to the above-cited symposium, also refers to the lack of direct support for the existence of operatory structures, but puts greater emphasis on the 'detached', 'one-sidedly cognitive' and abstract nature of Piagetian psychology. He considers that the lack of representativeness of the Piagetian tasks relative to the total *Lebenswelt* of the child is one of the reasons why Piagetian psychology is relatively useless for practical purposes. He even suggests political implications in what he considers to be a bias towards a one-sidedly intellectualistic and school-centred ideology. However, among his positive points for the theory, Smedslund acknowledges Piaget's accentuation of the role of organization of the person's activity, leading to the characterization of activity in terms of strategies, rather than in terms of specific linkages between behaviour and elements in the environment. This acknowledgement is at some slight variance with a third paper in the symposium.

The Role of Activity

Anthony, from a review of the literature, concludes that Piaget's insistence on the child's active manipulation of objects in intellectual development is excessive. It is concluded that activity is valuable but it has been overvalued and observation undervalued. Physical activity is often not what is needed for intellectual development: the child observing others in an appropriate context need not be wasting his time.

The Role of Learning

Siegel and Brainerd (1978), in their edited collection of critical essays entitled *Alternatives to Piaget*, maintain that 'the inconsistencies between empirical data and the theory's predictions are very serious. At the same time, analysis of the theory itself has revealed hitherto unsuspected logical problems with some of Piaget's key explanatory constructs. For these reasons, it now appears that a comprehensive reassessment and revision of the theory is in order.'

Piaget emphasizes the distinction between learning and development. Learning is subordinate to development. Although learning is acknowledged in an absolute sense, self-discovery training methods are considered to be particularly effective because 'active discovery is what happens in development', (Sinclair de Zwart, 1973). It is further maintained by the Geneva School that children cannot be taught a specific concept unless they already possess understanding to a degree—learning consisting of generalizing mental structures already developing. Brainerd concludes from an examination of research that: 'there is no reason to suppose . . . that the best procedures for training Piagetian concepts are those which imitate processes operating in everyday life . . . There is not the slightest reason to suppose that factors responsible for learning outside the walls of laboratories are, somehow, better attuned to the state of the organism than factors responsible for learning inside the walls of laboratories.' Further, Brainerd presents empirical findings with the claim that concrete operational concepts can be learned by children showing no evidence prior to training and further to pre-school subjects within the earlier half of the nominal age range for the pre-operational stage. Brown and Desforges (1979, op. cit.) endorse these contributions following a review of relevant research studies: 'Piaget's view of learning seems to require a great deal of special pleading to explain away the results of his critics'.

Educational Implications

It is evident that any theory of learning must have implications for education. Lawton and Hooper, in the above-cited Siegel and Brainerd collection of critical essays, continue to discuss possible artificial dichotomies between development and learning within the context of challenging the glib acceptance of Piaget's views as demonstrating *prima facie* validity and relevance for educational application. It is Lawton and Hooper's objective to develop programmes that are 'explicitly accountable in terms of straightforward behavioural objectives and associated requirements and, at the same time, designed in the spirit of Piaget's stated long-range goals for educational programmes'. Brown and Desforges (1977, op. cit.) emphasize that while Piaget's most convinced followers have been prepared to base whole curricula and teaching programmes upon Piagetian psychology, the most vociferous critics have taken the view that the theory has no implications whatsoever for instruction. Brown and Desforges conclude Piagetian theory to be 'less than adequate' as a basis for educational practice. It is of interest at this point to refer to Gallagher and Easley (1978) for a reminder in favour of the Piagetian perspective that Piaget's intention was to produce a theory of knowledge in terms of its genesis and not an exposition in pedagogy. Interpretation in terms of applications rather than implications has resulted in misapplications, trivializations and the development of ideas at variance with Piaget's position.

Novak (1978), in a paper entitled *An Alternative to Piagetian Psychology for Science and Mathematics Education*, emphasizes that much of the confusion in educational work based on Piaget's studies has derived from extrapolating ideas from his developmental psychology to the interpretation of learning events and to the design of instruction constrained by parameters of Piaget's developmental theory in a further critical essay.

Language

Moore and Harris (1978) outline the inadequacy of the Piagetian model for language development and the theories of Chomsky are suggested as a useful alternative. They conclude, '. . . a perusal of Piagetian literature on language acquisition, in conjunction with the data reported . . . provides scant evidence for the contention that language skills are a reflection of more general cognitive operations. Constant exposure to linguistic data affords children the opportunity to begin language learning early. They accomplish the task relatively quickly—by means of various inductive procedures and perceptual strategies, the nature of which is the focus of much ongoing research. If the origins of these learning skills exist within more general cognitive operations, it remains for Piagetian theory to stipulate what these universal operations are, and how they are invoked in the particular case of language learning. At a minimum, they must be as complex and as general as the strategies implicated in early language learning. Rather than defining language phenomena in such a way that extant theory can accommodate them, it is reasonable to expect that the theory be adapted to account for the data. In its present form, Piagetian theory looks like an unlikely candidate for the elucidation of language learning procedures', pp. 149—150.

Among his objections to Piaget's views, Rotman (op. cit.) posits that Piaget provides no adequate account of language; of what it means to think in and through symbols about, 'what he would have to call the unreal world of purely human meanings. Man makes himself through a variety of artifices and artefacts'.

Logic

Subsequent to earlier critiques (Parsons, 1960), more recently Ennis (1978), a logician, has highlighted the flaws inherent in Piaget's logical system within another collected critical essay. 'Finding no way to tell in Piaget's system whether someone can handle propositional logic,' he suggests that Piaget's claims in the area are false, untestable, and not about deductive logic. He proposes an alternative way of conceptualizing the area, the basis of which is a three-dimensional analysis of logical competence. Rotman (op. cit.), in relation to Piagetian theory, analyses the issue of 'whether it makes sense to think of logic or mathematics as an individual rather than as a social creation'.

Performance—Competence

Although Piagetian methodology has long received criticism, more intensive analyses have resulted recently in relatively more serious attacks. Siegel (1978, op. cit.) argues, on the basis of experimentation, that Piagetian results are primarily a consequence of the linguistic demands of his concrete-operational tests. Brown and Desforges (op. cit.) focus on the various aspects of the demands of a task which might defeat a child and lead to an underestimation of his competence: 'Piaget's tasks are cloaked in language'. Boden (op. cit.) also draws attention to such a difficulty particularly inherent in Piagetian theory: 'One of the methodological problems is to decide when a child's failure is due to a lack of Piagetian structures or general principles of thinking, and when it is due to other factors (such as ignorance, incomprehension or short memory-span). Some of these problems would arise in the interpretation of experimental results with respect to meticulously clearly expressed theories; but Piaget's relative obscurity, and his variability over different texts, do not help matters.'

Although acknowledging her indebtedness and influence in relation to Piaget, Donaldson (1978) argues that the evidence now compels a rejection of certain features of Piaget's theory. In her book, *Children's Minds*, she contends that young children's powers of reasoning are far greater than some of Piaget's claims would lead us to believe. When children are operating within a context where the intention is not clear to them they may well appear incompetent.

Other Theoretical Viewpoints

Siegel (1978, op. cit.) identifies a unifying theme throughout her collection of critical essays: the consideration of theoretical viewpoints other than Piaget's. 'When Piagetian theory cannot explain a particular set of findings, it is obvious that other theories must be considered.' It is, however, of interest that Siegel comments that 'no one theory predominates'. This identification would seem to lead to a focus on current counteraction to the aforementioned critiques.

CURRENT COUNTERACTION TO CRITICAL ANALYSES

To counterbalance the above, the edited book, *Toward a Theory of Psychological Development* (Modgil and Modgil, 1980), has provided relatively more favourable substantiation of the Geneva School. Theoretical analyses and accounts of research projects representing the most recent advances within the Piagetian framework were compiled, thereby attempting to accelerate the movement towards a comprehensive psychological theory. The construction of a generic theory needs to take into account: a wide range of psychological theories; branches of psychology; specific psychological issues; areas immediately related to psychology—philosophy, logic, mathematics and the sciences; applied areas, specifically education, representing a range of curriculum areas; and specific research methodologies—longitudinal and cross-cultural approaches to a range of psychological issues. Among such categorizations a wide range of disciplines are represented, each orientation of necessity making its own links with its own specific related disciplines.

The volume represents a substantial approach to the enterprise. From the specific projected categorizations arise areas of knowledge as far-reaching as child art, creativity, humanism, law, medicine, morality, psychopathology and psychotherapy. Each paper contains indications of how the particular orientation is seen to furnish interlocking mechanisms leading towards a theory of psychological development within the Piagetian framework.

Cognitive—Affective

Following the editors' introduction, the contributed papers are divided into a further seven sections. Part II illustrates the links to be made between cognitive and affective areas of development. Wolfe Mays, from the philosophical perspective, highlights

Piaget as showing as much interest in affectivity as any other psychologist. He analyses in depth the Freudian influences on Piaget's work, together with the lectures Piaget delivered at the Sorbonne in 1954: *'Les relations entre l'affectivité et l'intelligence dans le developpement mental de l'enfant'*. He further focuses on Piaget's account of the self and its relation with the other, involving moral considerations. Harley Shands, a psychiatrist, examines the development of a self: a 'self-describable' self. His objective is the formulation of a genetic affectology to complement Piaget's genetic epistemology: 'In learning to describe the *inner instructing* as well as the *outer behaving*, the person learns to "operate upon operations" to "describe describings" or, in computer terms, to describe the "program corresponding to the behavioural exhibition" . . . This stage of development seems to correspond, in affectological terms, to the formal operations of intelligence.' Melvin Weiner discusses a psychotherapeutic approach 'that achieves a Freudian and Piagetian rapprochement, and facilitates successful treatment through bringing about equilibration of assimilatory and accommodatory processes in psychotherapy'. Richards Peters, after philosophically analysing the main features that mark a man out as rational, examines Piaget's theory of development, focusing on the features bearing upon distinctions between 'rationality' and 'reasonableness', and on the relation between the development of reason and action and will.

The paper places the cognitive—affective issue in a wider context. Richard Kimball's chapter offers a theory of the psyche based mainly on the theories of Freud, Reich and Jung, and examines the effect of Piaget's contribution in relation to these and other theories.

Cognitive—Social

In Part III, Beryl Geber and Paul Webley look at the interface of social and cognitive-developmental psychology, and interrelate the insights each can give into the way in which the social world is constructed. Likewise, William Barker and John Newson suggest that developmental social psychology 'might establish itself at the interface between interaction and cognition, studying the way in which social activity is related to, and changes with, the beliefs, ambitions and frustrations of the people involved'. They focus on the research required to articulate the ways in which understanding develops as a function of the continually changing social context of children's lives. Transcendence of an individualist approach to cognition and society would be necessary: consideration of social cognitions alone would be inadequate. Appreciation of the relations between groups in which individuals arise would also be required. 'The study of people's responses to, and generation of, changes in social practices requires a systematic (Moscovici, 1972) approach to the sociality of individuals, and the inter-group character of society.' Howard Gruber's essay on the creative process, which is concerned with the development of thought in the individual case: 'creative thinking as an epigenesis, evolving through a series of structures', is also in this section.

Cognitive—Moral

In Part IV, Peter Tomlinson provides a comprehensive overview of Piaget's and Kohlberg's work on moral development, together with considerations of the emanating research. He reviews the chief criticisms levelled against Kohlberg's views and offers suggestions as to how the cognitive-developmental view might contribute, 'with suitable modifications, to a more integrated model of moral thought and action, ending with some brief perspectives on the practical relevance of this sort of view'.

June Pimm also reviews Piaget's theory of moral development, but she supports further the usefulness of the theory for the juvenile justice system. The contribution made by James Hemming emphasizes in the preamble that Humanism is not a closely defined body of doctrine, but a generalized attitude to life. He concentrates on themes which are to the fore in contemporary Humanist thinking, and demonstrates how they are illuminated by Piagetian insights. He includes considerations of: the process of development; the child's map of the world; individual fulfilment; social man and the moral dimension.

Abstract Models of Psychological Explanation

Piaget (1963) elaborates the notion that explanation by abstract model fulfils three functions: it makes precise otherwise imprecise deductions; it enables the discovery of new relations between general facts or laws which were not previously comparable; and it can supply causal links which were previously overlooked. This would appear to be synonymous with William Hoffman's use of category theory to express Piaget's theory of cognitive development in modern mathematical terms. His goal is to construct an adequate mathematical model, wherein deductions and inferences can be made, strictly from the mathematical structure itself, and then to emerge with interpretation hypotheses that are borne out by neuropsychological realities. David Dirlam presents 'informally a terminology for discussing classification', and secondly, he '. . . places classifier theory in the context of the current paradigm of research in cognitive development'. He considers that further development and application of the theory could have significant effects on much social science research. These considerations of abstract models of psychological explanation comprise Part V.

Longitudinal and Cross-cultural Research

Longitudinal and cross-cultural research methodologies are of significance for ascertaining the validity of a theory. Respectively, John Versey and Lita Furby provide surveys of researches carried out from a longitudinal perspective and cross-culturally, forming Part VI of the volume. Versey emphasizes the importance of longitudinal evidence and, after reviewing longitudinal studies pertaining to Piaget's theory, concludes that present 'evidence from both cross-sectional and longitudinal studies suggest that Piaget's theory of cognitive development will need adjustment and reformulation in the not too distant future'. However, much more evidence is needed before this takes place, but particular trends and discrepant features can be discerned and need to be pursued with further longitudinal studies. Furby's emphasis is on the general thrust of cross-cultural Piagetian studies and their implications for cognitive-developmental theory. One of her conclusions consists of the recognition that the theory has 'focused lopsidedly on the organism, and has neglected the role of environment'.

Education and Curriculum

Part VII comprises a comprehensive approach to education, incorporating a general approach to educational issues from the Piagetian perspective together with specific curricular orientations. Most contributors converge on the view that Piagetian developmental theory does not permit exact formulations for teaching, curriculum design or assessment. Frank Murray concludes that the only certain educational recommendation from a theory such as Piaget's is that schools should simulate 'natural' human development: schooling 'promotes intellectual growth best when it is based upon natural mechanisms of intellectual development'. Although educators cannot wait for empirical and theoretical issues to be resolved, they cannot ignore theoretical ambiguities and empirical obstacles. John Biggs also acknowledges the potential Piagetian theory has for profoundly influencing educational practice, but postulates that an intermediate body of theory is necessary. He draws a distinction between the hypothetical cognitive structures of Piagetian psychology and the structure of the learning outcome, 'psychology's educological offshoot'. Kevin Collis, within the mathematical curriculum, proposes that an information-processing model provides a fruitful way of looking at the problem of explaining the stage phenomena. A number of mathematical concepts are analysed and related to various Piagetian stages. Marcia Linn focuses on classroom learning experiences which might affect scientific reasoning or the ability to control variables. Michael Shayer, again within the science orientation, demonstrates the expediency of the Piagetian framework for 'prescribing the moves to make towards intellectual development' and for the testing process. Child art is discussed within the Piagetian ethos by Robert Schirrmacher and implications for the art teacher proposed.

In many publications the concluding section can be the terminus; in the volume under discussion, the conclusion increases the momentum. J. Jacques Vonèche, encircled by the Piagetian ethos and expertly conversant with the latest research endeavours of the Genevan School, comments on the difficulties of genetic psychology encountered in the preceding chapters of the volume, and then provides a reformulation of a theory of development around the dialectical interaction between the growing individual awareness of the self and the socializing forces. Part VIII then attempts to evaluate the effectiveness of the current project by promoting a number of characteristics of *A Theory of Psychological Development* within the Piagetian framework.

THE NEED FOR DEBATE

It will be noted that even more positive approaches to Piagetian theory identify a number of questionable elements and omissions. As Donaldson (op. cit.) argues, 'the evidence now compels us to reject certain features of Jean Piaget's theory . . . No theory in science is final; and no one is more fully aware of this than Piaget himself.' However, 'much that is said (in the later chapters of her book) . . . is, I believe, in no way incompatible with Piaget's views and has certainly been influenced by them in positive ways'. In similar vein Boden (op. cit.): 'In sum, despite all the criticisms, there is a rich store of psychological insights and theoretical speculations, and a profusion of intriguing empirical observations and remarkably ingenious experiments, to be found in Piaget's pioneering work . . . (so to someone attracted today to psychological or epistemological enquiry, one may say: "Read Piaget. Remember that he is usually vague and often wrong, and that there are still-uncharted dimensions of structural and procedural complexity within the mind that he seemingly has little inkling of. But yes— read Piaget.")' Therefore, in reiteration of Siegel and Brainerd (op. cit.) it would seem that 'the more prudent middle course lies somewhere between totally rejecting the theory and refusing to recognize its weaknesses'.

THE STRATEGY OF THIS BOOK

It was therefore proposed to provide in one single source the most recent 'crosscurrents and crossfire', to begin to clarify the contribution of Piaget to the evolution of the understanding of human development. Modgil (1974), Modgil and Modgil (1976) eight-volume series, and Modgil and Modgil (1980) bear witness to the number of experts in a wide variety of fields who see the potential of Piagetian theory. However, neo-Piagetians after many euphoric years have now to consider the discrepancies and the omissions, together with the various interpretations which are currently being highlighted. This volume provides theoretical analysis, often supported by research, of aspects of Piaget's theory presented predominantly either negatively or positively by *pairs* of distinguished academics representing particular areas of knowledge. Each paper includes an introductory consideration of the area of knowledge involved, together with discussion and analysis comprising a clear statement of how significant aspects of Piaget's theory within the framework of Piagetian theory in general are seen predominantly either negatively or positively to relate to the represented discipline. The *paired* contributions have been exchanged, thereby providing opportunity for both parties to refute the 'heart' of the opposing paper.

The development of a rationale for the ordering of contents seems unimportant for this particular collection of essays. However, in an attempt to adopt some strategy, areas of knowledge relating to the foremost inherent aspects of Piaget's theory have been placed first, with areas of application succeeding. Negative orientations within each area of knowledge receive first placing.

From a philosophical standpoint Phillips and Mays comprehensively analyse Piaget's theory in relation to philosophy, epistemology and sociology. Vonèche and Bovet, from the Genevan ethos, defend the psychological issues of Piagetian theory against 'attacks' from Siegel and Hodkin. From interest in teaching logic, Ennis argues that Piaget's logic is mistaken and defective; Tomlinson-Keasey, in refutation, illustrates the hindrance of progression in accounting for logical development to be due to a clash of structuralist paradigms. Elliot and Donaldson address themselves to the question of whether Piaget's theories of knowing are endangered by his relative lack of concern with language, and bring to light aspects not discussed by Piaget. Sinclair's access to Genevan archives permits her to draw attention to places where Piaget gives recognition to aspects of language acquisition which he does not usually stress. Wright and Weinreich-Haste, prominent in the moral sphere, focus on issues in Piaget's moral writings rarely receiving attention. Hofman and Elliott argue the merits and difficulties of attempting to psychometrize Piagetian theory. From a cross-cultural perspective, Buck-Morss claims Piaget's theory has a socio-economic rather than a cultural bias, whereas Ghuman supports the notion that Piagetian psychology can make a significant contribution towards the education of the third-world younger generation.

In application of Piagetian theory to education, Boyle presents the case that Piaget's theory has no discernible influence on educational practice, while Tamburrini considers to discuss Piaget's theory as being of no concern to education is to ignore a large body of experimental evidence relating to cognitive development which is one of the major concerns of education. In the applied area of science education, Novak promotes Ausubel's learning theory as more relevant and containing more interpretative power for a variety of important science and mathematics questions than Piaget's developmental psychology. Driver sees Piagetian theory as addressing a different problem in science education from that focused on by Novak and considers the two theories not in opposition but complementing each other. Fincham, concerned with special education, elaborates that until Piaget's theory of learning is clarified, it remains of limited value to the field of learning disabilities, while McFarland and Grant, from a more practitioner viewpoint, cannot agree with the assumption that usefulness of the theory cannot be considered prior to resolution of basic research questions.

A tabulated summary of the various debates, arranged in accordance with the areas of knowledge which the debators represent, has been provided at the end of the book. There has been no attempt to specifically focus on areas singled out in the introduction as being areas attracting 'attack' prior to this publication, but many of these aspects arise and receive further discussion and enlightenment within the adopted organization.

REFERENCES

Anthony, J. (1977) Symposium: Practical and theoretical issues in Piagetian psychology. *British Journal of Educational Psychology,* **47,** 18-23.

Barker, W. D. and Newson, J. (1980) The development of social cognition: definition and location. In Modgil, S. and Modgil, C. (Eds.) *Toward a Theory of Psychological Development.* Windsor: NFER.

Biggs, J. (1980) The relationship between developmental level and the quality of school learning. In Modgil, S. and Modgil, C. (Eds.) *Toward a Theory of Psychological Development.* Windsor: NFER.

Boden, M. (1979) *Piaget.* Glasgow: Fontana.

Brainerd, C. (1978) Learning research and Piagetian theory. In Siegel, L. S. and Brainerd, C. J. (Eds.) *Alternatives to Piaget.* London: Academic Press.

Brainerd, C. and Siegel, L. (Eds.) (1978) *Alternatives to Piaget.* London: Academic Press.

Brown, G. and Desforges, C. (1977) Piagetian psychology and education: time for revision. *British Journal of Educational Psychology,* **47,** 7-17.

Brown, G. and Desforges, C. (1979) *Piaget's Theory: A Psychological Critique.* London: Routledge and Kegan Paul.

Bryant, P. (1974) *Perception and Understanding in Young Children: An Experimental Approach.* London: Methuen.

Collis, K. (1980) School mathematics and stages of development. In Modgil, S. and Modgil, C. (Eds.) *Toward a Theory of Psychological Development.* Windsor: NFER.

Dirlam, D. (1980) Classifiers and cognitive development. In Modgil, S. and Modgil, C. (Eds.) *Toward a Theory of Psychological Development.* Windsor: NFER.

Donaldson, M. (1978) *Children's Minds.* Glasgow: Fontana.

Elkind, D. (1976) Elkind updates Piaget. *Day Care and Early Education,* **4,** 1, 9-10.

Elkind, D. (1976) *Child Development and Education.* New York: Oxford University.

Ennis, R. G. (1978) Conceptualization of children's logical competence: Piaget's propositional logic and an alternative proposal. In Siegel, L. S. and Brainerd, C. J. (Eds.) *Alternatives to Piaget.* London: Academic Press.

Flavell, J. (1977) *Cognitive Development.* Englewood Cliffs, New Jersey: Prentice-Hall.

Furby, L. (1980) Implications of cross-cultural Piagetian research for cognitive-developmental theory. In Modgil, S. and Modgil, C. (Eds.) *Toward a Theory of Psychological Development.* Windsor: NFER.

Gallagher, J. and Easley, J. A. (1978) *Knowledge and Development. Vol. 2 Piaget and Education.* New York: Plenum.

Geber, B. and Webley, P. (1980) Experience and society. In Modgil, S. and Modgil, C. (Eds.) *Toward a Theory of Psychological Development.* Windsor: NFER.

Gruber, H. (1980) The evolving systems approach to creativity. In Modgil, S. and Modgil, C. (Eds.) *Toward a Theory of Psychological Development.* Windsor: NFER.

Gruber, H. and Vonèche, J. (1979) *The Essential Piaget.* London: Routledge and Kegan Paul.

Hemming, J. (1980) Humanism and the Piagetian framework. In Modgil, S. and Modgil, C. (Eds.) *Toward a Theory of Psychological Development.* Windsor: NFER.

Hoffman, W. (1980) Mathematical models of Piagetian psychology. In Modgil, S. and Modgil, C. (Eds.) *Toward a Theory of Psychological Development.* Windsor: NFER.

Kimball, R. (1980) Affective and cognitive development, the psyche and Piaget. In Modgil, S. and Modgil, C. (Eds.) *Toward a Theory of Psychological Development.* Windsor: NFER.

Lawton, J. T. and Hooper, F. H. (1978) Piagetian theory and early childhood education: a critical analysis. In Siegel, L. S. and Brainerd, C. (Eds.) *Alternatives to Piaget.* London: Academic Press.

Linn, M. (1980) Teaching students to control variables. Some investigations using free choice experiences. In Modgil, S. and Modgil, C. (Eds.) *Toward a Theory of Psychological Development.* Windsor: NFER.

Mays, W. (1980) Affectivity and values in Piaget. In Modgil, S. and Modgil, C. (Eds.) *Toward a Theory of Psychological Development.* Windsor: NFER.

Modgil, S. (1974) *Piagetian Research: A Handbook of Recent Studies.* Windsor: NFER. (Japanese edition (1976 p. 488)).

Modgil, S. and Modgil, C. (1976) *Piagetian Research: An Appreciation and Theory of Cognitive Development and Sensorimotor Intelligence.* Vol. 1, pp. 171. Windsor: NFER.

Modgil, S. and Modgil, C. (1976a) *Experimental Validation of Conservation and the Child's Conception of Space.* Vol. 2, pp. 280. Windsor: NFER.

Modgil, S. and Modgil, C. (1976b) *The Growth of Logic: Concrete and Formal Operations.* Vol. 3, pp. 313. Windsor: NFER.

Modgil, S. and Modgil, C. (1976c) *School Curriculum and Test Development.* Vol. 4, pp. 331. Windsor: NFER.

Modgil, S. and Modgil, C. (1976d) *Personality, Socialization and Emotionality and Reasoning among Handicapped Children.* Vol. 5, pp. 381. Windsor: NFER.

Modgil, S. and Modgil, C. (1976e) *Cognitive-Developmental Approach to Morality.* Vol. 6, pp. 225. Windsor: NFER.

Modgil, S. and Modgil, C. (1976f) *Training Techniques.* Vol. 7, pp. 192. Windsor: NFER.

Modgil, S. and Modgil, C. (1976g) *Cross-Cultural Studies.* Vol. 8, pp. 239. Windsor: NFER.

Modgil, S. and Modgil, C. (Eds.) (1980) *Toward a Theory of Psychological Development.* Pp. 814. Windsor: NFER.

Moore, T. E. and Harris, A. E. (1978) Language and thought in Piagetian theory. In Siegel, L. S. and Brainerd, C. (Eds.) *Alternatives to Piaget.* London: Academic Press.

Moscovici, S. (1972) Society and theory in social psychology. In Israel, J. and Tajfel, H. (Eds.) *The Context of Social Psychology.* London: Academic Press.

Murray, F. (1980) The generation of educational practice from developmental theory. In Modgil, S. and Modgil, C. (Eds.) *Toward a Theory of Psychological Development.* Windsor: NFER.

Novak, J. D. (1978) An alternative to Piagetian psychology for science and mathematics education. *Studies in Science Education,* **5,** 1-30.

Parson, S. C. (1960) Inhelder and Piaget's The Growth of Logical Thinking, II, A logician's view point. *British Journal of Educational Psychology,* **51,** 75-84.

Peters, R. (1980) The development of reason. In Modgil, S. and Modgil, C. (Eds.) *Toward a Theory of Psychological Development.* Windsor: NFER.

Piaget, J. (1963) The multiplicity of forms of psychological explanations. *In Experimental Psychology: Its Scope and Method,* Fraisse, P. and Piaget, J. (Eds.) Vol. 1 Presses Universitaires de France. English translation, 1968, New York: RKP Basic Books Inc. Cited in Gruber, H. and Vonèche, J. (Ed.) (1979) *The Essential Piaget.* London: RKP.

Pimm, J. (1980) Piaget and the juvenile justice system. In Modgil, S. and Modgil, C. (Eds.) *Toward a Theory of Psychological Development.* Windsor: NFER.

Rotman, B. (1977) *Jean Piaget: Psychologist of the Real.* Sussex: The Harvester Press.

Schirrmacher, R. (1980) Child art. In Modgil, S.and Modgil, C. (Eds.) *Toward a Theory of Psychological Development.* Windsor: NFER.

Shands, H. (1980) The hunting of the self: toward a genetic affectology. In Modgil, S. and Modgil, C. (Eds.) *Toward a Theory of Psychological Development.* Windsor: NFER.

Shayer, M. (1980) Piaget and science education. In Modgil, S. and Modgil, C. (Eds.) *Toward a Theory of Psychological Development.* Windsor: NFER.

Siegel, L. (1978) The relationship of language and thought in the pre-operational child. A reconsideration of nonverbal alternatives to Piagetian tasks. In Siegel L. S. and Brainerd, C. (Eds.) *Alternatives to Piaget.* London: Academic Press.

Sinclair de Zwart, H. (1973) Recent Piagetian research in learning studies. In M. Schwebel and J. Raph (Eds.) *Piaget in the Classroom.* New York: Basic Books.

Sinclair de Zwart, H. (1977) Recent developments in genetic epistemology. *Genetic Epistemologist,* **6,** 1-4.

Smedslund, J. (1977) Piaget's psychology in practice. Symposium: Practical and theoretical issues in Piagetian psychology III. *British Journal of Educational Psychology,* **47,** 1-6.

Tomlinson, P. (1980) Moral judgement and moral psychology: Piaget, Kohlberg and Beyond. In Modgil, S. and Modgil, C. (Eds.) *Toward a Theory of Psychological Development.* Windsor: NFER.

Versey, J. (1980) Longitudinal studies and Piaget's theory. In Modgil, S. and Modgil, C. (Eds.) *Toward a Theory of Psychological Development.* Windsor: NFER.

Vonèche, J. (1980) Commentary and towards a developmental theory. In Modgil, S. and Modgil, C. (Eds.) *Toward a Theory of Psychological Development.* Windsor: NFER.

Weiner, M. (1980) Equilibration of structures in psychotherapy. In Modgil, S. and Modgil, C. (Eds.) *Toward a Theory of Psychological Development.* Windsor: NFER.

Chapter 2

Perspectives on Piaget as Philosopher: The Tough, Tender-minded Syndrome*

DENIS PHILLIPS

INTRODUCTION: DIMENSIONS OF THE TASK

> Whatever universe a professor believes in must at any rate be a universe that lends itself to lengthy discourse. A universe definable in two sentences is something for which the professorial intellect has no use. (James, 1960, Chap. 1, p. 18)

This wry comment by William James is singularly applicable to Professor Piaget—his universe certainly cannot be defined in two sentences. Indeed, a chapter devoted to his work as a philosopher barely suffices to scratch the surface.

Even to define the task requires moderately 'lengthy discourse'. Piaget has written a number of books with philosophical sounding titles: *Biology and Knowledge, Genetic Epistemology, Structuralism, Insights and Illusions of Philosophy,* and *Psychology and Epistemology,* to mention only a few, but a discussion of his philosophical work cannot rest with these. His philosophy is inextricably bound to his work in psychology, and hence one is also forced to take into account such volumes as *Six Psychological Studies, The Language and Thought of the Child, Judgment and Reasoning in the Child, Behaviour and Evolution,* and *Psychology of Intelligence.* In addition, his colleagues and students at Geneva have written important books and papers, and there is an enormous literature by fellow-travellers. In recent years, too, critics have been more vocal, and there are a number of philosophically-oriented analyses that have to be considered: the essays by Carol Feldman and Stephen Toulmin (1976), and D. C. Phillips and Mavis Kelly (1975); Brian Rotman's book (1977); Robert Ennis's critique of Piagetian logic (1978); the book by David Hamlyn (1978); and the symposium edited

*Helpful comments and criticisms have been provided by Nick Burbules, Jennie Nicolayev, Nel Noddings, Nancy Sanders, and Jeff Zorn.

by Theodore Mischel (1971). To these can be added those psychologically-based critiques which speak to some of the philosophical issues—the volume by Peter Bryant (1974) is one example.

FIRST IMPRESSIONS

Mere quantity of work, however, does not establish that an author has a claim to serious philosophical attention. And the fact is that even a cursory inspection of some of Piaget's key books would convince many readers that extensive study is not worth the effort.

There are three related defects that hamper the efforts of readers to master Piaget's arguments, and which may cause them to lose patience: (1) the material is convoluted; (2) it is often very badly argued; and (3) it often obfuscates or evades the central points at issue. Thus, the frustrated Theodore Mischel was led to write in a book review (1976, p. 164) that

> since the issues are not just empirical but heavily conceptual, their resolution requires the sort of skill in conceptual analysis that is the stock-in-trade of much recent Anglo-American philosophy. Piaget, perhaps because his European background inclines him to think of philosophy as general speculations which can have no resolution, has not concerned himself with work in analytic epistemology that would be directly relevant to the issues that do concern him.

Several examples will illustrate the dimensions of these related problems.

(1) *Convolution.* The following passage may well be making an interesting point, but nothing much is apparent because it is so dense. The parallels with passages from Hegel are startling. The quotation is taken from a recent exposition of the key explanatory concept 'equilibration':

> In the equilibration of the integration and the differentiation, the necessity for negations is equally clear. On the one hand, to differentiate a totality, T, in subsystems, S, means not only to confirm what each of these possesses but also to exclude, or deny, the characteristics each system does not have. On the other hand, to form (to integrate) a total system, T, means to free positively the characteristics common to all the S, but this also means to distinguish—this time negatively—the common features of special characteristics not belonging to T. In short, the differentiation is based on negations and then, in turn, the integration implies them. The totality T is modified and remains superior in rank to S, but within a new enlarged totality. (Piaget, 1977, p. 11)

In order to assess the holistic aspects of Piaget's thought, and also the explanatory theories he develops, one first has to decipher passages such as this, assuming, of course, that there is something here to be deciphered.

(2) *Paucity of argument.* This example is taken from a dialogue Piaget had with the psychologist Richard I. Evans in 1973. Piaget answered a question about the difficulties encountered in moving back and forth between the disciplines of psychology and philosophy:

> All epistemologists, of whatever school, are implicitly calling on psychology. Even if they maintain that they want to avoid any aspect of psychology, that is already a psychological position. The logical positivists, for example, claim to avoid psychology, in maintaining that logic can be reduced to language—to general syntax and semantics. Despite themselves, they have taken a psychological position. What we must keep in mind, then, is that every implicit psychological assumption could be, and should be, verified. This verification is what is missing from epistemology and philosophy. When you get into the field of verification, you are still concerned with the same problems, but they become more precise. Facts help to clarify them. (Evans, op. cit., p. 34)

Are the problems here rooted in the exposition, or do they result from weakness in the underlying position? In the first place, Piaget seems to be using the term 'psychology' rather broadly; only this way can a case be made that the avoidance of psychology (such as the refusal to allow psychological aspects into a theory about the nature of logic) is itself a 'psychological position'. In normal usage—the usage Evans clearly intended in asking his question—the avoidance of psychology is certainly a position, but it is a higher order or 'meta' or even philosophical position.

The problem is compounded when Piaget goes on to say that assumptions should be verified. It is not at all clear if he means that this should hold true also in epistemology and philosophy. It is not clear what even *counts* as verification in these fields and many epistemologists would oppose the suggestion—one that Piaget does make in various places, as will emerge later—that facts (including the facts that Piaget gathers in his interviews with children) help to clarify the problems of epistemology and philosophy. Of course, this is the very issue Evans was puzzled about and which he was discussing with Piaget. The latter's answer was merely begging the question.

(3) *Obfuscation*. The final example to illustrate the difficulties in dealing with Piaget's prose, and the philosophical thought which may (or may not) lie beneath it, is a footnote attached to a discussion of cognitive structures in *Genetic Epistemology* (p. 23):

> The reader may ask here whether 'structures' have real, objective existence or are only tools used by us to analyse reality. This problem is only a special case of a more general question: do relations have objective independent existence? Our answer will be that it is nearly impossible to understand and justify the validity of our knowledge without presupposing the existence of relations. But this answer implies that the word existence has to be taken to have a multiplicity of meanings.

Here Piaget attempts to have his cake and eat it too; after about eighty words the reader is no closer to understanding whether or not he thinks structures have 'objective reality'. The last sentence is a particularly delightful evasion that brings the reader back full circle. One wonders why Piaget bothered to put pen to paper at all.

Being charitable is a civilized virtue, and no doubt one could find reason to exercise it in Piaget's case. But charity also begins at home, and what is required is a sufficient reason—in the name of philosophy—to extend it to Geneva.

THE PHILOSOPHICAL INTEREST OF PIAGET'S WORK: AN INITIAL CHARACTERIZATION

If there is any philosophical merit in Piaget's writings, it cannot lie in the sophistication or ingenuity of many of his specific arguments and formulations, which too often are defective in the ways that have been illustrated. Rather, the interest must arise from the direction in which he was attempting to move. Light can be thrown on this by returning to William James.

In the classic opening chapter to his *Pragmatism*, James argued that on the basis of temperament one could divide philosophers into two broad categories—the 'tender-minded' and the 'tough-minded'. Most, he added, 'have a hankering for the good things on both sides of the line,' (1960, p. 23), but the classification nevertheless seems useful. Tender-minded philosophers tend to be rationalistic (to which James adds that they go by 'principles'), intellectualistic, idealistic, optimistic, religious, freewillist, monistic, and dogmatical. Tough-minded philosophers, on the other hand, are likely to be empiricist (they go by 'facts'), sensationalistic, materialistic, pessimistic, irreligious, fatalistic, pluralistic, and sceptical (ibid., p. 22).

Piaget falls among the tender-minded, even though, significantly, he is slightly tinged with toughness. Raised in the Continental rationalistic tradition, he sees serious 'gaps' in empiricism. And he has what Brian Rotman calls a 'Kant connection', (Rotman, op. cit., pp. 24-31), although he modifies the doctrines of the master in significant ways; it is here that his attempt at toughness, at 'going by the facts', is of great interest. Furthermore, he is a holist (not to mention, a structuralist) in the neo-Hegelian sense of this term (Phillips, 1976); it is relevant to note that William James wrote that 'rationalism means the habit of explaining parts by wholes', (James, 1971).

What is the chief way in which Piaget attempted to modify or toughen the tender-minded syndrome? To put it briefly and therefore crudely, like those in the Kantian tradition he holds that all human experience is mediated by categories (or, in his terms, structures). However, these are not innate but are developed or constructed by the individual as a result of interaction with the environment. Experimental psychology and biological theory are able to cast as much light on the nature and operation of these structures as can philosophical investigation. Hence the joining, in some of his book titles, of epistemology with psychology, biology, and genesis! Brian Rotman's words are worth quoting to help set the stage for the later discussion, although the picture is slightly oversimplified:

> . . . it is worth recalling in general terms how thoroughly Kantian Piaget's theory of mind is. Apart from his earliest studies, all of Piaget's work on children's cognitive structure is dominated by the Kantian picture of a cognizing mind constructing the world according to the intellectual categories and the forms of spatio-temporal intuition. Naturally Piaget presents his model of mind in terms not available to Kant, namely the structuralist language of algebraic groups of operations; but the organizing framework is precisely the same. It is true that within this framework Kant and Piaget diverge on method. Piaget's approach is concerned with the empirical question of how children and hence adults come to possess these faculties. (Rotman, 1977)

THE CONSTRUCTION OF STRUCTURES*

Initially, then, it seems relevant to focus upon Piaget's account of the development of cognitive structures in the individual child. To simplify the exposition, and also to highlight some features that will be crucial later, it will be a useful device to draw comparisons from time to time between the Piagetian child and the mature scientist.

Consider a scientist who is researching the behaviour of plastic materials under certain conditions of temperature and pressure. He will bring with him to his work what has been variously described as a paradigm, a disciplinary matrix, a conceptual scheme or a *Weltanschauung*. In the following discussion the expression 'scientific world-view' will be used as a label for this important, if abstract, entity.

The structure, and development, of scientific world-views has been the focus of interest in a great deal of recent work in philosophy, philosophy of science, and even philosophy of education. Although there is much disagreement, it is rarely if ever questioned that the scientist brings to his research a conceptual apparatus. For it is

---

*Some of the material in this, and the following, section is based upon D. C. Phillips' article, The Piagetian child and the scientist: Problems of assimilation and accommodation.

evident that he is able to use concepts such as mass, density, volume, viscosity, tensile strength, and elasticity; that he is acquainted with empirical laws, such as Boyle's law, Charles' law, and Hooke's law; that he is familiar with relevant theories, for instance, the kinetic theory of gases and quantum theory; that he commands mathematical techniques; and that he has a modicum of logical skill—he understands transitivity, implication, negation, and so on. Furthermore, it is also evident that he has some sense—although it is hard to describe—of when it is appropriate to apply particular concepts, or perform certain calculations, and so on.

Armed with this intricate intellectual apparatus, the scientist will work with his plastic materials. And if the research should prosper, his knowledge will grow. The oddities that he turns up—the appearance of unexpected properties or phenomena, the apparent breakdown of laws, or the failure of a theory to predict changes in the experimental material—will have to be accommodated.

Now, there are some striking similarities between our prototypical scientist, and the child as depicted by Piaget. For the Piagetian child, at whatever stage of development, brings with her to the activities of her daily life (such as playing with a ball of clay or Plasticine) a world-view with rather similar components to that of the scientist. The child's conceptual scheme will be far less sophisticated, and will perhaps be changing at a different rate to that of the scientist, but it will still be made up of concepts, rudimentary laws, theories and principles, and some elementary mathematics and logic.

Piaget, however, distinguishes between the parts of this world-view which involve 'knowledge of environmental data, which will eventually enable the subject to comprehend the exterior world objectively', and the parts which are logico-mathematical (*Biology and Knowledge*, p. 28). Concepts belonging to the first part are not merely 'copies' of reality, Piaget insists; concept formation is dependent upon the subject engaging in physical activity, and the process also involves 'co-ordination'. Sometimes Piaget refers to the resulting groups of concepts as 'causal structures' (*The Principles of Genetic Epistemology*, p. 24). The logico-mathematical structures, on the other hand, arise from the process of 'reflection' upon these co-ordinated actions rather than from the actions themselves. And, as Piaget points out, these latter structures, 'in the human child, are even to be observed in elementary form before there is any systematized physical knowledge (*Biology and Knowledge*, p. 28).* The following passage is a good summary:

> I should like now to make a distinction between two types of actions. On the one hand, there are individual actions such as throwing, pushing, touching, rubbing. It is these individual actions that give rise most of the time to abstractions from objects . . . Reflective abstraction, however, is based not on individual actions but on co-ordinated actions. Actions can be co-ordinated in a number of different ways. They can be joined together, for instance; we can call this an additive co-ordination. Or they can succeed each other in a temporal order . . . Now all these forms of co-ordinations have parallels in logical structures, and it is such co-ordination at the level of action that seems to me to be the basis of logical structures as they develop later in thought. (*Genetic Epistemology*, p. 18)

Armed, then, with a variety of structures, the child plays with some Plasticine, and in the course of ongoing experience she will turn up oddities that will need to be accommodated. (At this stage it would be possible to digress to discuss the highly 'inferential' nature of Piaget's conclusions; the evidence that a scientist possesses or lacks certain concepts and skills is direct compared with the evidence that a child possessor lacks such things. See for further discussion Phillips, 1976, pp. 5—6.)

---

*See also Piaget's *Psychology and Epistemology*.

THE STRUCTURE OF COGNITIVE STRUCTURES

It is important at this point to note that the scientist under scrutiny does not possess a disorderly array of concepts, laws, and logico-mathematical structures. There seems to be some *organization*. And although there is disagreement in the literature over the best way to characterize the organization of this scientific world-view, a number of people from diverse backgrounds have 'homed in' on one particular account. The pervasive image is a network. The more abstract theories and concepts of the world-view are located deep inside the mesh, while concepts and empirical laws closely related to the observable realm (for example, concepts such as temperature and volume which can easily be defined in terms of operations) are near to the edge of the network. Even if a small area within a particular science is taken for examination, the network analogy is appropriate. In the words of Carl G. Hempel (op. cit., p. 36):

> A scientific theory might therefore be likened to a complex spatial network: its terms are represented by the knots while the threads connecting the latter correspond, in part, to the definitions and, in part, to the fundamental and derivative hypotheses included in the theory. The whole system floats, as it were, above the plane of observation and is anchored to it by rules of interpretation. These might be viewed as strings which are not part of the network but link certain points of the latter with specific places in the plane of observation.*

A similar interpretation, but applied to the whole of a scientific world-view and not just to specific theories within the field of science, is held by W. V. O. Quine. In his influential paper 'Two Dogmas of Empiricism' (1961), Quine chose the image, not of a network, but of a forcefield:

> The totality of our so-called knowledge or beliefs, from the most casual matters of geography and history to the profoundest law of atomic physics or even of pure mathematics and logic, is a man-made fabric which impinges upon experience only along the edges. Or, to change the figure, total science is like a field of force whose boundary conditions are experience. (P. 42)

In Quine's view, the logico-mathematical portions of this 'field of force' are located well away from the boundaries.

In contrast to the scientist, a greater portion of the intellectual equipment of the Piagetian child is in a state of flux. Although her passage from infancy to adulthood forms a developmental continuum, for descriptive purposes it can be divided up into the well-known periods and sub-periods (it is this descriptive part of Piaget's work, of course, that has become so famous with lay people and educators). As the child progresses, it seems as if her mental structures—according to Piaget's account—become more comprehensive and better integrated or *equilibrated*:

> According to this point of view, intellectual operations, whose highest form is found in logic and mathematics, constitute genuine actions, being at the same time something produced by the subject and a possible experiment on reality. The problem is therefore to understand how operations arise out of material action, and what laws of equilibrium govern their evolution; operations are thus conceived as grouping themselves of necessity into complex systems, comparable to the 'configurations' of the Gestalt theory, but these, far from being static and given from the start, are mobile and reversible, and round themselves off only when the limit of the individual and social genetic process that characterizes them is reached. (*Psychology of Intelligence*, pp. 16—17)

Piaget does not specifically refer to the overall intellectual structure of the child as being in some sense 'layered', or as being a network with the relatively unchallengeable portions near the centre. As commented upon earlier, he does claim that there are two types of structures present in the mental equipment of the child—the logico-mathematical ones and the ones that embody concepts pertaining to the nature of the physical world. Even in one of his earlier books, *The Child's Conception of Physical*

---

*A similar image is presented in Pap, A. (1963) *An Introduction to the Philosophy of Science*, p. 52. London: Eyre and Spottiswoode.

Causality (first published in English in 1930), he distinguished between these, which he called the logical structures or formal category, and the real structures or category, and he pointed out that they had parallel and interacting courses of development.

A reader is hampered from forming a clear picture of the overall organization of these structures by severe terminological difficulties. A typical case is the following paragraph from *Six Psychological Studies*:

> Logic in the child (as in the adult) is evidenced in the form of operational structures; i.e. the logical act consists essentially of *operating*, hence of acting on things and toward people. An operation is, in effect, an internalized action which has become *reversible* and co-ordinated with other operations in a grouping, governed by the laws of the system as a whole. To say that *an operation is reversible* is to say that every operation corresponds to an inverse operation, as is true, for example, for logical or arithmetic addition and subtraction. An operation never exists in isolation. It is dependent on an operational structure such as the 'groups' in mathematics . . . or lattices or the structures that are more elementary than groups and networks, which we call 'groupings'. Each of these structures involves law of totalities which define the operational system as such and a particular form of reversibility (inversion in the group, reciprocity in the lattice, etc.). (P. 121, Piaget's emphasis)

The picture that can be built from all this shows the intellectual equipment of the Piagetian child (or for that matter, of the adult) as made up of a *number* of structures. Each of these structures is a system in the holistic sense that its parts are dynamically interrelated so that the 'whole is more than the sum of the parts'. Furthermore, in the child these structures are in a state of flux. They are changing or developing, moving always towards a more stable equilibrium. A slight alteration (or accommodating change) to any part of one structure will alter the whole structure; this follows as a corollary of Piaget's holism (for a critical discussion of the theses of holistic thought see Phillips, 1976). Finally, the various individual structures are not entirely independent, but are themselves dynamically interrelated. And to highlight the similarity and differences between Piaget's view and that of the philosophers and methodologists discussed previously, the logico-mathematical structure has, for Piaget, a somewhat privileged position. It is, to be sure, not safely enmeshed and protected the way it is depicted by Quine and others; on the contrary, it is much closer to the 'firing line' of contact with the physical surroundings. The privileged position of this structure lies in its primacy. The other structure, composed of concepts and relations directly pertinent to contact with the physical environment, would not be what it is were it not for the mediating influence of this logico-mathematical structure. As Piaget put it:

> Physical knowledge or experimental knowledge in general (including the geometry of the actual world) proceeds on the other hand by abstraction based on characteristics of the objects as such. We must therefore expect the role of perceptive fact to be greater in this second field. *But—and this is essential—in this field also, perception never acts alone. Only by adding something to perception do we discover the characteristic of an object.* And what we add is precisely nothing but a group of logico-mathematical limits which alone make perceptive reading possible . . . there is no experimental knowledge which can be qualified as 'pure', detached from all logico-mathematical limits consisting of classifications, functions, and so forth. (*Psychology and Epistemology*, pp. 72—73)

The words which have had emphasis added here have an unmistakable Kantian ring.

It appears that there are good grounds for the argument that there is only a trivial difference between Piaget and the views so far cited of many contemporary philosophers. This difference consists, basically, of a dispute over the best sort of pictorial representation for a world-view. The philosophers opt for something like a network, with the logico-mathematical elements lying near the centre, while Piaget opts for several networks, one of these being logico-mathematical in nature. In both images there exists the possibility that the concepts, laws and theories which are constructed to deal directly with the physical environment will reflect the influence of logico-mathematical portions of the world-view.

ACCOMMODATORY MECHANISMS AND THE PROBLEM OF CHANGE

For Piaget more than for Quine or Hempel, and certainly more than for Kant, questions of genesis and of change are primary. How do cognitive structures develop? What changes take place as the child has new experiences with the toys in her crib? Furthermore, if each individual constructs her own structures, then how is it that the process has the same results for everyone? To put it bluntly, Piaget faces a particularly severe form of the problem that has plagued all biologically and functionally-oriented positions in the social sciences—the problem of accounting for change.

A sceptical note can be introduced here in order to highlight the problem facing Piaget. It seems reasonable to suppose that not all adults accommodate to anomalous experience in the same way. Some of us, when challenged, rethink our presuppositions, but we rethink them differently from the way our friends rethink theirs; others adopt simple *ad hoc* hypotheses, or merely deny that the new evidence is relevant. Some become victims of groupthink, as Irving Janis calls it; some will sublimate; and for others the diverse processes known to resolve cognitive dissonance will bring relief. In such cases, our individual cognitive structures will change along different lines. If Piaget is right, however, there seems to be no such diversity among children. It is, perhaps, comforting but rather romantic to suppose that children are innately wiser, in that all of them unerringly select the 'most adequate' strategy by which to adjust, when those who begot them are so obviously floundering. We are entitled to ask Piaget about the 'homeostatic' mechanism that is at work in children, and to explain why it apparently stops functioning in adults.

Some light can be shed by considering again the scientist, who on the basis of his present world-view is making a prediction about the elasticity his plastic material will display when it is cooled a few degrees nearer absolute zero than he has ever chilled it before. He performs the experiment, and the results shatter his prediction. Which part of his scientific world-view requires adjustment? Contemporary literature on the philosophy of science contains an abundance of advice on this matter, but the overall thrust is that experience alone cannot dictate that a change be made to a specific portion of a scientific world-view. Various strategies are possible for dealing with 'recalcitrant experience'. To revert to the earlier metaphor, because the world-view is structured like a network, experience that seems to threaten a specific part of the net can—but need not—be dealt with by changing this part which is most closely 'aligned' with the experience. But it is equally possible to alter some other portion of the net to compensate, perhaps by adding *ad hoc* hypotheses, or by altering some law or theory, or perhaps by going deep into the net and changing the geometry (e.g. from a Euclidean to a non-Euclidean form) or even the logic. It all depends on which portions the scientist, or the scientific community, decides ought to be kept intact. Thus, if our scientist finds his prediction does not come true when his plastic is chilled near to absolute zero, he could abandon his hypothesis and be forced to change the part of his conceptual network containing his concept of the plastic material; but, alternatively, he could accommodate by altering the portion of his network pertaining to elasticity, 'the law of change of elasticity with temperature does not hold within x degrees of absolute zero', or he could hold that his measuring procedures fail at such extreme temperatures, and so on. These changes all preserve the stock of information already established in science, and they successfully accommodate the new experimental result—they successfully restore 'equilibrium'. They will, however, differ with respect to implications for future research, but this may not become apparent for some time.

This, in essence, is the message found in the writings of Imre Lakatos, Paul

Feyerabend, and W. V. O. Quine.* Feyerabend even stresses that it has sometimes been fruitful (in cases from the history of science) just to ignore evidence that challenges portion of the present world-view, in the hope that something will eventually turn up to account for it! Quine's words are a good summary of this general orientation:

> Any statement can be held true come what may, if we make drastic enough adjustments elsewhere in the system. Even a statement very close to the periphery can be held true in the face of recalcitrant experience by pleading hallucination or by amending certain statements of the kind called logical laws. Conversely, by the same token, no statement is immune to revision. Revision even of the logical law of the excluded middle has been proposed as a means of simplifying quantum mechanics . . . A recalcitrant experience can, I have urged, be accommodated by any of various alternative re-evaluations in various alternative quarters of the total system. (Op. cit., pp. 43—44)

In the light of these contemporary trains of thought, Piaget's discussion of the process determining the direction of change of the individual child's cognitive structures seems remarkably deficient. Consider the following passage from *Genetic Epistemology* (p. 15):

> To my way of thinking, knowing an object does not mean copying it—it means acting upon it. It means constructing systems of transformations that can be carried out on or with this object. Knowing reality means constructing systems of transformations that correspond, more or less adequately, to reality. They are more or less isomorphic to transformations of reality. The transformational structures of which knowledge consists are not copies of the transformations in reality; they are simply possible isomorphic models among which experience can enable us to choose. Knowledge, then, is a system of transformations that become progressively adequate.

At first sight, Piaget's acknowledgement that there are several 'possible isomorphic models' is reminiscent of the philosophers' argument that there are several ways a world-view can be constructed (or reconstructed) to cope with experience. But even without going further afield in Piaget's writings some problems emerge. In the first place, he stresses several times that these alternative models, or structures, which can be developed are isomorphic—isomorphic with reality, and hence, presumably, with each other. It is far from clear what is meant here, but the most straightforward interpretation would be that the models have the same 'logical structure', that is, the same arrangement of 'elements', otherwise, how could they possibly be isomorphic? In this case, the alternative models would be essentially the same, for it would be only a translation problem to move from one to another. The following two sentences are isomorphic in this straightforward sense; to arrive at the second from the first is a simple translation exercise:

(1) The cat is on the table.
(2) Rfc ayr gq ml rfc ryzjc.

Now, according to the position advanced by the philosophers, there is no question of isomorphism between the alternative world-views that can conceivably result when a scientific world-view is adjusted as a consequence of facing anomalous experience. One scientist might advocate the adoption of an exotic geometry in order to accommodate, while another may argue for the addition to the corpus of science a specific *ad hoc* hypothesis, and a third may suggest that some fundamental physical principle (like the conservation of parity) requires revision. The elements in these three world-views would not be the same; there would be no isomorphism. And yet all three world-views would presumably account for previously established scientific knowledge and explain the new and challenging experience.

---

*These writers disagree on many points, of course. See Feyerabend, P. K., (1970) Against method. In Radner, M., and Winokur, S. (Eds.) (1970) *Analyses of Theories and Methods of Physics and Psychology.* Minneapolis: University of Minnesota Press. Minnesota Studies in the Philosophy of Science, Vol. IV. The general position described here is sometimes summarized by the expression 'the under-determination of the theory of nature'.

CHANGING STRUCTURES: 'BIOLOGICAL KANTIANISM'

A related problem emerges from Piaget's claim that 'knowledge . . . is a system of transformations that become progressively adequate'. In various of his writings* he has acknowledged, like a good Kantian, the impossibility of obtaining an absolute gauge of external reality by means of which we could appraise the adequacy of our cognitive structures, for our contact with external reality is, of course, mediated by these same cognitive structures. So the test of adequacy becomes a functional—and in the final analysis, a biological—one.† It is central to much of Piaget's writing (as it was to Dewey's) that humans are part of physical (or external) reality, and have evolved within it. Piaget, like Dewey, believes that probably the most important of the adaptive mechanisms which have helped the human species to flourish is the capacity to exercise intelligence. In much of his voluminous work on this general issue, Piaget does not talk of the resulting knowledge (or the resulting intellectual structures) as being adequate mirrors of reality, but he prefers, not surprisingly, to use biological phraseology:

> It is in this sense that intelligence, whose logical operations constitute a mobile and at the same time permanent equilibrium between the universe and thought, is an extension and a perfection of all adaptive processes. Organic adaptation, in fact, only ensures an immediate and consequently limited equilibrium between the individual and the present environment. Elementary cognitive functions, such as perception, habit and memory, extend it in the direction of present space (perceptual contact with distant objects) and of short-range reconstructions and anticipations. Only intelligence, capable of all its detours and reversals by action and by thought, tends towards an all-embracing equilibrium by aiming at the assimilation of the whole of reality and the accommodation to it of action, which it thereby frees from its dependence on the initial *hic* and *nunc*. (*Psychology of Intelligence*, p. 9)

During these biologically oriented discussions Piaget seems never to consider seriously the possibility that, at any instant in time, there are a *number* of non-isomorphic, equally functional or 'adequate' ways in which the external world could be conceptualized; there may be several configurations of the child's network or world-view that allow the same answer to be given to questions put to children by a researcher. Or, to put it slightly differently, there seem to be no good grounds to support Piaget's assumption that there is only one particular configuration of a cognitive structure that will set it in equilibrium. If an individual is in a state of equilibrium when he or she has theories and beliefs (and so on) that facilitate 'satisfactory' dealings with the environment, and if rival sets of theories can function this way (as the principle that theories are underdetermined by nature indicates), then it follows that the process of equilibration alone is not sufficient to assure that individuals will come to construct identical (or even highly similar, on whatever criterion) cognitive structures.

There are passages—which again are hard to interpret—which indicate Piaget may have had further considerations in mind to account for the supposed fact that we all come to share the one set of physical concepts and interrelated logico-mathematical structures that he regards as truly adequate. He seems to postulate a biological link or chain between the cognitive structures of the adult and the realities in the external world, an aspect of his thought that is closely related to his alliance with contemporary structuralism.

---

*For example, see *Biology and Knowledge*, Section 23.
†This is a recurring theme throughout *Biology and Knowledge*, Section 23. Piaget's functionalism in its relation to his explanation of cognitive change is lengthily discussed by Theodore Mischel, Piaget: Cognitive conflict and the motivation of thought. In Theodore Mischel (ed.) (1971, *op. cit.*) Mischel's conclusion is a little less harsh than that reached in the present discussion.

The nature of this link is explicated in great detail in *Biology and Knowledge*, and it is conveniently summarized in the concluding paragraph of *The Child and Reality*. The conscious mechanisms of humans—what John Dewey somewhat vaguely called the capacity to think or carry out inquiries—are extensions of (and to Piaget are isomorphic with) biological or organic mechanisms that occur throughout the animal kingdom, but these in turn are determined by physico-chemical causes in the external world:

> This isomorphism of conscious implication and of organic causality can be conceived as a special case of correspondences between deduction and material reality which characterize the whole circle of sciences. Let us suppose the logico-mathematical structures placed in sufficient isomorphism with organic structures, then the latter explained causally in an efficient manner by a 'generalized' physico-chemistry . . . until the biological fact is encompassed. This physico-chemistry itself could not help becoming mathematical and deductive, thus based, as a point of departure, on its point of arrival . . . It is in the perspective of such a circle or, if we prefer, of such a constantly increasing spiral that it is probably fitting to situate the problems of relation between life and thought. *The Child and Reality*, p. 172)

One thing, at least, is very clear here: the argument involves an important confusion. By some sleight-of-hand, or slip of the argument, the mathematical description of the cognitive structures in the mind of the individual has become transformed into the mathematical structure of the physical (and biological) world. And this is not an isolated manoeuvre of Piaget's. There are many places where he confuses (or confounds or conflates) such things as: the structure of a part of the world, the structure of our theories dealing with the structure of this part of the world, and the structure of the psychological structures by which we master such theories or deal with such parts of the world.* There is no *prima facie* reason for believing these three things (if they exist) to be the same or even that they are tightly connected. If Piaget has convincing reasons, that is, if he is not confused, then he owes his readers a forthright account.

Carol Feldman and Stephen Toulmin point to essentially the same confusion in a related aspect of Piaget's work:

> Nowhere, it seems, are the differences between the problem involved in *formally representing* a theory and the problems involved in *empirically testing* it so difficult to keep separate as in the area of cognition. Just because the theoretical system in question can plausibly be presented as corresponding to some mental system in the mind of the actual child, we may be led to conclude that the formalism of the theoretical system must be directly represented by an isomorphic formalism in the mind of the child. In their account of the development of spatial knowledge, for example, Piaget and Inhelder (1956) deliberately blur the distinction between topology and Euclidean geometry as formal systems for describing (a) the spatial relations which constitute the phenomena the child copes with, and (b) the forms in the child's mind. In this way, ontological reality is assigned to the hypothetical mental structures of the theory simply on the basis of the formal expressions by which they are represented in the theory. (Op. cit., pp. 416—417)

There seems no escaping the conclusion, then, that notions like isomorphism and equilibration (and the related assimilation, accommodation and homeostasis) cannot do the work Piaget requires of them. There is a growing body of critical literature on

---

*For two examples located close together, see *Six Psychological Studies*, pp. 147, 152—153. The first involves confusion of the structure of part of the disciplines of logic and mathematics with structure of the psychological entities which enable an adolescent to think logically and/or mathematically; the second involves confusion between the behaviour of matter (clay), the theoretical structure humans have devised to deal with matter (the principle of conservation of matter), and the psychological structures the individual constructs as a result of playing with matter (clay). It is also interesting to note the similarity between the distinction made in the text of this paper and Karl Popper's *Three Worlds*.

these, which it is not necessary to summarize here.* One passage from Brian Rotman's lengthy discussion should suffice (op. cit., p. 118); it is taken from a context where Rotman has been attacking Piaget's 'biological Kantianism' for failing to recognize that any evolutionary-oriented account of the development of knowledge in the individual (Piaget does believe ontogeny closely recapitulates phylogeny) conflicts with the description of such development as a linear progression through a fixed series of stages (ibid., p. 106). On the notions of equilibrium and equilibration Rotman writes:

> But, as we have seen, there is no reason to suppose that increasingly stable equilibrium—whatever this is finally to mean—pursues a single path. Certainly the evolution of species, whether thought of in terms of equilibrium, or in any other way, cannot be described as a linear progression. There is, therefore, the question of which of the many paths forward from protozoa to their more complex descendants is the line of true progress, since presumably they have all evolved according to the identical laws of equilibrium. (Ibid., p. 116)

There are several routes for escape from this dilemma. One could acknowledge that individuals have different conceptual structures (and thus keep as central, if one was inclined, notions like equilibration); or one could stress more than Piaget does the importance of social pressures in determining the direction of cognitive development (this is the line taken by, among others, the Soviet psychologists Vygotsky and Luria, and David Hamlyn (op. cit., pp. 58—59) thinks it is the key to a significant conceptual weakness in Piaget); or one could fall back to a modernized version of Kantianism by stressing the existence of innate structures (which are, perhaps, produced by the genetic inheritance of our species). This last position is the one adopted by Noam Chomsky; he regards Piaget's viewpoint as 'obscure in crucial respects', and he argues:

> Piaget develops a certain 'constructive interactionism': new knowledge is constructed through interaction with the environment. But the fundamental question is evaded: *how* is this knowledge constructed, and why *just this kind* of knowledge and not some other? Piaget does not give any intelligible answer, as far as I can make out. The only answer that I can imagine is to suppose an innate genetic structure which determines the process of maturation. Insofar as he considers it wrong to give such an answer, he falls back into something like the empiricism that he wants to reject. What he postulates is nowhere near sufficient, it seems to me, to account for the specific course of cognitive development. (Op. cit., pp. 84—85)

THE ATTACK ON EMPIRICISM

This passage by Chomsky raises the issue of Piaget's attitude towards empiricism: why, indeed, did he reject it? In many of his books there are passing references to the matter, but perhaps the most detailed discussion is a paper written with Bärbel Inhelder: 'The Gaps in Empiricism'. This paper effectively dispels any lingering doubts about Piaget's philosophical acumen.

It rapidly becomes apparent that Piaget—and presumably his co-author—have little understanding of the empiricist philosophical tradition as it developed in the English-speaking world in the late nineteenth and twentieth centuries. There is no mention of Russell or Ayer or any of the dozens of others who might have been expected to be candidates for discussion. They do mention Herbert Spencer—one hopes that they do not consider him to have been the deepest representative of the tradition they are attacking; they refer to 'classical associationist empiricism' and to behaviourism; they mention Chomsky's successful attack on Skinner's theory of verbal behaviour; and

---

*See as an introduction to this literature: Mischel, 1971, op. cit.; Phillips, 1978, op. cit.; also Sophie Haroutunian (1979) Piaget: Adaptation and equilibration. Essay review in *Harvard Educational Review,* **49.**

they mention Quine. This latter, rather than being a sign of profundity, turns out to be their Achilles' heel:

> . . . the great logician Quine was able to show the impossibility of defending a radical dualism of analytic and synthetic judgments (this 'dogma' of logical empiricism, as Quine amusingly termed it). Moreover, a collective study by our Centre for Genetic Epistemology has been able to verify Quine's objections experimentally by finding numerous intermediaries between the analytic and synthetic poles. (Ibid., p. 123)

The point, of course, is that Quine was not putting forward a psychological or experimental hypothesis; he was making a conceptual point, and experimentally 'verifying' it is as much out of place as it would be if the proposition under consideration was that 'all black objects are black'. Anthony Quinton has a forthright statement of the general point that Piaget and Inhelder seem to have not grasped:

> As distinct from such earlier empiricists as Locke, Hume and Mill, the members of this tradition, which has been the standard or classical form of epistemology, in Britain at any rate, in this century, have been quite definite that their purpose is to give a logical analysis of knowledge as it actually exists and not a genetic or historical or psychological account of its growth. In Reichenbach's useful phrase, they are offering a rational reconstruction of our knowledge which sets out the reasons that logically justify our beliefs and not a narrative of the causes that in fact led us to adopt them. (Op. cit., p. 544)

Piagetians consistently overlook this issue of justification of knowledge-claims. In Chapter 4 of his book *Psychology and Epistemology*, for instance, Piaget discusses empiricism under the heading 'The Myth of the Sensorial Origin of Scientific Knowledge', and it is only the psychological issue of origin, rather than the modern epistemological issues of logical analysis and justification, that is identified as relevant.

So, in 'The Gaps in Empiricism', Piaget and Inhelder systematically misrepresent modern empiricism by psychologizing it; the bulk of their discussion focuses on associationism and behaviourism, and there is a deal of exposition of experimental studies. They start on this track in the first paragraph of their paper, where they introduce empiricism in these terms:

> . . . we find a central idea: the function of cognitive mechanisms is to submit to reality, copying its features as closely as possible, so that they may produce a reproduction which differs as little as possible from external reality. This idea of empiricism implies that reality can be reduced to its observable features and that knowledge must limit itself to transcribing these features. (P. 118)

This is no mere slip; the move of introducing the functioning of cognitive mechanisms is important, for it allows Piaget and Inhelder to link up the three main points they wish to make—the three 'gaps' they see in empiricism. If they had opened with a more philosophically-oriented account of empiricism (even the *Dictionary of Philosophy** would have given them nine alternatives to choose between), then at least two of their points (and possibly all) would have been discarded as irrelevant.

The first gap in empiricism, according to Piaget and Inhelder, is that 'biologists have shown that the relationship between an organism and its environment . . . is one of constant interaction' (ibid, p. 118). Here they are simply mistaken; as discussed earlier, this is no 'gap' at all, for empiricism relates not to the details of the processes by which knowledge is acquired, but rather it concerns the logical justification of knowledge-claims. There is no reason why an empiricist, *qua* empiricist, cannot accept the fact of organism—environment interaction.

The second 'gap' Piaget and Inhelder see in empiricism concerns mathematics, a field which they point out 'clearly escapes from the constraints of outer reality' (ibid., pp. 118 and 122—127). In their discussion, Piaget and Inhelder cover material they have

---

Dictionary of Philosophy, pp. 89-90. Dagobert Runes (Ed.) (1967) New Jersey: Littlefield Adams.

often presented before—the use of geometry by the Egyptians, Cantor's updating of mathematical procedures known to children and primitive societies, and the like. But again, the discussion is curiously uninformed about twentieth-century disputes in the philosophy of mathematics, or the views on mathematics by writers in the empiricist tradition—Bertrand Russell's name is conspicuously absent. The issue of rival geometries (Euclidean and non-Euclidean), and which of them is applicable to the universe, is never mentioned. Brian Rotman, himself a mathematician, concludes that 'Piaget's characterization of mathematics and of its creation is limited by certain misconceptions' (op. cit., p. 131).

The remaining 'gap' in empiricism is introduced in the following way:

> Thirdly, as man acts upon and modifies reality, he obtains, by transforming his world, a deeper understanding than reproductions or copies of reality could ever provide. Furthermore, cognitive activity can be shown to have structural properties. (*The Gaps in Empiricism*, pp. 118—119)

This, of course, is a reaffirmation of the Piagetian viewpoint rather than an argument against empiricism. But, once again, the crucial point is that empiricists need not deny that man may act upon (and even modify) 'reality'; and many have regarded empiricist philosophy as quite compatible with the development of 'deeper understanding' of the physical world. The issue is not the methods of inquiry that are adopted, but the logical justification or status of the knowledge that is obtained. To drive this home, it is worth quoting from Bertrand Russell's account of the nature of the physical world (although the overlap with Quinton's message earlier will be apparent):

> . . . we do not, in fact, experience many things that we think we experience. This makes it necessary to ask . . . in what sense physics can be based upon experience, and *what must be the nature of its inferences if it is to make good its claim to be empirically grounded.* (Op. cit., p. 128, my emphasis.)

In so far, then, as in his theorizing he stresses interaction with the environment, and eschews *a priori* or innate structures or categories, Piaget—as Chomsky pointed out—approaches close to the empiricism he thinks he has effectively criticized. Piagetian cognitive structures are modified (or undergo accommodatory changes) as a result of their facing recalcitrant experience, and equilibrium will only be attained (if ever) when there are no more surprises coming from further experience: the effectiveness of a structure is judged, in other words, in experiential terms. All this reeks of empiricism. It seems that, in trying to psychologize or biologize Kant, Piaget has innocently wandered across the border into tough-minded territory.

THE RELEVANCE OF PSYCHOLOGY FOR EPISTEMOLOGY

In his attacks on empiricism, then, Piaget misrepresents certain issues by psychologizing them. Does the same criticism apply more generally: has he erred in coupling epistemology with genesis, psychology, and biology (a coupling he flaunts in his book titles)?

At first glance it may seem that Piaget is advancing an exciting thesis. In the opening pages of his *Psychology and Epistemology* (pp. 7—8) he appears to hold a conception of epistemology that would be endorsed, not only by Quinton and Russell, but also by Popper, Reichenbach and many others:

> Epistemology is the theory of valid knowledge, and even if this knowledge is never in a state and always forms a process, this process is essentially the passage of a lesser to a greater validity.

He then goes on to make the bold assertion that psychology can make a contribution to epistemology thus conceived.

Several contemporary philosophers, who are well aware of the distinction between the genesis and the justification of beliefs and knowledge-claims, seem to have been favourably impressed by this Piagetian epistemological programme. As early as 1953 Wolfe Mays read an enthusiastic paper on precisely these issues to the Aristotelian Society (op. cit., pp. 49—76); and more recently Susan Haack has attempted to evaluate the arguments, pro and con, concerning the relevance of psychology to epistemology, and she comes down in support of Piaget's stance (as opposed to Popper's, which she takes as representative of the view that there is a well-nigh unbridgeable gulf between the two disciplines):

> But Piaget, unlike Popper, seems willing to include the historical, sociological and psychological questions which arise in the study of the growth of knowledge, as part of epistemology. The use of such locutions as 'developmental epistemology' and 'scientific epistemology' signals a generous view of the scope of epistemology . . . Piaget is committed to a thesis which Popper strenuously denies, viz. that psychological data can be relevant to questions of the validity of theories. (Op. cit., p. 175)

Unfortunately, a closer reading of Piaget's writings raises serious problems about his position. The last passage quoted from Piaget, which Haack also cites, is one of the few where he uses the term 'validity'. The examples he gives to flesh out this general statement—and certainly many of his other general discussions—indicate that he actually has something quite different in mind. In brief, he is concerned with the 'logical structure' of bodies of knowledge—with the architecture of cognitive structures—rather than with what Quinton, Popper, Reichenbach and others would call the validity or justification of the items of knowledge *qua* knowledge. This is clearly demonstrated in a passage, which occurs within two pages of the last quotation from Piaget, where he spells out what he takes to be involved in establishing the validity of 'norms' (by which, in this discussion, he means rules or principles such as conservation and transitivity):

> Next is the problem of the validity of these norms. The logician must now formalize structures suitable to these successive stages, properatory structures (without reversibility, transitivity, or conservations but with qualitative identities and oriented functions, likewise qualitative with corresponding but quite elementary, trivial MacLane type of 'categories') or operative structures (with 'group' or 'groupoid' characteristics). (*Psychology and Epistemology*, pp. 9—10)

For an alternative account of Piaget's position, consider the opening pages of *Genetic Epistemology*, where Piaget proceeds without using the term 'validity' at all. He starts by saying that genetic epistemology attempts to 'explain knowledge' on 'the basis of its history' and especially by the 'psychological origins of the notions and operations upon which it is based' (p. 1). Now, in this way one certainly can 'explain knowledge', in the sense of showing from whence it has come; but there is nothing so far in this account to show that the items under consideration are indeed knowledge—or, to put it in Dewey's terms, that the items have 'warranted assertibility'.

Piaget continues by pointing out that genetic epistemology, conceived in this way, 'runs into a major problem, namely, the traditional philosophical view of epistemology'. This looks promising, but it quickly becomes apparent that Piaget again is skirting around the issue of the validity or justifiability of the knowledge-claims:

> For many philosophers and epistemologists, *epistemology is the study of knowledge as it exists at the present moment; it is the analysis of knowledge for its own sake and within its own framework* without regard for its development. (*Genetic Epistemology*, pp. 1—2, my emphasis.)

The words that are emphasized here are amenable to interpretation in terms of analysis of validity of knowledge-claims, but Piaget does not clearly state that this is what he understands traditional epistemology to be concerned with. His words also can be interpreted as saying epistemology is concerned with analysis of the structural relations between the items of (so-called) knowledge. This second interpretation of Piaget's understanding of epistemological validity is made plausible by the preceding discussion in the present essay, which has highlighted Piaget's interest in the 'architecture' and dynamics of conceptual structures. Piaget's further discussion in *Genetic Epistemology*, and his examples here and also in *Psychology and Epistemology*, heavily tip the scales in this latter direction.

Piaget's answer to this 'major problem' his genetic epistemology faces at the hands of traditional philosophers is a triumph of obfuscation. He merely reasserts his original position, dressed up in different language so that it appears to be a rebuttal of the objection:

> Scientific knowledge is in perpetual evolution; it finds itself changed from one day to the next. As a result, we cannot say that on the one hand there is the history of knowledge, and on the other its current state today, as if its current state today were somehow definitive or even stable . . . Scientific thought is . . . a process of continual construction and reorganization. (Ibid., p. 2)

Thus, the structure of Piaget's argument early in *Genetic Epistemology* may be summarized as follows:

Piaget 1: Genetic epistemology considers genesis is relevant to understanding present knowledge.

Traditional objection: This is confused. Genesis is irrelevant to validity.

Piaget 2: It is not confused, because genesis is relevant to understanding how present knowledge evolved.

The examples Piaget uses to illustrate the genetic epistemological method do nothing to save the day. He again mentions Cantor's work in mathematics, Einsteinian and Newtonian physics, the structures developed by the Bourbaki group of mathematicians, time and speed in physics, the doctrine of object-permanence in the light of contemporary microphysics, and the notion of chance (ibid., pp. 3—8, and *Psychology and Epistemology*, pp. 7—21). In discussing these examples, he never shows how understanding genesis or psychological origin establishes the truth, validity, justifiability or warranted assertibility of these various knowledge-claims. In fact, it is far from clear what the examples do show; sometimes the point seems to be that the scientist or mathematician has made new use of primitive (or child-like) structures of thought, and sometimes Piaget seems concerned to explain why a piece of work overcame psychological barriers to its acceptance.

It is interesting to reflect upon what would have to be argued in order to establish that issues concerning genesis were relevant to whether or not knowledge-claims were valid or justifiable. It would need to be shown that there are some psychological or developmental processes, the unadulterated operation of which ensures that a true or valid or warrantedly assertable endpoint would be reached. Piaget is right in believing that the dominant tradition in epistemology denies that this can be shown, and recent writers have strongly reaffirmed this negative conclusion.* As indicated throughout the present essay, Piaget has not been able to make a breakthrough and he has often nimbly sidestepped the central issues.

CONCLUSION

Piaget's attempt to orient the foundations of epistemology towards biology and psychology—the attempt to toughen the tender-minded syndrome—must be rated as a

---

*For example, the work of Lakatos and Feyerabend on methodology in science suggests that no methods can be ruled out, or counted upon, in the search for scientific truth.

failure. And it is a little more than ironical to find the following words in his introduction to *Insights and Illusions of Philosophy* (p. xiii):

> . . . philosophy, as its name implies, is a 'wisdom', which man as a rational being finds essential for co-ordinating his different activities, but is not knowledge properly so-called, possessing safeguards and methods of verification characteristic of what is usually called 'knowledge'.

If this same insight had infused the rest of Piaget's work, a different conclusion might have been warranted for the present essay.

REFERENCES

Bryant, P. (1974) *Perception and Understanding in Young Children*. New York: Basic Books.

Chomsky, N. (1979) *Language and Responsibility*. New York: Pantheon Books.

Ennis, R. H. (1978) Conceptualization of children's logical competence: Piaget's propositional logic and an alternative proposal. In Siegel, L. S. and Brainerd, C. J. (Eds.) *Alternatives to Piaget*. New York: Academic Press.

Evans, R. I. (Ed.) (1973) *Jean Piaget: The Man and His Ideas*. New York: Dutton.

Feldman, C. and Toulmin, S. (1976) Logic and the theory of mind. *Nebraska Symposium on Motivation 1975: Conceptual Foundations of Psychology*. Lincoln: University of Nebraska Press.

Haack, S. (1975) The relevance of psychology to epistemology. *Metaphilosophy*, **6**, 175.

Hamlyn, D. (1978) *Experience and the Growth of Understanding*. London: Routledge and Kegan Paul.

Hempel, C. G. (1952) *Fundamentals of Concept Formation in Empirical Science*. Chicago: University of Chicago Press.

James, W. (1960) *Pragmatism; and Four Essays from The Meaning of Truth*. New York: Meridian.

James, W. (1971) *Essays in Radical Empiricism, and A Pluralistic Universe*. New York: Dutton. (A Pluralistic Universe, Lecture 1.)

Mays, W. (1953) The epistemology of Professor Piaget. *Proceedings of the Aristotelian Society*, **54**, 49-76.

Mischel, T. (Ed.) (1971) *Cognitive Development and Epistemology*. New York: Academic Press.

Mischel, T. (1976) Can genetic epistemology be divorced from epistemology? *Contemporary Psychology*, **21**, 164.

Phillips, D. C. (1976) *Holistic Thought in Social Science*. Stanford: Stanford University Press. London: MacMillan.

Phillips, D. C. (1978) The Piagetian child and the scientist: Problems of assimilation and accommodation. *Educational Theory*, **28**, Winter.

Phillips, D. C. and Kelly, M. E. (1975) Hierarchical theories of development in education and psychology. *Harvard Educational Review*, **45**.

Piaget, J. (1968) *Six Psychological Studies*. New York: Vintage Books. Tr. by Anita Tenzer.

Piaget, J. (1969) *Psychology of Intelligence*. New Jersey: Littlefield, Adams and Co.

Piaget, J. (1971) *Biology and Knowledge*. Chicago: University of Chicago Press.

Piaget, J. (1971) *Genetic Epistemology*. New York: W. W. Norton. Tr. by Eleanor Duckworth.

Piaget, J. (1971) *Insights and Illusions of Philosophy*. New York: Meridian. Tr. by Wolfe Mays.

Piaget, J. (1972) *Psychology and Epistemology*. New York: Viking Press. Tr. by Arnold Rosin.

Piaget, J. (1972) *The Child's Conception of Physical Causality*. New Jersey: Littlefield, Adams and Co.

Piaget, J. (1972) *The Principles of Genetic Epistemology*. London: Routledge and Kegan Paul. Tr. by Wolfe Mays.

Piaget, J. (1974) *The Child and Reality*. New York: Viking Press. Tr. by Arnold Rosin.

Piaget, J. (1977) *The Development of Thought*. New York: Viking Press. Tr. by Arnold Rosin.

Piaget, J. and Inhelder, B. (1972) The gaps in empiricism. In Koestler, A. and Smythie, J. R. (Eds.) *Beyond Reductionism: The Alfbach Symposium*. London: Hutchinson.

Rotman, B. (1977) *Jean Piaget: Psychologist of the Real*. Ithaca: Cornell University Press.

Quine, W. V. O. (1961) Two dogmas of empiricism. In his *From a Logical Point of View*. New York: Harper and Row.

Quinton, A. The foundations of knowledge. Reprinted in Chisholm, R. and Swartz, R. (Eds.) (1973) *Empirical Knowledge*. New Jersey: Prentice-Hall.

Russell, B. (1961) *An Outline of Philosophy*. New York: Meridian.

Chapter 3

Piaget's Sociological Theory

WOLFE MAYS

INTRODUCTION

Piaget has often been criticized for not taking sufficient notice of social factors in his account of the development of knowledge. This criticism, however, overlooks the sociological roots of Piaget's genetic epistemology. Although he does not give us a sociology of knowledge, he seems at times to come pretty close to it. The development of affective experience, logical, moral and legal thought are for him dependent on our relations with others: social co-operation plays an important role in the development of reason. Further, Piaget rejects Durkheim's holistic conception of society which imposes its social rules in the form of constraints upon the individual. Instead, he regards society as made up of individuals engaging in common activities: the technical actions of manufacture and use, economic actions of production and division of labour, moral and legal collaboration, actions of constraint and oppression, common research and mutual criticism.

Man's behaviour, Piaget contends, has both a psychological and a sociological aspect. From this point of view, he tells us, the positive fact is neither the individual nor the ensemble of individuals but relations between individuals: relations which continually modify our consciousness. The concept of a social system as a nexus of relationships which Piaget seems to espouse has, Dorothy Emmet (op. cit., p. 139) has pointed out, considerable similarities to an idealistic system of internal relations. Perhaps this is what his system of 'relativistic structuralism' has most affinities with.*

---

*It also resembles the view of the early Marx still under Hegel's influence. As Joseph O'Malley puts it, 'The being of society is not to be distinguished from the being of its members: nor is the essence of man in its actuality to be distinguished from the ensemble of social relationships of which he is focus and subject . . . In his individual existence he embodies his society'. (*Karl Marx: Critique of Hegel's Philosophy of Right*, p. xliv. Cambridge: Cambridge University Press (1970))

Piaget specifies the social relation which the self has to others, in terms of the notion of inter-individual exchange. This notion is not as novel as it sounds. It covers most forms of everyday behaviour—the way we exchange the time of the day with our neighbours, affection with our loved ones and friends, ideas and information with our professional colleagues, as well as the exchange of goods in the market place.

George Simmel, who was one of the first to explicate the social exchange theory of behaviour, pointed out that most relationships between men can be considered under this category. 'This is true of every conversation, of every love (even unrequited unfavorably), every game, every act of looking one another over . . . The ordinary vicissitudes of daily life produce a continuous alternation of profit and loss' (op. cit., pp. 43—44). Simmel brings out the element of reciprocity involved in social exchange when he remarks, 'All contacts among men rest on the schema of giving and returning the equivalence' (quoted in Blau, 1964, p. 1). But, he goes on, when such an equivalence cannot be legally enforced, gratitude enters in. Thus the actions between men, whether engendered by love, greed or gain, somehow live on in the sociological situation they have produced. In other words, after the exchange has taken place something remains in the minds of men—a feeling of gratitude, an obligation which leads us to return the equivalent of what we have received.

Peter M. Blau has more recently elaborated a somewhat similar theory of social exchange. In it he notes the way in which reciprocity is related to obligation. 'An individual', he tells us, 'who supplies rewarding services to another obligates him. To discharge this obligation the second must furnish benefits to the first in turn' (1964, p. 89). He continues, 'Only social exchange tends to engender feelings of personal obligation, gratitude, and trust; purely economic exchange as such does not' (ibid., p. 94). Blau's account of social exchange has, however, a somewhat utilitarian ring about it. Thus he speaks of benefits and the need to repay them by the person who has had a service rendered to him.

Despite Blau's attempt to distinguish social from economic exchange, the distinction he draws between them is more apparent than real. This comes out when he quotes with approval Homans' definition of social exchange, 'as an exchange of activity, tangible or intangible, and more or less rewarding or costly between at least two persons'.* Piaget takes up a similar position. He tells us, 'Exchange values comprise by definition all that which can give rise to an exchange, from objects used in our practical activities to ideas and representations involved in an intellectual exchange, as well as inter-individual affective values' (1965, p. 33).

In social exchange between individuals, feelings of obligation, gratitude and trust then play an important role. But in the case of economic exchange, where goods and services are exchanged for money, no such feelings of gratitude remain after the transaction has been completed, since the debts are then, as it were, cancelled out. In social exchange, on the other hand, where the items exchanged may be intangible ones, for example, ideas, promises or oaths of fidelity, the feeling of obligation engendered is assumed to be approximately equal in strength to the service rendered.

Piaget's first and most comprehensive paper on this topic, '*Essai sur la théorie des valeurs qualitatives en sociologie statique ('synchronique')*', (republished in 1965, op. cit., pp. 100—142) antedates both Blau's and Homans' social exchange theories, at least as far as publication is concerned. We know that Piaget lectured on sociology for

---

*George C. Homans, *Social Behavior: Its Elementary Forms*, p. 13. Homans points out that even the most commonplace behaviour can be taken as illustrating the principle of exchange, as when, for example, we say, ' "I found so-and-so rewarding"; or "I got a good deal out of him"; or, even "Talking with him took a good deal out of me".' (George C. Homans, *Sentiments and Activities*, p. 279.) It will be seen that these examples taken from everyday life to illustrate the process of social exchange, imply something like the economics of energy transfer.

many years, and that he was acquainted with the work of Marcel Mauss if not of Simmel. He certainly mentions Mauss's book *Le Don* which is concerned with the exchange of gifts in simpler societies. A central feature of Piaget's account is his positing of social exchange values which have a qualitative character as opposed to the quantitative nature of economic exchange.

Piaget illustrates what he means by a qualitative exchange value, by giving the following examples: the 'success' of a scientist, politician or apostle of some cause, the 'reputation' he has made for himself, the 'appreciation' the public has of his work or writings (ibid., p. 101). It thus covers our evaluations of others, which are based on the services they have rendered or can render us. Piaget argues that however important economic exchange values may be, and which may be quantified in monetary terms, they only form a fraction of the vast circulation of every kind of value which constitutes our social life, considered at a given moment of history.

The first part of Piaget's paper is largely taken up with the way in which in inter-individual exchange feelings for the other are formed. We are concerned here with the benefits and losses in the shape of satisfactions (positive and negative) engendered by the exchange. Piaget, however, also notes that in part these feelings are altruistic ones which lead not to enrichments or gains but to sacrifices—to gifts. One can, he tells us, find such spontaneous altruistic feelings in the very young child. Not all forms of social exchange can then be classified as profit and loss enterprises. This is the whole point of the second part of Piaget's paper when he discusses normative exchange where moral and legal norms enter in.

Piaget takes it as an elementary fact that in every society there exists a number of scales of value (ibid., p. 102). By a scale of values he means a comparison or ordering of our previously obtained satisfactions. Thus we might grade apples in accordance with their taste, for example, Cox's Orange Pippins as having a nuttier flavour than Worcester Permains. On a more aesthetic level, we might evaluate a Beethoven symphony as being more profound than one by Mendelssohn. We deal here with two different kinds of value scales. In one case, we are concerned with the comparison of pleasurable sensations, in the other, with aesthetic experiences. These values, Piaget tells us, originate from diverse sources, interests and individual tastes, fashion and prestige, and from moral and legal rules. They also include values corresponding to the needs of security, individual liberty and mutual confidence, without which no society is viable. We can, Piaget goes on, analyse these values at a determinate moment just as in economics we can reason about the average price of a commodity at a determinate time (ibid., p. 102).

THE INTER-INDIVIDUAL EXCHANGE OF VALUES

To simplify matters Piaget starts with an exchange between two individuals *A* and *B*, in which each partner evaluates and appreciates the actions of the other in terms of his own personal scale of values: they are useful to him, harmful or indifferent. Each such action will tend to give rise to a return action on the part of the individual. This may be either a material action (actual value), such as the transfer of objects in exchange for a service rendered, or what he terms a potential action (or value), for example, the gratitude one has for an earlier service, which can show itself as a return service at a later date (ibid., p. 104). This, Piaget points out, can already be seen in the behaviour of the very young child, as a spontaneous tendency to reciprocate—in the exchange of gestures, smiles, mimicry and imitation. Baldwin, he remarks, in his account of the way the child develops an understanding of the self and the other, is obviously largely concerned with this elementary fact of reciprocity.

Piaget now proceeds to give an axiomatization of the process of social exchange, which, he claims, enables him to describe the most varied social situations, for example, sympathy between individuals, as well as economic, moral, legal and logical behaviour. He finds a striking resemblance between qualitative exchange and certain economic laws. For example, the reputations of persons are, he tells us, like economic goods subject to the laws of supply and demand. Thus the same average literary ability will be valued differently in a small town where it enjoys a certain scarcity value than in a large one where it may go unnoticed (ibid., p. 113). Further, one can also find an equivalent to Gresham's law (that bad money drives out good money) during certain political and social crises, where new scales of value take the place of old ones, and where reputations are readily made and unmade (1973, p. 45).

Piaget symbolizes the actual and potential values occurring in the exchange process as follows (assuming that individuals A and B share a common scale of values):

rA = the action (or reaction) of A on B
sB = B's satisfaction engendered by A's action
tB = B's debt (obligation or gratitude) to A resulting from B's satisfaction
vA = B's valuation of A, resulting from B's obligation to A

Where the satisfaction engendered by A's action on B is equal to the effort, sacrifice of time, etc., which A has put into his action, we have the following equation:

Equation I* $$(rA = sB) + (sB = tB) + (tB = vA) = (vA = rA)$$

In other words, A's action, (rA), produces an equivalent satisfaction in B, (sB), and as a consequence B becomes obligated to A, (tB), so that his evaluation, namely, his esteem for him (vA) is correspondingly increased.

The service A renders to B can, Piaget points out, be regarded as a sacrifice for A, as he gives up something he possesses, and a benefit for B, as he receives something he did not previously have. This process may be illustrated by a number of examples: (1) A, in lending a book to B, temporarily gives it up, while B enjoys it; (2) a politician who by supporting his constituents against an unpopular government measure runs a risk, although his constituents will benefit from his support; and (3) a scientist or novelist who sacrifices his time and energy to work from which others derive intellectual or aesthetic satisfaction.

On the other hand, if B is grateful to A because of the book he has lent him, then A knows that he can on some future occasion obtain a similar benefit from B. Similarly, a politician who has acquired prestige or a moral position in society knows that his reputation will be of value to him one day. Piaget points out that we express these facts in ordinary language when we speak of the moral (or social) credit of an individual or of a debt of gratitude.

In the above examples we deal with a situation where neither partner loses or gains as a result of the exchange. But other cases are possible. Thus (1) A's action may involve a loss, since he fails to satisfy B; (2) A's action may produce a greater satisfaction in B than is commensurate with the effort he has put into his action; (3) A's action may produce a loss for him, but this time because B does not feel obligated to repay the benefits he has previously obtained; (4) A's action may be overvalued by B, namely, given a greater merit than it actually deserves.

Études Sociologiques, p. 106. I have somewhat modified Piaget's symbolism.

THE UTILIZATION OF POTENTIAL VALUES

Piaget now considers what might be termed the other side of the exchange relationship: the way in which an individual, once having acquired a social credit (or value), can as the result of the gratitude (or obligation) others feel towards him realize this credit. He may do this by asking for services in return for those he rendered earlier: he can also use his authority and prestige to make others comply with his wishes. In the case where B recognizes his obligations to A, we get the following equation, which illustrates the way A realizes his social credit:

Equation II* $(vA = tB) + (tB = rB) + (rB = sA) = (sA = vA)$

In other words, (1) if B recognizes a debt or obligation equivalent to the credit possessed by A and (2) if he pays his debt (fulfils his obligation) in the form of some equivalent service, and (3) if this service satisfies A in an equivalent fashion then (4) A's satisfaction will be equivalent to his credit.

Equation II expresses the return by B of a service equal to the one he originally received from A. Thus, to quote one of Piaget's examples: A may have given B information about his scientific work and techniques and B reciprocates by giving A similar information about his own. But other cases are possible. Thus B may not acknowledge his debt to A, and fail to return a service, or if he does acknowledge it, the service he returns may be greater or less than the one originally given to him by A. It will be observed that Equations I and II taken together illustrate the notions of distributive justice and reciprocity.

Piaget tells us, that the laws of economic exchange can be deduced as a special case of social exchange if one quantifies the values concerned (1965, c.f. pp. 110—113). Thus we might exchange three hundredweight of wheat for two hectolitres of wine. But, he goes on to note, with the exception of the economic exchange of quantities of goods and of certain specific cases of social exchange, such as etiquette and ceremonial protocol, one never claims all one's due and one never pays all one's debts. The circulation of social values is thus, Piaget remarks, based on a vast social credit continually increasing and being dissipated, and which disappears only as the result of a social revolution or a radical change (ibid., p. 110).

Piaget now considers the question of sympathy,† conceiving it as a social exchange between several individuals where both (or more) individuals reciprocally benefit: where their action produces a greater benefit (or satisfaction) for each other than the actual effort they have put into it. As he puts it, all that one partner does satisfies (benefits) the other more than it costs him and reciprocally (ibid., p. 110). However, in order for sympathy to occur, the individuals must also share a common scale of values. And this, he states, is what one means when one says of two individuals that they

---

*Ibid., p. 109.

†Antipathy, on the other hand, Piaget remarks, may be regarded as a situation where the partners reciprocally devalue each other.

We may compare Piaget's account of sympathy with Homans' statement that 'The open secret of human exchange is to give the other man behavior that is more valuable to him than it is costly to you and get from him behavior that is more valuable to you than it is costly to him.' (George C. Homans, *Social Behavior: Its Elementary Forms*, p. 62.) It will be seen that Homans' statement of the 'open secret of human exchange' is identical with Piaget's account of sympathy between individuals. Piaget's axiomatization of sympathy in inter-individual exchange applies both to his account and Homans.

These equations are (1965, p. 114):

(1) $(rA < sB) + (sB = tB) + (tB = vA) = (rA < vA)$; and
(2) $(rB < sA) + (sA = tA) + (tA = vB) = (rB < vB)$.

understand each other, that they agree or have the same tastes. But, as we shall see, the introduction of the latter condition does make sympathy a more complex relation than might appear from his simple equations, where he interprets it in terms of the mutual self-interest of the partners in the exchange.

In Piaget's account of sympathy in terms of social exchange, self-interest then plays an important role. Although each partner gains through the exchange neither loses. It is doubtful whether this somewhat cool attitude is what one usually means by sympathy or fellow-feeling, where we warmly identify ourselves with others. Altruism is certainly a component in fellow-feeling. As Max Scheler remarks, 'It is precisely *in the act* of fellow-feeling that self-love, self-centred choice, solipsism and egoism are first wholly overcome' (op. cit., p. 98). Piaget's account of sympathy here differs from his earlier account in *The Moral Judgment of the Child*, where he straightforwardly relates it to altruistic behaviour. Thus, when referring to jealousy in young children, he tells us, 'On the other hand, one can observe in conjunction with imitation and the ensuing sympathy, altruistic reactions and a tendency to share, which are of equally early date' (p. 317). Piaget's account of sympathy here then resembles much more Scheler's, than the one given by him in his theory of exchange which is concerned with prudential self-interest.

Piaget's attempt to formalize sympathy in terms of his theory of social exchange only applies in the special case where the values are prudential ones, where each party is concerned with achieving his own self-interest in the best way he can. It thus resembles Nietzsche's account of justice in its most elementary form, as 'good will among parties of approximately equal power to come to terms with one another, to reach an understanding by means of a settlement' (op. cit., p. 70). He spells out the nature of this understanding as follows: 'Each satisfies the other inasmuch as each receives what he esteems more than the other does. One gives another what he wants, so that it becomes his, and in return one receives what one wants' (ibid., p. 168).

Where, however, the personal scale of values is such that A is willing to make sacrifices for B without thought of his own self-interest, we would have something closer to Scheler's fellow-feeling. Scheler points out that in true fellow-feeling there is no reference to the state of one's own feeling. In commiserating with B, the latter's state of feeling is located in B himself; it does not filter across into A, the commiserator. Thus we suffer with others without feeling their suffering, and savour their joy without needing to get into a joyful mood ourselves (op. cit., pp. 41—42). If there is an exchange here, it is certainly not one which involves a *quid pro quo*. If it did, it would degenerate into the kind of sympathy described in Piaget's equations. Although sympathy as fellow-feeling occurs on an affective rather than moral level, it already has some of the characteristics of a moral feeling, since in it one puts oneself at one's partner's point of view, and, as it were, feels with him. And this seems to be the sort of sympathetic behaviour Piaget is discussing in *The Moral Judgment of the Child* when he states, 'the child's behaviour towards persons shows signs from the first of those sympathetic tendencies and affective reactions in which one can easily see the raw material of all subsequent moral behaviour' (p. 405).

Piaget explicitly makes this point in his later writings when he discusses Janet's account of sympathy. Janet held the view that we sympathize with people who do not make excessive demands on our time and emotional energy, where there is, as it were, a balance of emotional energy between the partners. Piaget's comment is that although this is a fair description of many everyday situations, for example, when we select travel or table companions, we would not, however, marry a woman just because she was economical on our time and energy and because we did not find her wearing. Indeed, two people in love might find each other extremely exhausting! (1973, pp. 39—41.)

VALUES AND SOCIAL RELATIONS

In order to forestall possible objections to his attempt to axiomatize the process of social exchange, Piaget emphasizes that his equations do not represent quantities, but qualitative relationships. 'Each person', he tells us, 'can take account of whether his actions are evaluated more or less than they have cost him in effort, whether there is an equivalence between the results of his actions and the effort he has put into them.' However much, he continues, these subjective valuations are without an objective basis (psycho-physiological), they are essential facts concerning social behaviour. We can analyse them exactly as the economist studies the laws of exchange without asking, for example, if the price of a precious stone corresponds to a real psycho-physiological utility for the buyer who attributes to it a subjective utility (1965, pp. 108—109).

On this view we are directly aware of the charisma of a public personality, for example, a politician or a film star, just as we are directly aware of the colour of his hair or the shape of his head. But unlike the public personality's physical features, social values need not have anything objective corresponding to them, just as the exchange value of gold may have little connection with its physical properties. Piaget points out that a patent medicine with an illusory effect can have a real exchange value for the person whose sufferings are alleviated independently of its objective medical properties. Similarly, the practice of magic in an African tribe can have a real exchange value for it, just as scientific predictions have value for us: during an eclipse the beating of the tomtoms is assumed to have the effect of frightening away the monster devouring the sun (ibid., p. 117).

Piaget tells us that his conception of social value is identical with Pareto's notion of 'ophelimity' (ibid., p. 62). Pareto used this notion to designate the abstract quality of things which satisfy a need or a desire whether legitimate or not. 'Gold', remarks Pareto, 'had a certain ophelimity for the Caribbean Indians. It was doubtful if it was *useful* to them, and certainly—in that it aroused the cupidity of the Spaniards—it became very harmful to them' (op. cit., p. 99). There are things, he notes, which are ophelimous to one man only, and others which are ophelimous for almost all men. In the last case ophelimity comes close to being an objective quality. For Pareto ophelimity applies not only to economic goods, but also to our activities. Thus, he tells us, 'The art of divination was ophelimous to a high degree for the armies in Ancient Greece; it was still ophelimous for Wallenstein; it is no longer so for armies today' (ibid., p. 100).

For Piaget, then, we evaluate persons and things much in the same way as we do commodities: wheat, wine or precious stones. Just as the price of a commodity arrived at in the market has such a quasi-objective character, so have the qualitative values which arise during the process of social exchange. Thus we can rate our politicians according to their success or popularity, and this will depend on the public appreciation of their services. Such preference ratings as used by public opinion polls can become an important instrument for the prediction of voting behaviour in an election.

What Piaget takes as experientially primitive is the ability on our part to compare and order intuitively such social values. Some examples (based on those given by Cohen and Nagel (op. cit., p. 289)) will illustrate further what Piaget has in mind here. Thus, we might advise people to 'Take Professor A's course, it's easier than Professor B's'; 'Travel by subway after 10 a.m., it's less crowded then'; 'Buy coffee X it's fresher than coffee Y'. In these cases we immediately grasp the difference between 'easy' and 'difficult', 'crowded' and 'uncrowded', 'fresh' and 'stale'. We have no difficulty in ordering our preferences in terms of the appropriate value-scale.

It has been argued against the social exchange theory as developed by Homans and

Blau, that for the valuation of one exchange item in terms of others to be effective, especially when they are intangible things such as feelings or ideas, would require a common measure of currency or unit of comparison. In terms of this currency, the values of different experiences '("getting a B$^+$ on an exam", "being kissed by one's sweetheart", "hearing a Beethoven quartet", "being served a cold beer")',* would need to be co-ordinated so that the value of one such activity can be related to the value of another. But, it is argued, such a common currency of value has not yet been identified. What, it is asked, would be the unit of comparison, the 'kiss', the 'quartet' or the 'cold beer'?

This sort of objection would not apply to Piaget's position. In any case, it is directed against a straw man, a crude hedonist concept of value on par with Bentham's statement 'pleasure being equal push-pin is as good as poetry'. In the first place, Piaget does not identify value with subjective utilities (or pleasures). Further, he would argue, one does not necessarily measure the social value of the exchange items in the way we measure quantities of economic goods exchanged against a common currency. Such a view assumes that in the field of qualitative values, there is only one scale or unit of measurement. But Piaget's point is that there is a whole variety of scales of value in our society, non-normative and normative; there are political, religious, literary and scientific scales. Indeed, his view presupposes something like a hierarchy of values, the normative ones being at a higher level than the non-normative ones.

In order that our value judgments may be coherent with each other, we would need to compare similar kinds of experience on self-identical scales. We would have to compare the pleasure obtained in kissing one's sweetheart with that obtained in kissing someone else's, the aesthetic enjoyment of listening to a Beethoven quartet with that obtained by listening to one by Mozart, and the pleasure of drinking cold beer with that of drinking warm beer. Only if we accept a crude form of utilitarianism, would we want to grade every value on the same hedonistic scale. Mill realized that some pleasures are higher than others, and that these are incomparable. Hence his doctrine 'better to be a man unsatisfied than a pig satisfied'.

Piaget also discusses collective or group values. He argues that they are derived from the valuations of the individuals constituting the social group. An example of such a collective value would be the prestige or reputation enjoyed by a politician. This Piaget regards as a composition of the fluctuating opinions of individuals: these would vary from appreciation to hostile criticism. Nevertheless, the overall consensus might be such that the politician would have a good measure of popularity and support. Piaget compares such fluctuations of social valuations to the fluctuations of economic values in a free-trade economy, where the price of the commodity results from a statistical equilibrium between supply and demand (1965, pp. 52—53). Thus in the sale of, say, wheat, the different bargains struck by individual buyers and sellers, and hence the price arrived at, would exhibit variations around a mean. This would stabilize itself in the form of a standard price for that commodity at a particular time.

Piaget's conception of society here resembles Pareto's view of it as a system of interacting forces (ibid., p. 42). These forces, Piaget points out, are, for Pareto, not constituted by norms or social concepts, but by residues or permanent instincts. Now, although Piaget is critical of Pareto's conception of residues as the motor of our behaviour, since he regards them as largely fictitious, he follows Pareto in describing social exchange on the synchronic level in terms of equilibrium structures. But Piaget replaces Pareto's mechanical model of society with a statistical one, in which the

---

*Deutsch, M. and Krauss, R. (1965) *Theories in Social Psychology*, pp. 114—115. New York: Basic Books. Quoted in Ekeh's *Social Exchange Theory: The Two Traditions*, p. 203.

multiplicity of fluctuating individual valuations takes on the character of collective values.

There is, however, this difference between Piaget's position and Pareto's. Whereas, for Pareto, ethical values are identified with a sort of meaningless chatter, whose function is to reinforce action,* for Piaget, moral and legal norms are meaningful concepts, and play a vital role in our social life. In order to explain the constitution of such norms, Piaget has recourse to the historical (diachronic) dimension, and here he follows Durkheim who saw a continuity between contemporary logical, moral, legal and religious concepts and those found in past and in more primitive societies. Piaget would, nevertheless, agree with Pareto that the sociogenesis of structures does not explain their function. Thus though our legal system has its roots in those of earlier societies, the validity of our legal rules is independent of their history. For example, we can show how the specific laws concerned with larceny are implied by the general legal principles relating to the preservation of private property in contemporary society.

MORAL NORMS AND EXCHANGE THEORY

For Piaget our behaviour towards others is not only actuated by feelings involving prudential self-interest: we are also obligated by moral values in our dealings with them. For example, to acknowledge after a certain lapse of time a service rendered assumes a moral attitude and this gives rise to a normative exchange, since we are obligated to return this service (ibid., pp. 121—131). In this connection Piaget analyses the simplest form of moral behaviour which is to be seen in the respect of the young child for his parents, which he terms unilateral respect. Thus if A is the parent and B the child, A's actions are valued more by B, than are those of B by A. The parent has a power and authority which the child has not got. He is felt as superior—as an object of affection and fear (i.e. respect).

This moral relationship, which is one of inequality, can be expressed formally as follows (ibid., p. 128):

$$(1) \qquad (rA < sB) + (sB = tB) + (tB = vA) = (rA < vA)$$
$$(2) \qquad (rB > sA) + (sA = tA) + (tA = vB) = (rB > vA)$$

(1) represents B's overevaluation of A insofar as he regards him as cleverer, wiser and stronger; and (2) A's underevaluation of B—A regards B as weaker and in need of both physical and moral protection.

We thus have an inequality or imbalance of moral attitudes. The child adopts the respected parent's scale of values, but the inverse is not true. The respect which the child has for the parent (i.e. vA) is translated by him into the form of the recognition of the parent's authority, and with this goes an obligation to conform to examples set him by his parents. Psychoanalysts have, Piaget points out, taken this up in their theory of the super-ego (ibid., p. 129). The super-ego, they would claim, encapsulates our early respect for our parents in the form of conscience.

The second form of respect described by Piaget, is that of mutual respect. It occurs at a later date in the child's development at adolescence, and is regarded, at least in our society, as a more mature form of moral behaviour. In this case the individuals A and B accept a common scale of values in which reciprocity plays a major role. Whereas unilateral respect arises from an inequality in the way two individuals value each other, mutual respect, on the other hand, he tells us, arises from an equivalence. Each partner

---

*Cf. *The Moral Judgment of the Child*, p. 110.

recognizes the other as his equal and treats him as an end rather than as a mere means. As opposed to the utilitarian goals of simple exchange, moral exchange has therefore a disinterested character (ibid., pp. 129—130).

But, Piaget asks, how can we explain the appearance of the normative dimension in social exchange? He finds the utilitarian attempt to explain the morality of conscience in terms of self-interest—the pleasure derived from the approval of others—unacceptable. A good man, he tells us, will prefer the dictates of his own conscience to that of public opinion. Nevertheless, he points out, the dictates of our conscience may yet be based on the moral views of our parents and friends, who have obligated us in the past (ibid., p. 126). Thus the introduction of norms which have an obligatory character in social exchange, is for Piaget only explainable as a function of their history. Piaget would, however, deny that he is committing the naturalist fallacy—trying to infer 'ought' from 'is' statements here. In keeping with his logical views, he would assert that the validity of moral norms can be considered quite independent of their genetic antecedents.

LEGAL NORMS AND EXCHANGE THEORY

Piaget next applies his exchange theory to the legal transactions between individuals or groups of individuals. He shows how both codified (State) law and uncodified law (that concerned with promises and contracts) can be expressed in terms of exchange theory. Legal exchange is of a more generalized nature than either spontaneous or moral exchange, since we are there concerned with legal persons and generalized rights and duties—with the legal relations which can exist between any individuals or groups of individuals (ibid., pp. 131—141 and pp. 172—202).

A good example of legal exchange may be seen in the law of contract, where individuals may exchange personal property, or promise to perform certain duties in return for money or services. For example, in the marriage ceremony, the nuptial pair promise to love, honour and obey each other. In such cases they are assumed to be responsible individuals who of their own free will enter into such a relationship. We have here a form of normative exchange behaviour where the conditions of the contract are binding on any such persons who enter into this relationship. Further, all social contract theories as to the origin of the State seem to have the character of an exchange. In Book II of the *Republic*, Glaucon stated it in its simplest form, in the form of men agreeing together not to injure one another in order to escape injury at the hands of their fellows.

Piaget, in his account, is largely concerned with the sociology of law, namely, with how society comes to construct rules considered by the social group as valid and obligatory.* In discussing the social origins of law he quotes the work of Pétrajitsky (a Polish sociologist of law) and that of Georges Gurvitsch: in their view legal rules are based on what might be termed legal emotions—legal convictions (ibid., p. 187). Piaget is himself sympathetic to this sort of approach. Prior to all codification of law, one cannot, he says, live with another person without recognizing his rights, and such recognition therefore constitutes an elementary legal feeling (ibid., p. 190). From the

---

*We cannot, Piaget says (*Études Sociologiques*, p. 201), draw a sharp distinction between morality and law in the so-called primitive societies which do not possess written laws. Thus if we consider such ritualized customs as potlatch, gift-giving, vengeance as well as rules relating to sex, it is difficult, he points out, to know whether they are of a legal or moral order. Even in our society, he goes on, although in practice it is easy to make this distinction, there is considerable difficulty formulating it in theory.

genetic point of view, he continues, the recognition of an authority is the condition of law, just as in morality respect precedes obligation (ibid., p. 191). Thus the child recognizes as valid the authority of adults before being obligated by precise duties.

Piaget sees a relationship between morality and law, and attempts to bring this out by means of an analysis of the feeling of respect in morality and the recognition of power and authority in law. However, as the latter kind of feeling is a more abstract and intellectualized one than the former, it cannot, he tells us, genetically precede it (ibid., p. 191). Further, as respect is the feeling of one person for another, it is essentially a personal feeling, whereas the recognition of an authority or a law is what Piaget calls a transpersonal feeling. In the latter case, we do not evaluate a person insofar as he is different from other persons, but only with respect to the function or service he performs within the social group. We can, Piaget says, obey a man because of his personal authority. In this case we deal with respect and obligation of a moral order. But if we obey his orders because he is the chief, we simply recognize a function, an obligation which differs from that occurring in morality (ibid., p. 192).

Piaget gives the following example of how the personal and the moral become differentiated from the transpersonal or legal. A particular child B respects his father A and will therefore obey him. The way in which this obedience shows itself will vary with the personalities of father and son. At a later date the son may no longer feel respect for his father and consequently moral obligation towards him. Nevertheless, he will recognize that his father has a legal right over him and he a duty towards him (ibid., pp. 194—195). Piaget therefore distinguishes between moral and legal relationships. In the former kind, the individuals A and B are not substitutable for any other person—we deal with persons *sui generis*. In the latter, we deal rather with legal persons, x and y: these can always be replaced by any father and son, who will have the same legal rights and duties to each other. Piaget therefore defines the notion of a transpersonal or legal relationship by the substitutable character of the terms, and the personal (moral) relationship by non-substitutability (ibid., pp. 195—196). In other words, anonymous or fictitious persons enter into the legal relationship, whereas only real persons enter into the moral relationship.

INDIVIDUALISTIC AND COLLECTIVISTIC THEORIES OF EXCHANGE

Piaget's sociological work can easily be related to some of his studies in the developmental field, since among other things he is concerned there with affective experience and logical, moral and legal thought and behaviour. What is not, however, immediately apparent is the relation of his social exchange theory to the various other kinds of exchange theory which have been developed by sociologists. As Piaget makes little reference to them, he would seem to have thought out his own theory largely by himself, although he would have been aware of Marcel Mauss's work in this field. It is therefore of interest to compare Piaget's theory with other such theories, especially as some of them were developed subsequently to his own, and without apparent reference to his work.

Two kinds of social exchange theory have been elaborated. These have been termed (1) the individualistic and (2) the collectivistic.* The former, largely associated with the names of Homans and Blau, is concerned with social exchange between pairs of individuals in face-to-face relations. As this theory emphasizes the psychological and

---

*For a full and very useful discussion of the differences between these two kinds of social exchange theory see Ekeh's *Social Exchange Theory: The Two Traditions*. I am much indebted to this book.

economic aspects of the social exchange process it has much in common with Piaget's own theory. For example, Blau considers both economic and social exchange as being part of a general phenomenon of exchange: economic exchange being regarded as a special case of this. Thus, he tells us, the expectation that benefits rendered will yield returns characterizes both economic and social transactions (1968, pp. 454—455, quoted in Ekeh, p. 172).

The collectivistic position covers those social exchange theories which accept Durkheim's view that society is an independent entity over and above its individual members, and that it imposes its rules in the form of constraints upon them. Marcel Mauss, who accepted Durkheim's position here, developed his theory of social exchange on the premise of the primacy of society over the individual. Starting from exchange in simpler societies, he argued that we do not find in such societies a simple exchange of goods among individuals. It is groups, or rather persons representing groups, who are involved in exchange and enter into agreements with each other. Individuals, when they take part in exchange transactions, do so as representatives of a family, clan or tribe, and not simply as individuals concerned with their own self-advantage (Ekeh, op. cit., c.f. p. 32).

The collectivistic position is to be seen at its clearest in the work of Levi-Strauss, who bases his ideas on some of Mauss's observations. Levi-Strauss was primarily concerned with marriage exchange in more primitive societies, with the way marriage partners are selected according to specific social rules. Thus, the selection of marriage partners or the exchange of gifts is not dependent on the desires of the individual, but has primarily a symbolic or cultural significance. In the case of the selection of marriage partners, choice may be limited by rules relating to exogamy and incest. In this way society increases the scarcity of marriageable women by excluding certain classes of women from eligibility.

Levi-Strauss is critical of the individualistic theory since by emphasizing self-interest, it tends to assimilate social exchange to economic exchange. A similar criticism was made by Malinowski, who could hardly have been described as a collectivist since he emphasized the psychological element in exchange. He argued that there is a fundamental human impulse to share, and a deep tendency to create social ties through the exchange of gifts: 'The giving of gifts seems to be a universal principle in all primitive societies' (op. cit., p. 175). And this, as we have seen, is something Piaget himself has observed in the altruistic behaviour of the young child. By implication Malinowski would seem to be saying that the concept of economic man who rationally balances gains and losses in terms of subjective utilities is a fiction of the economist.

The collectivistic view that social exchange is largely unrelated to economic exchange has, however, not gone unchallenged. The economic factor, it has been argued, is not absent in these examples of exchange which are said to have a symbolic or cultural value of which the giving of gifts is one. The utilitarian character of such gift-giving is, it is argued, masked by the time-factor—the delay in repaying the gift. Blau points out (1964, p. 99) that the custom of gift-giving at Christmas prevents us from reciprocating for an unexpected Christmas present until a year later, or until another suitable occasion arises. What custom seems to do in this case, is to regulate the time-interval during which an exchange can take place, without destroying its utilitarian character.

Sartre in his *Critique* makes a similar point: he quotes Levi-Strauss's attempt to show that potlatch is supra-economic in character. Levi-Strauss argues that, 'The best proof . . . is that . . . greater prestige results from the destruction of wealth than from its distribution, because however liberal it may be, distribution always requires a similar return' (p. 106). To this Sartre replies, 'in its destructive form (as seen in potlatch) the gift is not so much an elementary form of exchange as a mortgage of *the one* for *the other*, the period of time which separates the two ceremonies . . . masks their reversibility' (ibid., pp. 106—107). In other words, the first donor issues a challenge to the second to beat his performance, to sacrifice more of his goods, if he can, and so achieve greater prestige in the eyes of the tribe. Piaget seems to take up a similar position when he considers potlatch to be an exchange where the return is prestige rather than material wealth.

These practices are not confined to the Indians of North West America, but are to be found in contemporary society. The whole function of conspicuous consumption, 'keeping up with the Jones', would seem to be potlatch on a more genteel scale. It is clear that conspicuous consumption in which the competitive element plays an important role, has an economic as well as a cultural significance. Without the stimulus of mass advertising on the television and in the press, many industries producing luxury goods would fall on hard times. It has also been pointed out by Blau that the giving of alms to the poor, gifts to children and philanthropy in general, such as the endowment of Oxbridge colleges, has often a similar significance.

Piaget, who draws a sharper distinction than either Sartre or Blau between self-interested and moral behaviour, notes how the latter can become identified with the former. He points out that moral value is often popularly conceived as something like an economic exchange value. Thus we have been exhorted to perform good deeds now, for which the reward will come, if not in this world, then in the next. This kind of moral thinking, Piaget remarks, also assumes that the merit of such actions increases with the delay in their recompense. And this, he continues, reminds us of the economic concept of interest, conceived as the price of the difference between the actual value and the future value. The actual enjoyment constitutes a lesser satisfaction than the anticipated one (1965, p. 126). Piaget's point here is that in this type of moral thinking there is an economic component and in that sense it is a 'demoralization of morality'.

THE NOTIONS OF DISTRIBUTIVE JUSTICE AND EQUALITY

A fundamental assumption underlying Piaget's whole theory of social exchange, is that equality between individuals is a basic value in society, and that a balanced exchange is better and more durable than one which is unbalanced and unstable. Piaget assumes that social co-operation is an important factor in the development of the norms of equality and reciprocity, which are presupposed by the equalitarian theory of justice.

This position is developed in *The Moral Judgment of the Child*, where he argues that co-operation between equals constitutes the most deep-lying social phenomenon which has the surest psychological foundations. Now although Piaget believes that 'the idea of equality or of distributive justice possesses individual or biological roots', he points out that 'for true equality and a genuine desire for reciprocity, there must be born of the actions or reactions of individuals upon each other the consciousness of a necessary equilibrium binding upon and limiting both "alter" and "ego" ' (p. 317). Thus Piaget connects the notion of social equilibrium with the establishment of equality between partners as a result of their co-operation. Further, he assumes that this relation has its roots in a basic social experience—the awareness of a spontaneous tendency towards reciprocity.

Accepting as Piaget does the view that distributive justice has socio-psychological roots, he refuses to believe that it can be founded on any *a priori* theory of natural law. In this connection, he notes that most sociologists would agree that in each human society there exists a belief in justice higher than positive law. This belief, he continues, is not the expression of a factor prior to social evolution (i.e. due to natural law) but arises from the laws of equilibrium immanent in society. Piaget further elaborates on this theme when he says that whatever the rules of positive law holding in a given society, there is a permanent tendency in society towards greater equality, greater reciprocity and greater justice, because these are the forms of a better equilibrium (1965, p. 176).

Piaget identifies what he terms 'the aspiration for justice intrinsic to all human societies' with this tendency to achieve a better state of social equilibrium. In doing this, he would seem to be identifying the notion of equilibrium with a more harmonious, better balanced state of affairs; one in which, presumably, all individuals in that society have equal rights and duties. Despite the tautological flavour of the above argument, Piaget assumes that political and social equality, as it occurs in a democracy, is a better state of affairs morally than one of inequality (or dis-equilibrium). His position here is close to the early Greek view that the notion of harmony and proportionality applied indifferently as a physical and as an ethical principle. Euripedes epitomized this view as follows (c.f. George Sabine, op. cit., pp. 25—26):

> Equality, which knitteth friends to friends,
> Cities to cities, allies unto allies.
> Man's law of nature is equality.

However, there is this difference: Piaget takes the notion of equilibrium or equality as a limit concept towards which we strive socially, rather than as did the Greeks in the case of harmony as an *a priori* principle applying indifferently to the physical and moral realms.

Piaget's belief in the social origin of the concept of justice comes out in his statement that 'two or three individuals having always lived isolated on a desert island would necessarily arrive at the notion of justice without implying that they had it in advance (1965, p. 176). This view is in keeping with his assertion that human nature is socialized nature and that the sort of human nature attributed by Rousseau to his noble savage, endowed with moral virtues and rationality, is a pure fiction. The primitive roots of justice are for Piaget to be seen in the social sentiment of reciprocity in the child. Thus, he tells us, the sense of justice develops from 'the mutual respect and solidarity which holds among children themselves' (1932, p. 196).

The trouble, however, with Piaget's desert island example, is that if he was dealing with Robinson Crusoe and his Man Friday, the relation between them would be more like the Hegel Master/Slave relation—one of basic inequality. And such a relation would, as in Plato's *Republic*, be considered to be a perfectly just one, since both Robinson Crusoe and Man Friday perform duties appropriate to their proper station. Piaget could, of course, still argue that whatever the factual relationship was between them, the ideal relationship which they should aim at should be one of equality.

Piaget assumes that his basic equivalence relations, Equations I and II (which he equates with the achievement of social equilibrium), should be the ideal aimed at in the process of social exchange, whether it be non-normative or normative.* We have already noted that there can be inequalities or disequilibria in such an exchange. For example, when describing the intellectual exchange of ideas (or propositions) between partners in a discussion, he differentiates between what he terms a true equilibrium and

---

*Piaget regards the ideological norm of equality as something we should aim at in our moral education of children. Thus, he tells us, 'The modern idea is co-operation—dignity of the individual and respect for general opinion as elaborated in free discussion' (*The Moral Judgment of the Child*, p. 372). This, he argues, will give rise to the spirit of citizenship and humanity which is a feature of democratic societies. Piaget then believes that a democracy is morally a better society than say a meritocracy, which may be more efficient but where individuals might not be treated as ends in themselves.

a false one. In the former, the acceptance of a proposition (or argument) as true, results from the willingness of the discussants to co-operate—to come to an intellectual agreement. In the latter, the proposition or argument is accepted as true by one of the discussants, solely on the authority of the other, which is what is meant by indoctrination. There is, therefore, a basic inequality in the intellectual exchange relations. Piaget takes such a situation as being morally inferior to that in which the partners accept the truth of a statement as a result of an agreement arrived at by rational argument (1965, pp. 145—171).

However, not all accounts of distributive justice have been egalitarian. One has only to think of Orwell's slogan, 'All animals are equal but some are more equal than others'. For Plato, as we have seen, a just society was one in which inequality prevailed, where a person did the job he was best fitted for: the guardians governing, the soldiers defending, the workers working. In other words, each fulfilled the social role he was born into. Justice for Plato was giving every man his due. The notion of equal rights as we know it today (apart from women's rights) does not seem to have a place in Plato's *Republic*.

In the system of free competition, as it occurs in modern capitalist society, the individual's services become economic exchange items subject to the laws of supply and demand. Gouldner points out that the middle-class standard of utility implies that rewards should be proportional to the ability and effort one puts into one's personal work. It thus substitutes for the aristocratic ideal of rewarding an individual according to his social status, the bourgeois ideal of rewarding him according to his social usefulness (op. cit., pp. 62—63). Piaget's concept of distributive justice would seem to resemble that of the bourgeois ideal. He does tend to base the notion of equality, at least when dealing with spontaneous exchange between individuals, on the 'maximization of utilities'. In Piaget's view stable societies, as far as their non-normative exchange relations are concerned, are based on a balance of utilities, unstable ones on an imbalance.

Piaget's Equations I and II then maximize the joint advantage of the partners engaged in the exchange, so that it ends at reciprocal benefits. He makes this point when he says that 'the equilibrium which our Equations I and II formulate coincide in principle with the social equilibrium according to Pareto, since after the latter, the resultants X, Y, etc., of residues A, B, C, represent the "maximum of utility for society" when one chooses as a system of reference the "goals" (i.e. scales of values) of any individual *a* whatsoever' (1965, p. 116). The resultants, X, Y, etc., or social values, arise, however, for Piaget, from the process of exchange itself and not, as is the case for Pareto, from instincts or residues. The social equilibrium thus arrived at would exhibit Pareto's 'optimum welfare function': it would maximize the benefits of any individual *a* whatsoever in society. And this is another way of saying that everyone in that society would be better off and none poorer as a result of the exchange.

Nietzsche, in discussing the origin of justice, attempted to connect the concept of justice with something like an 'optimum welfare function', although he tended to restrict its functioning to an élite. He argued that the most primitive personal relationship is that between buyer and seller, creditor and debtor. From this, he goes on, originates the feeling of guilt, of personal obligation which precedes social groupings as such (op. cit., p. 70). The moral concern for justice and fairness, he argues, develops on such an elementary level among persons of equal power concerned to come to terms with one another. Justice has then the character of a trade and is derived from a prudent concern for self-preservation (ibid., p. 168).

Although Nietzsche's position here, as we have already seen, has much in common with Piaget's account of sympathy in his theory of social exchange, it is nevertheless opposed to Piaget's view that the normative concept of justice is genetically related to the altruistic elements in human nature. Piaget himself would regard such elements as being more primitive than the transaction of buying and selling. The whole notion of a fair economic deal already presupposes something like an intuitive sense of justice. Piaget's views on this matter tend to get obscured in his account of the utilitarian feelings occurring in individuals during spontaneous social exchange. Nevertheless, it is clear that he believes that the sense of justice is rooted in our altruistic emotions rather than in those of self-interest: in the disinterested approach of seeing others as ends in themselves—as equals. Piaget recognizes that not all values in society are utilities: there is a whole range of normative ones of which the injunction 'love thy neighbour like thyself' is one. Although the notion of reciprocity in the social exchange equations is conceived as a balance of gains and losses, reciprocity cannot endure beyond the initial transaction without the intervention of moral norms, and such norms are based on our early altruistic behaviour.

NORMATIVE RECIPROCITY AND SOCIAL ROLES

Piaget, in his account of social exchange, emphasizes face-to-face relationships of ego and alter, and then extends it to the relations existing between individuals and groups. But, as we have seen, in such exchanges there is no guarantee that the values will endure—people forget or are ungrateful—so that reciprocity may not hold. On the other hand, any action which has a norm or obligation behind it, leads to a new kind of relationship, one in which norms and hence disinterested attitudes motivate the individuals engaged in the exchange. And this can best be seen in the relationship of mutual respect, where the norms of equality and justice are exemplified in their most developed form.

So as to deal with institutionalized social behaviour where legal norms enter in, Piaget makes use of the notion of transpersonal relations, which are concerned, among other things, with the social function of persons within the group in which they live. In such functional relationships only an aspect of the real person is taken into account: we deal with legal or abstract persons. In the moral relationship, on the other hand, we are, according to Piaget, essentially concerned with unique individuals considered as ends in themselves.

Sartre has brought out the difference between the individual as a real existential individual and the social more general roles which he may play. He notes the stereo-typed thing-like character of social role-playing in his well-known remark, 'There is the dance of the grocer, of the tailor, of the auctioneer, by which they endeavour to persuade their clientèle, that they are nothing but a grocer, an auctioneer, a tailor' (1957, p. 59). The transition from the real person to his playing an idealized social role as a consequence of acquiring a social function or profession, is brought out perhaps unwittingly by the epitaph in a Scottish graveyard, 'Here lies the body of Tammas Jones, who was born a man and died a grocer'.*

Sartre's account of social roles does seem to be too restricted, as Dorothy Emmet notes (op. cit., p. 154), 'one man in his time plays many parts'.† In other words, he has

---

*Quoted by W. L. Sperry (1951) *The Ethical Basis of Medical Practice*. London: Cassells, p. 41. See Dorothy Emmet, *Rules, Roles and Relations*, p. 154.
†The quote is from Jacques' speech in *As You Like It*, Act II, sc. vii.

many functions: son, father, company-executive, churchwarden and golf-club member. In accordance with his different social functions which impinge on different aspects of his personality, he will have different social and legal obligations. In Piaget's view, when we refer to social institutions and even the State, we would seem to be referring to an assemblage of complex patterns of abstract idealized roles, underwritten, as it were, by legal norms.

An individual, according to Piaget, is thus involved in two sorts of exchange relations: the personal face-to-face relations occurring in spontaneous and moral exchange, and the transpersonal ones involved in the individual's relations to institutions and groups. Piaget notes the impersonalized character of such group behaviour, especially as it manifests itself in public opinion. For example, an individual may be constrained by public opinion to exhibit deference to a tribal chief or head of state. As he puts it, 'even if any individual whatsoever does not submit personally to the ascendency of the chief, he is obliged to fall in with the ensemble of transpersonal relationships which the other individuals of the group have to the chief . . . From whence the preponderance in the formation of a public opinion of such relations, in opposition to personal relations' (1965, p. 197).

It may be that the collectivistic rather than the individualistic form of exchange is more apparent in simpler societies than in modern ones, because the part played by the individual there is more circumscribed by social rules. And something similar might be said about the young child's behaviour which tends to be hedged around by restrictions, with little initiative left to himself. Piaget has shown that in the social behaviour of the young child as seen, for example, in such simple games as the playing of marbles, the rules of the game are handed down from one generation to another. He notes how children feel bound by such rules and harbour an almost mystical reverence for them.

In more primitive societies as a result of the pressure of social rules and taboos on the individual, and the need to conform to the tradition, there is, as Piaget notes, in contrast to modern society, little room for 'individualism and the functioning of personalities in the true sense'. This may perhaps be the reason why collectivistic theories usually take their examples of exchange from simpler societies, and are thus able to show that it is cultural or symbolic factors rather than economic ones which largely determine exchange transactions. On the other hand, the individualistic theory usually appeals to exchange as occurring in modern Western societies where the economic utilitarian motive is high.

Piaget, in his account of transpersonal relations, does not give a detailed discussion of such institutional relations. He is, however, fully aware, as we have seen, of the part played by rules in society even at an early age, as manifested in the games children play. In his sociological writings he is mainly concerned with the part played by legal rules, codified and uncodified, in our society. In modern society, as opposed to primitive societies, legal rules are usually clearly differentiated from moral ones. Hence, when we deal with legal exchange, we are not concerned with personal face-to-face relationships of ego and alter, but with legal persons and their relationships to each other and the group.

APPENDIX I

We have in this paper mainly dealt with Piaget's theory of exchange as it applies to affective and normative experience. Now, Piaget also regards the development of thought and rational argument as due to social factors, something often overlooked in discussions of his theory of concept formation. Piaget has told us that the need for proof in argument arises from 'the shock of our thought coming into contact with that of others, which produces doubt and the desire to prove'. This arises, he says, from the social need to share the thought of others and to communicate our own with success. He considers proof to be, therefore, the outcome of argument and logical reasoning as an argument which we have with ourselves and 'which reproduces internally the features of real argument' (1964, p. 204).

Piaget's belief that rational argument has its roots in an intellectual exchange between partners in a dialogue is reminiscent of Heidegger's emphasis on everyday discourse as being temporally prior to logical thought. Piaget goes on to assume that such rational argument is later internalized in the form of an argument with oneself. He is thus able to consider a dialogue between partners as a form of social exchange. In this case we deal with an intellectual exchange, and the exchange items are propositions whose truth or falsity is evaluated by us. From this point of view, Piaget tells us, an exchange of propositions is to be regarded as a system of valuations like any other (1965, *Les opérations logiques et la vie sociale*).

Piaget argues that in order for an intellectual exchange of ideas to become a normative exchange, namely, one which involves the application of logical rules to the exchange items, the discussants need to share a common scale of intellectual values. This is necessary if they are to express themselves in terms of a common idiom and in an unambiguous manner. The truth values in play must also remain constant throughout the discussion so that the discussants can refer back to them in case of dispute. This, he says, entails the constitution of two rules, which have the character of rules of communication or exchange. These are: (1) the principle of identity which maintains invariant the meaning of a proposition during the course of the discussion; and (2) the principle of contradiction which rules out the possibility of affirming and denying the proposition alternatively. It is the absence in the thought of the young child of such a rule which enables him to accept contradictory statements.

It must be noted that what Piaget is concerned with here is the way we use these rules in ordinary discussion, and not with their use in formal logical systems. His essential point is that a rational argument arises as a result of a dialogue between two partners and through their acceptance of common criteria in terms of which the propositions they communicate are judged to be true. When such an intellectual exchange or dialogue is formalized, Piaget claims that it takes the form of a system of *groupements* (i.e. a complex classificatory system). Its structure will therefore tend to coincide with the structures of the formal logic of propositions which is a purely ideal system, although not assuming it as its starting point.

APPENDIX II

One question we have not answered in this paper is: did Piaget's sociological interests influence his studies on cognitive development as they certainly did those on affectivity? We know that Piaget lectured on sociology over a lengthy period of time. His preparation for his sociology courses must have been undertaken at the same time as his studies on cognitive development. In his early writings one finds repeated references to the importance of the social factor in the development of thought and language. It therefore seems reasonable to assume that there was some cross-fertilization between his work on sociology and that in genetic psychology. For example, the notion of equilibrium seems to be used in his studies on cognitive development in a similar way to that in which it is used in his sociology.

Apart from an early paper on the relation between sociology and logic and the sociological discussions in *The Moral Judgment of the Child*, it was not until 1941 that his first paper on sociology appeared. In this paper he uses the notion of equilibrium in his exchange theory, to indicate a balance of the social values involved in the exchange cycle of 'action-satisfaction-obligation-return action'. He also relates such exchange transactions to the development of equality and the notion of distributive justice achieved through social co-operation.

Pareto in his sociology first used the notion of equilibrium in order to describe the functioning of a social system. Society was conceived by him as made up of social atoms, i.e. human individuals (on the model of particles in a mechanical system) interacting with each other. He used the notion of equilibrium to describe the manner in which regularities or laws arise in society, much in the same way as Kepler conceived his planetary laws as arising from the balancing of the forces exerted by the sun and planets acting on each other. Pareto believes that the mechanical model 'alone permits an understanding of the very complicated actions and reactions of social phenomena . . . and in this way affords us a precise conception of social and economic equilibrium (op. cit., pp. 31—32). The social scientist, he tells us, has to consider society as moving from one static equilibrium to another, in a continual series.

Piaget uses the notion of equilibrium in his exchange theory in a somewhat similar way to that in which it is used by Pareto, although his model is statistical rather than mechanical. Some such view is necessary if one conceives society under the form of a group of individuals interacting one with each other, rather than as a Durkheimian holistic system which imposes its laws on its individual members. In Piaget's view social regularities or laws have therefore the character of equilibrium structures arising as a result of such exchange transactions. In this sense his position may be described as a form of structuralism. He tries to show that the equilibrium structures, which can be axiomatically expressed in terms of the relations of equivalence (or non-equivalence), are applicable to the field of logical, moral and legal behaviour.

Further, when Piaget talks of stages in the child's cognitive development as equilibrium structures, he is looking at this development synchronically. From this point of view it consists of a series of equilibrium stages rather than a continuous process of development. And although Piaget describes his epistemology as a genetic one, this description can be misleading. He is not saying that the cognitive structures as they occur in the successive phases in the child's development are only to be described in historical or genetic terms. He would argue that on the synchronic level, such relations have also to satisfy certain formal criteria of validity.

REFERENCES

Blau, P. M. (1964) *Exchange and Power in Social Life*. New York and London: John Wiley.

Blau, P. M. (1968) Interaction: Social exchange. In Sills, D. L. (Ed.) *International Encyclopaedia of the Social Sciences*. Vol. 7. New York: Macmillan, Free Press.

Cohen, M. R. and Nagel, E. (1966) *An Introduction to Logic and Scientific Method*. London: Routledge and Kegan Paul.

Ekeh, P. P. (1974) *Social Exchange Theory: The Two Traditions*. London: Heinemann.

Emmet, D. (1966) *Rules, Roles and Relations*. London: Macmillan.

Gouldner, A. W. (1970) *The Coming Crisis of Western Sociology*. New York: Basic Books.

Homans, G. C. (1961) *Social Behavior: Its Elementary Forms*. New York: Harcourt Brace and World.

Homans, G. C. (1962) *Sentiments and Activities*. London: Routledge and Kegan Paul.

Malinowski, B. (1922) *Argonauts of the Western Pacific*. London: Routledge and Kegan Paul.

Nietzsche, F. (1969) *On the Geneology of Morals and Ecco Homo.* New York: Vintage Books. Tr. by Walter Kaufmann and R. D. Hollingdale.

O'Malley, J. (Ed.) (1970) *Karl Marx: Critique of Hegel's Philosophy of Right.* Cambridge: Cambridge University Press.

Pareto, V. (1966) *Sociological Writings.* London: Pall Mall Press. Tr. by Derick Mifin.

Piaget, J. (1932) *The Moral Judgment of the Child.* London: Routledge and Kegan Paul. Tr. by Marjorie Gabain.

Piaget, J. (1964) *Judgment and Reasoning in the Child.* New York: Littlefield, Adams and Co. Tr. by Marjorie Worden.

Piaget, J. (1965) *Études Sociologiques.* Geneva: Droz.

Piaget, J. (1973) *Main Trends in Interdisciplinary Research.* London: George Allen and Unwin.

Sabine, G. H. (1951) *A History of Political Theory.* London: Harrap.

Sartre, J. P. (1957) *Being and Nothingness.* London: Methuen. Tr. by Hazel Barnes.

Sartre, J. P. (1976) *Critique of Dialectical Reason.* London: N.L.B. Tr. by Alan Sheridan-Smith.

Scheler, M. (1954) *The Nature of Sympathy.* London: Routledge and Kegan Paul. Tr. by Peter Heath.

Simmel, G. (Ed.) (1971) *On Individuality and Social Forms: Selected Writings.* Chicago and London: University of Chicago Press.

Interchange

PHILLIPS REPLIES TO MAYS

To produce a sociological theory is, no doubt, an admirable thing in itself. It would be incredible academic narrowness not to rejoice that further advances had been made in this particular field. But when we are reminded that Piaget produced such a theory in years past, our pulses should quicken even more for there is hope that this work would be pertinent to certain of the important psychological and philosophical problems that have been identified in his better known (and, perhaps, more central) work.

Unfortunately such hopes are soon dashed: Professor Mays opens his discussion with the promising remark that 'Piaget has often been criticized for not taking sufficient notice of social factors in his account of the development of knowledge', but he returns to this broad theme only at the very end of his paper in Appendix II (and his discussion here primarily concerns the fact that the notion of equilibrium appears in both Piaget's psychological and sociological writings). In short, Professor Mays' paper does not exonerate Piaget from the charge that is cited, for he actually focuses on a much narrower issue—the development of *social* knowledge in the child.

It might be as well to lay out the key issues bluntly.

(1) Children acquire knowledge of social relationships, they acquire social skills, and they came to internalize social norms of various sorts (including moral codes). It would not be particularly surprising to find that these processes involve social interaction; furthermore, it is possible that an exchange theory could explain some of the phenomena and perhaps even a genetic account tracing the subsequent development of the child's primitive altruistic feelings could flesh out the story. Professor Mays' paper is primarily a favourably-oriented, non-critical exposition of Piaget's position on these matters; and the expositor is at some pains to tell us what Piaget *really* is getting at here, and to put Piaget's work in the context of other sociological writing (a thing which Piaget himself evidently has neglected to do).

(2) Those of us who criticize Piaget's failure to take sociological factors into account usually have something different in mind. We are focusing on general cognitive development, not the development of social knowledge. As indicated in my own contribution to the present volume, Piaget is faced with the problem of accounting for the regularities that, he claims, occur in the course of cognitive (and/or 'logical') development of *all* children. He denies complete genetic predetermination of cognitive structures, so apparently he is left with two possibilities— either certain 'biological' processes (assimilation, accommodation, equilibration, and so forth) are responsible, or social factors (such as socialization and education) play a central directing role. But the former are inadequate for the task, leaving the latter. And the fact is that Piaget does not discuss this alternative (in relation to cognitive development) in any detail, and neither does Professor Mays.

51

Enough of what Piaget and Professor Mays do *not* do. There are some puzzles about what *is* done. (The following remarks will not take up the issue of the adequacy of exchange theories in sociology, which would take us somewhat afield from assessing Piaget as a philosopher.)

The first puzzle concerns the status of many of Piaget's remarks, a puzzle which Professor Mays does not help the reader to resolve due to his reluctance to enter into critical assessment of his subject's writings. It seems that Piaget's sociological speculations are a mixture of empirical generalization (without it being clear what constitutes the relevant evidence), mixed with a liberal dose of the *a priori*, and topped with the attempt to formalize matters in quasi-mathematical terms. Thus, to cite as an example the set of issues which arise in the course of a few paragraphs in the second half of Professor Mays' paper:

(1) Is it a fact that all children have an altruistic sense? Is this an empirical claim, or is it some sort of necessary truth? What are the defining characteristics of altruism?

(2) What precisely is being claimed when it is said that, genetically, the sense of justice of the adult develops from (or 'is rooted in') the childhood altruistic elements? Are these latter necessary and sufficient conditions for the other? What is the evidence? Does the genetic account throw light upon the adult conception? (A critical reader might suspect the presence of the so-called genetic fallacy.) What would count as a refutation of such a claim?

(3) Would it, in principle, be possible to find a person who is altruistic but who has an entirely different sense of justice from the one discussed? And vice-versa?

Another important puzzle arises from a point that is tucked away in the first appendix. Professor Mays points out, with a straight face, that Piaget claims that the need for proof and rationality in argument arises from 'the shock of our thought coming into contact with that of others'. There is a lot that a philosopher could do with this, and it is puzzling that Professor Mays lets the opportunity pass. As the present discussion is only a commentary and not the occasion for a further essay, let it suffice to list again several of the relevant issues:

(1) Is Piaget making some logical or conceptual point, or is it merely an historical speculation? If the former, what is the actual argument (and is it valid)? If the latter, why is the point important, and on the basis of what evidence can it be assessed?

(2) There are many human intellectual pursuits where rationality (and/or proof) cannot be considered as mere appendages, added only after an unsuccessful bout of discussion with others. Rationality and proof are internal to (or constitutive of) some activities.

To sum up, then, Professor Mays gives us no reason to believe that Piaget's sociological theory successfully reinforces the other aspects of his life's work, nor does the discussion remove doubts as to Piaget's capabilities as a philosopher. Finally, the discussion does not even show that Piaget's work on sociology is acceptable *qua* sociology.

MAYS REPLIES TO PHILLIPS

I take it as a cardinal principle of interpretation that we ought, when dealing with the work of a thinker, important or otherwise, to try to understand him within his own framework of thought. We ought also to try to see whether his work is consistent rather than hunt for inconsistencies. The latter pursuit, a fashionable academic blood sport, as far as Piaget is concerned, will not necessarily lead to a better understanding of his work. From this stems my major criticism of Phillips' paper, namely, that being so convinced that Piaget's thought is confused he never attempts to understand it in terms of the latter's philosophical background. I will not discuss the numerous quotations taken from other Piagetian critics, which is a feature of Phillips' text. I will only say that not all the criticisms he catalogues will stand up to close examination. It seems to me that some are too simplistic, while others reflect radical misunderstandings of Piaget's position. Apart from the more general criticism I have already made of Phillips' approach, I will content myself with raising a number of more specific objections to the points he makes in his paper.

Phillips seems to believe that Piaget takes the world-view of the child to be a scaled-down version of that of the adult or scientist. He recognizes that the former is less sophisticated. 'But', he tells us, 'it will still be made up of concepts, rudimentary laws, theories and principles and some elementary mathematics and logic.' Although this may be the case for the older child, Piaget would argue that the very young child at least has not got a coherent theory of the world, that his thought is syncretic, that he is unable to carry out logical inferences and is relatively immune from contradiction. The very young child has not got another world-view than that of the adult. At this stage in his existence he has no world-view at all.

Phillips continues his criticism of what he takes to be the apparent invariant character of the structures of child thought which Piaget postulates. He notes that 'It seems reasonable to suppose that not all adults accommodate to anomalous experiences in the same way . . . In such cases our individual cognitive structures will change along different lines. If Piaget is right, however, there seems to be no such diversity among children'.

What is clear is that Phillips is talking about a different kind of cognitive structure than that posited by Piaget. Phillips is apparently referring to the way we adapt our methods and strategies, cognitive and otherwise, when we are faced with a new kind of problem. But this is a point Piaget has always made in his analysis of learning, as both the child and the adult solve problems by means of directed trial and error behaviour. The sort of cognitive structures Piaget refers to are much more general in character. For example, those of classification, seriation and simple inferences: structures which are involved in any sort of problem-solving.

In order to show further that such general structures are not as general as Piaget takes them to be, Phillips postulates three alternative world-views. He then correctly says that for models to have the same logical structure (i.e. be isomorphic) they need to have the same arrangement of elements. However, he continues, 'The elements of these three world-views would not be the same; there would be no isomorphism. And yet all these three world-views would account for previously established scientific knowledge and thus explain the new and challenging experience'.

But the notion of isomorphism does not depend on a similarity between elements. It is possible for there to be an isomorphism between any two systems, even though all the elements in each are different. This is the case with non-Euclidean geometries. Further, the Ptolemaic and Copernican systems, though radically different, are isomorphic with each other and explain the same phenomena. If in the three alternative world-views postulated by Phillips, some common laws of inference and some version of the law of non-contradiction did not apply, we would be unable to draw any inference at all— anything would imply anything else. Such a world would be 'a tale told by an idiot full of sound and fury signifying nothing'.

It needs to be made clear that Piaget does not believe that cognitive structures are found ready made in the child's mind. For Piaget there are no 'forms in the child's mind', at least not to start with. There is indeed no conscious self to contemplate such forms, as the self for Piaget only arises as the result of the child entering into social relations with others. Further, cognitive structures start off for Piaget as concrete reaction schemes and only take on an abstract intellectual character at a later date. When Piaget talks of topological or geometrical relations at this stage, he is largely concerned with the child's concrete handling of objects, with 'knowing how' rather than 'knowing that'. We might, of course, be able to read off such structures from the child's behaviour, just as we might be able to read off something like a syntax of movement from the galloping of a horse. But in neither case would we be dealing with 'forms in the mind'.

Following Rotman, Phillips argues that Piaget's developmental approach to knowledge involves him in a dilemma. He offers Piaget three possible escape routes, none of which Piaget seems to make use of. These are:

(1) He can acknowledge that individuals have different cognitive structures. We have seen Phillips' confusion on this point: between specific problem-solving techniques and the more basic classificatory and serial structures.

(2) Piaget could stress more than he does the importance of social processes in determining development. Piaget certainly takes account of social factors in his work, notwithstanding his critics.* The purpose of my paper included in this volume was to show precisely this. From his earliest work onwards Piaget has noted the influence of social factors on the development of reason and objective knowledge. He even claims that everyday practical logical thinking arises through the give and take of ordinary discourse with others.

(3) Piaget could fall back on a modernized form of Kantianism. In this context Phillips quotes Chomsky's question to Piaget, 'How is this knowledge constructed, and why *just this kind of* knowledge and not some other?' I might answer Chomsky by saying that for Piaget, apart from certain innate factors, this is largely due to the social and physical constraints of the world we live in. If we lived in a different sort of society, our moral values might be more authoritarian, our reasoning more paradoxical. As the inheritors of a twentieth century *Weltanschauung*, our material knowledge is different from that of Cro-Magnon man. But since certain basic social and physical environmental factors would be similar in both cases, some of the formal categories in terms of which we order the world and those in terms of which Cro-Magnon man did would probably be the same.

Further, it is doubtful whether Piaget can be said to biologize or psychologize Kant. As I have shown elsewhere, the influence of the Hegelianism of James Mark Baldwin, at least on the early Piaget, is probably greater than the alleged Kantian influence. For example, the self, for Piaget, is always a social self, and the development of knowledge also has a strong social component.†

Phillips is of the opinion that Piaget has little understanding of present-day empiricist trends among English-speaking philosophers. However, Piaget is not completely unaware of the analytic turn in philosophy. He relates an interesting discussion he had around 1926—1927 in Cambridge with G. E. Moore, arising from a lecture he gave there. Moore argued that as against the psychologist the philosopher is

---

*C.f. Mays, W. (1979).
†C.f. Mays, W. (1980).

solely concerned with true ideas. To which Piaget replied that 'the history of science is full of ideas which we judge today to be false: "How do you know, therefore, that your true ideas will not at a later date be judged to be inadequate?"' Moore's answer to this was, 'That's all the same to me, since my specific work is only concerned with the search for the true' (op. cit., p. 21). What this little dialogue brings out is the conceptual realism rather than the empiricism of Moore's position, a view shared I suspect by some other contemporary so-called empiricists. In any case, as Piaget was writing mainly for a French-speaking audience, he can hardly be blamed for not lavishly quoting Anglo-Saxon analytical philosophers or for that matter not writing in the style of Bertrand Russell.

Phillips, in referring to Piaget's experimental work on the analytic/synthetic question, remarks that Quine was making a conceptual point, and 'experimentally verifying it is as out of place as it would be if the proposition under consideration was that "all black objects are black".'

As I was responsible for suggesting to Piaget that we conduct the analytic/synthetic experiments, I ought to say what their objective was. Although most of us would agree that 'all black things are black' is a tautology, there has been a division of opinion among philosophers as to whether there is a sharp distinction between analytic and synthetic statements. Some have indeed argued that this distinction is merely a matter of convention and not based on any essential insight. It is of some interest to see whether this difference of opinion is also reflected in that touchstone of modern empiricism—ordinary discourse. I made the point (and here I imagine Piaget would agree) that this sort of investigation will not give us a logical justification of philosophical concepts. All that is claimed for it is that it may add another dimension to philosophical studies.* This work was suggested by Arne Naess's studies on the way the ordinary man uses such concepts as 'the true' and 'the certain' (op. cit.). I would have thought that an empiricist would have welcomed such an approach. Reichenbach, whose view of knowledge as a rational reconstruction Phillips presumably approves, argues that we must retain the notion of the descriptive task of epistemology by seeing that such reconstructions correspond to our actual thinking (op. cit., p. 6).

Consider Phillips' central criticism repeated in one form or another throughout his paper, that Piaget confuses genesis with validity. Piaget is, however, not at all concerned to show that genetic studies can establish the truth of normative statements. On the contrary, he has always drawn a clear distinction between the justification of logical, moral and legal norms, and the description of empirical facts. For Piaget, genesis and validity deal with two different approaches to the problem of knowledge— the diachronic and the synchronic. A genetic (diachronic) study of a particular concept, for example, that of time, would concern itself with tracing the development of this concept from its earliest appearance in the child to its later adult manifestations. A synchronic study of this concept or of a theory would among other things concern itself with its logical validity.

Piaget would argue that an account of the development of concepts in science and other fields of enquiry, needs to go hand in hand with a discussion of their validity. I doubt whether, for example, any physicist would wish to deny that the history of physics is completely irrelevant to our present knowledge of it. We can learn from both the insights and errors of past thinkers. And when we come to genetic studies of child thought this may enable us to see whether adult thought, has, for example, arisen as a consequence of social factors or whether it is largely due to innate dispositions. If we

---

*C.f. Mays, W. (1962).

equated philosophical relevance with formal validity without recourse to descriptive factors, we would not know whether our statements refer to actual, fictitious or absurd situations.

One of the difficulties Phillips has in understanding Piaget's position stems from a misunderstanding of how the term *épistémologie* is used in French philosophy. My guide here will be Lalande.

> This word designates the philosophy of the sciences, but in a more precise sense . . . it is essentially the critical study of principles, hypotheses and the results of the different sciences, with the object of determining their logical (non-psychological) origin . . . The English word 'epistemology' is very frequently used (contrary to its etymology) to designate what we call the 'theory of knowledge' . . . It seems to me that in distinguishing *épistémologie* from the theory of knowledge, it would be worth while enlarging the meaning of the former term, so as to include the psychology of the sciences, for the study of their actual development cannot without loss be divorced from their logical critique. (Lalande, op. cit., pp. 293—294)

What Lalande is saying here, and his view approximates to Piaget's, is that we ought not to divorce the study of the process of scientific discovery from its logical critique. This is something I assume Karl Popper would himself advocate. And I think that this sort of enquiry broadly corresponds to what Piaget means by the *épistémologie génétique*, namely, the logical critique of scientific concepts, principles and theories as seen against the background of their historic and genetic development. This leads me to my final remark: I would have thought that any critic of a French-speaking thinker would have tried to find out what the precise meanings of the terms he uses are in the original texts. It is sad that analytical critics of Piaget have not realized that it is necessary to do this. If they had, they might have seen that they were simply erecting Aunt Sallies in order to knock them down again.

REFERENCES

Lalande, A. (1962) *Vocabulaire Technique et Critique de la Philosophie*. Paris: PUF.

Mays, W. (1962) De-armchairisation. In Good, I. J. (Ed.) *The Scientist Speculates*. London: Heinemann.

Mays, W. (1979) Genetic epistemology and theories of adaptive behaviour. In Bolton, N. (Ed.) *Philosophical Problems in Psychology*. London: Methuen.

Mays, W. (1980) Affectivity and values in Piaget. In Modgil, S. and C. (Eds.) *Toward a Theory of Psychological Development*. Windsor: NFER.

Naess, A. (1953) *An Empirical Study of the Expressions 'True', 'Perfectly Certain' and 'Extremely Probable'*. Oslo: Kommisjon Hos Jacob Dybwad.

Piaget, J. (1971) *Insights and Illusions of Philosophy*. New York and Cleveland, Ohio: World Publishing Company.

Reichenbach, H. (1938) *Experience and Prediction*. Chicago: University of Chicago Press.

Chapter 4

The Garden Path to the Understanding of Cognitive Development: Has Piaget Led Us into the Poison Ivy?*

LINDA S. SIEGEL AND BARBARA HODKIN

The promise of understanding cognitive development has led psychologists to Piagetian theory and the voluminous, sometimes obscure, but always fascinating books and articles produced about the theory. In this chapter we will deal with the contributions of Piaget and his disciples to developmental psychology, and with the limitations of those contributions.

STAGES OF COGNITIVE DEVELOPMENT

Piaget and his co-workers have provided us with a broad theory of cognitive development. A basic tenet of this theory is that the development of human cognition is divided into a series of stages with increasingly more complex thought processes possible at each stage. This idea of stage is central to Piagetian theory. The major stages described are sensorimotor, pre-operational, concrete operational and formal operational.

But first, an historical digression. The concept of stages of cognitive development is used more extensively by Piaget than by other theorists, but the concept did not originate with Piaget. As Cairns and Ornstein (1979) have noted, the North American psychologist James Baldwin proposed a stage theory of development in 1906 when Piaget was 10 years old. Baldwin described three stages of cognitive development, 'prelogical, logical, and hyperlogical'. In the hyperlogical stage 'syllogistic forms come to have an independent or a prior force, and pure thought emerged—thought, that is, which thinks of anything or nothing'.

*We thank Jennifer Birrell for her dedicated and conscientious assistance. We also thank Shep, Rick, Laura, Jeffrey, Ann, Kristin and Bruna for their help.

Also, it is widely believed that Piaget introduced certain concepts in developmental psychology, for example, schema, assimilation, accommodation and circular reactions. Cairns and Ornstein noted that these ideas appear to have been developed by Baldwin who described them in 1894, two years before Piaget was born. The extent of Baldwin's influence on Piaget is unknown, and is a question we will leave to the historians.

Brainerd (1978b) has raised certain theoretical problems with the Piagetian position on stages of logical development. First of all, Piaget's stage concepts are largely descriptive rather than explanatory, because the conditions that explain or predict a child's behaviour in a particular stage are not known or specified. Without independent specification of the antecedent variables that lead to different stages, a definition of cognitive acquisition is not possible, and stages and stage transition are reduced to description. In addition, the universality of stage sequences is, at this point in time, a result of measurement procedures. There appears to be a sequence because tasks are such that 'lower level' skills are necessary components in 'higher level' tasks. For example, the understanding of number conservation requires that the child be able to construct a numerical correspondence. The sequence of concepts is a result of measurement operations, and is not necessarily characteristic of the process itself.

According to Brainerd, the concept of structures cannot be used as an independent criterion for stages. The concept of structure has been criticized in that it describes tasks and not behaviour (1974a, 1978b). Various tasks representing the same concept may be solved at different ages, because the structures may be operationally defined in many ways. We will show examples of this multiple definition throughout the chapter. These structures may appear to be present at different stages depending on the definition, so that structures cannot be used as criteria for stages.

A further problem with the Piagetian concept of stages is that the concept is sometimes not supported empirically. Results discrepant with the theoretical position are reported for the Piagetian stages of sensorimotor functions (Cornell, 1978), preoperational thought (Siegel, 1978), concrete operations (Brainerd, 1978a), and formal operations (Ennis, 1978).

The validity of the Piagetian concept of stages depends upon the validity of the procedures used to assess children's logical development. There are many methodological problems in the assessment of cognitive ability, and these problems bear on the issue of stages. We will show that the development of cognitive abilities appears to be a gradual process, dependent on stimulus and task variables, and that qualitatively different logical states, or stages, do not appear to be characteristic of children's thought processes.

METHODOLOGICAL PROBLEMS

The Piagetian theory of cognitive development, including the concept of stages, has provided us with an interesting and productive framework for research. However, there are many methodological problems in the study of cognitive development within a Piagetian framework. In this chapter, we will review some of these methodological problems with Piagetian theory and examine the alternatives that other investigators have proposed.

There are many methodological problems in assessing cognitive development with the traditional Piagetian tasks. In these tasks many variables are confounded, among them social factors, language, attention, memory and perceptual abilities. Investigators have not always been sufficiently appreciative of the fact that most cognitive tasks require abilities in addition to those they seek to measure. The multidimensional nature of the tasks makes performance difficult to interpret unless one attempts to control and study the other relevant factors.

SOCIAL PSYCHOLOGICAL CONTEXT EFFECTS

Studies of cognitive development are, typically, a conversational interaction between the child and experimenter. Children bring certain expectations to a situation, and experimenters do as well. Children's responses may be affected by the experimenter's behaviour in ways that have nothing to do with logical competence or incompetence. Direct demonstrations of the social psychology of the child—experimenter encounter are relatively rare, but there are some findings that lead us to believe that the social psychology of the cognitive development study is impossible to ignore.

From our own experience of testing young children, we have observed a number of difficulties. When a child is asked the same question several times, to assess the particular cognitive ability with different stimuli, the child may change the answer because he or she believes the adult is asking the question again because the first answer was wrong. Usually adults do not repeat a question when the answer is correct, but only when it is wrong. This response vacillation may be interpreted as a sign of unstable cognitive structures, but it may also reflect children's eagerness to provide the answers that they think the adult is seeking.

The effects of repeated questions are illustrated in the conservation task. In this task children may be shown, for example, two rows of five marbles each, equal in length, and asked whether or not the two rows have the same number. The experimenter, an obviously intelligent and competent adult, then transforms the array by making one row longer, and asks the child again whether the rows have the same number. Rose and Blank (1974) pointed out that asking the same question before and after the transformation suggests that the change made by the experimenter is important. From the child's perspective it is reasonable to assume that the situation has changed and, therefore, a new response is appropriate. To investigate this possibility, Rose and Blank tested children in the standard conservation task and in a task that omitted the initial equality question. In the alternate task, children simply saw a transformation and then made a conservation judgment. The children made significantly fewer errors in the latter condition, and thus showed more ability to conserve quantity when they were not confused by the experimenter repeating the question. Those children who received the one-question task first, did better on the subsequent standard conservation task than did the children who received the standard task initially.

It appears, then, that children's responses are influenced by the experimenter's behaviour and their interpretation of that behaviour. McGarrigle and Donaldson (1974/5) have provided an ingenious demonstration of this phenomenon. They argue that language is understood and interpreted in a particular context, often social. Natural language is not independent of context. The typical conservation situation may represent a dilemma for children, because the non-linguistic context and the logic of the adult's question appear to be in opposition. From an adult viewpoint, the behaviour of transforming the array is irrelevant to the logic of the repeated question. But children use non-linguistic cues to interpret language: the experimenter has changed the situation, so perhaps the child reasons that the experimenter is changing the question. As McGarrigle and Donaldson note, 'the non-linguistic behaviour is highly relevant for an utterance of a different type—one concerned with the length of the row rather than number. It could be that the experimenter's simple direct action of changing the length of the row leads the child to infer an intention on the experimenter's part to talk about what he/she has just been doing' (p. 343). In other words, the children may think that the experimenter has changed the referent from number to length. Of course, we do not know that children misinterpret the situation in this particular way, and we cannot ask them because young children's reflections on their thought are often non-existent and, at best, inaccurate (see Brainerd, 1973a, and Siegel, 1978, for evidence on this point).

McGarrigle and Donaldson devised a way to test this idea of misinterpretation by varying the agent who changes the array. In the standard condition the experimenter was the agent, and in a second condition a 'naughty' teddy bear 'accidently' transformed the rows. The children gave more correct responses in the 'accidental' condition than in the traditional task because, presumably, the social context did not mislead the children. The teddy bear had been introduced as mischievous, and so there was a ready explanation for the bear's behaviour. In the case of the experimenter in charge of the session, however, children were evidently disposed to evaluate his or her behaviour as being related to the experimental inquiry.

The socially based cognitions of adults, as well as those of children, can influence the assessment of logical development. Hunt (1975) reports a study in which several experimenters administered a conservation task to children aged two to four years. Some of the experimenters were led to expect that the children would be able to solve the task and others were told that the children would find it difficult. Significantly more correct responses were obtained from the children with experimenters who expected correct responses. Therefore, it appears that experimenter expectations affect experimenter—child interaction, which in turn affects logical assessment.

Another kind of social-psychological effect, seemingly related to conformity or co-operation, is reported by Rose (1973). She found that young children adopt an acquiescence response set, that is, they say 'yes' more than one would expect by chance. The children, aged three to six, were asked whether or not there were the same number of objects in rows that varied in several combinations of number, length and density. The correct answer to the equality question was 'yes' on half the trials, but the three- and four-year-olds answered 'yes' significantly more often than 'no'. This may reflect a general pattern of social interaction in which children are typically expected to say yes to adults.

Overall, we urge experimenters studying cognitive development to consider the child's interpretation of the experimental situation, which may differ considerably from that of the adult. The child's interpretation, however, is probably related in reasonable ways to the immediate social context and to the child's general social experience.

LANGUAGE AS A SOURCE OF DIFFICULTY

Piagetian theory holds that in early cognitive development language does not precede logic, and that, in fact, language is a symptom, or product, of logical growth (Inhelder and Piaget, 1964). Despite this position, one of the fundamental problems with Piagetian research in cognitive development is the amount of language comprehension and production that is required of children. There is ample evidence that young children have difficulty in understanding the language, for example, the relational terminology commonly used in tasks designed to assess cognitive development (see Siegel, 1978, for a discussion of evidence on this point). Children also have response, or production, difficulties that are based on language. Sometimes children are required not only to give the right judgment but to explain the logical basis for their judgment. When young children use rules to solve problems, they cannot always verbalize these rules. For example, three- and four-year-old children can learn to use a relational concept of 'more than' or 'same number', but they cannot justify their answers (Siegel, 1978). This observation is consistent with the Piagetian position on language and thought. In addition, Brainerd (1977b) has provided mathematical evidence that by using judgments as the only criterion, the error rates in classification of children's cognitive ability are lower than if correct explanations are also required.

Language problems in comprehension were illustrated by one seven-year-old who was shown an array of six red marbles and three green marbles, and asked the class-inclusion question, 'Are there more red ones or more marbles?' He knew the correct answer to the inclusion comparison, but thought the question 'so dumb that it must be a trick'. Linguistic difficulties in production were exhibited by a six-year-old who consistently made the correct inclusion judgment for eight different stimulus sets, but whose explanations of the judgments were not adequate. For example, with the set described above the child said there were more marbles and then explained, 'Cause there's six red ones and three green ones'.

When the questions asked are inappropriate, the children sometimes tell us indirectly that they do not understand. One of the ways they do this is to use a strategy that we have called the *recency strategy* (Siegel and Goldstein, 1969), in which the child selects the last alternative from a series. We hypothesize that a child uses this strategy if he or she either forgets the other alternative, or is confused by the language of the question and simply selects the alternative most recently heard. This phenomenon has been noted in young children in various logical tasks including conservation (Siegel and Goldstein, 1969), class inclusion (Kalil, Youssef and Lerner, 1974; Siegel et al, 1978; Hodkin, 1981) and moral judgments (Feldman et al, 1976). The fact that young children use recency strategy as much as 90 per cent of the time should provide us with one clue that there are problems with our assessment of cognitive development.

The theoretically postulated discrepancy between language and thought, and the empirically observed discrepancy between judgments and explanations, indicate that non-verbal investigation of cognitive development should be useful.

For example, Siegel (1978) found that young children could solve a non-verbal conservation task but not necessarily a verbal one. An ingenious non-verbal test for the conservation of liquid quantity has been used by Wheldall and Poborca (1979). They trained six- and seven-year-old children to press one button when shown two jars with equal amounts of water and to press another button when the jars contained unequal amounts of water. Once the children were able to make this discrimination correctly, they were asked to respond when one of two quantities judged equal was poured into a different jar. The children were able to answer correctly significantly more often in this non-verbal task than in the traditional verbally based task in which the experimenter asks, 'Do these two glasses have the same amount of water in them, or does this one have more water in it, or does this one have more water in it?' These data are evidence for the effect of language difficulties on conservation failure.

Young children can perform a non-verbal seriation task in which they must learn to select the second smallest from a series of randomly ordered bars of different heights (e.g. Gollin, Moody and Schadler, 1974; Griep and Gollin, 1978; Marschark, 1977; Siegel, 1972). This seriation concept also transfers to another dimension, for example, brightness instead of height. This type of procedure provides evidence for seriation in young children.

Even if one uses less verbal, rather than completely non-verbal tasks, there is evidence for the earlier attainment of cognitive concepts. There is some evidence that if one uses less complicated verbal tasks children possess complex reasoning skills before the Piagetian concrete operational period. For example, Greenberg, Marvin and Mossler (1977) found that children as young as four could reason from a premise to its logical conclusion. They asked children questions such as '[the experimenter] doesn't like to get wet, would he/she rather play in a puddle or read a book?' and as a check a nonsense question '[the experimenter] is very hungry, would he/she rather play with blocks or ride a bike?' Except for the three-year-olds, most of the children gave a correct answer and also gave a correct justification, that is, they related their answers to the premise. Some children were able to answer the nonsense question correctly, by saying that the experimenter 'would rather ride a bike so he/she could get home to eat'. This ability to reason runs counter to the accepted tenets of Piagetian theory, particularly because the criterion used in this study is a strict one: the children were required to have justifications for their answers. Considering the difficulty young children typically have in reflecting on their cognitive processes, these results indicate that with a child-appropriate task very young children can reason logically.

Some investigations have been reluctant to use non-verbal tasks, or have concluded that they are not useful or valid. For example, Larsen (1977) was critical of attempts to simplify logical tasks for children by reducing linguistic requirements. This kind of research is based on the assumption that performance failure is sometimes caused by language problems rather than cognitive deficiency, and Larsen says,

> . . . it is a question of whether the verbal deficiencies explain the cognitive behavior or whether, on the contrary, the cognitive processes explain the verbal deficiencies. If one takes the latter view, as the Genevans do, then to use the child's understanding of words to explain his cognition is to use the effect of a cause to explain the cause. (P. 1164)

We see a problem with Larsen's analysis. The 'cognitive behavior' referred to is children's task performance, which is *not* equivalent to 'cognitive processes', or to 'cognition'. Consistent with the Genevan position that cognitive growth leads to language development, we argue that both cognitive processes and language skills are necessary for success with traditional research tasks, and that the language skills may lag behind the cognitive processes.

Larsen raised a serious charge against research that attempts to control factors like language, attention and memory, and that often uses different criteria for evaluating performance. He suggested that the alternative tasks become 'qualitatively different tasks'. We note, however, Larsen's concern about 'defining the notion of understanding the concept . . .' (p. 1163). That is exactly the point. Piagetians have defined a set of mental operations or structures, and have used certain operational definitions of these structures. Other investigators have used other procedures, that is, *different operational definitions*. Science involves operational definitions that express the properties of the concept in question in reasonable ways, and the use of different operational definitions is important to assess the generality and the validity of our research findings. We think the non-traditional operational definitions are reasonable expressions of the concepts being studied, that is, it seems to us that children must use the logical ability in question to succeed at the alternative tasks. To support the opposite position, that success with the alternative tasks does not depend upon the same logical ability as that required by the Piagetian tasks, one should be able to describe how children might succeed at the alternative tasks without using that logical ability. Non-verbal alternatives to tasks such as conservation and seriation have not been successfully criticized on these grounds.

In a review of studies that reduced language in the assessment of Piagetian concepts, Miller (1976) found current results somewhat modest. He concluded, however, that the general attempt was worth pursuing because it may lead to more precise evaluation of cognitive development, and the results may also bear on issues such as the sequencing of various cognitive attainments, stages of cognitive development and processes which underlie cognitive abilities.

EFFECTS OF PERCEPTION, ATTENTION AND MEMORY

There is evidence that in addition to social and linguistic factors, perception, attention and memory influence the assessment of cognition. There is much variation in the level of the cognitive responses depending on the nature of the perceptual information in stimulus materials and the demands on attention and memory. (See Miller, 1978, for a review of the evidence on this point.) For example, children find conservation easier with smaller numbers (Winer, 1974b), with candy as stimuli (Calhoun, 1971), and with their own fingers as stimuli (Curcio, Robbins and Ela, 1971). They also find conservation easier if the transformation occurs behind a screen instead of within their view (Miller and Heldmeyer, 1975). In these research situations the perceptual information is varied, but Miller claims that the concept of attention may also help to explain these findings. It may be that the child's ability to filter out irrelevant information is developing, but the cognitive processes, or logical thinking, may not be changing. Thus, young children with immature attentional capacity can perform better with simple or familiar materials.

Silverman, Vanderhorst and Eull (1976) have shown that conservation and perceptual abilities are related. Children who received training for length conservation improved in ability to judge the length of sticks in a complex illusion situation. Clearly conservation is not independent of perceptual aspects of a situation, but is closely related to those aspects.

Memory is sometimes an important component of cognitive development tasks. In the study of moral judgment, Piagetian theory proposes a sequence in understanding the role of intentionality in behaviour (Piaget, 1932). According to Piagetian theory, younger children tend to judge an act by its consequence, and older children by the intention of the doer. The younger child thinks that a boy who breaks several plates while helping his mother set the table commits a worse act than another boy who breaks one plate reaching for a forbidden cookie jar. However, Austin, Ruble and Trabasso (1977) found recency effects in children's moral judgments with the most recent alternatives being recalled more frequently. They also showed that if one made sure the children remembered all the alternatives, children in kindergarten and first grade were able to understand intentionality as well as children in second and third grades. In addition, Bryant and Trabasso (1971) have shown that memory influences the assessment of ability to make transitive inferences. When memory factors were controlled, young children made correct inferences.

Central to Piagetian theory is the belief that cognitive operations develop in a sequential fashion. Once an operation develops it is presumably available to the child, and by a strict interpretation should not vary with the situation. Of course, this is not the case. For example, Elkind (1961) has shown that the conservation of mass develops significantly earlier than the conservation of weight which in turn develops significantly earlier than the concept of volume, although presumably these conservations should develop simultaneously as they are all characterized by the same process. Piagetians also report this variability based on stimulus dimensions, and the concept of decalage has been postulated to account for this phenomenon. But it is not clear from Piagetian theory why this occurs, and the theory needs other postulates for completeness. Odom (1978) has proposed one possibility, the perceptual change position; he suggested that what changes with development is the child's ability to process perceptual information such as dimensionality. In support of this position, Odom, Astor and Cunningham (1975) reported that children found it was easier to solve a double-classification matrix when the task involved more salient dimensions.

Evidence from these studies indicates that perception, attention and memory affect children's performance on cognitive developmental tasks. Further, the variability in task success as a result of perceptual, attention and memory effects does not support the stage model of cognitive development.

TRAINING AS A METHODOLOGICAL ISSUE

In the preceding material, we pointed out that assessment of cognitive ability is often confounded by effects from non-logical sources. One research approach that can help in evaluating this situation is the use of training studies. When training succeeds we know that children can learn to demonstrate the logical ability, and sometimes training research can indicate the basis for difficulties the children have with the task initially.

Piagetians assert that, in general, training does not help children to acquire basic logic, although it may speed the transition between logical stages. Inhelder and Piaget (1964) asked children questions designed to make explicit the relationships between hierarchical classes. This series of logical questions did not improve the children's performance with class-inclusion questions. In another study, Sinclair and Inhelder (reported in Sinclair de Zwart, 1969) tried to teach non-conserving children to produce language like that of children who could conserve. The effect of this training on later conservation behaviour was negligible, and the authors suggested that only children who were already in the process of acquiring conservation were affected.

Non-Piagetian researchers, however, have pursued the question of logical training, and this is not simply a result of the North American proclivity to make everything bigger and better, including children's minds. It is, we believe, a reflection of the idea that cognition development is not independent of specific experience. Children's understanding of space, time, number, classification and, in fact, any cognitive process, depends on specific experience with certain environmental events and materials.

By training a concept, we can examine the specific experiences that might be relevant, and the specific non-logical factors that may impede children in demonstrating understanding of the concept. Sometimes in training we attempt to provide children with some background so they can understand what is being tested or required. That is, if an investigator wants to test class inclusion by asking if there are more animals or dogs, in an array of six dogs and three cats, the child must first understand that dogs and cats are both animals. This type of strategy was used by Siegel et al (1978), and in the non-verbal tasks described in Siegel (1978). The important point about training is that it can be used to provide investigators with a better understanding of cognitive development. We feel that training is not begging the issue of cognitive assessment, but is an attempt to ascertain whether a child can learn a concept with a minimal amount of instruction. The critical question in this kind of research is not the absolute presence or absence of the concept, but whether or not the child can benefit from experience to learn the concept.

According to Piagetian theory, training procedures are effective only when the training follows the course of spontaneous concept development, and the children already possess the rudiments of the concept to be trained. Brainerd (1978a) argues that there is no reason to assume that training methods must imitate spontaneous concept development. Several methods of training, for example, simple correction and rule teaching, improve performance on a variety of Piagetian tasks, and these are not the self-discovery or spontaneous methods thought effective by Piaget. Tutorial methods are as effective as self-discovery methods and perhaps even more so.

With regard to the Piagetian assertion that only children in logical transition can be trained, there are studies in which children who showed no evidence of concepts such as conservation or class inclusion were successfully trained. Piaget's hypothesis that learning will be constrained by the child's level of cognitive development has not received empirical support (Brainerd, 1978a). On the basis of Piaget's theory, pre-operational children should not be able to profit from instruction. However, Brainerd has reviewed the evidence from a number of studies, and concluded that three- and four-year-olds can be trained to solve conservation problems. Similarly, we have found that three- and four-year-old children can be trained to solve class inclusion (Siegel et al, 1978). Furthermore, the learning does not differ in quality from that of older children, as measured by the ability to transfer to novel stimulus material.

OVERVIEW OF METHODOLOGICAL PROBLEMS

The results of the various studies discussed show that in cognitive development tasks we are studying more than logical ability. Ignoring the effects of social context, language, perception, attention and memory is particularly illogical when one wants to infer, as many investigators do, the lack of a cognitive operation from an incorrect response. There are many possible reasons for an incorrect response and unless one considers this in interpretation, serious errors of inference will be made.

FOCAL AREAS IN COGNITIVE DEVELOPMENT

We will now examine methodological problems and alternative experimental approaches in some specific content areas.

The Case of Infant Development

One of Piaget's most substantial contributions to developmental psychology has been his description of infant behaviours. Piaget's description of infant development is an extensive and comprehensive one. The concepts have become useful to psychologists in a variety of ways. These concepts include such abilities as the understanding of objects, space, causality and imitation. Piaget charted these in detail. Uzgiris and Hunt (1975) have developed an infant assessment device based on the Piagetian system. For example, Piaget describes the development of the concept of the permanent object, the understanding that objects still exist even when they disappear from sight. There have been many studies of the object concept since Piaget described it (e.g. Bower, 1967; Bower and Paterson, 1972; Butterworth, 1975; Corman and Escalona, 1969; Gratch, 1976; Gratch et al, 1974; Landers, 1971; Webb, Massar and Nadolny, 1972).

Piaget's theory has led to some interesting studies. One in particular tested the infant's awareness of object permanence and avoided many of the usual methodological pitfalls in cognitive development research by an ingenious procedure. Lecompte and Gratch (1972) hid a toy watched by 9-, 12- and 18-month-old infants, and then, unknown to the children, they substituted a different toy. Within this age range there was an increase in the degree of puzzlement showed by the infants when they were confronted with a different toy from the one that had disappeared under the washcloth. They were, of course, surprised that the same toy did not reappear.

Piaget's descriptions were based on observation of his own children, the traditional way in which the science of developmental psychology began. As these were very significant observations, North American psychologists used them and subjected them to rigorous examination and testing. Sometimes the observations have not been supported. Consider the case of the object concept. Unfortunately the assessment of this ability has methodological problems because in order to demonstrate this ability the infant must visually follow an object or reach for an object. Memory, attention and eye-hand co-ordination all enter into this process. Cornell (1978) has shown that the development of various object concept skills can be learned. By a gradual increment in task difficulty Cornell was able to train infants to reach for an object hidden behind two screens. Invisible displacement, that is an object screening another object from the infant's view, was also a factor, as the infant showed less search during invisible displacement and paid more attention to its mother's face so it was distracted from the task. Or consider what Piaget (1954) describes as the Stage 4 error (called the AB error) in the development of the object concept. When a child has found something at one location A and it is hidden at another location B, the child continues incorrectly to search at A. Gratch et al (1974) found that if there was no delay, that is, if the child was allowed to search as soon as the object was hidden, then children made fewer errors. Therefore, the reason for errors may have been forgetting. Memory is involved in these tasks and must be controlled before inference is made about failure of cognitive performance.

Piagetian theory assumes that manipulation of objects is important in the development of cognitive ability, particularly during the sensorimotor period. The co-ordination of reaching and looking is an example of a process that is important for cognitive development. Kopp and Shaperman (1973) report on the case of a child who was born with the complete absence of any limbs and whose interactions with objects consisted of 'looking and listening and batting and rolling objects with his head and trunk' (p. 43). In spite of the very limited interaction with the environment, which was based entirely on distance receptor, this child showed normal cognitive and language ability at the age of three.

The significance of early interactions with objects, according to Piagetian theory, is that they allow the co-ordination of various aspects of the environment. Suppose an individual was paralysed from birth; he or she would not be able to engage in the simple behaviour with objects that would be important for cognitive development. Jordan (1972) and Segalowitz (1980) discuss just such a case of a woman in her early 40s with a head the size of an adult's, a body the size of an infant's, with completely nonfunctional limbs. This woman could read and talk well and was considered quite intelligent. This degree of non-interaction should retard cognitive development, which, according to Piagetian theory, would never advance past the early sensorimotor stage. But the Piagetians argued that she had normal visual and oral activity and that the development of these senses should be enough for sensorimotor development. However, as Jordan argues, Piaget considers sensorimotor co-ordinations very important, and such limited environmental actions should have a significant effect on cognitive development. Segalowitz argues that eye movements alone do not allow a secondary circular reaction of the type described by Piaget, for example, a child attempting to reach a doll with his or her hand and getting feedback from these actions, so that Piaget's theory cannot explain development in this case.

The Case of Class Inclusion

We feel that Piagetians have not paid enough attention to the structural character-istics of the tasks used to assess cognitive development. This problem can be illustrated with class inclusion, a typical Piagetian task. In inclusion tasks children are shown two subclasses that form a superordinate class, and they are asked to compare the numerosity of the larger subclass and the superordinate class. For example, given three dogs and two cats the Piagetian inclusion question is, 'Are there more dogs or more animals?' This type of question requires simultaneous consideration of the subclass and the superordinate class. Correct answers presumably demonstrate understanding of the relationships between hierarchical classes, and thus Piagetians consider inclusion the critical test of classification ability in the concrete operational stage.

Inhelder and Piaget (1964) reported that inclusion competence is exhibited between ages eight and twelve. Piagetians conclude that when children are not able to simultaneously compare the superordinate class and its included subclass, the children often resort to comparison of the two subclasses and choose the larger subclass. In other words, the erroneous strategy of comparing subclasses with each other results from logical deficit. However, errors in performance may reflect other factors in addition to logical deficit. For example, children may sometimes have language-related problems, such as difficulty in understanding what the inclusion question means. Older people may also misinterpret the question: Winer (1974a) asked college students 'In the whole world are there more dogs or more animals?' and found that 31 per cent assumed that the requested comparison was between dogs and other animals.

There have been various attempts to reduce the language difficulties that children may experience with the standard class-inclusion problem. For example, Niebuhr and Molfese (1978) used a modified version of the class-inclusion task in which, rather than making verbal responses, children used the mathematical symbols for 'greater than' and 'less than' to indicate the relationship between the superordinate and subordinate class. This version with a non-verbal response was significantly easier than the standard task for children in grades one to three.

Siegel et al (1978) postulated that young children might understand an inclusion question that did not contain the word 'more' because this kind of relational term is difficult at an early age. As well, Siegel's question may be more interesting to children than the Piagetian question: she asked, 'Do you want to eat the Smarties or the candies?', in contrast to the standard form, 'Are there more Smarties or more candies?' Four-year-olds gave more correct inclusion responses to Siegel's question than to the Piagetian question. These very young children often demonstrated logical ability with the question in a form that they could understand.

Shipley (1979) reported that children performed relatively better with an inclusion question in which 'all' modified the superordinate and 'only' modified the subclass, providing the children with two linguistic cues to meaning. Shipley's questions were of the type, 'Which is more, only the Smarties or all the candies?' Hodkin (1981) has shown that the single modifier 'all' is sufficient to improve performance. Children gave more correct responses to the question, 'Are there more Smarties or more of all the candies?', than to 'Are there more Smarties or more candies?' Further investigation with control questions showed that children did not give more right answers to the all-modified question because they simply chose the class modified by all, and the effect was not caused by referencing all the items without an inclusion comparison. The all-modified inclusion question conforms to natural language use, and children are able to understand that this linguistic form refers to the subclass and the entire superordinate class. Because they understand the request, they are able to demonstrate inclusion logic when it is available.

Piagetians claim that when children are not able to compare a superordinate class and its included subclass, the children resort to comparison of the subclasses. That is, logical deficit is responsible for comparison of subclasses, a strategy that systematically leads to wrong answers because the larger subclass is always used in the inclusion question. We have shown, however, that the linguistic form of the Piagetian inclusion question predisposes children to subclass comparison strategy. A performance function below 50 per cent correct response is evidence of this strategy, and in our work this has occurred only with the standard Piagetian question. There was no evidence that children were comparing the subclasses in Siegel's inclusion question or in the all-modified inclusion question (Siegel, 1978; Hodkin, 1981). Consistent findings are provided by a detailed mathematical analysis of response in an inclusion study with a reduced language question and the standard Piagetian question (Hodkin, 1979). With the Piagetian question a large proportion of response was based on comparison of subclasses, but with the reduced language question very little response was based on this strategy. These results show that inclusion performance is a function of linguistic factors as well as logical ability. More specifically, the subclass comparison error is caused by the language used in the Piagetian inclusion question and is not based on logical deficit.

Winer (1980) has pointed out that more information is needed about the reasons why language manipulations affect children's inclusion performance. Some of that information is now available. Compared to other language forms, the Piagetian question predisposes children to the error of comparing the subclasses, and thus it is reasonable to conclude that the language of the Piagetian question suggests that the subclass comparison is intended. The investigation of reasons for the effect of the all-modified inclusion question eliminated certain non-logical possibilities, and these results support the idea that children are able to understand the intended comparison of subclass to superordinate class.

The studies reported here, with alternative forms of the inclusion question, cast serious doubt on the inference that young children cannot understand a hierarchical classification schema. Often they can demonstrate such understanding, if the question is asked in a manner appropriate to their linguistic level.

To the extent that class-inclusion performance is related to linguistic clarity we might expect success with verbal training procedures that increase the comprehensibility of the inclusion question. Ahr and Youniss (1970) and Winer (1974a) both used expanded forms of the inclusion question, mentioning the smaller subclass along with the larger subclass and the superordinate, and children gave more right answers with the expanded form than with the standard Piagetian question. However, Ahr and Youniss found that experience with the expanded form did not improve subsequent performance with standard inclusion questions, although children who received simple verbal feedback training with standard questions did maintain higher performance in post-testing. We suggest that when children received the expanded form of the question, specifying both subclasses and the superordinate class, they immediately understood the comparison asked for, but this advantage of understanding the question did not transfer to the non-expanded Piagetian form. But when the children received verbal feedback to the non-expanded Piagetian question they learned the meaning of that question, and this advantage was maintained when feedback was no longer available.

Several methods of training for class inclusion have been successful. Kohnstamm (1968) used feedback and detailed explanation with five-year-olds and Sheppard (1973) trained six-year-olds with a procedure based on physical manipulation of classes and discussion of the relationships between classes. Simple verbal feedback about the correctness of the children's answers was used by Brainerd (1974b) with four- and five-year-olds, and by Siegel et al (1978) with three- and four-year-olds. Judd and Mervis (1979) made kindergarten children aware of the contradiction between their answers to the class-inclusion question and their counting of the subordinate and superordinate classes. Hodkin (1980) replicated the logical discussion, feedback and counting and contradiction studies, using post-tests with novel stimulus sets. The results indicated that all three training approaches were successful with children in the first grade.

In the training studies reported here there was improvement in inclusion performance, and the authors concluded that verbal training was effective in the sense that many children learned to make the inclusion comparison. However, it could be that some children already possessed inclusion logic, and the training was successful for these children because it made clear to them what the inclusion question meant. Of course, inclusion training and question clarification may have jointly contributed to improved performance. Further work is needed to clarify the basis for training effects, but it is clear that children considered pre-operational can be trained to demonstrate class-inclusion reasoning.

In recent years there have been several studies of perceptual effects on inclusion, and it appears that certain perceptual conditions may allow children to understand the inclusion question more easily. For example, Tatarsky (1974) varied the salience of the superordinate class with three sets of stimulus materials. Wooden blocks painted all blue or all red were used in the 'two-dimension, unequal salience' condition which represented the standard inclusion condition; with these materials the superordinate attribute, i.e. wooden, was not visible. In the 'two-dimension, equal salience' condition the blocks were half painted either red or blue, and the other half was unpainted wood so that the superordinate attribute was visible. In the 'one-dimension' condition all of the blocks were painted half yellow, with the other half either blue or red; in this case subclass and superordinate attributes were equally visible and were from the same dimension, colour. Compared to the standard 'two-dimension, unequal salience' condition, children of ages five to eight gave more right answers to the 'two-dimension, equal salience' questions, and performance was even better with the 'one-dimension' questions. Tatarsky concluded that demonstration of inclusion ability increases as the superordinate class becomes more salient.

Wilkinson (1976) also manipulated the salience of the superordinate class, comparing a standard inclusion question and an inclusion question that referred to distinctive features of the subclass and the superordinate class. Given drawings of women with a chair and a picnic basket and men with a chair but no picnic basket, the standard inclusion question was 'Are there more mothers or grown-ups?', and the distinctive features question was 'Are there more grown-ups who have a picnic basket or more grown-ups who have a chair?' With the standard question pre-school children gave the correct answer 23 per cent of the time, but when specific identifying features were used for the classes the children were correct 60 per cent of the time. Wilkinson suggested that children's first counting strategy includes a prohibition against counting items twice, making correct inclusion response impossible with the standard question. The distinctive features question allows young children a way around the double-counting prohibition because they can, for example, count picnic baskets and chairs rather than double-counting mothers. However, Wilkinson's argument about counting strategy is weakened by Tatarsky's earlier finding that children did better in a 'one-dimension' condition than in a 'two-dimension, equal salience' condition. If the effects of superordinate salience, or distinctiveness, were based only on counting strategy, then children should do just as well comparing wooden to blue halves as comparing yellow to blue halves.

Tatarsky's position was based on salience of the superordinate class, and Wilkinson used a counting strategy explanation. Another interpretation of these results is based on the operationalization of the classes, and raises a serious possible objection to considering these as studies of inclusion logic. In the conditions of interest, Tatarsky's equal salience conditions and Wilkinson's distinctive features condition, separate features defined the subclass and the superordinate class, and children may have been treating these as exclusive classes rather than as superordinate class and included subclass. This argument suggests that children were comparing blue halves to wooden halves instead of comparing wooden-blocks-with-blue to wooden blocks, and they were comparing picnic baskets to chairs instead of comparing adults-with-baskets to adults-with-chairs. If this was the case, these conditions did not facilitate inclusion performance but rather removed the requirement to make an inclusion comparison.

This criticism does not apply to McGarrigle's manipulation of both superordinate and subclass salience (McGarrigle, Grieve and Hughes, 1978). Superordinate class salience was increased by asking 'Are there more black cows or more sleeping cows?' in comparison to 'Are there more black cows or more cows?' Subclass salience was increased in the question 'Are there more red steps to go to the chair or more steps to go to the table?' compared to 'Are there more steps to go to the chair or more steps to go to the table?' The same stimulus materials were used for each set of two questions. Compared to the standard question forms, pre-schoolers gave more right answers when the superordinate class was salient and fewer right answers when the subclass was salient. These studies are not subject to the distinctive features argument, because sleeping was not separate from cows and red was not separate from steps. Perceptually it would have been very difficult for children to treat the subclass and the superordinate as exclusive classes, and thus McGarrigle's results show that the salience of class levels is important in inclusion performance.

It may be that increasing the perceptual salience or distinctiveness of the super-ordinate *makes clear* to children the comparison that is requested. Perhaps questions involving salient superordinate classes help children to understand that in fact the inclusion comparison is required, while questions with salient subclasses diminish that understanding. In other words, these studies may have been effective because in certain conditions children's misunderstanding of the question was either reduced or increased.

In a series of experiments Isen et al (1975) and Trabasso et al (1978) have contributed to the inquiry into perceptual effects in class inclusion. For example, they found that children's performance improved when items outside the stimulus set were used. The children gave more right answers to the inclusion question, 'Are there more dogs or more animals?' when fruit was also present than they did when only the animals were displayed.

In a second procedure in the Trabasso studies, some of the children were asked all pair-wise contrasts for the two superordinate classes, for example, 'more dogs or more apples', 'more dogs or more fruit', 'more animals or more fruit', and so on. This use of multiple comparisons facilitated inclusion performance at ages five, seven and nine in comparison to single-class (standard) inclusion questions that did not include multiple contrasts.

Even more striking than the effects with a contrasting class and multiple contrasts is the evidence obtained from the comparison of a subclass to an unrelated superordinate level class, for example, 'more dogs or more fruit'. In both of the Isen et al studies there was no difference in correct response between the question, 'Are there more dogs or more animals?' and the question, 'Are there more dogs or more fruit?' This is a surprising finding. Piagetian theory would not predict difficulty with the comparison of a subclass and an unrelated superordinate, because the two classes are distinct and there should be no problem with simultaneous consideration. The task analysis provided by Trabasso et al does account for the finding of equivalent difficulty for the two types of questions. This model proposes that given the display with the two superordinate classes, animals and fruit, the children encode only the subordinate classes, dogs, cats, apples and oranges. Thus when asked to compare dogs and fruit, the children do not have an accurate estimation of fruit, but must use either apples or oranges, which results in incorrect response.

In addition to linguistic and perceptual effects, class-inclusion performance has been found to depend upon the specific stimuli used in terms of category typicality or atypicality. Certain items are more central than others as examples of a category. For example, a horse is a more prototypic animal than a fly, at least to children if not to entomologists. Carson and Abrahamson (1976) found that children were more likely to answer class-inclusion questions correctly if the content represented a 'good' example of a category. Thus, questions comparing horses and animals were easier than those comparing flies and animals.

Markman (1973) and Markman and Seibert (1976) investigated language effects by examining the semantic aspect of superordinate class salience. They have shown that children in kindergarten and first grade perform better on inclusion questions when the superordinate class is labelled with a collective noun like family or pile than when a class noun like dogs or blocks is used. Markman and Seibert pointed out certain key distinctions between collections and classes: collections are defined by the relationship of the members, while classes are defined by a common attribute possessed by each member; in a collection, the parts are not representative of the whole as is true for a class; and collections have an internal organization which is lacking in classes. Because of these differences Markman and Seibert concluded that collections are more coherent psychological units than classes. This greater 'wholeness' on the part of collections allows children to preserve the superordinate class better when it is labelled with a collective noun, so that children are less likely to make a disjunctive comparison of the subclasses. It appears that when a collective noun is used in the question children understand that an inclusion comparison is requested.

The research surveyed here clearly indicates that when we study class inclusion we are not assessing inclusion competence independent of the child's experience in the world. There are many factors which affect children's response to inclusion questions. The context of the questions is important, and this includes the kind of class content used, the salience of the attributes that define subclasses and superordinate class, and the presence or absence of contrasting classes. Quantification skills available to the children, and the use of multiple comparisons may affect response. Linguistic factors are significant, especially with regard to whether or not the children understand what it is that we are asking them to do. If English-speaking adults were asked the inclusion question in Greek, most would fail the question.

The Case of Animism

From his interviews with children, Piaget concluded that there was a substantial amount of animism in the thinking of children. He described four stages of the development of the differentiation between animate and inanimate objects. According to Piaget's scheme, the child in Stage 1 believes that if something is intact and in good condition, it is alive, but if it is damaged, it is not. A whole dish is alive and a broken one is dead. In Stage 2, if a thing moves it is alive, if it is stationary it is not. A child at this stage will say a stone is dead and the sun is alive. Stage 3 thinking attributes life to anything that moves without apparent assistance, for example, a dog or the moon, but life is not attributed to anything that needs something else to make it move, for example, an automobile or bicycle. At the most mature level, Stage 4, only animals and plants are seen to have life, and sometimes only animals. Studies such as those of Russell (1940) and Russell and Dennis (1939) confirmed the existence of these stages. In these studies children from 3 to 16 years old were asked questions about whether objects such as stones, buttons, pencils, dogs, birds and flowers were alive. In order to explore the child's concepts of life more fully and to partially alleviate the problem of the child's answer to the Piaget-type questions being dependent on the child's interpretation of the word life, Russell (1940) asked the children about the stages of 'knowing' and 'feeling' in objects that they had judged to be alive or not alive. Children were asked such questions as 'Does the button know where it is? Does the pencil feel when it touches something? Does the dog feel anything when I touch it?' The children's concept of life included an understanding that knowledge and feeling were correlated with life.

Many of Piaget's results were replicated in a study of five- to twelve-year-olds by King (1961). The majority of the five- and six-year-olds thought that all things that move are living, although the children could differentiate between some living and non-living objects. Most six-year-olds knew a bird and a dog were alive and by the age of seven most of the children knew that an aeroplane was not living. There were some animistic responses at all ages. The status of the sun gave the children the most trouble; even many children (35 per cent) as old as eleven judged the sun to be alive.

Piaget's claims about child animism have not been universally accepted. In a very early refutation, Margaret Mead (1932), the famous anthropologist, argued that animistic tendencies such as the attribution of personality and will to inanimate objects are a result of educational and environmental influences, not the structure of the child's thought. She tested the degree of animistic thought in primitive children, the Manus of the Admiralty Islands, to determine whether this type of thinking was universal and whether it disappears in adults in our society because of education or because of an intrinsic developmental process. Mead thought that it is especially important to distinguish between spontaneous animism which appears in the child without any training and the kind of pseudo-animism that is found in children's thinking as a result of imitating adult responses. The latter kind cannot be considered an innate part of the child's thinking. For example, the attribution of events and actions to ghosts is a common part of the culture of the Manus, and so a child who talks about ghosts is not displaying spontaneous animism, but rather is echoing what adults have said. But a child who personalizes the sun or the moon or who talks to an imaginary playmate is showing spontaneous animism because these things are not specifically part of the culture. Mead studied the drawings and conversations of Manus children and found no spontaneous animism and no tendency to personalize things that had not been given personalities by adults. Mead also tested the animism of these children by presenting them with some standardized situations; she asked them to explain how her typewriter worked, what caused a Japanese paper flower to expand rapidly in water, and she tried to get them to blame their pencil for a drawing that they did not like. Even in these cases, the children did not resort to animism or magical explanations. They resisted the explanation that a little man in the typewriter did the writing, they did not want to blame the pencil for their bad drawings, and they understood the action of the water on the paper flower ('the water got inside and made it bigger').

As a matter of fact, Mead goes one step further. Her data show that animistic thinking is not an intrinsic part of children's thought and that sometimes children specifically *reject* the non-logical magical concepts of adults. One example she cites is that the adult Manus believe that if their reflection falls on water, then part of their soul will leave their body, and they will have to redeem it through the use of magic. The Manus do not take their children out in boats because the children ignore the taboo and insist on looking at their image in the water. The children reject the adults' magical concept that the image is part of the body. Mead attributes the lack of animistic thinking by the Manus children to the fact that they are encouraged to learn as much as possible about the physical world, so they have alternative concepts to magical ones. In any case, the nature of animism cannot be studied independently of the culture and environment and, according to Mead, animism cannot be viewed as a universal characteristic of thought.

Huang and Lee (1945) also objected to Piaget's concept of animism, for two reasons. First of all, the child may have a problem in understanding the term 'living' and, second, when the child does display animism it may be a function of not being completely acquainted with the properties of the object. To study the problem in greater detail they asked three- to nine-year-old children a variety of questions about objects: 'Was it living? Did it have life? Did it feel pain if pricked with a pin? Could it want things? Could it be good or bad?' They found relatively little animism, but even when the children made animistic responses they were not likely to endow the inanimate objects with qualities typically associated with life, such as goodness and pain. They were most likely to be correct about pain and least likely to be correct in answer to the question 'Does it have anything that it must do?' Huang and Lee concluded that animism is not general but based on limited knowledge about certain objects. Animism is a result of overgeneralization because inanimate and animate objects share some of the same properties.

All of the questions designed to test animism require a high level of understanding of language. Language has been found to be a factor in the measurement of animism. Klingberg (1957) found that the wording of the question made a difference. 'Does it have life?' was more likely to be answered correctly than 'Is it living?' Klingensmith (1953) also investigated this problem of possible lack of language skills interfering with assessment of the concepts. In this study, children were shown such objects as a lighted candle, an alarm clock that ticked loudly, a goldfish, a broken dish. They were asked questions like 'Is it alive?', 'Does it feel pain?', 'Does it grow?', 'Does it hear?', 'Does it see?' Many children answered the question about being alive incorrectly but did not endow the inanimate objects with sensory capacities. They knew that a comb or a broken dish did not grow, hear or see. The children were most likely to be wrong on the candle and the clock, probably because they showed activity. Therefore animism may not be as universal as one would expect from Piaget's theory. The children's understanding that inanimate objects do not have sensory capacities suggests that the problem may be with the understanding of the term *alive*, not with the failure to understand the nature of the objects. As a matter of fact, the youngest children were more likely to be right about the clock and the candle than the older ones. Perhaps this was a reflection of the fact that the older ones understood the function of these objects and confused life with function.

Jahoda (1958) tested children's animism in a more experimental way. He attempted to control the specific educational and environmental factors which could be producing animism. He provided some West African school-children with the demonstration of a record player. The children had not been exposed to Western technology and had never seen anything like a record player. When he asked them how it worked most of the children did not resort to any sort of animistic thinking. They specifically resisted the suggestion that there was a man inside who did the singing when the experimenter suggested that explanation as an alternative. However, one of the children was confused by the RCA trademark (a dog) and said 'There is something like a dog on it, so when you put the nail on, the dog sings through the nail and we hear it.' But, for most of the children, there was very little animism.

Piaget also described prelogical non-rational thinking when the young child is asked to explain various phenomena of the natural world. Piaget asked the children such questions as 'Why do the clouds move?', 'Why does the river move?' At first the child relies on magic explanations, for example, 'We make the clouds move by walking'. Later the child demonstrates what Piaget calls artificialism, indicating that cloud movement is caused by external forces, 'men' or 'God'.

Piaget's claims that children resort to magical thinking were challenged by Huang (1943) and Huang, Yang and Yao (1945) who hypothesized that children would use logical explanations with appropriate materials. They showed the children some magical situations and asked the children for an explanation of what they had seen. In one of these situations, for example, the child broke a toothpick and the experimenter wrapped the broken toothpick in the handkerchief. When the handkerchief was taken away, the toothpick was whole again. In all these situations, the children were surprised and understood the strangeness of the event. They did not, as Piaget would expect, offer non-logical magical solutions but instead tried to explain the events in a rational way, such as 'the toothpick was not really broken', or 'the toothpick was only bent, not broken', or 'there were two toothpicks'. Many of the explanations that the children offered were naïve and incorrect, but there was evidence of many attempts to use physical principles rather than magical notions. Berzonsky (1971) reported similar findings.

One explanation for the use of magical explanations by children is that they are unfamiliar with the phenomena that they are asked to explain. Presumably they would use magical explanations if they were unfamiliar with the phenomena. Berzonsky tested this by asking children to explain familiar events (e.g. what makes a clock tick . . . a kite fly), and more remote events, (e.g. what makes the wind blow . . . the stars shine . . . it get dark). Children gave more naturalistic explanations for the familiar events but used magical explanations for the more remote events. The structure of a child's thinking is very much dependent on the material and the child's experience, and cannot be thought of as magical or logical in absolute terms. Smith and Dougherty (1965) found that children were more likely to use naturalistic explanations when they watched demonstrations than when they were asked questions. After experience of manipulating materials children were more likely to offer naturalistic explanations (Mogar, 1960). Berzonsky (1970) found that children gave more naturalistic, non-magical explanations if the experimenter questioned them in greater depth and probed the reason for their responses. Nass (1956) found that the form of the question made a difference in the type of responses that the children gave; *how* questions (how does a car move) resulted in less magical and animistic explanations than *why* questions. *Why* questions imply that the child should search for some motivational and intentional qualities, that is, qualities of life, on the part of the object. *How* questions do not have this connotation. The degree of animism and non-rational thinking described by Piaget is at least open to question.

LONG-TERM MEMORY: IMPROVEMENT OR NOT?

Piagetians report data summarized in Piaget and Inhelder (1973) which show children's memory improving over the course of time, six to eight months, in a period that their cognitive development is also presumably improving. For example, children, when asked to draw what they remember of a seriated array of sticks, are sometimes better after six months than they were immediately after they had seen the original. The memory for the array improved, according to Piaget and Inhelder, because the children were able to understand the operation of seriation. This surprising finding fascinated developmental psychologists; unfortunately they have been preoccupied with replicating the original finding in a variety of situations rather than examining the basic assumptions of the theory. In one study examining the relationship between the improvement in an individual child's memory and the actual change in seriation ability for the same child, no relationship was found between operational improvement and memory improvement (Maurer et al, 1979). This particular situation illustrates the problems of uncritically accepting a theory instead of testing the theory's postulates. It is this blind acceptance of Piagetian theory that has led investigators of cognitive development astray. Piaget cannot be blamed for this. History has repeatedly shown us that disciples are more dogmatic than the master.

EGOCENTRISM OR NOT?

Piaget's theory has led us to believe that the young child is egocentric, that is, does not understand another's point of view. However, there are a number of studies which show that this may not be the whole story. In a series of experiments, Borke (1971, 1972, 1975, 1978) has shown that children as young as three can identify emotions such as sadness and anger in others and have the ability to understand another's visual perspective if the task is simplified. Borke's studies have been criticized on the grounds that the child may associate certain feelings with situations without specifically understanding a perspective different from his or her own. With this criticism in mind, Mossler, Marvin and Greenberg (1976) designed a task in which the child knew something different from his or her mother, because of immediate prior information. The two-year-olds did not understand the task and the three-year-olds had difficulty with it. However, the four-, five-, and six-year-olds behaved non-egocentrically and generally expressed understanding of what their mothers did and did not know, although they often could not justify their responses. Again we have a situation where children manifest a cognitive skill but cannot explain it.

As an example of egocentrism, Krauss and Glucksberg (1969) have found that young children performed poorly in tasks in which they had to communicate to another child on the other side of the screen which one of several forms they had in mind. Maratsos (1973) used a simpler version of this task in which he had three- to five-year-old children describe a toy to someone who could see or who could not see (an experimenter with his eyes closed). Children gave more explicit verbal descriptions (rather than non-specific references or gestures) in the case where the experimenter could not see, demonstrating that children did have non-egocentric communication skills.

Young children may in fact have role-taking skills. The heavy emphasis on cognitive skills that is characteristic of most assessments of perspective-taking may mask the child's social awareness. While it is probably not fair to blame Piaget for the stress on the cognitive aspects of social behaviour, few investigators have simplified the tasks and situations sufficiently to be able to assess adequately egocentrism or the lack of it in the young child. But some studies have shown non-egocentric behaviour in the child below six and seven, the age at which Piaget postulates that the process of decentring begins (Piaget and Inhelder, 1956). For example, Fishbein, Lewis and Keiffer (1972) found that pre-school children were able to demonstrate another's perspective if the response involved turning a complex display to depict the experimenter's view, which was different from their own. Performance on this task was virtually errorless even for very young children.

The methodology of Fishbein et al differed from previous studies in that they did not use hypothetical questions, such as, 'If a doll could see . . .'. Similarly, Masangkay et al (1974) had the child and the experimenter in different parts of the room, and asked the child, 'What do you see?' and 'What do I see?' They found that children as young as two years could understand that the experimenter saw things differently than they did.

Young children adjust their language to the characteristics of a speaker. For example, four-year-olds use simpler language to a two-year-old than to a four-year-old (Shatz and Gelman, 1973). Masur (1978) found that four-year-olds adjusted their speech to the linguistic level of the two-year-old listener when the four-year-olds had to explain how a toy worked to 'high verbal' two-year-olds or 'low verbal' two-year-olds. The difference between these groups of two-year-olds was in mean length of utterance but not in behaviour or cognitive ability. The four-year-olds' speech was responsive to the characteristics of the listener in that they produced longer and more complex utterances to speech that was more responsive. A kind of conversational fine tuning occurred that indicated that the four-year-olds were responsive to the verbal productions of the two-year-old, which is hardly egocentric.

Wellman and Lampers (1977) have shown that children as young as two years old can adapt their language to the speaker and can respond to feedback. In free play, the children made many attempts to get their message across clearly by doing such things as taking the referent to the speaker or trying to get the speaker's attention. They also made attempts to recommunicate their message when the listener indicated a lack of understanding. These two-year-olds appeared to be successful communicators 80 per cent of the time. We doubt that adults would do much better. Menig-Peterson (1975) examined the verbalizations of children of ages three to five in two conditions in which the listener either was or was not present when certain experiences occurred. In the condition in which the listener was naïve, the children used more specific language and appropriately introduced more new elements of the situation. That is, the children modified their language to take account of the listener's knowledge. Pre-school children have been able to modify their language to take account of the listener's perspective, behaviour which is not egocentric.

Flavell, Shipstead and Croft (1978) found that 2½- to 4-year-old children could hide an object so another person could not see it even if the object was visible to the child himself. Therefore, the children could distinguish between their own perceptions and the perceptions of others. Marvin, Greenberg and Mossler (1976) have shown that two- to six-year-old children could distinguish between several points of view. They played a game with each child and mother in which one of the participants closed his or her eyes and the other two selected one of two toys as the correct one (the secret). The children could correctly say whether or not they knew the secret and whether their mother and the experimenter did. Again, a simpler and more child-oriented task demonstrated non-egocentric abilities.

Liben (1978) has shown that while young children may fail certain complex perspective-taking tasks, they do demonstrate non-egocentric abilities in one very interesting situation. The child and/or the experimenter wore sunglasses with yellow or green lenses. When asked what colour a white card looked like to the child and to the experimenter, many four- and five-year-olds and most six- and seven-year-olds could answer correctly. They did not make egocentric errors of thinking the adult saw the same colour that they did. Hoy (1975) demonstrated that the degree of egocentrism exhibited by young children depended on the nature of the message and the characteristics of the listener. For example, it was easier when the child could observe the listener's behaviour and talk to him or her than when the child could do neither. These results suggest that a child may have the ability of competence to produce language in referential, non-egocentric communication, but may fail to do so because of situational variables. This discrepancy is the competence—performance problem noted in discussions of cognitive development (see Siegel and Brainerd, 1978, Introduction).

When relating a personal experience to adults in the course of a conversation, children aged 3½ to 9½ were able to introduce the listener to the situation and provide much necessary background information such as what objects and people were involved and how the events took place (Menig-Peterson and McCabe, 1978). Again this type of communication ability is not the egocentric speech that the Piagetian system attributes to young children. Green (1977) has demonstrated non-egocentric role-taking ability in kindergarten children who were able to label the emotion happiness, sadness, fear or anger shown in a film clip, and could give a correct reason for the emotion. This task was more realistic and less complex than many others because the children could non-verbally indicate the person or object that caused the emotion in order to demonstrate non-egocentrism.

Rheingold, Hay and West (1976) have shown that children at 14 to 20 months demonstrate a great deal of sharing behaviour by giving and showing toys and objects to their parents and even to unfamiliar persons. This sharing behaviour demonstrates a level of social awareness that cannot be called egocentric. Non-egocentric communication can be trained in young children, for example, children can be trained to be more effective listeners in a referential communication task (Patterson, Massad and Cosgrove, 1978). Children were given a strategy in which they could ask questions to help them when they thought they did not understand the speaker's message. Apparently egocentric communication in children can be facilitated through this minimal training procedure. Cox (1977) was able to train spatial perspective-taking skills in five-year-old children. The successful training involved confronting the child with a picture of what the experimenter saw or giving verbal feedback about the correctness of the child's response. Allowing the child to actually move to the experimenter's position was less successful. A retention test showed the effect of training persisted at least as long as 15 weeks. Burns and Brainerd (1979) have shown that preschool children's cognitive and affective perspective-taking ability can be improved by cognitive and role-taking skills in play.

These demonstrations of non-egocentric behaviours are not anomalous findings. The findings represent the behaviour of children in situations which are comprehensible and meaningful to children, in contrast to complex and artificial experimental situations. It appears that experimenters have often been egocentric in failing to see that children may not understand their language and behaviour. In the study of egocentrism Piagetian theory has led us down the wrong path.

THE CASE OF FORMAL OPERATIONS

Ennis (1978) proposes problems in Piaget's logical system and provides evidence that children can sometimes engage in complex logical thinking prior to adolescence. Danner and Day (1977) gave subjects a Piagetian bending rods task involving their ability to isolate variables in a formal operational sense, that is, to find which of several variables determine whether a rod will bend. Some subjects were given a suggestion for a strategy, 'to find out what makes a difference in bending, make sure everything is the same except the one thing you're testing', p. 1057. With this sort of prompt formal operational procedure improved, and the effect generalized to other tasks. The authors do not regard this as training but as an attempt to reveal a latent formal operation ability. Lowenthal (1977) has shown that in a game-like situation children as young as nine can operate with a complex logical system and display formal operational structures.

Arlin (1975) proposed a stage of cognitive development beyond the Piagetian formal operational stage. She called the stage problem-finding, a stage based on the ability to formulate questions and problems. She claims that problem-finding requires the development of formal reasoning strategies but is not an invariant consequence of those strategies. The evidence for the development of problem-finding is contradictory (Cropper, Meck and Ash, 1977; Fakouri, 1976), so further analysis will depend on future research. Should there be reliable evidence for the problem-finding stage, this will present a serious challenge to Piagetian theory.

CONCLUSIONS

This survey indicates that certain aspects of the Piagetian position are not empirically supported. For example, human cognitive skills develop gradually, not in qualitatively different logical stages. Cornell (1978) has demonstrated this gradual development for the object concept, Borke (1978), Odom (1978) and Siegel (1978) for pre-operational and concrete operational concepts, and Ennis (1978) for formal operations. In addition, accurate conclusions about the course of cognitive development cannot be drawn without studying the simultaneous development of language, perception, attention and memory. It is also important to study the manner in which a child's thinking changes with training, as this may tell us how a child learns and may help with some of the measurement problems in cognitive development.

We conclude that theories, like roses, have their thorns and aphids as well as blossoms. Piaget has generated the most significant theory in the field of cognitive development. This theory has provided a framework and a stimulus to much of the research in cognitive development, including our own. There are, however, problems with Piagetian methodology and interpretation. If investigators adopt this methodology uncritically, if they are not open to alternative explanations of task performance, if they do not consider alternative and perhaps more appropriate definitions of Piagetian operations, then those investigators are doing themselves, the theory and the science of developmental psychology a disservice. Alternatives and challenges are the necessary nutrients for the growth of understanding, and without them this field of investigation remains fallow.

REFERENCES

Ahr, P. R. and Youniss, J. (1970) Reasons for failure on the class-inclusion problem. *Child Development,* **41,** 131-143.

Arlin, P. K. (1975) Cognitive development in adulthood: A fifth stage? *Developmental Psychology,* **11,** 602-606.

Austin, V. D., Ruble, D. N. and Trabasso, T. (1977) Recall and order effects as factors in children's moral judgments. *Child Development,* **48,** 470-474.

Berzonsky, M. D. (1971) The role of familiarity in children's explanations of physical causality. *Child Development,* **42,** 705-715.

Borke, H. (1971) Interpersonal perception of young children: Egocentrism or empathy? *Developmental Psychology*, **5**, 263-269.

Borke, H. (1972) Chandler and Greenspan's 'Ersatz egocentrism': A rejoinder. *Developmental Psychology*, **7**, 107-109.

Borke, H. (1975) Piaget's mountains revisited: Changes in the egocentric landscape. *Developmental Psychology*, **11**, 240-243.

Borke, H. (1978) Piaget's view of social interaction and the theoretical construct of empathy. In Siegel, L. S. and Brainerd, C. J. (Eds.) *Alternatives to Piaget: Critical Essays on the Theory*. New York: Academic Press.

Bower, T. G. R. (1967) The development of object permanence: Some studies of existence constancy. *Perception and Psychophysics*, **2**, 411-418.

Bower, T. G. R. and Paterson, J. G. (1972) Stages in the development of the object concept. *Cognition*, **1**, 47-55.

Brainerd, C. J. (1973a) Judgments and explanations as criteria for the presence of cognitive structure. *Psychological Bulletin*, **79**, 172-179.

Brainerd, C. J. (1973b) Neo-Piagetian training experiments revisited: Is there any support for the cognitive-developmental stage hypothesis? *Cognition*, **2**, 349-370.

Brainerd, C. J. (1974a) *The concept of structure in cognitive-developmental theory*. Paper presented at the annual convention of the American Psychological Association, New Orleans, August—September.

Brainerd, C. J. (1974b) Training and transfer of transitivity, conservation, and class inclusion of length. *Child Development*, **45**, 324-334.

Brainerd, C. J. (1977a) Cognitive development and concept learning: An interpretative review. *Psychological Bulletin*, **84**, 919.

Brainerd, C. J. (1977b) Response criteria in concept development research. *Child Development*, **48**, 360-366.

Brainerd, C. J. (1978a) Learning research and Piagetian theory. In Siegel, L. S. and Brainerd, C. J. (Eds.) *Alternatives to Piaget: Critical Essays on the Theory*. New York: Academic Press.

Brainerd, C. J. (1978b) The stage question in cognitive-developmental theory. *The Behavioural and Brain Sciences*, **2**, 173-213.

Bryant, P. E. and Trabasso, T. (1971) Transitive inferences and memory in young children. *Nature*, **232**, 456-458.

Burns, S. M. and Brainerd, C. J. (1979) Effects of constructive and dramatic play on perspective-taking in very young children. *Developmental Psychology*, **15**, 512-521.

Butterworth, G. (1975) Object identity in infancy: The interaction of spatial location codes in determining search errors. *Child Development*, **46**, 866-870.

Cairns, R. B. and Ornstein, P. A. (1979) Developmental psychology. In Hearst, E. (Ed.) *The First Century of Experimental Psychology*. Hillsdale, N.J.: Lawrence Erlbaum Associates.

Calhoun, L. G. (1971) Number conservation in very young children: The effect of age and mode of responding. *Child Development*, **42**, 561-572.

Carson, M. T. and Abrahamson, A. (1976) Some members are more equal than others: The effect of semantic typicality on class-inclusion performance. *Child Development*, **47**, 1186-1190.

Corman, H. H. and Escalona, S. K. (1969) Stages of sensorimotor development: A replication study. *Merrill-Palmer Quarterly*, **15**, 351-361.

Cornell, E. H. (1978) Learning to find things: A reinterpretation of object permanence studies. In Siegel, L. S. and Brainerd, C. J. (Eds.) *Alternatives to Piaget: Critical Essays on the Theory*. New York: Academic Press.

Cox, M. V. (1977) Perspective ability: The conditions of change. *Child Development*, **48**, 1724-1727.

Cropper, D. A., Meck, D. S. and Ash, M. J. (1977) The relation between formal operations and a possible fifth stage of cognitive development. *Developmental Psychology*, **13**, 517.

Curcio, F., Robbins, O. and Ela, S. S. (1971) The role of body parts and readiness in acquisition of number conservation. *Child Development*, **42**, 1641-1646.

Danner, F. W. and Day, M. C. (1977) Eliciting formal operation. *Child Development*, **48**, 1600-1606.

Elkind, D. (1961) The development of quantitative thinking: A systematic replication of Piaget's studies. *Journal of Genetic Psychology*, **98**, 37-46.

Ennis, R. H. (1978) Conceptualization of children's logical competence: Piaget's propositional logic and an alternative proposal. In Siegel, L. S. and Brainerd, C. J. (Eds.) *Alternatives to Piaget: Critical Essays on the Theory*. New York: Academic Press.

Fakouri, M. E. (1976) 'Cognitive development in adulthood: A fifth stage?' A critique. *Developmental Psychology*, **12**, 472.

Feldman, N. S., Klosson, E. C., Parsons, J. E., Rholes, W. S. and Ruble, D. N. (1976) Order of information presentation and children's moral judgments. *Child Development*, **47**, 556-559.

Fishbein, H. D., Lewis, S. O. and Keiffer, K. (1972) Children's understanding of spatial relations: Co-ordination of perspectives. *Developmental Psychology*, **7**, 21-33.

Flavell, J. H., Shipstead, S. G. and Croft, K. (1978) Young children's knowledge about visual perception: Hiding objects from others. *Child Development*, **49**, 1208-1211.

Gollin, E. S., Moody, M. and Schadler, M. (1974) Relational learning of a size concept. *Developmental Psychology,* **10,** 101-108.

Gratch, G. (1976) On levels of awareness of objects in infants and students thereof. *Merrill-Palmer Quarterly of Behaviour and Development,* **22,** 157-176.

Gratch, G., Appel, K. J., Evans, W. F., Lecompte, G. K. and Wright, N. A. (1974) Piaget's stage IV object concept error: Evidence of forgetting or object conception? *Child Development,* **45,** 71-77.

Greenberg, M. T., Marvin, R. S. and Mossler, D. G. (1977) The development of conditional reasoning skills. *Developmental Psychology,* **13,** 527-529.

Griep, C. and Gollin, E. S. (1978) Interdimensional transfer of an ordinal solution strategy. *Developmental Psychology,* **14,** 437-438.

Hodkin, B. (1979) *Class inclusion: Analysing the bases of response.* Paper presented at the biennial meeting of the Society for Research in Child Development, San Francisco, March.

Hodkin, B. (1980) *Reanalysis of training studies in class inclusion.* Paper presented at the University of Waterloo Conference on Child Development, Waterloo, May.

Hodkin, B. (1981) Language effects in assessment of class-inclusion ability. *Child Development,* **52.**

Hoy, E. A. (1975) Measurement of egocentrism in children's communication. *Developmental Psychology,* **11,** 392.

Huang, I. (1943) Children's conception of physical causality: A critical summary. *Journal of Genetic Psychology,* **63,** 71-121.

Huang, I. and Lee, H. W. (1945) Experimental analysis of child animism. *Journal of Genetic Psychology,* **66,** 69-74.

Huang, I., Yang, H. C. and Yao, F. Y. (1945) Principles of selection in children's 'phenomenistic' explanations. *Journal of Genetic Psychology,* **66,** 63-68.

Hunt, T. D. (1975) Early number 'conservation' and experimenter expectancy. *Child Development,* **46,** 984-987.

Inhelder, B. and Piaget, J. (1964) *The Early Growth of Logic in the Child.* New York: Harper and Row.

Isen, A. M., Riley, C. A., Tucker, T. and Trabasso, T. (1975) *The facilitation of class inclusion by use of multiple comparisons and two-class perceptual displays.* Paper presented at the meeting of the Society for Research in Child Development, Denver, Colorado, April.

Jahoda, G. (1958) Child animism: A critical survey of cross-cultural research. *Journal of Social Psychology,* **47,** 197-212.

Jordan, N. (1972) Is there an Achilles' heel in Piaget's theorizing? *Human Development,* **15,** 379-382.

Judd, S. A. and Mervis, C. B. (1979) Learning to solve class-inclusion problems: The roles of quantification and recognition of contradiction. *Child Development,* **50,** 163-169.

Kalil, K., Youssef, Z. and Lerner, R. M. (1974) Class-inclusion failure: Cognitive deficit or misleading reference? *Child Development,* **45,** 1122-1125.

King, W. H. (1961) The development of scientific concepts in children. *British Journal of Educational Psychology,* **31,** 1-20.

Klingberg, G. (1957) The distinction between living and not living among 7—10-year-old children with some remarks concerning the so-called animism controversy. *Journal of Genetic Psychology,* **90,** 227-238.

Klingensmith, S. W. (1953) Child animism: What the child means by 'alive'. *Child Development,* **24,** 51-61.

Kohnstamm, G. A. (1968) An evaluation of part of Piaget's theory. In Sigel, I. E. and Hooper, F. H. (Eds.) *Logical Thinking in Children: Research Based on Piaget's Theory.* New York: Holt, Rinehart and Winston.

Kopp, C. B. and Shaperman, J. (1973) Cognitive development in the absence of object manipulation during infancy. *Developmental Psychology,* **9,** 430.

Krauss, R. M. and Glucksberg, S. (1969) The development of communication: Competence as a function of age. *Child Development,* **40,** 255-266.

Landers, W. F. (1971) Effects of differential experience on infant's performance in a Piagetian Stage IV object-concept task. *Developmental Psychology,* **5,** 48-54.

Larsen, G. Y. (1977) Methodology in developmental psychology: An examination of research on Piagetian theory. *Child Development,* **48,** 1160-1166.

Lecompte, G. K. and Gratch, G. (1972) Violation of a rule as a method of diagnosing infants' level of object concept. *Child Development,* **43,** 384-396.

Liben, L. S. (1978) Perspective-taking skills in young children: Seeing the world through rose-coloured glasses. *Developmental Psychology,* **14,** 87-92.

Lowenthal, F. (1977) Games, graphs and the logic of language acquisition—a working hypothesis. *Communication and Cognition,* **10,** 47-52.

Maratsos, M. P. Non-egocentric communication abilities in pre-school children. *Child Development,* **44,** 697-700.

Markman, E. (1973) The facilitation of part-whole comparisons by use of collective noun 'family'. *Child Development,* **44,** 837-840.

Markman, E. and Seibert, J. Classes and collections: Internal organization and resulting holistic properties. *Cognitive Psychology,* **8,** 561-577.

Marshark, M. (1977) Lexical marking and the acquisition of relational size concepts. *Child Development,* **48,** 1049-1051.

Marvin, R. S., Greenberg, M. T. and Mossler, D. G. (1976) The early development of conceptual perspective-taking: Distinguishing among multiple perspectives. *Child Development,* **47,** 511-514.

Masangkay, Z. S., McCluskey, K. A., McIntyre, C. W., Sims-Knight, J., Vaughn, B. E. and Flavell, J. H. (1974) The early development of inferences about the visual precepts of others. *Child Development,* **45,** 357-366.

Masur, E. F. (1978) Pre-school boys' speech modifications: The effect of listeners' linguistic levels and conversational responsiveness. *Child Development,* **49,** 924-927.

Maurer, D., Siegel, L. S., Lewis, T. L., Kristofferson, M. W., Barnes, R. A. and Levy, B. A. (1979) Long-term memory improvement? *Child Development,* **50,** 106-118.

McGarrigle, J. and Donaldson, M. (1974/5) Conservation accidents. *Cognition,* **3,** 341-350.

McGarrigle, J., Grieve, R. and Hughes, M. (1978) Interpreting inclusion: A contribution to the study of the child's cognitive and linguistic development. *Journal of Experimental Child Psychology,* **26,** 528-550.

Menig-Peterson, C. L. (1975) The modification of communicative behaviour in preschool-aged children as a function of the listener's perspective. *Child Development,* **46,** 1015-1018.

Menig-Peterson, C. L. and McCabe, A. (1978) Children's orientation of a listener to the context of their narratives. *Developmental Psychology,* **14,** 582-592.

Mead, M. (1932) An investigation of the thought of primitive children, with special reference to animism. *Journal of the Royal Anthropological Institute,* **62,** 173-190.

Miller, P. H. (1978) Stimulus variables in conservation: An alternate approach to assessment. *Merrill-Palmer Quarterly,* **24,** 143-160.

Miller, P. H. and Heldmeyer, K. H. (1975) Perceptual information in conservation: Effects of screening. *Child Development,* **45,** 588-592.

Miller, S. S. (1976) Non-verbal assessment of Piagetian concepts. *Psychological Bulletin,* **83,** 405-430.

Mogar, M. (1960) Children's casual reasoning about natural phenomena. *Child Development,* **31,** 59-65.

Mossler, D. G., Marvin, R. S. and Greenberg, M. T. (1976) Conceptual perspective-taking in two- to six-year-old children. *Developmental Psychology,* **12,** 85-86.

Nass, M. L. (1956) The effects of three variables on children's concepts of physical causality. *Journal of Abnormal Social Psychology,* **53,** 191-196.

Niebuhr, V. N. and Molfese, V. I. (1978) Two operations in class inclusion: Quantification of inclusion and hierarchical classification. *Child Development,* **49,** 892-894.

Odom, R. D. (1978) A perceptual-salience account of decalage relations and developmental change. In Siegel, L. S. and Brainerd, C. J. (Eds.) *Alternatives to Piaget: Critical Essays of the Theory.* New York: Academic Press.

Odom, R. D., Astor, E. C. and Cunningham, J. G. (1975) Effects of perceptual salience on the matrix task performance of four- and six-year-old children. *Child Development,* **46,** 758-762.

Patterson, C. J., Massad, C. M. and Cosgrove, J. M. (1978) Children's referential communication: Components of plans for effective listening. *Developmental Psychology,* **14,** 401-406.

Piaget, J. (1932) *The Moral Judgment of the Child.* London: Routledge and Kegan Paul.

Piaget, J. (1954) *The Construction of Reality in the Child.* New York: Basic Books.

Piaget, J. and Inhelder, B. (1956) *The Child's Concept of Space.* London: Routledge and Kegan Paul.

Piaget, J. and Inhelder, B. (1973) *Memory and Intelligence.* London: Routledge and Kegan Paul.

Rheingold, H. L., Hay, D. F. and West, M. J. (1976) Sharing in the second year of life. *Child Development,* **47,** 1148-1158.

Rose, S. A. (1973) Acquiescence and conservation. *Child Development,* **44,** 811-814.

Rose, S. A. and Blank, M. (1974) The potency of context in children's cognition: An illustration through conservation. *Child Development,* **45,** 499-502.

Russell, R. W. (1939) The development of animistic concepts in the child. *Psychological Bulletin,* **36,** 600.

Russell, R. W. (1940a) Studies in animism: II. The development of animism. *Journal of Genetic Psychology,* **46,** 353-366.

Russell, R. W. (1940b) Studies in animism: IV. An investigation of concepts allied to animism. *Journal of Genetic Psychology,* **57,** 83-91.

Russell, R. W. and Dennis, W. (1939) Studies in animism: I. A standardized procedure for the investigation of animism. *Journal of Genetic Psychology,* **55,** 389-400.

Segalowitz, S. J. (1980) Piaget's Achilles' heel: A safe soft spot? *Human Development,* **22,** 137-140.

Shatz, M. and Gelman, R. (1973) The development of communication skills: Modifications in the speech of young children as a function of listener. *Monographs of the Society for Research in Child Development,* **38,** (5, Serial No. 152).

Sheppard, J. L. (1973) Conservation of part and whole in the acquisition of class inclusion. *Child Development,* **44,** 380-383.

Shipley, E. F. (1979) The class-inclusion task: Question form and distributive comparisons. *Journal of Psycholinguistic Research,* **8,** 301-331.

Siegel, L. S. (1972) Development of the concept of seriation. *Developmental Psychology,* **6,** 135-137.

Siegel, L. S. (1978) The relationship of language and thought in the pre-operational child. In Siegel, L. S. and Brainerd, C. J. (Eds.) *Alternatives to Piaget: Critical Essays on the Theory.* New York: Academic Press.

Siegel, L. S. and Brainerd, C. J. (1978) *Alternatives to Piaget: Critical Essays on the Theory.* New York: Academic Press.

Siegel, L. S. and Goldstein, A. G. Conservation of number in young children: Recency versus relational response strategies. *Developmental Psychology,* **1,** 128-130.

Siegel, L. S., McCabe, A. E., Brand, J. and Matthews, J. Evidence for the understanding of class inclusion in pre-school children: Linguistic factors and training effects. *Child Development,* **49,** 688-693.

Silverman, I. W., Vanderhorst, G. N. and Eull, W. H. (1976) Perception as a possible source of conservation: Evidence for length conservation. *Child Development,* **47,** 427-433.

Sinclair de Zwart, H. (1969) Developmental psycholinguistics. In Elkind, D. and Flavell, J. H. (Eds.) *Studies in Cognitive Development.* New York, London, Toronto: Oxford University Press.

Smith, F. and Dougherty, J. H. (1965) Natural phenomena as explained by children. *Journal of Educational Research,* **59,** 137-140.

Stone, C. A. and Day, M. C. (1978) Levels of availability of a formal operational strategy. *Child Development,* **49,** 1054-1065.

Tatarsky, J. H. The influence of dimensional manipulations on class-inclusion performance. *Child Development,* **45,** 1173-1175.

Trabasso, T., Isen, I. M., Dolecki, P., McLanahan, A. G., Riley, C. A. and Tucker, T. (1978) How do children solve class-inclusion problems? In Siegler, R. S. (Ed.) *Children's Thinking: What Develops?* New York: Halsted Press.

Uzgiris, I. C. and Hunt, J. McV. (1975) *Assessment in Infancy: Ordinal Scales of Psychological Development.* Urbana: University of Illinois Press.

Webb, R. A., Massar, B. and Nadolny, T. (1972) Information and strategy in the young child's search for hidden objects. *Child Development,* **43,** 91-104.

Wheldall, K. and Poborca, B. Conservation without conversation? An alternative, non-verbal paradigm for assessing conservation of liquid quantity. *British Journal of Psychology,* in press.

Wilkinson, A. (1976) Counting strategies and semantic analysis as applied to class inclusion. *Cognitive Psychology,* **8,** 64-85.

Winer, G. A. (1974a) An analysis of verbal facilitation of class-inclusion reasoning. *Child Development,* **45,** 224-227.

Winer, G. A. (1974b) Conservation of different quantities among pre-school children. *Child Development,* **45,** 839-842.

Winer, G. A. (1980) Class-inclusion reasoning in children: A review of the empirical literature. *Child Development,* **51,** 309-328.

Chapter 5

Training Research and Cognitive Development: What do Piagetians Want to Accomplish?*

JACQUES VONÈCHE AND MAGALI BOVET

INTRODUCTION

The present chapter is divided into three parts. The first and longest part is devoted to a restatement of Piagetian theory in such terms as to elicit the biological foundations of the theory as well as to reinstate the basic tenets of genetic epistemology. The second part attempts to show that various methodologies stem from various epistemologies and that different methodologies accomplish very different tasks in science. They should not be confused with one another, and there should not be any sort of worshipping of any specific method regardless of the aims of the epistemology in which it is instrumental. This is part of the means—ends hierarchy. The third part consists of a selective review of the literature in the domain of training. It demonstrates how researchers outside the Piagetian tradition have confused the issues. Performances have been taken for competences and achievements for processes to the point of making further research pointless by removing the cognitive problem at stake by removing the so-called irrelevancies. The conclusion attempts to bring back the baby in the tub as well as the water out of which the empiricists as well as the idealists wanted to bleach the polluting Piagetian slovenliness in a generous attempt at epistemological purity. The danger with purity, as Mary Douglas pointed out in *Purity and Danger* (1966), is that it eliminates the ambiguities from life and nature instead of explaining how we come to make our peace with them.

Dr Magali Bovet took ill during the preparation of this paper so that I am solely responsible for the final stage of the manuscript. Dr Bovet would certainly have taken out a number of abrasive remarks and comments as well as smoothed out the general tenor of the argument with her usual kindness, of which I am incapable.

83

Now, a word of caution to the reader is in order. We do not think that Piagetian psychology is *the* answer to all problems in developmental theory and practice. We even consider that it presents very great difficulties in grounding knowledge in biological homeostatic or homeorhesic models as well as in formal logical mathematical groups. But these difficulties do not seem to preoccupy the majority of developmental psychologists, although they should really be more concerned with them than with stages, social processes or trainability in children's development, all issues which are not central to Piagetian thinking as Gruber and Vonèche have pointed out in *The Essential Piaget* (1977).

THEORY

Since the aim of this book is to present arguments for and against Piagetian theory instead of firing our usual cartridges against empiricism, we would like to present the reader of that tradition with a Piaget who speaks to their condition.

As an example of what we should be doing, we would like to give an excerpt of M. Donaldson's *Children's Minds* (1978).

> Piaget was originally trained as a zoologist, and when he studies human behaviour he tries to place it in the wider context of behaviour of other living things. For him the key question is: how do animals adapt to their environment? Human intelligence is then considered as one means of doing this.
>
> It is important to recognize that the focus of attention is not on the ways in which people differ from one another—hence not on 'intelligence testing' as ordinarily understood. Piaget wants to discover—and explain—the normal course of development. For he believes that there *is* a normal course: a sequence which we all follow, though we go at varying speeds and some go further than others.
>
> This focus on what is common to us all is related to the fact that, as well as being a zoologist, Piaget is an epistemologist: that is, he is concerned with general questions about the nature of knowledge. He believes that these questions cannot be answered without taking account of how knowledge develops and grows. So both of his interests—the biological and the epistemological—converge in the study of human intellectual development.
>
> Clearly this development can be studied as it occurs in individual lives; or it can be studied as it occurs in the history of the species in the development of bodies of knowledge like mathematics or the sciences. Piaget is interested in both of these topics. But we shall be concerned here only with his claims about the developments that take place within an individual life-span.

Five points seem noteworthy for our purpose.

(1) Animal adaptation and human intelligence.
(2) Biology and knowledge.
(3) The close relation between ontogeny and phylogeny.
(4) Insistence on developmental mechanisms.
(5) Focus on commonalities and not differences.

Let us take these points one by one.

Animal Adaptation and Human Intelligence

> Cognitive processes seem, then, to be at one and the same time the outcome of organic autoregulation reflecting its essential mechanisms, and the most highly differentiated organs of this regulation at the core of interactions with the environment so much so that, in the case of man, these processes are being extended to the universe itself. (Piaget, 1971, p. 34)

Cognitive processes are 'organs'? At first reading, this seems like a kind of objective idealism giving material reality status to ideas. On a second reading what Piaget seems to mean is simply that cognition cannot be said to occur in any one of the conventionally defined organ systems of the body, but draws upon them and reorganizes them into a new set of functional relations. Thus 'cognitive autoregulation makes use of the general systems of organic regulations such as are found at every genetic, morpho-genetic, physiological and nervous level, and forthwith adapts them to their new situation . . . This situation constitutes the exchanges with environment that form the basis of behaviour' (ibid., pp. 36—37).

But, for Piaget, there are some crucial differences between cognition and organic functioning: 'The outstanding characteristic of cognitive organizations is the progressive dissociation of form and content' (ibid., p. 153). In at least four ways, then, Piaget's formulation seems to have a ring of philosophical idealism: the teleological note of autoregulation (Piaget would say teleonomical instead of teleological), the assertion that cognitive processes are 'organs', the claim of their universality and completeness, and the ultimate separation of form and content. But Piaget strongly believes that modern developments in systems theory and cybernetics provide the conceptual tools for understanding a growing, self-regulating, adaptive system without giving way to teleology.

Biology and Knowledge

Biology and Knowledge (Piaget, 1967) which is an essay on the relations between organic regulation and cognitive processes raises the question of how the various forms of knowledge can be seen as differentiated organs of the regulations of functional exchanges with the external world. Piaget justifies his hypothesis that cognitive functions constitute a specialized organ for regulating with the external world by the use of five different arguments: (1) the relationships between life and truth; (2) the shortcomings of the organism; (3) the relations between instinct, learning and logico-mathematical structures; (4) the bursting out of instinct; (5) the relation between knowledge and society.

Life and truth

These two concepts seem to be opposed, since the property of knowledge is the attainment of truth, whereas the property of life is simply survival. This opposition seems in contradiction to Piaget's idea of the continuity between life and knowledge. However, one could consider truth as a copy of reality and say that life and truth coincide since both deal with the same reality. But the problem remains in such a view that in order to copy the model, one needs to know what is being copied. Thus, knowledge constantly anticipates itself in this world-view.

If truth is not a copy of reality, it can only be the result of the organizing activity of a subject. Philosophers in search of an absolute have had recourse to some transcendental subject way above human nature, which is also contradictory to the local historical conditions in which humans have to search for truth, as evidenced in the progress of knowledge. Thus one should not escape from nature into absolutism, but penetrate nature and see how truth has appeared as an output of just surviving. This is a biological question: the question of the construction of the different stages allowing the passage from survival to the formation of an internal/external necessity which we call truth.

Shortcoming of the organism

Life is a system of exchanges with the environment; therefore the organism tries to extend as far as the environment as a whole does, but it does not succeed. This is where knowledge comes in and assimilates functionally the entire universe. The forms of knowledge relay the forms of life and bring them beyond their actual physiological limits that make them unstable and perishable, by extending these material forms into a system of conservations. Thus the shortcomings of the organism are clearly due to the fact that physiological regulations are always locally determined by their here and now interaction with the external world. On the contrary, the forms of thought bring in stability and simultaneously reversible mobility. Their very mobility allows the forms of thought to be more and more independent of actual external pressure and internal imbalances. The problem is now to understand how the forms of thought can surpass organic regulation.

Instinct, learning and logico-mathematical structures

The first device by which the organisms bring a certain stability to their organization is heredity. Instincts follow this pattern. Instincts link together in one capsule hereditary dispositions of the organism and phenotypic accommodations. This process cannot be corrected if either environmental or organic conditions change drastically in the course of the animal's life. It is, thus, a form of adaptation that will burst out in the dissociation of its two components, hereditary dispositions and phenotypic accommodations. Phenotypic accommodations will lead to learning, and hereditary dispositions to cognitive regulations that will separate progressively forms from contents by recognizing those aspects of experience that can be transformed and generalized from one situation to the next. This process of differentiation is for Piaget at the roots of logico-mathematical structures.

The bursting out of instinct

One of the basic characteristics of anthropoids is the almost total disappearance, in their case, of instinct. The 'logic' of instinct is that, thanks to a programme, it links together in one stable unit organic hereditary dispositions and phenotypic accommodations. In anthropoids, this programme dissolves and leaves room for a new mode of interaction between the organism and its environment: intelligence. The main characteristic of intelligence is that it replaces programming by construction. The differences between programme and construction are many: a programme cannot be corrected in the course of action, whereas a construction must correct itself constantly by definition; a programme results from the fixation of one given state of the organism to one given state of the environment; its range of variation and adaptation is limited, whereas a construction resulting from an equilibrium between the subject and the environment is infinitely adaptive. Last but not least, by separating strongly organic dispositions from phenotypic accommodations, the constructions of intelligences allow for two opposite and complementary directions of development: interiorization in the direction of its sources and exteriorization in the direction of learned, experimental adjustments.

Relation between knowledge and society

If such a complete reconstruction is possible, it is because, when abandoning the support of hereditary apparatus and developing constructed and phenotypic regulations, intelligence gives up the transindividual cycles of instinct in order to adopt inter-individual or social interaction. Anthropoids work only in groups. Social environment does for intelligence what population does for genetics: it provides an effective support for co-operation, namely the co-ordination of view points into a reversible mobile system.

The Close Relation Between Ontogeny and Phylogeny

Piaget's hypothesis in his book *Adaptation Vitale et Psychologie de l'Intelligence: Sélection Organique et Phénocopie* (1974) (not yet translated) is that the changes in the genome can be viewed as an extension of the self-regulating activities of the organism. Piaget's critique of neo-Darwinism bears on two key points. First, in neo-Darwinism, mutation is considered as being a random process, in the sense that a given mutation, when it occurs, has no relation to the adaptive needs of the organism. Second, natural selection is a process in which the organism is essentially passive; it is the environment that responds to the mutation that has happened to the organism.

Piaget raises three objections to this picture of phylogeny. First, the sheer improbability of the evolution of complex organs on the basis of chance alone. Second, the genome is not sealed off from the rest of the body. It is known to control the functioning and the development of the organism during its embryological life. It is implausible to think of this relation as one way. Third, each individual gene is not sitting there simply waiting for a mutation to happen to it or not, as chance decrees. It is interacting with other genes, influencing them and being influenced by them. So, the organism is perpetually active. It is hard to imagine that, for Piaget, such an organism does not take the initiative of the mutation as part of a total process of organized self-regulation. In such a perspective, selection is not only natural, but also organic in the sense given to it by J. M. Baldwin (1896—1902). Baldwin noticed that many structural changes occur in an organism when they are not yet useful. There is thus a phenomenon of anticipation, as Piaget calls it, that is concomitant with the influence of the past, so much so that there is a continuity from memory to anticipation such that a given scenario can be run either backward in memory or forward in anticipation. For Piaget, this is made possible by *phenocopy*. The phenocopy hypothesis proposes that there are both exogenous and endogenous variations in phenotypes. A variation appears by chance exogenously. Once the exogenous form is established, the organism reinvents it by changing itself in such a manner as to produce endogenously the same phenotypical result. This process of replacement of an exogenous phenotype by an endogenous genotype of the same form is what Piaget calls *phenocopy* and Lorenz *genocopy*. This process should be clearly distinguished from Lamarckism. The heredity of acquired characteristics in Lamarckism consists in a mere internalization of the exogenous into the endogenous. It corresponds to behaviourism in psychology. On the contrary, the phenocopy hypothesis supposes an endogenous reconstruction of the exogenous. So, at each level, from the genome to the more abstract cognitive structure, the organisms have an inner system for sensing perturbations in their functioning. If something is not working properly, a process of variation begins in the form either of a mutation or of groping until a response occurs that solves the problem by either nullifying the perturbation or anticipating it as a subsystem of the organism's interaction with the environment, both at the biological and cognitive levels.

In such a view, the link between phylogenesis and ontogenesis is very strong indeed, since individual variations are always concomitant with species variations. So much so, that the only way for Piaget to understand the missing links between historical and prehistorical men is the study of today's children. This could appear as a return to the famous recapitulation hypothesis of phylogeny into ontogeny. This would be mistaken, because, for Piaget, the relationship existing between phylogeny and ontogeny is subsumed under common mechanisms of construction, as in phenocopy. What he says is simply that if we are going to understand developmentally the unfolding of cognitive processes, the only way 'to fill the gaps in our knowledge at the level of phylogenesis is a recourse to embryo- or to ontogeny' (Apostel et al, 1973, p. 230, our translation). 'If we are to ask from history the secret of formative mechanisms, we should then be able to reconstitute the most elementary processes of prehistorical man and the intellectual stages of the formation of man' (ibid., p. 230).

Thus, for Piaget, the child is the real primitive among us, the missing link between prehistorical men and contemporary adults.

Insistence on Developmental Mechanisms

It should be clear by now that the focus of Piaget's attention is upon development at every level. Ontogenetic development is only part of the picture, since it makes sense only by relation to phylogenesis. In the same way, cognitive changes in the child make sense only by reference to their biological, phylogenetic origins. According to Piaget, questions in general psychology such as the place of learning, the nature of intelligence, etc., could be answered only developmentally. Moreover, epistemological questions about the nature of knowledge could also be answered only developmentally. So much so that Piaget transformed Kant's original question: how is knowledge possible, into a question that has a developmental answer: how is the growth of knowledge possible? This changed formulation is important. It avoids the unanswerable question of distinguishing between a state of absence of knowledge and one in which knowledge is already there, by transforming it into one about distinguishing stages of lesser and better knowledge.

Focus on Commonalities and not Differences

It should be obvious by now that individual differences are not important for somebody who is looking for the general subject of history: phylogenesis and 'epistemogenesis' (genetic epistemology). At the biological level, Piaget is interested in forms and their variations. His theoretical position is from this view point noteworthy. Contrary to the main Mendelian position that distinguishes between fluctuating and hereditary variations, of which the former is due to changes in the intensity of some environmental variables and the latter to the introduction of a wholly new factor—mutation, Piaget considers that all variations are adaptive changes which, if continued, become irreversible or hereditary in the Mendelian sense. The point, here, is not that there are hereditary and fluctuating species, but that a continuing fluctuating variation becomes hereditary. The consequence of this is twofold: (1) the change is never sudden but always gradual; (2) the explanation for the change lies in the process of becoming itself.

The explanation by genesis is also present at the psychological level in Piaget's theory. Although he grew interested in the development of intelligence thanks to a standardization of Binet's tests of intelligence, Piaget looked immediately for what was common to all children of the same age, namely, their criterion for truth. This led him later on to the discovery of conservation and other invariants of behaviour. In *The Moral Judgment of the Child*, Piaget looked also for commonalities in the application of norms that change with the developmental level of the child, but which are universally respected by the children of the same age. In a forthcoming book with the physicist Garcia, he is trying to treat history of science in the same way, i.e. to discover a hierarchy of truth criteria universally respected by each period of science. The subject in which Piaget is interested with regard to biological, psychological and scientific knowledge is the so-called epistemic subject, a subject that is representative of a mode of thinking of the world and not the individual subject, who could be at various developmental levels in the different domains of human action.

METHODOLOGY

The very fact that Piaget insists upon commonalities rather than on differences raises an interesting methodological question for the study of learning. In order to assess the effectiveness of learning upon a given child, one would need a method by which the exact individual performance of that given child could be measured before and after training. Hence a differential methodology. Apparently, there is no such a thing in Piaget's approach. How is the effect of learning to be measured then?

To understand the specificity of the Genevan approach, one must understand clearly the relationship existing in Piaget's psychology between learning and development. For Piaget, learning is different from development but at the same time subsumed under the latter. The main limitation to learning, in this view, is the fact that it can only enlarge a specific segment of the total process of development, by showing how mental structures generate each other, and how schemata are reco-ordinated with each other.

This does not mean at all that Piaget is an idealist for whom development is purely endogenous. On the contrary, it means a very strong form of interactionism, because the kind of reconstruction that takes place under learning conditions is explained in terms of cognitive conflicts. A cognitive conflict supposes an interaction between the existing schemata of the subject and observable, environmental data that do not fit the existing representational model of the child at that moment. 'A living creature does not merely react, it also *takes action*' (Donaldson, M., her italics, op. cit., p. 131). Taking action upon the environment entails a reco-ordination of internal schemata.

It should be clear by now that such a cognitive conflict is the opposite of empiristic methodologies imagined, for instance, by P. Bryant and J. Bruner (among others), in which the attainment of conservation or invariance is made possible by removing so-called irrelevant cues and sharpening relevant ones. It seems to the present authors that the very concept of relevance refers necessarily to certain cognitive expectations made by the subject on the basis of a certain unformulated 'theory' about the nature of the world.

Removing the conflict between incompatible cues (for example, length and number in the conservation of number) also removes the problem.

Cognitive conflict is also different from the quantitative methodologies that attempt to measure the differences in performance *before* and *after* a certain training. Usually, these methods are based upon classical differential tests such as IQ for instance. Their aim is to compare two scores and look for the statistical differences. If the difference is significant beyond a certain probability level, it is concluded that the given training has been effective.

In contrast to this, the concern of the Genevan method is to see what happens during the training procedure. How does the subject move from one set of schemata to another? How does the child perceive a contradiction and try to solve it? By superseding it, or by compromising between the different sets of schemata, or by reducing the posed problem to one for which he or she already has a solution? These are some of the questions asked by the Genevan School. They are very different from the questions generally asked by learning psychologists who want the animal or the child to solve the problem that they, as experimental psychologists, have asked, and in addition, to do so in the way they want them to do so. Such a way of reasoning is radically different from the Genevan one. The Piagetians are interested in discovering what the child thinks about a given question and not how the child could achieve more and better performances. Sometimes it has been said that the Piagetian preoccupation with what the child thinks has led psychologists of that persuasion to complicating excessively a simple straightforward problem for which there is a straightforward response into a lengthy and involved interview that brings the child to the verge of boredom or nervous breakdown. This criticism could be answered in the following way: the assessment of the exact position of the child relative to a given problem needs time and accuracy. Often, a given child will need a certain 'breaking-in' into the sphere of preoccupation that the psychologist wants him or her to espouse. In addition, a number of counter-suggestions have to be made in order to assess the degree of stability, reliability and structuralization of the concept attained by the child. In such a perspective, which is centred around the cognitive processes that children use to answer a problem, it is obvious that children from five to twelve can be presented with the same difficult problem, instead of a sequence of graduated straightforward questions that can be answered successfully at different ages. It should be understood that if one is persuaded that the subjects act upon environment and not just respond to it, then, it becomes tremendously important to show how these subjects structure the problem asked of them according to their cognitive level. Such a strategy necessarily entails that the children are given full opportunity to experiment with the material, to muddle it up, to mess around with it, in short, to make errors, since the experimenter's goal is not performance nor achievement but the manifestation of the cognitive processes at work in the problem-solving situation. Thus the very status of errors is drastically different in Piaget's approach from what it is in classical learning theories. S-R psychologists go to great lengths to avoid errors during learning, since errors are supposed to prevent the subjects from reaching criterion in the most rapid fashion. In contrast, Piagetian psychologists find errors very informative about the internal structure of the mind and they would call on examples such as Dunlap's (1931) experiment in training typists, where learning occurred best when the trainees were deliberately encouraged to let errors happen (a practice that even those trained otherwise seem to continue). In fact, lacunae, mistakes and insufficiencies are often the very basis of a developmental classification; they are the dark side of growth.

The Piagetian learning research paradigm differs considerably from the S-R paradigm in that primarily it does not compare levels of performance before and after training, but focuses upon what has been transformed *in the course of training*. It is the occurrence of novelty which is the main focus of attention and not the fight against the nul hypothesis, an idea imported from R. A. Fisher's agricultural statistics into psychological research where too little is known about the nature of the beast to apply that method intelligently. Once again, the worship of a method leads to trivial results or unguaranteed assertions. The before/after paradigm overlooks the processes by which learning occurs in favour of a score. Such an approach fuses performance and competence instead of looking at the feedback of performance upon competence. In fact, very little research, if any, has been carried out into how trainers train trainees to become independent from them in their learning. Bearison's (1975) study on the long-term effects of his own training method of conservation showed practically no after-effects three years after. The subjects of the experimental group apparently did not learn how to learn, which is the point of all learning research.

SELECTED REVIEW OF THE LITERATURE

In a recent review of learning research and Piagetian theory, Brainerd (1978) mentions a number of articles showing that the tutorial method is as efficient as the Genevan's 'self-discovery' approach, if not more. Let us analyse the major studies he mentions.

The first is a doctoral dissertation presented in 1969 by Rochel Gelman. The study is based on a three-phase design: a training initiated within two weeks of pretesting, a post-test after the last day of training and a second post-test two or three weeks later. A subject was defined as a nonconserver if he/she gave no correct answer or explanations, or one or two correct answers but no correct explanations or one or two correct answers but no correct explanation for any of the right items. The test items retained for learning were the conservation of length, liquid and mass. Three training conditions were devised: (1) discrimination learning-set with length and number stimuli; (2) the same conditions without feedback about correct answers after discrimination; (3) discrimination learning-set with 'junk' stimuli. Each problem consisted of three stimuli, two of which containing identical stimuli, and one containing different ones. There were 16 problems and six trials for each, presented for two consecutive days. The same situation served as pretest, training and post-test. During the post-test, the experimenter also measured the training transfer to a slightly modified situation (for example, for length conservation, the Muller—Lyer illusion).

The results showed that 'impressive improvements in both number and length conservation were observed' (Brainerd, 1978, p. 86). But what had been learned in the process? The understanding of 'same' and 'different' was most likely acquired before training. In addition, the subjects in oddity control training made virtually no errors in training. In the learning-set training, the subject began to learn immediately, reaching an asymptotic performance afterwards. What is the effect of learning here? In the non-feedback situation, the young children did not learn very much, showing that what had been learned was the giving of a verbal answer of a certain type.

Now, compare this sort of training with a truly Piagetian task: in the Piagetian situation, children are not given any feedback, but counter-suggestions. In addition, they are supposed to transform a puzzling situation into a problem that they can solve. According to their logic of thinking, the solution will be different. Such a situation has nothing in common with such things as animal training, discrimination learning, or researching a criterion decided by the experimenter.

To the extent that conservation is reduced to a problem of attention and discrimination, nobody would need Piagetian theory. A simple conditional and learning theory is sufficient to account for the results. Unfortunately, the tasks devised by Gelman had nothing to do with conservation. She measured only something relevant to classical learning theories and she called it 'conservation'. To us, this is an abuse of language. Hatano and Suga (1969) did the same.

In Murray's study (1972), using conformity training à la Ash, we find another example of changing the problem of logical conservation into social conformity. Yielding to the pressure of the majority is quite a different thing from having attained conservation, as evidenced in Ash's original situation where the minority of 'one' gave answers that they knew were incorrect. Miller, Schwartz and Stewart (1973) pretested young adults (median age 20) on weight conservation with the expected result of 100 per cent success. Then, they trained the subjects in experiments in which the experimenter cheated reality by adding or subtracting surreptitiously small quantities of matter during the transformation. In the post-test, 14 subjects out of 46 gave non-conservation responses. Interestingly enough, these responses are not at all pre-operatory.

The 'nonconserving' subjects accounted for the pseudo-nonconservation of matter thanks to strictly formal operational forms of reasoning. Thus, once again one should clearly distinguish between the results of the subjects and the processes by which they are attained. It is pitiful that with his immense experimental training Frank B. Murray did not try to test the power of this result by imagining a counter-experiment à la Miller and Schwartz. Thanks to such a Popperian falsification procedure, he would have been able to show experimentally that there is a complete independence between social manipulation of responses and mental operations.

A third example is provided by Sheppard's studies on quantity conservation and class inclusion trainings conducted respectively in 1973 and 1974. In the quantity conservation experiment, the subjects were trained by the self-discovery method which focuses on the learning of a compensation rule for the two dimensions of a container (what is gained in width is lost in height and vice-versa). The results indicated 30 to 40 per cent of progression from non-conservation to perfect performance among subjects who were passive observers of the transformations made by the experimenter and agreed with his or her comments about the results.

Brainerd makes a point out of the fact that Sheppard got better results than Inhelder, Sinclair and Bovet (1974) who studied a similar situation where the subjects (and sometimes pre-conservers) were active. But there is no point to be made here, because, once again, Brainerd confuses drill training with human learning and growth. It would take the most stupid children not to be capable of predicting correctly what will happen to the water level, the sausage, etc., after having *actually* seen *several times* what has happened to the very same material about which they made wrong predictions the first time around. Who is kidding whom here?

Sheppard's experiment on class inclusion shows even more shortcomings, since, in addition, it confuses logical sequence with direction of attention: the child is not supposed to show any *understanding* of the logical sequence involved in this sort of class inclusion but to follow certain behavioural rules dictated by the experimenter. Again, what does this have to do with the growth of knowledge? It is mere drill training within the capability of any mammal and not only of children. Sarah, the chimpanzee who made Premack famous, 'conserves' in the very same way as Sheppard's subjects.

If one examines, then, a broader range of learning studies as we did earlier (Bovet and Vonèche, 1977), one is led to conclude that the subjects who benefited the most from training were also described by the experimenters as older, more mature, or more articulate than those who did not. This is not surprising, since the natural growth of thinking takes so much time to happen, but it casts some doubts on the validity of the categorization system by which children are classified as conservers and non-conservers. There is, here, a confusion between genetic psychology and differential psychology. It should be clear that the methods of each of these two fields are intended to bring about different outcomes. Differential psychology is interested in individual differences and not so much in the way these differences are formed, which is the object of genetic psychology. Thus, using the methods of one field to get results in the other seems somewhat strange and rather imprudent as a procedure. In fact, when progress is reported, it could be due entirely to the fact that subjects who attained the stage of conservation after learning were just on the verge of getting there naturally.

In addition, most of the studies do not meet three basic criteria of the valid attainment of conservation: (1) temporal stability of the acquisition; (2) amount of intertask transfer; (3) construction of more complex structure. This is especially true for the studies reported by Brainerd. In an interesting follow-up study, Bearison (1975), testing the subjects who had been trained in his learning experiment for advances in operatory development, discovered that those who were naturally ahead of their age group were still more advanced three years after but that those who had benefited from learning were back at the natural average level, showing that training had no lasting effect. If these results were to be generalized, they would show the pointlessness of training studies for cognitive development. In fact, who wants short-term effects in education?

CONCLUSION

What seems misunderstood in learning research about operatory concepts is the necessity of an equilibration between two co-ordinated dynamic factors: (1) the internal regulatory forces; and (2) the external argumentative powers. Only the latter is amenable to direct pressure from the environment, be it physical or social. The former depends on the integration of different levels of cognitive development within a given individual. But it is by means of argumentation that subjects make their own cognitive structure known, as well as take into consideration the viewpoint of others. Therefore, we think it absolutely necessary to let children argue and even to encourage them in this activity by a special procedure that we call the 'clinical' or 'critical' method. Argumentation is central to the understanding of the causal aspects of cognitive growth and as such is superior to other training methods. But we certainly rejoice in observing that those researchers who do not share our theoretical concerns nevertheless record the same findings as those of Piaget and his followers. We welcome the polemical methodological discussions between us, because they will help us to clarify our approach and improve our experimentation in many ways so that our results become more widely acceptable to developmental psychologists of different persuasions. The advantage of a discussion such as this is that it contributes to making our field more scientific and less philosophical in the sense that scholastic crossfires and personal paradigms are substituted by general consensus.

REFERENCES

Apostel, A. (1973) *L'Explication dans les Sciences.* With others including J. Piaget. Paris: Flammarion.
Baldwin, J. M. (1896) A new factor in evolution. *The American Naturalist,* **30,** 441-451 and 536-553.
Baldwin, J. M. (1902) *Development and Evolution.* London: G. Allen. New York: McMillan.
Bearison, D. J. (1975) Induced versus spontaneous attainment of concrete operations and their relationship to school achievement. *Journal of Educational Psychology,* **67** (4) 576-580.
Bovet, M. C. and Vonèche, J. J. (1977) Is child stimulation effective? In Oliverio, A. (Ed.) *Genetics, Environment and Intelligence.* Amsterdam: Elsevier.
Brainerd, C. J. (1978) Learning research and Piagetian theory. In Siegel, L. and Brainerd, C. J. (Eds.) *Alternatives to Piaget: Critical Essays on the Theory.* New York: Academic Press.
Donaldson, M. (1978) *Children's Minds.* London: Fontana.
Douglas, M. (1966) *Purity and Danger.* London: Routledge and Kegan Paul.
Dunlap, K. (1934) quoted in Murchison, C. (Ed.) *Handbook of General Experimental Psychology.* Worcester: Clark University Press.

Gelman, R. J. (1969) Conservation acquisition. *Journal of Experimental Child Psychology,* **9,** 167-187.

Gruber, M. E. and Vonèche, J. (Eds.) (1977) *The Essential Piaget.* New York: Basic Books.

Hatano, G. A. and Suga, Y. (1969) Equilibration and external reinforcement in the acquisition of number conservation. *Japanese Psychological Research,* **11,** 17-31.

Inhelder, B., Sinclair, H. and Bovet, M. C. (1974) *Learning and the Development of Cognition.* Cambridge: Harvard University Press.

Miller, S. A., Schwartz, L. C. and Stewart, C. (1973) An attempt to extinguish conservation of weight in college students. *Developmental Psychology,* **8,** 316.

Murray, F. B. (1972) Acquisition of conservation through social interaction. *Developmental Psychology,* **6,** 1-6.

Piaget, J. (1957) *Le Jugement Moral Chez l'Enfant.* Paris: Presses Universitaires de France.

Piaget, J. (1967) *Biologie et Connaissance.* Paris: Gallimard.

Piaget, J. (1974) *Adaptation Vitale et Psychologie de l'Intelligence: Sélection Organique et Phénocopie.* Paris: Hermann.

Sheppard, J. L. (1973) Conservation of part and whole in the acquisition of class inclusion. *Child Development,* **44,** 380-383.

Sheppard, J. L. (1974) Compensation and combinatorial systems in the acquisition of class inclusion. *Child Development,* **45,** 717-730.

Interchange

SIEGEL AND HODKIN REPLY TO VONÈCHE AND BOVET

Vonèche and Bovet deal with several controversies between Piagetians and non-Piagetians. One of these issues concerns the role of learning in development. Vonèche and Bovet appear to treat learning as a passive, mechanistic process. We believe that this conception of learning is an inaccurate one. Learning is not inherently passive, but can be an active and creative process. Learning involves response-produced changes in the organism's perception of and reaction to the environment, and is not a static process. The learner changes with each environmental encounter so that the process is one of organism—environmental interaction.

The authors refer to most attempts at training as 'drill training'. The implication is that this training is merely some sort of rote learning. However, studies such as those of Sheppard (1973, 1974) and Hatano and Suga (1969) have examined the generality of training and have found that, for many children, the training does generalize to other situations. This would seem to be a significant form of learning. It seems both interesting and important to demonstrate that such learning takes place.

There is the implication that psychologists who study learning are interested only in the outcome not the process. Perhaps there are some that fit this stereotype but there are many who do not. For example, Cornell (1978) has examined the *manner* in which babies acquire the concept of object permanence.

Learning psychologists are not interested in only immediate performance. Obviously one must look at the long-term effects of training and its transfer to other similar tasks. Brainerd (1978) has reviewed many studies that do so. But one cannot ignore these obvious gains.

The point of the learning experiments is that if the learning can take place easily through observation or experimentation the concept of the child as pre-operational has little meaning. The child's status, or, if one prefers, responses, can be easily changed (at least in some cases). This malleability is important for both theoretical and empirical reasons. Theoretically, the ease with which learning can take place casts doubt on the strict structuralist position. Empirically, it means that the whole idea of the assessment of the level at which a child is functioning is not merely a matter of presenting him or her with a task and noting the behavioural and verbal responses but also involves examining the susceptibility to training of certain cognitions. A concept that can be easily trained cannot be said to be absent in a child.

One of the issues raised in this paper is the competence—performance problem. The argument of the Piagetians seems to be that just because a child can do a non-traditional version of Piagetian task it does not mean that the child really understands the concept. Vonèche and Bovet call these performances that 'have been taken for competences'. However, when we show that a child can do a non-traditional version of a Piagetian task, we believe that we are demonstrating that a child has some competence. The point is that there are different operational definitions of the same concept; the Piagetian version is not the only one. We must look for the reasons for the differences, not just say that one task is the right one and another is the wrong one. The point has been argued before (e.g. Siegel, Brainerd, 1978) but the Piagetians have ignored it.

The authors speak of the need for counter-suggestion as a technique to study. But children, especially younger ones, want to please an adult. They may, indeed, agree that the flattened ball of clay has a smaller amount of clay, if the adult suggests it. But they may be doing it to please the adult. At least investigators must be sensitive to this possibility. The child—experimenter interaction must be viewed from a social psychological perspective.

Piaget and his collaborators have provided us with a useful theoretical approach and careful observations of children's behaviour. What we do say is that the Piagetian tradition has not considered alternative approaches. For example, the other research methods often yield a different picture of cognition. We believe the Piagetian system must consider the results of these studies and incorporate these data into their theoretical model.

REFERENCES

Brainerd, C. J. (1978) Learning research and Piagetian theory. In Siegel, L. S. and Brainerd, C. J. (Eds.) *Alternatives to Piaget: Critical Essays on the Theory.* New York: Academic Press.
Cornell, E. (1978) Learning to find things: A reinterpretation of object permanence studies. In Siegel, L. S. and Brainerd, C. J. (Eds.) *Alternatives to Piaget: Critical Essays on the Theory.* New York: Academic Press.
Hatano, G. and Suga, Y. (1969) Equilibration and external reinforcement in the acquisition of number conservation. *Japanese Psychological Research,* **11,** 17-31.
Sheppard, J. L. (1973) Conservation of part and whole in the acquisition of class inclusion. *Child Development,* **44,** 380-383.
Sheppard, J. L. (1974) Compensation and combinational systems in the acquisition of class inclusion. *Child Development,* **45,** 717-730.
Siegel, L. S. and Brainerd, C. J. (1978) Preface. In Siegel, L. S. and Brainerd, C. J. (Eds.) *Alternatives to Piaget: Critical Essays on the Theory.* New York: Academic Press.

VONÈCHE AND BOVET REPLY TO SIEGEL AND HODKIN

As immodest as it might be, I would like to refer the authors to my interview with Jean Piaget to appear in a book edited by John Broughton and John Freeman-Moir with the provisional title of Baldwin. There, Piaget recognizes a convergence between his and Baldwin's ideas; nothing more. This seems evident from the papers published by Piaget before he encountered Baldwin's ideas via his meeting with Pierre Janet in Paris. Now, let us examine the core of the chapter.

Stages or not?

As Gruber and myself have written in *The Essential Piaget* (1977), the concept of stage does not serve a central function in Piaget's theory. It is essentially a descriptive concept that accounts for the fact that any change, in order to be perceived at all as *change*, must be dually composed of invariance and transformation. It is only when this dialectical process of change is understood, that development can be posited as a process of ideal ordering of organizations, systems or principles. Other definitions of change would not guarantee the orthogenetic principle according to which development is the progression from a state of relative indifferentiation to one of relative differentiation marked by an improvement in hierarchical integration. Without such a general principle, any change on the basis of time would be considered as development (with the sorry corollary that some developments would be revolting ones). Chronology should not be confused with development, history with evolution and progress with history.

Piaget sees such an orthogenetic principle in his law of equilibration. The fact that so many researchers have obtained the same results as his initial ones, shows that real changes are conforming to Piaget's ideal order of development.

Methodological traps

Piaget was never interested in the social context of his experimental situations, because his interest in the child's 'life-world' is limited to the ways in which it is transformed into the world of scientific thought through development. The social psychology of cognitive development is beyond Piaget's scope and this has been expressed clearly by him in several places. One should not be blamed for not doing what one never claimed to be doing.

Language as a source of difficulty

Piaget never denied that language was a source of important difficulties. But once again, the study of psycho-linguistics is not his purpose.

Perception, attention and memory as factors

Once again, Piaget is not a child psychologist but a genetic epistemologist using children for his own purposes and not for their own sake.

Nevertheless, he had Gréco (1960) shown that conservation was easier with small numbers than with large ones and that 'numerosity' anteceded number concept. In *La Genèse des Structures Logiques Élémentaires* (1959), a book on classification and seriation published by Inhelder and Piaget, it was demonstrated that children found it easier to solve double-matrix problems some twenty-five years before the study of Odom, Astor and Cunningham (1975) made the same point.

In *The Mechanisms of Perception* (1961) Piaget showed, long before Silverman, Vanderhurst and Eull (1976) that conservation and perception presented some interesting partial isomorphisms.

As far as the concept of decalage is concerned, one should not forget that these decalages are the mark that the dissociation between form and content is not yet complete.

To train or not to train

This point receives adequate treatment in our own chapter here.

The case of infant development

Piaget cannot be wrong at the same time for not paying enough attention to the senses *and* for putting too much emphasis on sensorimotor co-ordinations. One must choose one's argument here. Either the manipulation of objects is irrelevant for cognitive development in infancy and therefore Piaget put too much attention on attention, memory and perception, or, sensory development has not been studied enough by Piaget and more object manipulations should be introduced by further researchers in their studies of infancy. This seems only logical. One cannot argue both ways.

The case of class inclusion

Once again, Piaget's point is not to have the child *respond* to saliency but to observe the child *produce* it spontaneously. A parrot responds to human language but never produces it. By all sorts of artefacts such as linguistic changes or the introduction of specific stimuli, a clever enough experimenter could change the age of attainment of all sorts of concepts, but then these concepts would not be the same any more either.

Inhelder and Piaget (1959) made the distinction between class and collection some twenty-five years before Markman and Seibert (1976).

The case of animism

The point of animism was made by Piaget early in his career and was never taken up again in further researches on causality and Piaget conducted more than one hundred of them. Obviously, this point was not central to his thinking. Nevertheless, from this observation to the simple denial of animism in children, the step is too big for me to take.

Long-term memory improvement or not?

This criticism is well taken. There is no good reason to postulate a necessary relation between operational improvement and memory improvement. The only advantage of operational improvement is to alleviate somehow the memory load in certain situations.

Egocentrism or not?

I never understood fully the long controversy between Piaget and Wallon on this topic, since, to me, egocentrism meant only in the end that children are less articulate than adults in describing absent things, in role-taking and in other communicative abilities.

The case of formal operations

Siegel and Hodkin argue the case for formal operational attainment before the age of 11 to 12, whereas so many authors (see Gruber and Vonèche, 1976) argue the opposite, namely that about one-third only of the young adolescents and adults reach the stage of formal operations. This shows the plasticity of concept attainment as measured by cognitive psychologists of different persuasions and raises an important theoretical issue, which does not receive an adequate treatment here.

This question is intimately linked with another issue that has not been raised by the authors of this chapter, namely that Piaget's stages of development stop when the institutions that Western societies have devised for the protection of childhood stop rearing children. This question was discussed in relation to formal operations by Gruber and Vonèche (1976) and Vonèche alone in 1979. These authors postulate a life-long cognitive development, provided that one remains healthy and wealthy enough to enjoy a good life. So, instead of fighting each other's personal paradigms of cognitive development, I would propose that psychologists of all schools unite in their efforts to secure these minimum conditions of life-long development for the children of the world especially in these times when so many children are abused, tortured, starved or killed.

REFERENCES

Greco, P. (1960) Recherches sur quelques formes d'inférences arithmétiques. In *Problèmes de la Construction du Nombre*. Paris: Presses universitaires de France.

Gruber, H. E. and Vonèche, J. J. (1976) Réflexions sur les opérations formelles de la pensée. *Archives de Psychologie*.

Gruber, H. E. and Vonèche, J. J. (Eds.) (1977) *The Essential Piaget*. New York: Basic Books.

Inhelder, B. and Piaget, J. (1959) *La Genèse des Structures Logiques Élémentaires*. Neuchâtel: Delachaux et Niestlé.

Vonèche, J. J. et al (1979) *Effets Économiques et Sociaux de l'Enseignement*. Vevey: Delta.

Vonèche, J. J.: Evolution, development and the growth of knowledge: a consideration of Baldwin's biological ideas. In Broughton, J. and Freeman-Moir, J. (Eds.) *Baldwin*, to be published by Ablex, New York.

Vonèche, J. J. Piaget on Baldwin: an interview. In Broughton, J. and Freeman-Moir, J. (Eds.) *Baldwin*, to be published by Ablex, New York.

Chapter 6

Children's Ability to Handle Piaget's Propositional Logic: A Conceptual Critique*

ROBERT H. ENNIS

Ennis, Robert H., Children's ability to handle Piaget's propositional logic. Vol. 45, No. 1, *Review of Educational Research*. Copyright © 1975, American Educational Research Association, Washington, DC.

People have a variety of reasons for their interest in the extent of children's logical ability. Mine has developed from an interest in the teaching of critical thinking. I have earlier argued (Ennis, 1962) that deductive logic plays an essential role in all aspects of critical thinking. This is not to claim that deductive logic is in itself sufficient to deal properly with the range of decisions and choices we must make, rather that it is a necessary tool.

If this is so, then both the efforts to teach critical thinking to students and the expectations of previous critical thinking attainment by students assume a degree of facility in deductive logic on the part of the students. If such facility is absent, then the efforts will fail and the expectations will be wrong; thus, postponement or abandonment, or some successful teaching of the required logical facility will be necessary.

To be more specific: if a person is attempting to show students that the occurrence of several successful predicted instances does not by itself prove a generalization, that person should be interested in whether the students know that a proposition does not imply its converse (though the students need not put the knowledge in that language); a person who wants to show students the import of the failure of a prediction from a hypothesis should be interested in whether the students know about the bearing of the denial of a consequent upon an antecedent.

Since Piaget's work dominates the literature on children's logical capacities, a person with my interests should therefore expect to look to Piaget for guidance. I have found none. In this article I attempt to explain why. First I focus on Piaget's propositional

*Helpful suggestions were made by Joe Burnett, Stephane Dausse, J. A. Easley, Jr., Walter Feinberg, L. L. Gross, W. R. Kenzie, Jana Lucas, Thomas Knapp, Lawrence Kohlberg, James Roberge, Robert Rumery, Barbara Moor Sanner, Edward Smith, Patrick Suppes, Eric Weir and Lauren Weisberg.

logic and urge that this propositional logic is a defective logic. Then I argue that Piaget's claim that children of 11 to 12 and under cannot handle propositional logic is either untestable or false or otherwise defective, depending on one's interpretation of the claim.

Clarity of presentation requires an introduction to standard propositional logic. Readers familiar with standard propositional logic, the paradoxes of material implication, and the distinction between propositions and propositional functions might well skip to the second section after glancing at Table 6.1 and reading the last paragraph of this section.

STANDARD PROPOSITIONAL LOGIC

Propositional logic is generally taken to be one basic kind of deductive logic, one which is exemplified by the following valid argument, using content from an Inhelder—Piaget example (1958) that will be examined further.

> *Example 1.*
> Premises:
> 1. If this rod is thin, then it is flexible.
> 2. This rod is thin.
> Conclusion:
> 3. This rod is flexible.

The argument is called 'valid', because the conclusion follows necessarily from the premises.

Basic Units and Logical Operators

In the argument there are two different simple propositions involved, which remain essentially unchanged throughout the argument. The propositions are 'this rod is thin' and 'this rod is flexible'. Using the labels 'p' and 'q':

> let 'p' = 'this rod is thin'; and
> let 'q' = 'this rod is flexible'.

In standard propositional logic, the basic units are propositions (like 'this rod is thin' and 'this rod is flexible') that can stand alone (as in lines 2 and 3 in Example 1), or that can be joined or modified by logical operators (like 'if' and 'then' in line 1), *but that remain essentially unchanged throughout the course of an argument.* The shift from 'it is flexible' in line 1 to 'this rod is flexible' in line 3 is not regarded as an essential change since the two mean exactly the same in the context of this argument. In line 1, the word 'it' is not free to refer to anything but *this rod*.

The argument in Example 1 can be symbolized as follows:

> *Example 2.*
> 1. If p, then q
> 2. p
> ———————
> 3. Therefore q

Often one finds 'p $\supset$ q' or 'p$\rightarrow$q' used to represent, 'If p, then q' Piaget uses 'p$\supset$q'.

Table 6.1 *Basic Valid and Invalid Propositional Argument Forms*

	Valid Forms	Invalid Forms
Implication Forms[a]	1. Detachment: If p, then q p ——————— Therefore q	6. Particular conversion: If p, then q q ——————— Therefore p
	2. Particular contraposition: If p, then q not q ——————— Therefore not p	7. Full conversion: If p, then q ——————— Therefore if q, then p
	3. Full contraposition: If p, then q ——————— Therefore if not q, then not p	8. Particular inversion: If p, then q not p ——————— Therefore not q
	4. Particular transitivity: If p, then q If q, then r p ——————— Therefore r	9. Full inversion: If p, then q ——————— Therefore if not p, then not q
	5. Full transitivity: If p, then q If q, then r ——————— Therefore if p, then r	
Alternation Forms	10. Denying alternant: p or q not p ——————— Therefore q	11. Affirming alternant: p or q p ——————— Therefore not q[b]
Conjunction Forms	12. Affirming a negajunct:[c] Not both p and q p ——————— Therefore not q	14. Denying a negajunct: Not both p and q not p ——————— Therefore q (or not q)
	13. Proving a negajunction by denying a negajunct: Not p ——————— Therefore not both p and q	
Negation Form	15. Double negation equivalence: Not not p ——————— Therefore p } and vice versa	

[a]Names for the implication forms have been selected with an eye to an approach I am developing for describing logic achievement.

[b]Some people hold that there is a reading of 'p or q' that justifies a conclusion of 'not q' from an affirmation of 'p'. This reading is called the 'strong "or"', as distinct from the 'weak "or"' interpretation given here.

[c]A negajunct is one part of a negated conjunction.

In the proposition, 'If p, then q', the stated relationship between 'p' and 'q' is called implication, because of the words, 'if' and 'then'. In that implication relationship, 'p' is called the *antecedent*, and 'q' the *consequent*, by virtue of their positions with respect to 'if' and 'then'. In an implication, the antecedent implies the consequent. Furthermore, the antecedent in an implication is a *sufficient condition* for the consequent. I call a proposition expressing the claim that something is a necessary and/or sufficient condition a *conditional*.

The negation of a proposition is not regarded as a change in the proposition, but rather as an external operation upon the proposition. Thus, 'It is not the case that this rod is thin' represents an external negation operation upon the proposition, 'this rod is thin', the negation being represented by the words, 'it is not the case that'. Generally the wording 'this rod is not thin' is treated as equivalent to 'it is not the case that this rod is thin', although this sort of simplification occasionally produces problems. The negation of the proposition 'p' is represented by various devices, including '—p', 'p̄', and 'not p'. Piaget uses 'p̄'.

A third logical operator is the symbol 'or' (often together with 'either') as used in:

> *Example 3.*
> Either Jim will lengthen the rod, or the rod will not bend.

Assigning letters as follows:

> 'p'—'Jim will lengthen the rod'
> 'q'—'the rod will bend'

Example 3 is symbolized as follows:

> 'p or not q'.

If I had assigned 'q' to 'the rod will *not* bend', then Example 3 would be symbolized this way:

> 'p or q'.

Often the symbol 'v' is used instead of the word 'or': 'p v q'. Piaget uses the 'v'. Most logicians (and Piaget) attach the name 'disjunction' to a statement of the form, 'p or q', although I shall be using the name 'alternation', because of its greater affinity to the usage of our students, and because it is not associated in the literature with material implication, a subject to be examined later.

A fourth logical operator is the conjunction, 'and', as used in:

> *Example 4.*
> This rod is thin and it is flexible.

Symbolized, Example 4 becomes 'p and q'. Often the 'and' is replaced by a dot or a caret: 'p.q' or 'p^q'. Piaget uses the dot.

In sum, the four basic logical operators are the *implication* operator, the *negation* operator, the *alternation* operator, and the *conjunction* operator. Propositional logic ordinarily is concerned with the validity of arguments utilizing propositions standing alone or under the influence of one or more of these four logical operators.

Basic Propositional Argument Forms

A number of common propositional logic argument forms are organized in Table 6.1 according to whether they are valid or invalid, and whether they use an implication, an alternation, a conjunction, or a double negation. There is redundancy in the table from a logical viewpoint, because of the convertibilities and implications of the operators, but I am not here trying to be elegant, only to be clear and to avoid prejudging some ticklish issues.

The argument given in Example 1 is, as can be seen from Table 6.1, an example of 'detachment', so called because affirming 'p' entitles one to *detach* (and affirm) the 'q' of 'If p, then q'. Other names given to this form, incidentally, are 'affirming the antecedent' and 'modus ponens'.

This set of argument forms, although it contains some logical redundancy, gives one an idea of most of the basic moves that propositional logic entitles one to make. One additional but controversial move (to be discussed next) often rounds out the traditional system. Complex and elegant ways have been developed to combine and build all these moves into a logically simple total system. But, for present purposes, it is best to leave the exposition at the level of Table 6.1 with the exception of the discussion of the controversial move just mentioned.

A Controversial Topic in Contemporary Propositional Logic: Material Implication

Material implication is that interpretation of the implication relationship that holds 'if p, then q' to be equivalent to the negajunction, 'not both p and not q'; regards the latter (and thus the former) as shown true by either showing the truth of 'q', or the falsity of 'p'; and regards them as shown to be false by the combination of the truth of 'p' and the falsity of 'q'. Thus the conditional, 'If this rod is *thick*, then it is flexible' would be judged equivalent to 'It is not the case both that this rod is thick and that this rod is inflexible'. Both would therefore be shown to be true by showing either one of the following:

1. This rod is flexible (q).
2. This rod is thin (not p). (Here 'p' represents 'this rod is thick'.)

In case (1), showing that the rod is flexible (q) shows that not both of the following are true (since the second is not true): 'the rod is thick' and 'the rod is inflexible'. In case (2), showing that the rod is thin (not p) shows that not both are true, since the first, 'the rod is thick', is not true. Putting it only in terms of letters, if 'q' is true, then it must also be true that not both p and not q. If 'p' is false, then not both p and not q. The falsity of either negajunct proves the negajunction (Form (13) in Table 6.1).

A number of people have balked at this sort of result (e.g. Strawson, 1952; Piaget, 1967), because, for example, showing that a rod is thin does not by itself seem sufficient to prove that if it were thick, it would be flexible. Defenders of the result would note that, in putting the challenge, I changed from the indicative 'is' to the subjunctive 'were' and would hold that the odd result does not matter anyway, since, by assumption, the rod is in fact thin; thus, no mistaken conclusion can be drawn from the result, 'if the rod is *thick*, then it is flexible'. They also note the elegance achievable by incorporating the given equivalence into the system.

Such results are called the 'paradoxes of material implication', material implication being the label for implication defined in terms of negajunction. Parallel paradoxes exist for alternation, for universal statements in class logic (the nonexistence of A's allegedly commits one to the claim that all A's, are B's), and for set theory (anything is allegedly true of the empty set). I shall not here discuss these parallel paradoxes, but should like to note that these paradoxes are absent from the logic propounded by Piaget, and from the logic of Table 6.1 (so long as the negajunction of Argument Form (13) is regarded as establishable by the establishment of the falsity of either negajunct, *regardless* of its relationship to the other negajunct, and is regarded as saying no more than that). The paradoxes are discussed in detail in philosophical literature (including Lewis, 1912; Strawson, 1952; Russell, 1960; Faris, 1962; Clark, 1971; and Young, 1972).

That completes this brief exposition of propositional logic. One might find further enlightenment in one or more standard logic texts. In order of increasing difficulty, texts by Ennis (1969), Fisk (1964) and Strawson (1952) are some that attempt to avoid the paradoxes; and (again in order of increasing difficulty) texts by Black (1952), Beardsley (1966), Copi (1961), and Quine (1960) incorporate the paradoxes at least to some extent. Incidentally, the standard use of truth tables (which I shall not explain, but which are explained in the last four works mentioned) does involve one in the paradoxes of material implication.

Unless it is otherwise qualified, I shall henceforth use the term 'propositional logic' to refer to the logic indicated in Table 6.1, without the material implication interpretation of the 'if—then' relationship. When speaking of a propositional logic that incorporates material implication and of Piaget's propositional logic, I shall so indicate.

PIAGET'S PROPOSITIONAL LOGIC

In some respects, Piaget's propositional logic is like the standard system. He does use the standard notation of the propositional calculus developed by logicians within the last century. See pp. 293—303 of *Growth of Logical Thinking from Childhood to Adolescence* (Inhelder and Piaget, 1958), which will henceforth be referred to as *GLT*. He uses the letters 'p', 'q', 'r', etc. He represents implication by 'p⊃q', alternation (which he and most logicians call 'disjunction') by 'p v q', and negajunction (which he calls 'incompatibility') by 'p/q'. These are standard symbolizations. He treats 'if p, then q' as equivalent to 'not p, or q' (GLT, p. 298), a standard equivalence in propositional logic. Thus,

> *Example 5.*
>   'If this rod is thin, then it is flexible.'
> would be equivalent to
>   'Either this rod is not thin, or it is flexible.'

Furthermore, he treats both 'if p, then q' and 'not p or q' as equivalent to the combination, 'p.q v p̄.q v p̄.q̄' (GLT, pp. 296 and 297), as is done in material-implication propositional logic. This last is a crucial equivalence, bearing further scrutiny, particularly of the meaning that Piaget attaches to the combination, 'p.q v p̄.q v p̄.q̄', and to others like it. But before looking at Piaget's meaning for such combinations, we should examine his general combinatorial system and his method of generating the total set of sixteen of these combinations. This set also fits into the tradition of material-implication propositional logic (even though his interpretation, as I shall later show, does not).

The Combinatorial System of Sixteen Binary Operations

Piaget's combinatorial system of sixteen binary operations is a crucial feature of his propositional logic. What is this system? It is best explained by showing how it is generated, building with the letters 'p' and 'q'.

There are four different ways in which the symbols, 'p' and 'q', 'p̄' and 'q̄', can be combined in pairs, without repeating either symbol (or either letter) in a pair:

(1) p.q (2) p.q̄ (3) p̄.q (4) p̄.q̄

Following Piaget, let us call each of these four pairs an 'element'.

These elements can nonredundantly be joined together by the symbol, 'v', in sixteen different ways, if we count single appearances of an element and the absence of any element. Each of these sixteen combinations is a 'binary operation'. In order to see how to get sixteen, let each element be represented by a letter, 'a', 'b', 'c', or 'd', and make a list sixteen items long, as in Table 6.2, combining the letters in accordance with the possibilities allowed by the above plan. The idea for this method of explanation comes from John Flavell (1963, pp. 213—214).

Table 6.2 *Method of Construction of the Sixteen Combinations from Four Elements Represented by 'a', 'b', 'c' and 'd'*

1.	a	9.	bd
2.	b	10.	cd
3.	c	11.	abc
4.	d	12.	abd
5.	ab	13.	acd
6.	ac	14.	bcd
7.	ad	15.	abcd
8.	bc	16.	0 (for the absence of any element)

Using the order used by Piaget in his presentation in GLT (pp. 293—303), Table 6.3 presents the sixteen binary operations that are possible, starting with two letters. (Starting with three letters, there are 256; with four letters 65 536. The formula is 2^{2^n}.) These combinations, which he calls 'operations', make up his combinatorial system.

Table 6.3 *Piaget's System of Sixteen Binary Operations, as Presented in GLT (pp. 293—303)*

Piaget's Name and Number	Constructed Combination	Corresponding Construction Table 2	Piaget's Logical Shorthand
1. Complete affirmation	p.q v p.q̄ v p̄.q v p̄.q̄	abcd	p∗q
2. Negation of complete affirmation	nothing	0	0
3. Conjunction	p.q	a	p.q
4. Incompatibility	p.q̄ v p̄.q v p̄.q̄	bcd	p/q
5. Disjunction	p.q v p.q̄ v p̄.q	abc	p v q
6. Conjunctive negation	p̄.q̄	d	p̄.q̄
7. Implication	p.q v p̄.q v p̄.q̄	acd	p⊃q
8. Nonimplication	p.q̄	b	p.q̄
9. Reciprocal implication	p.q v p.q̄ v p̄.q̄	abd	q⊃p
10. Negation of reciprocal implication	p̄.q	c	p̄.q
11. Equivalence	p.q v p̄.q̄	ad	p = q[a]
12. Reciprocal exclusion	p.q̄ v p̄.q	bc	p vv q
13. Affirmation of p	p.q v p.q̄	ab	p [q]
14. Negation of p	p̄.q v p̄.q̄	cd	p̄ [q]
15. Affirmation of q	p.q v p̄.q	ac	q [p]
16. Negation of q	p.q̄ v p̄.q̄	bd	q̄ [p]

[a]He also uses 'p ⊋ q' for 'equivalence'.

In this binary operation system, the equivalences going across the lines are the standard ones of material-implication propositional logic (e.g. in line 7, treating 'p⊃q' as equivalent to the combination 'p.q v p̄.q v p̄.q̄', and calling it 'implication' is standard).

Furthermore, by assuming that two negatives equal a positive, we can transform the right-hand column 'operations' into one or more others or their negation, just as one can do in standard material-implication logic. For example, an implication can be transformed into a disjunction (although the antecedent turns out to be negated in the disjunction):

Example 6.

Step:		Comment:
1.	p⊃q	1. Assumed starting point.
2.	p.q v p̄.q v p̄.q̄	2. The equivalent combination of (1).
3.	p̄.q v p̄.q̄ v p.q	3. Simply a rearrangement of (2).
4.	p̄.q v p̄.q̄ v p̄.q	4. Substitution of 'p̄' for 'p' in the third element of (4). This achieves a denial of 'p̄' in the third element of (4).
5.	p̄ v q	5. (4) is the combination for the disjunction in (5), treating 'p̄' (instead of 'p') as the left-hand disjunct.

Piaget notes this sort of transformation: 'But implication can be expressed in at least three equivalent ways: p⊃q; p̄ v q and p = p.q' (GLT, p. 298).

The crucial differences between Piaget and others is in the meaning and justification of the *combinations* in Column 2. Since implication is so basic, I shall concentrate heavily on the combination for implication in my exposition of Piaget's approach to the meaning and justification of these combinations.

The Meaning and Justification of Combinations, with Emphasis on that of Implication

In material-implication propositional logic, 'p.q v p̄.q v p̄.q̄' means that *at least one* of the three conjunctive elements ('p.q', 'p̄.q', and 'p̄.q̄') is true, producing the material implication situation in a somewhat different form, but again the truth of 'q' or the falsity of 'p' establishes the truth of the whole. Consider the first alternative (the truth of 'q'). The truth of 'q' establishes (if 'p' be true) the first element or (if 'p' be false) the second element. Since 'p' must be either true or false (a standard assumption in this sort of logic), then either the first or second element is established by the truth of 'q'. Since the truth of any of the elements establishes the whole, the truth of 'q' establishes the whole—and therefore establishes its equivalent, 'if p, then q'. Similarly, the falsity of 'p' establishes the whole—and thus also the implication, 'if p, then q'. Thus, we have material implication built into the crucial equivalence, on the standard interpretation of combinations.

But Piaget does not interpret them that way, thus avoiding material implication and its paradoxes, a fact about which he is pleased (1967, p. 273). For him, the way to show that 'p.q v p̄.q v p̄.q̄' is true is to show that *all three* elements, not just any one, hold, and that the fourth possibility, 'p.q̄', does not hold. Now this is impossible if we continue to treat 'p' and 'q' as propositions, since the first conjunctive element holds 'p' to be true and the second holds it to be false. Either this rod is thin or it is not thin. It cannot be both.

But Piaget does not treat 'p' and 'q' as propositions in the sense defined in the second section of this paper. He does not treat them as able to stand alone. Instead he treats 'p' and 'q' as sentences (call these sentences 'propositional functions') containing variables for which one may substitute references to different objects (e.g. 'rod x is thin', 'rod x is flexible'). These propositional functions cannot meaningfully stand alone since 'rod x' does not have a referent. There is no way to tell whether the propositional function, 'rod x is thin', is true (when it stands alone), since we do not know what rod is rod x.

However, Piaget's propositions, although unable to stand alone meaningfully, can be made meaningful by adding either 'for any x . . . ' or 'there exists an x such that . . .'. In contemporary logic these additions are called respectively the 'universal quantifier' and the 'existential quantifier'. I shall illustrate the use of each.

> *Example 7.*
> (Assuming the domain of rods)
> For any x, rod x is thin (meaning 'All rods are thin').
> There exists an x, such that rod x is thin (meaning 'There is at least one thin rod').

Furthermore, propositional functions can meaningfully stand together in sentences like the following:

> *Example 8.*
> 1. For any x, if rod x is thin, then rod x is flexible;
> or in other words:
> 2. If a rod is thin, then it is flexible.

Example 8 is a generalization about all rods within the realm under consideration. Thus, it is basically different from the conditional of Example 1, which is about one rod only. It incorporates a universal quantifier to make a generalization. Piaget's implications are generally of this form.

His combinations (like 'p.q v $\bar{p}$.q v $\bar{p}$.$\bar{q}$') have an implicit existential quantifier attached to each element so that the appearance of an element means that the existence of at least one of the indicated sort of case is claimed. For example, the appearance of the element, 'p.q', in the above combination amounts to a claim that there is at least one case such that p and q, or, in terms of our example, there is at least one object such that it is a thin rod and it is a flexible rod. Or, less awkwardly, there is at least one thin flexible rod. Similarly, to include the element, '$\bar{p}$.q', in terms of our example, is to claim that there is at least one thick (non-thin) flexible rod, and the element, '$\bar{p}$.$\bar{q}$', that there is at least one thick inflexible rod. Thus, all three elements can hold, since they are about different cases. The inconsistency that one would face in standard propositional logic by asserting all three elements does not exist for Piaget, since he makes existential claims using propositional functions. And the elements can stand alone, since they have an implicit existential quantifier attached.

There are two other crucial features of Piaget's combinations: (1) on the simplest reading, the 'v' that joins the elements in a combination is to be read 'and' rather than 'or'; and (2) there is, in addition to the presented combination, an implied denial of the existence of any unmentioned kind of case, in the implication combination, a denial of any fitting the description 'p.$\bar{q}$', or in our example, a denial of the existence of any thin rods that are not flexible.

Thus, in terms of our example, the combination for implication is to be read as follows:

> *Example 9.*
> There is at least one rod that is thin and flexible (p.q); and
> there is at least one rod that is thick and flexible ($\bar{p}$.q); and
> there is at least one rod that is thick and inflexible ($\bar{p}$.$\bar{q}$); and
> there are no rods that are thin and inflexible (no p.$\bar{q}$'s).

When Piaget says, '(p⊃q) = (p.q) v (p̄.q) v (p̄.q̄)', (*Traité de Logique*, 1949, p. 233; also GLT, p. 297), he is implying that Example 8 (either (1) or (2)) is equal to Example 9.

We now have the means to interpret any Piagetian propositional logic formula: if it is in operator form as found in the right-hand column in Table 6.3 (e.g. 'p⊃q'), we convert it to its combination form in the second column of Table 6.3 (e.g. 'p.q v p̄.q v p̄.q̄'). Then using the strategy just outlined, we can say that the formula implies the existence of at least one of each of the kind of cases described in each element (e.g. 'p.q') of the combination, *and* implies the nonexistence of any cases coming under any one of the four possible elements ('p.q', 'p.q̄', 'p̄.q', 'p̄.q̄') that are not mentioned in the combination.

Furthermore, we have the means to prove and disprove Piagetian propositional logic formulae. By establishing the content of Example 9, for example, we prove (in Piagetian logic) the implication relationship specified in Example 8. And by showing that one or more of the conditions specified in Example 9 fails, we show (in Piagetian logic) that the implication relationship in Example 8 does not hold. These methods for proving and for disproving play a significant role in judging and describing children's logic in GLT.

The Accuracy of this Interpretation

Does Piaget really mean that the assertion of a combination means that there is at least one case of each of the mentioned elements and that there are no cases of the unmentioned elements? I believe so, both because his detailed interpreters say so and because a number of things he says in *Traité de Logique* and GLT indicate this interpretation.

The presented interpretation of combinations is given to Piaget's propositional logic by Charles Parsons, a hostile critic and a logician (1960, pp. 76—77), and also by John Flavell, a friendly summarizer (1963, p. 215), by Seymour Papert, an interpreter and defender (1963, pp. 109 and 117), and by Herbert Ginsburg and Sylvia Opper (1969, pp. 181—196). Piaget's apparent citation of the Papert article in support of Piaget's propositional logic also counts in favour of the interpretation. (I say 'apparent' because Piaget gives no citation, only mentioning Papert's name.) More explicitly Piaget (1967, p. 273), in defence against Parsons, refers to two points that Papert makes in the article by Papert that I mentioned—that Piaget's propositional logic can be self-consistent and that it avoids the paradoxes of material implication. And Piaget presumably does not disagree with Papert's interpretation. To cite in your defence someone else's demonstration that your system is consistent without agreeing with the basic lines of that person's interpretation of your system would be odd.

Then a number of things that Piaget says strongly support the interpretation.

(1) He defines implication in *Traité de Logique* (1949) in a way that makes any other interpretation implausible.

Implication: (p⊃q). If the conjunctions (p.q); (p̄.q) and (p̄.q̄) are true while p.q̄ is false, there is then implication in the sense (asymmetric) 'p implies q':

$$(p \supset q) = (p.q) \lor (\bar{p}.q) \lor (\bar{p}.\bar{q})$$

In terms of classes, implication corresponds with inclusion P<Q, which leaves empty the class (PQ̄).

Example: if p = 'x is a mammal (P)' and q = 'x is a vertebrate (Q)', one has then only three true cases: PQ (mammals that are vertebrates), P̄Q (vertebrates other than mammals), and P̄Q̄ (nonmammalian nonvertebrates). But the class

P$\bar{\text{Q}}$ is null because mammals that are not vertebrates do not exist: the class P is included in Q, from which p $\supset$ q by exclusion of p.$\bar{\text{q}}$ (p. 233, author's translation). See Figure 6.1.

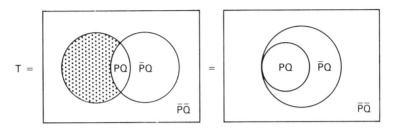

(Piaget, 1949, p.233)

Figure 6.1

The word 'and' in the first sentence of the passage suggests that all three must hold (although he did not say 'if and only if'). Otherwise why should he say 'and'? And how else can all three hold unless there is at least one case of each? Further-more, the example fits the interpretation: at least one member to fit each of the three elements and none to fit the fourth.

Piaget's exposition in *Traité de Logique* is the place to which he and Inhelder refer us 'for a more detailed presentation of the symbolism of propositional operations . . .' (GLT, p. xxiv). Hence the above definition of implication is particularly significant.

(2) He illustrates 'complete affirmation' with a case in which he notes that:

> In the flexibility experiment . . . when the subject classifies the rods into brass or non-brass and circular or noncircular sections, he discovers that all four possible associations occur. (GLT, p. 293)

The only plausible interpretation of 'all four possible associations occur' appears to be 'there is at least one case of each of the four pairs of propositional functions, "p.q", "p.$\bar{\text{q}}$", "$\bar{\text{p}}$.q", and "$\bar{\text{p}}$.$\bar{\text{q}}$"'.

(3) In discussing the possibility of integrating the expression 'p.q' into larger combinations, like the one for implication, he speaks of the 'occurrence of p.q':

> In particular the stage III subjects struggle against the temptation to conclude from the occurrence of p.q the assertion of an equivalence p $\underset{C}{\supseteq}$ q or of a simple implication p$\supset$q. (GLT, p. 294)

The phrase, 'the occurrence of p.q' seems to mean the occurrence of at least one case fitting the description, 'p.q'.

(4) In discussing incompatibility, he speaks of the *presence* and *absence* of the 'characteristics denoted by p and q' and of those denoted by 's' and 't':

> The inverse of the operation of conjunction p.q is incompatibility (p/q = p.$\bar{\text{q}}$ v $\bar{\text{p}}$.q v $\bar{\text{p}}$.$\bar{\text{q}}$), which means that the characteristics denoted by p and q are never conjunctive—that is to say, that where one is present, the other or both are absent. Thus in the colour experiment the

> subject discovers as follows that one of the liquids bleaches the mixture . . . If s states the presence or absence of the fourth liquid, the subject ascertains that only the combination s.$\bar{t}$ v $\bar{s}$.t. v $\bar{s}$.$\bar{t}$ is verified. (GLT, p. 295)

Here the appearance of an element can mean nothing other than that there is at least one case fitting the description.

(5) He says that observing three associations establishes an implication:

> After he [a subject] has established . . . [an] implication p $\supset$ q by observing three associations, p.q, $\bar{p}$.q, and $\bar{p}$.$\bar{q}$. (GLT, p. 305)

For some reason he does not here mention the lack of the fourth association, p.$\bar{q}$, but he must include this idea, so presumably he just forgot to say it here. The important thing is that 'observing three associations' (plus denying the fourth) establishes an implication. To observe an association is to have seen at least one case fitting the description.

(6) Lastly he speaks of 'the observation of p.$\bar{q}$' and makes a statement about non-implication that is puzzling unless one accepts the total interpretation:

> Before concluding on the basis of observation of p.$\bar{q}$ that it must be a case of nonimplication, the stage III subject assures himself that he has eliminated all other combinations which include not only p.$\bar{q}$ but also p.q. (GLT, p. 299)

Why must one 'eliminate p.q' in order to establish nonimplication? Why is 'observing p.$\bar{q}$' not enough? The answer lies in the formula for interpretation of combinations: there must be at least one case of each of the mentioned elements *and no cases of the unmentioned elements*. Since the element, 'p.q', is unmentioned in the one-element combination, 'p.$\bar{q}$' (which is defined as nonimplication), the subject has to eliminate 'p.q'.

Although the above six quotations and cited testimony by other interpreters make a strong case for the interpretation I have presented of Piaget's propositional logic, Piaget's style does not readily lend itself to precise interpretation. Sometimes he says one thing, sometimes another; and often his language is vague.

For example, he (or perhaps Inhelder; they do not specify) says:

> The implication p $\supset$ q is . . . equivalent to establishing that the case (p.$\bar{q}$) never occurs. Still in order to establish this it is necessary to consider the four possibilities (p.q) v (p.$\bar{q}$) v ($\bar{p}$.q) v ($\bar{p}$.$\bar{q}$); in any case, the implication is nothing more than the addition of three possibilities (the first, the third, and the fourth) combined by the operation (v) which signifies 'or'—i.e. it is an addition of what is possible and not of 'realities'. (GLT, p. 17)

This quote suggests that each of the three elements must be shown to be *possible* not that each must have an example. This alternative interpretation has difficulties similar to those I shall offer, but it is a different interpretation from the one I have given. One faces this kind of problem in attempting to make sense out of Piaget's logic.

Some Problems with Piaget's Propositional Logic

I have gone to some length to establish the given interpretation because of the problems engendered by this logic. One wants to be confident of an interpretation that results in the difficulties I am about to enumerate, which come under two headings: (1) some paradoxes of Piagetian logic; and (2) the lack of safeguards against overgeneralization. Parsons (1960) perceived a number of these difficulties, but his discussion has not received due notice, because, I believe, of its compactness and the typographical errors in the published version.

Paradoxes

Some paradoxes of Piagetian logic are (1) the specified requirement of the existence of mentioned cases and nonexistence of unmentioned cases; (2) the incompatibility between 'if p, then q' and 'if q, then p', and (3) the incompatibility between the affirmation of 'p' and the affirmation of 'q'. These paradoxes, which I shall elaborate, do not destroy his system. It can still be self-consistent. But the system, whether we treat it as normative or descriptive, is not about the implication, etc., that we (and children and adolescents) know.

The requirements of the positive and nonexistent cases. Although the case-existence problem crops up in a variety of places, I shall focus on its appearance in the implication combination, 'p.q v p̄.q v p̄.q̄'. The problem is that it is unreasonable to require the existence (I shall consider possibility later) of at least one of each of the three kinds of case. This is most clear for the second kind, symbolized by 'p̄.q'. It does not make sense to require that there be at least one *thick* (non-thin) flexible rod for it to be the case that if a rod is thin, it is flexible. There might not be any thick flexible rods. But that should not falsify the implication, 'If a rod is thin, it is flexible'.

Next, consider the requirement of the first kind of case ('p.q') for the implication statement, 'If anyone grabs those two wires, that person will be shocked'. Because of my rudimentary electrical knowledge, I know that generalization to be true of two wires in my house, but there is no case of 'p.q', that is, of a person who has grabbed the two wires and was shocked. And there might never be such a case. According to the given (existence, not possibility) interpretation of Piaget's combinations, the lack of such a case shows that the implication is mistaken. This should not be.

With respect to the requirement of a case of 'p̄.q̄' consider the statement, 'If a body has inertia, then it is in principle detectable'. Let 'p' = 'body x has inertia' and 'q' = 'body x is in principle detectable'. Let the domain be bodies. Now the statement represented by 'if p, then q' might be true, and it might be false. I am inclined to accept it. But the fact that there are no bodies that do not have inertia (and thus no cases of the first half of the element 'p̄.q̄'—and thus no cases that satisfy the whole element) should not prove it wrong. The requirement of a case fitting 'p̄.q̄' is thus mistaken.

The requirement that there be no cases of the unmentioned elements is all right for implication but not for nonimplication. Earlier I noted that Piaget required the nonexistence of any case fitting 'p.q' in order that we have a case of nonimplication, 'p.q̄' (GLT, p. 299). In the pendulum experiment described in GLT, an increase in weight does not imply an increase in the period of the pendulum. This is what we would ordinarily call a case of nonimplication. And we would call it that on the ground of a clear case of an increase in weight without a change in the period of the pendulum (other things being equal). We would do this even though we did have a case of 'p.q', that is, a case of an increase in weight that *was* accompanied by an increase in the period. This could easily happen if the length of the pendulum were increased at the same time that the weight was increased. Thus, the requirement of no 'p.q's is inappropriate for nonimplication in the ordinary sense of 'nonimplication'.

Now the specification of the four requirements enables Piaget to avoid the paradoxes of material implication and their analogues. But, unfortunately, his requirements are themselves paradoxical.

On the interpretation that he requires *possibility of existence*, rather than *existence*, of the cases, the problems remain. With respect to the element, 'p̄.q', it seems unreasonable to require that it be possible for there to be a thick flexible rod in order that it be true that if a rod is thin, it is flexible. More strikingly, it seems unreasonable to require that it be possible for there to be a case of an increase in the period of a pendulum without an increase in length, in order that it be true (at a given point on this earth) that, if the length is increased (p), the period is increased (q). Certainly none of their pendulum subjects in GLT could have shown such possibility, yet some were credited justifiably with inferring to the generalization, if the length is increased, the period is increased.

With respect to the element 'p.q', it seems unreasonable to require the possibility of someone's grabbing both wires in order that it be true that, if anyone grabs the two wires, that person will be shocked. The wires might be deliberately placed twenty feet apart because we realized that, if anyone grabs both, he will be shocked. Placing them twenty feet apart makes it impossible to grab them both. If, in reply, someone makes the assumption that it is possible for a person to develop who has a twenty-foot reach, then the counter is that, on this interpretation of a possibility (logical possibility), anything is possible, and the Piagetian requirement under the possibility interpretation becomes empty.

It is similar with the element, 'p̄.q̄'. I do not think it possible for there to be a body without inertia. This does and should not stop me from believing that if a body has inertia it is, in principle, detectable.

Under the possibility interpretation applied to nonimplication, the requirement of the nonexistence of a case of 'p.q' would remain: that the element(s) not mentioned 'never occurs'. Again, the pendulum experiment shows the difficulty. A case of an increase in weight accompanied by an increase in the period does occur, as was shown by the subjects in the experiment, even though the appropriate conclusion was that an increase in weight does not imply an increase in the period.

Thus, the requirements remain paradoxical under the possibility interpretation, as opposed to the existence interpretation of the Piagetian combinations. In avoiding material implication and its analogues, Piaget introduced problems that are at least as serious.

The clash between 'If p, then q' and 'If q, then p'. According to the given interpretation of Piaget's combinations 'if p, then q' requires the existence of at least one case of 'p̄.q'; but 'if q, then p' requires the nonexistence of any case of 'q.p̄', which is equivalent to 'p̄.q'. Thus, both implications cannot be true. In terms of our example, the following cannot both be true:

1. If a rod is thin, then it is flexible.
2. If a rod is flexible, then it is thin.

The first conditional requires the existence of a thick flexible rod. The second requires that there be no flexible rods that are thick (that is, no thick flexible rods).

This is not necessarily an inconsistency within his system, but it is not in accord with the way people use the word 'if' in their everyday valid reasoning. I should not like to have students judged for their reasoning prowess according to his idiosyncratic use of 'if'. And on the view that takes Piaget as only describing children's reasoning, one must respond that children (and adults too) often do take those two implications as equivalent—but never incompatible (Ennis and Paulus, 1965; Ennis et al, 1969; O'Brien and Shapiro, 1968; Ryoti, 1972).

Piaget does not recognize this inconsistency between one-way implication and other-way implication (he calls them 'reciprocals' of each other), saying in *Traité de Logique*, 'q ⊃ p is compatible with p ⊃ q even though one implication is not necessarily entailed by the other' (p. 234). In GLT he says 'In the pendulum experiment (Chapter 4), the increase in length (stated by p) corresponds to an increase in oscillation rate (stated by q), and the converse is also true' (p. 301). The clause, 'and the converse is also true', implies that an implication each way can be true.

Since his allowing implication to be true each way is inconsistent with the basic structure of his system, it appears that here is an aberration that must be resolved. He can do so by simply declaring that implication, as he means it, is incompatible with its converse, and both are incompatible with two-way implication. Thus, his 'if p, then q' would mean something like 'if, but not only if, p then q', etc.; and the compatibility quotes in the previous paragraph would just be about ordinary implication, not Piagetian implication. This resolution would be as paradoxical as the paradoxes of material implication that he is trying to avoid, but the system would then be internally consistent.

The clash between the affirmation of 'p' and the affirmation of 'q'. The affirmation of 'p' is defined as 'p.q v p.q̄', which requires that there be no cases fitting 'p̄.q'. The affirmation of 'q' is defined as 'p.q v p̄.q', which requires that there be a case fitting 'p̄.q'. In terms of an example, to affirm that men are mortal ('p' = 'x is a mortal') is inconsistent with the affirmation that men are vertebrates ('q' = 'x is a vertebrate') when the population under consideration is men. The first affirmation requires the nonexistence of immortal vertebrates; the second affirmation requires the existence of immortal vertebrates. This paradoxical result also arises under the possibility interpretation. I do not see how to resolve this paradox.

Lack of overgeneralization safeguards

The lack of safeguards against overgeneralization is a ticklish problem, especially since the subjects' reasoning described in GLT is inductive reasoning from evidence to generalizations. The Piagetian logic that I have sketched out might well be regarded as an inductive logic since it takes us from observation of cases to generalizations. For example, the inference to 'If a rod is thin, then it is flexible' from an examination of individual cases is inductive. How does the invitation to overgeneralization arise? Consider this short, simple list of steps in generalizing from data—without commitment to the order in which the steps are presented.

One step, which I shall call Step 1, is that of observing cases. Step 2 consists of checking cases against the generalization to see whether they contradict it or are instances of it. Step 3 consists of judging whether the cases selected are typical or representative of all the cases covered by the generalization. If they are typical or representative, we can generalize.

In the immediately preceding discussion, I suggested problems with Piaget's approach to Step 2, noting that he had too many necessary conditions. The problem here is in Step 3.

It is an old problem: how to justify the inductive leap from observed data to a conclusion that goes beyond the data. In terms of our example, the problem is how to justify the leap from the observation of a small number of cases of rods to the generalization, 'If a rod is thin, then it is flexible'. One way to handle the problem is to deny that the generalization goes beyond the data—to claim that the generalization is only about the data that have so far been gathered. This approach effectively eliminates the leap, but makes the generalization relatively useless. It does not give any indication of what to expect of the next thin rod we encounter, not even what to expect of already-examined thin rods the next time they are examined. If Piaget chooses this resolution, he is talking about a relatively useless process. That he does not choose this resolution is suggested by a comment about implication and a description of what he holds to be a Stage II (7—8 to 11—12) inadequacy:

> The most important of these operations, or at least the one which nearly always orients the substage III-A subjects' analysis at the beginning of the experiment, is the formal operation of implication by which the subject assumes that a determinate factor produces the observed consequences in all cases. At stage II, a comparable causal relationship was established by simple correspondence—for example, the longer the rod, the more flexible—but this type of reasoning cannot be legitimately generalized to all cases. (GLT, pp. 58—59)

It sounds here as if he does not want to limit the subject's conclusion to the examined cases only. That is, it appears that he is talking about reasoning to generalizations that go beyond the data. How else can we explain his use of the phrase, 'in all cases'?

The crucial phrase in his definition of implication is that stating the fourth necessary condition: in GLT (p. 16) it is specified as follows, 'one also has to establish the . . . falsehood of p.q̄ for p⊃q . . .;' in *Traité de Logique* (p. 233) it is specified as 'while p.q̄ is false'. Does that mean that in all the *examined* cases there are no cases fitting 'p.q̄' (this is the more likely interpretation and the one offered by interpreters Ginsburg and Opper, 1969, pp. 187, 188, 191, 193, and 194), or does it mean that in all examined *and unexamined* cases there are none fitting 'p.q̄' (the less likely interpretation)?

If he means that the set of *examined* cases must contain none fitting 'p.q̄', then we have a condition that can be satisfied by observation, but the formula for the meaning of implication becomes a generator of overgeneralizations. Consider the following argument produced by the anti-feminist political sage who claims that United States presidents will always be males. Put in the language of implication between propositional functions, this claim becomes, 'If x is a United States President, then x is a male (for every x)'.

According to Piaget's definition of implication in terms of a combination that claim would be made true by the following facts:

1. There is a case of a president who is male. (George Washington.)
2. There is a case of a nonpresident who is male. (Alexander Hamilton.)
3. There is a case of a nonpresident who is not a male. (Martha Washington.)
4. There is no case of a president who is not a male. (There is none at the time of writing.)

All these conditions are satisfied. But surely that does not prove the anti-feminist correct.

The Piagetian combination gives us a set of conditions that are presented as jointly sufficient and separately necessary for an implication. The fourth condition leads us into difficulty when we take all four as sufficient. On the examined-cases interpretation, the condition leads us to produce overgeneralizations.

This invitation to overgeneralization is either accepted or at least felt by Piagetian interpreters, Ginsburg and Opper (1969). Using the examined-cases interpretation, as I indicated earlier, Ginsburg and Opper characterize the 'adolescent's conclusions [as] certain and necessary . . . since the experiments have been designed properly' (p. 188). That even properly designed experiments lead to conclusions that are certain and necessary should be anathema to any experimenter, especially in view of the fact that the Piaget—Inhelder adolescents spent not more than an hour or so on their experimental work with pendulums.

On the examined- and unexamined-cases interpretation, the fourth condition holds that there must be no cases of 'p.q̄', past, present, and future. Thus, an inductive leap must already be made in order that one be able to satisfy the fourth condition of the formula. Yet the formula for implication ('p.q v p̄.q v p̄.q̄, and no cases of p.q̄') appears to be an inductive guide for going from data to generalizations. It appears to be a formula for induction, yet to satisfy the formula one must already have performed the crucial induction.

In other words, one crucial feature of the inductive leap from examined to unexamined cases is the judgment that the examined cases are typical. Piaget's logic neglects the problem of typicality in extending the examined cases to cases not found in the experimental setup contrived by Inhelder. Yet the conclusions discussed cover cases not found in those experimental setups. 'If a rod is thin, then it is flexible' covers more than the rods Inhelder provided. It covers the aerial to my television set and a glass stirring rod in my chemistry laboratory.

I could go on conceiving of possible alternative interpretations, since Piaget's style is not conducive to clear understanding. The evidence I have put forward adequately supports, I believe, the interpretation I have offered. Alternatives are open to someone who does not accept this interpretation, but one must stop somewhere. A person who seeks to offer another interpretation is obligated to defend it textually and to see whether what Piaget says, under *that* interpretation, is defensible. The types of problems that I have raised with the interpretation I have offered are among those that should be considered. The basic question is this: Does Piaget's logic commit us to conclusions that we should not be committed to, and does it prevent us from drawing conclusions that we are entitled to draw? On the interpretation I have offered, Piaget's logic fails on both counts.

THE TESTABILITY AND SIGNIFICANCE OF PIAGET'S CLAIM THAT CHILDREN 11—12 AND YOUNGER CANNOT HANDLE PROPOSITIONAL LOGIC

Consider this assertion in GLT (p. 1):

> If we are to explain the transition from the concrete thought of the child to the formal thought of the adolescent, we must first describe the development of propositional logic, which the child at the concrete level (stage II: from 7—8 to 11—12 years) cannot yet handle. Experimentation shows that after a long period during which only operations appropriate to class and relational groupings and to the numerical and spatiotemporal structures which resulted from them are used, the beginnings of stage III (substage III-A, from 11—12 years to 14—15 years: and substage III-B, from 14—15 years onward) are distinguished by the organization of new operations performed on the propositions themselves and no longer only on the classes and relations that make up their content.
>
> To study the questions raised by this development, we must analyse how children or adolescents at stage III go about solving problems which appear purely concrete but which experiments indicate can be resolved only at stage III and which actually presuppose the use of interpropositional operations. Part I of the present work will be devoted to this analysis.

Although the authorship of the quotation is not explicitly attributed to Piaget or to Inhelder, I shall speak as if Piaget is the responsible party. The thoughts expressed in the quote are in accord with his writings elsewhere and with the chapters of GLT explicitly attributed to him in the preface of GLT. Furthermore, the quote is a broad claim about child development and is the sort of thing for which Piaget is very well known. Lastly, all people to whom I have talked about the matter take the view expressed in the quote to be Piaget's view.

In the above quotation Piaget explicitly asserts that children 'from 7—8 to 11—12 . . . cannot yet handle . . . propositional logic'. He also suggests that propositional logic facility develops with the onset of Stage III, which appears to start at '11—12'.

There is a vagueness here since it is not clear what he is saying about children who *are* either 11 or 12. Perhaps he is allowing for individual differences, in which case the vagueness seems appropriate at least in the early-development stages of this theory.

The problem that I want to raise is about the *meaning* of 'handle propositional logic', regardless of how he deals with the loose boundary. A rough indication of a boundary somewhere around 11 or 12 will enable us to consider this meaning problem, which is more fundamental than the question of the precise location of the boundary.

Since the claim about those 11 to 12 and below is initially clearer than the one about children 11 to 15 and above, and since my ultimate concern is whether he is saying anything in this key quotation (and others like it), I shall focus on the more explicit claim, that children 11 to 12 and younger 'cannot yet handle . . . propositional logic'.

Given the previous analysis of Piaget's propositional logic, it is tempting to say that we are glad that children do not handle his propositional logic, and hope and believe that adolescents and adults as well do not exercise their alleged capacity, since the logic is so implausible. So we should ignore the claim and get on with our work. But the problem is not that simple.

For one thing, the logic is correct in some respects (e.g. the following two principles are correct and implicit in his logic: (1) there must be no cases fitting 'p.q̄' for p to imply q*; and (2) the implication 'if p, then q', does not imply the implication 'if q, then p'). It would be useful to know whether children of 11 to 12 and under act in accord with these correct principles, if Piaget's claim gives this sort of information. Furthermore, if children over 11 to 12 actually do operate in accord with the principles of Piaget's propositional logic, bad as this way of thinking may be, then it would be valuable to know that about them, and it would be valuable to know that children of 11 to 12 and under are different in this respect.

Some Initially Puzzling Features of Piaget's Claim

In my experience, persons who are acquainted with the propositional logic tradition are puzzled when first faced with this claim of Piaget's. If 'handle propositional logic' means to master the propositional calculus as taught in most contemporary logic courses, then the question is why should Piaget have picked on such young children as lacking this ability, and indicated (as he and Inhelder do in GLT, pp. xxii, 1, 43, 296, etc.,) that adolescents can handle propositional logic; for most college students cannot handle propositional logic; in that sense. If, on the other hand, the claim is that practically no children can reason in accord with any of the forms of propositional logic presented earlier in Table 6.1, then whose who also have current or recent acquaintance with children feel that the claim is just false. This feeling is substantiated by a variety of studies including ones by Burt (1919), Hill (1961), Ennis and Paulus (1965), O'Brien and Shapiro (1968), Roberge (1970), Shapiro and O'Brien (1970), Ennis (1971), and Ryoti (1972).

These studies as a group also show that children are considerably worse at making judgments about invalid forms of arguments than about valid forms. But adolescents also are considerably worse at making judgments about invalid forms than valid forms (Ennis and Paulus, 1965; Gardiner, 1965; Howell, 1965; Martens, 1967; Paulus, 1967; Miller, 1968; Carroll, 1970; Roberge, 1970; Shapiro and O'Brien, 1970; Ryoti, 1972; and Flener, 1973).

What is it that children allegedly cannot do that adolescents can do? Both have ability to reason in accord with at least some of the principles of propositional logic, and both have considerable trouble with logical fallacies.

---

*Interpreting 'p' and 'q' as propositional functions.

Perhaps one might expect on the basis of Piaget's claim that there is some quantum jump in propositional logic ability from childhood to adolescence. This is a difficult suggestion to evaluate for both logical and practical reasons: The logical ones are the vagueness of the boundary line to which I referred earlier and the vagueness of the size of the difference needed to count as a quantum jump. A significant practical difficulty is that of gathering data on a large enough representative sample, data generated by using the same (or quite comparable) test (or other evaluation method) with each child repeatedly over a period of approximately ten years—longitudinally from, perhaps, age 7 to 17. The reason that the data should be gathered longitudinally is that the alleged quantum jump might well occur at quite different ages for different children. To group the children cross-sectionally by ages or grades would tend to mask such spaced-out quantum jumps. No study exists that satisfies this practical problem, and Piaget has left us rather in the dark about the logical problems.

There is a group of three studies that come out of one tradition, use somewhat similar tests, and cover cross-sectionally a range of years. I shall indicate the results of these studies but then suggest that, however these studies had turned out and however even the ideal study turns out, they probably would not defeat what I take to be Piaget's claim, because his claim appears to be about some total logical characteristic, some holistic ability—not the ability to reason in accord with a set of principles of propositional logic. I shall also suggest that there appears to be no way to tell whether this total logical characteristic is possessed by a child, and thus that his claim is not of use to someone interested in explaining and predicting children's logical behaviour.

The three studies are those by Ennis and Paulus (1965), Roberge (1970), and Ennis (1971). Percentage summaries of their results appear in Table 6.4. Ennis and Paulus used the *Cornell Conditional Reasoning Test* (in Ennis and Paulus, 1965) with grades 5, 7, 9, and 11, and Roberge used the *Paulus Conditional Reasoning Test* (in Paulus, 1967) with grades 4, 6, 8 and 10. The tests used in these two studies had items of the following form (modelled after the description by Roberge, 1970):

> Suppose you know that:
> If _____, then _____
> Another premise (or two)
> then would this be true?
> Proposed conclusion.

The possible responses which the students could select were 'A. Yes', 'B. No', or 'C. Maybe'. The meaning of these possible answers was explained to the students as follows:

A. YES, it must be true.
B. NO, it can't be true.
C. MAYBE, it may be true or it may not be true. You weren't told enough to be certain whether it is 'YES' or 'NO'.

Both studies used an operational definition of 'mastery of a logical principle' modelled after Ennis (1964), but even then the results are not quite comparable, because they had different standards of mastery. Ennis and Paulus required at least five out of six items correct, and Roberge required at least eight out of twelve.

The Ennis (1971) study used the *Smith—Sturgeon Conditional Reasoning Test* (in Ennis et al, 1969) with grades 1, 2, and 3. This test, although based on the same approach as the other two, was designed for use with children who cannot read and was administered individually in the presence of concrete objects about which children were asked to reason. At least five out of six correct was the standard for mastery. (A judgment of 'correct' here required an adequate justification by the student for his

Table 6.4 *Percentages of Some Students in Grades 1 to 11 Mastering Some Basic Conditional Logic Principles*

N	Grade Level			Percentage Mastering a Principle					
	Ennis (1971)	Ennis and Paulus (1965)	Roberge (1970)	Detachment	Particular Conversion	Particular Inversion	Particular Contraposition	Transitivity[a]	Full Contraposition
30	1			b	00	20	40	13	b
28	2			b	11	43	64	29	b
29	3			b	07	31	62	45	b
57			4	53	02	02	35	28	33
102		5		51	02	03	30	25	34
57			6	54	00	00	23	28	33
99		7		56	03	06	41	45	40
57			8	95	00	00	74	81	84
80		9		66	04	05	35	40	35
57			10	100	19	05	65	82	44
78		11		62	03	12	35	58	33

[a]Particular transitivity for grades 1 to 3; full transitivity for grades 4 to 11.
[b]Not evaluated in this study.

Notes: 1 One should, in particular, beware in comparing grades 1 to 3 with the rest because of the different type of testing used with grades 1 to 3.
2 The Ennis-led studies used 'at least five out of six' as sufficient for indicating mastery. The Roberge study used 'at least eight out of twelve'.
Some more noncomparability is thereby introduced.

answer.) Because of the different method of administration, one cannot expect a developmental continuity between the results of this study and the other two. If one were to ignore this difference in testing methods, one would get what appears to be a significant retrogression from grade 3 to the next grade tested (4 or 5, depending on the study examined). This illustrates the difficulty that permeates the literature—the use of different tests in different studies; and the difficulty appears here even though the tests arise out of the same tradition.

Be that as it may, the results of these studies fail to support the suggestion that there is a quantum jump at some particular point in a child's development. However, they do not conclusively prove that there is no quantum jump. As I indicated earlier, a series of extensive longitudinal studies would be needed to settle the matter. In any case, it is clear that many young children do reason in accord with at least some principles of propositional logic, that many adolescents fail to reason in accord with the basic principles of invalidity, and that there is general progress as children grow older.

A Holistic Quality: Working Within the Combinatorial Systems

I mention these studies for the benefit of those who think, as I once did, that such empirical research has a bearing on Piaget's claims. I do not now think that it does, because a close reading of Piaget suggests that the quality supposedly distinguishing adolescents from children, and equivalent to ability to handle propositional logic, is quite elusive.

This quality, a holistic one, seems to be the ability to work within the combinatorial system that I described in some detail earlier. Piaget's emphasis on working within this combinatorial system comes through clearly in the following quotes:

> [T]he subject's reasoning no longer operates in a simple formulation of relationships or concrete correspondences but requires a formal combinatorial system. (GLT, p. 42)

> Such a composition of relations requires that we must resort to what we have called in Chap. 1 the 'structured whole' (the combinations having 0, 1, 2, 3, and 4 conjunctions) . . . (GLT, p. 43)

> To arrive at this analysis the subject would have to use a complete combinatorial system . . . (GLT, p. 54)

> This complete combinatorial system is precisely the mark of formal thought. (GLT, p. 55)

> The combinatorial system which constitutes propositional logic. (GLT, p. 55)

> The combinatorial method inherent in formal thinking and adolescent propositional logic. (GLT, p. 93)

> We are not exaggerating when we claim that it is possible for subjects at this level [stage III-B] to work in turn with each of the 16 binary combinations of propositional logic. (GLT, p. 104)

> So the main feature of propositional logic is not that it is verbal logic, but that it requires a combinatorial system. (GLT, p. 254)

> Thus we would not want to speak of incompatibility p/q (a propositional operation) except for those subjects capable of placing this combination in opposition to the set of 15 other combinations in the system or to the principal ones among these (p.q, p v q, p ⊃ q, etc.,) . . . However, the stage III subjects, who utilize a complete combinatorial system in their experimental trials on the colourants and who also express the results by means of adequate statements, are able to place their combination in opposition to the 15 others. (GLT, p. 296)

It is somewhat disturbing to a close reader of Piaget to find so many explicitly different things said about the significance of the combinatorial system for handling propositional logic. For convenience I use the phrase, 'Working within the combinatorial system', letting that refer to whatever it is that Piaget equates to handling propositional logic. However, it is still unclear what Piaget is saying children cannot do, because it is not clear how to tell whether children are working within the combinatorial system (that is, whether they are 'handling' Piaget's propositional logic).

Possible Criteria for Determining Whether Children Are Working Within the Combinatorial System

Since the phrase, 'working within the combinatorial system', does not have an immediately obvious meaning, one must cast about for possible criteria for its application. In my search I came up with four candidates, but, as I shall try to show, none rendered Piaget's claim about children useful to someone interested in children's deductive logic ability. It is, of course, open to any Piaget interpreter to come up with some other criterion, but I could find no others with any degree of plausibility.

The following four criteria for telling whether someone is working within the combinatorial system can be found discussed by Piaget in GLT: (1) the use of the language of propositional logic; (2) suppositional reasoning; (3) distinguishing one operation from another; and (4) isolating the variables. I shall deal with each in turn.

The use of the language of propositional logic

One's first impulse might be to look at the language children use and understand to see whether they express themselves in terms like 'if . . . then', 'either . . . or', 'implies', 'not both', etc., and can reason correctly with propositions containing such terms, since these terms have direct translations into the symbolism of the combinatorial scheme of 16 binary operations. This was and is my impulse. It is followed in the earlier-mentioned research that some might think conflicts with Piaget's claim. But Piaget explicitly rejects this as a way of telling whether a child is working within the combinatorial system:

> But it is fruitless to look for an exclusively verbal or linguistic criterion—e.g. considering all statements containing the words 'if . . . then' as implications . . . (GLT, p. 279)

> Now, we readily admit that on the basis of language alone we cannot tell whether an isolated statement is concrete or formal . . . There is no doubt that it is always possible to express propositional operations in the language of classes at the formal level . . . Conversely, the operations inherent to these groupings (classifications, etc.,) could be expressed in propositional language. (GLT, p. 280)

On the other hand, Piaget or Inhelder (they do not identify), in one of the places where an attempted connection between what children do and their working within the combinatorial system appears most clearly, apparently makes use of this linguistic criterion. An attempt is made to show, for a subject referred to as GOU, that each of the sixteen binary functions 'can be distinguished in his protocol' (GLT, p. 103). But the person doing the distinguishing is Piaget/Inhelder—not GOU. In treating each binary operation, Piaget/Inhelder show to their own satisfaction that GOU's protocol for each binary operation either contained the wording of the binary operation (e.g. 'It's either the distance or the content (or both)', the quotation marks being supplied by Piaget/Inhelder), or it contained a thought that Piaget/Inhelder expressed in the language of that binary operation (e.g. 'Implication $(p \supset q) = (p.q \lor \bar{p}.q \lor \bar{p}.\bar{q})$; if a magnet is attached to the disk, it will stop in front of the boxes containing iron', quotation marks being supplied by me). In this demonstration that GOU 'uses propositional rather than concrete operations', Piaget or Inhelder did not refer to GOU's reasoning suppositionally, nor to GOU's distinguishing each operation from all fifteen others, nor to GOU's isolation of the variables. The linguistic criterion was used exclusively.

Incidentally, Bynum, Thomas, and Weitz (1972) have contended that the GOU protocol contained only eight of the sixteen binary operations. What Piaget/Inhelder see other people do not see when looking at the same data. Such radical disagreement lends support to the desire to get some fairly clear and plausible categories and concepts to use in describing children's knowledge of logic.

If the linguistic criterion were used to identify propositional logic, then Piaget's claims would be false, even about his own kind of experiments. Weitz et al (1973), using a strictly linguistic criterion for identifying the binary functions, replicated the magnetism experiment from which the GOU protocol springs. They found no significant difference in the extent of use of the binary functions among nine-, twelve-, and sixteen-year-olds.

> All age groups used the same five operations [and no one used more than five]: conjunction, implication, disjunction, converse implication, and independence of p in relation to q. Of these five, only two were used with any regularity: conjunction and implication . . . The more developed reasoner used the *same* operations as the less developed reasoner, but the former used those operations in a more complex and sophisticated manner. (Op. cit., p. 283)

Piaget's rejection of the linguistic criterion insulates him against such results, but makes one wonder what would count as a test of his theory. As Piaget/Inhelder showed in the analysis of the GOU protocol, the linguistic criterion for identifying cases of propositional logic is attractive. When deprived of this criterion, one must look elsewhere for some basis for making predictions from his theory.

Suppositional reasoning

Shortly following one of the above-presented quotes rejecting the linguistic criterion, Piaget offers a semi-linguistic criterion that I shall call the suppositional-reasoning criterion:

> When a subject says, 'if it were (such and such a factor) that played a part, then you should find (such and such an unobserved consequence),' one can be sure of the hypothetico-deductive and consequently propositional nature of the operations involved. (GLT, p. 279)

This criterion is also presented in his earlier work, *Judgment and Reasoning in the Child* (1959), though there it is offered as a characteristic of the possibly broader trait, *formal* reasoning ability:

> The child cannot reason from premises without believing in them. Or even if he reasons implicitly from assumptions which he makes on his own, he cannot do so from those which are proposed to him. Not till the age of 11—12 is he capable of this difficult operation, which is pure deduction. (Ibid., p. 252)

The suppositional trait is that of being able to reason from that which the reasoner believes to be untrue, or at least does not believe to be true.

There are two problems here. First of all, many children under 11—12 do have this trait (Ennis, 1971); thus, his view would be false if this criterion were used. Second, even if many children under 11—12 did not have this trait, there is no reason to think that the trait is connected with the ability to work within Piaget's combinatorial system. What could be the connection?

Distinguishing one operation from another

Frequently Piaget mentions the subject's ability to distinguish one operation from the others as the way to tell whether the subject is working within the combinatorial system:

> But the operation does not take on propositional meaning until it is placed in opposition to the other possible combinations. (GLT, p. 293)

> Thus we would not want to speak of incompatibility p/q except for those subjects capable of placing this combination in opposition to the set of fifteen other combinations in the system or to the principal ones among these (p.q, p v q, p ⊃ q, etc.). (GLT, p. 296)

> The discovery of implication as such consists of differentiating it from the other possible combinations (p v q, p = q, etc.). (GLT, p. 298)

However, this criterion is not helpful, because Piaget does not tell us how to tell whether someone is distinguishing one operation from the fifteen others; thus untestability is again suggested. It is somewhat ironic that Piaget/Inhelder, in commenting about GOU's protocol (reported earlier), did not check to see whether GOU distinguished each from the fifteen others, but rather held that Piaget/Inhelder could do the distinguishing.

A seemingly plausible way to tell whether someone is distinguishing each from the others would get us back to the verbal criterion explicitly rejected by Piaget: we would look to see whether a person reasons correctly from and to statements that contain such terms as 'if . . . then' and 'either . . . or'. If, for example, they conclude 'If a rod is thin, then it is flexible' rather than 'Either a rod is thin or it is flexible' when the former is the appropriate conclusion, then we judge them to have successfully distinguished, given that both were alternatives that were presented to them. Similarly, when given a particular-contraposition kind of argument, if they draw the correct conclusion, then we can be fairly sure that they treated the 'if . . . then' statement as an 'if . . . then' statement, rather than an 'either . . . or' statement. Again, there is evidence of distinguishing. But this approach depends on the rejected verbal identification of the different propositional statements.

Isolating the variables

The ability to isolate variables and hold all but one constant in making an empirical inquiry is offered by Piaget as a sure sign of the combinatorial system:

> Whether he tries to separate out the variables. The latter implies both hypothetico-deductive reasoning and a combination system . . . (GLT, p. 279)

> The isolation of variables necessarily leads the subject to combine the base associations among themselves n-by-n and thus to substitute for the simple multiplication and correspondence operations which give rise to the base associations the combinatorial system . . . (GLT, p. 288)

> Isolation of variables . . . necessarily ends up at a combinatorial system. (GLT, p. 288)

His reasoning, although difficult to explicate, seems to go like this (reconstructed from the discussion in GLT, pp. 284—288): the base associations or elements (of which there are four for two variables: 'p.q', 'p.q̄', 'p̄.q', and 'p̄.q̄') are not rich enough to interpret the results of separating variables and holding some constant. One also needs combinations of these base associations (e.g. 'p.q v p̄.q v p̄.q̄', the combination for implication). Let 'r' mean 'rod x is made of brass' and 'p' and 'q' mean 'rod x is thin' and 'rod x is flexible' respectively. By holding r constant, one might get a case of 'p.q', a case of 'p̄.q', a case of 'p̄.q̄', and no cases of 'p.q̄', although, had r not been held constant, one might have obtained a case of 'p.q̄' (a thin rod that did not bend because it was made of glass). Thus, one would be entitled by virtue of the fact that r was isolated and held constant to conclude 'if p, then q' other things being equal. The strategy of isolating and holding variables constant can only make sense if one is striving to ascertain the truth of such combinations as the one for implication, rather than uncombined base associations of elements. Hence, separating variables implies a combinatorial system.

If this explication of his argument is correct, then his crucial (and I believe mistaken) assumption is that the base associations are inadequate for the problems, but that the *combinations* of the base associations are adequate. He puts it as follows:

> We have shown that these associations . . . are inadequate for the solution of the problems we posed, although of course they must be established before further reasoning is possible. Only afterwards, when these base associations have been structured, can the subject choose the crucial combinations from the total number of possible ones. Thus it must be at this point that the combinatorial system makes its appearance. (GLT, p. 287)

The question is whether Piaget has shown that the base associations are inadequate and that combinations made from them are adequate. The burden of my earlier remarks about Piagetian logic is that the combinations, in fact, misrepresent the propositional-function relationships; thus, isolating variables (a correct procedure) could not imply the use of combinations (an incorrect procedure). That the base associations are by themselves inadequate nobody would deny, since one must take account of context, existing knowledge, reasonableness of attempts to falsify, sampling procedures, etc. But the same requirements exist for combinations. Furthermore, the base associations *do* represent all possible combinations of the variables under consideration.

One must be careful, in dealing with this aspect of Piagetian argument, not to indulge in an ambiguous use of the term, 'possible combination'. There are the possible combinations of variables (e.g. a thin, flexible rod evidences one combination of variables), and the possible combinations of the Piagetian elements ('p.q v p̄.q v p̄.q̄' is one of the combinations). The four base associations represent all the possible combinations of the variables, 'p' and 'q' (assuming, as Piaget does, only two values for each variable). A subject's thinking of all four base associations as the possible combinations (of variables) is not the same as a subject's thinking of the sixteen possible combinations of Piagetian elements. That a subject thinks of the possible combinations of variables, as one might well do who isolates the variables for purposes of varying them one at a time, would suggest, by trading on an ambiguity, that the subject is thinking of the possible combinations of Piagetian elements. Thinking of the possible combinations of Piagetian elements could perhaps be taken as working within Piaget's combinatorial system. Thinking of the possible combinations of variables would be evidenced by isolating the variables. There is a danger of trading on an ambiguity in inferring from someone's isolating the variables to someone's working within the combinatorial system.

The result of this discussion is that, if ability to isolate variables is a characteristic limited to children over 11—12 (a limitation denied in a study by Anderson, 1965), there is no reason to believe that from this it follows that the combinatorial system is limited to children over 11—12. There appears to be no connection between isolating variables and possessing the combinatorial system. Hence, even though Piaget offers isolation of variables as a criterion for the presence of the combinatorial system, there is no reason to accept it as a criterion. One could with as much reason offer it as a criterion for the presence of class reasoning, which Piaget assigns to children between 7—8 and 11—12.

Of course, one can insist that it is Piaget's theory and that he has a right to interpret his terms any way he chooses. The result, then, is that Piaget is talking about isolating the variables when he uses the phrase, 'handle propositional logic'. There is an Alice-in-Wonderland air about such a way of talking, but if we accept it, we must still remember that he would not then be talking about what we are interested in when we express an interest in children's deductive-logic ability.

Piaget's Treatment of Some Apparent Counter-examples

Based upon the foregoing analysis of Piaget's theory,* it appears that the claim that children 11—12 and under cannot handle propositional logic is a false, untestable, or otherwise defective claim. Piaget's response to a question asked in 1965 by Patrick Suppes at a Paris conference fails to modify this impression. Suppes said:

> I would like to ask Dr Piaget how he feels about the exhibition of the use of logical structures by children, in their very sophisticated and very subtle command of their own language. In experiments on children of age 6, 7, and 8 years, they show without training a remarkable facility with problems of the following sort: 'If John is in school, then Mary is in school. John is in school. What can you say about Mary?' A somewhat more difficult problem should be *tollendo tollens*: 'If John is in school, then Mary is in school. Mary is not in school. What can you say about John?' Or syllogisms of the sort: 'All children in the third grade have been to the circus. John is in the third grade. What can you say about John?' In other words, we have found that the natural logic of ordinary language, which is also the logic of intuitive mathematics, is already under good command of children at a relatively young age, given that the sentences or words one uses are familiar to the child and are not too foreign either in content or direction of intent. (Piaget, 1967, p. 277)

Piaget answered:

> Thank you for that question which is fundamental. I think that in order to respond to it, one must be careful in experimentation to dissociate that which comes from language and that which language permits the imagination to evoke concretely ['ce que le langage permet comme évocation concrète par l'imagerie en général' is how Piaget put this last phrase]. In your examples it is a question of relatively simple situations that the language describes. The problem is to know how the child reasons. Does he reason by means of situations that he can evoke, or imagine, or does he reason by means of combinations of terms? In the case that you have given, the reasoning that you call verbal seems precocious to me. But I know other cases. (1967, pp. 277—278, my translation.)

There appear to be three facets of Piaget's reply. One is to suggest that Suppes' situations are relatively simple. This is true, but one wonders how that is related to Piaget's theory. The simplicity of situation criterion is like the isolation of variables criterion; each is more or less identifiable, and in each, sophistication probably develops with age. But what is their connection with the combinatorial system and propositional logic?

A second facet is the attribution of precociousness to the reasoning of Suppes' children. This feature of Piaget's reply suggests untestability. Children who appear to go against his theory are just precocious.

If Piaget did not mean to avoid the counter-example impact of Suppes' examples by attributing precociousness to the children's reasoning, then perhaps he meant that Suppes was misinterpreting the reasoning that occurred. Piaget's distinction, the third facet of his response, would then be called upon to show how what might appear to be one thing was really something else, for Suppes' first two examples are propositional logic in the standard sense of 'propositional logic' and these examples were handled by children well under the age 11—12. Whether or not Piaget was avoiding the counter-examples by calling the reasoning precocious, application of his distinction might also be a way of dealing with them.

The distinction appears, on the face of it, to be one between reasoning by means of language (Piaget's words: 'that which comes from language', 'by means of combinations of terms') and reasoning by means of images ('that which language permits the imagination to evoke concretely', 'by means of situations that he can evoke, or

---

*I have not considered having Piaget's INRC structure as a possible interpretation of working within the combinatorial system or handling propositional logic, because having that structure for implication, for example, seems only to require distinguishing and relating $(p \supset q)$ (I) from and with $p.\bar{q}$ (N), $q \supset p$ (R), and $\bar{p}q$ (C), rather than the fifteen other combinations (Beth and Piaget, 1966, pp. 181-183), thus neglecting the important p v q, p.q and p/q. Lunzer (1965, p. 30) has noted other problems with Piaget's applying the INRC structure to children's thought.

imagine'). Although Piaget does not specify which side of the distinction applies to children 11—12 and under, presumably they are the ones who reason by means of images, reasoning by means of language being reserved for adolescents.

Applying the distinction to Suppes' examples, a first inclination is to think that Piaget meant that, although Suppes' children might appear to be reasoning by means of language, they were only reasoning by means of concrete images—and thus they fit Piaget's theory. Testability questions, on this interpretation, immediately arise, for one wonders how Piaget would know that these children were reasoning by means of images without assuming his theory to be correct in the first place.

Perhaps Piaget meant that Suppes' children were working with images, though not reasoning. The testability-or-falsity problem would arise here, for one wonders what right he has to say that these children were not reasoning. My associates' experiences and my own (Ennis, 1971) with six- to nine-year-olds, including interviews and observations of their justifications of their conclusions, strongly suggest that many do reason—and reason correctly—with 'if—then' statements.

On the other hand, one wonders what it is that these children were not doing, if it was suggested that they were not reasoning by means of language. What have they failed to do? What is reasoning by means of language?

Perhaps 'reasoning by means of language' is reasoning that operates through an understanding of the *meaning* of the language used, and in particular, of an understanding of the *meaning* of the logical operators involved—in Suppes' first two cases, 'if—then' and 'not'. One wonders on what ground Piaget can deny this description to Suppes' children (if he does so). Age is a ground that makes the theory look untestable.

In sum, then, Piaget's simplicity-of-situation response appears irrelevant to the propositional-logic question. His precociousness response, if he means it the way it sounds, pushes his claim towards untestability. If he means his precociousness response some other way, then his distinction between reasoning with images and reasoning with language fails to allay the impression of untestability. Perhaps there are other interpretations, but the only ones that occur to me are quite implausible.

Incidently, after Piaget's responses to Suppes' question, Anatol Rapoport attempted a defence of Piaget by suggesting that children would not be successful with examples with similar content, but in which nothing necessarily followed:

> I would be more impressed if the question were put in such a way as not to suggest the correct answer, for example: 'If John is in school, then Mary is in school, Mary is in school, what can you say about John?' The answer is, 'Nothing'. But many children, I am sure, of 6 and 7, will say, 'John is in school'. (Piaget, 1967, pp. 279—80)

I take Rapoport to have been suggesting that Suppes' examples were of a special sort and not representative of (propositional?) logic, or at least were answerable on other grounds than propositional logic.

Suppes' first two examples are of the forms, detachment and particular contraposition, both valid forms (see Table 6.1). Rapoport's example is of the form, particular conversion, an invalid form. More examples were produced in the exchange, but Suppes' were all of valid forms and Rapoport's of invalid forms. The Hill (1961), O'Brien and Shapiro (1968), and Ennis (1971) studies suggest that both are right, that children in the six-to-eight range do fairly well with the valid forms, but poorly with the invalid forms.

However, Rapoport's point does not help Piaget's position, since (as I indicated earlier) adolescents also do poorly on the invalid forms, contrary to what one would expect from the Piaget-claimed ability of Stage III-B. If lack of mastery of the invalid forms should count against young children's knowledge of propositional logic, then it should count against adolescents' knowledge of propositional logic. Rapoport's examples can help one part of Piagetian theory only at the expense of another part.

But Rapoport's point does advance the discussion by focusing it, Piaget's response leaves me with a strong impression of untestability. An untestable theory does not tell us anything and cannot be a basis for predictions.

PIAGET'S LOGIC: A DESCRIPTIVE OR NORMATIVE SYSTEM?

It might be urged, in reply to my criticisms of Piagetian logic as a system of logic, that he was only using the symbolism of logic, but was not attempting to offer a way of judging the validity of reasoning: that Piaget's system is a descriptive system, not a normative one. Ginsburg and Opper (1969) suggest this approach:

> Piaget's major question, of course, is not whether the adolescent can come up with the 'right' answer. Rather the issue is whether and how his thought differs from that of the younger child. (Op. cit. p. 182)

It is, of course, true that Piaget is attempting to offer a descriptive system. Otherwise my previous suggestion of the untestability of his system would be irrelevant. But his descriptions involve statements about the presence or absence of traits that Piaget judges normatively by his logic:

> We have shown that these associations or multiplicative correspondences are *inadequate* for the *solution* of the problem we posed . . . (GLT, p. 287, emphasis added.)

> In particular the Stage III subjects struggle against the *temptation* to conclude *too quickly* from the occurrence of p.q the assertion of an equivalence $p \underset{C}{\supset} q$ or of a simple implication $p \supset q$. (GLT, pp. 294—295, emphasis added.)

> [Stage III-B subjects] *know* when they see an elementary association, p.q or p.q̄, etc., that it *may be* included in any one of several combinations (p∗q, p[q], or p ⊃ q, for example), and *they can verify its truth or falsehood more or less systematically.* Conversely, when they assume a complex combination such as p ⊃ q as a hypothesis, they *know how to verify it by* going back to its elements p.q and p̄.q or by looking for a *counterproof* in the *falsehood* [sic] of p.q̄. (GLT, p. 304, emphasis added.)

Thus, his system is an attempt to describe, to state empirical truths, but the empirical statements are about ability to do what Piaget construes as good or bad logic. His claim about children's ability to handle propositional logic, thus, has both normative and descriptive dimensions.

SUMMARY

In this article I have suggested that the normative dimension of Piaget's claim (that is, Piaget's logic) is mistaken, because it prohibits certain inferences one is entitled to make, because it invites overgeneralization, and because of other odd results. Since Piaget uses this logic to judge the adequacy of children's thinking, as well as to attempt to describe the thinking, these inadequacies in the logic are a significant flaw.

The descriptive dimension (the claim about what children and adolescents can and cannot do) appears defective as well. I mentioned evidence that would, on the most obvious interpretation of the claim, falsify it, but also suggested that Piaget probably did not intend that interpretation. Unfortunately, many people take the claim in that interpretation, making recommendations based upon it.

In a search for a satisfactory interpretation of the claim, I considered four possible criteria for judging whether someone is working within Piaget's combinatorial system (and thus handling propositional logic): (1) using the language of propositional logic; (2) doing suppositional reasoning; (3) distinguishing binary operations from each other; and (4) isolating the variables. No matter what the interpretation, I have concluded that the claim is either false, or untestable, or not about deductive logic.

It is open to others to unearth new interpretations (I could find no other plausible ones), and to consider the truth and application of the claim, sticking to the unearthed interpretation. The danger lies in attempting to justify the claim using one interpretation, and then applying or predicting from the claim, using another interpretation.

REFERENCES

Anderson, R. C. (1965) Can first graders learn an advanced problem-solving skill? *Journal of Educational Psychology,* **56**, 283-294.

Beardsley, M. (1966) *Thinking Straight.* (3rd Ed.) Englewood Cliffs, N.J.: Prentice-Hall.

Beth, E. W. and Piaget, J. (1966) *Mathematical Epistemology and Psychology.* Dordrecht, Holland: D. Reidel Publishing.

Black, M. (1952) *Critical Thinking.* (2nd Ed.) Englewood Cliffs, N.J.: Prentice-Hall.

Burt, C. (1919) The development of reasoning in school children. *Journal of Experimental Pedagogy,* **5**, (2 + 3), 68-77, 121-127.

Bynum, T. W., Thomas, J. A. and Weitz, L. J. (1972) Truth-functional logic in formal operational thinking: Inhelder and Piaget's evidence. *Developmental Psychology,* **7**, 129-132.

Carroll, C. A. (1970) *Low achievers' understanding of four logical inference forms: an analysis of difficulties and of the effect of instruction.* (Doctoral dissertation, Columbia University) Ann Arbor, Michigan: University Microfilms. No. 71-6151.

Clark, M. (1971) Ifs and hooks. *Analysis,* **32**, 33-39.

Copi, I. (1961) *Introduction to Logic.* (2nd Ed.) New York: Macmillan.

Ennis, R. H. (1962) A concept of critical thinking. *Harvard Educational Review,* **32**, 81-111.

Ennis, R. H. (1964) Operational definitions. *American Educational Research Journal,* **1**, 183-201.

Ennis, R. H. (1969) *Ordinary Logic.* Englewood Cliffs, N.J.: Prentice-Hall.

Ennis, R. H. (1971) Conditional logic and primary children. *Interchange,* **2**, 126-132.

Ennis, Robert H. (1975) Children's ability to handle Piaget's propositional logic. *Review of Educational Research,* **45**, No. 1. Copyright 1975, American Educational Research Association, Washington DC. Reprinted by kind permission.

Ennis, R. H. and Paulus, D. H. (1965) *Critical thinking readiness in grades* 1-12 (Phase 1: *Deductive reasoning in adolescence*), (Coop, Research Project, No. 1680), Ithaca, N.Y.: Cornell Critical Thinking Readiness Project.

Ennis, R. H., Finkelstein, M., Smith, E. and Wilson, N. (1969) *Conditional Logic and Children.* Ithaca, N.Y.: Cornell Critical Thinking Readiness Project.

Faris, J. A. (1962) *Truth-functional Logic.* New York: The Free Press of Glencoe.

Fisk, M. (1964) *A Modern Formal Logic.* Englewood Cliffs, N.J.: Prentice-Hall.

Flavell, J. H. (1963) *The Developmental Psychology of Jean Piaget.* Princeton, N.J.: D. Van Nostrand.

Flener, F. O. (1973) *A comparison of reasoning with general and singular propositions by fifth, seventh, and ninth grade students.* (Doctoral dissertation, University of Illinois) Ann Arbor, Michigan: University Microfilms.

Gardiner, W. L. (1965) *An investigation of understanding of the meaning of the logical operators in propositional reasoning.* (Doctoral dissertation, Cornell University) Ann Arbor, Michigan: University Microfilms. No. 66-4109.

Ginsburg, H. and Opper, S. (1969) *Piaget's Theory of Intellectual Development.* Englewood Cliffs, N.J.: Prentice-Hall.

Hill, S. (1961) *A study of logical abilities in children.* (Doctoral dissertation, Stanford University) Ann Arbor, Michigan: University Microfilms. No. 61-1229.

Howell, E. N. (1965) *Recognition of selected inference patterns by secondary school mathematics students.* (Doctoral dissertation, University of Wisconsin) Ann Arbor, Michigan: University Microfilms. No. 65-14,886.

Inhelder, B. and Piaget, J. (1958) *The Growth of Logical Thinking from Childhood to Adolescence.* New York: Basic Books.

Lewis, C. I. (1912) Implication and the algebra of logic. *Mind,* 522-531.

Lunzer, E. (1965) Problems of formal reasoning in test situations. In Mussen, P. H. (Ed.), European research in cognitive development. *Monographs of the Society for Research in Child Development,* **30**, 19-46.

Martens, M. A. (1967) *Use of selected rules of logical inference and of logical fallacies by senior high students.* (Doctoral dissertation, The University of Wisconsin) Ann Arbor, Michigan: University Microfilms. No. 67-16,980.

Miller, W. (1968) *The acceptance and recognition of six logical inference patterns by secondary students.* (Doctoral dissertation, University of Wisconsin) Ann Arbor, Michigan: University Microfilms. No. 68-13,651.

O'Brien, T. and Shapiro, B. (1968) The development of logical thinking in children. *American Educational Research Journal,* **5**, 531-541.

Papert, S. (1963) Sur la logique Piagetienne. In Apostel, L., Grize, J. B., Papert, S. and Piaget, J., (Eds.) La filiation des structures (Vol. XV of Études d'Epistémologie Génétique). Paris: Presses Universitaires de France, pp. 107-129.

Parsons, C. (1960) Inhelder and Piaget's the growth of logical thinking. II: A logician's viewpoint. *British Journal of Psychology,* **51**, 75-84.

Paulus, D. H. (1967) *A study of children's abilities to deduce and judge deductions.* (Doctoral dissertation, Cornell University) Ann Arbor, Michigan: University Microfilms. No. 67-16,365.

Piaget, J. (1959) *Judgment and Reasoning in the Child.* Patterson, N. J.: Vittlefield, Adams & Co., (first published in 1928).

Piaget, J. (1949) *Traité de Logique.* Paris: Libraire Armand Colin.

Piaget, J. (1953) *Logic and Psychology.* Manchester, England: University of Manchester Press.

Piaget, J. (1967) Logique formelle et psychologie génétique. (Including discussion by Piaget, J. F. Richard, P. Suppes, M. Reuchlin, A. Rapoport, P. Fraise, H. Simon and F. Restle). In Les modeles et la formalization du comportment *(Proceedings of the International Colloquium of the National Center for Scientific Research,* Paris, July 5-10, 1965), pp. 269-283.

Quine, W. V. O. (1960) *Methods of Logic.* (Rev. Ed.) New York: Henry Holt.

Roberge, J. J. (1970) A study of children's abilities to reason with basic principles of deductive reasoning. *American Educational Research Journal,* **7**, 583-595.

Russell, L. J. (1960) Formal logic and ordinary language. *Analysis,* **21**, 25-34.

Ryoti, D. E. (1972) *Student responses to equivalent inference schemes in class and conditional logic.* (Doctoral dissertation, University of Illinois) Ann Arbor, Michigan: University Microfilms.

Shapiro, B. J. and O'Brien, T. C. (1970) Logical thinking in children ages six through thirteen. *Child Development,* **41**, 823-829.

Strawson, P. F. (1952) *An Introduction to Logical Theory.* London: Methuen.

Weitz, L. J., Bynum, T. W., Thomas, J. A. and Steger, J. A. (1973) Piaget's system of 16 binary operations: An empirical investigation. *Journal of Genetic Psychology,* **123**, 279-284.

Young, J. J. (1972) Ifs and hooks: A defense of the orthodox view. *Analysis,* **33**, 56-63.

Chapter 7

Structures, Functions and Stages: A Trio of Unresolved Issues in Formal Operations*

CAROL TOMLINSON-KEASEY

INTRODUCTION

Inhelder and Piaget's (1958) classic work on adolescent thought processes, *The Growth of Logical Thinking from Childhood to Adolescence*, has altered our entire view of the phenomena of adolescent cognition. Wallace (1965) comments on the paucity of earlier work describing cognitive growth in adolescence and touts Inhelder and Piaget's book as 'nothing short of a revolution' in the area. Such a contribution would, by itself, warrant our close attention. But the fact that formal operational thought represents the final period in a comprehensive view of the development of logical skills only magnifies its impact on all of the fields that are centrally concerned with cognitive development. Few theorists have attempted to account for the whole of logical development. That Piaget and his colleagues have ventured boldly into such a difficult and complex area is reason enough for a tribute. That they have altered the course of developmental psychology and revitalized other areas of investigation is a far greater tribute. That they have been enormously successful in describing the course of logical thinking is an awesome achievement.

Inhelder and Piaget's (1958) assessment of the fragments of adolescent thinking skills might, under other circumstances, have been left as amusing anecdotes. With Piaget's theoretical genius at the helm, they were woven into a comprehensive view of how adolescents approach logical tasks. To cap this achievement, Piaget has integrated this final, logical pattern of thought with the thinking skills of earlier years. When such a rare and important contribution is made by any major theorist, it is always followed

*The author would like to acknowledge the valuable criticisms and suggestions made by Edith Neimark and David Moshman as this chapter was being written and revised.

131

by decades of research to clarify, verify, extend, or deny the many parts of the theory. In terms of formal operations, this research has just begun. For years developmental psychologists have replicated and extended many of Piaget's observations, a fact recorded by the many areas being considered in this volume. In the areas of infancy, language acquisition, and concrete operations, Piaget's theoretical guidance has primed researchers to investigate new phenomena and formulate new views of old phenomena. Although the research in formal operations has been slow getting started (Ausubel and Ausubel, 1966), in recent years interest in this period of thought has mushroomed and the literature in developmental psychology is filled with accounts of experimental studies of logical processing in pre-adolescents and adolescents.

It is the purpose of this chapter to review the research pertinent to the period of formal operational thought, and to assess the strengths and weaknesses of the theory proffered by Inhelder and Piaget. This task is made considerably easier by the availability of several excellent reviews of the formal operations research (Ausubel and Ausubel, 1966; Neimark, 1975a; Modgil and Modgil, 1976; Keating, 1979). Edith Neimark's chapter, in addition to reviewing the area, offers a brief, but accurate and understandable summary of the Genevan position that readers are referred to for more information on the structural elements of formal operations. By assuming, as a minimum, the background provided by Neimark's review, this chapter is free to concentrate on three critical theoretical components of Piaget's theory. These are, after Overton (1972), the structural component, the functional component, and the stage component. In succeeding sections, these components will be described, the literature relevant to each component will be reviewed, and an attempt will be made to integrate the findings from differing points of view.

THE STRUCTURAL COMPONENT

The first component to be examined is the *structure d'ensemble* that Inhelder and Piaget have proposed as a model for thought. This general concept has evoked as much controversy as any of the concepts that Piaget has introduced during his career. Underlying this controversy, which has become more heated in recent years, is a philosophical division that is often overlooked. If the formal operational structures posited by Piaget are to be fairly evaluated, this philosophical division must be acknowledged. In the following discussion, then, the epistemological tenets of structuralism will be contrasted with a more elementaristic stance. The comments made here are necessarily brief, and are directed ultimately toward a consideration of formal operations. However, the philosophical differences appear repeatedly in the conflicts between continental and American psychologists. The reader interested in a more general and more comprehensive treatment is referred to Langer (1969), Gardner (1973), Steiner (1974), Feldman and Toulmin (1975), Reigel and Rosenwald (1975), Overton (1975, 1976) and Lunzer (1976).

Gardner (1973) traces the rich French intellectual and philosophical traditions that foreshadow modern structuralism. René Descartes, Jean Jacques Rousseau, Claude Henri Saint-Simon, August Comte, and Emile Durkheim, are a few of the structuralists who have influenced several generations of philosophers and social scientists both directly through their writings and indirectly through their students. In each succeeding generation, the students of these masters become convinced of the validity of some of their mentors' ideas, revise others, and discard those that are no longer useful. The work of each generation, although distinctive in many ways, reflects the ideas and force of their predecessors. Certainly Piaget is one of the current structuralists whose epistemological position incorporates many of the features of the French structuralist tradition.

Any excursion into this tradition, no matter how brief, should note that the criticisms levelled at structuralists have not changed (Gardner, 1973). Like Piaget, structuralists of the past were taken to task by their colleagues, students, and critics, for their anti-empirical position, for relying on introspection, for circular reasoning and for overgeneralizing. The fact that these criticisms appear repeatedly through the centuries should serve notice that the issues and questions being debated are long standing and not easily resolved.

What is structuralism and why does it generate such controversy? The basic tenets of structuralism are deceivingly simple and can be applied to any field (Gardner, 1973). Structuralists are distinguished first by their conviction that there is a pattern or organization underlying mental functioning; second, by their belief that this structure can be discovered through orderly analysis; and finally, by their notion that structures have a generality and cohesiveness that extends beyond a specific instance. A structure then, is the representation of the form or pattern of the phenomena under study.

Part and parcel of a structuralist approach to any subject matter consists of abstracting from the data. Such abstractions are, of course, common in scientific endeavours in many fields and have guided scientists to atoms, genes, and the organization of the solar system. What, then, is distinctive about structuralists that is not true of scientists in general? The distinctiveness of structuralism comes from positing an organization as a primary construct that is necessary to further description and explanation. Structures introduced at this very early point in scientific endeavours show a commitment to 'function or activity as primary over substance; to emergent holism; to dialectic causation and change; and to various constructivist epistemologies' (Overton, 1975, p. 64).

Piaget's structuralism is, obviously, a primary example of the former philosophical tradition, emphasizing wholeness, transformations and self-regulation (Piaget, 1970c). Throughout the present chapter his position will be labelled structuralism. The second position outlined is more characteristic of American and British psychological traditions than it is of Continental psychology. This opposing viewpoint will be labelled elementarism. These two positions are variously labelled 'holistic structuralism' and 'elementaristic structuralism' (Overton, 1975); 'rationalist' and 'empiricist' (Pascual-Leone, 1978); 'structural/developmental' and 'taxonomic/sequential' (Moshman, 1978) by various authors. They all refer basically to the paradigms being contrasted here.

The structuralist paradigm necessitates the specification of activities and functions under study. Piaget's theory specifies the functional invariants and describes a variety of logical skills that are present during different phases of development. These skills are then scrutinized for an underlying organization, or what Piaget prefers to call the *structure d'emsemble*. The next phase of most structurally oriented analyses is concerned with relationships between the organizational factors that have been posited. At this point 'the whole or organization, is . . . necessarily, not contingently, prior to the parts' (Overton, 1975, p. 66). To try to reduce this holistic construct to its component parts is to change the nature of the structure from an entity that explains to one that is explained by component parts.

The second paradigm, labelled elementarism, views these steps in the structuralist approach as circular and untestable. Scientists who embrace this paradigm accuse the structuralists of armchair theorizing and overgeneralizing. This is understandable since, in the elementaristic paradigm, the construct or structure never assumes a primary or guiding role. Since a structure can always be reduced to more basic concepts, these component parts are the important aspects of the scientific enterprise (Van den Daele, 1974; Brainerd, 1975, 1978; and Ennis, 1975, 1976, 1978). This paradigm is often accused of being reductionistic, atheoretical, and mindlessly empirical.

Charting these different views of the scientific enterprise provides perspective on a clash that has continued throughout modern scientific history. The paradigms used differ in such basic ways that the questions asked, the methods employed, the theorizing that results and the interpretation of the data are affected. In some sense, the disputes between these opposing viewpoints can only be settled by an evaluation of paradigms. Since such a tangent is more compatible with a chapter on the history and philosophy of science, it will not be explored here. (See Feldman and Toulmin, 1975; Riegel and Rosenwald, 1975.)

With this background, we can turn our attention to the structures posited by Inhelder and Piaget as representative of formal operational thought. These specific structures—the lattice and the INRC group—are derived from a formal logico-mathematical system. Even the use of such a system is a major point of contention. Piaget notes the power of formal representations when he says that logic is 'at present perhaps the most exact discipline in terms of the rigour of its demonstrations' (Piaget, 1973, p. 28). The advantages of a formal system come from the precision that the language of mathematics or logic bestows. Such precision has served the physical sciences well and structuralists argue that psychology might be able to eliminate some of the ambiguities and misinterpretations from their concepts by casting them in this more explicit form. The complexity of current cognitive theories 'is far more manageable . . . if expressed in a systematic mathematical manner, precisely because the relationships between the elements in a mathematical system are carefully and explicitly defined' (Feldman and Toulmin, 1975, p. 415).

The above arguments favour the representation of logical operations in a formal way. There are, however, very real dangers involved in casting imprecise constructs in a formal system. One can focus on the formal representation and its working and thus lose sight of the more basic skills. From the description already given, it is apparent that the structuralist is much more likely to get lost in the formal system, because of its primary importance, than the elementarist. Blumstein describes this error in the field of structural linguistics: 'The formal machinery has become more and more complex, all in the name of simplicity . . . ' (Blumstein, quoted in Overton, 1975, p. 67).

It has also been argued that the formalisms that Piaget uses reintroduce elementarism into a structuralist perspective. Discussing the set of elements which comprise the formal system introduces this atomistic viewpoint on a level far removed from the data. Piaget defends such an examination of a structure (1970b); but to others, it is the equivalent of armchair theorizing. 'Therefore the constant and ubiquitous tension between holism and elementarism continues' (Overton, 1975, p. 68).

Another danger is a confusion of what the relationship is between the structure and behaviour. A series of papers by Bynum and his colleagues (Bynum, Thomas and Weitz, 1972; Weitz et al, 1973) evidence this confusion. This group began a search for the behavioural equivalents of all 16 binary operations of truth functional logic in the protocols of adolescents solving logical tasks. Their results, that the subjects used only five of the 16 operations and that even Inhelder and Piaget's account (1958) only demonstrated the use of eight operations, has been interpreted as a severe criticism of the theory (Ennis, 1978). And it is from an elementaristic viewpoint. But the structuralist sees these 16 operations as 'ideal' (Inhelder and Piaget, 1958; Inhelder, 1962) possibilities. The primacy of the structure is foremost in the structuralist's consideration, and that structure, when complete, has 16 possible binary operations. In this sense, it does not matter whether or not all 16 are demonstrated by adolescents solving tasks.

This lack of concern with the relationship between theory and behaviour tasks is difficult for investigators operating from a more elementaristic framework. In fact, the ground rules for what constitutes evidence are altered significantly in the structuralist position because the actual behaviour of subjects is passed through a structural lens. The paradigm, whether it be structuralistic or elementaristic, guides not only the questions being asked, but the nature of the data being collected and what is considered appropriate data. Whether or not there is an isomorphic relationship between structures and behaviours has important implications for the whole field of psychology and is widely debated (Flavell, 1963; Gardner, 1973; Pitt, 1976; Brainerd, 1978; Keating, 1979). Those who argue that isomorphism is required reason as follows: if there is no isomorphic relationship between behaviour and structure then any conclusions based only on behaviours do not apply to structures. Hence the theoretical structure is both unjustifiable and unverifiable (Ennis, 1975, 1976, 1978).

The controversy surrounding the relationship between the structure and behaviour, reflects another aspect of the different status given to structures by the Geneva group. The structuralists are much less concerned with such isomorphism because their explanatory power comes from the construct. Flavell (1963) characterizes this distinction nicely: 'This approach is distinctly logical rather than empirical; in itself it says nothing whatever about whether children in fact think this way' (Flavell, 1963, p. 188).

The elementarists demand isomorphism between constructs and behaviour because their constructs stand or fall on these one-to-one comparisons. Piaget sets the tone for the different way he uses constructs in the following:

> We try . . . to translate into abstract language the structures of intellectual operations evidenced by the behaviour of subjects and we use for this purpose various logico-mathematical structures . . . What we discover is of course no longer an abstract structure, but a set of intellectual rules or norms which take the form of impressions of logical necessity. (Piaget, 1973, p. 19)

Although Piaget and his colleagues have repeated this position on several occasions (Piaget, 1970b, 1970c), psychologists of a more elementaristic persuasion are still prone to attribute to the adolescent characteristics that are only applicable to the structure (Feldman and Toulmin, 1975).

The obvious question, given the lack of isomorphism between structures and behaviours, is: how does one evaluate these structures? Are formal structures simply a philosophical totality that one accepts or rejects on the basis of epistemological persuasions rather than empirical terms? Feldman and Toulmin (1975) attempt to answer this question in terms of cognitive development and draw a lengthy parallel between the history of theoretical physics and what actually occurs in nature. There is, for example, no visible line at the equator; yet in theoretical physics the role of the equator is accepted. This parallel is meant to demonstrate the role of the structure, and to point out that a description of the structure usually precedes any empirical documentation.

> The task of demonstrating that a representation is adequate *simply as a representation* is temporally prior to, and logically distinct from, the task of investigating which (if any) formal features of the representation have physical counterparts in the empirical world. And it may always turn out that, although formally elegant and satisfactory, a particular system of logical structure does not lend itself appropriately to the task of representing the actual, empirical phenomena in the particular field of science concerned. (Feldman and Toulmin, 1975, p. 433)

In this comment Feldman and Toulmin neatly define the issue and reflect the current two-pronged discussions on the viability of formal operational structures. Piaget and his colleagues are trying to assess the adequacy of the structural representation they have proposed (Karmiloff-Smith, 1978), and their detractors are looking for the behavioural equivalents of a line where the equator is supposed to be.

There is no denying that at some point an empirical component must be found if there is ever to be a rapprochement between the formal propositions and actual behaviour. But the two paradigms even disagree on the form of that empirical component. Feldman and Toulmin (1975) would like structuralists to demonstrate how structures come into existence by presenting a fairly detailed description of the sequence of structures as well as some notion of the mechanism that prompts development. In addition, these authors are interested in the kinds of performances that indicate the existence of structures. Surely no one would deny that Piaget has attempted to describe the sequence of structures. His entire career has focused on the ontogenesis of logic and he has provided several accounts of how these structures come into being, beginning with the newborn and continuing through adolescence (Piaget, 1952, 1954; Inhelder and Piaget, 1958, 1964). While these accounts are global, many investigators have fleshed out the behavioural components of the schemas and structures that have been described.

In order to document empirically how the operational structures of the concrete and formal period emerge, we must first develop appropriate behavioural assessments of the structure and then trace the behavioural changes that occur. In the realm of concrete operations, we have spent more than 20 years devising appropriate behavioural assessments of the structure. Only a handful of longitudinal studies have used those assessments to chart behavioural changes (Almy, Chittenden and Miller, 1966; Wohlwill, Fusaro and Devoe, 1969; Almy et al, 1970; Little, 1972; Stephens, 1974; Hooper, Toniolog and Sepple, 1978; Tomlinson-Keasey et al, 1979). One longitudinal study by Tomlinson-Keasey et al (1979) traces the behavioural components of the concrete operational structure over four years and concludes that the skills that emerge over this period are related and can be characterized as a *structure d'ensemble*.

In the area of formal operations, progress has been much more limited. We currently do not have acceptable behavioural assessments of the structure we are trying to document. Bart (1971, 1972, 1978) and Neimark (1978) have both commented that the tasks used by Inhelder and Piaget may not provide the behavioural assessments we need. Although many investigators have turned to tasks requiring propositional logic, Osherson (1975b) cautions that such tasks may not be appropriate behavioural analogues of the formal operational structure.

Since we are so far from acceptable measures of the behaviour that might represent the structure, it is little wonder that there has been only one longitudinal attempt to assess changes in the behaviour (Neimark, 1975b). This single study detects 'marked shifts to higher performance scores' when a subject's strategy becomes more general; and prompts Neimark to conclude that 'This evidence provides extremely strong support for Piaget's stage theory' (Neimark, 1975b, pp. 211—212). Certainly Neimark's data is a welcome compliment to the cross-sectional studies, and begins the process of following individuals through time. Still, it seems that judgment on how formal operational structures come into existence must be held in abeyance until (1) more agreement on behavioural assessments is reached, and (2) more longitudinal studies are reported.

The second question raised by Feldman and Toulmin concerns the mechanism which guides development. Here again Piaget has offered several commentaries (Piaget, 1970c, 1970d; Piaget, 1975) and a variety of researchers have devised experiments to test the mechanisms he suggests (Kuhn, 1972; Inhelder, Sinclair and Bovet, 1974; Kuhn, 1978).

The final question raised by Feldman and Toulmin concerns behaviours that document the existence of structures. Their position, echoed by Brainerd (1978) and Ennis (1978) is that one must define empirically the components of a structure, not merely infer them from the formal structure. Similar demands regarding the nature of scientific explanations are made by the positivist tradition that prevails in American psychology. Explanatory force comes from establishing causal relationships between antecedent or stimulus variables and the consequent, response variables. In a structuralist view, such isolation of variables and the demand for independent measurement of the two variables is less appropriate. A stimulus variable is only meaningful in the sense that it is interpreted by the organism and the response variable must consider the goal of the organism. In this sense there can be no explanation without an understanding of the structure.

Bruner (1976) brings this point to life in his comment, 'The position of a piece on a chessboard, the function of a word in a sentence, a particular facial expression, the colour or placement of a [traffic] light, then cannot be interpreted without reference to the person's internalized rules of chess or language, the conventions he holds concerning human interaction, the traffic rules in force in his mind' (p. 4). Independent variables, in reality, depend on the structure of the organism. Because of this inter-dependence, structuralists have abandoned an empirical system that imposes artificial independence on variables; and prefer an empirical system organized around a structure. In short, each of these paradigms rejects the empirical procedures advocated by the other.

The fact that the empirical requirements of the two paradigms are at odds should not deter us from a consideration of the data that has been gathered. It should serve, rather, as a caution to interpret that data from both a structuralist and an elementarist perspective. With this caution in mind, we can turn to a consideration of the empirical studies.

Since the objective in this section is to demonstrate how the clash in paradigms permeates all phases of the scientific enterprise, there will be no attempt to review all of the empirical studies. Instead, two areas of continuing interest are selected as representative of the research in formal operations. Specifically, the work of information-processing theorists and reports of experiments using propositional logic will be examined.

Propositional Logic

Tasks involving propositions and requiring deductive reasoning were first used to study formal operations by Wason (1960, 1961). Wason and his colleague Johnson-Laird have continued to use propositions to investigate the ability of students to use deductive reasoning (Wason and Johnson-Laird, 1972; Johnson-Laird and Wason, 1977; Wason, 1977). The typical format of these now familiar tasks is to present students with a set of four cards with either a letter or a number on each card. A rule describing a relationship between numbers and vowels is presented. 'If a card has a vowel on one side, then it has an even number on the other side.' The students are then asked to turn over the cards that will indicate whether the rule is true or false. Only five of 128 university students were initially able to perform this task (Johnson-Laird and Wason, 1970). In modifications that involve less abstract materials Johnson-Laird, Legrenzi and Legrenzi (1972) presented fronts and backs of envelopes with and without a 5d stamp on it. In this situation 21 of the 24 students were able to identify which envelopes would have to be examined to determine whether 'a sealed envelope has a stamp on it'. Obviously the nature of the task is critical to whether or not subjects are successful. This point has also been made by Osherson (1975a) and Kuhn (1977).

Other studies by Hill (1961), Ennis et al (1969), Knifong (1974) and Kuhn (1977) also required conditional reasoning. In these studies reviewed in detail later in this chapter, the inferences did not demand the integrated combinatorial system (Kuhn, 1977). If the falsifiability of an argument or if several interdependent statements had to be evaluated, the likelihood of success seemed to be minimal before the eighth grade (Kuhn, 1977; Moshman, 1979).

The use of tasks requiring propositional logic is appealing, seemingly because it mimics the structure proposed by Piaget. As we have seen, however, this strategy often confuses the theoretical structure with behavioural responses. Osherson's caution that 'standard logical derivation techniques do not accurately mirror the mental derivations of subjects' (1975a, p. 88) seems worth repeating. He argues that standard logic should not be used as a competence model since such a system requires acceptance of a class of statements that people intuitively reject. Perhaps this intuitive rejection of some arguments explains why the university student's performance is so variable on Wason's tasks. In searching for an adequate competence model, Osherson suggests that we would profit from finding and documenting the rules that people use in solving logical problems. In a volume on adolescent reasoning he takes this advice to heart and conducts a meticulous series of experiments examining the rules adolescents use in making deductive inferences (Osherson, 1975b). Along the way, he demonstrates that (1) inferences relying on causal content are not responded to in the same manner as inferences involving artificial content; (2) information overload is not as viable an option for explaining the performance of adolescents as it is with younger subjects; and (3) propositional logic and the logic of classes cannot be subsumed under a more general mental schematism. Osherson's goal, at the beginning of the volume, was to investigate 'whether adolescence brings a reorganization of the mental operations underlying logical competence' (1975b, p. 5). The partial answers that he obtains tend to favour a positive response to this question. However, Osherson is a careful and conservative investigator whose assessment of his own model includes certain reservations and acknowledges its extremely restricted scope, so he is content to withhold judgment. Clearly, Osherson is interested in exploring a variety of explanations for the development of logic; and he includes Inhelder and Piaget's model as one plausible option.

What conclusions can be drawn from the studies of propositional logic? We can see first of all that there is substantial disagreement about the relationship between these tasks and formal operational structures. The disagreement derives, in part, from the different lenses—either structuralist or elementarist — that investigators look through to view the data. The kinds of analyses performed by Knifong (1974), Kuhn (1977) and Ennis (1978) illustrate how structuralists and elementarists view the link between the behaviour and the structure. Still these and the studies requiring a range of tasks (Osherson, 1975b; Kuhn, 1977; Moshman, 1977; Staudenmayer and Bourne, 1977) give us some picture of the behaviours that might document the existence of a structure. Osherson's (1975b) effort and Neimark's (1975b) longitudinal study are probably the strongest data for inferring a structure. Yet, as observed earlier, the evidence from these studies can certainly be interpreted from other perspectives.

Information Processing

Another tack taken by current investigators is to examine a functionalist model. On the face of it, such an emphasis would seem to be entirely consistent with Piagetian theory.

After all, activity is basic to Piaget's system and the functional invariants are operative through all of the stages he describes. However, some investigators argue that the Genevans emphasize structures to the exclusion of functions. To redress this alleged imbalance, Pascual-Leone (1969, 1975) and Case (1972, 1974, 1975) began a series of studies emphasizing the functional nature of knowledge acquisition. These investigators hoped to demonstrate that a model emphasizing functional aspects would make the systems that are operative in cognitive development explicit. To date, however, the period of formal operations has received limited attention in these attempts.

One might expect such a functionalist view to sidestep the whole structural issue. But a recent exchange between Pascual-Leone (1978) and Trabasso (1978; Trabasso and Foellinger, 1978) suggests that Pascual-Leone's model is not entirely elementaristic. Pascual-Leone complains that his position is being misconstrued because of the general neglect of epistemology that characterizes American models and because his general 'rationalist model' is being mistaken for an 'empiricist local' model. At least in his mind, there is a clash of paradigms.

Robert Siegler is another information-processing theorist whose primary interest is examining the functional aspects of logical skills. Unlike Case and Pascual-Leone, his work has focused on formal operational skills. Siegler's work is also distinctive in that it does not use propositional logic as its starting point, but relies on problems adopted from or very similar to Inhelder and Piaget's formal operational tasks (Siegler, 1977).

Siegler focuses on processing variables which are not unlike the functional variables Pascual-Leone examines. In one series of experiments, Siegler (1976) investigated three aspects of the answers children gave to the balance task; (1) the child's existing knowledge, (2) the benefits the child derived from experience; (3) how the child understood the problem. In his results and discussion Siegler reports that all of these are found to be important variables in the child's solutions. In the positivist tradition, he has isolated antecedent and consequent variables that affect formal operational skills.

Siegler, like the other information-processing theorists, purposely sidesteps the issue of structure. Yet the structures that the child uses might well be used to explain all three of the factors he describes. Certainly, the Genevans would argue that structures determine the child's existing knowledge, how the child understands the task, and how the experience is interpreted. Such an argument is really not germane to Siegler's and Trabasso's more elementaristic view and is only mentioned to underline the very different paradigms being used.

As with the propositional logic, it is clear that this work is important to a complete understanding of the development of logical skills. Siegler, Pascual-Leone, Trabasso and Case have isolated variables that enhance or impair task performance. Unlike those working with propositional logic, these investigators have less inclination to evaluate their models in structural terms. Yet all of them include variables that, it could be argued, reflect an underlying structure.

In essence then, the structuralists begin their investigation of the acquisition of knowledge from a very different perspective than the elementarists. These different perspectives shape the whole scientific enterprise and it is not surprising that the two viewpoints generate different questions to investigate, rely on different methods for obtaining information and disagree about the kinds of data that are relevant. This clash of paradigms is not new but each generation of scientists must confront it anew. In the area of formal thought, a close look at the arguments being presented and the issues being debated reveals yet another version of this ancient clash.

THE FUNCTIONAL COMPONENT

The functional component of Piaget's theory consists of all of the processes that spur the child to interact with the environment and to translate that interaction into progressively more consistent and stable patterns of thought. The processes to be considered include both the physical manipulations that dominate the first few years of life and the mental activity that surrounds reformulating a problem, pondering conflicting evidence, etc. The focus on both the physical and mental activity of the child is shown in the processes that Piaget outlines as important to the development of intelligence—assimilation, accommodation, and equilibration (Piaget, 1952). All of these involve the organism acting, reacting, adapting, and organizing—in other words being active. Contrast these with more static functional variables that are often related to intelligence—existing knowledge, understanding of the problem. These variables minimize both the actual activity of the organism and the dynamic quality of the organism—environment interaction that Piaget emphasizes. A flavour of the importance Piaget places on the activity of the organism is obtained from his introductory remarks in a volume about education:

> . . . action is only instructive when it involves the concrete and spontaneous participation of the child himself with all the tentative gropings and apparent waste of time that such involvement implies. It is absolutely necessary that learners have at their disposal concrete material experiences (and not merely pictures) and that they form their own hypotheses and verify them (or not verify them) themselves through their own active manipulations. The observed activities of others, including those of the teacher, are not formative of new organizations in the child. (Piaget, 1974, pp. ix—x)

This statement has triggered a number of objections from researchers who do not regard active manipulation as important (Ross et al, 1976; Anthony, 1977). They interpret activity in a very literal and restricted way to mean actual manipulation. Such an extreme interpretation of Piaget's position is clearly untenable; but Piaget never intended for activity to exclude the active reformulations and mental assessments that accompany learning. In fact, this mental activity is the basis of operational thought processes.

Inhelder, Sinclair, and Bovet (1974) describe various ways in which the activity of an organism affects thought processes, and reiterate the role of activity in Piaget's formulations.

> . . . being cognitively active does not mean that the child merely manipulates a given type of material; he can be mentally active without physical manipulation; just as he can be mentally passive while actually manipulating objects. Intellectual activity is stimulated if the opportunities for acting on objects or observing other people's actions or for discussions correspond to the subject's level of development. (1974, p. 25)

If the development of logic is understood as fundamentally an active process, then there are two logical corollaries. The first asserts that the activities of the organism result in the construction of a framework or organization for understanding the world. This constructive process, then, becomes one of the functional components of Piaget's theory. The second corollary asserts that this activity is regulated by the organism. Hence exploring and constructing are mediated and guided by the child in a self-regulating or self-directed manner. In essence, this position suggests that parents, teachers, and philosophers cannot accurately assess how any particular child will construct an experience. Conclusions that seem obvious to adults may be totally lost on a concrete operational child. Likewise, experiences that seem trivial may coalesce many fragments of ideas into more logical wholes. The fact that logical growth must be regulated this way follows from a view that places such a high premium on the active involvement of the organism. If activity is basic, then how the child constructs the world must flow from that activity.

These related concepts—the active organism, a constructionist view of how logic is acquired and a self-regulating organism—form the core of the functional component of Piaget's theory and will be used to guide the review of the empirical literature. These core concepts have led to two sets of deductions in the area of formal operations. The first surrounds the issue of self-regulation. If self-regulation is necessary for children to develop the logical foundations of knowledge, then children who are allowed to explore, discover and invent their own organization should gain a more complete understanding of a concept than children who are supplied with answers to someone else's questions.

There is an extensive literature on the advantages and disadvantages of discovery learning in young children (Bruner, Jolly and Sylva, 1976). Many of these studies outline the critical role that exploration and discovery seem to play (Hutt and Bhavani, 1972; Sylva, 1976). However, the importance of discovery and exploration in learning seems to be regarded very differently in high school and college. Once through the primary grades, didactic learning, lecturing, and experiencing phenomena through books, movies, pictures, and lectures become recommended methods of teaching (but see Karplus et al, 1977b).

In a study that deals directly with self-regulation, Kuhn (1978) exposed fourth and fifth graders who showed no reasoning above the concrete level to problems requiring the combinatorial scheme and an isolation of variables scheme. Each pair of subjects consisted of an experimental subject who directed the experiments and activities that took place during a session, and a yoked control who observed exactly the same manipulations but did not direct them. After eleven weeks of problem-solving, she compared the yoked subjects on the highest problem they had mastered in the intervention sequence and on overall post-test performances. The experimental subjects made significantly greater progress than their yoked controls, and performed better than the controls on the more complex tasks included in the post-test. The results were interpreted as demonstrating that subjects who direct their own activity are better able to make use of the data yielded by their experiments. Both of these groups of subjects made significant progress in formal operational skills. Hence observing by itself was useful; but not as useful as directing the experiment.

Another set of data on the role of activity comes from a variety of intervention programmes at the college level (Lockhead, 1977; Tomlinson-Keasey and Eisert, 1978; Tomlinson-Keasey, Fuller and Campbell, 1978). These programmes cannot really be classified as training studies since they involve the redirection of the entire curriculum. The scope of these multidisciplinary, year-long curricular innovations also makes specific causal variables difficult to isolate. Typically, the programmes are designed to (1) begin instruction at the level of the student; (2) to require students to explore a variety of subjects; and (3) to let students regulate their own learning. The ADAPT programme (Accent on Developing Abstract Processes of Thought) is one such attempt that encouraged freshmen to become involved in the content of six different disciplines during the freshman year. In the ADAPT programme, classes and modules of material were designed with an exploration phase, a discovery phase, and an application phase (Karplus, 1974). In the exploration phase, for example, students groped with sets of blocks of different densities; sets of poems representing couplets, limericks, and blank verse; and limited incomes that were to be allocated to a variety of expenses, investments, etc. After this exploration, students were encouraged to draw inferences, rules and concepts from their data. The final phase in each module involved applying or generalizing the concepts discovered.

A comparison of students in this programme and students completing a typical freshman year indicated that all freshmen made considerable progress on formal operational thinking during the course of the year. However, the ADAPT students made significantly more gains in the realm of logical and abstract thinking than a matched group of control students (Tomlinson-Keasey and Eisert, 1978). Similar results were demonstrated in a second year of the programme, and when the programme was transplanted to another college (Tomlinson-Keasey, Fuller and Campbell, 1978). These studies, like most curriculum modifications, are subject to a variety of confounds (Tomlinson-Keasey and Eisert, 1978). Nevertheless, the fact that students who are actively involved make more gains in logical skills and seem to conceptualize issues in a more differentiated way serves to underscore the role of activity and replicates the gains Kuhn reported in her controlled experimental setting. There is no denying that students can make gains in a variety of settings. But settings that allow students to explore relevant variables may well have a greater impact than more indirect methods.

Two studies that try to look more specifically at the self-regulation model are Lawson and Wollman (1976), and Kuhn and Angelev (1976). Lawson and Wollman used four training sessions over a two-week period to train higher level thought processes. Their experimental methods combined rule learning and exploration; and both fifth and seventh graders made greater gains in logical thinking than a control group. However, the now common result of minimal transfer of learning (Brainerd and Allen, 1971; Tomlinson-Keasey, 1972; Keating, 1979) was evidenced.

Kuhn and Angelev (1976) have conducted a training study that benefits from the lessons learned during two decades of similar studies in the area of concrete operations. Their intervention was spread over 15 weeks and their design incorporated a post-test one month later, and a delayed post-test four months later. In addition, they avoided the assumption, implicit in other studies, that experiences leading to higher level functioning indicate how students should be taught and how a curriculum should be designed. These are really very separate issues, and should be clearly delineated in the literature. The history of science abounds with examples of interventions that were effective at some level, but told us little about what might happen in less contrived settings. A casual reading of educational practices in less industrialized cultures suggests that much of what we do in western countries in the name of education is similarly contrived.

Kuhn and Angelev wanted to test the efficacy of self-regulation in a learning situation. Hence, they used a design that left students to their own devices in a problem-solving environment. One group of pre-adolescents—the self-regulation group—exercised their own strategies and set up their own experiments during the training sessions. No strategies were suggested to them; instead they were left in a 'problem rich environment' to explore and evaluate as they pleased. A second group received a demonstration of how to approach and solve the problems. Post-test comparisons demonstrated that the students who were allowed to exercise their cognitive skills performed at the same level as students receiving direct instruction. Of interest, too, is the fact that if the training sessions occurred only once every two weeks, the students did not make more progress than no treatment controls. It seems a minimum amount of continuity is necessary for such exploration to lead to cognitive growth. Kuhn and Angelev conclude that providing a rich problem environment that enables subjects to exercise their cognitive skills approximates more closely natural developmental processes and demonstrates that these are as effective as didactic training. This study also underlines the constructive nature of cognitive structures and suggests that self-regulation is a viable and researchable mechanism for explaining progressive change.

Turning to more typical training studies, we find several attempts to facilitate formal operational thought. Ross et al (1976) compared cognitive conflict training, concept formation training, and didactic training. After a 30 to 50 minute session in which college students were trained on separating variables, the authors found that only students given didactic training had made significant progress. Their study demonstrates that to teach something quickly, one must cut down on the trial and error and false starts that accompany exploration and provide, instead, a specific and clear conceptual framework. However, this study and others in the same vein (Siegler, Liebert and Liebert, 1973; Siegler and Liebert, 1975; Siegler and Atlas, 1976) provide little insight into the self-regulation model.

The studies reviewed here, although not exhaustive, are representative of investigations that examine the effect that training can have on formal thought. There is little doubt that a variety of procedures can lead to improved performance. It is less obvious that there is much generalization from the short-term training studies. Self-directed activity and the individual construction of experience are shown to promote higher level functioning in many settings. A final important point to emerge from these studies, especially given the impasse that exists regarding the structural component, is that the functional components can be operationalized and investigated using elementaristic methods.

In summary, the functional components of Piaget's theory have received some attention and the results obtained have generally supported the view that self-regulation and the active involvement of the student contribute to cognitive progress. There is, however, much work to be done in this area. It is heartening that investigators agree on one point—the mechanisms outlined by Piaget should become the focus of future research (Case, 1974; Kuhn, 1978; and Pascual-Leone, 1978). Given that the clash in paradigms assumes less importance in investigations of functional variables (for a different view see Overton, 1976), real progress might be made in illuminating the mechanisms of development if researchers began investigating the functional components in earnest.

THE STAGE COMPONENT

In what sense is it meaningful to speak of stages of cognitive development? This question, asked in 1978 by Brainerd, had been addressed in 1971 by Flavell, and in 1969 by Pinard and Laurendeau. All of these authors have recommended making major changes in the concept of stage or dispensing with the concept altogether. Yet the fact that major articles continue to appear discussing stages suggests that this concept has a certain tenacity (see, for example, the rebuttals to Brainerd's 1978 statement). Perhaps, then, it is appropriate to begin our evaluation of the stage component of formal operations by considering whether or not it makes sense to distinguish between a stage of concrete operations and a stage of formal operations.

The picture coming from Geneva regarding stages has been very consistent through the years. However, as we shall see, the interpretations of this position by other psychologists has ranged from conceiving of stages as discontinuous and biologically controlled to seeing stages as continuous, highly dependent on experience, and probabilistic. A naïve interpretation is that stages are the central concept and the mainstay of Piaget's theory of development. Piaget has never intended to place stages in that kind of spotlight. Stages are more properly seen as heuristic descriptions of structures that emerge as the child interacts with the environment. They are, in a sense, a by-product of the ongoing processes of assimilation, accommodation, and equilibration (Karmiloff-Smith, 1978). Piaget's discussion of stages, however, is often taken out of the context of the invariant processes of development. This leads to exaggerating the importance of stages and minimizing other equally important theoretical tenets. With the caution not to separate stages from the functional invariants, we can turn to a consideration of Piaget's conception of stage.

Perhaps Piaget's most succinct statement on what a stage is comes from a chapter published in 1960. In this chapter, Piaget outlines five different criteria for stages that have served as a jumping-off point for many discussions of stages (Brainerd, 1978; Pinard and Laurendeau, 1969). In essence, Piaget's definition of a stage requires (1) that there be an invariant sequence to the stages; (2) that each stage consist of a *structure d'ensemble* that characterizes the total aspects of a stage; (3) that stages be integrated into the following stage; (4) that each stage supply the foundation for the following stage; and (5) that each new stage constitute the culmination of what is prepared in the preceding stage (Tanner and Inhelder, 1960).

Notice that this statement of stage criteria does not imply that a child's behaviour is discontinuous. Perhaps because stages are often set in the biological analogue of metamorphosis, psychologists expect stages to include major discontinuities in behaviour. If such discontinuities exist, one can conclude that a stage has been defined. But the Genevan position on discontinuities, as revealed in the following remarks made by Inhelder, make it clear that abrupt discontinuities in a child's behaviour are not necessary to a stage formulation.

> A theory of stages remains incomplete, however, as long as it does not clarify the contradiction between two concepts of development—the one stressing the complete continuity, and the other, the absolute discontinuity, of stages. It seems to us, however, that this contradiction is more apparent than real . . . Indeed, it seems as if during the formation of a structure of reasoning . . . each new procedure depends on those the child has just acquired. Once achieved, this structure serves as a starting point for new acquisitions. The latter will then be relatively independent of the formative process of the former structure. It is only in this sense that there would be discontinuity in passing from one stage to another. (Inhelder, 1962, p. 24)

The point is that behavioural discontinuity and structural discontinuity are not the same. Structural discontinuity is evident in the different approaches that guide problem-solving. Behavioural discontinuity may be evident, but is not necessary. Two children solving the same problem may arrive at the same solution through very different means. Their behavioural similarity does not imply structural similarity. The confusion between behavioural discontinuity and structural discontinuity is another reflection of the paradigm clash discussed in the first section of this chapter. To elementarists, behaviours must reflect structures and hence behavioural continuity must infer structural continuity. Hence, evidence of behavioural continuity is construed as a refutation of stages. To a structuralist, the existence or nonexistence of behavioural continuities is irrelevant. The important focus is the structural discontinuity, and the use of stages highlights that structural discontinuity.

The passage from Inhelder's monograph quoted above speaks to issues other than the discontinuity issue. It argues, as mentioned earlier, that stages are a heuristic device. It also discusses growth within a stage after the initial inklings of a stage are present. This growth has been integrated into the stage notion by Flavell (1971). In his look at stage-related properties of development, Flavell included the notion of immediate functional maturity in his 'caricature' of a stage. But this caricature does not reflect and was not intended to reflect Piaget's view. Since formal operational thought reportedly begins between 12 and 15 years of age and continues for years as a person's aptitudes become progressively more differentiated, 12-year-olds are not likely to be as skilful in their application of logic as 25-year-olds (Piaget, 1972). The stage of formal operations, then, does not require an abrupt break from concrete operational thought, nor does it demand that a new logical skill be fully functional immediately. What a stage of formal operations does propose is that problem-solving and thought are now guided by a qualitatively different set of more abstract principles than those used in concrete operational thought.

In looking at the criteria that Piaget does suggest, the one that has received the most comment and investigation is the notion that stages must follow an invariant sequence. There are now scores of studies that document this general progression (for reviews see Neimark, 1975a; Modgil and Modgil, 1976; and Keating, 1979). Many of these studies could be loosely classed as replication studies since they rely on the tasks pioneered by Inhelder and Piaget. Since Neimark's review, investigators have tended to focus on somewhat different issues and replication studies, *per se*, are no longer popular. However, there are several recent studies that use the Inhelder and Piaget tasks and report the kind of progression from concrete operations to formal operations that the Genevan studies found (Somerville, 1974; Webb, 1974; Chapman, 1975; Schwebel, 1975; Webb and Daurio, 1976; Danner and Day, 1977; Martorano, 1977; Stone and Day, 1978). Particularly illuminating are the series of careful descriptive studies published by Karplus and his colleagues (Karplus et al, 1977a; Adi et al, 1978; Karplus, 1978a, 1978b; Karplus, Adi and Lawson, in press). Other investigators have developed their own formal operational tasks or adapted Piagetian tasks for their research. Some of these that are not discussed in length in other sections of the chapter are Case (1974), Shayer, Kuchenmann and Wylam (1976), Ronning (1977), Green (1978) and Shayer and Wylam (1978). Without exception, these studies report the general progression from concrete to formal thought outlined by Inhelder and Piaget (1958).

As in the research on concrete operations, the replication studies have often shown that the age at which a particular skill is acquired varies; but no study, that I am aware of, has shown the sequence from concrete to formal functioning to be reversed. If an investigator were to find that a child could use the skills defined as formal operational while demonstrating no skill with concrete operational thought, then the stage notion would have to be abandoned. Such results are as unlikely as a person being five-feet tall and then being two-feet tall; or of a person mastering the logic of multiplication before the logic of addition is mastered.

Given the robustness of the general progression, one might think that the criterion that stages constitute an invariant sequence had been reasonably well established. But Brainerd in a 1978 paper argues that because invariant sequences are logically necessary in the theory, it becomes tautologous to argue that these can be used to verify the notion of stages. In a more pragmatic sense, however, the documentation of the invariant sequence from concrete operational thought to formal operational thought can be used to assess the general validity of Piaget's characterization of the development of operational thought. In this context, these studies have been extremely valuable.

The relationship between concrete operational thought and formal thought has been the subject of other studies that are satisfied with the general sequence described by Inhelder and Piaget but which want to examine particular logical skills. Case (1974), for example, reports satisfactory training of certain formal skills before conservation of weight or the combinatorial scheme is present. He does not, however, regard this evidence as detrimental to a stage position. Rather he concludes:

> that the acquisition of any particular item of knowledge does not depend on the match between the formal structure of that knowledge and the formal structure of the knowledge which the child already possesses. Rather it depends upon the match between the pragmatic structure of the situation in which the child first has a chance to construct that particular item of knowledge, and the functional limitations of his thought processes at the stage in his life when he encounters such a situation. (Case, 1974, p. 572)

Case's data demand a more variegated and specifically defined view of stages such as the one outlined by Flavell (1971).

Studies demonstrating that young children can perform the skills that are theoretically required in propositional logic have also been used to question the notion of an invariant sequence. To illustrate this argument, a series of studies that seemingly demonstrate that young children are capable of using conditional reasoning will be examined (Hill, 1961; Ennis, Finkelstein, Smith and Wilson, 1969). Typically these studies present logical tasks in the following format:

> If this is room 9, then it is the fourth grade.
> This is room 9.

The child is then asked if it is a fourth-grade class. On such tasks a majority of the six-, seven- and eight-year-olds answered the simple conditional statements correctly. These results appear to shatter the notion that propositional logic is reserved for adolescents. Knifong (1974), however, analyses these tasks from a structural perspective and presents a convincing argument that such tasks require only transductive reasoning. To solve these problems the child need not form a propositional statement from which deductions are made; but need only make associative connections. In Karmiloff-Smith's view the seven-year-old alters these statements into a concrete form and reasons 'that . . . "each time x, then most of the time y", leading to a correct but only "plausible" conclusion' (1978, p. 189).

Kuhn (1977) disputes Knifong's analysis of conditional reasoning. She argues instead that a concrete operational child can generate the four products of a proposition involving two variables (1) p and q, (2) not p and q, (3) p and not q, and (4) not p and not q, if they are presented in a concrete and conversational mode. In her sample of first, second, third and fourth graders, she finds that 100 per cent of the first graders answer the $(\bar{q}.p)$ form of the syllogism correctly and 50 to 80 per cent of the fourth graders answer all four forms of the syllogism correctly. These percentages are even higher than earlier studies and Kuhn uses these to support her position that the concrete operational child has the skill to deal with individual items requiring conditional reasoning.

Ennis (1978), too, objects to Knifong's interpretation. Since transduction is a form of propositional logic, and since many of the younger children did respond correctly to fallacy arguments, Ennis asks plaintively 'What is the distinctive thing that adolescents can do, but that children cannot do?' (1978, p. 232). Kuhn offers a response when she asserts that concrete operational children cannot 'comprehend a given combination of p × q products in the context of all of the possible conditional relations between p and q' (1977, p. 358). In fact, Kuhn found no case in which subjects were able to transform all of the sample statements correctly until the eighth grade. It is this totality of reasoning involving multiple transformations of information that differentiates formal operational reasoning from concrete operational reasoning, not isolated examples of concrete transformations.

Piaget has also answered investigators who report propositional logic in very young children. In reply to a study presented by Patrick Suppes, Piaget countered that the logic required was relatively simple and that it is important to know whether the reasoning used requires combinations of terms (Piaget, 1967, p. 277). In his view, the stage of formal operations represents a higher level integration of the earlier skills typically exemplified by the simpler concrete transformations.

This sequence of studies looking at conditional reasoning, as well as other investigations of conditional reasoning (O'Brien and Shapiro, 1968; Shapiro and O'Brien, 1970; Bourne and O'Banion, 1971; Roberge and Paulus, 1971; Kodroff and

Roberge, 1975), points out several problems that are endemic to Piagetian research. The first is that Piaget's position on formal operations is extremely complex and changes in his position are inevitable (Piaget, 1970a; Beilin, 1977). What logical skills are actually reserved for formal operational functioning? What forms do these skills take at earlier stages? Are these earlier forms evidence of concrete or formal skills? In some of his writings Piaget seems to take the position defended by Knifong (Piaget, 1928). In others, the position taken by Kuhn is presented (Inhelder and Piaget, 1958; Piaget, 1967).

A second problem pinpointed by this series of studies of conditional reasoning is the enormous difference in performance depending on whether the problem is presented in a familiar day-to-day context or an abstract and unfamiliar one. After arguing that college students were often unable to solve problems requiring falsification (Wason and Johnson-Laird, 1972), several investigators revised the tasks to include meaningful content (Gilhooley and Falconer, 1972; Bracewell and Hidi, 1974). Such changes led to dramatically increased estimates of the level of thinking employed by subjects. Kuhn and Brannock (1977) have also documented a difference in the context of problems used. The unavoidable conclusion is that how one evaluates logical skills depends on the manner of presentation as well as the specific transformation being assessed. This revision complicates the picture and makes a simple notion of stages hard to abide. Whether one invokes the competence and performance distinction (Moshman, 1977) or retreats behind the notion of horizontal decalage, the problem remains. Although Piaget has paid lip service to this problem, there is as yet no satisfactory resolution. What is needed to settle the issue is a chronicling of the acquisition of a host of formal operational skills. American and British psychologists seem, in recent years, to be working on such a description.

A third problem is a methodological one. Many of these studies have focused on a single transformation or task. The typical paradigm is to assess a particular transformation or task in several age groups. This method is likely to emphasize the continuous aspects of logical thought and is less likely to detect the more integrative hierarchical aspects of the *structure d'ensemble* of formal operations. When investigators have looked at a range of problems (Staudenmayer and Taddonio, 1974; Staudenmayer and Bourne, 1977; Moshman, 1979); when they have assessed all eight forms of the conditional argument (Kuhn, 1977); or when the task has required integrating elements (Siegler and Vago, 1978); the results have, in general, agreed with Piaget's view that formal operations represent a higher level integration of concrete operational thought.

Piaget also has a legitimate complaint with elementaristic methodologies. In an effort to standardize the often wandering responses of children, the possible answers the child can give are limited and the probes for the logic underlying the answer are standardized. Often, the results obtained with such changes in the method do not conform, at least on the surface, with predictions made from the theory. There is little doubt that seven-year-olds and twelve-year-olds will perform in similar ways on many logical tasks (Joffe-Falmagne, 1977). But the heart of the Genevan argument is that these answers are arrived at with very different types of logic and one must probe the logic to determine its nature (Johnson-Laird, 1977).

To sum up, the postulated sequence from concrete to formal operational functioning has been documented repeatedly in a global fashion. More specific statements about particular concrete operational skills in relation to formal operational functioning have been less clear cut. Hence the position that seems most attractive is the one outlined by Flavell (1971) that there might be a subset of concrete operational skills that are necessary before any formal operational skills are apparent. As this subset of concrete operational skills reaches a functionally mature level, some of the basic formal operational skills will be apparent. Despite the appearance of basic formal operational skills, growth and generalization of concrete operational skills will continue.

Does such a position constitute a death knell for stages? Certainly it does if stages are conceived of as discontinuous entities that emerge full-blown according to a biologically preprogrammed schedule. If, however, stages are seen as descriptive, they would retain some value in this capacity. Unfortunately, the kind of detailed description called for by Flavell's model is not currently available. What seems to be needed is a series of longitudinal studies following children through concrete and formal operational functioning and presenting a variety of tasks to these children. Such a study would yield a representative view of the sequence of skills that emerge as children make the transition from concrete to formal functioning.

The criticism that stages are global concepts that are somewhat ill defined is difficult to refute. There are, however, a variety of ways to handle these criticisms. One can throw the concept out entirely, one can treat stages as heuristic and descriptive, or one can try to define the stages more specifically and then evaluate their usefulness. It seems that Piaget and his colleagues have selected the second option, and Piaget's critics, depending on their epistemological persuasions, have chosen the first or third alternatives.

CONCLUSION

This chapter has dealt with three issues that are currently the focus of a large portion of the research in formal operations. An examination of the data and arguments relevant to these three questions has not, as some might have hoped, led to any obvious resolutions. What does seem clear is that there is not likely to be any resolution of the structural issue in the near future. Such a resolution would require more agreement among investigators from different theoretical perspectives on the relationship between behavioural assessments of formal operations and the structures that they elucidate.

More progress is likely to be evident in the functional assessment of formal operational skills. The investigations of self-regulation, the studies that focus on performance variables, and the information-processing studies have all contributed to a more detailed picture of formal operational functioning and to a better understanding of the processes a child goes through in evaluating information.

Whether or not there are stages and what constitutes evidence of these stages is a worn issue. However, the question keeps reappearing in the literature primarily because of the link between stages and structures. Piaget's structural viewpoint argues that the form of the structure changes during development. The differing forms that the structure takes during ontogenesis are the stages that are so widely debated. Twenty years of research on the thought processes that are labelled concrete has taken a lot of the mystery out of this stage of development and we now have an adequately detailed picture of the different skills and operations that children acquire while learning to order and classify their world. A similarly detailed description of the skills and operations of formal thought is not available. Hence the mystery of this stage of thought remains. Perhaps as more information is acquired the stage issue will recede in importance and investigators will be able to chart the structural changes in logical reasoning without having to defend a rigid, discontinuous stage view of development.

The structural, functional and stage aspects of Piaget's theory merge, in the structuralist view, into one inseparable explanation of development. Artificially separating them, as has been done in this chapter, is a serious disservice to the totality and interdependence of the three components. The functional processes yield organizations which are abstracted into more static structures. As an abstraction these structures are scrutinized for explanatory power, and from these, stages characterized by modal behaviours can be described.

The theoretical edifice constructed from these three components has an elegance and general serviceability unmatched in the history of developmental psychology. Still the need for revisions and changes will continue as will the need for a more specific understanding of the relationships between and within the components. Unfortunately, the continuing explication of facets of the theory is hindered by a clash in paradigms of the sort discussed by philosophers of science. Some tolerance of divergent paradigms is necessary if the data generated by each paradigm are to be woven into a powerful, as well as elegant, explanation of development.

REFERENCES

Adi, H., Karplus, R., Lawson, A. and Pulos, S. (1978) Intellectual development beyond elementary school VI: Correctional Reasoning. *School Science and Mathematics,* **8,** 675-683.

Almy, M., Chittenden, E. and Miller, P. (1966) *Young Children's Thinking: Studies of some Aspects of Piaget's Theory.* New York: Teachers College Press.

Almy, M. C., Dimitriovsky, L., Hardeman, M., Gordis, F., Chittenden, E. and Elliott, D. L. (1970) *Logical Thinking in the Third Grade.* New York: Teachers College Press.

Anthony, W. S. (1977) Activity in the learning of Piagetian Operational Thinking. *British Journal of Educational Psychology,* **47,** 18-24.

Ausubel, D. P. and Ausubel, P. (1966) Cognitive development in adolescence. *Review of Educational Research,* **36,** 403-413.

Bart, W. M. (1971) The factor structure of formal operations. *British Journal of Educational Psychology,* **41,** 70-77.

Bart, W. M. (1972) Construction and validation of formal reasoning instruments. *Psychological Reports,* **30,** 663-670.

Bart, W. M. (1978) Issues in measuring formal operational reasoning. *The Genetic Epistemologist,* **7,** 3-4.

Beilin, H. (1977) Constructing cognitive operations linguistically. In Reese, H. W. (Ed.) *Advances in Child Behavioral Development Vol. II.* New York: Academic Press.

Bourne, L. E. and O'Banien, K. (1971) Conceptual rule learning and chronological age. *Developmental Psychology,* **5,** 525-534.

Bracewell, R. J. and Hidi, S. E. (1974) The solution of an inferential problem as a function of stimulus materials. *Quarterly Journal of Experimental Psychology,* **26,** 480-488.

Brainerd, C. J. (1975) Structures-of-the-whole and elementary education. *American Educational Research Journal,* **12,** 369-378.

Brainerd, C. J. (1978) The stage question in cognitive-developmental theory. *Behavioral and Brain Sciences,* **2,** 173-213.

Brainerd, C. J. and Allen, T. W. (1971) Experimental inductions of the conservation of 'first order' quantitative invariants. *Psychological Bulletin,* **75,** 128-144.

Bruner, J. S. (1976) Psychology and the image of man: Herbert Spencer Lecture. *Times Literary Supplement,* 17 December.

Bruner, J. S., Jolly, A. and Sylva, K. (1976) *Play: Its Role in Development and Evolution.* London: Penguin.

Bynum, T. W., Thomas, J. A. and Weitz, L. J. (1972) Truth functional logic in formal operational thinking: Inhelder and Piaget's evidence. *Developmental Psychology,* **7,** 129-132.

Case, R. (1972) Learning and development: A neo-Piagetian interpretation. *Human Development,* **15,** 339-358.

Case, R. (1974) Structures and strictures: Some functional limitations on the course of cognitive growth. *Cognitive Psychology,* **6,** 544-574.

Case, R. (1975) Social class differences in intellectual development. *Canadian Journal of Behavioral Science,* **7,** 244-261.

Chapman, R. H. (1975) The development of children's understanding of proportions. *Child Development,* **46,** 141-148.

Danner, F. W. and Day, M. C. (1977) Eliciting formal operations. *Child Development,* **48,** 1600-1606.

Ennis, R. H. (1975) Children's ability to handle Piaget's propositional logic: A conceptual critique. *Review of Educational Research,* **45,** 1-41.

Ennis, R. H. (1976) An alternative to Piaget's conceptualization of logical competence. *Child Development,* **47,** 903-919.

Ennis, R. H. (1978) Conceptualization of children's logical competence: Piaget's propositional logic and an alternative proposal. In Siegel, L. S. and Brainerd, C. J. (Eds.), *Alternatives to Piaget: Critical Essays on the Theory.* New York: Academic Press.

Ennis, R., Finkelstein, M., Smith, E. and Wilson, N. (1969) Conditional logic and children. New York: Ithaca. Cornell Critical Thinking Readiness Project (ERIC Document Reproduction Service No. ED 040 437).

Feldman, C. F. and Toulmin, S. (1975) Logic and the theory of mind. In Cole, J. K. and Arnold, W. J. (Eds.) *Nebraska Symposium on Motivation,* **23,** 409-476.

Flavell, J. H. (1963) *The Developmental Psychology of Jean Piaget.* Princeton, New Jersey: Van Nostrand.

Flavell, J. H. (1971) Stage related properties of cognitive development. *Cognitive Psychology,* **2,** 421-453.

Gardner, H. (1973) *The Quest for Mind.* New York: Knopf.

Gilhooley, K. J. and Falconer, W. A. (1972) Concrete and abstract terms and relations in testing a rule. *Quarterly Journal of Experimental Psychology,* **24,** 193-199.

Green, M. G. (1978) Structure and sequence in children's concepts of chance and probability: A replication study of Piaget and Inhelder. *Child Development,* **49,** 1045-1053.

Hill, S. (1961) *A study of the logical abilities of children.* Doctoral dissertation, Stanford University.

Hooper, F. A., Toniolog, T. A. and Sepple, T. S. (1978) A longitudinal analysis of logical reasoning relationship: Conservation and transitive inference. *Developmental Psychology,* **14,** 674-682.

Hutt, C. and Bhavani, R. (1972) Predictions from play. *Nature,* 237.

Inhelder, B. (1962) Some aspect of Piaget's genetic approach to cognition. In Kessen, W. and Kuhlman, C. (Eds.) Thought in the Young Child. *Monographs of the Society for Research in Child Development,* **27.**

Inhelder, B. and Piaget, J. (1958) *The Growth of Logical Thinking from Childhood to Adolescence.* New York: Basic Books.

Inhelder, B. and Piaget, J. (1964) *The Early Growth of Logic.* London: Routledge and Kegan Paul.

Inhelder, B., Sinclair, H. and Bovet, M. (1974) *Learning and the Development of Cognition.* Cambridge, Massachusetts: Harvard University Press.

Joffe-Falmagne, R. (1977) The development of logical competence: A psycho-linguistic perspective. Workshop on developmental models of thinking. Kiel, West Germany, September, 1977.

Johnson-Laird, P. N. (1977) Models of deduction. In Johnson-Laird, P. N. and Wason, P. C. (Eds.) *Thinking: Readings in Cognitive Science.* Cambridge: Cambridge University Press.

Johnson-Laird, P. N. and Wason, P. C. (1970) A theoretical analysis of insight into a reasoning task. *Cognitive Psychology,* **1,** 134-148.

Johnson-Laird, P. N. and Wason, P. C. (1977) A theoretical analysis of insight into a reasoning task. In Johnson-Laird, P. N. and Wason, P. C. (Eds.) *Thinking: Readings in Cognitive Science.* Cambridge: Cambridge University Press.

Johnson-Laird, P. N., Legrenzi, P. and Legrenzi, M. (1972) Reasoning and a sense of reality. *British Journal of Psychology,* **63,** 395-400.

Karmiloff-Smith, A. (1978) On stage: The importance of being a nonconserver. *The Behavioral and Brain Sciences,* **2,** 188-190.

Karplus, R. (1974) *Science Curriculum Improvement Study: Teachers Handbook.* Berkeley, California: Lawrence Hall of Science.

Karplus, R. (1978a) *Intellectual development beyond elementary school IX. Functionality, a survey.* Advancing education through science-oriented programs ID-51. Berkeley, California: Lawrence Hall of Science.

Karplus, R. (1978b) Proportional reasoning in the People's Republic of China. A pilot study. *The Genetic Epistemologist,* **7,** 5-6.

Karplus, R., Adi, H. and Lawson, A. E. Intellectual development beyond elementary school VII. Proportional probabilistic, and correlational reasoning. *School Science and Mathematics,* **80,** 673-683.

Karplus, R., Karplus, E., Formisano, M. and Paulsen, A. (1977a) A survey of proportional reasoning and control of variables in seven countries. *Journal of Research in Science Teaching,* **14,** 411-417.

Karplus, R., Lawson, A. E., Wollman, W. T., Appel, M., Bernoff, R., Howe, A., Rusch, J. J. and Sullivan, F. (1977b) *Science Teaching and the Development of Reasoning.* Berkeley, California: University of California.

Keating, D. P. (1979) Adolescent thinking. In Adelson, J. P. (Ed.) *Handbook of Adolescence.* New York: Wiley.

Kimball, R. L. (1968) *A Background Concept Study in Malawi.* Domasi: Science Centre.

Knifong, J. (1974) Logical abilities of young children—two styles of approach. *Child Development,* **45,** 78-83.

Kodroff, J. and Roberge, J. (1975) Developmental analyses of the conditional reasoning abilities of primary grade children. *Developmental Psychology*, **11**, 21-28.

Kuhn, D. (1972) Mechanisms of change in the development of cognitive structures. *Child Development*, **43**, 833-845.

Kuhn, D. (1977) Conditional reasoning in children. *Developmental Psychology*, **13**, 342-353.

Kuhn, D. (1978) *The role of self-directed activity in cognitive development*. Unpublished paper. Graduate School of Education, Harvard University.

Kuhn, D. and Angelev, J. (1976) An experimental study of the development of formal operational thought. *Child Development*, **47**, 697-706.

Kuhn, D. and Brannock, J. (1977) Development of the isolation of variables scheme in experimental and 'natural experimental' contexts. *Developmental Psychology*, **13**, 9-14.

Langer, J. (1969) *Theories of Development*. New York: Holt, Rinehart and Winston.

Lawson, A. E. and Wollman, W. T. (1976) Encouraging the transition from concrete to formal cognitive functioning—an experiment. *Journal of Research in Science Teaching*, **13**, 413-430.

Little, A. (1972) A longitudinal study of cognitive development in young children. *Child Development*, **43**, 833-844.

Lockhead, J. (1977) *A profile of the cognitive development of freshmen engineering students.* Paper presented at Annual Convention of American Psychological Association. San Francisco, August.

Lunzer, E. A. (1976) An appreciation of Piaget's work. In Varma, V. P. and Williams, P. (Eds.) *Piaget, Psychology and Education.* London: Hodder and Stoughton.

Martorano, S. C. (1977) A developmental analysis of performance on Piaget's formal operations task. *Developmental Psychology*, **13**, 666-672.

Modgil, S. and Modgil, C. (1976) *Piagetian Research: Compilation and Commentary. Volume 3. The Growth of Logic—Concrete and Formal Operations.* Windsor: NFER Publishing.

Moshman, D. (1977) Consolidation and stage formation in the emergence of formal operations. *Developmental Psychology*, **13**, 95-100.

Moshman, D. (1978) Logical reasoning in young children: Case study of a paradigm clash. *The Formal Operator*, **1**, 9-10.

Moshman, D. (1979) Development of formal hypothesis—testing ability. *Developmental Psychology*, **15**, 104-112.

Neimark, E. D. (1975a) Intellectual development during adolescence. In Horowitz, F. D. (Ed.) *Review of Child Development Research, Volume 4.* Chicago: University of Chicago Press.

Neimark, E. (1975b) Longitudinal development of formal operations thought. *Genetic Psychology Monographs*, **91**, 171-225.

Neimark, E. (1978) On the measurement of formal operations. *The Formal Operator*, **1**, 10-11.

O'Brien, T. and Shapiro, B. (1968) The development of logical thinking in children. *American Educational Research Journal*, **5**, 531-543.

Osherson, D. N. (1975a) Logic and models of logical thinking. In Falmagne, R. J. (Ed.) *Reasoning: Representation and Process.* Hillsdale, New Jersey: Lawrence Erlbaum Associates.

Osherson, D. N. (1975b) *Logical Abilities in Children, Volume 3.* Hillsdale, New Jersey: Lawrence Erlbaum Associates.

Overton, W. F. (1972) Piaget's theory of intellectual development and progressive education. In Squire, J. R. (Ed.) *A new look at progressive education.* Washington: Association for supervision and curriculum development, pp. 88-115.

Overton, W. F. (1975) General systems, structure, and development. In Riegel, K. F. and Rosenwald, G. C. (Eds.) *Structure and Transformation: Developmental and Historical Aspects.* New York: John Wiley.

Overton, W. F. (1976) The active organism in structuralism. *Human Development*, **19**, 71-86.

Pascual-Leone, J. (1969) *Cognitive development and cognitive style: a general psychological integration.* Doctoral dissertation. Geneva University, Geneva, Switzerland.

Pascual-Leone, J. (1970) A mathematical model for the transition rule in Piaget's developmental stages. *Acta Psychologica*, **32**, 301-345.

Pascual-Leone, J. (1975) A view of cognition from a formalist's perspective. In Riegel, K. F. and Meacham, J. (Eds.) *The Developing Individual in a Changing World.* The Hague: Mouton.

Pascual-Leone, J. (1978) Compounds, confounds, and models in developmental information-processing: A reply to Trabasso and Foellinger. *Journal of Experimental Child Psychology*, **26**, 18-40.

Piaget, J. (1928) *Judgment and Reasoning in the Child.* New York: Harcourt, Brace.

Piaget, J. (1952) *The Origins of Intelligence in Children.* New York: International University Press.

Piaget, J. (1954) *The Construction of Reality in the Child.* New York: Basic Books.

Piaget, J. (1965/1967) Logique formelle et psychologie génétique, including discussion by Piaget, J., Richard, J. F., Suppes, P., Reuchlin, M., Rappoport, A., Fraise, P., Simon, H. and Restel, F. In *Les modèles et la formalization du comportement. Proceedings of the International Colloquium of the National Center for Scientific Research.* Paris, July 5-10, 1965. Paris, 1967, 269-283.

Piaget, J. (1970a) Piaget's theory. In Mussen, P. H. (Ed.) *Carmichael's Manual of Child Psychology*. New York: Wiley.

Piaget, J. (1970b) *Psychologie et Epistémologie*. Paris: Gonthier.

Piaget, J. (1970c) *Structuralism*. New York: Basic Books.

Piaget, J. (1970d) General problems of interdisciplinary research and common mechanisms. In *Main Trends of Research in the Social and Human Sciences*. The Hague: Mouton.

Piaget, J. (1971) *Biology and Knowledge*. Chicago: University of Chicago Press.

Piaget, J. (1972) Intellectual evolution from adolescence to adulthood. *Human Development, 15,* 1-12.

Piaget, J. (1973) *Main Trends in Interdisciplinary Research*. New York: Harper and Row.

Piaget, J. (1974) Foreword. In Schwebel, M. and Raph, J. (Eds.) *Piaget in the Classroom*. London: Routledge and Kegan Paul.

Piaget, J. (1975) *L'Équilibration des Structures Cognitives: Problème Central du Développement*. Paris: Presses Universitaires de France.

Pinard, A. and Laurendeau, M. (1969) Stage in Piaget's cognitive-developmental theory: Exegis of a concept. In Elkind, D. and Flavell, J. H. (Eds.) *Studies in Cognitive Development*. New York: Oxford University Press.

Pitt, R. B. (1976) Toward a comprehensive model of problem-solving: Application to solutions of chemistry problems by high school and college students. Unpublished doctoral dissertation. University of California, San Diego.

Reigel, K. F. and Rosenwald, G. C. (1975) *Structure and Transformation: Developmental and Historical Aspects*. New York: John Wiley.

Roberge, J. and Paulus, D. (1971) Developmental patterns for children's class and conditional reasoning abilities. *Developmental Psychology, 4,* 191-200.

Ronning, R. R. (1977) Modeling effects and developmental changes in dealing with a formal operations task. *American Education Research Journal, 14,* 213-223.

Ross, R. J., Hubbell, C., Ross, C. G. and Thompson, M. (1976) The training and transfer of formal thinking tasks in college students. *Genetic Psychology Monographs, 93,* 171-187.

Schwebel, M. (1975) Formal operations in college freshmen. *Journal of Psychology, 91,* 133-141.

Shapiro, B. and O'Brien, T. (1970) Logical thinking in children ages six through thirteen. *Child Development, 41,* 823-829.

Shayer, M. and Wylam, H. (1978) The distribution of Piagetian stages in British middle and secondary school children 11—14/16 year olds and sex differentials. *British Journal of Educational Psychology, 48,* 62-70.

Shayer, M., Kuchemann, D. E. and Wylam, H. (1976) The distribution of Piagetian stages of thinking in British middle and secondary school children. *British Journal of Educational Psychology, 46,* 164-173.

Siegler, R. S. (1976) Three aspects of cognitive development. *Cognitive Psychology, 8,* 481-520.

Siegler, R. S. (1977) The twenty questions game as a form of problem-solving. *Child Development, 48,* 395-403.

Siegler, R. S. and Atlas, M. (1976) Acquisition of formal scientific reasoning by 10- and 13-year-olds: Detecting interactive patterns in data. *Journal of Educational Psychology, 68,* 360-370.

Siegler, R. S. and Liebert, R. M. (1975) Acquisition of formal scientific reasoning by 10—13-year-olds: Designing a factorial experiment. *Developmental Psychology, 11,* 401-402.

Siegler, R. S. and Vago, S. (1978) The development of a proportionality concept: Judging relative fullness. *Journal of Experimental Child Psychology, 25,* 371-395.

Siegler, R. S., Liebert, D. E. and Liebert, R. M. (1973) Inhelder and Piaget's pendulum problem: teaching pre-adolescents to act as scientists. *Developmental Psychology, 9,* 97-101.

Somerville, S. C. (1974) The pendulum problem: Patterns of performance defining developmental stages. *British Journal of Educational Psychology, 44,* 266-281.

Staudenmayer, H. and Bourne, L. E. Jr. (1977) Learning to interpret conditional sentences: A developmental study. *Developmental Psychology, 13,* 616-623.

Steiner, G. (1974) On the psychological reality of cognitive structures: A tentative synthesis of Piaget's and Bruner's theories. *Child Development, 45,* 891-899.

Stephens, B. (1974) Symposium: Developmental gains in the reasoning, moral reasoning and moral conduct of retarded and nonretarded persons. *American Journal of Mental Deficiency, 79,* 113-126.

Stone, C. A. and Day, M. C. (1978) Levels of availability of a formal operational strategy. *Child Development, 49,* 1054-1065.

Sylva, K. (1976) Play and learning. In Tizard, B. and Harvey, D. (Eds.) *The Biology of Play*. Philadelphia: Lippincott.

Taplin, J. E., Staudenmayer, H. and Toddonio, J. L. (1974) Developmental changes in conditional reasoning: Linguistic or logical? *Journal of Experimental Child Psychology, 17,* 360-373.

Tanner, J. M. and Inhelder, B. (1960) *Discussions on Child Development Volume 4*. London: Tavistock Publications.

Tomlinson-Keasey, C. (1972) Formal operations in females from eleven to fifty-four years of age. *Developmental Psychology,* **6,** 364.

Tomlinson-Keasey, C. and Eisert, D. (1978) Can doing promote thinking in the college classroom? *Journal of College Student Personnel,* **19,** 99-105.

Tomlinson-Keasey, C., Fuller, R. G. and Campbell, T. (1978) *You know more of a road if you travel it.* Paper presented at 8th annual Symposium of the Jean Piaget Society. Philadelphia, Pa., May 18, 1978.

Tomlinson-Keasey, C., Eisert, D., Kahle, L., Hardy-Brown, K. and Keasey, B. (1979) The structure of concrete operational thought. *Child Development,* **50.**

Trabasso, T. (1978) On the estimation of parameters and the evaluation of a mathematical model: A reply to Pascual-Leone. *Journal of Experimental Child Psychology,* **26,** 41-45.

Trabasso, T. and Foellinger, D. B. (1978) Information-processing capacity in children: A test of Pascual-Leone's model. *Journal of Experimental Child Psychology,* **26,** 1-17.

Van Den Daele, L. D. (1974) Infrastructure and transition in development analysis. *Human Development,* **17,** 1-23.

Wallace, J. G. (1965) *Concept Growth and the Education of the Child.* Windsor: NFER.

Wason, P. C. (1960) On the failure to eliminate hypotheses in a conceptual task. *Quarterly Journal of Experimental Psychology,* **12,** 129-140.

Wason, P. C. (1961) Response to affirmative and negative binary statements. *British Journal of Psychology,* **52,** 133-142.

Wason, P. C. (1977) Self-contradictions. In Johnson-Laird, P. N. and Wason, P. C. (Eds.) *Thinking: Readings in Cognitive Science.* Cambridge: Cambridge University Press.

Wason, P. C. and Johnson-Laird, P. N. (1972) *Psychology of Reasoning: Structure and Content.* London: Batsford.

Webb, R. A. (1974) Concrete and formal operations in very bright 6—11-year-olds. *Human Development,* **17,** 292-300.

Webb, R. A. and Daurio, S. P. (1976) *Formal operations in very bright 8—14-year-olds.* Mimeographed paper.

Weitz, L. J., Bynum, T. W., Thomas, J. A. and Steger, J. A. (1973) Piaget's system of 16 binary operations: An empirical investigation. *Journal of Genetic Psychology,* **123,** 279-284.

Wohlwill, J. F., Fusaro, L. and Devoe, S. (1969) *Measurement, seriation, and conservation: A longitudinal examination of their relationship.* Paper presented at the meeting for the Society for Research in Child Development. Santa Monica, California, March 1969.

Interchange

ENNIS REPLIES TO TOMLINSON-KEASEY

A THIRD PARADIGM: THE WHAT-WOULD-COUNT-AS-EVIDENCE APPROACH

In attempting to present both sides of an issue, Professor Tomlinson-Keasey offers two alternative paradigmatic approaches to viewing Piaget's structuralism: the structuralist approach and the elementarist approach. It is unfortunate that she limits herself to two alternatives.

According to her, elementarists are reductionists, they insist on isomorphism between structures and behaviours, and they seek behavioural equivalents of Piaget's theoretical concepts. (These are three similar ways of characterizing hard-line positivistic behaviourism.) Since I think that there are strong arguments against such elementarism (Ennis, 1964), I regret that elementarism is the only other category she gives besides structuralism, and regret that my approach is classified by her as elementarist.

Two essential features of a third approach are:

(1) The insistence that there be an indication of the kind of empirical evidence that would *count for*, and the kind of evidence that would *count against* a theory.
(2) The refusal to attempt the reduction of theoretical concepts to observational terms.

Elementarism and the third approach share the first feature in a way, since, although elementarism insists on reduction, it does as a result insist on, among other things, an indication of the kind of evidence that would count for and against a theory. But the elementarists' requirement that a concept be exhausted by (that is, be reducible to) some set of specified behaviours is explicitly rejected by this third approach. (I am here ignoring the problems inherent in the concept *behaviours* in order to bring out in at least rough form the distinction in the broad empiricist tradition between insisting on reduction and not doing so.)

If the requirement is violated that there be an indication of what would count as evidence for and against a theory or a hypothesis, then the theory or hypothesis cannot play the crucial role we expect of it in telling us about the world and in generating even loose predictions about the future. I am not sure why Tomlinson-Keasey did not see that this was the requirement that I was applying (among other places) in expressing my disappointment with the Piaget/Inhelder treatment of the GOU protocol (Ennis, 1975, p. 30 (this volume, p. 122); Inhelder and Piaget, 1958, p. 103). I said, 'Piaget's rejection . . . makes one wonder *what would count as a test* of his theory' (italics added for emphasis). Tomlinson-Keasey said that I 'interpreted as a severe criticism of the theory' the claim by Bynum, Thomas and Weitz (1972) that GOU only exhibited eight of the sixteen combinatorial operations and that their adolescent subjects exhibited only five. My criticism is not that there were only eight here and five there, but that Piaget does not tell us *how to see* how many there are—or *how to see* whether any are there—or *how to see* whether a person is operating 'within the combinatorial system'. He (or Inhelder) sees all sixteen in the GOU protocol. Bynum, Thomas and Weitz see only eight. One wonders how Piaget (or Inhelder) gets sixteen—especially since he explicitly rejects the linguistic criterion as a way of identifying a case of the handling of propositional logic (e.g. using the appearance of the word 'if' to indicate implication; Ennis, 1975, p. 30 and this volume, p. 123; Inhelder and Piaget, 1958, pp. 279-280). The point is not that the GOU protocol and the additional Bynum evidence prove Piaget wrong, but rather that if they do not prove him wrong, then he owes us an account of what sorts of thing, if they occurred, would count for and against his view, and an account of how one would identify them.

The problem can be seen again in Tomlinson-Keasey's interpretation of the Kuhn (1977) work, which Tomlinson-Keasey thinks to be a 'response' to the question I asked, 'What is the distinctive thing that adolescents can do, but that children cannot do?' (1978, p. 232; a similar question is in 1976, p. 915). Kuhn considered all the possible ways in which two propositions, p and q, and their negations, could be combined in an implication relationship, and produced the following eight possibilities:

(1) $p \to q$ (3) $\bar{p} \to q$ (5) $q \to p$ (7) $\bar{q} \to p$
(2) $p \to \bar{q}$ (4) $\bar{p} \to \bar{q}$ (6) $q \to \bar{p}$ (8) $\bar{q} \to \bar{p}$

Eight possible combinations is not sixteen possible combinations, a fact that should suggest that this set is not Piaget's sixteen binary combinations, working within which is a crucial feature of handling propositional logic. Furthermore, using Piaget's interpretation of implication (and most contemporary interpretations) the last four reduce to the first four. (Each item in the last four is a contrapositive of an item in the first four.)

So we have *four* possible logically-different combinations, the number, incidentally, that Piaget ascribes to class logic (Inhelder and Piaget, 1958, p. 275, 287). Is the success that Kuhn found only among eighth graders then to be called success in class logic, or in propositional logic? Since Piaget denies our use of the linguistic criterion, how do we know that these eighth graders were doing propositional logic in Piaget's sense? Why should we predict from Piaget's theory that children do not do what Kuhn found they did not do, and that adolescents can do what the eighth graders did. Piaget does not help to answer the question because he does not tell why such behaviour as Kuhn found in the eighth graders should be regarded as evidence that they can handle propositional logic. And this is because he does not give us reason to think that the logic they were doing is propositional logic in his sense.

An adherent of the third approach does not insist on a reductive-behavioural definition of a theoretical term. Rather he or she asks for an indication of the meaning of the theoretical term by means of a specification of the kinds of evidence that would count for, and the kinds of evidence that would count against a theory containing the term. Without such a specification, one cannot make predictions from such a theory (for if one could, then the satisfaction of the predictions generally would count as evidence for the theory, and the failure of the predictions generally would count as evidence against it), and the theory has not been shown to be empirically meaningful.

I realize that there is much more to be said on the topic of testability in this context, but since Tomlinson-Keasey eschewed philosophy of science, the above discussion constitutes an attempt to lure her into a more thorough consideration of the topic of testability and meaning, and a recognition of this third approach as a possible way of thinking about Piaget. Classic discussions of comparative merits of the elementarist and third approaches include those by Rudolph Carnap (1956), Michael Scriven (1956), and Noam Chomsky (1959).

That Tomlinson-Keasey has at least some sympathy with the third approach is evidenced by her question towards the end of her essay, 'Are these earlier forms *evidence of* concrete or formal skills?' (italics added), p. 147 this volume. Another indicator of sympathy is her mention of 'Piaget's predictions'. She apparently feels, as I do, that one should be able to make predictions from Piaget's theory (predictions that need the theory to help generate them).

That Tomlinson-Keasey had this third approach as an alternative paradigm explicitly available to her is suggested by her attributing views to Feldman and Toulmin that sound like it. I quote her: 'The ground rules for *what constitutes evidence* are altered significantly'; 'structuralist must demonstrate . . . *what kinds of performance indicate* the existence of structures' (italics added). Why she did not give this third approach as a paradigm for viewing Piaget is thus a puzzling question. Since she did not, I invite her to do so. It might seem then to her and her readers a more reasonable approach than the two she depicted.

REFERENCES

Bynum, T. W., Thomas, J. A. and Weitz, L. J. (1972) Truth functional logic in formal operational thinking: Inhelder and Piaget's evidence. *Developmental Psychology*, **7**, 129-132.

Carnap, R. (1956) The methodological character of theoretical concepts. In Feigl, H. and Scriven, M. (Eds.) *The Foundations of Science and the Concepts of Psychology and Psychoanalysis* (Vol. 1 of the Minnesota Studies in the Philosophy of Science). Minneapolis: University of Minnesota Press.

Chomsky, N. (1959) A review of B. F. Skinner's *Verbal Behavior*. *Language*, **35**. Reprinted in Broudy, H., Ennis, R. and Krimerman, L. (Eds.) *Philosophy of Educational Research*. San Francisco: McCutchan.

Ennis, R. H. (1973) Operational definitions. *American Educational Research Journal*, **1**, 183-201. Reprinted in Krimerman, L. I. (Ed.) (1969) *The Nature and Scope of Social Science*. New York: Appleton-Century-Crofts. Also in Broudy, H. S., Ennis, R. H. and Krimerman, L. I. (Eds.) *Philosophy of Educational Research*. San Francisco: McCutchan.

Ennis, R. H. (1975) Children's ability to handle Piaget's propositional logic: A conceptual critique. *Review of Educational Research*, **45**, 1-41. Also in this volume.

Ennis, R. H. (1976) An alternative to Piaget's conceptualization of logical competence. *Child Development*, **47**, 903-919.

Ennis, R. H. (1978) Conceptualization of children's logical competence: Piaget's propositional logic and an alternative proposal. In Siegel, L. S. and Brainerd, C. J. (Eds.) *Alternatives to Piaget: Critical Essays on the Theory*. New York: Academic Press.

Inhelder, B. and Piaget, J. (1958) *The Growth of Logical Thinking from Childhood to Adolescence*. New York: Basic Books.

Scriven, M. (1956) A study of radical behaviorism. In Feigl, H. and Scriven, M. (Eds.) *The Foundations of Science and the Concepts of Psychology and Psychoanalysis* (Vol. 1 of the Minnesota Studies in the Philosophy of Science). Minneapolis: University of Minnesota Press.

Tomlinson-Keasey, C. Structures, functions, and stages: a trio of formal operational constructs. This volume.

TOMLINSON-KEASEY REPLIES TO ENNIS

Tomlinson-Keasey acknowledges Ennis's paper in her chapter.

Chapter 8

Piaget on Language

ALISON ELLIOT AND MARGARET DONALDSON

With regard to the language-learning child, Piaget often stands accused of neglect or partial interest. He does not propose a theory of language development: the closest he comes to adopting child language as the object of a developmental study is in *Play, Dreams and Imitation in the Child* where he outlines an account of conceptual development and the role of language in this. Even here, he seems to approach the task with a certain reluctance, referring to the intervention of language with the words 'collective verbal signs coming to interfere with the symbols we have already analysed'. However, Piaget's treatment of language cannot be put into its proper perspective unless we recognize that he is not so much a developmental psychologist as a genetic epistemologist. That is, the interest in epistemology is for him primary. He is not concerned to review all aspects of development, and there is no reason why he should be. His guiding aim is to contribute to our understanding of the nature of knowing.

To embark on a criticism of Piaget's theoretical writings on language is therefore to run the risk of imposing false challenges on him. The main question must be whether his theories about knowing are in any way endangered by his treatment of language. If they are not, it is unimportant that this treatment is somewhat cavalier.

There are at least two ways in which Piaget's relative lack of concern with language might put the main body of his theorizing at risk. First, he might wrongly assess the role of language in the development of thinking; and second, to the extent that he uses language in his own experiments, he might misinterpret his findings by failing to take due account of how the linguistic component is affecting the outcome.

In considering these issues, it is important to note that Piaget's views on language appear to be largely offshoots of his epistemological position. That is, he does not seem to ask what is known about language and then see what this can contribute to epistemology. Rather he first adopts an epistemological position and then considers what it implies about language. Consequently if he were wrong about language (in so far as he does have things to say about it) this might either be because of his basic epistemological beliefs or because he had wrongly assessed their implications.

There are obvious limits to the inferences about the nature and function of language which can be made from a starting point in epistemology. Clearly, inferences about language in general will be easier to make on this basis than inferences about features specific to particular languages. And, indeed, it is only about the former that Piaget has anything positive to say. In regard to the latter, Piagetian theory can at most suggest certain constraints on development, without explaining positively how progress might come about. And here the constraints that have been proposed rest mainly on the general notion that mastery of a specific linguistic structure will have to wait on mastery of some relevant cognitive structure. However, the theory lacks any precise indication of how such cognitive structures can be recognized in language and so it lacks the ability to predict language development in any detail.*

If we now turn rather to a consideration of the universal nature of language, the Piagetian position is briefly as follows. Language is one manifestation of much more general adaptive mechanisms having to do with representation, that is, with the distinction of 'signifiers' from that which they signify. Thus language belongs, in its beginning, with other varieties of symbolic functioning like deferred imitation and make-believe; and its advent in the second year of life is not to be attributed to some sudden coming-into-play of a highly specific innate device. Rather, like the other representational modes, it grows out of and depends upon the achievements of the sensorimotor period. Thus it is linked, both horizontally and vertically so to speak, with other adaptive functions. It has no special pride of place. And, above all, it is not the *source* of intelligent thought or knowledge. For Piaget, the origins of thought are to be found in action.

All of this appears to stem from one key epistemological belief, namely, that knowledge, at least of the most important kind, is not something which can be 'given' by one human being to another. Piaget is concerned to maintain that the development of the kind of knowing which lies at the heart of human intelligence—the kind that crucially distinguishes a mature from an immature mind—is something which each one of us must construct for himself.

This is not to say that Piaget denies the importance of social influences (which is a common misunderstanding).† On the contrary, he sometimes stresses the significance for intellectual progress of the encounter with another person's 'point of view'. But nevertheless that progress, if it occurs, will be because of active processes that have been stimulated by the encounter and not because of anything passively received. Knowledge is not something that can be handed over.

Now from this basic tenet Piaget draws the conclusion that you cannot make people more intelligent by telling them things. You can, of course, pass on *some* pieces of knowledge in this way, such as, for instance, the knowledge that Paris is the capital of France. But you cannot influence the operational structures of the mind, unless perhaps in a negative way by telling a child something prematurely and so reducing the likelihood that he will find it out for himself in the kind of way that entails a genuine constructive gain.

---

*It is, however, true that a number of attempts to use Piagetian principles in the detailed study of language development have been made by researchers other than Piaget himself. (See, for instance, Beilin, 1975 and Sinclair, 1969, 1978.)

†For instance, we find him saying that the most generalized forms of thought are 'forms of cognitive exchange or of inter-individual regulation as well as being produced by the common functioning which is a necessary part of every living organization' (Piaget, 1971, p. 360).

This argument is persuasive—until one becomes aware of a curious omission. The whole emphasis is on the *receptive* aspect of interpersonal verbal exchange, on the child as passive recipient. But what of the *active* use of language as a means of finding things out? What of the child as questioner?

For some reason, Piaget pays little attention to this aspect of interpersonal language. To use his own terminology, he centres upon the notion that knowledge verbally transmitted is knowledge passively received. He does not decentre from this to the complementary notion that knowledge verbally requested is knowledge actively sought. And so his arguments remain in this regard curiously unbalanced and incomplete. If it were the case that the child was always, linguistically, a passive recipient, one might indeed conclude that Piaget's basic epistemological position implies a very restricted role for language in the development of thought. But to the extent that a child uses language to find things out at least as actively as he uses motor exploration of the world this line of reasoning collapses. One could, of course, perfectly well imagine a race of beings who were passive recipients of linguistically conveyed information long before they used language actively to formulate questions that could contribute to a search for knowledge. But these beings would not be human.

Thus it is possible to agree with Piaget that language is not the original source of thought and to agree with him further in stressing the active nature of the development of thought without denying to language a genuinely constructive role in that process. In limiting this role to the extent that he does, Piaget goes much too far.

We turn now to the question of the ways in which Piaget uses language in his methods for studying thought. And here, perhaps, the first thing to recognize is that he has become, with the passing of time, more wary of relying on it. In his later work, indeed, he seldom relies on it exclusively. Yet still in most of that work language figures in two ways: in the giving of instructions or asking of questions by the experimenter and in the giving of answers and justifications by the child. Given that this is so, and given that Piaget sets great store by the empirical dimension of his work, he has to adopt an attitude to the value of the things children say to him and the extent to which children understand what is being said to them. In the following pages, therefore, we shall examine Piaget's attitudes to some aspects of child language and assess how justified they are in the light of current work in experimental studies of language development. From this, we shall conclude that there is reason to believe that Piaget's assumptions about the dynamics of interaction with a pre-school child may be faulty. As a result, his interpretations of much of his data are called into question and so his theories are threatened.

It is essential once again to make a distinction between the receptive and the expressive control of language. In considering the child's receptive control of language Piaget is remarkably sanguine. He believes that 'children assimilate the language they hear to their own semantic structures, which are a function of their level of development' (Inhelder and Piaget, 1964, p. 3). This accords with what we have already seen to be a fundamental tenet. It follows that children's understanding of language will never be in advance of their understanding of the cognitive structures expressed by the language or embodied in it and so there will be no danger that they will understand, through language, phenomena which they have not already come to understand through their own actions. Consequently, children's receptive control of language does not threaten to overestimate their level of operational development.

Does it, on the other hand, perhaps underestimate that level? Since Piaget makes no suggestion that attainment of a given level of cognitive development is *sufficient* to guarantee control of the corresponding features of linguistic development, he would presumably have to allow that a child's linguistic understanding might on occasion be delayed relative to his non-linguistic abilities. But this would either be a matter of an individual child's departure from the population norm, or else it would be a function of aspects of the particular language being learned. In either case it would be of limited interest for him. There seems to be no feature of his theorizing that might alert him to any general risk of underestimating children's logical or conceptual competence by relying for evidence on the use of tests that involve language. If children at a given stage show a regular tendency to interpret the experimenter's words in ways which differ from the adult interpretation, then the Piagetian notion is that this is because the cognitive systems differ. The difference is not to be looked for in ways of interpreting language. We shall return to this topic later, for it is a crucial one.

Meanwhile Piaget's trust in the child's receptive language has to be contrasted with the suspicion with which he approaches expressive language at the pre-operational stage. Like many another diarist he indicates the mismatch between the function of the child's early words for the child and their function in adult language. He continues to elaborate his own account of vocabulary development whereby word meanings do not acquire full objectivity and true conceptual status until the onset of concrete operations (Piaget, 1951). He devotes special attention to the child's use of relational terms, such as kinship terms, logical conjunctions and quantifiers (Piaget, 1926, 1928; Inhelder and Piaget, 1964), and demonstrates that the appearance of these words in children's speech does not guarantee that they are supported by a full adult semantic analysis. In the face of examples where the child's use of the terms is confused (as in the intriguing claim by a nine-year-old that 'I am not well, because I'm not going to school') Piaget's attitude is ambivalent, arguing now that 'verbal confusion . . . is always a sign of logical confusion' (1928, p. 77), now that 'the child will admit on the verbal plane certain illogicalities which he would deny to concrete reality' (1928, p. 83). 'Vertical decalage' can be invoked to clarify some of these problematic examples but the difficulties surrounding the interpretation of children's linguistic errors serve to reinforce Piaget's rejection of expressive language as a reliable indicator of the child's knowledge.

There is another aspect, however, to Piaget's attitude to the child's expressive language. When it is free of confusion and when it accurately expresses the understanding of a phenomenon which has already been demonstrated in the child's actions, it represents a higher intellectual attainment than the non-verbal attainment of an operation because it indicates a level of conscious realization of knowledge that was previously unconscious. Piaget has always valued this articulation of knowledge and, for example, reserves the accolade of 'conserver' for those who can justify their decisions as well as make the correct ones. Recently, he has been exploring the steps by which children become conscious of their actions and come to articulate their knowledge (Piaget, 1977, 1978); and he has been demonstrating that the process is not merely an automatic mapping from one level to another but has rules of construction of its own. Thus Piaget's attitude to the child's expressive language has two sides to it: during the development of a structure, a child's use of language can give a misleading estimate of his level of understanding, but once adequate understanding has been demonstrated, the child's verbal expression of this understanding is in itself a later development which is a reliable indicator of an even higher level of conscious understanding.

We have seen, then, that verbal exchanges between child and adult continue to play a crucial role in the collection of most of Piaget's data and that he makes certain assumptions about the validity of these as a source of evidence. If he were to be seriously wrong in so doing, his theories would be vulnerable. We shall therefore now consider the extent to which recent work in developmental psycho-linguistics calls his assumptions into question.

Students of child language have been interested for some time in the respective contributions which studies of comprehension and of production may make to knowledge of the development of linguistic competence. The changes in accepted views about this over the past few years are relevant to our present concern.

A decade ago, tests of comprehension were believed to be relatively free from theoretical difficulties of interpretation although there were thought to be certain known risks in their design. Study of the child's language production, on the one hand, suffered more acutely from Chomsky's (1964) reminder that it was merely performance data and, particularly in the child's case, was multiply distorted in known and unknown ways from the underlying competence. On the other hand, productive *control* of a linguistic structure was held to be a later development than its comprehension and somehow a more complete achievement. However, recent experimental and theoretical studies have shown that the issues are more complex than was at first supposed.

Comprehension studies of language development usually centre on a particular linguistic contrast, such as active and passive sentences, opposite pairs of adjectives, verbs, prepositions, contrasting quantifiers, comparative and superlative adjective forms and so on. A task is constructed which involves the child's making some judgment or performing some action in response to statements or instructions given verbally by the experimenter. Pairs of instructions are then formulated which differ only with respect to the key words characteristic of the distinction being tested and which, when slotted into the task, would elicit distinct actions or judgments from an adult who understands the linguistic distinction.

For example, Macrae (1976) set out to test whether children understood that, in certain circumstances, the verbs *go* and *come* should be discriminated, in that *go* refers to a movement which does not have as its goal the position occupied by the speaker at the time of utterance, while *come* can refer to movement towards the speaker. She introduced three dolls to the children—Peter, Alice and their pet tortoise, Terry. She placed them on a table, equidistant from each other, and placed a chair beside Peter and an identical chair beside Alice. The children were told that Terry was an obedient tortoise and that Alice and Peter were ordering him around. They were told 'Alice says to Terry: Come to the chair', or 'Alice says to Terry: Go to the chair' and they had to make Terry do as he was told. For adults and for older children, the appropriate responses to these instructions differ, involving movement to Alice's chair for the 'come' instruction and movement to Peter's chair for the 'go' instruction. It was therefore assumed that this would be an adequate test of children's ability to handle the deictic distinction between the verbs, i.e. the distinction which is tied to the relation between the position of the speaker at the moment of utterance and the end-points of the movement.

Over the last fifteen years, studies of this design have proved a popular way of investigating language development, particularly within the pre-school age-group. On the face of it, they appear to be a relatively fast and clean way of accessing the child's growing competence because, although psychologists and linguists have of necessity to base their theories on language performance, testing of comprehension seems a better way of determining what language is for the children than searching their spontaneous speech for regularities. Evidence appears to be given directly of the children's grasp of the distinction to the extent that the tasks considered sample representatively the manifestation of the distinction in adult speech. However, this trust in comprehension studies of child language has been short-lived and for reasons which are instructive in the context of an assessment of Piaget's position.

From the start, certain precautions had to be taken in the design of the experiments. These involved ensuring that both responses were equally salient, that, in the absence of the distinction being tested, either response would be appropriate and that no means were available for making the correct discrimination other than understanding of the words being tested. In the illustration given above, which tested discrimination of deictic verbs, these standard precautions of experimental design were observed. Both Alice and Peter were used as speaker, so as to check that the children were prepared to produce both the responses of interest, viz. movement towards each chair. Had the speaker said 'Walk to the chair', an instruction which is deictically neutral, then either response would have been appropriate, by adult standards. Finally, it was difficult to see what alternative basis for discrimination could have been used by the children other than the one being tested, which was based on speaker deixis. It was fair to assume that if a child reliably produced the correct adult responses, then he could discriminate the verbs according to this adult role of application.

Assumptions were also made, however, about how the child approached the task and these guided the interpretation given to response profiles which did not fit the adult pattern. These assumptions could be stated quite simply: the child approached the task in the same way as an adult would. For an adult, the task would be to listen to the language used and base his responses on his understanding of the language. For an adult, the materials of the task would merely be a vehicle for the linguistic test and so would be subordinated to the rules of application of the language. For an adult, therefore, the precise method of testing the distinction would be of secondary importance. And so it was assumed that, if a subject gave the same response for both verbs, he must have confused the verbs and thought they meant the same as the one for which he was producing the correct answers. Finally, it was assumed, on the adult model, that if he did not understand what was expected of him he would either say so or would respond randomly to the instructions. These are the assumptions which underlie many of the studies used to probe the comprehension process with adult subjects (see, for example, Clark, 1976). It soon became obvious that the same assumptions were being made in the developmental studies as well.

Now, whether or not these assumptions are valid in the case of adult subjects, they led the interpretation of the developmental studies to some peculiar conclusions. In the illustration quoted, there was an overwhelming tendency for the children to move Terry towards the speaker, irrespective of the verb in the instruction, a response which coincided with that appropriate for the verb *come*. Thus it was tempting to conclude that the children understood *come* and confused *go* with it. However, this conclusion proved to be untenable, because a slight change in the presentation of the task led to an opposite result. If Terry, Alice and Peter were replaced by three other dolls, Mary and her brothers Tom and David, and the children were told 'Tom says to Mary: Come to your brother', they were more likely to avoid moving towards the speaker, irrespective of the verb, so producing the correct response for *go* items and the incorrect one for *come* items. Yet another presentation of the distinction, where the speaker stood halfway up a flight of steps and the instructions were of the form 'Come up the steps, etc.', led to the children ignoring the speaker altogether and producing patterns of responses unlike those expected for either verb. In addition, in this latter condition the children behaved the same way whether the verb was *go, come* or one of the non-deictic verbs, *run, jump* and *walk*.*

Thus it began to appear that when children did not discriminate the verbs, their decisions were guided more by features of the wider setting of the experiment than by

---

*In these experiments, it was not until the children were about eight years old that they demonstrated that they could handle the distinction. This agrees with the findings of Clark and Garnica (1974) who also tested comprehension. Richards (1976), on the other hand, found that when children *produced* the verbs, the distinction was present at an early age.

any incipient or partial understanding of the distinction the experiment was designed to test. So it became difficult to use such a test of comprehension as an instrument to probe the *development* of the target distinction.

Over the last six or seven years numerous studies have led to similar conclusions. Clark (1973) reported that when children's understanding of locative prepositions was tested, their responses were better described as dependent on features of the materials used in the task than as consequent upon changes in the linguistic forms used. Donaldson and McGarrigle (1974) and Donaldson and Lloyd (1974) showed that when children were asked to judge quantified statements, such as 'All the cars are in the garages', they frequently based their decision on whether the set of garages was full or not, something irrelevant for the adult's decision. And there is now a substantial body of work confirming that the conclusion is quite general. When young children are asked questions or given instructions about some visible material array, their responses are apt to be influenced by features of this array which are irrelevant to what an adult would regard as 'the meaning' of the language. How are we to take theoretical account of this fact? What is the difference between child and adult?

We should notice, first of all, that 'adult' here actually means an intellectually sophisticated adult in our kind of culture; and such people have developed certain very special skills. In the course of their education they have become aware of language as a vehicle for the expression of 'timeless meaning'—meaning that transcends any particular context of occurrence. They have learned to think of what utterances mean in abstraction from any particular communicative endeavour.*

However, it seems clear that, in the beginning, (both individually and culturally speaking) language is not regarded in this way. Rather it is one component of a total situation, and the interpretation of it is not separated (perhaps not separable) from the wider attempt to make sense of the totality. When a child tries to make sense of instructions given to him or questions asked of him, his knowledge of the language is only one of various considerations that will determine his interpretation and hence his response.

Now, at first sight, this might not seem very different from the Piagetian claim that children 'assimilate the language they hear to their own mental structures' (Inhelder and Piaget, 1964). But the crucial question is this: what grounds have we for supposing that we know enough about how such 'assimilation' works to be able to say that a 'mental structure' which does not manifest itself when a particular bit of language is interpreted is therefore absent? For instance, if a child, looking at two rows of objects, interprets a question about number as if it were a question about length, what entitles us to conclude that this shows a concept of number to be lacking or defective?

The truth is that at the moment we know that certain non-linguistic variables interact with linguistic ones to determine interpretation, but we know little in detail about the nature of this interaction or its developmental history. We do know that the precise effects of context change over the course of development, between, say age two and age seven or eight, but we do not know exactly how or why. (See, however, a paper by Sinha (1978 unpublished manuscript) which makes interesting proposals.)

As to the nature of the non-linguistic variables, these seem to fall into at least two broad categories.

First, there are impersonal features of the physical array which the child is asked to consider. For instance, Donaldson and her colleagues (Donaldson and Lloyd, 1974; Donaldson and McGarrigle, 1974) found that the sight of an empty garage seemed to

---

*Of course, even intellectually sophisticated adults do not ignore context in their everyday uses of language. On the contrary, they rely on it heavily (see, for instance, Ziff, 1972); but the point is that they *can* concentrate on the meaning of decontextualized words, and they know when they are supposed to do so.

be curiously salient. However, we agree with Grieve, Hoogenraad and Murray (1977) that, while the child's response is constrained by physical features of the array, the important consideration may not be these features *per se* but 'his experience of the material, partially determined by the cultural environment'.

Second, there are the interpersonal variables. If, as we said earlier, the child's aim is to make sense of the total situation, then it should come as no surprise that another and perhaps specially powerful source of influence will be what the child takes to be the intention of the speaker. And in judging this he will attend to what the speaker does as well as to what he says.

Now in a typical Piagetian conservation task, the experimenter asks if two objects are the same in some respect, and he gets an answer. Then *making sure that the child notices what he is doing*, he changes one of these objects. And he repeats his question. What could be more reasonable than that the child should think he is *meant** to take account of this change, given that language for him is embedded in its context, given that it does not have the separateness and primacy which it later attains?

McGarrigle and Donaldson (1974/1975) studied the effect of using a variant of a conservation task in which the crucial transformation was carried out not by the deliberate act of the experimenter but by the intervention of a 'naughty' teddy bear. Thus the transformation was presented to the child as accidental, something that could well be ignored. Under this condition, significantly more children between the ages of four and six gave conserving responses than in a traditional version of the task.

This result has since been replicated by Dockrell, Neilson and Campbell (1980) and by Light, Buckingham and Robbins (1979). In the same paper Light and his colleagues go on to report a further interesting experiment where the transformation is not so much accidental as incidental to the ostensible purpose of the child's activity.

The subjects in this study, who worked in pairs, were given the task of putting small pasta shells into the cells of a grid as quickly as possible, the first child to use up all his shells being the 'winner'. Thus, if the game was to be fair, each child must start with an equal quantity of shells.

The shells were placed in two beakers of similar dimensions and the tester adjusted the contents until the children agreed that they were equal. Then, however, the tester pretended he had suddenly noticed that the rim of one beaker was chipped (as indeed it was). The damaged beaker was then declared to be unsafe to use because of the risk of cutting one's fingers. Another beaker had therefore to be found—and the only one available turned out to be of a larger size. The experimenter poured the pasta shells into this larger beaker and then asked whether the children were satisfied that the original equality had been preserved.

The results obtained under this 'incidental' condition were dramatically different from those obtained in a corresponding standard task. Differences significant at the 0.001 level were found.

When Light et al discuss these findings they take the view, as we do, that the differences probably arise from the fact that in one case the child receives the message: *this transformation is important*; while in the other he receives the message: *this transformation is irrelevant*. From this, Light et al are inclined to conclude not that the traditional conservation task underestimates the child's cognitive level (as did McGarrigle and Donaldson, 1974/1975) but rather that conservation tasks are simply not a good way of finding out what that level is.†

---

*Notice that, in English, the verb 'to mean' also has the meaning 'to intend'. And in French the use of *vouloir dire* is even more explicit.

†On the other hand, ironically enough, Sinha (1978) concludes that conservation tasks provide 'an ideal vehicle for the study of the acquisition and development of communicative competence'.

There is certainly something to be said for this point of view, if one looks at the results of these studies of conservation task variants alone. False positives might certainly occur as well as false negatives. However, other work (for instance, Gelman and Gallistel, 1978) is now available to support the view that a good deal of under-estimation has indeed been going on for a long time. The present position can thus be summarized as follows.

Piaget's data concerning the cognitive development of 'pre-operational' subjects must be reinterpreted in the light of the new evidence which shows that, in his own interpretations, he has not taken enough account of the extent to which language, for children, is embedded in context. It is now clear that many errors in tasks of conservation, class inclusion and the like have their source in what (from a formal point of view) are misinterpretations of questions or instructions by the child. And it is no longer possible to claim that these misinterpretations are simply reliable signs of the immature state of whatever 'cognitive structure' the test purports to assess.

However, it does not follow that *all* errors in such tasks arise from misinterpret-ations of the kind we have been considering. It does not follow that children do not *also* encounter difficulties of the kind that Piaget postulates.* And, most certainly, the recognition that some of the results obtained are due to the child's habitual modes of interpretation does not throw us back on the notion that concepts like class and number are innate. To the extent that the Piagetian account of these concepts becomes suspect, we are simply faced with the need to study them anew.

CONCLUSION

We conclude that the studies outlined here indicate that it is essential to have a highly interactive model of the way in which a pre-school child approaches an experimental test of his comprehension. They point to the difficulty of interpreting the behaviour of a child who has not yet achieved adult competence or at least who does not demonstrate it in his responses. It is therefore not the time to be as sanguine about children's understanding of language as Piaget appears to be. The studies we have reviewed point to the dangers of assuming that it is possible to direct the child's attention to an isolated feature of the total communicative act between himself and the adult. They therefore make it difficult to conclude, along with Piaget, that while both systems are developing, language follows cognition at a respectful distance.

It may be paradoxical to suggest that Piaget, who has done so much to emphasize the qualitative differences between the child and adult mind, has been guilty of too adult-centred an approach to his data collection. And yet close inspection of some recent investigations appears to support this claim.

---

*However, there is other evidence, having nothing specifically to do with language and so not reviewed here, that Piaget's explanations in terms of centration and decentration are unsatisfactory. See Donaldson (1978).

REFERENCES

Beilin, H. (1975) *Studies in the Cognitive Basis of Language Development.* New York: Academic Press.
Chomsky, N. (1964) Comments in Bellugi, U. and Brown, R. (Eds.) *The Acquisition of Language.* SRCD Monographs, **29**, No. 1.
Clark, E. V. (1973) Non-linguistic strategies and the acquisition of word meanings. *Cognition,* **2**, 161-182.

Clark, E. V. and Garnica, O. K. (1974) Is he coming or going? On the acquisition of deictic verbs. *Journal of Verbal Learning and Verbal Behavior,* **13,** 556-672.

Clark, H. H. (1976) *Semantics and Comprehension.* The Hague: Mouton.

Dockrell, J., Neilson, I. and Campbell, R. N. (1980) Conservation accidents revisited. *International Journal of Behavioural Development,* **3,** 423-439.

Donaldson, M. (1978) *Children's Minds.* London: Fontana.

Donaldson, M. and Lloyd, P. (1974) Sentences and situations: Children's judgements of match and mismatch. In Bresson, F. (Ed.) *Problèmes Actuels en Psycholinguistique.* Paris: Centre National de la Recherche Scientifique.

Donaldson, M. and McGarrigle, J. (1974) Some clues to the nature of semantic development. *Journal of Child Language,* **1,** 185-194.

Gelman, R. and Gallistel, C. R. (1978) *The Child's Understanding of Number.* Cambridge, Mass: Harvard University Press.

Grieve, R. Hoogenraad, R. and Murray, D. (1977) On the child's use of lexis and syntax in understanding locative instructions. *Cognition,* **5,** 235-250.

Inhelder, B. and Piaget, J. (1964) *The Early Growth of Logic in the Child: Classification and Seriation.* London: Routledge and Kegan Paul.

Light, P., Buckingham, N. and Robbins, A. H. (1979) The conservation task as an interactional setting. *British Journal of Educational Psychology,* **49,** 304-310.

Macrae, A. J. (1976) Meaning relations in language development: a study of some converse pairs and directional opposites. Unpublished Ph.D Dissertation. University of Edinburgh.

McGarrigle, J. and Donaldson, M. (1974/1975) Conservation accidents. *Cognition,* **3,** 341-350.

Piaget, J. (1926) *Language and Thought of the Child.* London: Routledge and Kegan Paul.

Piaget, J. (1928) *Judgment and Reasoning in the Child.* London: Routledge and Kegan Paul.

Piaget, J. (1951) *Play, Dreams and Imitation in the Child.* London: Routledge and Kegan Paul.

Piaget, J. (1971) *Biology and Knowledge.* Edinburgh: Edinburgh University Press.

Piaget, J. (1977) *The Grasp of Consciousness.* London: Routledge and Kegan Paul.

Piaget, J. (1978) *Success and Understanding.* London: Routledge and Kegan Paul.

Richards, M. M. (1976) *Come* and *go* reconsidered: children's use of deictic verbs in contrived situations. *Journal of Verbal Learning and Verbal Behaviour,* **15,** 655-665.

Sinclair, H. (1969) Developmental psycholinguistics. In Elkind, D. and Flavell, J. H. (Eds.) *Studies in Cognitive Development: Essays in Honour of Jean Piaget.* London: Oxford University Press.

Sinclair, H. (1978) Conflict and progress. In Miller, G. A. and Lenneberg, E. (Eds.) *Psychology and Biology of Language and Thought.* New York: Academic Press.

Sinha, C. (1978) The development of word meaning. Unpublished thesis. University of Bristol.

Ziff, P. (1972) *Understanding Understanding.* Ithaca, New York: Cornell University Press.

Chapter 9

Piaget on Language: A Perspective

HERMINA SINCLAIR

Piaget's views on language have often been analysed, discussed, lauded and lamented, though they play only a comparatively minor part in his monumental *oeuvre*. As an epistemologist, Piaget is concerned with the nature of knowledge, and, more specifically, with the ways in which knowledge changes. As he has often emphasized, Piaget is only secondarily a developmental psychologist. That he is a psychologist at all is due to his conception of epistemology: in his opinion, the nature of knowledge cannot be studied through philosophical reflection alone, or through historical research into the different fields of science alone, but only through a combined study of present-day knowledge and scientific method, their history, and the development, in the child, of the basic concepts and operations that underlie all epistemologically important knowledge.

As is discussed in other chapters of this volume, Piaget's epistomological theory is, according to his own characterization, biological, constructivist and interactionist. As such, it stands as a refutation of empiricism, and, in a certain sense, it is also opposed to rationalism or nativism.

Language enters into Piaget's studies in several ways. At the most superficial level, language is used in psychological experiments, by way of dialogues and question-and-answer sequences, in order to discover children's beliefs and concepts. His early work (*Le Langage et la Pensée Chez l'Enfant*, 1923; *Le Jugement et le Raisonnement Chez l'Enfant*, 1924) was almost exclusively based on verbal interviewing techniques. Later, much more use is made of experimental situations involving the manipulation of objects, though questions and dialogue remain important. Interesting though they may be, methodological questions about talking with children as an experimental device will not be discussed in this paper. At the deepest level, language is discussed in Piaget's work as a possible constructive factor in the development of thought, and this is the main point I intend to elaborate here. At the deepest level, language is discussed by Piaget in his argumentation against logical positivism, the doctrine that reduces all logic, and, finally, all mental operations to language, and that for Piaget is a direct prolongation of empiricism.

Let me start with what should, perhaps, be the ending. From an epistemological point of view, Piaget considers the creation of new knowledge, inventions and discoveries not to be due to language, but to abstractions, of different kinds and at different levels, from actions and, more importantly, from their co-ordinations. It should be clearly understood that Piaget is concerned with the creation and elaboration of knowledge in the various sciences. He is not concerned with creation in the arts, which presents a different problem. The overriding importance Piaget attaches to the subject's activity as the source of knowledge about the world in which he lives, and about his own and other people's reasoning processes, is made abundantly clear in such works as *L'Épistémologie Génétique* (1970), *L'Équilibration des Structures Cognitives* (1975), and *Recherches sur l'Abstraction Réfléchissante* (1977).

My discussion of Piaget's views on language will fall into two parts: the relation between language and thought; and the implications of his theory for the study of language acquisition. The first part will be based, in the main, on the two most explicit articles he has written on the topic of language and thought, which date respectively from 1954 and 1963. His preface to Ferreiro's study (1971) adds some useful clarifications. More recent general texts such as *La Psychologie de l'Enfant* (1966), *Le Structuralisme* (1968), *L'Épistémologie Génétique* (1970) and *L'Équilibration des Structures Cognitives* (1975) do not indicate any change in Piaget's position. The second part will mainly refer to the older volume dealing with symbol construction in general (*La Formation du Symbole Chez l'Enfant*, 1946) and to an article entitled 'Problèmes de psychologie génétique' (1956).*

THE RELATION BETWEEN LANGUAGE AND THOUGHT

Though the relation between language and the operations of intelligence is an eminently epistemological issue, Piaget's 1954 article is written directly from a psychological point of view; the 1963 article starts with the epistemological problem of the status of language in theories of knowledge mainly in relation to logical positivism; however, after having briefly referred to Carnap, Tarski and Morris, he asserts that the problems raised by their theories 'are psychological issues' (1963, p. 53), and proceeds to treat them as such.

Why, may we ask, does Piaget, in the case of language, not follow his own epistemological method of weaving together history, analysis of the present state of a scientific discipline and fact from child development in order to decide on an issue of construction of knowledge? Because, I would guess, the origins of language remain shrouded in mystery, and the present state of general linguistics (despite remarkable recent achievements) does not yet allow far-reaching epistemological conclusions.

Before giving an account of the psychological arguments adduced in the 1954 and 1963 papers, I must enter a word of caution: Piaget does not provide a definition of what he means by 'language', and the reader has to infer this meaning from the context. On the whole, *language* in the quoted texts means 'natural language', i.e. one of the very many languages spoken today. *Langage courant*, everyday language, is opposed to *langages artificiels ou techniques*, artificial or technical languages; but the

---

*The original editions of the 1954 and 1956 papers are now difficult to obtain; both were reprinted in 1964 (*Six Études de Psychologie*), and my page references are to this more recent edition, though for the sake of chronology I continue to refer to the 1954 and 1956 papers.

latter are said to be 'psychologically also languages' (1963, p. 52). Piaget also uses *langue* (1963, p. 53) and *parole* (1963, p. 56), though he does not seem to make the distinction which is frequently made by French-speaking authors between these expressions, derived from de Saussure.

Transposed into psychological terms, the problem of language and its relations to thought is treated by Piaget as two separate questions: is language a sufficient condition for the development of thought, i.e. has thought its origins in language? and if not, is language nevertheless a necessary condition for the development of thinking, i.e. can the basic cognitive operations be elaborated without the help of language?

In the papers mentioned, and on other occasions as well, Piaget starts off by saying that he is aware of the important contributions 'language' makes to thought, and that 'very probably' complex mental operations cannot be achieved without its help, but that these contributions have often been analysed by other authors, and that he himself will mainly point out its insufficiencies (1963, p. 52). Moreover, and this fits in with his epistemological concerns, Piaget's arguments mainly concern the relation between language and logic, few authors having proposed theories which reduce to language the knowledge of the physical or social world.

Is Language the Source of Thought

Piaget's answer to this first question is an unqualified 'no'. In the first place, the action-patterns ('schèmes') of the pre-verbal, sensorimotor period can be shown to be functional equivalents of the later operations of thought, exhibiting parallel structures and similar developmental dynamics. The evidence for this point comes from Piaget's observations and analyses of his own children's behaviour during their first two years of life, noted and discussed in great detail in two of his most important works, *La Naissance de l'Intelligence Chez l'Enfant* (1936) and *La Construction du Réel Chez l'Enfant* (1937). The infant searches for and finds regularities in the ways objects and people behave, he discovers new relations between their behaviour, he invents new means for obtaining interesting effects—in short, he is an organizer, an inventor and a discoverer before he becomes a talker. And the ways in which he organizes his actions so as to deal with his (admittedly still very restricted) world show a striking isomorphism with the organization underlying his later thinking: the reasoning activities of the toddler, school-child and adolescent (logic), the experimental approaches to the world of objects (natural sciences), and the insights into other people's motivations, beliefs and ideas (psychology, sociology, etc.). As Oléron suggested in his discussion of Piaget's 1963 paper, and as Piaget wholeheartedly agreed (1963, pp. 63 and 71), the infant is not only a pre-logician, but also a pre-physicist, pre-psychologist, etc. Recently, other researchers, working with larger groups of subjects and in more experimental settings, have strikingly confirmed and on some points amplified Piaget's analyses (Moreno et al, 1976; Foreman et al, 1975).

Thinking, in the sense of the operations and concepts that make it possible to absorb information, to fit it into a meaningful framework and to go beyond it towards new discoveries and inventions, has its roots in activity, not in language. The fundamental structures and mechanisms of thought are prefigured in the infant's behaviour well before the appearance of language (1963, p. 54).

In this argument, Piaget uses the word 'language' in the sense of the production of the first 'words' and utterances recognizable by the infant's environment as belonging to the mother tongue and as having, apparently, a more or less stable meaning.

Another argument Piaget uses in order to show that the child does not derive his mental operations directly from language is the following: natural languages, in their everyday use, incorporate lexical and syntactical structures that reflect conceptual structures, but once the child has acquired language, he is still far from capable of dealing with problems such as class inclusion and intersection, conditions and consequences, etc. (1963, p. 58). Frequent everyday use of nouns such as 'poodles', 'dogs' and 'animals', or quantifiers such as 'all', 'more' and 'some', of conditionals such as 'if . . . then' might be thought to lead directly to the corresponding operations, but this is not the case. In a series of experiments discussed in *La Genèse des Structures Logiques Élémentaires* (1959), Inhelder and Piaget showed that operations such as hierarchical class inclusion, intersection and seriation are not fully acquired until much later. In some of these experiments the use of quantifying words was avoided in the instructions and questions (e.g. the intersection task, p. 178 sqq), but in others it was not. This raises a problem of interpretation which has been discussed by e.g. Donaldson and Lloyd (1974) and Karmiloff-Smith (1977).

Piaget seems to accept that by the age of five (if not before) children have essentially mastered the main morphosyntactical structures of their mother tongue as well as its most generally used categorial and quantifying terms. And, indeed, by that age, children certainly appear to understand utterances such as 'I'll give you some of my pencils, but you can't have them all' or 'A guinea-pig is a little furry animal', etc. They also sometimes produce such utterances, in a perfectly appropriate context. Apparently, Piaget's expression 'once the child has acquired language' is to be taken along these lines. His conclusion, in this argument, is that whatever information the ordinary use of language provides about class relationships, such information is only assimilated when the child has become capable of additive and multiplicative operations; and the latter are co-ordinated actions that have been interiorized, thereby becoming reversible and atemporal (unlike the real actions of uniting, separating, re-uniting in different ways, etc., which can only be effected in temporal and successive ways). Language, says Piaget (1963, p. 58), may help the interiorization process, but neither creates nor directly transmits logical structures.

Is Language Necessary for the Development of Thought?

Although at the beginning of the 1963 article Piaget affirms that language no doubt remains a necessary condition for the completion of logical structures (p. 51), he goes on to argue against a constructive role of language *per se* in this respect. Complex structures such as lattices, combinatorials and mathematical groups, he points out, cannot even be formulated in ordinary language, yet are within the grasp of adolescents, as is clear when young people deal with problems involving double-reference systems, or proportions or combinatorial probabilities. These complex structures, he adds, do not seem to be implicit in language itself, though a better understanding of the possible links between the structure of language and that of formal logical thought will have to await further work following 'the various trends of linguistic structuralism (Hjelmslev, Togeby, Harris)' (1963, p. 59).* When he wrote the 1963 paper, Piaget did not know of Chomsky's work, which he discusses in later publications (c.f. *Le Structuralisme*, 1968). Piaget has not published any further explicit discussions on the particular point of possible structural resemblance between

---

*All quotations from French texts are given in my own translation, though English editions of some of these texts are listed in the bibliography.

logical and linguistic operations, and, as far as I know, the problem has hardly been raised by Chomsky apart from a short passage (1965, p. 55) where he argues that 'according to the theory of transformational grammar, only certain kinds of formal operations on strings can appear in grammars—operations that, furthermore, have no *a priori* justification'.

Thus far, the conclusion from the article quoted, as from many other passages in Piaget's works, seems inescapable: language as such, i.e. language in its specifically linguistic structural aspects, cannot be seen to exert a constructive influence on the development of thought.

However, language also has functional aspects: it serves representation and communication, and the possibility has to be considered that its constructive influence on thought is found in its functions rather than in its lexical and grammatical structures.

Language as a Means of Representation

Piaget has mainly considered the representative function of language, emphasizing the fact that it shares this function with mental images, symbolic play, 'pretend' behaviour, followed by drawings, etc. (*La Formation du Symbole Chez l'Enfant,* 1946; *Mémoire et Intelligence,* 1968; *Les Mécanismes Perceptifs,* 1961; Piaget and Inhelder: *La Psychologie de l'Enfant,* 1966). Representation has its roots in imitation, according to Piaget, and has very modest beginnings: recognition memory; imitation by contagion during the first weeks of life; accommodation, e.g. of the act of grasping an unfamiliar object, where, before it actually grasps, the hand 'imitates' the object's size or shape. Imitation develops some time during the second year of life into a more specific capacity for representation which allows the child to evoke persons, objects and events in their absence. As such, this capacity transforms sensorimotor intelligence into what can properly be called thought, and extends its powers far beyond the (already remarkable) capacities for organization, discovery and invention proper to the pre-representational period. At this point in development, the representational capacity is called the semiotic (or symbolic) function by Piaget, and its role in cognitive development is essential.

The representational capacity develops hand-in-hand with, and, under the guidance of, intelligence. In Piaget's own, typically dialectical formulation, ' . . . (the semiotic function) makes thought possible by providing it with an illimited field of applications in contrast with the restricted boundaries of sensorimotor intelligence and of perception, but it develops only under the direction and with the help of thought or representative intelligence' (1966, p. 72). When taxed with the apparent circularity of statements such as the above, Piaget often answers by agreeing to the circularity, but by calling it a 'genetic circularity' or a 'dialectical spiral' and by pointing to the importance of such phenomena in biology.

The hand-in-hand development of the representational function and intelligence is an essential part of Piaget's biological constructivist view of human development: it allows him not only to find the roots of conceptual development in the co-ordinations of actions during infancy, but also to emphasize the functional continuity of life-span development while distinguishing structural stages in this development.

Piaget therefore concludes that neither language in its representational function, nor representation in general are sufficient conditions for the development of thought, though they play an important role. Moreover, since language is not the only medium for representation, it may not even be a necessary condition. Piaget points out that the crucial evidence in this respect comes from experiments with deaf children who have little or no knowledge of a natural language nor of an equivalent sign language such as Ameslan. In the 1963 article, Piaget quotes the experiments carried out by Vincent-Borelli (1956), and Oléron and Herren (1961), which show that profoundly deaf children are perfectly capable of constructing the essential operations (seriations, classifications, etc.) with only slight retardation as compared to hearing children. Since then, Furth's experiments (1966) have proved this point beyond doubt. This does not mean, of course, that deaf children with no special training to provide them with sufficient proficiency in a conventional system of symbolization (sign language, or written natural language, or even, in some cases, lip-reading and speaking) do not lack an important source for the acquisition of information in many fields of knowledge; but it does mean that the basic mental constructs which are necessary for meaningful apprehension of such information are elaborated without the help of what for hearing children is an important representational medium. Language, in the sense of utterances and written texts which one produces oneself or receives from others, provides food for thought, it does not create thought.

Language as a Means of Social Interaction

Social interaction and, more specifically, language as a means of communication, has been comparatively little studied or discussed by Piaget. In his detailed observations of his own children in natural settings, other people and particularly the closest adults obviously come into the picture continuously. Yet, in *La Naissance de l'Intelligence Chez l'Enfant* and *La Construction du Réel Chez l'Enfant*, though not completely absent, few analyses of social interaction occur comparable to the analyses of the infant's interaction with objects. Observations of older children's verbal exchanges are found in *Le Langage et la Pensée*, and from these are derived the much discussed concepts of 'egocentric speech' and 'collective monologue'. The only extensive study of social interaction among children is to be found in *Le Jugement Moral Chez l'Enfant*, in Piaget's fascinating analysis of how children of different ages organize and conceptualize their play with marbles.

This comparative paucity, however, does not allow us to infer that Piaget minimizes the influence of social interactions on the development of thought. On the contrary, in both the 1954 and 1963 papers, Piaget concludes that language is necessary for the development of thought, and is thus indeed a constructive factor, even if it cannot be the source of thought; and the constructive power of language lies in its communicative aspect. As regards the relationship between the transformation of sensorimotor intelligence into thought during the second year of life and social interaction, we find the same genetic circle as in the relationship between this transformation and representation: the question, says Piaget (1954, p. 52), 'is like asking whether it's the chicken that makes the egg or the egg that makes the chicken, since all human behaviour is at the same time social and individual'.

Moreover, Piaget makes a stronger case for social interaction as a fundamental constructive influence than he does for representation. In several passages in *La Construction du Réel Chez l'Enfant* he even appears to attribute explanatory power to social interaction as regards the constitution of the representational function. In a passage where the child's conceptualization of space is discussed we find the following reflections (p. 322): ' . . . why does the subject, at a certain stage of his mental development, try to construct a representation of spatial relations instead of simply acting on them? Obviously, in order to communicate to others, or to obtain from others, some information concerning a real object or event that has to do with space.

Apart from social interaction no reason for the transition from action to pure representation can be found . . . representation and the detachment from one's own action are underpinned by adaptation to others and social co-operation'. And, in the same chapter, the dialectic relationship between social interaction and thought is emphasized: ' . . . as soon as language appears, the socialization of thought can be witnessed in the elaboration of concepts, of relations and rules, that is to say, a structural development (takes place) . . . indeed, it is due to co-operation with others that the human mind comes to make observational judgments, since the recording of facts implies a presentation or an exchange and has no meaning in itself for the individual's own activity. Whether thought becomes rational because it is social, or inversely, the interdependence of the search for truth and socialization is, in my opinion, undeniable' (p. 316).

The first passage quoted is a direct contradiction of a point in Bronckart's otherwise excellent account of Piaget's views on language (1977, p. 57): ' . . . for Piaget, and the constructivists, reference to representation is sufficient to explain the emergence of language'. In fact, Piaget says just the opposite: the representational function is to be explained by social interaction. Piaget has not modified his views on this point, except to emphasize that verbal discussion is preceded by, and finds its source in, collaboration and interpersonal exchanges in action. However, unlike representation, which also at adult age can take many forms (drawings, graphs, formulas, etc.), Piaget appears to regard language, i.e. discussion and dialogue, as the main means of personal exchange beyond the earliest stages of development, and it is in this sense that he accords to language an essential and necessary role in the construction of mental operations.

At the conclusion of this account of Piaget's views on language and its relations to thought, I would like to add a few remarks. In the first place, it has to be emphasized that in all the above quotations Piaget refers to mental operations in so far as they are considered to be universal, and similarly, when speaking about language, he refers to both its structural and its functional aspects that are thought to be universal. The universality of mental operations has often been attested (c.f. Dasen et al, 1978), and the idea of the existence of cognitive universals also appears intuitively acceptable. Certainly, at the adult level, mathematicians, physicists, chemists develop the same kind of theories and work with similar scientific methods. Superficially, the same does not seem to be true for social interaction in general and for language in particular, as the enormous variety of natural languages eloquently attests.

The question of linguistic universals has fairly recently been reintroduced as an important problem by Chomsky (1965, p. 27, sqq), but no linguistic theory is explicit on this point, just as there is no consensus among linguists comparable to the consensus among physicists, chemists, etc. Also, intuitively, many people feel that modes of social interaction differ more profoundly in the different cultures than do cognitive structures (2 and 2 make 4, and not a little bit less or a little bit more; apples, oranges and lemons fall to the ground; sugar dissolves in hot water—everywhere on earth). I think that this state of affairs may well be one of the reasons for the almost total absence of experimental studies in Piaget's own work on social interaction and language, apart from his personal predilection for other aspects of development. As regards the main point discussed here, i.e. the constructive influence of early interchanges in action, and later language, on the development of thought, a series of observational studies carried out by a Piaget-oriented research group in Paris, under the direction of M. Stambak, on infants from the age of nine months onwards is beginning to fill the experimental gap. Many other researchers have also begun to study social interaction among infants, though not from the point of view of its influence on the development of thought. It looks as if in the near future a large body of experimental fact will be available leading to clarification of this important issue.

PIAGET'S THEORY AND LANGUAGE ACQUISITION

In recent publications, most authors writing on the acquisition of language and especially on the very early period, make reference to Piaget's theory. Slobin (1973, p. 180) was probably among the first to do so in a detailed manner and also to point out that the relevance of Piaget's work on cognitive development for problems of language acquisition resides most obviously in the child's meaning-intentions—in other words, in the content the child tries to convey. Indeed, Piaget's own, rather brief, discussion of the beginnings of language (*La Formation du Symbole Chez l'Enfant*, p. 228, sqq) is written from this point of view. Undeniably, to know what kinds of meanings the young child is intellectually capable and desirous of expressing is a psycho-linguist's prerequisite for trying to understand the child's utterances and is in turn a prerequisite for a theory of language acquisition. However, to study the content of the child's messages and the content he searches for and finds in other people's utterances is not the same thing as studying the development of the structure of his utterances or the mechanisms by which the child gradually discovers and re-creates the structural properties of his mother tongue. Does Piaget's work on the development of mental operations and on the structural and dynamic aspects of its origins, i.e. sensorimotor intelligence, provide us with a basis for a theory of language acquisition in the latter sense?

Sensorimotor Intelligence as a Heuristic Model for Language Acquisition

Piaget himself has said very little on this point. However, he stresses the fact that speaking and understanding speech are actions, and as such they partake in the mechanisms and structures of other actions. Piaget's view corresponds to that of Janet (1936, pp. 259—260), in Ferreiro's words: 'It is not a matter of reducing language to thought, but of deriving both from the general organization of action within the framework of a developmental theory of cognitive activity' (Ferreiro, 1971, p. 12). Many of the Genevan psycho-linguistic studies have been carried out with this basic premise in mind. (For a recent overview, see Sinclair et al, 1976, and for some more recent developments, Berthoud and Sinclair, 1978.) However, the idea that the construction modes and final structure of sensorimotor intelligence provides the child with a powerful heuristic model necessary to start the acquisition of his mother tongue is no more than a very general hypothesis. At various times I have speculated on how this heuristic model is used by the child (1971, pp. 126—127; 1973, p. 411; 1975, pp. 223—238).

In a very general sense I think that the hypothesis must be true: intelligence is phylogenetically and ontogenetically prior to language; language is a product of the human mind, and its universal structural principles must be related to the subject's organizational principles of dealing with the immediate, *hic et nunc* environment, all the more so since these principles ultimately are based on biological, and particularly neural, regulations and co-ordinations. The only way to reject the premise is to suppose the existence in human beings of a specific genetic endowment for language, as Chomsky appears to do. I do not know of any neurological evidence that would plead for such an initial compartmentalization of the human brain; what appears to be attested is a gradual specialization. At this level, the question cannot be decided before further progress in neurology furnishes decisive evidence.

Intellectual and Communicative Universals

To return to the psychological level: the important controversy bears on the choice of basic organizational principles. From his epistemological point of view, Piaget concentrated on certain structures and described how they develop into the logical instruments essential for the organization of all human knowledge. My speculations concerned these same fundamental structures. However, recent research in language acquisition has raised the profound problem of whether these structures and the processes by which they are elaborated are the only important ones for language. To my knowledge, McNeill (1969, p. 150) was the first to ask this question and to suggest the existence of 'communicative universals', which may or may not have the same form as 'intellectual universals', but may have a separate origin.

The question can be rephrased as follows: does the communicative function of human language impose particular constraints on its (universal) structure, just as its function of representing the human organization of reality does? And if so, what does this imply for the processes by which the child acquires language? These questions do not simply reiterate the accepted fact that the child learns his language in a communicative setting—they go far deeper.

As regards the structures of social interaction (of which language is a particular case), Piaget himself seems to have foreseen some such questions. In the following passage (Piaget, 1956, p. 148) he proposes a functional identity between inter-individual and intra-individual operations: 'The form of collective interaction that intervenes in the constitution of logical structures is essentially the co-ordination of inter-individual actions in collaboration and in verbal exchanges. Indeed, when one analyses this collective co-ordination of actions, it is seen to consist also of operations, but inter-individual and not intra-individual ones: what one person does may, for instance, be completed by somebody else (addition), or it may correspond to what several others are doing (multiplicative correspondences); or what one person does may be different from what others are doing, but certain cues may point to a relationship between the different points of view (reciprocity), etc. In strife and opposition, negations and inverse operations are at work, etc.'

Indeed, all the various aspects of Piaget's theory suppose a strong parallelism between what is individual and what is interpersonal. However, the parallelism is only briefly referred to in his writings, and moreover, language may well be a special case, in which the demands of supple and economic communication impose both structural characteristics and acquisition processes not found in other types of social interaction.

Researchers in language acquisition are beginning to struggle with these essential problems (Bates, 1976; Snow and Ferguson, 1977; Lieven, 1978, and others). The most explicit proposal for the derivation of linguistic structural principles from communicative interaction comes, I think, from Bruner (1975, 1978). However, in my opinion, a great deal of work has to be done before we can do more than speculate on these issues; in particular, far more attention will have to be paid to comparisons between acquisition data in different languages. This point is also argued by Slobin in a recent paper (1979), who, moreover, presents both theoretical and methodological proposals for attacking the problems outlined above.

Much research will have to be carried out, many words spoken and many texts written before the mystery of the child's acquisition of his mother tongue is unveiled. Piaget's contribution, small as it is in comparison with what he has done for our understanding of the development of thought, will, I believe, remain important, because of the profound issues he has raised and the often passionate controversies his writings have triggered.

REFERENCES

Bates, E. (1976) *Language and Context: the Acquisition of Pragmatics.* New York: Academic Press.

Berthoud, I. and Sinclair, H. L. (1978) L'expression d'éventualités et de conditions chez l'enfant. *Archives de Psychologie,* **XLVI**, No. 179, pp. 205-233.

Bronckart, J. P. (1977) *Théories du Langage: Introduction Critique.* Bruxelles: Mardage.

Bruner, J. S. (1975) The ontogenesis of speech-acts. *Journal of Child Language,* **2**(1), 1-19.

Bruner, J. S. (1978) On prelinguistic prerequisites of speech. In Campbell, R. N. and Smith, P. T. (Eds.) *Recent Advances in the Psychology of Language: Language Development and Mother—Child Interaction.* New York: Plenum Press.

Chomsky, N. (1965) *Aspects of the Theory of Syntax.* Cambridge, Mass: M.I.T. Press.

Dasen, P., Inhelder, B., Lavallée, M. and Retschitzki, J. (1978) *Naissance de l'Intelligence Chez l'Enfant Baoulé de Côte d'Ivoire.* Berne: Hans Huber.

Donaldson, M. and Lloyd, P. (1974) Sentences and situations: children's judgments of match and mismatch. In *Problèmes Actuels de Psycholinguistique.* Paris: Editions du Centre National de la Recherche Scientifique.

Ferreiro, E. (1971) *Les Relations Temporelles dans le Langage de l'Enfant.* Genève: Droz.

Forman, G. E., Kushner, D. and Dempsey, J. (1975) *Transformations in the manipulations and productions performed with geometric objects: an early system of logic in young children.* Publication of the Center for Early Childhood Education, School of Education, University of Massachusetts, Amherst.

Furth, H. G. (1966) *Thinking Without Language.* New York: Free Press.

Inhelder, B. and Piaget, J. (1959) *La Genèse des Structures Logiques Élémentaires.* Neuchâtel: Delachaux and Niestlé. English edition (1964) *The Early Growth of Logic in the Child.* London: Routledge and Kegan Paul.

Janet, P. (1936) *L'Intelligence Avant le Langage.* Paris: Flammarion.

Karmiloff-Smith, A. (1977) More about the same: children's understanding of post-articles. *Journal of Child Language,* **4**, 377-394.

Lieven, E. (1978) Turn taking and pragmatics: two issues in early child language. In Campbell, R. N. and Smith, P. T. (Eds.) *Recent Advances in the Psychology of Language: Language Development and Mother—Child Interaction.* New York: Plenum Press.

McNeill, D. (1969) In Koestler, A. and Smythies, J. R. (Eds.) *Beyond Reductionism. The Alpbach Symposium.* New York: Hutchinson.

Moreno, L., Rayna, S., Sinclair, H., Stambak, M. and Verba, M. (1976) *Les Bébés et la Logique.* Paris: CRESAS.

Oleron, P. and Herren, H. (1961) L'acquisition des conservations et le langage. *Enfance,* **4**, 201-219.

Piaget, J. (1923) *Le Langage et la Pensée Chez l'Enfant.* Neuchâtel: Delachaux and Niestlé. English edition (1926) *The Language and Thought of the Child.* London: Routledge and Kegan Paul.

Piaget, J. (1924) *Le Jugement et le Raisonnement Chez l'Enfant.* Neuchâtel: Delachaux and Niestlé. English edition (1926) *Judgment and Reasoning in the Child.* New York: Harcourt and Brace.

Piaget, J. (1932) *Le Jugement Moral Chez l'Enfant.* Paris: Alcan. English edition (1932) *The Moral Judgment of the Child.* New York: Harcourt.

Piaget, J. (1936) *La Naissance de l'Intelligence.* Neuchâtel: Delachaux and Niestlé. English edition (1952) *The Origins of Intelligence in Children.* New York: International University Press.

Piaget, J. (1946) *La Formation du Symbole Chez l'Enfant.* Neuchâtel: Delachaux and Niestlé. English edition (1951) *Play, Dreams, Imitation in Childhood.* New York: Norton.

Piaget, J. (1954) Le langage et la pensée du point de vue génétique. In Revesz, G. (Ed.) *Thinking and Speaking.* Amsterdam: North Holland Publishing.

Piaget, J. (1956) *Problèmes de Psychologie Génétique.* Moscow: Voprossi Psykhologuii.

Piaget, J. (1961) *Les Mécanismes Perceptifs: Modèles Probabilistes, Analyse Génétique, Relations avec l'Intelligence.* Paris: PUF.

Piaget, J. (1963) Le langage et les opérations intellectuelles. In Ajuriaguerra (de), J., Bresson, F., Fraisse, P., Inhelder, B., Oléron, P. and Piaget, J. *Problèmes de Psycholinguistique.* Paris: PUF.

Piaget, J. (1964) *Six Études de Psychologie.* Genève: Gonthier. English edition (1967) *Six Psychological Studies.* New York: Random House.

Piaget, J. and Inhelder, B. (1966) *La Psychologie de l'Enfant.* Paris: PUF: (Que sais-je.) English edition (1969) *The Psychology of the Child.* New York: Routledge and Kegan Paul/Basic Books.

Piaget, J. (1968) *Le Structuralisme.* Paris: PUF. (Que sais-je.) English edition (1971) *Structuralism.* London: Routledge and Kegan Paul.

Piaget, J., Inhelder, B. and Sinclair, H. (1968) *Mémoire et Intelligence.* Paris: PUF. *Memory and Intelligence.* London: Routledge and Kegan Paul.

Piaget, J. (1970) *L'Épistémologie Génétique.* Paris: PUF. (Que sais-je.) Genetic Epistemology. In *Norton Paperbacks on Psychiatry and Psychology.* New York: Norton. 1971.

Piaget, J. (1975) *L'Équilibration des Structures Cognitives: Problème Central du Développement.* Paris: PUF.

Piaget, J., et al (1977) *Recherches sur l'Abstraction Réfléchissante.* Paris: PUF. 2 volumes.

Sinclair, H. (1971) Sensorimotor action patterns as a condition for the acquisition of syntax. In Huxley, R. and Ingram, E. (Eds.) *Language Acquisition: Models and Methods.* New York: Academic Press.

Sinclair, H. (1973) Language acquisition and cognitive development. In Moore, T. E. (Ed.) *Cognitive Development and the Acquisition of Language.* New York: Academic Press.

Sinclair, H. (1975) The role of cognitive structures in language acquisition. In Lenneberg, E. H. and Lenneberg, E. *Foundations of Language Development,* Volume I. New York: Academic Press.

Sinclair, H., Berthoud-Papandropoulou, J., Bronckart, J. P., Chipman, H., Ferreiro, E. and Rappe Du Cher, E. (1976) *Recherches en psycholinguistique génétique.* Archives de psychologie, **XLIV**, No. 171.

Slobin, D. (1973) Cognitive prerequisites for the development of grammar. In Ferguson, C. and Slobin, D. (Eds.) *Studies in Language Development.* New York: Holt, Rinehart and Winston.

Slobin, D. (1979) Invited address to the Fiftieth Annual Meeting of the Eastern Psychological Association, Philadelphia, April.

Snow, C. and Ferguson, C. (1977) *Talking to Children: Language Input and Acquisition.* Cambridge: Cambridge University Press.

Verba, M., Stambak, M., Rayna, S. and Bonica, L. (1979) *Les Échanges dans une Situation d'Expérimentation Physique.* Paris: CRESAS.

Vincent-Borelli, M. (1956) La naissance des opérations logiques chez les enfants sourds-muets. *Enfance,* **4,** 222-238, et *Enfance,* **9,** 1-20.

Interchange

ELLIOT AND DONALDSON REPLY TO SINCLAIR

We welcome the clear account which Professor Sinclair gives of Piaget's views on language. The way in which she has made use of the distinction between structure and function in communicating the essence of his ideas seems to us to be very helpful. She has also drawn attention to some places where Piaget gives recognition to certain aspects of language acquisition which he does not usually stress.

Professor Sinclair confines herself largely to an exegesis of Piaget's writings and does not make much comment upon them. With her interpretation of his views we have no quarrel.

SINCLAIR REPLIES TO ELLIOT AND DONALDSON

Piaget's assessment of the role of language in the development of thought is the first point discussed by Elliot and Donaldson. Throughout their paper they take 'language' in the sense of interpersonal verbal exchange. As I showed in my own paper, it is precisely to language in this sense that Piaget attributes a constructive role in the development of thinking, just as Elliot and Donaldson do. The latter, however, consider that 'in limiting this (constructive) role to the extent that he does, Piaget goes much too far'. They appear to argue that Piaget did not give enough weight to interpersonal verbal exchange, because he neglected 'the child as a questioner' and because he 'did not decenter . . . to the notion that knowledge verbally requested is knowledge actively sought'. This is astounding, for nobody to my knowledge has paid more attention than Piaget to children's spontaneous search for knowledge and their verbal questions. In *Le Langage et la Pensée Chez l'Enfant* Piaget devotes an entire chapter to the analysis of 1125 spontaneous questions asked by one child over a period of 10 months and starts by stating: 'There is no better introduction to the study of children's logic than a study of their spontaneous questions.' And indeed, from this first collection of questions and many others as well, Piaget sketched the outline of his theory about the development of logical implication on the one hand and causal explanation on the other. Moreover, Piaget's experimental method (called the 'clinical' and, later, the 'critical exploratory' method, but whose essential characteristics have not changed) assigns an important part to children's spontaneous questions as is quite clear from the very first detailed description he gave of his interviewing technique. To quote from *La Représentation du Monde chez l'Enfant* (p. 8): 'The detailed study of children's spontaneous questions reveals their interests at different ages and shows us many problems they are concerned with which we might never have thought of or which we would never have formulated in the same terms . . . We may thus state the first rule of our method: when a particular type of explanation given by children is to be studied, the questions we will ask them will be determined in content and in form by the spontaneous questions asked by children of the same age or younger.' One may regret, as I do, that Piaget did not devote more of his time to the study of interpersonal verbal exchange, but one cannot reproach him with not having paid attention to the child as a questioner.

The second point discussed by Elliot and Donaldson concerns Piaget's use of language in psychological experiments. This is, indeed, an interesting problem. As long ago as 1963, Flavell (pp. 434—438) gave an excellent survey of the issues raised by (to use the same terms as Elliot and Donaldson) the receptive and expressive language of the child who is being interviewed. In contrast with Flavell's clear exposé, Elliot and Donaldson's argumentation is, in my opinion, confusing. The confusion is partly due to the fact that though they often refer to 'misinterpretations of questions and instructions by the child' that are supposed to occur during Piaget-type interviews, the examples they give concern, with one exception (Donaldson's and Lloyd's 1974 study, already quoted in my paper), the total dynamics of the adult-experimenter cum child-subject situation rather than its linguistic aspect. But the confusion is mainly due to two misconceptions the authors entertain: concerning the nature of the Piagetian experiments and the different methods by which the results have been obtained.

The various conservation concepts are key notions in physics, and the history of science shows us their gradual, often difficult, elaboration by scientists. Piaget and Inhelder had the brilliant idea to study the construction of some of these concepts by the (epistemic) child-subject: theirs was an epistemological concern, not a desire to construct a new set of tests to determine children's cognitive levels. The same can be said about the other tasks designed by Piaget and his collaborators. Many of the tasks are presented in a non-verbal form as well as in a verbal one; unfortunately the former are much less well known. The interested reader should consult *L'Image Mentale Chez l'Enfant* and *Mémoire et Intelligence* for striking constructions and drawings by non conservers showing the same 'mistaken' theories as can be inferred from their verbal exchanges with the experimenter. The mistaken yet constructive theories can only be brought to light under certain experimental conditions. When shown two identical bottles filled with liquid, one of which is emptied into an ordinary glass, and when asked to point to where the liquid from the other bottle will come up to in another, tall and thin glass, children at a certain stage will carefully put the two glasses together and show a level in the second glass identical with the level in the first— to be very surprised indeed when the level actually goes up much higher. When asked, before pouring, whether there will be the same amount to drink in the thin glass as in the other, they will answer: 'Of course; the bottles are the same, and you say you are going to pour it all.' In the first situation, the child gives a 'non-conserving' answer; in the second, as in most real-life situations, he gives a 'conserving' answer because nothing in the general context of the question activates a conflicting theory based on the (often correct) idea that 'going further means winning'. How can results such as the pointing to an identical level in the two glasses of different shape be considered 'errors . . . [that] have their source in what (from a formal point of view) are misinterpretations of questions or instructions by the child' (Elliot and Donaldson)? In individual cases and in dialogue-type tasks, misunderstandings may very well occur, but the enormous bulk of data, both in verbal and non-verbal tasks obtained with many thousands of children speaking many different languages, show clearly the type of pre-theories children have about epistemologically important notions.

Thus, the tasks are meant to study the epistemic development of certain concepts in the child, not to determine the cognitive level of a particular child or group of children. It is true that the tasks can be used in situations where it is important to assess the cognitive level of a particular subject or of a group of subjects, as may happen in learning studies or in studies of pathology. In such instances, the experimenter has to proceed very cautiously, using the freedom of the exploratory method but keeping the situation and the questions constant as far as possible across subjects, and he may have to modify certain of the 'traditional' aspects of the tasks (c.f. Inhelder et al's critique of the traditional class-inclusion questions for a learning study, 1974). What should not be done is to transform the tasks into tests whose results can be subjected to statistical treatment (such as 'differences significant at the 0.001 level', quoted with approval by Elliot and Donaldson). Used this way, I cannot but agree that the tasks are 'simply not a good way of finding out what the [child's cognitive] level is'.

The fact that under certain conditions children do better than under others raises different issues, which can also be interesting, just as it is interesting that children do indeed progress during learning sessions or that nowadays Genevan children appear to attain certain conservation concepts earlier than their counterparts 30 years ago. But such results are no challenge to the theory. The theory would be challenged if it could be shown that the key concepts are elaborated in a way that is very different from the developmental stages described by Piaget. If it turned out that children before a certain age simply have no theories at all and answer haphazardly, or that they do not have some kind of 'going-beyond-means-more' theory, but an idea such as 'rough objects always weigh more than smooth objects' (to invent a more specific example), or if they were found to master proportions before numerical equivalence, the theory would indeed have to be revised. But until now, such findings have not been reported. Results of the kind discussed by Elliot and Donaldson may clarify certain points, bring to light aspects of child development not discussed by Piaget and his co-workers, and add useful information (generally of a more psychological than epistemological nature), but they are not in contradiction with the theory.

REFERENCES

Flavell, J. (1963) *The Developmental Psychology of Jean Piaget.* Princeton: Van Nostrand.
Piaget, J. (1923) *Le Langage et la Pensée Chez l'Enfant.* Neuchatel: Delachaux and Niestlé.
Piaget, J. (1926) *La Représentation du Monde Chez l'Enfant.* Paris: P.U.F.
Piaget, J. and Inhelder, B. (1966) *L'Image Mentale Chez l'Enfant.* Paris: P.U.F.
Piaget, J. and Inhelder, B. (1968) *Mémoire et Intelligence.* Paris: P.U.F.

Chapter 10

Piaget on Morality: A Critical Perspective

HELEN WEINREICH-HASTE

INTRODUCTION

Longevity presents problems to the critic. Because Piaget was until very recently still active and still developing his theory, it is usual to refer to his latest work in a particular area. Most of his studies of forty or fifty years ago on thought and language have been expanded or subsumed by later writings. *The Moral Judgment of the Child*, however, was not followed up; it remained an aside. Some of the issues raised by the studies, for example, egocentrism, were explored in other contexts, but Piaget never developed the main theoretical issues. In the monograph he hypothesized a parallel relationship between moral and conceptual development, which his later studies could have elaborated, but he never integrated his moral and his conceptual studies. It has been left to others to do this.

The monograph has been very influential and has generated many replications and critical studies. As Wright (1982) has pointed out, 'it is a relatively easy task to point out the obscurities, inconsistencies and idiosyncrasies in Piaget's thinking'. While this is true, it is surprising that the majority of criticisms have concentrated on selected issues and methodology; few have taken the theory as a whole and critically explored its implications. Therefore, in this chapter I intend to review the major criticisms, but my main focus will be on three issues, two of which have received relatively little attention. Firstly, I shall consider Piaget's main thesis, which is essentially social-psychological, and which has largely been ignored by subsequent writers. Secondly, I shall consider the implications of Piaget's definition of morality. Thirdly, I shall consider the empirical and theoretical material in the monograph which relates to the development of moral judgment. In my final section I shall consider how later theoretical work in the area has moderated or expanded Piaget's work.

It is worth locating the historical context of *The Moral Judgment of the Child* by reference to its contemporaries. It was published two years after Freud's *Civilization and Its Discontents*. In America, the prominent psychologists were Terman, Gesell and Lashley; the full tide of learning theory had barely begun. Hartshorne and May had just published their character study. The dominant interest of many psychologists was the development of quantitative assessment techniques of personality and intelligence. Simultaneously, on both sides of the Atlantic, there was lively interest in psycho-analytic theory and research. The implications of both approaches were being explored in educational practice and theory. It was a period of practical experiments in non-authoritarian education, based on a variety of interpretations of Rousseau and Freud. Piaget refers with favour to French examples, the 'Activity Schools' (Hilgard, 1958; Flugel, 1964).

One area where the historical context merits examination is methodology. Piaget's attitude to methodology strikes the present-day psychologist as odd. Today we feel obliged to justify the use of qualitative methods, and implicitly or explicitly validate them by reference to some form of quantification. Piaget constantly apologises for using any quantitative data at all, on the grounds that only through qualitative techniques can we understand the processes of the child's thinking. It is not surprising that a major criticism of Piaget's work has come from American and British psychologists trained in the positivistic, statistical tradition. It is only relatively recently that anglophone psychologists have rediscovered process and structure, and the limitations of positivistic methods for examining these.

Piaget's orientation to methodology arises from his attitude to the importance of epistemology, and the close relationship between psychology and philosophy—a relationship which behaviourist psychologists explicitly severed. Yet, at the time he was writing the monograph, dogmatic empiricism was not entrenched even in America; clinical and statistical techniques, later brought into confrontation (Meehl, 1954; Miller, 1962), largely existed side by side as alternative, if debated, methods.

To criticize with historical awareness, therefore, demands some circumspection. The temptation is to take a present-day perspective and criticize the writer in terms of that. Disciples as well as critics may be selective in this way. It is a salutary experience to return to the original and attempt to work within its own parameters, and to find things that were taken for granted at time of writing, but which have recently been *re-discovered* in psychology.

PIAGET'S THESIS: A SUMMARY

Piaget's prime concern in the monograph was an examination of the psychological implications of the theories of the sociologists, Durkheim, Fauconnet and Bovet, about societal morality and its transmission to the next generation. He was engaging in a social psychological exercise: the description of developmental change was an integral part of his social psychological explanation, but the implications of the evidence for a theory of developmental processes were largely incidental to his main purpose.

The main argument of the monograph concerns one paradox: how can individual, autonomous morality develop out of the necessarily imposed morality of the 'adult' world? This is the paradox which Piaget argues that Durkheim had failed to solve, and which he himself attempts to solve by reference to developmental and social psycho-logical explanation. His primary explanation is in terms of the interaction between the child, the parent and peers, and developmental changes which are manifested in 'the two moralities of the child'; the morality of constraint and the morality of co-operation. Piaget's main thesis is that the form of 'respect' changes, from a unilateral respect for authority to a mutual respect for peers, and that this change is consequent upon peer interaction, and upon the changing cognitive perspectives which this interaction facilitates. Fauconnet's work on objective and subjective responsibility, and Bovet's work on respect, are invoked as explanations of the processes involved in the developmental changes which Piaget demonstrated.

Central to the thesis and its exegesis is Piaget's implicit moral theory, which he shared with Durkheim. Both are part of the rationalist tradition of Kant and Rousseau. To quote a later Kantian: 'moral learning is not so much a matter of supplying missing motives as one of the free development of our innate intellectual and emotional capacities according to their natural bent. Once the powers of understanding mature and persons come to recognize their place in society and are able to take up the standpoint of others, they appreciate the mutual benefits of establishing fair terms of social co-operation . . . natural sympathy for other persons and innate susceptibility to the pleasures of fellow feeling and self-mastery . . . provide the affective basis for the moral sentiments once we have a clear grasp of our relations to our associates from an appropriately general perspective. Thus this tradition regards moral feelings as a natural outgrowth of a full appreciation of our social nature' (Rawls, 1971, pp. 459—460). Rawls relies quite heavily on Piaget in elaborating his own model for the development of a sense of justice. Rawls contrasted the Kantian, rationalist model with the Humean model that moral development is about the development of appropriate *motives*. His preference for the former is explicit: '(it) presents a happier picture, since it holds that the principles of right and justice spring from our nature and are not at odds with our good, whereas the other account would seem to hold no such guarantee' (op. cit., p. 461). This viewpoint is implicit in Piaget's work, and, indeed, the monograph is directed towards demonstrating how those principles evolve.

SUBSEQUENT RESEARCH AND THE MAJOR CRITIQUES

Subsequent research has largely ignored Piaget's main thesis. Researchers have, on the whole, concentrated on the account of developmental changes in moral thinking, and have focused upon particular aspects of the original study. The areas which have had particular attention are the absolute versus relative nature of moral judgment, the belief in immanent justice, and intentionality (the development of subjective responsibility), (Lickona, 1976; Modgil and Modgil, 1976). Most of the research replicating or extending Piaget's study has confirmed his general findings, though there have been differences in the rate of growth found.

The monograph has been heavily criticized, particularly on empirical grounds. These criticisms, to some extent, reflect changing preoccupations and models in developmental psychology. In 1969 Lickona enumerated the various 'misinterpretations' which characterized much of the criticism of the monograph. These misinterpretations arise in several cases from a conceptual gap between the critic and the framework within which Piaget was working. In the 1950s, certain fundamental differences in assumptions made Piaget's work essentially incomprehensible to the anglophone psychologist of the positivist tradition. 'Intelligence', for example, for most anglophone psychologists of the period meant 'a hereditary potential for intellectual growth which experience can develop, but only within genetically set limits' (Lickona, 1969). Intelligence, therefore, was a *measurable, independent variable*. Piaget, in contrast, regarded intelligence as a *process*.

Criticisms that Piaget ignored demographic factors such as sex, culture and social class reflect different approaches to explanation, and different models of the person.

Implicit in Piaget's work is a model of the person as active, seeking to comprehend, learning through experimentation and through the development of increasingly complex categorization and organization of experience. In learning theory, the implicit model of the person is passive. One of the rationales for the individual differences approach is that, by isolating all the variables involved in a phenomenon, one eventually arrives at a valid construct and, at the same time, identifies the determining characteristics. The tradition within which Piaget operated, emphasizes structure and process, and starts, therefore, with the phenomenon itself; not with its contingencies and antecedents. An example of the learning theory perspective is the criticism of Bandura and Macdonald, who attempted to demonstrate that the order of stages of development could be inverted by reinforced role-modelling. In a sense they succeeded, in that some subjects did conform to the adult model. However, their theoretical assumption was that the malleability of the child's thinking in this social situation was evidence that the *whole* of the child's thinking originated from reward and punishment. An alternative to Bandura and Macdonald's conclusions is that the child behaved entirely in accordance with known characteristics of conformity behaviour. Le Furgy and Woloshin (1969) and Cowan et al (1969) replicated Bandura and Macdonald's study and argued that only situational, not developmental, conclusions could be drawn from their findings.

Many psychologists have had difficulties with the concept of an invariant sequence of stages. The concept of maturation, a biological phenomenon translated into child psychology, particularly by Gesell, has frequently been invoked as the explanation of Piaget's stages. A number of psychologists, including Bandura and Macdonald, pitted a social learning theory model against Piaget because they regarded him as a hereditarian. For psychologists who accept the evidence of the invariant sequence and prefer to interpret it in terms of maturation, there remains the problem of accounting for a 'biological' basis of morality. Wilson has recently attempted a socio-biological analysis of stages of moral reasoning (1978).

Criticism of the sequence or nature of *stages* of moral development is also in several senses a misinterpretation. Relatively few studies have failed to replicate the order and form of the change in moral thinking, but many have found differences in the rate of development. Others have also demonstrated inconsistency; the child appears to be at a heteronomous 'stage' in one area but show autonomous thought elsewhere. However, Piaget never claimed consistency or other 'stage' properties of moral thinking; he explicitly refers to 'phases'. While he argued for qualitative changes between the two moralities, he did not consider that development in this area had the same characteristics as cognitive development.

The social-psychological questions which are Piaget's main thesis have virtually been ignored; the majority of studies have focused on the developmental changes in specific areas of moral reasoning—especially intentionality, immanent justice, objective responsibility. Researchers have not tested the wide range of moral thought, nor examined the theoretical basis. The conception of rules is fundamental to Piaget's theory and is certainly the most adequately documented area in the monograph, yet it has hardly been studied by subsequent researchers. Lickona cites one unpublished paper in the area, Modgil and Modgil cite none. I have been unable to trace any work. Some studies have tackled the developmental hypotheses, egocentrism and decentration, for example (Ugurel-Semin, 1952; Stuart, 1967), and some attention has been paid to the relationship between cognitive processes and moral reasoning (Lee, 1971; Hardeman, 1972). The central hypothesis about the effect of social and authority relations has, however, been tested only by indirect measures. Some researchers have examined the effect of authoritarian versus non-authoritarian environments—either parental or school—on the level of moral reasoning (Macrae, 1954; Johnson, 1962).

Others have examined the effect of peer interaction—frequently via an indirect measure of the child's sociability and popularity (e.g. Kohlberg, 1958). One variation is the work of Breznitz and Kugelmass, who investigated the differences between kibbutz versus urban children in intentionality judgments (1967); they found none.

The methodological critiques of the monograph have on occasion been used to dismiss the findings and by implication the whole theoretical framework. Recently, Kurtines and Greif (1974) wrote a substantial methodological critique of Kohlberg's research which they dismissed on the grounds that it used unsound 'projective' techniques. This is an inaccurate description of Kohlberg's and Piaget's methods, and reflects again a misunderstanding arising from positivistic assumptions (Broughton, 1978). On the whole, however, it is recognized that there is no adequate alternative to the open-ended method of eliciting the processes of moral reasoning (Pittel and Mendelsohn, 1966; Rest, 1974).

A further critique which reflects basic differences in assumptions is that moral judgment fails to correlate with moral behaviour. This critique is best considered in the wider context of the relationship between attitudes and behaviour. One theoretical assumption is that attitudes are interesting to psychologists primarily as a mediation between stimulus and behaviour; if attitudes do not predict behaviour, their functions are unclear and the methodological problems attached to their measurement not worth overcoming. While this criticism is rarely expressed in such crude terms in social psychology, it does appear in the area of moral development. If moral judgments do not predict moral behaviour, of what interest can they possibly be? Yet the argument that attitudes predict behaviour has long been questioned. Mainstream social psychology has for a long time focused on situational factors in behaviour and attitudes as post-hoc reflections upon behaviour, as cognitions, explanations or justifications (Festinger, 1957; Moscovici, 1978; Semin and Manstead, 1979).

These criticisms arise from a tradition of psychology which also equates moral development with the acquisition of habits and the inculcation into the child of the conventional beliefs and habits of her culture. If socialization is successful, according to this view the articulated belief must be validated by behaviour. This model of morality and socialization is a combination of the Humean model of morality and the social-learning model of development. The acquisition of guilt, in particular pre-transgression anxiety, is the prime focus of this approach. Guilt is a motive which (1) can be seen as classically conditioned, and (2) as a prevention, therefore a predictive contingency of anti-social or immoral action (Eysenck, 1976). The one area in which a clear correlation between behaviour and moral reasoning has been established is conformity. Using Kohlberg's measures, several studies have demonstrated that the highest and lowest stages of moral reasoning correlate with non-conformity—though only the highest stages correlate with refusing to conform on matters of principle. It is the middle stages of moral thinking which correlate with conformity to conventional behaviour (Milgram, 1965; Salzstein, Diamond and Belenky, 1972; McNamee, 1977). Traditional socialization models cannot adequately account for these results. (See Weinreich-Haste 1979(b).)

THE PRESENT CRITIQUE

I shall consider three areas, which have, in my view, been overlooked in the existing critiques. First, I shall consider the main thesis of Piaget which has largely been ignored. Second, I shall consider the definition of morality which is implicit in Piaget's work, and the limitations which this definition places on analysis and theory. Third, I shall consider the research which Piaget described in the monograph, and examine the evidence and arguments for developmental stages of moral thinking. Finally, I shall consider the implications for Piaget's work of the subsequent work of Kohlberg, Damon and Selman.

Piaget's Thesis

Subsequent fragmentation of the themes which Piaget investigated has tended to obscure the wholeness of the original. Piaget's main purpose was to criticize Durkheim's basic position, that morality is always 'imposed by the group upon the individual and by the adult upon the child'. Therefore, in the monograph, Piaget was less interested in the actual moral development of the *child*, and more interested in the social-psychological question: What are the mechanisms operating between individual and society in the transmission of morality? He utilized the developmental material as a means of pursuing this thesis. My argument is that he failed in this, but that he made a contribution to developmental psychology almost by default. The emphasis of subsequent research, of course, reflects the success of his developmental material. However, it is arguable that developmental social psychology has been impoverished by its failure to attend to Piaget's social psychological insights, incomplete though they were.

Authority was the central concept of Durkheim's sociological perspective. Another commentator has written that Durkheim was 'engrossed in the problem of authority—that is, social authority—and its relation to state, economy, and other major spheres. It is not extreme to say that Durkheim was obsessed by authority. His entire approach to the understanding of religion, of morality, of reason itself, stems from his profound sense of the role of social authority in human lives. Each of these is, in its most imposing form, itself a type of authority; each emanates from that larger authority which is the social bond' (Nisbet, 1974, p. 438).

Piaget criticized Durkheim's perspective on a number of points, concerned with social-psychological issues involved in the processes of moral transmission. For example, he picked up an important and unresolved paradox inherent in Durkheim's position. If all morality is imposed, there is an inevitable confusion of the morality of constraint and the morality of co-operation. Further, there can be no distinction between 'is' and 'ought'. If what is transmitted is the orthodoxy, there can be no gap between the actual and the ideal; the 'good' must be that which is established. This paradox involves the distinction between duty and the good. If morality is constrained, then the good must of necessity be identical to duty.

Piaget argued that the solution is to look at the developmental change in the understanding of morality, a change which he claimed is from the simple acceptance of the voice of power to a morality of respect and co-operation. The consequence of this change is the development of 'true' morality, and morality which is autonomous but functional to individual and society. The *definition* of morality is therefore of great importance. Morality is a *method of reasoning*. 'In the midst of the network of groupings which constitute our present society, individuals agree, not so much to preserve a set of dogmas and rites, as to apply a "method" or set of methods. What we affirm is verified by the others; what is done is tried out and tested by the others. The essence of experimental behaviour—whether scientific, technical or moral—consists, not in a common belief, but in rules of mutual control. Everyone is free to bring in innovations, but only in so far as he succeeds in making himself understood by others and understanding them' (Piaget, 1932, p. 347).

The method 'implies that certain provisional truths have been established but above all . . . there is more to discover'. He criticized Durkheim for conceiving of morality as consisting of givens, and argued that '"common morality" does not consist in a "thing" given to individuals from without, but in a sum of relations between individuals. Common morality would thus be defined by the system of laws of perspective enabling one to pass from one point of view to the other, and allowing in consequence the making of a map . . . in this case each individual perspective could be different from the others and at the same time adequate' (p. 352).

This definition of the method of morality integrates a social psychology of inter-action with a cognitive model of social construction. Morality becomes not the rules as such, but the *understanding* of rules, roles and relations. Co-operation, therefore, is the *manifestation* of morality, but for Piaget, co-operative *behaviour* was also a necessary precursor and antecedent of articulated, conscious cognition of rules.

The process which, according to Piaget, links morality of constraint and morality of co-operation is *respect*, and here again Piaget departed from Durkheim in his definitions. The essence of the authority relationship is the respect which the child has for the adult or the powerful peer. Piaget accepted Bovet's much more individualized notion of respect, which allows for mutual, (not simply unilateral) respect, born of equality and co-operation; 'it is sufficient in (Bovet's) view that there should be contact between two individuals for one to respect the other, and for those moral values to appear which are born of this respect' (p. 375). Respect, and the developmental changes in its form, was thus the central issue in Piaget's developmental study. His developmental material did indeed demonstrate just such changes; the child orientates initially to the voice of authority at least in *justification* and *explanation* of the rule (even though she may not actually *obey* the adult).

The evidence of forms of respect is substantial ammunition against Durkheim's position. Unfortunately, Piaget's thesis was that changes in the form of respect and in the reasoning of the child with regard to rules arise from the *social situation* surrounding the transmission of values, that unilateral respect is the consequence of constraint exercised by adults, and that mutual respect is the consequence of peer interaction. For this Piaget produced no evidence. His developmental material demonstrated that the implications of Durkheim's position are not tenable, but he failed to demonstrate the social psychological mechanisms which were presented as alternatives to those of Durkheim. His social psychological thesis depends on an analysis of the role of the parent or authority figure, firstly in imposing a constraint, and secondly in creating the psychological environment in which the child may be free to develop a morality of co-operation. The interaction processes which instigate the development of a morality of co-operation require analysis of the peer relationships. Despite the centrality of this to his thesis, Piaget in fact made no attempt to test it. He frequently *asserted* the importance of both parent and peer behaviour, and cited exemplars of the kind of regime which he considered conducive to development, but nowhere did he test this. Most subsequent research has been within a developmental psychological framework, treating the relevant variables as determinants of individual development, rather than as manifestations of the wider social-psychological question of the transmission of morality. Some studies do bear indirectly on the social-psychological hypotheses. Researchers have demonstrated that authoritarian environ-ments are on the whole more likely than 'progressive' ones to slow down the movement from heteronomous to autonomous thinking, but the evidence suggests that this is particularly due to the strong emphasis on the values of rule-following and obedience, rather than on limitations on the opportunities for peer interaction (Boehm and Nass, 1962; Breznitz and Kugelmass, 1967; Baumrind and Black, 1967). Two studies, however, have been of value in illuminating the *processes* involved.

The work of Hoffman on the effects of parental techniques on the form of moral reasoning and motivation in young people provides indirect support for Piaget's propositions. The subjects in the study were considerably older than Piaget's, and under investigation was the *type*, not the *stage*, of moral reasoning. Hoffman found evidence that inductive techniques produced more rational, independent and autonomous morality, and techniques involving either physical or psychological power relationship were more conducive to an immature, affect-bound form of morality. These findings have some relevance for the social-psychological variables involved in the transmission of morality (Hoffman, 1963, 1970).

Bronfenbrenner's well-known studies of the contrasts between US and Soviet methods of 'character education' did highlight the theoretical approach of Makarenko which has much in common with Piaget's conception of the importance of peer relations (Bronfenbrenner, 1962; Garbarino and Bronfenbrenner, 1976). Bronfenbrenner found striking evidence in the Russian system of the effectiveness of peer allegiance, even against adult pressures, and of the way in which teachers utilized this, in fact, to transmit effectively the 'adult-approved' value system. The children in his studies had a powerful conception of ingroup allegiance and intergroup competition, and strong shame reactions associated with 'letting the side down'. This data is, of itself, demonstration of the significance of peer interaction at the relevant age, but not specifically of the developmental processes which Piaget postulated in association with peer interaction. As Piaget himself noted, there is little difference between power-asserted constraint by parents and by peers, and it is possible to argue that co-operation is easily confused with constraint in the setting Bronfenbrenner described. A further objection has subsequently been put forward by Bronfenbrenner (Garbarino and Bronfenbrenner, 1976), that the Soviet system is *monolithic*; although the peer group is the agent for instilling and maintaining co-operation, the message is identical to that which the adults would choose to put over, if they were acting as constraints; Western society in contrast is *pluralistic*; the child receives conflicting messages from various sources, and the growth process is facilitated by the child learning to negotiate these conflicts. In view of Piaget's avowedly dialectical model, it is likely that he would agree with the spirit if not the letter of Bronfenbrenner's later, revised ideas.

It is perhaps unfortunate that Piaget invested so much of his theoretical resource in the monograph in the sociological and social-psychological theory. He spent relatively little time extending the theoretical—as opposed to the descriptive—aspects of development. The interesting theoretical issues are scattered in the monograph. He reiterated a number of points, for example, on respect, throughout the monograph, but in terms of their social rather than their developmental implications. For example, the most complete of his studies, both empirically and theoretically, is the first section on the rules of games. It is also the one area where there is actually some evidence of the effect of experience and peer interaction. Yet it is not until the last pages of the monograph that the significance of the inclusion of rules in his definitions of morality becomes explicit: 'As for sympathy, it has of itself nothing moral in the eyes of conscience. To be sensitive alone is not to be good; sympathy must be canalized and steadied . . . sympathy is natural to the self. But before this sympathy can acquire a moral character there must be a common law, a system of rules' (p. 395). These sentiments are virtually identical to Rawls' position, quoted earlier: the rule defines the good and the moral.

It is essential to Piaget's position *vis-à-vis* Durkheim that the rule is not simply a reflection of adult morality, but something which develops of itself, changing with the child's changing consciousness and conceptualization. Following Baldwin, he identified three phases of rule consciousness: firstly, the law is the voice of command within the self—the adualistic, egocentric parent internalized, but not differentiated from the self; secondly, the law is generalized to others, and thirdly, the content of the law is elaborated through practical intelligence and autonomous reasoning. The egocentrism of the first phase has parallels in logical thinking: 'In the psychology of the intellect it is this egocentrism that seems to us to explain the logic and the causality peculiar to the child: his difficulty in handling relations and in forming objective causal series, etc. From the social and moral point of view, it is this egocentrism which explains why, though he is so absorbed in others, that he conforms to examples and commands received from without, yet the child introduces into every piece of collective behaviour an irreducible element of individual interpretation and unconscious deformation. Hence, the *sui generis* attitude found among the smaller children with regard both to rules of games and to their parents' commands—an attitude of respect for the letter of the law and of waywardness in its application' (p. 399).

The above is an example of the tantalizing way in which Piaget introduced major insights about the relationship between cognitive and moral processes. Instead of pursuing the precise developmental analysis which he began, and for which he undoubtedly had the data and material available, he returned to invoking his vaguer and more limited social-psychological perspective. Subsequent development beyond the externality and imperativeness of the law, he said, must depend on something more 'than a mere ratification on the part of individual intelligence: there must be relations of a new type between individuals who meet as equals, relations founded on reciprocity, relations that will suppress egocentrism' (p. 401). In contrast, in a brief analysis of the egocentrism of the child's early rule conception, he did not invoke the parental variable, instead he concentrated on the processes of the child's thinking, and this analysis has a clarity and richness which is provocatively brief—a mere couple of pages.

Another exciting aspect of his developmental theory which was only fragmentarily examined, in several different parts of the monograph, is the notion of *conscious realization*. This process is fundamental to the cognitive theory. Action upon the world occurs first developmentally, and only after the passage of time does this become articulated conceptually. Sensorimotor action precedes and is the foundation for symbolic action.

Table 10.1 demonstrates clearly the parallel but sequential development of *motor*, or *habit* rules and their conscious realization. But it is only again at the end of the monograph that Piaget explored some of the theoretical issues in the process of conscious realization, in this case of the development of self-consciousness, and the progress out of egocentrism. It is really the only place in which he explored the processes of conscious realization, and it is particularly interesting that his account is a clear statement of a *dialectical* process: 'as the shuttle flies backwards and forwards between ejection and imitation, equilibrium is maintained between consciousness of self and awareness of others. "Moral consciousness" appears when the self is no longer in a state of harmony, when there is opposition between the various tendencies that constitute it' (p. 394). And later: 'In order to discover oneself as a particular individual, what is needed is a continuous comparison, the outcome of opposition, of discussion, and of mutual control, and indeed consciousness of the individual self appears far later than consciousness of the more general features in our psychological make-up. That is why a child can remain egocentric for a very long time . . . while participating on all points in the minds of others' (p. 410).

This brief exploration encapsulates many concepts which were to become central to Piaget's main cognitive thesis, and which have perhaps had their most recent elaboration in *The Grasp of Consciousness* (1977) in which Piaget elaborated in great detail the processes by which consciousness (or 'cognizance') of motor actions comes

Table 10.1 *Summary of the data presented by Piaget and*

Age [N.B.: ages in the data are frequently *approximate*][a]

N.B. Only in the Rules of the Game and Lying were children under 5 studied.

Age	Rules of the Game			Responsibility	Immanent Justice	Lying
	Marbles (boys)	Consciousness of Rule	Hide-and-seek (girls)			What are 'lies'
<5	Motor behaviour; individual, ritualized.	Rules not coercive in character— motoric, or, later, exemplary.	Egocentric, imitative.	Objective responsibility, culpability = amount of damage, etc.		
5	Play is egocentric, imitative, not co-operative. Child is aware of set of codified rules.	Rules respected as sacred and untouchable, emanating from adults and lasting forever. Alternatives seen as transgression.	Rules change but ritual is important. Similar view as boys regarding origin of rules.			Confusion of oaths and lies.
6					86%	
7	Co-operative play. Tries to win. Shows concern with mutual control and unitary set of rules.		Co-operative and competitive. New rules acceptable if practicable and agreed by group.		73%	Awareness of difference between lies and mistakes, but both 'lies'.
8						Distinction between lies and mistakes made explicitly.
						Average age for 'objective' response for lies: the bigger and less credible, the 'worse'.
9	Groups of players agree on the rules of the game, but appreciate variations in rules.	Rules as laws arising from mutual consent. Respected through loyalty, but changeable through negotiation.		Subjective responsibility, intention taken into account.	54%	
10						Average age for 'subjective' lie: blatant lies less bad because less credible. Distinction between lie and joke or exaggeration.
11	Rules codified. Procedure fixed and observed by whole group.					Intention to deceive as criterion of 'lie' made explicitly.
12+					34%	

[a]A line across the column indicates that Piaget divided his sample into groups

his associates in *'The Moral Judgment of the Child'*, 1932.

Lying / Punishment for Lying	Punishment and Retributive Justice	Distributive and Retributive Justice
Lies naughtier if punished at once: punishment *defines* naughtiness.	(Where offender in class is known to group.) Everyone should be punished because by not owning up/ telling everyone is guilty.	(Where offender is not known to group.) Everyone should be punished because wrong-doing requires punishment, even if innocent suffer.	70% believe it fair to reward 'good' child at expense of bad.
Lies naughty because they break *rule*.			
Deceipt destroys trust, so worse to lie to friend than to adult.	Everyone should accept punishment as an act of solidarity by group.	No-one should be punished because more unjust to punish innocent than to let guilty go.	40% believe it fair to reward virtue (older children also perceive instrumental advantage of equality: no revenge, better behaviour in response to love, etc.).
			25% believe it fair to reward virtue.

Punishment for Lying column:

30% mentioned reciprocity in punishment; general view that 'severest is best'.

49% mentioned reciprocity punishment as simple reciprocity. *Lex talionis*, emphasis on *equality*.

82% mentioned reciprocity punishment should be suitable, connected to, and proportional to, fault. Emphasis on *equity*.

Rotated marginal notes (Lying):
- 81% believe it is worse to lie to an adult than a child.
- 51%—equally bad to lie to adult and child.
- 17%—worse to lie to companion.

Rotated marginal notes (Punishment for Lying):
- Unanimously in favour of punishment as deterrent.
- Increasingly in favour of reasoning as more effective than punishment *per se*.

Rotated marginal notes (Distributive and Retributive Justice):
- Should report miscreant.
- Justice subordinated to adult authority.
- Should not report miscreant—even lie to parent or teacher to avoid 'sneaking'.
- Progressive egalitarianism.
- Equity

divided at that age. No line indicates that ages represented are approximate.

(Table 10.1 continues on p. 192)

Table 10.1 *(Continued)*

Age [N.B.: ages in the data are frequently *approximate*][a]

N.B. Only in the Rules of the Game and Lying were children under 5 studied.

Age	Justice and Fairness																	
	'What is unfair'				Treatment for Accidental Loss			Response to Unfair Order				Talion for Injustice			Cheating			
	[Acts which are 'forbidden']	[Going against rules of game]	[Inequality of treatment]	[Social injustice]	[Punish child for loss]	[Give child another to equal with siblings]	[Give child another because smallest (equity)]	[Just: should obey]	[Unjust: child defends equality (Rambert's study)]	[Just (Piaget's study)]	[Unjust]	[(Paying back a bully) right (Rambert's study)]	[Reasons based on authority]	[Reasons based on equality]	[Naughty because forbidden]	[Against rules of game]	[Makes co-operation impossible]	[Against equality]
6	64%	9%	27%	0%	48%	35%	17%	95%	5%	75%	25%	19%	100%	0%	64%	6%	0%	30%
7								55%	45%	15%	85%	33%						
8								33%	66%			65%	84%	16%				
9	7%	9%	73%	11%	3%	55%	42%	16%	83%			72%						
10								10%	90%			87%	68%	26%	8%	24%	20%	48%
11								5%	95%			91%	32%	62%				
12+					0%	5%	95%	0%	100%			95%	15%	62%				

about. The essence of the concepts of assimilation and accommodation are there, though expressed in different form, and Piaget was already exploring the notion of equilibration and its essentially dialectical nature.

As has been noted, subsequent research has selected and extracted, not taken Piaget's package as a whole. To understand what Piaget was trying to do, it is necessary to consider the logic of his package and, additionally, his implicit definition of morality. It is not immediately obvious why he chose the range of elements which he reported in the monograph, and why he excluded others. Apart from the centrality of rules, which, as we have seen, is a legacy of Piaget's Kantian inheritance, the rest of the package appears to be largely a collection of conventional moral precepts and avoidances. It can be argued that 'moral' is an arbitrary criterion. Piaget has, for example, used an essentially non-moral example to make substantial social and developmental points about rules. The rules of the game of marbles turn out to be an excellent means of investigating how children relate in a collaborative activity, and how the child comes to comprehend these relationships and the criteria by which they may be regulated. In many ways this is a straightforward extension of the earlier work, *The Child's Conception of the World*, in which Piaget explored the child's understanding of social and physical phenomena.

In other areas of the moral 'package', such as lying and causing damage, Piaget treated it as implicit that the *rules* governing them are transmitted from the adult culture to the child in the same way that the rules of marbles are transmitted from older to younger children. He demonstrated that the *attitude* of the child to these rules is similar to her attitude to the rules of marbles or hopscotch. His primary interest in these areas of 'morality' lay in the changing conception of 'fairness' or 'wrongness'.

Immanent justice, intentionality and responsibility have subsequently been investigated both as aspects of moral thinking and as examples of social and attribution processes. The findings do not, in fact, substantiate a change of morality from a morality of *constraint* to a morality of *co-operation*. They do, however, demonstrate a change from a morality of egocentric absolutism to a morality based on a relativistic conception, in which the child is able to take the perspective of others. In other words, the social-psychological thesis is not demonstrated, but the developmental-cognitive thesis is.

Piaget's failure to answer his own social-psychological questions should not blind us to the vital importance of the questions he did raise in trying to bridge sociology and psychology. These questions have not been adequately answered since. Indeed it is only recently that social psychologists have again begun to ask them: how does individual consciousness arise from collective or social consciousness and how does the reciprocal relationship between these two develop and change? The study of social or collective consciousness has been, and still is, the province of sociologists and political scientists. The study of individual consciousness has largely been the province of the psychologists, but in largely isolation from sociological issues. This narrowness of perspective has come under considerable criticism recently (e.g. Riegel, 1978).

For the 'passive' model in psychology there is no problem; the individual belief system reflects an increasingly 'accurate' absorption of the collective consciousness. For the 'active' model of the person, the problem is: How does the individual develop a differentiated mode of consciousness which is both a translation and an individualization of the collective mode? The individual initially has access to the collective consciousness via authority figures and later additionally through her own experience. But reception and comprehension of the collective knowledge is limited and distorted by the limitations of the individual's cognitive capacities. Piaget's work in the cognitive field examines just this process; the stages represent increasing comprehension of the physical world and by implication the individual ultimately arrives at a 'true' and accurate capacity for perceiving and conceiving. The parallel questions in the moral sphere are how the individual translates and develops an increasingly sophisticated conception of morality. As I shall later discuss, to some extent Kohlberg's work does just this, with specific reference to justice.

However, this is *not* the question which Piaget asks, but to some extent it is the question which he answers. His questions are: How does morality in society change and develop, and how does the individual come to understand ('respect') the rules of morality? This is explicit in the very first page of the monograph; 'All morality consists in a system of rules and the essence of all morality is to be sought for in the respect which the individual acquires for these rules . . . the doctrines begin to diverge only from the moment that it has to be explained how the mind comes to respect these rules' (p. 1). This is why Piaget talks about the moralities of *constraint and co-operation*, and not, as subsequent writers in the field have done, of heteronomous and autonomous morality. The former has social-psychological connotations implying something about interpersonal interaction. The latter focuses on the child's cognitive frame of reference and cognitive organization; the developmental change is from an undifferentiated self and other to a self differentiated from others but cognizant of interaction with them.

Although Piaget failed to answer his social-psychological questions, his research generated a great deal of valuable data and a mass of insights and concepts which are significant contributions to developmental psychology. Many have been brought to full fruition in his cognitive work, but not reapplied to social and interpersonal areas. He failed to take up the questions about 'social cognition' which the moral research generated, apparently because he regarded those as a mere postscript to his work reported in *The Child's Conception of the World*. It is perhaps a moot point as to whether the logical operations of moral and social cognition could ever be expressed with the *precision* that physical and mathematical reasoning can be, but subsequent researchers have elaborated more fully the structure and processes of moral reasoning and interpersonal cognition. They have done so, however, largely by selecting specific elements for investigation, rather than taking the 'package' as a whole, and they have been far more interested in the developmental than the social issues.

The Implicit Definition of Morality

Piaget's 'package' reflected a particular view of morality, determined largely by his dominant preoccupation with the processes involved in the change from constraint to co-operation. Many of the elements are only tenuously related via this main theme. Intentionality, for example, has very little relevance to the understanding of rules, but it is central to notions of responsibility and culpability. The elements of Piaget's moral package were (1) rules, (2) the nature of responsibility, (3) retributive justice, and (4) distributive justice. Under these general headings, he investigated the understanding of various forms of conventional 'wrongness'—lying, cheating, causing damage, disobedience—and various aspects of 'fairness'. 'Fairness' encompasses retributive and distributive justice in adult—peer relations, and rules of interaction in the game situation.

It is easy to argue that, even within the Kantian paradigm, this is a curiously narrow definition of morality. Although Kohlberg, for example, ignores both rules and distributive justice, he does include a large area of morality which Piaget ignores, namely rights and obligations. Piaget spoke of 'duty versus good', but confined this to the issue of obedience to adults. He restricted the concept of obligation to conformity to mutually agreed rules in the game. Kohlberg, but not Piaget, investigated contract and the conditions of its application, not merely contract as an alternative form of rule.

Piaget also ignored the contractual element of affect-based relations such as friendship and love, which both Kohlberg and Damon have subsequently found to be central to the child's reasoning about social and moral issues (Kohlberg, 1976; Damon, 1977). Peer-group relations were defined solely in terms of the criteria for negotiation of the rules of play and the distribution of rules and favours. Damon (1977) argues that *friendship* is a psychologically separate category from justice and of considerable importance in children's judgments.

There have, of course, been innumerable criticisms of Piaget's moral perspective simply because it is based on justice and roles. Other perspectives, which place greater emphasis on the development of motive, have had considerable influence on moral psychology in both social-learning and psychoanalytic paradigms. Philosophers of education as well as psychologists have argued that morality should be grounded in sympathy, love or empathy (Wilson, Williams and Sugarman, 1967; Peters, 1978). Piaget, as has been noted, specifically rejected sympathy as the source of *moral* principle. Some psychologists have moved towards something of a compromise between the two positions. Hoffman argues that there is a case for empathy as the *origin* of impulses which, when formalized through increased cognitive sophistication, become the respect for rules that Piaget and other justice-oriented psychologists concentrate on (Hoffman, 1976).

Possibly it is more salient to ask whether the definition of morality with which Piaget was working, was adequate for its main purpose, the critique of Durkheim's position. My conclusion is that neither the definition, nor the ways that Piaget used it, were adequate. For example, let us consider rules. To study the rules of a child's game has certain great advantages. The child, within the span of a few years, moves from being the receiver and obeyer to being the giver and maker of rules. Further, the creation of, as well as the obedience to, rules is a peer activity, and it can be studied in action. However, Piaget failed to ask *why* rules should be obeyed or not; he asked only what rules were, and *whether* they should be obeyed. This is a striking omission and Kohlberg's later studies have demonstrated the usefulness of this question. In measures of fairness, Piaget asked only whether punishment was fair or not, not what its purpose was—thus failing to elicit the underlying reasoning about the nature of 'fair'. He took it for granted that the child would regard punishment as an *inevitable* consequence of naughtiness. In asking about the deterrent effect of various forms of punishment, which implies a purpose, he asked only about the efficacy, not the rationale.

While it may be valid to begin with the *child's* view of normality, it is limiting to take for granted only one definition of naughtiness. Breaking the rules is a primary category of immorality because Piaget's model emphasizes the priority of the rule in the definition of morality: the restoration of order is a return to rule-following. If punishment is perceived as a means to this end—by the theorist as well as the child—it will, not surprisingly, form a dominant part of the discourse. The consequence of this emphasis on punishment for 'wrongness' has prevented Piaget from examining other forms of sanction besides those imposed by adult power or, to a lesser extent, by peer pressure. For example, while negotiation is considered within the context of rule-creation or change, it is not considered in the context of retributive justice, yet both Kohlberg and Damon have subsequently shown that this is a lively area of debate among children.

Another striking omission is the analysis of any *positive* aspects of morality. Piaget concentrated on what is wrong and what is unfair—he did not consider even the positive distributive justice of sharing. Justice is the central implicit tenet of the Kantian model, but this implies a positive as well as a negative element. Piaget's preoccupation with the power relations between adult and child obscured these broader issues of morality.

Let us consider in detail one issue, 'fairness', which has different definitions at different points in the monograph. It has often been pointed out that the inconsistencies and obscurities in the monograph are an easy target, but in view of the centrality of this concept to the dominant theme of justice, it is worth examining the variations in detail. 'Fair' is a catch-word which seems to be used as an implicit universal criterion for justice; in the interrogatory, 'fair' is the testing-point for the child's judgment of 'right' or 'morally OK'. In a sense this is quite legitimate; 'fair' is a powerfully rhetorical word and universally used by children in just this way (Breakwell, 1982).

However, Piaget seemed to have taken it for granted that the universality of the rhetoric precludes the necessity for defining it. In my view this is a critical mistake, because to understand the child's definition of 'fairness' and its applications would be a considerable advance in understanding the child's conception of justice. In fact, the material for analysing 'fairness' is present in the data, but Piaget ignored its significance, in particular he ignored the importance of the disparate and sometimes contradictory definitions which the concept yielded.

Fairness is first introduced in the monograph in the context of innovating rules in the game of marbles. It is clear that fairness here simply means a 'better game', without any implications of justice or egalitarianism. For the child at the egocentric stage, fair means *accurate* and *right*. At the next stage, fair means that skill and not simply luck is involved—equal opportunities for competition exist. However, the 'fairest' rules are those best known among the peer group, and familiarity, along with long-establishment, of rules is fair because it diminishes cheating. For girls, *practicability* of rules is also a criterion of fairness.

A shift in the concept of fairness is clear; the young child identifies fair with accuracy, a good game is one which conforms to the official rules. Later, fairness is whatever facilitates the most effective interaction between players. Piaget rightly stressed that this is evidence of a powerful principle of *reciprocity*. But what he did not stress is that there is no 'moral' implication in the second stage of fairness. It is not even distributive justice; it is simply pragmatism. Only the possibility of cheating, in that one person may gain disproportionately, suggests a remote connection with distributive justice.

Fairness is also examined in relation to retributive justice. The younger child considers the fairest punishment to be the most severe. For the youngest children, in fact, punishment is seen to be *fairer* than leniency or 'sportingness'. By about eight years old the child comes to think of the effectiveness of punishment as contributing to its fairness, but only at about thirteen does the child come to consider distributive justice—that the punishment should be proportional to the fault. Fairness is also legitimacy; to the young child the adult is seen as having an absolute right to inflict punishment. This changes to the right to engage in simple retaliation for pragmatic reasons. There is plenty of evidence that fairness is confused with 'authority'. For the young child it is 'fair' that the bridge should fall under the wrongdoer, and 'fair' to tell on the naughty brother. This equation of fairness with 'rightness' echoes the equation of fairness with accuracy reported earlier.

Piaget did ask children to give examples of what was 'not fair', and found a relationship with age. For younger children, overwhelmingly, 'not fair' meant engaging in forbidden acts; only a quarter mentioned inequality, which was the main criterion for the older children. (See Table 10.1.) Piaget interpreted this as 'justice subordinated to adult authority'; in my view, it is better interpreted as a lack of a concept of *distributive* justice altogether, and an equation of *retributive* justice with adult authority. It is clear that the child does not differentiate 'rightness' from 'fairness'; to me this demonstrates a lack of conception of fairness rather than a different use of the term. Clearly, Piaget did not choose to recognize the different *kind* of justice indicated by the children's responses.

While my main concern is with conceptual issues rather than empirical refutations, it is worth noting that other researchers have subsequently found that children do operate with a concept of fairness, both in action and in justification and explanation of action. Ugurel-Semin (op. cit.) found that children did engage in distribution of goods (nuts) in ways which increasingly manifested equality and equity. Damon (op. cit.) also studied sharing behaviour and found that children over four years old did justify their distribution according to some recognizable criterion of 'fairness'.

Responsibility is also a central issue in Piaget's moral definition, and some similar problems exist here. Piaget's interest in the concept of responsibility was kindled by Fauconnet's anthropological analysis of differences between 'primitive' and 'modern' conceptions. Fauconnet identified a historical shift from collective or 'objective' responsibility to individual, 'subjective' responsibility. Piaget found in this close parallels with the change from authority-based to peer-based morality. He identified the unilateral respect of the child for the adult with a conception of objective responsibility; if damage or hurt has been done, it must be *assuaged* and *punished* (not specifically *made good*, but *expiated*). Crime is pollution or infection. The collective effect of the act is of greater importance than the individual's culpability in a moral sense.

Piaget saw the link as being via obedience, a necessary component of constraint morality; 'under the effect of adult constraint the child cannot conceive the laws of the physical universe except in the guise of a certain obedience rendered by things to rules' (p. 340). Thus the child attributes causality *and* obligation to natural phenomena, such as the wind, the sun and the clouds. The distinction between moral obligation and social causality, and physical causality and the regularity of events, is not apparent to the child who holds a morality of constraint.

Responsibility was studied in several ways. Immanent justice, the idea that natural justice is in some way equivalent to divine justice, is a manifestation of 'objective' responsibility. However, the main investigation of the changing conception of responsibility was through intentionality. The shift from judgments in terms of objective criteria (the amount of damage done) to the subjective criterion of the individual's moral culpability is amply demonstrated by Piaget's and by subsequent findings. It is of note that neither Piaget nor subsequent researchers found such a clear relationship in the case of immanent justice; though immanent justice does decline with age, it is not a sudden conceptual transformation as is manifest in the case of intentionality (Medinnus, 1959; Gutkin, 1973).

However, intentionality is only partly a 'moral' question. Piaget focused on the moral because of his concern with his critique of Durkheim. The evidence cited above also suggests that there are wider implications also for the child's conception of causality, and that the changing conception of causality—responsibility is a precondition for awareness of the implications of retributive justice. The child who holds an egocentric perspective of the world attributes animistic characteristics to her environment, and she also holds absolutist and generalized conceptions of punishment, whether divine or parental. 'It is wrong because it is punished', or 'it is wrong because it comes into the category of things forbidden', are conceptually no different from the conception that a bicycle is alive because it moves, or that the sun 'has to' rise or the moon to set when the day comes. Obligation confuses moral and physical regularity and cause.

An interesting final irony is that Piaget's implicit model of morality focuses very much on 'conventional' moral behaviour, rules and duties. The rationalist tradition in which Piaget was working is basically in opposition to the view that moral psychology is about socialization and the acquisition of correct habits. Despite the implications that the morality of co-operation is about autonomy Piaget's emphasis on the understanding of punishment and wrongness can be seen as a rationalist perspective on the socialization of impulse control. Perhaps this is not surprising; Durkheim was concerned with the transmission of moral rules and the moral code, by implication a monolithic and restrictive notion. In so far as Piaget tried to question this, he was inevitably drawn into the same assumptions about the *content* of morality arising from such a conception. Possibly it is only the subsequent evidence from Kohlberg's work demonstrating that mature moral reasoning is frequently in conflict with 'conventional' morality which makes us surprised when we examine Piaget's implicit model of morality.

The Developmental Sequence

The developmental sequence of moral reasoning has received the most attention from subsequent researchers, and it is my contention that it is the most successful, but least theoretically explored, aspect of the monograph. It has, however, been much misunderstood. The enthusiasm of empirical psychologists has been for piecemeal replication, not for analysis of the theoretical implications of the original evidence. A notable lack in nearly fifty years of research has been serious efforts to link Piaget's cognitive and moral theories. Despite the overlapping processes (e.g. centration, decalage, etc.) only a handful of studies have concentrated on these, the majority of researchers confining themselves to elaborating the description of the developmental sequence and the effects of independent variables (Ugurel-Semin, 1952; Stuart, 1967; Lee, 1971).

However, Piaget produced a considerable amount of empirical evidence scattered through the monograph, and this evidence can be presented in orthodox tabular form (see Table 10.1). In this form certain patterns emerge. For example, it is immediately apparent from the Table that the age range of subjects in the study of rules of the game is exceptional; in most studies the age range was six to twelve. In most of the studies, the subject group was arbitrarily divided by Piaget into 'younger' and 'older' at age nine. This is misleading because in the qualitative material that Piaget presents, it is frequently apparent that changes take place at seven to eight, rather than nine; in other words, roughly contemporaneous with the movement into concrete operational thinking. The difficulties, therefore, of making theoretical statements about the *order* or significance of the changes reported in quantitative form are considerable.

It is clear from the Table that, in the heteronomous phase, or the morality of constraint, there is a unity of conceptualization; objective conceptions dominate all areas of thinking and limit the definition of morality narrowly. The characteristic of the morality of co-operation, or autonomous morality, is *diversity*. One major criticism of Piaget, in my view, is that he did not appear to appreciate the significance of this change from unity to diversity; by concentrating on the type of morality, i.e. 'co-operation', he ignored the subtleties of the second phase, which have considerable implication for the reasoning processes of moral judgment. Subsequent researchers, because they tend to concentrate on only one area of morality, on the whole also miss the significance.

Firstly, let us consider *reciprocity*, which Piaget argues is the central principle of the second phase of morality. Peer orientation and mutuality may be manifested in two ways; through behavioural co-operation with others and through egalitarian attitudes expressed in reasoning. The child *behaves* co-operatively in a game-playing situation, demonstrating an implicit understanding of the need for a common set of rules. Later, she becomes able to negotiate changes in the rules, not merely able to negotiate between disputed interpretations of the rule. These behavioural abilities become explicit as *cognitions* some two years after they are apparent as behaviours.

The expression of reciprocity as a principle (or rhetoric) of egalitarianism is evident in both distributive and retributive justice. However, Piaget concentrated solely on the perception of justice *vis-à-vis* parents' treatment of children, especially in relation to punishment. He said very little about reciprocity and the relationship between peers.

In my view, peer orientation can be considered separately from reciprocity. It is part of Piaget's thesis that peer orientation is the origin of mutual respect and the morality of co-operation. The evidence for peer orientation as such, is somewhat fragmented. In the middle childhood period—about nine to ten—the child is powerfully oriented towards her peers, demonstrating group solidarity in opposition to the adult world. You should not give your friend away, even if this means the whole class is punished; you should protect your sibling against your parent, even if you have to lie. Lying to a peer is worse than lying to an adult. These responses have an interesting quality; in contrast with many other areas, it is clear that here the child is speaking from commitment, not theory or analysis. Rhetoric is rampant; solidarity *is* a categorical imperative. Clearly, a distinction can be made between developmental change in rhetorical moral statements and in conceptual comprehension. It is not at all apparent that they are the same thing.

Secondly, let us consider conceptual changes. Piaget argues that the *volte-face* from adult to peer is the consequence of interaction and the development of mutual respect. But an alternative interpretation is that changes in moral *conceptualization* are demonstrably cognitive. An increase in cognitive complexity is clearly evident in the case of rules. In addition to a marked decrease in *behavioural* egocentricity, the child becomes increasingly aware of alternative rules, and is able to handle the relativism involved in this consciousness. In judgments about lying, there are two, parallel developments, increasing understanding of subjective responsibility (intention), and increasing capacity to differentiate between swear-words, lies, mistakes and exaggeration. Perceiving the intentions of the actor is one important aspect of this, but it is also evident that the child is demonstrating increased capacity for cognitive differentiation and logical exclusion.

Thirdly, tabular representation of the whole range of Piaget's findings, as in Table 10.1, scotches a frequently perpetuated myth. Reviewers of Piaget's work tend to discuss Piaget's *three stages of moral reasoning*, the third stage being 'equity'. Reference to equity is to be found only, in passing, with regard to one study of retributive justice and one study of distributive justice. The study of rules refers to a parallel development in the codification of rules, which implies sophisticated relativism. Piaget did not actually discuss the possibility of an 'equity' stage until three-quarters of the way through the book. He considered it simply as a more relativistic extension of equality; it really does not have the status of a 'stage' or 'phase' at all.

This is interesting, because, in fact, Piaget's own evidence *does* suggest some significant changes; a close analysis of the justice material indicates that equitable thinking is in *opposition to*, not merely an extension of, egalitarian thinking. The material on older children's understanding rules demonstrates a very sophisticated legislative and judicial skill, and with it a shrewd and complex understanding of the processes of group negotiation and co-operation. Piaget himself noted that, in the rules of the game of marbles, the person of fourteen has considerably more subtlety and complexity of thought than the average adult has about the broader social and political issues. The child in her early teens, in relation to childhood games, is child-as-adult, and precocious in the comprehension of rules because she is the law-giver, not simply because the rules of marbles are somewhat less complex than political rules. Piaget reflected briefly upon this interesting developmental question, but perhaps because, in his view, it was not central to his main thesis about the morality of constraint and co-operation he did not pursue its theoretical importance.

Fourthly, *respect* is a central issue in the change from the morality of constraint to that of co-operation. Piaget, Bovet and Durkheim all argue that respect is initially for the individual, and only consequently for the law which the individual represents. It was Piaget's position that the child's early unilateral respect for authority gives way to mutual respect, especially for peers, as a consequence of interaction. Consequent upon this change develop reciprocity, relativity of justice and subjective responsibility. Piaget expressed his perspective on respect in a somewhat circular fashion: 'The mere fact of individuals living in groups is sufficient to give rise to new features of obligation and regularity in their lives. The pressure of the group upon the individual would thus explain the appearance of this *sui generis* feeling which we call respect and which is the source of all religion and morality . . . A rule is, therefore, nothing but the condition for the existence of a social group; and if to the individual conscience rules seem to be charged with obligation, this is because communal life alters the very structure of consciousness by inculcating into it the feeling of respect' (p. 96).

A number of difficulties are apparent in this conception. 'Unilateral respect', for example, has connotations of obedience and unquestioning acceptance of the parental point of view, which are certainly not evident in the *behaviour* of the young child. An alternative interpretation has been suggested by Lickona (1976); 'the child's early obedience orientation in moral thinking appears to be based less on respect for the moral status of adults than on simple recognition of their superior powers' (p. 240). This would be a more parsimonious interpretation; it would fit the notion that the child accepts the authority perspective because she is not aware of having any *choice*. But *if* authority is omnipotent, 'respect' is an irrelevant or inappropriate concept.

If we focus on Piaget's original implication that respect is a dynamic of cognitive organization, then an examination of the cognitive changes illuminates some of the issues. It becomes clear that a rejection of adult authority is only an element of the second phase of thinking. It is more that the child has learned to attend to more than one version of events, and to do this requires social and conceptual negotiation. The development of mutual respect is coincidental with increased relativism in other areas of thinking. Decreasing egocentricity, both social and cognitive, increases the capacity of the individual to perceive what alternatives are available and also to be more open to influences and channels of information.

The case of lying provides an interesting illustration because the changes are well documented in Piaget's evidence. Lying is a conceptually sophisticated concept; to comprehend it, the child must establish several new categories in addition to relaxing her unilateral respect. Initially the child has a very general concept that all 'bad' utterances are lies—bad being defined as 'punishable'. Then she becomes aware that there is a difference between a lie and a mistake, but still contends that both are 'lies'. Concurrently, the child has a simple, objective view that the bigger the lie, the more it is punished and the greater the sin is perceived to be. Then the child begins to distinguish between lies and mistakes, but still regards lies as wrong because they break a *rule*. Later, lies are defined as an explicit intention to deceive (that being the locus of the sin), and about the same time the child begins to distinguish between 'credible' lies and non-credible lies and exaggerations. The latter are not so bad because no-one would be deceived; they have the status of a 'joke'. It seems that only later still does the child perceive consciously the *social* implications of lying, that it destroys trust between people. This appears to develop somewhat later than the view that you should not lie to a companion because it is counter to the ethos of solidarity.

It is difficult to interpret these findings simply in terms of lessening of unilateral respect, if by respect we mean a reaction to power or authority. An alternative is to look at the cognitive implications of unilateral respect. One way of looking at unilateral respect is that it is a failure to differentiate superordinate and subordinate categories, a lack of decentration. The child focuses on one aspect of the problem only and cannot incorporate any other. This means that the child does not perceive a moral *dilemma*. This is clearer in Kohlberg's data than in Piaget's, because Kohlberg set 'dilemmas' with genuinely alternative answers. Piaget set problems which do not have alternative 'correct' answers; in most of Piaget's stories, the 'wrong' answer denoted heteronomous thinking *per se*.

A final aspect of development to be derived from the data is *egocentrism*. Piaget stresses that egocentrism is essentially *social*. It is not that the child is solely wrapped up in her own thoughts, it is that she does not differentiate between her own thoughts and those of others. She is unable to distinguish between internal and external sources of knowledge. In the chapter on rules, Piaget describes the paradox that the child cannot distinguish between what she has always known, and new knowledge. Even apparently spontaneous ideas appear to the child to be coming from somewhere, being part of a collective wisdom to which she already has access. The Elders of Neuchâtel, guardians of wisdom to Piaget's subjects, were able to put ideas into the child's mind. It is as though the child cannot conceive of the non-existence of knowledge; everything is known, everything has rules. As soon as the child is given access to that knowledge, it is absorbed and undifferentiated from other, longer established knowledge. The source and justification of knowledge is authority; even if the child creates something new in a game, the child will invoke authority to support the innovation. Authority 'must have known about it'. It is as though the child regards her new insight as simply another *access* to the vast cornucopia of Knowledge. She is like St. Joan, whose imagination was not differentiated from a hot-line to the saints (Shaw, 1958).

The development of both behavioural and conceptual egocentrism is most evident in the study of rules. It is only in this study that evidence of the parallels between motor and conscious activity are available. Initially the child does play egocentrically, with no reference even to rules. She manifests ritual only. By about five she behaves imitatively with regard to the rules, but it is some time later that she begins to behave in a way which indicates that she understands the compelling nature of the rule, which is the full manifestation of social play. Later still, co-operative negotiation becomes possible.

Several researchers have criticized the implications of Piaget's views on egocentrism. A number of researchers have noted that non-egocentric behaviour precedes the expression of non-egocentric concepts. Others have argued that Piaget's theoretical view should logically extend to *affective* egocentricity. If the child cannot take the role of the other, then sympathy and altruism should not be possible. Yet there are many studies which do indicate that the child as young as fifteen months will manifest empathic and altruistic acts in the presence of another's distress (Borke, 1971, 1978; Hoffman, 1976).

Secondly for Piaget the issue of egocentricity has closely related the change from unilateral to mutual respect; mutual respect can only develop as egocentricity wanes (though the causal direction is not at all clear). What then is going on in the transition from one form of morality to the other? Is the ability to take the perspective of the other necessary to conceptualize (1) alternative perspectives and models, (2) the behaviour and interactions of others in a co-operative situation, or (3) to generate conclusions from these about the nature of rules, roles and relationships? It seems from the evidence that (2) clearly develops first. The child develops 'empathic' behaviour which, however, seems not to be formally co-operative.

RECENT THEORY AND ITS IMPLICATIONS

The foregoing has concentrated on criticisms of the monograph which, in my view, have been ignored or underexplored. I have examined these criticisms, especially those with theoretical relevance, rather than attempting to make the connections and fill in the gaps in Piaget's thesis, though to some extent this can be done utilizing his own data. I have also engaged in a critique within the terms of Piaget's own perspective, that of cognitive-developmental theory. It is, of course, possible to criticize every stage of Piaget's theoretical and empirical work, if one starts from completely different theoretical premises. The extent to which this is useful can perhaps be judged from the evidence presented of social learning theorists' attempts. I have confined myself to taking Piaget's basic problem and asking whether he succeeded in solving it. My contention is that he has not. Furthermore, he focused on a social-psychological problem and consequently ignored the implications and many interesting questions which his developmental material generated. Ultimately, he left his social-psychological thesis unfinished because he could not test his primary hypothesis, ignoring some exciting developmental psychological questions because of his social-psychological focus.

As has been discussed, subsequent research has been very selective. Some of this research has considerably modified Piaget's conclusions about the age at which the child develops certain concepts, and the rate of growth generally (e.g. Borke, 1971, 1978; Donaldson, 1978). Other research has added considerably to an understanding of the variables associated with development. However, relatively few researchers have taken the *whole* thesis, nor have they examined the conceptual problems associated with 'moral' development.

I shall now consider three researchers who have made some attempt to tackle the theoretical issues. Each has been selective, and none has come to terms with Piaget's social-psychological questions, but each has made a significant contribution to the developmental aspects of the thesis, and by doing so has underlined some of the conceptual problems of the original. The three are Selman, Damon and Kohlberg.

Selman's studies have taken up the difficult question of role-taking and its relation to moral thought. Although he worked with children contemporary in age to Piaget's subjects, he nevertheless makes comparison with Kohlberg's rather than Piaget's theoretical model. He regards himself as an ego development theorist and as such is not particularly concerned with cognitive processes or problem-solving. His definition of role-taking is social perspective; 'the child's structuring of his understanding of the relation between the perspectives of self and others' (1976).

His studies demonstrate unequivocally that social perspective-taking is a prerequisite for moral reasoning. He has, therefore, separated out two variables which Piaget consistently confused, and demonstrated their sequential relationship. This does not necessarily imply a causal relationship—it may mean that role-taking is a *key element* in moral reasoning which must develop before further progress on moral issues is possible. It is not, however, evidence for Piaget's main hypothesis because Selman does not really tackle the issue of a social interactive origin of role-taking skills. He has concentrated on breaking down analytically the role-taking process (Selman, 1980).

Damon's studies are extensive investigations of social understanding, in particular the child's perceptions of interrelationships. Moral issues arise in two ways, in the context of obligations between persons, and in the central concept of justice. His studies indicate clearly defined *separate* categories of justice, obedience and authority relations, friendship and the understanding of social convention.

His work on obedience and authority is particularly relevant to Piaget's thesis. He concluded from his findings that the development of justice 'bypassed any subservient reliance on the moral commands of authority'. 'In children's early justice reasoning and conduct we found a set of moral principles entirely different from the authority-obeying values that the predominant theories present as characterizing primitive morality' (p. 169). In contrast with Piaget, Damon proposes 'a rather simple developmental hypothesis: that a person's moral knowledge (assumed to be a justice function) grows out of his early reflections on common justice problems, rather than solely out of his early experience with adult constraint . . . in this perspective, authority becomes but one of the many social relations with which the child must learn to deal. It is not, as has been assumed by many, a general starting-point for all moral principles' (p. 171).

The implications of Damon's work are considerable. If social understanding and moral principles derive from social interaction and experience *per se* and not as a consequence of a shift away from authority constraints, then Piaget's whole social psychological thesis is brought into question. Damon's evidence reveals a much more complex and differentiated range of reasoning about social and moral issues than Piaget's somewhat arbitrary definition of morality would imply. His findings elaborate considerably the developmental theory of Piaget in this area by demonstrating interrelationships, as well as important distinctions, between concepts.

Kohlberg's studies have been with older children and adults. This imposes some limitations as to their direct relevance to Piaget's theory. However, there is undoubted overlap—some would say unity—between Kohlberg's first two stages and Piaget's heteronomous and autonomous stages. There is some significance in the fact that Kohlberg found children up to fourteen using stage 1 thinking, and many adults still operate with stage 2 thinking. Kohlberg's stages 3 to 6 can be seen as an elaboration and extension of Piaget's very sketchy stage of equity, but the developmental importance of Kohlberg's work is that it demonstrates the *ongoing* nature of moral development, that it is a life-span process, not a matter of significant changes at the age of about eight. Like Damon, Kohlberg's studies extend and substantiate the developmental aspects of Piaget's thesis, but then pay little attention to the social-psychological ones.

Kohlberg, furthermore, has a different implicit definition of morality from Piaget. Piaget's concentration on 'justice' was largely in terms of the differences in reasoning between an authority-based morality of constraint, and the mutual respect basis of morality of co-operation. His definition was tied closely to the conception of 'wrongness' and fairness really only insofar as it related to wrongness and retributive justice. Kohlberg's conception of justice as a core concept in moral development differs from Piaget's. Kohlberg is largely uninterested in the concept of the *rule*, except in terms of law. In this he differs fundamentally from Piaget. On the other hand, Kohlberg pays much more attention than Piaget to *contractual* rights and obligations, based on affect or civil relations. Whereas Piaget appeared to have conceived of moral development as increased understanding of the rule and its applications, Kohlberg is more concerned with the development of principles and the conflict between legal and moral definitions of duty and right.

These three theorists have various implications for Piaget's position. Each has extended the developmental perspective well beyond Piaget's description, and each is a theoretical advance. Their evidence of a wide range of separate functions and areas of reasoning which have been loosely linked by the global term 'moral', has both extended the definition of morality and facilitated the understanding of the processes involved in moral reasoning. Studies of the correlates of moral reasoning, as well as of the components of moral and social reasoning, confirm the interlocking relationship between moral thinking and social reasoning—both in the sense of understanding social conventions and understanding the relationship between individuals, and individuals and wider society (Haan, Smith and Block, 1968; Weinreich-Haste, 1982). This evidence has considerable implication for social as well as developmental psychology, particularly the issue of how the child acquires rules, and the processes by which the child comes to construe and order her understanding of the world.

However, to date, subsequent theoretical development has not tackled Piaget's social-psychological thesis adequately. The cognitively based, active model of the person represented by the three researchers cited emphasizes the processes of individual judgment and the way in which judgments are organized and reorganized in the course of development. This approach is highly individualistic and ignores the social psychological processes which are implicitly present in Piaget's social-psychological analysis. There remains a need to return to the social psychological questions which Piaget posed.

REFERENCES

Armsby, R. (1971) A re-examination of the development of moral judgments in children. *Child Development,* **42,** 1241-8.
Bandura, A. and Macdonald, F. J. (1963) The influence of reinforcement and the behaviour of models in shaping children's moral judgments. *Journal of Abnormal and Social Psychology,* **67,** 274-281.
Baumrind, D. and Black, A. E. (1967) Socialization practices associated with dimensions of competence in pre-school boys and girls. *Child Development,* **38,** 297-327.
Berg-Cross, L. G. (1975) Intentionalist, degree of damage, and moral judgments. *Child Development,* **46,** 970-974.
Boehm, L. and Nass, M. L. (1962) Social class differences in conscience development. *Child Development,* **33,** 565-574.
Borke, H. (1971) Interpersonal perception of young children. *Developmental Psychology,* **5,** 263-269.
Borke, H. (1978) Piaget's view of social interaction and the theoretical construct of empathy. In Siegel, L. S. and Brainerd, C. J. (Eds.) *Alternatives to Piaget.* London: Academic Press.
Breakwell, G. M. (1982) Moralities and conflicts. In Locke, D. and Weinreich-Haste, H. (Eds.) *Moral Judgment and Moral Action.* London: Wiley.
Breznitz, S. and Kugelmass, S. (1967) Intentionality in moral judgment: developmental stages. *Child Development,* **38,** 469-479.
Bronfenbrenner, U. (1962a) The role of age, sex, class and culture in studies of moral development. *Religious Education,* **57** (supp), 3-17.
Bronfenbrenner, U. (1962b) Soviet methods of character education. *American Psychologist,* **17,** 550-564.
Broughton, J. (1978) The cognitive-developmental approach to morality: a reply to Kurtines and Greif. *Journal of Moral Education,* **7,** 81-97.
Cowan, P., Langer, J., Heavenrich, J. and Nathanson, M. (1969) Social learning and Piaget's cognitive theory of moral development. *Journal of Personality and Social Psychology,* **11,** 261-274.
Crowley, P. (1968) Effect of training upon objectivity of moral judgment in grade-school children. *Journal of Personality and Social Psychology,* **8,** 228-232.
Damon, W. (1977) *The Social World of the Child.* San Francisco: Jossey-Bass.
Donaldson, M. (1978) *Children's Minds.* London: Croom Helm.
Eysenck, H. J. (1976) The biology of morality. In Lickona, T. (Ed.) *Moral Development and Behavior.* New York: Holt, Rinehart and Winston.
Festinger, L. (1957) *A Theory of Cognitive Dissonance.* Stanford: Stanford University Press.
Flugel, J. C. (1964) *A Hundred Years of Psychology.* London: Methuen.
Freud, S. (1930) *Civilization and Its Discontents.* London: Hogarth Press.
Garbarino, J. and Bronfenbrenner, U. (1976) The socialization of moral judgment and behavior in a cross-cultural perspective. In Lickona, T. (Ed.) *Moral Development and Behaviour.* New York: Holt, Rinehart and Winston.
Gutkin, D. C. (1972) The effect of systematic story changes in intentionality in children's moral judgments. *Child Development,* **43,** 187-195.
Gutkin, D. C. (1973) An analysis of the concept of moral intentionality. *Human Development,* **16,** 371-381.
Haan, N., Smith, M. B. and Block, J. (1968) Moral reasoning of young adults. *Journal of Personality and Social Psychology,* **10,** 183-201.

Hardeman, M. (1972) Children's moral reasoning. *Journal of Genetic Psychology,* **120,** 49-59.

Harrower, M. R. (1934) Social status and the moral development of the child. *British Journal of Educational Psychology,* **4,** 75-96.

Hilgard, E. R. (1958) *Theories of Learning.* London: Methuen.

Hoffman, M. L. (1963) Child rearing practices and moral development: generalizations from empirical research. *Child Development,* **34,** 295-318.

Hoffman, M. L. (1970) Conscience, personality and socialization techniques. *Human Development,* **13,** 90-126.

Hoffman, M. L. (1976) Empathy, role-taking, guilt and development of altruistic motives. In Lickona, T. (Ed.) *Moral Development and Behavior.* New York: Holt, Rinehart and Winston.

Johnson, R. C. (1962) A study of children's moral judgments. *Child Development,* **33,** 327-354.

Kohlberg, L. (1958) The development of modes of moral thinking and choice in the years ten to sixteen. Unpublished Ph.D. Thesis, University of Chicago.

Kohlberg, L. (1976) Moral stages and moralization; the cognitive-developmental approach. In Lickona, T. (Ed.) *Moral Development and Behavior.* New York: Holt, Rinehart and Winston.

Kurtines, W. and Greif, E. B. (1974) The development of moral thought. Review and evaluation of Kohlberg's approach. *Psychological Bulletin,* **81,** 453-470.

Lee, L. C. (1971) The concomitant development of cognitive and moral modes of thought; a test of selected deductions from Piaget's theory. *Genetic Psychology Monographs,* **83,** 93-146.

LeFurgy, W. A. and Woloshin, G. W. (1969) Immediate and long-term effects of experimentally-induced social influence on the modification of adolescent's moral judgments. *Journal of Personality and Social Psychology,* **12,** 104-110.

Lickona, T. (1969) Piaget misunderstood: a critique of the criticisms of his theory of moral development. *Merrill-Palmer Quarterly,* **16,** 337-350.

Lickona, T. (1976) Research on Piaget's theory of moral development. In Lickona, T. (Ed.) *Moral Development and Behavior.* New York: Holt, Rinehart and Winston.

MacRae, E. (1954) A test of Piaget's theories of moral development. *Journal of Abnormal and Social Psychology,* **49,** 14-18.

McNamee, S. (1977) Moral behaviour, moral development and motivation. *Journal of Moral Education,* **7,** 27-32.

Medinnus, G. R. (1959) Immanent justice in children; a review of the literature and additional data. *Journal of Genetic Psychology,* **94,** 253-262.

Meehl, P. E. (1954) *Clinical v Statistical Prediction.* Minneapolis: University of Minnesota Press.

Milgram, S. (1965) Some conditions of obedience and disobedience to authority. *Human Relations,* **18,** 57-76.

Miller, G. A. (1962) *Psychology, the Science of Mental Life.* Harmondsworth, London: Penguin.

Modgil, S. and Modgil, C. (1976) *Piagetian Research, Vol. 6.* Windsor: NFER.

Moscovici, S. (1978) *Social Influence and Social Change.* London: Academic Press.

Nisbet, R. (1974) *The Social Philosophers.* London: Heinemann.

Peters, R. S. (1978) The place of Kohlberg's theory in moral education. *Journal of Moral Education,* **7,** 147-57.

Piaget, J. (1929) *The Child's Conception of the World.* London: Routledge and Kegan Paul.

Piaget, J. (1932) *The Moral Judgment of the Child.* London: Routledge and Kegan Paul.

Piaget, J. (1977) *The Grasp of Consciousness.* London: Routledge and Kegan Paul.

Pittel, S. M. and Mendelsohn, G. A. (1966) Measurement of moral values: a review and critique. *Psychological Bulletin,* **66,** 22-35.

Rawls, J. (1971) *A Theory of Justice.* London: Oxford University Press.

Rest, J., Cooper, D., Coder, R., Masanz, J. and Anderson, D. (1974) Judging the important issues in moral dilemmas. *Developmental Psychology,* **10,** 491-501.

Riegel, K. F. (1972) Influence of economic and political ideologies on the development of developmental psychology. *Psychological Bulletin,* **78,** 129-141.

Salzstein, H. D., Diamond, R. M. and Belenky, M. (1972) Moral judgment and conformity behaviour. *Developmental Psychology,* **7,** 327-336.

Selman, R. (1976) Towards a structural analysis of developing interpersonal relations concepts: research with normal and disturbed pre-adolescent boys. In Pick, A. (Ed.) *Tenth Minnesota Symposium on Child Psychology.* (Ed.) Minneapolis: University of Minnesota Press.

Selman, R. (1976) Social-cognitive understanding: a guide to educational and clinical practice. In Lickona, T. (Ed.) *Moral Development and Behavior.* New York: Holt, Rinehart and Winston.

Selman, R. (1980) *The Growth of Interpersonal Understanding.* New York: Academic Press.

Semin, G. and Manstead, A. (1979) Social psychology: social or psychological? *British Journal of Social and Clinical Psychology,* **18,** 191-203.

Shaw, G. B. (1958) *St. Joan.* Harmondsworth, London: Penguin.

Stuart, R. B. (1967) Decentration in the development of children's concept of moral and causal judgment. *Journal of Genetic Psychology,* **111,** 59-68.

Ugurel-Semin, R. (1952) Moral behaviour and moral judgment in children. *Journal of Abnormal and Social Psychology,* **47,** 463-474.

Weinreich, H. E. (1975) Kohlberg and Piaget, aspects of their relationship in the field of moral development. *Journal of Moral Education,* **4,** 201-213.

Weinreich-Haste, H. E. (1979) Moral development. In Coleman, J. (Ed.) *The School Years.* London: Methuen.

Weinreich-Haste, H. E. (1982) Social and moral cognition. In Locke, D. and Weinreich-Haste, H. *Moral Judgment and Moral Action.* London: Wiley.

Wilson, J., Williams, N. and Sugarman, B. (1967) *Introduction to Moral Education.* Harmondsworth, London: Penguin.

Wilson, E. O. (1978) *On Human Nature.* Cambridge, Mass.: Harvard University Press.

Wright, D. S. (1971) *The Psychology of Moral Behaviour.* Harmondsworth, London: Penguin.

Wright, D. S. (1982) 'The Moral Judgment of the Child' revisited. In Locke, D. and Weinreich-Haste, H. (Eds.) *Moral Judgment and Moral Action.* London: Wiley.

Chapter 11

Piaget's Theory of Moral Development

DEREK WRIGHT

INTRODUCTION

In this chapter I wish to focus upon certain central ideas in Piaget's treatment of moral development. These ideas are expressed in his original monograph *The Moral Judgment of the Child*. Though Piaget has reiterated these ideas in subsequent publications, he has not developed them further: hence I shall be mainly confined to a discussion of that monograph.

The justification for doing this is twofold. In the first place later investigators who have built on Piaget's work have been mainly concerned with his empirical findings, and those will not be discussed here. Those who have built upon his theoretical position and who have contributed most to what has come to be called the cognitive-developmental approach to morality, notably Kohlberg, have explicitly or implicitly ignored certain key notions in Piaget's original formulations and have as a consequence arrived at certain theoretical difficulties which might have been avoided had these notions been taken more seriously. The second reason is that Piaget's formulations in this monograph are frequently unsystematic, imprecise, confusing and even contradictory. The question the student of Piaget so often faces, namely, 'What does Piaget really mean?' is even more pressing in this area than in the main body of his work precisely because he has not subsequently attempted to elaborate upon his theory.

There are, therefore, two policies which might be adopted in a chapter of this kind. The first is to make it an exercise in Piagetian exegesis, attempting to make explicit 'what Piaget really said'. This policy will not be followed, partly because of the unresolved obscurities in his formulation, but mainly because the question of what Piaget really meant is less important than the more substantive issue of how we might most profitably conceive the process of moral development. Instead, I shall try to present and defend an account of a perspective on moral development which is rooted in Piaget's ideas, and which remains faithful to the spirit of his work, but which in certain respects involves reformulating what he has said and making explicit what he has left implicit, and at one point arguing for a statement of his theory which is at variance with that usually derived from his monograph. It should be emphasized that I shall not be concerned with the issue of whether or not the theoretical presuppositions are true, in the sense of being empirically supported, nor with the issue of how they might be operationalized in empirical research, but simply with the clarification of a stance which could be adopted in the attempt to understand moral development.

At the outset there is a respect in which Piaget's approach differs somewhat, at least in emphasis, from those who have been mainly responsible for developing the cognitive-developmental approach since his monograph (e.g. Kohlberg, 1973; Turiel, 1973). These investigators have studied empirically the development of the child's moral judgment and reasoning through the use of hypothetical problems of a moral kind and shown that there is a clear developmental progression in the child's moral thought. They have then applied to this progression the full conceptual apparatus of structure and stage transformation which Piaget has developed in his studies of intellectual development. The consequence has been to pose the relationship between moral thinking and action in a way that contrasts with that of Piaget.

PRACTICAL AND THEORETICAL MORALITY

As is now well known, Kohlberg found evidence of a developmental sequence of at least five stages of moral reasoning. His assertion that later stages are to be preferred over earlier ones is partly based upon the claim that later stages exhibit more than earlier ones those characteristics which distinguish good from bad reasoning in any context, such as making relevant discriminations and relating these in a rational and coherent way. The problem then arises of conceiving how these stages of reasoning derived from hypothetical problems are related to real-life moral action. Now since Kohlberg conceives his stages as analogous to Piaget's stages of intellectual development, that is, as a sequence of structures moving towards greater equilibrium through successive qualitative transformations, he cannot escape the implication that moral action is the *application* of an individual's stage of moral reasoning. Of course, many other factors are present in a real-life situation demanding moral decision: but since the claim is that the stages refer to relatively deep structural aspects of a person's moral thinking their presence in real-life moral action must be presumed—otherwise, of course, the stages do not refer to enduring structural aspects of moral thought. In accounting for progression through the stages, Kohlberg has recourse to the principle of cognitive conflict. But it is clear that the conflict induced by no means necessarily has to arise out of real-life moral situations: it can as well be induced by other people's moral problems, hypothetical dilemmas, and discussion with other people. Thus the problem for Kohlberg, theoretically speaking, is to explain how the individual applies a level of moral reasoning, which may have been reached in relative independence of his own moral experience, to his moral decision-making. Kohlberg has done this, at different times, through invoking stage specific motivations or through the concept of ego strength.

Piaget poses the problem, again from a theoretical point of view, in exactly the opposite way. His primary concern is to understand practical morality, by which he means the total process of moral judgment, decision and action. His interest in theoretical morality, or the way a child answers an experimenter's questions about his moral beliefs or copes with hypothetical moral issues, is as a means of understanding practical morality better. His speculative theorizing is focused firmly on practical morality, and he was very conscious of how remote the child's theoretical morality could be from it. As he observes 'a moral problem presented to the child is far further removed from his moral practice than is an intellectual problem from his logical practice' (MJ, p. 108). It is interesting to note in this respect that Kohlberg's use of the dilemma for which there can be no unequivocal answer, a method Piaget does not use, gives Kohlberg's tasks a stronger element of the logical problem than can be found in Piaget's tasks.

The problem for Piaget is this: given the fact that the child first develops a practical morality how does he subsequently arrive at a theoretical morality? His discussion of the matter is tentative and speculative, though also subtle and rooted in experience with children. (See MJ, pp. 107—116.) It is useful to distinguish three levels: A, the level of practical morality where the child, immersed in his social situation, makes largely intuitive moral judgments which guide his action; B, the level at which the child reflects more or less articulately to himself at a purely verbal and ideational level about the morality of his own and other people's actions; and, C, the level of the communication of his judgments, beliefs and reasonings to others. As Piaget was well aware, movement from level B to level C is much influenced by factors like linguistic ability and the pressures of the social situation. The more significant process for Piaget is the movement from level A to level B, and, as is well known, he invokes the concept of conscious realization which he had found useful in other contexts. The child reconstructs at the representational level the morality he is living at the practical level. We might put the point more generally by saying that the child tries to make sense to himself of his own moral experience. Since this 'making sense' necessarily follows the experience, there is an inevitable time-lag between them.

Piaget is far from clear why and how conscious realization occurs; indeed, the meaning of the term seems to vary with the context in which he uses it. But one stable element in his usage would lead us to infer that the experience of the problematic in the moral life would be a major stimulus to such conscious realization. Moreover, he is explicit that social interaction is a necessary condition: 'the individual is not capable of achieving this conscious realization by himself' (MJ, p. 407). This would seem self-evident when morality is an aspect of social interaction, but one form such socially induced problematic experience can take is when the moral prescriptions of others conflict with the individual's own moral experience (conversely we would expect the moral prescriptions of others to be accepted only when they coincide with his own moral experience).

The conceptual concerns of Piaget and Kohlberg have been presented as contrasting, at the expense of some injustice to both, in order to show that they are really complementary. Piaget focuses on movement from level A to level C and Kohlberg from level C to level A. For both, level B is pivotal. Kohlberg has shown how level C theoretical morality develops through the discussion and the examination of moral issues that are not immediately personal for the individual to more rational and coherent systems. But the impact of such reasoning upon the practical morality of the individual depends upon whether it rings true with his conscious realization of his own moral experience at level B, that is, whether key elements are seen as 'self-evident'. For Piaget, it is level B which is not only made possible by social interaction but which also permits the child to contribute to the moral problems of his society and be actively concerned with general moral issues.

The point of this discussion is to offer some justification for the idea that by returning to Piaget's original conceptions the reasoning—action problem raised by

Kohlberg's theory can be seen in a different light. It is at least implicit in Kohlberg's theory that the hypothetical moral dilemma used in his scaling device is in fact to moral practice what the intellectual problem is to logical practice, an assumption which Piaget, starting from a theory of practical morality, explicitly rejects. The argument could perhaps be put most simply as follows: the practical moral life is about relating to persons and situations; theoretical morality, which Kohlberg has studied, is about the relationships between persons *as ideas*, in situations which are also ideas, that is to say, it is wholly representational; relating to the idea of a person is a very different matter from relating to a person. Of course, there are situations of a political or institutional kind where moral decisions are made by an agent in relation to the ideational representation of persons, and a developed theoretical morality is clearly important for such occasions. Moreover, theoretical morality may not be irrelevant to moral decisions made in relation to actual persons. But not only is the idea of persons derived from relating to them and dependent upon the nature of that relating, but to relate to a person as if he were an idea is not to relate to him as a person. Finally and most important, moral life originates in relation to persons, not in relation to the idea of persons, and it is here that only a theory of practical morality is relevant. Piaget's theory is, above all, a theory of practical morality and it is to that theory we must now turn.

MORAL MOTIVATION

Providing an inclusive definition of the moral which will serve to delineate for the psychologist of moral development the area of his concern is notoriously difficult and will not be attempted here. What is hardly disputable is that central to that concern is the making of prescriptive judgments of the kind 'I ought to do this', 'he ought to do that', and 'this state of affairs ought to exist'. It is not, of course, the verbal uttering of such prescriptions that indicates moral awareness; the prescriptive judgments must themselves be expressive of an action tendency consistent with them. To be a moral person then, whatever else it may involve, means making moral judgments of the kind 'I ought' and being impelled to act in accordance with it, such that if the ensuing action is not consistent, the consequence is guilt, conflict, self-blame and the like. As for prescriptions of the kind 'he ought to', or 'this state of affairs ought to exist', these become expressions of the individual's own moral action when he derives 'I ought' prescriptions from them. In short, the hallmark of a moral being is the presence of what for convenience I shall call the 'ought motive', a conception which encompasses both moral obligation and moral aspiration.

Of course, many more complexities need to be built in if this account is to be satisfactory. The motive may vary in strength both between individuals and within the same individual from one kind of situation to another. It may be in conflict with other motives or allied with them, or may be regulative of conflict between other motives. The cognitive discriminations which shape the motive will vary between individuals and developmentally within the same individual. And so on. The question for the moment is how this ought motive is to be understood and explained within psychology.

Hitherto there have been three dominating perspectives; psychoanalysis, learning theory and sociological approaches. Each, of course, has numerous variants but all have two features in common: the cognitive structuring of moral motivation, the prescriptive component, is seen as received and accepted by the child either from adults or from the norms of social groups; and the motivating element is seen as deriving from the reinforcement contingencies that adults and social groups administer. In short, moral obligation is understood by being subsumed under more general processes of socialization and social control. Now what is not in question here is that these three theoretical perspectives refer to actual processes that occur, nor that they have, in their different ways, an essential role to play in a comprehensive explanation of the moral life. What is in question is whether they are adequate as explanations of the essentially moral component in the moral life, what is here called the ought motive.

There are certain philosophical considerations which suggest they may not be. It has to be admitted that philosophical issues are seldom settled definitively. But the logical analysis of that universe of discourse we call moral, with its concepts of right, wrong, rights, duties, ought and ought not, does permit at least two provisional conclusions. It appears beyond serious doubt that it is impossible to deduce a prescriptive conclusion from descriptive premises; to do so there must be at least one prescriptive assertion among the premises. Thus it does not follow from the assertion 'my parents tell me I ought to do this' that 'I ought to do it' unless a second premise is added, namely, 'I ought to do what my parents tell me to do'. Now it is impossible to deduce this second premise from any assertion about my parents, such as 'my parents tell me I ought to do what my parents tell me I ought to do'. The assertion 'I ought to do what my parents tell me' is one which, logically, I alone can make; it must originate from me. To put the point more generally, the universe of moral discourse is not one that I can be logically compelled to enter, but must, so to speak, step into voluntarily. Then the concept of ought itself, which is central to prescriptive utterance, is not reducible to, or translatable into, concepts of fearing, desiring or wanting and the like. It exists so to speak *sui generis* and the kind of work it does is distinctively different from other motivational concepts.

The relevance of the logical analysis of moral concepts for the psychological study of moral processes is far from clear. However, there are reasons why we should not ignore it. Consider first a typical learning theory analysis of the acquisition of the rule against stealing. As a consequence of parental training, certain acts are repeatedly defined as stealing and through punishment are associated with aversive responses in the child. Later, when faced with an act he is about to commit which he has to construe as stealing, this construing of the act evokes the conditioned aversive responses in the individual which inhibit him from acting. He has been trained not to steal, a training which is generalized through the cognitive constructions he has been taught to put upon his actions. Assuming that such a training process does in itself produce an inhibition against stealing, then the only accurate account the individual can give is of the form 'I have a conditioned aversion against stealing'. He cannot, that is, claim with truth that his resistance to the temptation to steal was determined by his sense of moral obligation. The learning theorist could, of course, argue that nevertheless in fact the individual may learn to use prescriptive cognitive structures when the dynamic involved is anxiety. But this is to deny that concepts reflect experience. It seems probable that people have evolved the conceptual universe of moral prescription precisely because human experience has demanded it; because moral obligation is experienced as qualitatively different from fear, anxiety and the like.

The relation between logical and psychological analysis needs much more detailed treatment than can be given here. All that is claimed here is the relatively weak conclusion that the logical analysis of moral concepts provides a reason for exploring a different way of conceiving moral obligation than that dominant in psychology. And, of course, this alternative way of looking at it is present in Piaget's formulations.

The alternative approach can be simply stated. Because the concept of 'ought' is *sui generis* it is reasonable to postulate that psychologically there is an ought motive or sense of moral obligation which is likewise *sui generis*, in the sense that it is not derived from other motives but emerges in its own right under appropriate conditions as a qualitatively distinct form of human motivation. It is so to speak elemental. In talking of a motive we are asserting that it is an indissoluble unity of cognition, affect and action tendency, and that it is, or becomes, an enduring disposition. An analogy might be the motive of curiosity, which, given appropriate conditions, emerges spontaneously, and which is likewise a unity of cognition, affect and action tendency. And just as curiosity may, on occasion, be compounded with sexuality or aggression, so the ought motive may be compounded with other motives.

For some reason psychologists have been strangely reluctant to consider moral development in these terms, with the notable exception of Piaget. Of course, in the total process of socialization the ought motive, as understood here, must be regarded as one element which interacts with many other processes of conditioning, social learning, identity formation and the like. But since this particular approach conceives it as the distinctively moral element in the whole complex process of personality development, then we need first to consider it in isolation. The question then is how we understand the conditions under which the motive emerges and is strengthened, and how the cognitive structuring of the motive develops through progressive discriminations and organization.

In approaching Piaget's account, it is important to remember that his whole structural theory is a particular example of general systems theory. A system has been defined as a set of elements which exist in relation to each other such that the functioning of the system as a whole exhibits features which cannot be attributed to the functioning of any particular elements or to some additive or cumulative effect of the functioning of the elements. Systems can be more or less open, more or less hierarchical in organization, but are always in some measure autoregulative and self-conserving. Piaget's operational structures of the intellect exhibit these characteristics. Since they are developmental, they move through a process of equilibration to ever more stable equilibria; and since they are intellectual, one of the functions exhibited by the systems as a whole is the experience of logical deduction, the compulsion of entailment, or, as Piaget calls it, moments of 'acquired self-evidence'. Now though Piaget does not make his position unequivocally explicit, and, indeed, his treatment of moral development preceded the fuller elaboration of his theory, there are signs that he is applying essentially the same approach to the embryonic beginnings of moral obligation. Morality exists between people. It is when the child first forms relationships with others that he experiences obligation. These relationships themselves can be regarded as systems, developing towards greater equilibrium, one function of which is the generation of moral obligation. It is in this sense that the sense of obligation generated within relationships can be regarded as the analogue of logical deduction within intellectual systems. This is at least one interpretation that can be put upon Piaget's otherwise perplexing statement that 'logic is the morality of thought just as morality is the logic of action' (MJ, p. 404). For the child who is party to such relationship systems, his conscious realization of the nature and form of the obligation he experiences creates for him those cognitive structures that relate to morality. Through his conscious realization he structures for himself the functioning of the relationship as a whole in so far as it concerns obligation.

For the very young child, says Piaget, there is a spontaneous pleasure in regularity. 'But we must distinguish carefully between the behaviour into which there enters only the pleasure of regularity, and that into which there enters an element of obligation. Now this element of obligation . . . intervenes as soon as there is society, i.e. a relation between at least two individuals' (MJ, p. 23). In other words, the ought motive is a function of the relationship between people and cannot be adequately accounted for in terms of processes of the individual's psychology alone. As Piaget says, the real theoretical conflict 'lies between those who want to explain the moral consciousness by means of purely individual processes (habit, biological adaptation, etc.) and those who admit the necessity for an interindividual factor' (MJ, p. 100). Rules become 'charged with obligation' because 'communal life alters the very structure of consciousness by inculcating into it the feeling of respect' (MJ, p. 96). Because Piaget also talks about types of relationship and the degrees of equilibrium they can manifest, it is clear that it is not simply social interaction which is primary for moral obligation but relatively enduring interindividual relationships. It follows, too, that the absence of such relationships in early life would have the effect of impairing the moral development of the child. On the other hand, the subsequent development of the child's morality will depend upon the kind of relationships he experiences and how he construes the obligations they generate for him.

RELATIONS OF UNILATERAL AND MUTUAL RESPECT

Piaget proposes a dimension along which personal relationships can be compared, from unilateral respect at one end to mutual respect at the other. Unilateral respect relationships are highly asymmetrical. One party to the relationship has power, status, authority and prestige, and imposes beliefs and rules on the other. The other is submissive, obedient, constrained and coerced, 'looks up' to the dominant partner, is dependent, and his opinions, beliefs and reasonings do not count. It should be noted that Piaget considers the moral impact of such relationships only from the point of view of the submissive partner; the implications for the dominant partner raise interesting questions which he does not explore. In mutual respect relationships the parties are equal, on the same footing, and relate to each other in such a way that the autonomy of each is affirmed by the relationship. Each values the opinions, judgments and reasonings of the other as he values his own. Decisions are arrived at through discussion in which reciprocity ensures that each plays an equal part in the process. The keynote of mutual respect relationships is co-operation.

Piaget's theory of the relevance of these relationships for the moral life is usually summarized as follows. The young child first experiences relationships of unilateral respect with his parents. These induce in him a morality of duty, that is, a sense of obligation to keep parental rules and an understanding of those rules as authority based and therefore unchangeable (moral realism). Morality is heteronomous, that is, something external to be obeyed. Later, the child begins to experience relationships of mutual respect with peers; these make possible for the child the experience of co-operation and lead to the morality of the good, that is, to the morality of moral aspiration and autonomy. Morality is now internalized. The child originates moral judgments rather than applying parental judgments, and displays the cognitive signs of the morality of co-operation, such as taking account of intention and understanding rules as based upon mutual agreement. The basic formula is that morality is first heteronomous and subsequently autonomous. Such an account of Piaget's position is accurate enough as far as it goes and certainly can be defended by reference to his monograph. However, his position is a good deal more complex than this. Indeed, it is possible to find unresolved tensions, even contradictions, in what he says so that the way is open for a somewhat revised interpretation.

Unilateral and mutual respect are modes of relating; both can be present at different times within the same ongoing relationship and there are modes intermediate between the two extremes. 'Constraint is never unadulterated, nor, therefore, is respect ever purely unilateral: the most submissive child has the feeling that he can, or could, argue, that a mutual sympathy surrounds relationships that are most heavily charged with authority. And conversely, co-operation is never absolutely pure: in any discussion between equals, one of the disputants can always exert pressure on the other by making overt or hidden appeals to custom or authority' (MJ, p. 84). Just as unilateral relatedness, moral realism and the morality of constraint can be found among adults, so 'the earliest social relations contain the germs of co-operation'. Piaget very explicitly rejects the equation of mutual respect with peer relationships and unilateral respect with adult relationships. Not only can parents create mutual respect with their children from a very early age, but Piaget urges them to do so. He says 'one must place oneself on the child's own level, and give him a feeling of equality by laying stress on one's own obligations and one's own deficiencies' . . . and 'in this way the child will find himself in the presence, not of a system of commands requiring ritualistic and external obedience, but of a system of social relations such that everyone does his best to obey the same obligations, and does so out of mutual respect' (MJ, p. 134). Conversely, the child's relation to the peer group can be one of unilateral respect. 'Either respect is directed to the group and results from the pressure exercised by the group upon the individual, or else it is directed to individuals and is the outcome of relations of individuals amongst themselves' (MJ, p. 95).

Though Piaget asserts that mutual respect is in the form of equilibrium towards which unilateral respect tends, and therefore implies a developmental progression, he also stresses the radical difference between the two. 'If mutual respect derives from unilateral it does so by opposition' (MJ, p. 93). The very nature of the respect involved is qualitatively different. Piaget contrasts the love and quasi-physical fear that are present in unilateral respect with the love and moral fear present in mutual respect. By moral fear he means the fear of losing the moral respect of the other.

Piaget seems to accept without question from Durkheim and Bovet the assumption that relationships of unilateral respect with authorities generate a form of moral obligation. Yet his own observations and theorizing constantly undermine this position. This is most clear in relation to justice, which for Piaget is central to morality. For he asserts that relations of unilateral respect inhibit the development of the sense of justice. 'Authority as such cannot be the source of justice, because the development of justice presupposes autonomy' . . . 'unilateral respect, then, does, *by the very nature of its mechanism,* constitute an obstacle to the free development of the sense of equality' (MJ, p. 279). This does not mean that the adult cannot influence the development of justice but that he only does so through mutual respect relatedness. 'In so far as he practises reciprocity with the child and preaches by example rather than by precept, he exercises here, as always, an enormous influence' (MJ, p. 318). 'Adult authority even if it acts in conformity with justice has therefore the effect of weakening what constitutes the essence of justice', namely, autonomy (MJ, p. 318). 'It is often at the expense of the adult and not because of him that the notions of just and unjust find their way into the youthful mind' (MJ, p. 196).

It is not only in relation to justice that unilateral respect relatedness is, to say the least, irrelevant. It is also true of truthtelling. 'One must have felt a real desire to exchange thoughts with others in order to discover all that a lie can involve' (MJ, p. 163). Such interchange is by definition impossible within unilateral relatedness. 'If the desire for truthfulness does not correspond to something very fundamental in the child's nature, the adult's command, in spite of the nimbus that surrounds it, will always remain external, "stuck on" as it were to a mind whose structure is of a different order' (MJ, p. 163). More generally Piaget says, 'The unique contribution of co-operation to the development of the moral consciousness is precisely that it implies the distinction between what is and what ought to be, between effective obedience and an ideal independent of any real command' (MJ, p. 391).

These considerations suggest that though Piaget continued to follow Durkheim and others in asserting the reality of a heteronomous morality of duty, his own thinking was moving towards a position which denies the possibility of such a morality, or, perhaps more accurately, denies that a purely heteronomous duty can be a moral duty. Certainly the logical point made earlier in this chapter implies that a heteronomous morality is a contradiction in terms, because no-one can be commanded to enter the moral domain; entry into it can only be through the individual's own autonomous recognition of its validity. Piaget explicitly accepts that autonomous recognition is the condition of being moral; he does not *explicitly* recognize that therefore there cannot be a heteronomous morality.

The problem lies in the two elements which Piaget recognizes as constituting unilateral respect, namely, quasi-physical fear and love. A relationship of pure constraint in which power is asserted over the child and his obedience is induced by fear is not a condition for the emergence of moral obligation. But normally anyway, relationships with parents have a strong element of mutual sympathy and affection. Sympathy, Piaget says, is part of the 'instinctive foundation of morality'. 'The primary condition of the moral life is the need for reciprocal affection'. But it is precisely 'spontaneous mutual affection' which is 'the starting point for a morality of good', that is, the morality of co-operation (MJ, p. 173). 'It is from the moment that it replaces the rule of constraint that the rule of co-operation becomes an effective moral law' (MJ, p. 62). Elsewhere Piaget says 'there is nothing in the actual form of duty that forces its content to conform with good. Duties are not obligatory because of their contents but because of the fact that they emanate from respected individuals. There may, therefore, be duties that have nothing to do with morality' (MJ, p. 389). If in this quotation we understand duty in a non-moral sense entirely (from a psychological point of view), and if we substitute 'feared' for 'respected', then Piaget's position becomes consistent. In so far as the parent—child relationship is characterized by power assertion and constraint, it may result in conformity but it cannot result in moral obligation; on the other hand, to the extent that it is characterized by reciprocal affection, it does generate moral obligation through the mutual respect which is contingent upon mutual and reciprocal affection.

Piaget's main empirical ground for inferring a heterogenous morality lies in his findings concerning the child's theoretical morality. He claims a functional link between the young child's moral realism and respect for authority and his intellectual egocentrism. Now even if we accept Piaget's account of egocentrism, we would expect precisely that it would not show itself in the child's practical morality. For by the age of two the child is said to be thoroughly decentred in his overt activity, most of which is social, and that it is only at the representational level that he exhibits this egocentricity again. If we suppose that the child's relationship with his parents is characterized by occasions of authoritarian assertion by the parent against a background of continuing mutual affection, we would expect the former to be more salient in the child's mind when he makes his first attempts at consciously construing the justification for his intuitive moral judgments.

MUTUAL RESPECT AND THE DEVELOPMENT OF MORAL COGNITION

Piaget is no more explicit about mutual respect relationships than he is about unilateral. But his general conception is clear enough and intuitively understandable. The relationship presupposes that, at least while interacting in this mode, people are equal in respect to each other with regard to authority, status and the like; or, perhaps more accurately, such differences in status and power as may exist are irrelevant to this mode of relating. The autonomy and equal value of each party to the relationship is affirmed by it. At the intellectual level, the mutual respect approach to others is nicely exhibited by Beth when he says that his viewpoint is 'characterized by the continual effort to understand every other viewpoint as reasonable', without, of course, abandoning his right to his own point of view (Beth and Piaget, 1966, p. 4). To the extent to which mutual respect characterizes an ongoing relationship, it necessarily implies a measure of mutual sympathy and affection. As such it corresponds to what we might call personal relationship as distinct from hierarchically structured role relatedness or the deindividuated submergence of the individual in a social group or collective.

Piaget plainly attaches a great deal of importance to such relationships in the development of the child. At the intellectual level they facilitate conscious cognitive decentring, the attainment of objectivity of thought and logical structures, and, in general, the socialization of the intellect. They are an important condition of personality development for they make possible the differentiation of the self from others and the situating of the self in relation to others through role-taking. They encourage self-respect and the sense of being of equal worth to others. And, of course, they make possible the emergence of the ought motive or sense of obligation, and the origination of moral judgments.

They also play a crucial role in the development of the child's theoretical morality. The theoretical morality a child presents to others is obviously a function of many factors, such as his intellectual skills in rationalizing what he has been told by others and what he sees as expected of him by others. But the extent to which this morality is personally authenticated is measured by the extent to which it is the conscious realization of his own moral experience.

Piaget draws an important distinction between constituted and constitutive rules. The former result from the agreement reached by conscious discussion between people within a relationship of mutual respect. It is not clear whether constituted rules in this sense can be regarded as moral, or, more accurately, whether they will correspond to moral rules when they are the conscious realization of constitutive rules. Constituted rules can obviously include the rules of games and of conventions and, of course, laws. These may not in terms of their content be what we would call moral. The moral dimension is present when the breaking of such rules is also a violation of constitutive rules. Constitutive rules are those which are fundamentally implicit in the structure of mutual respect relationships themselves, which are the conditions of the maintenance and development of such relatedness. In so far as they are consciously realized they have a quality of self-evidence about them. They are not so much rules reached by agreement as the principles which make the reaching of agreement possible. Piaget has called them principles of procedure, but that is perhaps not too happy a way of putting it. They include justice and fairness, truthtelling, keeping promises and agreements, concern for the welfare of others, respect for their judgments and beliefs, and the assertion of the worth of people, including the self. In short, they are the basic moral concerns, and one way or another can be regarded as the conditions of mutual respect relatedness between people. The heart of moral development can then be defined as the prolonged and continuing experience of mutual respect relationships such that the conscious realization of the constitutive rules of such relatedness is charged with moral obligation and the rules themselves systematized and universalized to all people and situations. The function of Kohlberg's developmental scheme in the process of progressive universalization of moral prescription can be readily seen. The contribution of Piaget's conception of practical morality to Kohlberg's formulations would seem to lie in the fact that the continuance of personal relatedness of a mutual respect kind throughout adult life is needed so that the highly generalized morality of the adult can retain its roots in obligation and personal authentication. The question of how the individual achieves a universalized morality that retains its roots in moral obligation is one which Piaget does not discuss; but it would seem to involve some degree of conscious realization and universalization of the foundation of mutual respect relatedness, namely, sympathy and good will.

CONCLUSION

It cannot be stressed too much that Piaget's theory of moral development is unfinished, often incoherent and sometimes apparently contradictory. This chapter is intended as a re-affirmation of his central ideas, and, of course, underlying that re-affirmation is a conviction of their relative validity. At the same time, there has been some restatement of his position, but it is hoped, one that remains faithful to his general ideas. This restatement reduces effectively to the claim that his morality of duty is not truly moral but corresponds to those aspects of the process of socialization and social control which other theories have dealt with and which accounts for the facts of conformity but not for the facts of moral obligation. At the same time, it is argued that he offers a uniquely valuable way of conceiving the nature and origins of moral obligation.

REFERENCES

Beth, E. and Piaget, J. (1966) *Mathematical Epistemology and Psychology.* Dordrecht Reidel.
Kohlberg, L. (1973) *Collected Papers.* University of Harvard: Center for Moral Education.
Turiel, E. (1973) Stage Transition in Moral Development. In Travers, R. M. (Ed.) *Second Handbook of Research on Teaching.* Chicago: Rand McNally.
Piaget, J. (1932) *The Moral Judgment of the Child.* London: Routledge and Kegan Paul.

Interchange

WEINREICH-HASTE REPLIES TO WRIGHT

In his chapter, Wright has set out to make explicit certain points in Piaget's monograph on *The Moral Judgment of the Child*, and to consider the implications of extending those points beyond Piaget's explicit position. In doing this Wright has made three major points. The first point is that the relationship between thought and action— practical and theoretical morality—is conceived very differently by Piaget and by those, such as Kohlberg, who have ostensibly extended the 'Piagetian tradition' in moral psychology. Wright argues that the essential basis of Piaget's developmental theory, in moral as well as logical fields, is the process of conscious realization; cognitive representation is a reflection upon already existing actions. Kohlberg, on the other hand, focuses upon the representation of the moral concept and its usage in problem-solving: the direction of relationship is that thought in some sense *predicts* action. The implication is that, for Kohlberg, the moral force arises from the conceptualization of the moral issue, and is translated into action to a greater or lesser degree. The implication of Piaget's position, according to Wright, is that the child experiences a sense of obligation to others and acts increasingly co-operatively in the social context, and, as a consequence of the conscious realization of these events, comes to develop a morality based upon mutual respect.

Wright's second point concerns the nature and development of the sense of obligation. Piaget argued that obligation arose inevitably from the experience of social interaction, and from obligation arose respect, initially unilateral, subsequently mutual. Wright has extended this idea so that the *motive* of obligation is for him central to the conception of a 'moral being'. Additionally, Wright makes explicit the 'systems theory' implications of Piaget's theory; a sense of obligation is the *equilibrating factor* which strengthens and maintains relationships; hence, obligation has a developmental and a social function.

Following from this interpretation, Wright argues that heteronomous morality is not in any recognizable sense 'morality' at all. There are a number of reasons for this position, some of which are inherent in Piaget's formulations, some are not. Firstly, a morality of constraint implies, of course, no autonomy; to act on command is not to act on the basis of moral motives. On the other hand, Piaget recognizes that an understanding of the rules, if not the reasons for them, is a form of morality. Secondly, Wright's definition of morality is specifically geared to interpersonal relationships; obligations arise from interactions, they are, in Wright's view, obligations between *people.* Therefore obligations to conform to a rule (or even a role) do not seem to conform to this, and morality can only be said to begin when the child has a motive of obligation as between persons. His criticism of Kohlberg arises from the same position;

218

the implicit morality about which Kohlberg theorizes is concerned not with people and interaction, but with *ideas* of people, and principles *about* relationships, rather than with relationships themselves.

Wright's approach has generated some striking insights; he can, indeed, claim that by going beyond Piaget in certain areas, and by focusing on little-explored obscurities in Piaget's monograph, he has made explicit some of Piaget's underlying assumptions. However, I would take issue with Wright on some points. It seems to me that Wright is, perhaps deliberately, conflating two issues which Piaget separated, at least overtly. Piaget's monograph is ostensibly about the transmission of morality from one generation to the next, and the question to which he addressed himself, which has both social and developmental factors, was the way in which a morality of constraint (based on unilateral respect) can become a morality of co-operation (based on mutual respect). For Piaget, the social and developmental mechanisms of this psychological process concerned interaction with others, both peers and elders. However, his definition of *morality* seems to be implicit in the kinds of questions he posed to his subjects and concerns various definitions of 'justice', in particular retributive justice and distributive justice to some degree. His primary criterion is fairness, and his empirical studies were to a large measure directed towards demonstrating how the child's idea of fairness changes. In discussing 'morality' Piaget concentrates in particular on justice.

In other words, it seems to me that Wright is focusing on a different definition of morality from Piaget. Wright explicitly asks the questions about how the individual becomes a 'moral being' and he utilizes Piaget's developmental theory as a means of examining this question, deriving insights from the theory which provide a cognitive dimension. However, the origins of a 'moral motivation' theory, as Wright acknowledges, do not lie in any existing *cognitive* theory; they derive from trait- or affect-based theories—which tend to lack a cognitive dimension. Cognitive theories have concentrated on how the child comes to understand certain moral concepts (usually justice); only recently have some writers (e.g. Damon, Selman) begun to ask how the child conceives of relationships between people. Such theoretical approaches do not ask how the individual becomes a 'moral being', but how the individual comes to understand the moral or conventional rules offered to it by society. Wright may legitimately argue that such an approach tells us little about moral behaviour, or even about the basic motives which affect how the child construes certain situations as 'moral'. He may also argue that by taking Piaget's conception of the development of mutual respect a stage further, he can ask relevant questions about the *implications* of this for the development of the moral motive. However, I think it is a fundamental departure from Piaget's position.

WRIGHT REPLIES TO WEINREICH-HASTE

Weinreich-Haste has presented a most thorough review of Piaget's work on moral development and placed it in the context of other and more recent contributions. In my view, it is the most comprehensive and useful review to have been written for some time. Her critique of Piaget's monograph is cogent and convincing, and she has pointed up certain weaknesses of argument that had not been noticed before. In effect, she has given substantial and detailed support for the assertion that Piaget's monograph is tentative, limited and often confused.

It is impossible in a short response to do justice to the many points raised in her lengthy chapter. In the main I find myself in agreement with what she says. The points I wish to raise may not be regarded as particularly substantial in the light of the main thrust of the monograph but, to my mind, they are important if we are looking for points of departure in Piaget's theorizing rather than attempting, as Weinreich-Haste has done, a balanced assessment of the work itself. Precisely because Piaget's theorizing in this field is unfinished and fragmentary, the reader has some freedom in making his own synthesis for purposes of criticism or support.

A preliminary point, which is peripheral to a discussion of Piaget but which needs to be said, is that Piaget, and apparently Weinreich-Haste too, is less than fair to Durkheim. Durkheim is presented by Piaget as the advocate of unilateral respect and the morality of constraint. In fact, his position is much more subtle than this. He has argued strongly that autonomy is an essential ingredient of a moral person. Though he can perhaps be criticized for incoherence and inconsistency, it cannot be denied that he has, by implication, laid the basis for the importance of those relationships of mutual respect which Piaget saw as his own major contribution.

One of the most central conceptual distinctions that Piaget draws is between practical and theoretical morality. Though Piaget at times appears to forget the distinction, his readers should not. The child's first tentative theoretical morality tends to take the form of the morality of constraint, and the presumption is that this represents the conscious realization of an earlier practical morality. The fact that young children invariably are under the control and direction of adults lends plausibility to this. But there is so far no evidence that the young child's practical morality takes this form, and Piaget's later work in other areas shows that conscious realization is initially a process which is highly subject to error. Whether the young child's embryonic sense of *moral* obligation is a function of unilateral respect remains therefore an open question. Piaget's own suggestion, which informal observation of very young children would seem to endorse, is that regularities of a social kind become changed with obligation whatever the character of the social relationships.

More important, and a point which Weinreich-Haste does not in my view stress enough, Piaget saw unilateral and mutual respect as in conflict. Mutual respect emerges in spite of unilateral respect, and it is itself of a different order. Moreover, mutual respect according to Piaget can, and to some extent usually does, exist from the earliest years and alongside unilateral respect. Development is less a transition from one to the other than the increasing salience of mutual respect and the decreasing salience of unilateral. This is held by Piaget to be a feature of the child's developing practical morality, even though his first attempts at theoretical morality imply a dominance of unilateral respect. My point is simply that Piaget's position is more subtle, or confused, than a simple account in terms of a constraint morality superseded by a morality of co-operation would imply.

A concept embedded in Piaget's theory which has not received enough attention, and which Weinreich-Haste does not pick up and discuss, is that of *relationship*. It appears that moral philosophers and psychologists have tended to understand morality in terms of attributes of, or processes in, the individual. Sociologists and many social psychologists have tended to see it as an aspect of the induction of children into social structures and the processes which induce conformity to the norms of those structures. Very recently some psychologists have begun to recognize that the category of relationships cannot be subsumed under either such concepts as attitude and social interaction, nor those of social structure. It is a curious fact, though one not wholly unexpected in terms of Piaget's later work on conscious realization, that though we have good reason to think that relationships of mutual affection and love are crucial for the development of the child's practical morality, it is not until the child is much older that considerations of love and caring appear in his theoretical morality. It is to Piaget's credit that the concept of relationship is at the heart of his theory, even if he did not develop it with any precision.

And so my main response to Weinreich-Haste is to say that though she has done very effectively what she set out to do, her examination of Piaget does not do justice to those elements in his thinking that can be taken as starting points for further elaborations of a relatively novel kind.

Chapter 12

Potential Sources of Structural Invalidity in Piagetian and Neo-Piagetian Assessment*

RICHARD J. HOFMANN

THE HORIZONTAL DECALAGE AS A MANIFESTATION OF STRUCTURAL INVALIDITY

A major problem, not unfamiliar in the field of clinical psychology, is one of attempting to operationalize the theory and work of a 'great man' when it is not totally clear whether it is the great man who makes the theory work, in which case lesser men cannot make the theory work, or whether it is a great man with a great theory. Clearly, Jean Piaget is a great man; the true greatness of his theory remains to be demonstrated. That is, Piaget's work must be judged as being functional without Piaget. His work must demonstrate a validity beyond the Genevans. Piaget himself has suggested this point:

> I have the conviction, illusory or well founded . . . and only the future will tell whether this conviction [Piaget's theory] is partly true or only the result of obstinate pride . . . that I have laid bare a more or less evident general skeleton which remains full of gaps so that when these gaps will be filled the articulations will have to be differentiated but the general lines of the system will not be changed. The history of experimental sciences is full of examples that illustrate my point. When a theory succeeds another theory the first impression is often that the new theory contradicts the older and eliminates it. But later research often shows that more has to be retained of the older theory than could be foreseen. The better theory turns out to be the one that retains most of the preceding theory. (Sinclair De Zwart, 1977.)

*This essay was written in its entirety while the author was a Faculty Research Fellow at Miami University. A number of unpublished studies served as a basis for this essay. These unpublished studies were carried out with the kind support of the William Holmes McGuffey Laboratory School. Finally, the author wishes to acknowledge the extensive and provocative critiques of the penultimate draft of this essay provided by Barry Wadsworth and William Gray. I profited greatly from their scholarly comments Needless to say, we disagree on some points, and so this acknowledgment should not be regarded as implying that they endorse my essay in all respects.

223

Generalizing or operationalizing Piaget is analogous to filling in the above mentioned gaps. One potential approach for operationalizing at least a part of Piaget's theory is the psychometric or assessment approach. Yet, Piagetian psychology did not evolve through the study of individual differences, a basic goal of psychometrics. Rather it evolved through the study of individual similarities. Piaget himself has never had any great interest in 'psychometrizing' his work (Wadsworth, 1978). Piagetian psychology and psychometrics are clearly strange 'bedfellows' whose offspring may bear little resemblance to its parents.

The research literature on the replication and extension of Piaget, utilizing his *méthode clinique* or objective refinements thereof, has achieved only approximate success (see Green, Ford and Flamer, 1971; or Smedslund, 1977; or Beilin, 1965; for numerous discussions and references to problems). One perspective on these failures and approximate successes can be seen in the research that has been done that is relevant to the time-lag within structures generally referred to as horizontal decalage (Piaget, 1962). Piaget (1967, 1971, 1973) has noted that children, on the average, are able to solve quite specific problems at certain ages. However, if one alters the problem, say by changing the material or the situation, or by using an apparently equivalent problem, then time-lags of several months or even several years may be observed. For example, a child may demonstrate a grasp of the principle of invariance by demonstrating conservation of weight at approximately nine years of age, but may not demonstrate conservation of volume until 11 years of age. Similarly, class-inclusion problems show considerable time-lags depending upon the object class used (Lovell, 1961; Feinberg and Laycock, 1964; Inhelder and Piaget, 1964; Inhelder, 1971; Piaget, 1971). Piaget (1975) has noted time-lags as great as two years between successes when asking children to show him where the water would be in a glass that is half full and where the water would be in a glass that is half empty. These problems of time-lags represent a serious obstacle for those who wish to operationalize Piaget (see Inhelder, Sinclair and Bovet, 1974). As noted by Droz and Rahmy (1976), time-lags 'call for intuition on the part of the reader' (p. 64) and they optimistically anticipate that a further understanding will be obtained through empirical investigation. Piaget's works and writings span half a century. During that period of time he has been extremely prolific and has enjoyed the scholarly companionship of numerous prolific colleagues. His works over this period of time may be thought of as being evolutionary in the sense that his newer works sometimes contradict his older works but more frequently represent, in part, extensions of his older works (Droz and Rahmy, 1976). Thus reader intuition, as advocated by Droz and Rahmy, must be tempered by the chronology in which Piaget is read. Only the most astute Piagetian scholars will have this necessary intuition.

A more general way of viewing time-lags is through a consideration of the general task structure utilized in the assessment process. A child responds in one way in one situation and in another way in a second situation that 'appears to be' logically equivalent to the first situation as far as task structure is concerned. In general, the logical task structure does not seem to be a good predictor of behaviour across situational task variation (Smedslund, 1977). That is, variation in the structure of what appear to be logically equivalent tasks will frequently result in response variation. Tasks that result in such response variation may be thought of as being structurally invalid if the potential for response variation is not recognized when the tasks are being used in an assessment process. Structural invalidity is a term that is intended to imply that the structure of a task(s) is invalid in so far as providing for legitimate generalization. Legitimate generalization refers to inferences regarding the presence of, or absence of, a cognitive structure as a function of an individual's performance on a task or set of tasks.

When operationalizing Piaget by utilizing a psychometric approach, structural invalidity will exist if the results of an assessment of an individual do not show a substantial relationship with the results of a second assessment that is assumed to be logically equivalent, or if the general age associated with mastery performance on the assessment is greater or less than expected. The objective of this brief essay is one of explicating eleven sources of structural invalidity in Piagetian and neo-Piagetian research.

Although this essay is critical of the present state of the art regarding Piaget and psychometrics, there is evidence suggesting that the assessment of Piagetian cognitive structures provides information not provided by the more traditional cognitive assessment procedures (Uzgiris and Hunt, 1975; DeVries and Kohlberg, 1977; Wadsworth, 1978, Pt. IV; Tuddenham, 1979, personal communication; Wachs, 1979, personal communication). The spirit of this essay is one of being critical of the present state of the theory regarding Piaget and psychometrics with the realization that such a critical discussion will lead to methodological research resulting in a stronger, pragmatic approach to Piagetian assessment.

BASIC SOURCES OF STRUCTURAL INVALIDITY IN PIAGETIAN AND NEO-PIAGETIAN ASSESSMENT

In attempting to determine the presence and nature of cognitive structures, Piaget originally developed and utilized a procedure referred to as the *méthode clinique* (clinical method) (Wadsworth, 1978). Although he presented a discussion of this technique in one of his early works (Piaget, 1929), it has undergone adaptive modification through the years, yet is still largely intact. The replication literature on Piaget is rich in providing descriptions and criticism of a variety of Piagetian and neo-Piagetian assessment procedures. In the section to follow, these assessment procedures will be integrated to define a general structure for Piagetian and neo-Piagetian assessment.

Virtually all of Piaget's work may be thought of as being hierarchical. The term hierarchical is used here to convey the idea of a relatively fixed sequence; therefore, any general structure for assessment must necessarily include the logic of hierarchies or sequences.

In discussing assessment there are two general categories of concern: stimulus and response. The stimulus represents anything that is done or presented to an individual and the response represents anything that the individual does or says in return. At a more basic level, one must consider how the stimulus is presented and how the response is returned. Piaget and neo-Piagetians have used at least four possible modes of presenting stimuli and have used at least five response modes.

Stimulus Presentation Mode

Disregarding the specific content of the stimulus, Piaget has utilized a visual mode of presentation (Inhelder and Piaget, 1964), a tactile mode of presentation (Inhelder and Piaget, 1964), a kinaesthetic mode of presentation (Inhelder, 1968; Piaget and Inhelder, 1974), and an auditory mode of presentation (Piaget, 1929). There is a very clear hierarchical relationship among these four modes of presentation. Assuming, for convenience of presentation, a single attribute seriation (sorting) task (Piaget and Szeminska, 1952), it is possible to provide empirical evidence that the age at which a child can demonstrate a presence of the seriation structure will vary as a function of the mode of stimulus presentation.

Utilizing a collection of 10 rods of different lengths, Inhelder and Piaget (1964) demonstrated that seven-year-old children were successful in visually seriating the rods—a visual presentation. Similar results have been obtained in replication studies (Lovell, Mitchell and Everett, 1962; Elkind, 1964; Mansfield and Clark, 1977). With similar collections of rods, Inhelder and Piaget (1964) demonstrated that eight- to nine-year-old children were successful in seriating the rods from shortest to longest 'by touch', that is, the rods were presented beneath a screen so that the children could not see them—a tactile presentation. According to Piaget (1967), it is not until about the age of nine or ten that the child can serially order weights (balls of the same size but of different weight that are sorted from lightest to heaviest)—a kinaesthetic presentation. Similar seriation results following a kinaesthetic presentation have been noted elsewhere (Inhelder, 1968; Piaget and Inhelder, 1974). Although Piaget has not investigated single-attribute seriation utilizing an auditory presentation, our own informal work with seriation at our McGuffey Laboratory suggests that successful single-attribute seriation following an auditory presentation occurs at a later age than it does following a kinaesthetic presentation. With a collection of 11 different tone bars we have been able to demonstrate with a sample of approximately 100 children that successful auditory seriation occurs at about 12 years of age.

If one could use all four modes of stimulus presentation for assessing the presence of cognitive structures, the general order of sequence in which their presence could be inferred across age levels would be visual, tactile, kinaesthetic and auditory. That is, a cognitive structure will appear at an earlier age following a visual presentation than it will following a kinaesthetic presentation, assuming both presentation modes are viable.

When one uses a particular presentation mode and does not consider the potential consequences of using other modes of presentation, there is a danger of improperly generalizing the effects associated with the presentation mode. It is quite possible that such effects might be either more or less apparent with other presentation modes, depending upon the hierarchical placement of the original presentation mode.

Structural invalidity source (1). When the hierarchical placement of the stimulus presentation mode utilized with a particular assessment procedure is not clearly delineated, the results of the assessment procedure are subject to improper generalization.

Stimulus presentations are also utilized in pairs, double or multiple seriation. With such a task either one of two possible orientations is used. Either two different stimulus presentation modes are used (e.g. a child may be asked to sort a set of balls by weight, kinaesthetic presentation, as well as by colour intensity, visual presentation), or two different dimensions within a single-stimulus presentation mode are used (e.g. a child may be asked to sort a collection of cut-out leaves by colour intensity, visual presentation, and by size, visual presentation). A correct multiple seriation results in a multiplicative seriation matrix (see Inhelder and Piaget, 1964).

In their research, Inhelder and Piaget (1964) appear to use two different dimensions within a visual stimulus presentation mode. They note that prior to successful multiple seriation, a child may demonstrate successful seriation within either dimension independently of the other dimension; that a child may demonstrate successful seriation within one dimension but not within the other dimension. Although there does not appear to be any published Piagetian research on the use of multiple-stimulus presentation modes, such research would represent a logical extension of the Inhelder and Piaget research on multiple seriation within the visual stimulus presentation mode.

Great care should be exercised when using two presentation modes. If two stimulus presentation modes are used, it is quite likely that they will interact to produce a unique effect. Such an effect may have little relationship to the effects that would occur with either stimulus presentation mode used independently of the other. Furthermore, the hierarchical placement of various paired presentation modes is somewhat vague. The ambiguity of paired presentation modes and their possible interaction effects are noted in a rather extensive review of cross-modal functions provided by Freides (1974). If paired presentation modes are to be utilized in developing an assessment procedure, the effects of their possible interaction should be noted. If possible a discussion of the effects should be couched within the context of the expected independent effects of each presentation mode. Finally, an effort should be made to determine the hierarchical placement of the paired presentation modes within either a single presentation mode hierarchy, or within a hierarchy defined by the possible paired presentation modes, or, ideally, within a hierarchy defined by the combination of single presentation modes and paired presentation modes.

Structural invalidity source (2). When paired presentation modes are used with a particular assessment procedure and are either not recognized as representing a possible interaction between two independent presentation modes or not delineated within a hierarchical context, the results of the assessment procedure are subject to improper generalization.

Performance Response Mode

Disregarding the specific content of the response, Piaget has used three general levels of performance response: recognition, construction and graphic reproduction. Recognition requires no overt production on the part of the respondent as the correct response is selected from a collection of responses. Recognition responses are used extensively in Piaget's memory research (Piaget, Inhelder and Sinclair de Zwart, 1973), as well as in other research, multiplicative classification (matrices) (Inhelder and Piaget, 1964), certain haptic perception work (Piaget and Inhelder, 1956), and mental imagery (Piaget and Inhelder, 1971), to note just a few. Construction responses involve the use of certain materials to construct something, i.e. matchsticks to construct a triangle (Piaget and Inhelder, 1956), fragments of a regular geometric figure to construct the figure (Piaget and Inhelder, 1971), or wooden dowels to construct the memory of a seriation task (Piaget, Inhelder and Sinclair de Zwart, 1973). Graphic reproductions or graphic responses are simply drawings that represent responses, i.e. drawing simple geometric figures to study characteristics of spatial representation (Piaget and Inhelder, 1956), drawing seriated arrays to demonstrate memory (Piaget, Inhelder and Sinclair de Zwart, 1973), drawing 'anticipated figures' in the study of mental imagery (Piaget and Inhelder, 1971). As with stimulus presentation modes, there is a very clear hierarchical relationship amongst these three performance response modes. The age and extent to which a child can demonstrate the presence of a given structure will vary as a function of performance response mode.

In several references, Piaget notes a very distinct hierarchical relationship amongst response modes. Generally, presence of a cognitive structure will occur at an earlier age when a recognition response is required, rather than when a construction or graphic reproduction is required. Construction responses typically precede graphic reproductions chronologically (Piaget and Inhelder, 1956; Blackstock and King, 1973; Piaget, Inhelder, Sinclair de Zwart, 1973).

At least one of the sources of structural invalidity that occurs with stimuli presentations will occur in an analogous fashion with performance response modes. When one uses a particular performance response mode and does not either note the particular consequences of the other performance response modes or discuss their effects within a hierarchical context relative to the other performance response modes, there is a possibility of improperly generalizing the results.

Structural invalidity source (3). When the hierarchical placement of the performance response mode utilized with a particular assessment procedure is not clearly delineated, the results of the assessment procedure are subject to improper generalization.

Unlike stimulus presentations, performance response modes are not used jointly. It does happen frequently, however, that more than one performance response mode is used with an assessment procedure. When more than one performance mode is used, the modes are used sequentially, e.g. a recognition response is required and then a manipulation response is required from the same child. Inhelder and Piaget (1964) have noted that when graphic reproduction precedes construction in single-attribute seriation, there is a certain amount of practice effect which actually facilitates the manipulative construction response of the seriation task. Thus, those children who first participate in graphic reproduction of a single-attribute (length) seriation task actually do better at seriating the task than do similarly aged children who do not initially participate in anticipatory graphic reproduction.

Structural invalidity source (4). When two or more performance response modes are used in a fixed order with some particular assessment procedure there may be an order effect that distorts the results of the assessment to the extent that the results of the response modes appear either more similar than they actually are or more dissimilar than they actually are. In either case the effects of one or more performance response modes are subject to improper generalization when they are used in a fixed order.

If one suspected an order effect and if one was trained in experimental design, one might decide to use a procedure called 'counterbalancing' (Campbell and Stanley, 1966) to eliminate the effects of order. When counterbalancing, the order of the performance response modes is randomized so that randomly different respondents respond according to different orders of response modes. Whereas structural invalidity source (4) essentially results in a constant effect for all respondents, a counterbalanced presentation, random order for performance response mode would have a very irregular effect. Such an irregular effect would manifest itself as an inflated estimate of individual differences within certain performance response modes because certain respondents, determined by random selection, would benefit from a practice effect associated with a particular order of response modes to which other respondents were not exposed. When the particular response mode associated with an order effect is evaluated independently of order, there will be greater individual differences associated with this particular response mode than there would be if the response mode were actually used independently of other response modes with the same respondents. Thus, some performance response modes would falsely appear to be much more sensitive to individual response differences in a counterbalanced presentation format than they would appear to be if used independently. Such performance response modes would also falsely appear to be more sensitive to individual differences than other performance response modes used in the same counterbalanced design.

Structural invalidity source (5). When two or more performance response modes are used in a random order with some particular assessment procedure, there may be an irregular order effect that distorts the apparent sensitivity of certain response modes to individual differences. Such irregular effects result in an improper generalization of the sensitivity of the response modes involved.

Verbal—Non-verbal Response Mode

It is well established that Piaget's primary method of interacting with children is verbally through the *méthode clinique* (Piaget, 1929). The *méthode clinique* was developed by Piaget as an improvement over standardized testing (see Wadsworth, 1978). In particular, it was developed to probe the thinking and reasoning of a child in order to determine the presence and nature of cognitive structures (schemata). Piaget has modified his assessment procedure over time, eventually merging it with experimentation to define a procedure that is now referred to as 'the method of critical exploration' (Inhelder, Sinclair and Bovet, 1974).

The method of critical exploration requires a child to respond to questions and to verbalize about phenomena that have been produced. It is an interrogation of the child and it varies as a function of the type of cognitive structure being assessed and the response of the individual child. Contradiction is introduced into the assessment procedure in an effort to have the child verbalize the reasoning process that is being used. Because different questions, different contradictions and different situations arise as a function of the cognitive structure(s) being assessed and as a function of a child's response, Inhelder, Sinclair and Bovet (1974, p. 21) indicate that the method of critical exploration, 'Yields reliable data only if the interviewer has acquired a very thorough theoretical background and mastery of the interviewing technique'.

Piaget utilizes all of the previously noted performance response modes and then requires verbalization following the performance response. The adequacy of the performance response is evaluated in conjunction with the verbalization which follows it. Such verbalizations are referred to as justifications by Inhelder, Sinclair and Bovet (1974) and as explanation criteria by Brainerd (1973, 1977).

Brainerd (1973) contends that Piagetian theory does not justify explanation criteria and that explanations are a sufficient but not necessary condition for the presence of structures. In discussing age discrepancies within Piagetian replication work, Brainerd notes that Piagetian research has somewhat inflated age norms because of its rigid adherence to explanation criteria. Such criteria, when considered within the context of individual respondents, will on occasion, suggest, incorrectly, that a child does not possess the cognitive structure that is being assessed; that is, explanation criteria are very conservative.

Structural invalidity source (6). When utilizing an explanation criterion with a particular performance response mode, certain respondents may be erroneously categorized as not possessing the cognitive structure being assessed when really they do. Explanation criteria may result in inflated age norms.

Brainerd (1973, 1977) argues that the explanation criterion should be replaced with a judgment criterion. When a judgment criterion is used, the non-verbal, or minimally verbal, response, as provided by the performance response mode, is evaluated for evidence or a lack of evidence of the presence of the cognitive structure of interest. From an objective psychometric position, judgment criteria are very desirable as they are dichotomous and relatively objective. Actually, it is the judgment criterion that is followed by the explanation criterion in the method of critical exploration. The judgment criterion is the minimum necessary evidence required to demonstrate the presence of a cognitive structure, although some might argue that a more accurate statement would be that a judgment is necessary, but not sufficient evidence. Judgment criteria may be evidenced by a variety of responses which make them susceptible to at least three types of errors that do not typically occur with explanation criteria: guesses, direct perception and irrelevant hypotheses (Smedslund, 1969; Brainerd, 1973). While

Brainerd (1973) correctly argues that such errors can be controlled and eliminated, when such errors are not eliminated, judgment criteria are extremely liberal. When considered within the context of individual respondents, liberal criteria will on occasion suggest, incorrectly, that a child possesses the cognitive structure that is being assessed. The consequence of such errors will be liberal or depressed age norms (see Braine, 1959).

Structural invalidity source (7). When utilizing a judgment criterion with a particular performance response mode, certain respondents may be erroneously categorized as possessing the cognitive structure being assessed. Judgment criteria may result in liberal age norms.

It would seem that either response criterion, judgment or explanations, would result in a source of structural invalidity. Which source of errors does one wish to make? In addressing this question, Brainerd (1977) states that normally there will be a differential error rate as a function of the response criterion and that one ought to select the criterion with the lowest error rate. He provides a discussion based upon probability demonstrating that the lower error rate is usually associated with a judgment criterion. This is an especially important finding in that a judgment criterion does not require a sophisticated, trained examiner and it is an objective criterion that is much easier to implement than an explanation criterion.

In summarizing the research literature on judgment and explanation criteria, Brainerd (1977) presents a rather astonishing discovery that follows quite logically from his probability discussion. He notes that there is not a single Piagetian or neo-Piagetian research study in which cognitive structures emerge non-sequentially with judgment criteria and sequentially with explanations. Yet, when two cognitive structures are observed to develop sequentially, the research literature shows that either the sequence is observed with both types of criteria or it is observed with judgments only criteria. Bingham-Newman and Hooper (1975) as well as Brainerd and Hooper (1975) have provided evidence that certain cognitive structures, identity and equivalence, which are confirmed as being sequential when using a judgment criterion, are rejected as sequential when using an explanation criterion.

Structural invalidity source (8). When utilizing an explanation criterion with a particular response mode, one may conclude that a collection of cognitive structures are not sequential; yet when using a judgment criterion with the same response mode, one may conclude that the same collection of cognitive structures are sequential.

This source of invalidity is particularly perplexing in that much of Piagetian theory assumes hierarchical or sequential relationships amongst certain cognitive structures. As with the stimulus presentation mode and performance response mode, there is a hierarchical relationship amongst judgment and explanation criteria. Put simply, judgment criteria are less conservative (more liberal) than explanation criteria. A *single* cognitive structure will generally appear at an earlier age following a judgment criterion than it will following an explanation criterion.

A FACETED DEFINITION OF A GENERAL PIAGETIAN AND NEO-PIAGETIAN ASSESSMENT TASK STRUCTURE

In the previous sections, Piagetian and neo-Piagetian assessment procedures were discussed within the general context of assessment task structure. Eight sources of structural invalidity were identified as being associated with their hierarchical relationships. By collectively considering the three modes—stimulus presentation, performance response and verbal—non-verbal response—it is possible to specify a general assessment task structure.

The term mode can also be referred to as a facet in the sense of Guttman (1965). The three modes or facets will define a Cartesian space into which any method of Piagetian or neo-Piagetian assessment may be placed. In Table 12.1 each mode is referred to as a major facet A, B or C, with subscripted lower case letters representing the elements of a facet. The three facets of Table 12.1 will define 24 possible combinations of three elements each ($4 \times 3 \times 2$), one from each facet. The Cartesian product of the three facets is written as ABC and each three-element profile defines a sub-universe or particular assessment procedure.

Frequently, when determining a faceted definition of a universe, the elements within a facet can be ordered or sequenced. When the elements can be sequenced within facets, the resulting sub-universes within the Cartesian product can be sequenced meaningfully. With regard to facet A, the stimulus presentation mode, there is a formal sequencing, $a_1 < a_2 < a_3 < a_4$. The symbol '<' is used to signify that what is to the left of the symbol precedes what is to the right of the symbol in the total sequencing within the facet. In the classic Guttman (1954) scaling sense, presence of the cognitive structure, a_2, implies presence of the cognitive structure, a_1, assuming all else to be equal. In theory, it is then assumed that facet A defines a perfect Guttman scale. Similarly, the elements within facet B, the performance response mode, and facet C, the verbal—non-verbal mode, may be assumed to define perfect Guttman scales: $b_1 < b_2 < b_3$; $c_1 < c_2$.

Having defined the three assessment modes and the hierarchical relationships or structuring within modes, it is possible to produce and structure the 24 sub-universes defined by the Cartesian product ABC.

Table 12.1 *Facets and elements of facets for defining a general Piagetian and neo-Piagetian assessment task structure*

Facets	Elements of Facets
A = stimulus presentation mode	a_1 visual a_2 tactile a_3 kinaesthetic a_4 auditory
B = performance response mode	b_1 recognition b_2 construction b_3 graphic reproduction
C = verbal—non-verbal mode	c_1 judgment c_2 explanation

In Figure 12.1, a general Piagetian and neo-Piagetian assessment task structure is portrayed. The connecting arrowed lines between sub-universes in Figure 12.1 identify those sub-universes between which the relation '<' holds. For the two sub-universes $a_1b_1c_1$ and $a_1b_2c_1$, the relationship $a_1b_1c_1 < a_1b_2c_1$ will hold if and only if at any one time $a_1 \leq a_1$, $b_1 \leq b_2$, and $c_1 \leq c_1$. For example, ($a_1b_1c_1 < a_1b_1c_2 < a_2b_1c_2 < a_2b_2c_2 < a_3b_2c_2 < a_4b_2c_2 < a_4b_3c_2$) represents an assessment sequence or scale that involves seven sub-universes.

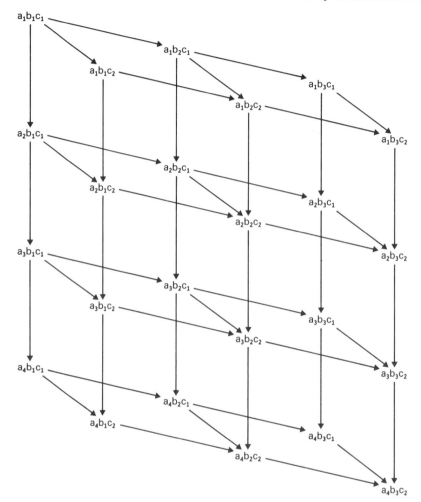

Figure 12.1   A facet design of a general Piagetian and neo-Piagetian assessment task structure.

The first eight sources of structural invalidity are a function of not knowing where an assessment procedure is located within the faceted assessment task structure portrayed by Figure 12.1. The sequencing is between sub-universes rather than within sub-universes. Each connected sub-universe differs from its predecessor sub-universe on only one facet. Each sub-universe can be modified in either two or three ways to move to a 'higher' or more difficult assessment sub-universe, so each has two or three lines branching down from it. The first sub-universe might be thought of as the assessment procedure on which the presence of a cognitive structure will be noted at the earliest possible age—a visual presentation requiring a non-verbal or judgment recognition response. The most advanced sub-universe defines the assessment procedure on which the presence of a cognitive structure will be noted at the latest age—an auditory presentation requiring an explanation of a graphic response.

Figure 12.1 defines all logically possible sub-universes, but that does not mean that all sub-universes are practical within the context of a particular cognitive structure. The universe defined by Figure 12.1 may also be expanded to include such things as content variation (to be discussed in the section to follow). The universe defined by Figure 12.1 would expand threefold when 'mapped' onto conservation of matter, weight and volume because of the hierarchical relationships amongst matter, weight and volume. Similarly, if one were to consider mapping seriation strategies (Piaget, Inhelder and Sinclair de Zwart, 1973) which also have a demonstrated hierarchical relationship onto Figure 12.1, it would expand. There are a number of hierarchical distinctions that could be further imposed on Figure 12.1 in order to refine it for very specific assessment procedures, i.e. figurative—operative representations, topological—Euclidean projective properties, to name just a few. As additional hierarchical relationships are identified in conjunction with a particular cognitive structure, Figure 12.1 can be mapped onto them to define a specific structural universe for a particular cognitive structure.

Depending upon how one operates, there are a number of statistical properties implicit in Figure 12.1. As previously indicated, the descending paths of connected lines define scales. It is also possible for variation to occur within a sub-universe in Figure 12.1, as a function of mapping it onto some other facet not yet noted. The relations between sub-universes can be expressed using ordinary correlation coefficients. Although it is not possible to predict the magnitude of the sub-universe correlations, it is possible to predict the pattern of the relative magnitudes. Such predictions follow from the logic of the facet model and have been discussed in great detail elsewhere (e.g. Gabriel, 1954; Guttman, 1954). The pattern of the correlations define what is properly referred to as a simplex correlation matrix. This matrix has a number of interesting properties which will not be discussed here other than noting that if the sub-universes are ordered from least complex to most complex (following a descending path of connected lines in Figure 12.1), the largest 'correlations are all next to the main diagonal, and taper off as one goes to the upper right and lower left of the table' (Guttman, 1954, pp. 270—271).

Verbally, Guttman (1959) identifies the simplex as being based on the *contiguity hypothesis*. Within the context of a faceted definition of the general Piagetian and neo-Piagetian assessment task structure those sub-universes defining a simplex correlation matrix are represented by sub-universes along any descending path of connected lines. The contiguity hypothesis indicates quite simply that the closer two sub-universes are on this path the higher will be the magnitude of their relative correlation.

With empirical data, *approximations* to simplexes should be obtained if the faceted definition is correct (see Guttman, 1959, pp. 324—328, and Davison, 1977, for a discussion of a less than perfect empirical approximation to a simplex), but one should neither expect total perfection with real data nor attempt to compute intercorrelations between sub-universes where there is but a single binary task. An alternative approach that may be used when one is representing a sub-universe with a single task is the Guttman scaling approach.

CONTENT VARIATIONS

The final sources of structural invalidity to be identified are associated with the actual content of the tasks themselves. In those assessment procedures where task content appears to influence the age of acquisition of cognitive structures, three sources of content variation have been identified: dimensional variation, perceptual variation and cultural variation.

Whereas the previous sections discussed well-defined sources of structural invalidity, this section is a 'catch-all'. It is the last general source of structural invalidity to be discussed because it is not yet well understood. Future research will without a doubt extend our present knowledge of the sources and effects of content variation. In particular, the sources and effects of cultural and environmental variation will enlarge quite rapidly with concentrated research.

Dimensional Variation

Piaget and Inhelder (1962) and Piaget (1973), in discussing the conservation of matter, weight and volume, have noted a four-year lag between conservation of matter and conservation of volume, with conservation of weight occurring approximately two years after conservation of matter and two years prior to conservation of volume. Analogous results occur with regard to the conservation of length, area and geometric volume (Piaget, Inhelder, and Szeminska, 1960). Conservation of length is demonstrated approximately six years earlier than conservation of geometric volume, with the conservation of area occurring approximately two years after conservation of length and approximately four years prior to conservation of geometric volume. These time-lags in conservation are quite robust with respect to cultural variation. Indeed, Piaget (1973) indicates that his findings with conservation of matter, weight and volume have been replicated in France, Poland, England, the United States, Canada and Iran. Piaget and Inhelder (1962) indicate that these lags are quite logical and that they demonstrate 'the primacy of operations over perception'. These time-lags may occur as a function of the number of geometric dimensions necessitated by the operation. Such task variation can be referred to as dimensional variation. A simple hierarchical relationship must necessarily exist amongst geometric dimensions. This relationship simply stated is that cognitive structures will appear at earlier ages on single dimension tasks than they will on higher dimensional tasks. Not all Piagetian assessment procedures can involve multiple geometric dimensions. Such assessment task variations as multiple seriation and multiplicative classification involve multiple attributes, but they do not involve multiple geometric dimensions. Dimensional variation is then a 'natural', in the sense of being universal, source of task variation, and is so well documented that it does not provide a real source of structural invalidity, unless a naïve researcher devises multiple dimension tasks but assumes the tasks to be unidimensional.

Perceptual Variation

Inhelder and Piaget (1964) note in their work on seriation that they might have found a marked improvement in the seriation of length had they used fewer elements or if the attribute, length, difference between the elements had been greater. Several years ago we developed at our McGuffey Laboratory an objective scoring procedure for use in assessing a child's ability to represent spatial relationships. We had a group of approximately 100 children from our McGuffey Laboratory draw the geometric figures presented by Piaget and Inhelder (1956) as well as those by Bender (1938). The scoring procedures, when adapted to the Piagetian figures, had some very compelling statistical properties: extremely high, above 0.95, internal consistency; the subscale intercorrelations defined a simplex of the form that was hypothesized on the basis of Piagetian theory. These statistical properties deteriorated considerably when the scoring procedures were adapted to the Bender figures! However, a closer evaluation of the scoring procedures and the figures indicated that the procedures only deteriorated when they were applied to the Bender figures that did not have 'good form'. Both of these examples as well as others noted by Smedslund (1969) address the role of perceptual complexity of the stimulus presentation on task difficulty. In particular, the age at which a cognitive structure appears may be inflated as a function of a perceptually complex stimulus presentation. If the objective of a Piagetian or neo-Piagetian assessment is one of determining the nature and presence of a cognitive structure, then the stimulus presentation should be perceptually simple enough to allow the structure to appear.

Structural invalidity source (9). When utilizing a perceptually complex stimulus presentation, one may erroneously conclude that a cognitive structure is not present.

While Piagetian research strives to use a perceptually simple stimulus presentation, the perceptual complexity of much of the replication and neo-Piagetian research is questionable. Often the publications simply report what the author thought was being assessed and provide at best a brief note on the assessment materials (see Fogelman, 1970), making it impossible to evaluate the perceptual complexity of the stimulus presentation. A more extensive discussion of perceptual variation is provided by Feigenbaum (1963), Smedslund (1969) and Odom (1978).

Cultural Variation

Inhelder and Piaget (1964), in dealing with inclusion, 'all' and 'some', note that there is an age gap of several years between success on the task of comparing the number of tulips with all of the flowers in a bouquet and success in comparing the number of swallows with all of the birds in a flock. Piaget (1971), in discussing this lag, speaks of the children of Geneva as having more difficulty with animals than with flowers, but he does not offer any explanation for this lag. In a later publication calling for comparative, cross-cultural research, Piaget (1973) suggests that social, cultural or educational factors varying from one society to another may exert hitherto unrecognized influences on assessment task procedures for certain cognitive structures. He indicates that comparative studies are necessary to address the questions of: the generalizability of stage sequencing; the generalizability of the average age at which various cognitive structures emerge; the generalizability of the rate at which structures are acquired. Goodnow and Bethon (1966) report that the combinatorial task is very sensitive to the effects of schooling or experiences. They report a conversation with one Chinese boy who explained that 'a catty of rice may come in different shaped bags, but it is always a catty; he has carried them and knows' (p. 581). The thrust of the Goodnow and Bethon (1966) article is one of noting the effects of schooling and experience on Piagetian tasks by using comparative cross-cultural studies. In studying the hierarchical relationship amongst conservation of quantity, weight, volume and length across various cultures, discrepant results have been obtained regarding the conservation of weight, quantity and length (Dasen, 1972).

The notions of cultural influence on the acquisition of cognitive structures is not necessarily restricted to Western *vs* non-Western comparisons. Indeed, comparisons between rural and urban children in the same geographic areas, or between any environmentally different groups, may result in time-lags, more so than sequence changing (see Modgil and Modgil, 1976). It is only recently that researchers have shown an awareness of the effects of environmental differences on the time-lags associated with particular cognitive structures. Smedslund (1977) provides an example of the effects of the home environment on a particular boy, ' . . . a little boy in one of my pilot studies who failed in most of the tasks . . . was superb in the task of measuring length. The boy's father turned out to be a carpenter, and the boy had been allowed to help and watch his father many times' (p. 3). Exactly how specific environmental differences affect cognitive structure remains to be determined.

Although it has never been reported as a published study, it would be most informative to study the previously mentioned two inclusion problems near Capistrano in Southern California. Supposedly migrating swallows have returned to the Capistrano mission on approximately the same date for the past 500 years. Every year as the date draws near newspapers throughout America tell the story of the swallows of Capistrano.

Structural invalidity source (10). If one does not address the effects of cultural or environmental variation on the assessment of certain cognitive structures, it is possible that the estimated age of acquisition of the structure will be in serious error.

Although Piaget (1973) indicates that stage sequencing may be influenced by cultural variation, one ought not to be concerned with this as a potential source of structural invalidity, as the sequencing of Piagetian stages has generally been well replicated. Alternatively, if an empirically based difficulty hierarchy or Guttman scale has been established for an assessment procedure, it may be extremely sensitive to cultural variation.

Structural invalidity source (11). If the tasks of an assessment procedure are defined as being sequential as a function of empirically derived task difficulties, the task order may change as a function of cultural or environmental variation.

SUMMARY

This essay has noted eleven sources of structural invalidity in Piagetian and neo-Piagetian assessment procedures. The first eight of these sources of invalidity were discussed within three general modes of assessment: stimulus presentation, performance response, and verbal—non-verbal response. A faceted definition of a general Piagetian and neo-Piagetian assessment task structure was given using the elements of the stimulus presentation mode, performance response mode, and verbal—non-verbal response mode. The facet design delineated the hierarchical relationships within modes and between combinations of modes, assessment sub-universes. It was noted that the first eight sources of structural invalidity are a function of not knowing where an assessment procedure is located within the faceted task structure.

An additional three sources of structural invalidity were noted as occurring within the context of task content variation. Three sources of content variation were discussed: task variation as a function of geometric dimensions; task variation as a function of perceptual variation; task variation as a function of cultural or environmental variation. Unlike the stimulus—response modes, content variation is somewhat ambiguous and not fully understood. The faceted task structure could be mapped specifically onto any one of the three sources of content variation to define a more content-specific task structure (which was suggested for geometric dimensions). But the hierarchical relationships within the particular source of content variation would have to be well understood in order to establish a valid task structure.

While preparing this essay, I struggled continually with the notion of discussing 'task understanding' as a source of structural invalidity. Smedslund (1977) has succinctly stated the problem associated with task understanding, 'In order to decide whether a child is behaving logically or not, one must take for granted that he [the child] has correctly understood all instructions and terms involved' (p. 3). He points out that there is a circular relation between logic and understanding, with each presupposing the other. Thus, researchers must make a choice of which one to take for granted and which one to study. Smedslund implies that Piagetian psychologists focus on logic as a variable to be studied, thereby implying that a child understands a task and any failure on a task is simply a non-logical performance on the part of the child not a failure to understand the task. All sources of structural invalidity have a particular commonality; once one is aware of a source of structural invalidity, its effects can be recognized and understood within the context of a specific task. Task understanding does not have this commonality, as a child can appear to perform either logically or illogically on a task that is not understood as well as on a task that is understood. For these reasons task understanding has not been identified as a source of structural invalidity. Implicitly, task understanding is included in the debate dealing with judgment and explanation criteria that led to structural invalidity source (8).

Finally, it must be noted that what has been presented herein has been distilled from numerous references. Yet this essay is by no means comprehensive. It should be viewed as a first attempt to impose a general psychometric structure on Piagetian theory. Piaget has chosen to ignore such a structure, yet by so doing he has not weakened his theoretical position. Rather he has made it quite difficult for others to operationalize his theory psychometrically. There can be little doubt that additional research will clarify the general topic of content variation, with the end result being quite specific mappings of the faceted task structure of Figure 12.1. Such content-specific task structures will be invaluable in operationalizing Piaget.

REFERENCES

Beilin, H. (1965) Learning and operational convergence in logical thought development. *Journal of Experimental Child Psychology, 2,* 317-339.

Bender, L. (1938) A visual motor Gestalt test and its clinical use. *Research Monographs, American Orthopsychiatric Association,* No. 3.

Bingham-Newman, A. M. and Hooper, F. H. (1975) The search for the woozle circa 1975: Commentary on Brainerd's observation. *American Educational Research Journal, 12,* 379-387.

Blackstock, E. G. and King, W. L. (1973) Recognition and reconstruction for seriation in four- and five-year-olds. *Developmental Psychology, 9,* 255-259.

Braine, M. D. S. (1959) The ontogeny of certain logical operations: Piaget's formulations examined by non-verbal methods. *Psychological Monographs, 73* (5, whole No. 475).

Brainerd, C. J. (1973) Judgments and explanations as criteria for the presence of cognitive structures. *Psychological Bulletin, 79,* 172-179.

Brainerd, C. J. (1977) Response criteria in conceptual development research. *Child Development, 48,* 360-367.

Brainerd, C. J. and Hooper, F. H. (1975) A methodological analysis of developmental studies of identity conservation and equivalence conservation. *Psychological Bulletin, 82,* 725-737.

Campbell, D. T. and Stanley, J. C. (1966) *Experimental and Quasi-experimental Designs for Research.* Chicago: Rand McNally.

Dasen, P. (1972) Cross-cultural Piagetian psychology. *Journal of Cross-Cultural Psychology, 3,* 23-39.

Davison, M. L. (1977) On a metric, unidimensional unfolding model for attitudinal and developmental data. *Psychometrika, 42,* 523-548.

DeVries, R. and Kohlberg, L. (1977) Relations between Piagetian and psychometric assessments of intelligence. In Katz, L. G. (Ed.) *Current Topics in Early Childhood Education: Volume 1.* Norwood, New Jersey: ABLEX.

Droz, R. and Rahmy, M. (1976) *Understanding Piaget.* New York: International Universities Press. Tr. by J. Diamanti.

Elkind, D. (1964) Discrimination, seriation, and numeration of size and dimensional differences in young children: Piaget replication study VI. *Journal of Genetic Psychology,* **104,** 275-296.

Feigenbaum, K. D. (1963) Task complexity and IQ as variables in Piaget's problem of conservation. *Child Development,* **34,** 423-432.

Feinberg, I. and Laycock, F. (1964) Ability of blindfolded children to use landmarks to locate a target. *Child Development,* **35,** 547-558.

Fogelman, K. R. (1970) *Piagetian Tests for the Primary School.* London: NFER.

Freides, D. (1974) Human information-processing and sensory modality: cross-modal functions, information complexity, memory and deficit. *Psychological Bulletin,* **81,** 284-310.

Gabriel, R. G. (1954) The simplex structures of the progressive matrices test. *British Journal of Statistical Psychology,* **7,** 9-14.

Green, D. R., Ford, M. P. and Flamer, G. B. (1971) *Measurement and Piaget.* New York: McGraw-Hill.

Goodnow, J. J. and Bethon, G. (1966) Piaget's tasks: the effects of schooling and intelligence. *Child Development,* **37,** 573-582.

Guttman, L. (1954) A new approach to factor analysis: the radex. In Lazarsfeld, P. F. (Ed.) *Mathematical Thinking in the Social Sciences.* Glencoe, Illinois: Free Press.

Guttman, L. (1959) A structural theory for intergroup beliefs and action. *American Sociological Review,* **24,** 318-328.

Guttman, L. (1965) A faceted definition of intelligence. *Studies in Psychology, Scripta Hierosolymitana,* **14,** 166-181.

Inhelder, B. (1968) *The Diagnosis of Reasoning in the Mentally Retarded.* New York: John Day. Tr. by W. B. Stephens.

Inhelder, B. (1971) Developmental theory and diagnostic procedures. In Green, D. R., Ford, M. P. and Flamer, G. B. (Eds.) *Measurement and Piaget.* New York: McGraw-Hill.

Inhelder, B. and Piaget, J. (1964) *The Early Growth of Logic in the Child.* London: Routledge and Kegan Paul. Tr. by E. A. Lunzer and D. Papert.

Inhelder, B., Sinclair, H. and Bovet, M. (1974) *Learning and the Development of Cognition.* Cambridge: Harvard University Press.

Lovell, K. (1961) *The Growth of Basic Mathematical and Scientific Concepts in Children.* New York: Philosophical Library.

Lovell, K., Mitchell, B. and Everett, I. R. (1962) An experimental study of the growth of some logical structures. *British Journal of Psychology,* **53,** 175-188.

Mansfield, R. S. and Clark, K. S. (1977) The effects of age and irrelevant stimulus variation on a simple seriation task. *Journal of Genetic Psychology,* **131,** 51-57.

Modgil, S. and Modgil, C. (1976) *Piagetian Research: Compilation and Commentary, Volume 8, Cross-cultural Studies.* Windsor: NFER.

Odom, R. D. (1978) A perceptual-salience account of decalage relations and developmental change. In Siegel, C. S. and Brainerd, C. J. (Eds.) *Alternatives to Piaget.* New York: Academic Press.

Piaget, J. (1929) *The Child's Conception of the World.* New York: Harcourt, Brace. Tr. by J. and A. Tomlinson.

Piaget, J. (1962) Introduction. In Laurendau, M. and Pinard, A., *Causal Thinking in the Child, a Genetic and Experimental Approach.* New York: International Universities Press.

Piaget, J. (1967) *Six Psychological Studies.* New York: Random House. Tr. by A. Tenzer and D. Elkind.

Piaget, J. (1971) The theory of stages in cognitive development. In Green, D. R., Ford, M. P. and Flamer, G. B. (Eds.) *Measurement and Piaget.* New York: McGraw-Hill.

Piaget, J. (1973) *The Child and Reality: Problems of Genetic Psychology.* New York: Grossman. Tr. by A. Rosin.

Piaget, J. (1975) *Correspondences and Transformations.* Presentation at the Fifth Annual Meeting of the Jean Piaget Society, Philadelphia.

Piaget, J. and Inhelder, B. (1956) *The Child's Conception of Space.* London: Routledge and Kegan Paul. Tr. by F. J. Langdon and E. A. Lunzer.

Piaget, J. and Inhelder, B. (1962) *Le Developpement des Quantités Physiques Chez l'Enfant.* Neuchatel: Delachaux et Niestlé.

Piaget, J. and Inhelder, B. (1971) *Mental Imagery in the Child. A Study of the Development of Imaginal Representation.* London: Routledge and Kegan Paul. Tr. by P. A. Chilton.

Piaget, J. and Inhelder, B. (1974) *The Child's Construction of Quantities.* London: Routledge and Kegan Paul. Tr. by A. Pomerans.

Piaget, J. and Szeminska, A. (1952) *The Child's Conception of Number.* London: Routledge and Kegan Paul. Tr. by T. Gattegno and F. Hodgson.

Piaget, J., Inhelder, B. and Sinclair de Zwart, H. (1973) *Memory and Intelligence.* London: Routledge and Kegan Paul. Tr. by A. J. Pomerans.

Piaget, J., Inhelder, B. and Szeminska, A. (1960) *The Child's Conception of Geometry.* New York: Basic Books. Tr. by E. A. Lunzer.

Sinclair de Zwart, H. (1977) Recent developments in genetic epistomology. *The Genetic Epistemologist,* **6,** 1-4.

Smedslund, J. (1969) Psychological diagnostics. *Psychological Bulletin,* **71,** 234-248.

Smedslund, J. (1977) Symposium: Practical and theoretical issues in Piagetian psychology—III Piaget's psychology in practice. *British Journal of Educational Psychology,* **47,** 1-6.

Uzgiris, I. and Hunt, J. (1975) *Assessment in Infancy: Ordinal Scales of Psychological Development.* Chicago: University of Illinois Press.

Wadsworth, B. (1978) *Piaget for the Classroom Teacher.* New York: Longman.

Chapter 13

The Measurement Characteristics of Developmental Tests

COLIN ELLIOTT

This paper is addressed to the problem of constructing tests based on theories of development. Such tests may be assessment devices or, in certain circumstances, they may produce unidimensional measurements. The paper was written late in relation to others in this volume and the author had the benefit of being able to read Hofmann's paper beforehand. Although written primarily from a negative standpoint, Hofmann makes a number of important points which should be taken into account by constructors of developmental tests, and I believe that nothing in this paper is incompatible with the points he has made.

The present paper is written primarily from the standpoint of relating Piagetian and neo-Piagetian tasks to measurement theory, and, in particular, to latent trait theory. Although the author was briefed to accentuate the positive and eliminate the negative (to coin a phrase), the reader may perceive that the paper is by no means wholly positive. There are difficulties in applying psychometrics to developmental tasks, and these difficulties must be faced. Some of the difficulties lie in the inferences that we may draw from children's responses to such tasks, and Hofmann deals fully with these. Other difficulties arise out of the characteristics of the data itself, i.e. the item-by-person response matrix. This paper is addressed primarily to the latter problems. However, although the author will emphasize some statistical points of measurement theory, he believes, along with Levy (1973), that what we need are more tests about theories and fewer theories about tests.

Measurement should always develop from theory and from careful observation. Given these prior requirements, the author will argue that while some developmental tests—often quite deliberately—do not have measurement properties, other developmental tests do. In consequence, it is possible in certain cases to reconcile the requirements of psychometric and developmental theory.

MEASUREMENT AND ASSESSMENT

In science, the term 'measurement' is used to denote the use of a numerical scale representing a single dimension.* That dimension may involve more than one component variable, as in the measurement of density, in which case the dimension is defined in terms of the relationship between the components. Thus, if we were asked to evaluate a number of motor cars, we could, for each car, provide measurements for a wide range of features such as aspects of size, power output and performance characteristics. No doubt we could place the cars in rank order on a measurement scale for each feature. If, however, we were then asked to provide 'measures' of the cars in terms of 'dimensions' such as value-for-money or technical excellence, we would undoubtedly have difficulties in defining, and consequently measuring, the dimensions. Even if one person were to define each dimension in terms of a weighted composite of other measurements, it is unlikely that all people would agree on the definition of the weighted composite, and even more unlikely that this definition would be considered appropriate when applied to ranges of cars which were more or less expensive than the ones presently being evaluated. Thus, all one could hope to do is to provide an assessment, rather than a measurement, of the cars in terms of these complex dimensions.

Many tests in psychology and education come into the assessment rather than the measurement category of observation. Even IQ figures—being multidimensional and having no generally agreed definition in terms of components—are probably best thought of as assessments of individuals' average rankings in the population rather than being measurements, although it seems that they are usually considered to be in the latter category. It is certainly true that people who obtain the same IQ score, even on the same test battery, may obtain it in different ways (e.g. Eysenck, 1967). For example, person A may be strong on verbal tasks and weak on non-verbal, while B shows the opposite pattern; C may be strong on short-term memory but relatively weak on reasoning; D may be quick but careless, while E may be slower but more accurate: yet all of them obtain the same IQ. Such a situation is inconceivable in measurement in other sciences. For example, if two substances X and Y are of the same density, X cannot be relatively heavy for its volume and Y be relatively light. I repeat, many tests in education and psychology—not just IQ tests—have problems like these, and tests based on Piagetian and neo-Piagetian theories of development are no exception to this position.

This initial discussion of the characteristics of measurement has concentrated upon the need for measurement to be related to a single dimension. It is pertinent at this point to state briefly what this might mean in educational and psychological measurement.

A unidimensional test requires two broad conditions to be satisfied. The first condition relates to the content of the test items. The test constructor should be satisfied theoretically that all the items are measuring the 'same thing': that is, that they require the same combination of processes from the testee for their response, and that the responses to a single item or to different items should not be qualitatively different. A good example of a unidimensional test is one of word reading. In such a test, each

---

*The author recognizes that many authorities such as Stevens (1951) and Guilford (1954) distinguish the four levels of *nominal*, *ordinal*, *interval* and *ratio* measurement. In this paper, in common with most scientific usage, the term 'measurement' will denote the last two of these levels. The term 'assessment' will generally refer to the classificatory and simple ranking procedures denoted by the first two levels.

item consists of a printed word which a child looks at and to which an oral response is made. It is clear that this is a complex task: it involves many cognitive processes, including visual perception, search and retrieval from long-term verbal memory stores, and verbal encoding of the response—and all of these processes are in themselves complex. Yet the test is unidimensional in that each item broadly requires the operation of the same set of processes. The test constructor ensures that these are as uniform as possible by deleting items which sample some other process or area of knowledge, such as a foreign language. In the construction of Piagetian and neo-Piagetian tests, content control is perhaps more difficult and certainly less self-evident than in the example of the word reading test above. There may also be problems in classifying and scoring a range of qualitatively different responses to an item. If the test is to be unidimensional, however, it is essential that the items and the responses of people to them should be potentially quantifiable along a single dimension.

A thorough content analysis of a test, while necessary, is not of itself sufficient to ensure unidimensionality. The second condition which needs to be satisfied is a statistical one. This will be dealt with in more detail later in this paper. Once again, this is a necessary, but not in itself sufficient, condition for unidimensionality. At this point in the paper, it is merely necessary to note that this criterion is concerned with establishing that the items in a theoretically unidimensional test keep their relative difficulty values across all groups of individuals for whom the test is intended.

THE CONCEPT OF DEVELOPMENT

Development is a term that can be used in two senses. The first refers to growth along one dimension. Thus we may refer to an individual's development or growth in vocabulary, number concepts or spatial ability. The second sense in which the term is used is when it refers to the movement of an individual through an invariant succession of qualitatively different stages. In this sense, a certain level of achievement or performance at one stage is a necessary but not sufficient condition for progression to the next stage.

The two senses are not incompatible. To postulate an invariant sequential progression through stages is not necessarily to deny the existence of individual differences in performance within a stage. It is evident that even though a child can operate at a certain stage with one class of problems, he may not be able to do so with other problems. In this context, Piaget (e.g. 1971) emphasizes the existence of horizontal decalage, or time-lags, within a stage of development, where a child is able to solve problems in some content areas but not in others. Such individual differences within a stage may be attributable to various factors, such as differences in cultural or educational experience, differences in information-handling capacity, differences in verbal comprehension or expressive ability and so on.

Inspection of the content of tests and their method of scoring often reveals an implicit definition of development. Most tests probably represent development one-dimensionally. A vocabulary or a spatial test covering a wide age and difficulty range can be thought of in terms of models of knowledge acquisition or skill acquisition which postulate quantitative growth rather than qualitative changes. These tests contrast with tests based on developmental theories in which qualitative differences in responses are recognized. Some tests of this type may quantify scores within a stage, as in tests of conservation or of formal operational thinking. Other tests, say of science reasoning or of moral development, look at performance across stages of development; they enable the test user to make an assessment of an individual's developmental level, but recognize that the quantification of qualitatively different responses is meaningless. For example, if low-level responses to items were scored 1, medium level 2, and so on, and the item scores were summed to obtain a total score for the test, this total score would, by implication, represent a single, but difficult-to-interpret, dimension.

This very problem occurs in some tests in which a test author has conceived of a single dimension on which low- and high-level responses are scored in the manner described above. Thus a score of 2 on one item is characterized as being equivalent to two scores of 1 on two items. Despite this, developmental psychologists may point out that, according to their theories, the low- and high-level responses represent qualitatively different types of response which characterize different stages of development. For example, in response to the question, 'How are an apple and an orange alike?', two common responses are, 'Because they have skins and pips,' and, 'Because they are fruit'. One way of dealing with such responses is to treat them quantitatively, by assigning 1 or 2 points to them respectively, as Wechsler does in WISC-R Similarities (Wechsler, 1974). This assumes that both responses can be placed in quantitatively different positions on the *same* dimension. However, such responses can also be thought of as representing two qualitatively different dimensions, such as concrete and formal operational thinking, after Piaget, or the following of subordinate and superordinate rules of equivalence, after Bruner (1966).

Those who prefer to conceive of development as a unidimensional process of skill acquisition and integration (e.g. Brown and Desforges, 1977) may be happy to use the total scores that children obtain on such a test as an index of such development. Such an interpretation is unlikely to be wholeheartedly accepted by those who adhere to stage concepts of development. It is up to the former group to demonstrate to the latter not only that their concept of development is plausible, but also that such a test is unidimensional in terms of the statistical criterion which was alluded to earlier in this paper and which will be covered in more detail later.

PIAGET'S INFLUENCE ON TEST DEVELOPMENT

Despite the popularity of Piagetian theory in the curriculum of institutions concerned with training in education, there remain doubts in some quarters about the direct relevance of the theory for classroom practice. Indeed, Inhelder, Sinclair and Bovet (1974), having worked for years with Piaget, state that 'Piaget's theory and the extensive experimentation attached to it can be applied to educational practice only in a very indirect way, as many educators have been forced to admit' (p. 30). Biggs (1980), recognizing the problem, has suggested that an intermediate body of theory—'educology'—is necessary to link Piagetian theory with educational practice. Biggs hopes that this intermediate body of theory would be more understandable and useful to teachers than the original theory. The plethora of publications purporting to present Piagetian principles to pedagogues provides further evidence that teachers find it hard to link the theory to practice.

However, these problems have not prevented the theory from being used extensively as a basis for curriculum design (for a review, see Modgil and Modgil, 1976). It has been applied in such areas as mathematics (e.g. School Mathematics Project, 1969;

Nuffield Mathematics Project, 1970, 1973; Schools Council, 1972; Howell, Walker and Fletcher, 1979) and science (Nuffield Combined Science, 1970; Science Curriculum Improvement Study, 1974; Nuffield Chemistry, 1978; Shayer, 1979).

Similarly, Piaget's influence upon psychometrics has been quite inadvertent, as Jensen (1980) has noted. As in the case of curriculum design, difficulties exist in using Piagetian theory as a basis for test construction, many of which were expressed in Green, Ford and Flamer (1971). Despite these difficulties, tests have been published covering the whole developmental range from sensorimotor tests (Uzgiris and Hunt, 1975), concrete operational conservation tests (Goldschmid and Bentler, 1968), tests spanning the whole range of concrete and formal operational thinking (Shayer, Kuchemann and Wylam, 1976; Shayer and Wylam, 1978; Wylam and Shayer, 1980), to tests purely of formal operational thinking (Ward, 1972; Ward and Pearson, 1973; Elliott, Murray and Pearson, 1979).

Returning to the earlier distinction made between tests as measurement or assessment tools, the majority of Piagetian tests are probably within the latter category. This is for two major reasons: the problem of assessment across stages and the problem of horizontal decalage.

Assessment Across Developmental Stages

Any test purporting to assess the developmental stage reached by a person is by definition a non-unidimensional test and is therefore, according to our definition, an assessment rather than a measurement device. This is not to say that such tests do not pose a range of technical and theoretical problems which are all broadly related to the inferences one may draw from the responses of a person to this type of test.

If the range of items within a test covers more than one developmental stage, the resulting person x item matrix may be expected to approximate to a simplex (Guttman, 1955) or a 'twisted pear' distribution (Jensen, 1970). In such a distribution, persons who pass a given item can pass all easier items, and those who fail a given item also fail all harder items.

In view of the likelihood that Piagetian items designed to cover a number of developmental stages will form a simplex scale, or something closely resembling a simplex, a number of attempts have been made to reconcile the Piagetian and psychometric approaches. Bentler (1971, 1973) has developed psychometric procedures for the ordinal analysis of test items and responses which span qualitatively different levels of development. Symposia edited by Dockrell (1970) and by Green, Ford and Flamer (1971) have considered the problem of the integration of developmental theory and techniques of measurement, and present the position as it appeared in the late 1960s. More recently, Modgil (1974, 1976) has produced reference works listing and reviewing studies in this area. The impression received from such reviews and symposia is that while advances have been made in developing Piagetian tests, some scepticism exists about the practicability of measuring developmental stages using standardized tests (see, for example, comments by Elkind, Nivette, Ayers and Sticht in Green, Ford and Flamer, 1971). In commenting on a fairly recent symposium on reasoning, moral judgment and moral conduct in retarded and non-retarded persons (Stephens, 1974), Kohlberg (1974) expressed the opinion that 'Piagetian tasks do define a domain irreducible to psychometric concepts'. On the other hand, Hunt (1974), another discussant, argued strongly in favour of ordinal scales of development, preferably criterion referenced rather than norm referenced, and, indeed, has subsequently published a number of such ordinal scales for infant assessment (Uzgiris and Hunt, 1975).

Examples of tests which come into this category are the tests described by

Tuddenham (1970, 1971), covering the pre-operational and concrete operational stages; Uzgiris and Hunt (1975), covering six stages within the sensorimotor period; Wylam and Shayer (1980), covering science reasoning over the concrete and formal operational stages; and Pearson and Elliott (1980), covering various stages of social reasoning. For all of these tests it would be possible to produce total scores which might well be scalable to estimate a person's ability on a single higher-order trait (such as 'g'). However, the chief purpose of such tests is to enable the tester to examine the qualitative pattern of scores across items, for it is these that indicate the developmental level reached by the child. Hence the search for simplex scales in which the patterns of scores within the test are easily interpretable and hopefully give valuable information to such people as teachers and parents.

Such simplex techniques, however, do not enable objective estimates of ability to be made *within* a stage. It is commonly observed that while an individual can operate at a certain stage with one class of problems, he may not be able to do so with other problems which, for example, have different content or have a different modality of presentation. Piaget (e.g. 1971) himself emphasizes the existence of horizontal decalage, or time-lags, within a stage of development. In the use of ordinal scales of development across stages, such decalage is usually ignored or treated as error.

The Problem of Decalage

Decalage can be broadly categorized into that which is consistent and common to most individuals within a population, and that which is inconsistent and individual specific. If a test is constructed to measure performance within a stage, the total score of the individual is meaningful if the standardization population shows consistent fluctuations in performance on the various items in the test. For example, if all children were to find conservation of length easier than conservation of number, which in turn was easier than area or volume, one would be able to give a clear interpretation of a score on a test of conservation in terms of general conservation ability.

If, however, the relative difficulty of the various items was not consistent for all children, a total score on a conservation test could not be treated as a measurement, and it would, indeed, be inadvisable to use it. In such a case, it would be necessary to refer to an individual child's performance on the separate items of the test, concluding, perhaps, that he can conserve length and volume, but not number or area. In the case of the test with consistent decalage, we would be using a measurement device. In the inconsistent case, the test would provide us with an assessment but not measurement. Such an assessment would often be thought of as criterion referenced (e.g. Wylam and Shayer, 1980), although it could also be evaluated normatively.

How are we to decide whether the items in a test which purports to measure *within* a stage show consistent or inconsistent decalage? An answer to this question may be provided by the application of a measurement model which was first made explicit by Rasch (1960). The model and its measurement characteristics will be outlined in the next section. This will be followed by two examples of the model applied to Piagetian test items.

THE ITEM—PERSON RESPONSE MODEL FOR UNIDIMENSIONAL SCALES

The model is commonly known as the Rasch model because it was first made explicit by Rasch (1960, 1966). However, its assumptions have been implicitly accepted by test users from the earliest days of educational and psychological testing.

The model states that when a person is given a test item, only two things determine the probability of the person getting the item right. These are (1) the ability of the person, and (2) the difficulty of the test item. Those readers unfamiliar with the model are advised to pause and reflect on the audacious simplicity of this idea! For a given item, people who have more ability have a higher probability of passing it than people of lower ability. Similarly, if we take a group of people of the same ability, they would have a higher probability of passing an easy item than one which is more difficult. Note here that the term 'ability' means 'ability to do the items in the test': it does not refer to any other sort of ability, although we know that people's abilities over a wide range of cognitive tasks are often highly correlated.

How do we estimate the abilities of persons and the difficulties of items? As we might expect from such a simple model, (1) the total number of items in the test which a person gets right is used to estimate his ability, and (2) the total number of people in a sample who get an item right is used to estimate its difficulty. The actual parameter estimation procedures are not the province of this article. Most test constructors using this model employ computer routines developed by Wright (e.g. Wright and Panchapakesan, 1969). Full descriptions of the model, including formulae, now abound in the literature. The Summer, 1977, issue of the *Journal of Educational Measurement* contains articles (e.g. Wright, 1977) and references to the use of the Rasch model in the context of latent trait models in general. British work using the Rasch model is outlined and discussed by Wilmott and Fowles (1974), Dobby and Duckworth (1979), Choppin (1976, 1979), Goldstein (1979) and Elliott (1981, a and b).

Let us assume that the abilities of people in a sample and the difficulties of items in a test have been estimated. We can then use a simple formula—which takes these ability and difficulty estimates—to calculate the expected probability of persons of a given ability passing a given item. We can plot this expected probability across all abilities of persons in the sample. This has been done in Figure 13.1 for two different items.

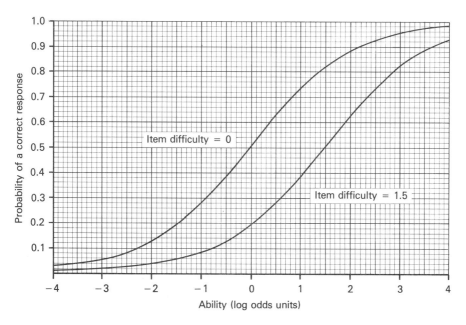

Figure 13.1 Expected probabilities of a correct response for persons of varying ability when given two items of differing difficulties.

Note that the curves given in Figure 13.1 are *expected* curves. In practice, we often find that the *actual proportion* of persons of a given ability who get an item right is not the same as the expected proportion. The difference between the observed and expected proportions might be within acceptable limits of measurement error. If it is outside these limits, we would normally conclude that some other factor is responsible— ambiguity of instructions or scoring, guessing, some distinctive ability or domain of knowledge being required, and so on. Whatever the reason, it is apparent that it is not solely ability and difficulty which are determining the probability of people being correct: the items are not unidimensional.

The point is illustrated by the Item Characteristic Curves (ICC) in Figure 13.2. Here are plotted the obtained proportions of persons passing two items, both of which are estimated to have the same overall difficulty. The solid line shows the expected probability or proportion of passes at each ability level. Item A shows observed proportions which deviate very little from the expected. Item B shows marked deviations from the expected curve. In particular, it appears that persons of low ability get item B right more often than expected, and persons of high ability fail on it more often than expected.

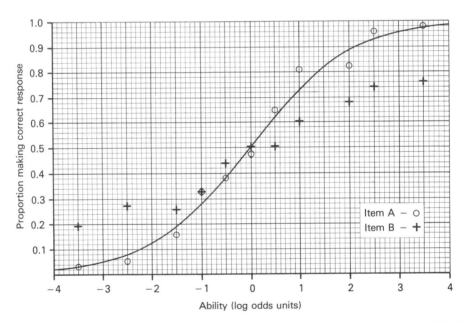

Figure 13.2 Expected (curve) and obtained proportions of correct responses to two items of identical overall difficulty (difficulty = 0 log odds).

It would seem that item B cannot belong to a unidimensional test in which all items are measuring the same attribute. In a unidimensional test, all ICC should have the same slope, i.e. they should not intersect (see Figure 13.1). In other words, the *ordering* of items in terms of their relative difficulty should be the same for persons of different ability. In our example, item A is harder than item B for persons of low ability, but is easier than item B for persons of high ability. It is inconceivable that such a situation could exist in physical measurement. How, using two weights, could one be lighter than the other when weighing heavy objects, becoming heavier than the other when the object being weighed is lighter?

When items are measuring one dimension, test data will fit the Rasch model (Lumsden, 1978). Fit to the model involves an evaluation of the extent to which the observed responses of persons to items deviate from the expected probabilities. Once again, further detailed consideration of the unidimensionality assumption, together with methods of testing goodness of fit to the Rasch model, may be found in previously cited references.

Goodness of fit to the Rasch model is, therefore, a necessary but not sufficient criterion of test unidimensionality. As outlined earlier in this paper, a prior content analysis in terms of a theory is also necessary if a unidimensional test is to be constructed.

If on the basis of a developmental theory, we are satisfied that the items in a test measure development within a stage, their goodness of fit to the Rasch model can then be assessed. If the items show consistent decalage, they will fit the model. If inconsistent, they will not fit. Two examples of fitting and non-fitting tests will now be described.

THE MODEL APPLIED

The two examples of tests based on Piagetian theory are tests of conservation and formal operational thinking. Both were administered to large samples of children during the standardization of the British Ability Scales and are published as part of that test battery (Elliott, Murray and Pearson, 1979).

Formal Operational Thinking

The items in this scale were written on the basis of Piaget's theory that at the stage of formal thought, the individual is able to reason about hypothetical propositions. The items represent thirteen of the sixteen logical propositional combinations of p and q (Piaget and Inhelder, 1969, p. 134). An array of picture cards is shown to the child. Each card shows a boy and a girl holding hands. The boy may have yellow hair (p) or red hair ($\bar{p}$) and the girl may have yellow hair (q) or red hair ($\bar{q}$). After an extended teaching sequence to ensure that the child understands the nature of the task, arrays of cards are presented which show various combinations of boys' and girls' hair colours. For example, in a four-card array, two cards may show red-haired boys holding hands with yellow-haired girls and two may show yellow-haired boys with red-haired girls. The child (who is told that the hair colours have nothing to do with real life!) is asked to say, on the basis of the cards presented, how boys' and girls' hair colours go together. A concrete operational response would be tied to the cards presented. In our example, such a response would not go beyond something like, 'Boys with red hair go with girls with yellow hair and boys with yellow hair go with red-haired girls'. A formal response, on the other hand, would show clear evidence of handling propositional operations, as in, 'Boys go with girls of the opposite hair colour', or, 'Boys don't choose girls with the same colour of hair as themselves'. Full details of the method of administration and scoring of the items are given in the test manual (Elliott, Murray and Pearson, op. cit.).

For each item, a child making a formal operational response would score 1, other concrete or pre-operational responses scoring zero. As might be expected, some of the propositional combinations are more difficult than others. A single pairing is relatively easy, whereas when three different pairs are presented (with only one missing pair), this is relatively difficult. Children who have even odds of success on the easier items have odds of over 50 to 1 against making a correct response to the most difficult items.

The items in the scale, which was administered to 1573 children between the ages of eight and seventeen years, were tested for goodness of fit to the Rasch model. All the items fitted satisfactorily, the probability of the worst fitting item being 0.14. The overall fit of the whole scale, with a probability of 0.2, was also satisfactory.

Figure 13.3 shows the observed proportions of children at different ability levels who get the worst fitting item right, in comparison with the expected curve. Despite some fluctuation at the upper and lower ends of the curve, the observed points show a reasonable conformity to expectation.

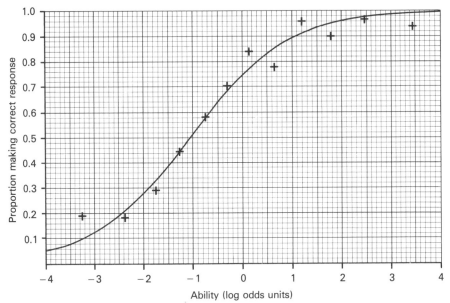

Figure 13.3 Expected (curve) and obtained proportions of correct responses for the worst fitting item in the Formal Operational Thinking scale (difficulty = −1.03 log odds).

It is, therefore, reasonable to conclude that the items in the formal operational thinking scale form an internally consistent, homogeneous, unidimensional set; that quantitative individual differences in scores on the scale represent quantitative differences in ability to reason about hypothetical propositions; and that the results indicate that the attempt to fit a psychometric model with strong assumptions to a Piagetian test seems to have been successful.

Conservation Items

This group of seven items formed part of a larger scale aimed at measuring the development of number concepts. The items in the larger scale failed to fit the Rasch model (although further development work by one of my postgraduate students has produced a successful scale of basic number skills (McNab, 1980, to be published in 1981). Despite the poor fit of the number concept items, it was decided to examine the consistency of a set of conservation items which, at face value, looked as if they might form a unidimensional set. The items test conservation of length (two items), number (two items), area, volume and weight.

All items follow basically the same procedure. Firstly, the correspondence of the objects to be compared (e.g. the number of bricks in two lines) is established with the child's agreement. Secondly, the objects are transformed in front of the child (e.g. the bricks are spatially rearranged). Thirdly, the child is asked three questions of similar form (e.g. 'Are there more blue bricks than green bricks?' 'Are there more green bricks than blue bricks?' 'Are there the same number?'). Having asked these questions, a second transformation is carried out on the materials and the three questions are repeated.

A child scores 1 for each item if *all six* questions are answered correctly, zero otherwise. Full details of the method of administration and scoring of the items are given in the test manual (Elliott, Murray and Pearson, op. cit.).

The items showed variations in difficulty, although these were nowhere near as broad as the difficulty range of the items in the formal operational thinking scale. Children who have even odds of success on the easier items (conservation of area and number) have odds of about 3 or 4 to 1 against making a correct response on the most difficult items (conservation of length).

The order of difficulty may be surprising, but it should be remembered that the absolute range of difficulty is relatively narrow. The unusual order of difficulty cannot be attributed to order effects in the presentation of items, as this was randomized at the time of standardization.

The conservation items were administered to 1714 children between the ages of 3½ and 11 years. As might be expected, over one thousand of the children obtained zero or maximum raw scores. The items were tested for goodness of fit to the Rasch model using the remaining 549 children. They failed to fit the model satisfactorily, the probability of the worst fitting item being less than 0.001 that it fitted the model. Similarly, when the whole set of items was tested for fit, the probability was less than 0.001 that they fitted the model.

Figure 13.4 shows the observed proportions of children at different ability levels who get the worst fitting item right, in comparison with the expected curve. Considerably greater fluctuation exists at all ability levels than in the item illustrated in Figure 13.3. Furthermore, the fluctuation appears to be inconsistent: the observed ICC is neither too flat nor too steep in general, but rather wavy. The reasons for this fluctuation are obscure, and other items show similar wavy patterns.

Let us look at this fluctuation another way. The fluctuation must mean that the items do not keep their order of difficulty relative to each other across children of all abilities. The order of difficulty for the seven items in the test is shown in Table 13.1 for each group of children who obtained a particular raw score on the test. Thus, for children who got three items right, item 7 was the easiest, item 3 the next easiest, and so on, until we reach item 1 which was the hardest. Inspection of Table 13.1 indicates fairly gross fluctuations in the order of item difficulty for each of the raw score groups.

It seems that these conservation items show such a level of fluctuation in fit to the Rasch model that they must be considered to provide an example of inconsistent decalage. As a result, they cannot be treated as a unidimensional set; and individual differences in total scores on the test must be interpreted with considerable caution, as the items are not all measuring a common dimension. For such a set of items, it would indeed be preferable (if the child does not fail or pass them all) to describe his or her performance on individual items rather than in terms of an overall score.

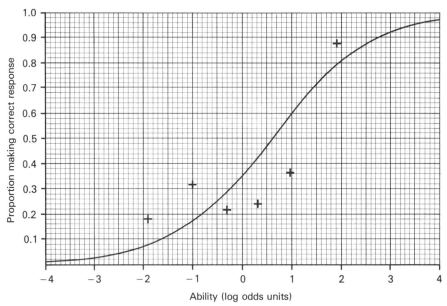

Figure 13.4 Expected (curve) and obtained proportions of correct responses for the worst fitting of the conservation items (difficulty = 0.64 log odds).

In passing, it would be interesting to have the results of a Rasch analysis on the Goldschmid and Bentler (1968) conservation items, as these are in fairly common usage and are often held to be an example of the successful application of psychometrics to Piagetian items.

DISCUSSION

The earlier sections of this paper made a number of points. These may be conveniently summarized as follows: (1) tests which are devised to elicit responses from children across more than one developmental stage are not unidimensional; (2) non-

Table 13.1 *Order of difficulty of the seven conservation items for each raw score group (zero and maximum scores excluded)*

		Raw Score					
		1	2	3	4	5	6
	Easiest	7	4	7	3	3	3
		1	3	3	7	7	2⎱
Order of		5	1⎱	5	4	4	5⎰
Difficulty		6	7⎰	4	6	5	7
of Items		3	2⎱	6	5	6	1⎱
		4	6⎰	2	1⎱	1	4⎰
	Hardest	2	5	1	2⎰	2	6

unidimensional tests can only provide relatively crude estimates of developmental level and should be considered as assessment devices and not as measuring instruments; (3) the term 'measurement' implies unidimensionality; (4) in order to construct a unidimensional test, the proper procedure is to set up a strict specification of the item type and follow this with tests of the specification, as Lumsden (1976) has also suggested. In particular, when devising a test in relation to a developmental theory, the test constructor needs to be satisfied *both* that the items represent a homogeneous content area (in developmental tests, this would be a content area within a developmental stage), *and* that the items are consistent in terms of their relative difficulty for all ability levels of persons taking the test. This latter criterion is satisfied if the items fit the Rasch item-person response model, which is the only unidimensional latent trait model.

The two example tests which have been used to demonstrate the use of the Rasch model indicate that the goodness of fit of items to the model provides an indication of the consistency or inconsistency of horizontal decalage. The tests may, of course, be criticized as not being valid tests of the Piagetian constructs that they are designed to measure. Clearly, the sources of structural invalidity which Hofmann describes in relation to Piagetian tests may apply to these as to any others. Whether this is so or not, the main points of the argument in this paper still hold.

A substantial and growing number of tests have been developed which have as their inspiration Piagetian and neo-Piagetian theory. A number of these (e.g. Uzgiris and Hunt, 1975; Wylam and Shayer, 1980) are intended to be no more than assessment devices enabling a range of responses to be made over a number of developmental stages. Such responses are evaluated mainly in a criterion-referenced fashion and the tests are intended to be of more relevance to educators than the results from more traditional psychometric tests. Other tests, such as the formal operational thinking and the conservation tests outlined earlier, are intended to provide more traditional measurements of performance within a developmental stage. Sometimes these may provide psychometrically satisfactory unidimensional measures, but sometimes not.

The whole enterprise of constructing tests based on Piagetian and neo-Piagetian theory is subject to concerns regarding the inferences which may be drawn from children's responses to the test items. Provided that we are satisfied with various aspects of their content validity, measurement theory can then provide us with a valuable means of evaluating their dimensionality which can then inform our decisions on the interpretation of test scores.

REFERENCES

Bentler, P. M. (1971) An implicit metric for ordinal scales: implications for assessment of cognitive growth. In Green, D. R., Ford, M. P. and Flamer, G. B. (Eds.) *Measurement and Piaget.* New York: McGraw-Hill.

Bentler, P. M. (1973) Assessment of developmental factor change at the individual and group level. In Nesselroade, J. R. and Reese, H. W. (Eds.) *Life-span Developmental Psychology.* New York: Academic Press.

Biggs, J. B. (1980) The relationship between developmental level and the quality of school learning. In Modgil, S. and Modgil, C. (Eds.) *Toward a Theory of Psychological Development.* Windsor: NFER.

Brown, G. and Desforges, C. (1977) Piagetian psychology and education: time for revision. *British Journal of Educational Psychology,* **47,** 7-17.

Bruner, J. S. (1966) *Toward a Theory of Instruction.* Cambridge, Mass: Harvard University Press.

Choppin, B. H. (1976) Recent developments in item banking: a review. In de Gruijter, D. N. M. and van der Kamp, L. J. T. (Eds.) *Advances in Psychological and Educational Measurement.* London: Wiley.

Choppin, B. H. (1979) Item banking and the monitoring of achievement: an introductory paper. *Research in Progress*, 1. Slough: NFER.

Dobby, J. and Duckworth, D. (1979) *Objective Assessment by means of Item Banking*. Schools Council Examination Bulletin, No. 40. London: Evans/Methuen.

Dockrell, W. B. (1970) (Ed.) *On Intelligence*. London: Methuen.

Elliott, C. D. (1981a) *The British Ability Scales, Manual 1: Introduction and Rationale* (in preparation).

Elliott, C. D. (1981b) *The British Ability Scales, Manual 2: Technical Information* (in preparation).

Elliott, C. D., Murray, D. J. and Pearson, L. S. (1979) *The British Ability Scales*. Windsor: NFER.

Eysenck, H. J. (1967) Intelligence assessment: a theoretical and experimental approach. *British Journal of Educational Psychology*, 37, 81-98.

Goldschmid, M. L. and Bentler, P. M. (1968) *Concept Assessment Kit—Conservation*. San Diego: Educational and Industrial Testing Service.

Goldstein, H. (1979) Consequences of using the Rasch model for educational assessment. *British Educational Research Journal*, 5, 211-220.

Green, D. R., Ford, M. P. and Flamer, G. B. (1971) (Eds.) *Measurement and Piaget*. New York: McGraw-Hill.

Guilford, J. P. (1954) *Psychometric Methods*. New York: McGraw-Hill.

Guttman, L. (1955) A generalized simplex for factor analysis and a faceted definition of intelligence. *Psychometrika*, 20, 173-192.

Howell, A., Walker, R. and Fletcher, H. (1979) *Mathematics for Schools: Teacher's Resource Book, Level 1*. (2nd Edition.) London: Addison-Wesley.

Hunt, J. McV. (1974) Discussion: developmental gains in reasoning. *American Journal of Mental Deficiency*, 79, 127-133.

Inhelder, B., Sinclair, H. and Bovet, M. (1974) *Learning and the Development of Cognition*. London: Routledge and Kegan Paul.

Jensen, A. R. (1970) Hierarchical theories of mental ability. In Dockrell, W. B. (Ed.) *On Intelligence*. London: Methuen.

Jensen, A. R. (1980) *Bias in Mental Testing*. London: Methuen.

Kohlberg, L. (1974) Discussion: developmental gains in moral judgment. *American Journal of Mental Deficiency*, 79, 142-146.

Levy, P. (1973) On the relation between test theory and psychology. In Kline, P. (Ed.) *New Approaches in Psychological Measurement*. London: Wiley.

Lumsden, J. (1976) Test theory. *Annual Review of Psychology*, 27, 251-280.

Lumsden, J. (1978) Tests are perfectly reliable. *British Journal of Mathematical and Statistical Psychology*, 31, 19-26.

McNab, I. C. (1980) *A basic number skills scale for the British Ability Scales*. Unpublished M.Sc. thesis, University of Manchester.

Modgil, S. (1974) *Piagetian Research: a Handbook of Recent Studies*. Windsor: NFER.

Modgil, S. and Modgil, C. (1976) *Piagetian Research: Compilation and Commentary*. Windsor: NFER.

Nuffield Chemistry Project (1978) *Revised Nuffield Chemistry Teacher's Guide II*. London: Longman.

Nuffield Combined Science Project (1970) *Teacher's Guides I and II*. London: Longman/Penguin.

Nuffield Mathematics Project (1970) *Checking up 1*. London: Chambers/Murray.

Nuffield Mathematics Project (1973) *Guide to the Guides*. London: Chambers/Murray/Wiley.

Pearson, L. S. and Elliott, C. D. (1980) The development of a social reasoning scale in the new British Ability Scales. *Journal of Moral Education*, 10, 40-48.

Piaget, J. (1971) The theory of stages in cognitive development. In Green, D. R., Ford, M. P. and Flamer, G. B. (Eds.) *Measurement and Piaget*. New York: McGraw-Hill.

Piaget, J. and Inhelder, B. (1969) *The Psychology of the Child*. London: Routledge and Kegan Paul.

Rasch, G. (1960) *Probabilistic Models for some Intelligence and Attainment Tests*. Copenhagen: Danish Institute for Educational Research.

Rasch, G. (1966) An item analysis which takes individual differences into account. *British Journal of Mathematical and Statistical Psychology*, 19, 49-57.

School Mathematics Project (1969) *S.M.P. Books A—H*. Cambridge: Cambridge University Press.

Schools Council (1972) *Mathematics in Primary Schools: Schools Council Curriculum Bulletin No. 1*. (4th Edition.) London: HMSO.

Science Curriculum Improvement Study (1974) *S.C.I.S. Teacher's Handbook*. Berkeley: Lawrence Hall of Science, University of California, Berkeley.

Shayer, M. (1979) Has Piaget's construct of formal operational thinking any utility? *British Journal of Educational Psychology*, 49, 265-276.

Shayer, M., Kuchemann, D. E. and Wylam, H. (1976) The distribution of Piagetian stages of thinking in British middle and secondary school children. *British Journal of Educational Psychology*, 46, 164-173.

Shayer, M. and Wylam, H. (1978) The distribution of Piagetian stages of thinking in British middle and secondary school children, II: 14/16 year-olds and sex differentials. *British Journal of Educational Psychology*, 48, 62-70.

Stephens, B. (1974) Symposium: developmental gains in reasoning, moral judgment and moral conduct of retarded and non-retarded persons. *American Journal of Mental Deficiency,* **79**, 113-115.

Stevens, S. S. (1951) Mathematics, measurement and psychophysics. In Stevens, S. S. (Ed.) *Handbook of Experimental Psychology*. New York: Wiley.

Tuddenham, R. D. (1970) A Piagetian test of cognitive development. In Dockrell, W. B. (Ed.) *On Intelligence*. London: Methuen.

Tuddenham, R. D. (1971) Theoretical regularities and individual idiosyncrasies. In Green, D. R., Ford, M. P. and Flamer, G. B. (Eds.) *Measurement and Piaget*. New York: McGraw-Hill.

Uzgiris, I. C. and Hunt, J. McV. (1975) *Assessment in Infancy: Ordinal Scales of Psychological Development*. Urbana: University of Illinois Press.

Ward, J. (1972) The saga of Butch and Slim. *British Journal of Educational Psychology,* **42**, 267-289.

Ward, J. and Pearson, L. S. (1973) A comparison of two methods of testing logical thinking. *Canadian Journal of Behavioural Science,* **5**, 385-398.

Wechsler, D. (1974) *Wechsler Intelligence Scale for Children—Revised*. New York: Psychological Corporation.

Willmott, A. S. and Fowles, D. F. (1974) *The Objective Interpretation of Performance: The Rasch Model Applied*. Windsor: NFER.

Wright, B. D. (1977) Solving measurement problems with the Rasch model. *Journal of Educational Measurement,* **14**, 97-116.

Wright, B. D. and Panchapakesan, N. (1969) A procedure for sample-free item analysis. *Educational and Psychological Measurement,* **29**, 23-48.

Wylam, H. and Shayer, M. (1980) *C.S.M.S. Science Reasoning Tasks: General Guide*. Windsor: NFER.

Interchange

HOFMANN REPLIES TO ELLIOTT

Important common assumptions of Hofmann and Elliott

There is perhaps no better summary of the problems of traditional psychometric methods applied to Piagetian theory than that given by Piaget (1928—Introduction). He certainly would agree with many of the problems discussed by both myself and Elliott. Indeed, Elliott and I clearly agree on a number of points; yet we appear to be at odds on several others.

Both Gray and Wadsworth (see acknowledgment of Hofmann essay) were critical of my decision to eliminate statistical discussions from my essay. In the discussion to follow, I shall attempt to avoid statistical discussions but the reader should be aware that the Hofmann essay is based upon a Guttman scaling model (see Hofmann, 1980) while the Elliott essay is based upon the Rasch model. My concerns with Elliott's essay are concerns with the Rasch model applied to development.

One major point of agreement between Hofmann and Elliott is so important that I feel I must preface my comments here with a concise statement of the point. A major assumption of my essay as well as of Elliott's essay is that a well-constructed instrument should minimize the effects of a psychometric problem that may be referred to as composite confusion. Ideally, any particular score obtained by a psychometric procedure is unique in the sense that it can be obtained in but one way. There are many instruments that violate this assumption. To wit, with a simple ten-item objective instrument, there are at most 30 240 combinations of five correct items. If a composite score is determined simply as the number of acceptable responses, then there will be 30 240 possible ways to obtain a score of five. As the number of ways to obtain a given composite score increases, the score interpretation becomes more confusing, i.e. composite confusion. The magnitude of the validity of an instrument is inversely related to the extent to which an instrument displays composite confusion. Elliott and I directed our attentions to procedures that will reduce composite confusion on a Piagetian-based instrument.

A second important point was stated explicitly by Elliott and assumed by Hofmann, the distinction between assessment and measurement. Assessment implies the property of greater than or less than (ordinality) as well as the property of different from or similar to (nominality). Measurement assumes all of the properties of assessment as well as the properties of a true zero point and comparable intervals.

I have assumed that no social science instrument is a measurement instrument; rather, there exist, at best, assessment procedures. I believe, however, that Elliott assumes that by using the Rasch model a measurement procedure will result.

Redefinition of development

Development refers to the movement of an individual through an invariant succession of hierarchical steps, such that a certain level of performance at one step is a necessary but not sufficient condition for progression to the next step. What is not clear in Piagetian theory is where one stage stops and the next one starts. To be sure, there are qualitative distinctions between the major Piagetian stages but a child does not jump from one stage to the next, rather a child progresses 'slowly' from one stage to the next (Pinard and Laurendeau, 1969; Piaget, 1971).

Inherent in the discussion of structural invalidity was the assumption that tasks or items within an assessment procedure should always be hierarchical and that the hierarchy should remain invariant from sample to sample. To the extent that a hierarchical ordering of tasks is obtained, the composite confusion of the assessment procedure will be reduced and the validity enhanced.

Following from this assumption and definition of development is the expectation that a person-by-task matrix should approximate a simplex, even if the tasks do not cover more than one developmental stage. Contrary to Elliott, I believe that quantitative distinctions within a stage on a hierarchical test are reasonable estimates of relative ability within the stage. The spirit of my essay was one of implying that when there is task-difficulty variation within a stage (i.e. on logically equivalent tasks) the variation typically occurs because of structural invalidity; that structural invalidity is *not bad*, especially if you understand it. To understand structural invalidity is to generalize Piagetian theory to content.

Glaser and Nitko (1971) indicate that the ideal criterion-referenced test will be hierarchical and that hierarchical tests will by necessity be criterion referenced. Furthermore, they indicate that although all criterion-referenced tests are easily normed, most norm-referenced tests are not criterion referenced. They imply that the perfect criterion-referenced test will be a Guttman scale with a reproducibility of unity.

To the extent that the tasks within a Piagetian assessment are logically equivalent, with content variation and *no* task-difficulty variation the assessment may very well be a mastery test of a particular developmental level. One can make a compelling argument that such a test will sort the respondents into just two groups: the non-masters, who are not within the developmental level being assessed by the tasks, and the masters, those who are operating beyond the level being assessed by the tasks. There is possibly a third group of respondents who represent those operating at the developmental level being assessed. I would argue that with any statistical sampling continuity there would not only be task-difficulty variation for this third group of respondents but there would also be a hierarchical ordering of the tasks which would generally hold for all of the respondents within this group. How does such a discussion reconcile Elliott's problems with the conservation test?

Statistical inconsistencies or process of cognition

I am a bit uneasy about Elliott's conservation example. His results seem neither to conform with Piagetian expectations nor appear to occur as a function of any of the discussed sources of structural invalidity. Whether or not such results, inconsistent decalage, occur with any regularity is difficult to determine, as they would not be publishable by traditional publication standards. However, we have had a somewhat similar experience in a study conducted in our McGuffey Laboratory School. It is this experience that forms the basis for this section of my comment.

In a comparative study of graphic representational space skills of three groups of similar aged children (visual learning disabled, non-visual learning disabled and normal) an inconsistent decalage was hypothesized and observed (see Hofmann and Schmidt, 1979, for a brief report). Specifically, it was noted that children with visual learning disorders were unable to represent certain topological relationships; yet they were able to represent more advanced Euclidean relationships. Such an inconsistent decalage was not observed with the non-visual learning disabled and normal children. A brief summary of the structural logic leading to the study is reported elsewhere (Hofmann, 1977). The objective of the study was to demonstrate that developmental inconsistencies might for some special groups of children be a function of a learning disorder, as opposed to either an inconsistency in the psychological theory or measurement theory. (For elaboration of this point see Inhelder, 1968; Schmid-Kitsikis, 1973.)

One property of the Guttman scaling model is that a reproducibility can be obtained for a collection of tasks, for the tasks separately and also for each respondent. If the response pattern of a particular respondent does not conform to the idealized response pattern associated with a unique task hierarchy, the Guttman reproducibility associated with the respondent will be low. The respondent level Guttman reproducibility is a direct index of the extent to which the respondent's composite score is contaminated by composite confusion. It seems to me that the Rasch model, as Elliott discusses it, does not consider respondent characteristics. It would be interesting to look at the respondent's statistical characteristics for Elliott's conservation data. Piagetian theory, as I understand it, does not appear to be sensitive to learning disorders that might be disruptive to developmental sequences.

Epilogue

As I read Elliott's essay, it was apparent that we agreed on a number of points. My suspicion is that our interpretations of Piaget are tempered by the psychometric models to which we adhere. I firmly believe that any differences in our thinking would be reconciled through personal discussion.

REFERENCES

Glaser, R. and Nitko, A. J. (1971) Measurement in learning and instruction. In Thorndike, R. L. (Ed.). *Educational Measurement.* (2nd Edition.) Washington: American Council on Education.

Hofmann, R. J. (1977) Reproducibility and learning hierarchies. *Journal of Science Teaching,* **45**, 387-390.

Hofmann, R. J. (1980) Multiple hierarchical analysis. *Applied Psychological Measurement,* **4**, 91-103.

Hofmann, R. J. and Schmidt, P. (1979) A Piagetian-based assessment procedure for identifying children with visual learning disorders. In Poulsen, Miki and Lubin, G. (Eds.) *Piagetian theory and its Implications for the Helping Professions: Proceedings of the Eighth Interdisciplinary Conference Volume II.* Los Angeles: University of Southern California Press.

Inhelder, B. (1968) *The Diagnosis of Reasoning in the Mentally Retarded.* (2nd Edition.) New York: John Day.

Piaget, J. (1928) *Judgment and Reasoning in The Child.* New Jersey: Littlefield, Adams.

Piaget, J. (1971) The theory of stages in cognitive development. In Green, D. R., Ford, M. P. and Flamer, G. B. (Eds.) *Measurement and Piaget.* New York: McGraw-Hill.

Pinard, A. and Laurendeau, M. (1969) 'Stage' in Piaget's cognitive-developmental theory: exegesis of a concept. In Elkind, D. and Flavell, J. H. (Eds.) *Studies in Cognitive Development: Essays in Honour of Jean Piaget.* New York: Oxford University Press.

Schmid-Kitsikis, E. (1973) Piagetian theory and its approach to psychopathology. *American Journal of Mental Deficiency,* **77**, 694-705.

ELLIOTT REPLIES TO HOFMANN

Elliott's reply to Hofmann has been incorporated in Elliott's chapter.

Chapter 14

Socio-economic Bias in Piaget's Theory and its Implications for Cross-culture Studies*

SUSAN BUCK-MORSS

(This article is reproduced by kind permission of S. Karger, Switzerland, from Volume 18 of their journal *Human Development*.)

The cross-cultural application of Piaget's tests has generated a tangled controversy due to the fact that Western children appear to undergo a more rapid cognitive development than their non-Western peers (Bruner, Olver and Greenfield, 1966; Price-Williams, 1969; Berry and Dasen, 1974). Participants in the controversy tend to fall into two groups: psychological universalists, who stress the subjective universality of human psychology, and cultural relativists, who emphasize the objective, cultural and environmental variables in psychological development. I spoke recently with psychologists in several African countries* where Piaget's tests have been administered frequently to children of the first post-independence generations (Evans, 1970, pp. 75-83), and where, with education a major issue of national policy, the controversy has an implicit political content. Yet this content is obscured by the fact that the ideological implications of the two positions are not unequivocal. The psychological universalist position—which is taken, with qualifications, by Piaget (1966) himself—assumes that a general theory of cognition is possible, and thus appears to stand squarely opposed to ideologies of biological racism; but it cannot account for the frequent chronological 'lag' in test performance of non-Western samples and the fact that members of some cultures never 'reach' certain levels of logical operations (Dasen, 1974) without implying another kind of ethnocentrism, the cultural superiority of the West. Cultural relativists, sensitive to this problem, point to a plethora of cultural variables both within the tests (method of testing, equipment used, language and translation) and

---

*My thanks are due to the following people for their friendly reception. I dedicate this article to them without holding them in any way responsible for its contents. C. A. Duruji, University of Nigeria, Nsukka; J. O. O. Abiri, E. A. Yoloye, University of Ibadan; Dr Taiwo, Provost, University of Lagos; E. W. K. Adjei, H. C. Bulley, Mrs M. Williams, University of Ghana, Legon; R. A. LeVine, H. Odera Oruka, Okot P'Bitek, C. Super, University of Nairobi; J. McGovern, M. Mbiliyni, M. v. Freyhold, University of Dar-es-Salaam.

among those tested (literacy level, child-rearing, parental occupation), and claim that the test results are therefore culturally biased. On the level of theory such relativism maintains it moral and political purity, but in practice it cannot avoid contamination: here anthropological tolerance can become a veil for paternalism. For, however much respect is given to 'traditional' cultures, unless the children of these new nations become capable of performing the kind of abstract thinking Piaget has identified, they will have difficulty in competing on an international level where Western 'culture' controls the playing field and has already determined the rules of the game. This argument, in turn, has its problems, however, as it runs into that dilemma which structures so much of third-world intellectual debates: acknowledgment of a need to imitate the West in order to achieve 'equal' cognitive skills can encourage another kind of psychological inequality by feeding the subjective sense of inferiority which Franz Fanon so perceptively analysed and which the cultural movement of *négritude* was designed to overcome.

Of course, it can be argued that intellectual activity can close its eyes to these problems, as its goal is the search for truth regardless of the latter's political implications. But the fact is that these considerations are not merely extrinsic to theoretical ones. On the one hand, the vast number and diversity of cultural variables which the relativists have identified (what Cole and Scribner, 1974, call 'trees in search of a forest') threaten to so splinter the Piagetian effort to develop a general theory that they force it into silence: in an attempt to correct deficiencies of the theory, such 'radical relativism' (Berry, 1974) challenges the very possibility of valid cross-cultural comparisons. On the other hand, if the general theory is maintained—and at least so far as the sequence of stages is concerned most of the evidence points in its favour—the whole linear conception of genetic development with its metaphors of progression and regression, advance and retardation, creates a context in which, if cultural chauvinism is rejected, the problem of a time-lag remains unexplained and unexplainable.

ABSTRACT, FORMAL COGNITION AND THE STRUCTURE OF COMMODITIES

Social scientists in the West and non-West may not be aware that the debate in which they are involved has specific historical origins: it is a continuation of the philosophical controversy between scientism and relativism which first preoccupied European theorists at the turn of the twentieth century. In 1923 (when Piaget was busy with Binet tests) the Hungarian Communist Georg Lukács published *History and Class Consciousness* (Lukács, 1971), a group of essays which shifted the controversy to a radically different axis. These essays were Marxist and passionately partisan (reason why 'neutral' intellectual circles have largely ignored them) and yet the uniqueness of Lukács' approach owed as much to Max Weber (who was his teacher) as it did to Marx, and far more than it did to Engels.* His theory of the relationship between psychology and society (in Marxism, the substructure—superstructure problematic) centred around two crucial premises: first, that the correlation between consciousness and reality was a structural one (rather than reflecting isolated economic, environmental or

---

*One of Lukács' express purposes was to argue against Engels' interpretation of Marxism as a dialectic of nature, and because of its unorthodoxy, his book was denounced as revisionist by the Russian Communist Party. Lukács yielded to Party pressure and openly renounced the book himself in 1934.

socio-cultural variables); second, that abstract formalism was the particular logical structure of Western capitalism in its present industrial stage, that it characterized both the socio-economic mode of production and the mode of consciousness.

This understanding of the interrelationship between subjective and objective factors sets the present Piaget controversy in a new light.* For underlying both the cultural-relativist and the psychological-universalist positions has been the premise of a duality between cognition and society and the assumption that formal structures of thought are universal precisely because they are abstract, while particular content, separate from form, is unessential, contingent on cultural and environmental factors. What Lukács tried to demonstrate was that there was a structural identity between mind and society and that the logical structure of abstract formalism, far from universal, is itself the product of history, that *the form of cognition is itself social content.*

Abstract formalism and abstraction are not the same thing. The ability to abstract is a cognitive skill fundamental to human language competence (Chomsky, 1968), but formalism is a particular kind of abstraction. It is the ability to separate form from content, and the structuring of experience in accord with that distinction. Its model is the supra-empirical, purely formal language of mathematics.

Of course, it was Marx who first argued that abstract formalism was the organizing principle structuring the social relations of production and commodity exchange within Western industrial capitalism. In the first chapter of *Capital*, he outlined the decisive characteristics of this 'commodity structure': abstraction of form from content which cancelled out qualitative distinctions such as social use value (the 'exchange principle'); abstraction of objects from the processes of their production and reproduction ('reification'); abstraction of phenomena from history so that they appear as universal constants divorced from the possibility of temporal transformation ('fetishism') (Marx, 1967). The importance of Lukács' contribution was to demonstrate that the structure of commodities had become 'the central structural problem of capitalist society in all its aspects', including the formal patterns of cognition (Lukács, 1971, p. 83). To illustrate, he gave a critical analysis of Kant's philosophy which, in various 'neo-Kantian' forms, has dominated technical and theoretical thinking in the West since the late nineteenth century. Lukács argued that Kant's formalism, which attributed cognitive value to the abstract structure of verbal judgments and the rational forms of time, space and causality, regardless of particular, concrete content, paralleled the capitalistic concern for abstract exchange value rather than social use value; Kant's insistence that reality could never be known reflected the reified appearance of commodities in the marketplace, cut off like fetishes from the social process of their production, and resulted in the necessity in Kantian philosophy of distinguishing between the knowable 'appearance' and the unknown 'essence' (the thing-in-itself); Kantian dualism, the separation of formal mental operations from the perceptual objects which provided the content of thought, was the cognitive counterpart of the alienation of workers from the object of their production (Lukács, 1971, pp. 110—149). This kind of abstraction was, to be sure, not new. Mathematics and the Aristotelian categories and forms of classification were hardly inventions of Western capitalism. What was new, however, was that under capitalism this logic provided the

---

*It should be noted that Erich Fromm (who considers himself a Marxist humanist) did pioneering work in analysing the interaction between social structure and psychological development (1936, 1941), and has recently stressed its importance in cross-cultural psychological comparisons (Fromm and Maccoby, 1970). Fromm's primary interest has been in that structure's relevance to the structure of character rather than cognition. But see the articles by his colleagues, Maccoby and Modiano (1966, 1969).

structural base of social and economic relations and, within thought, so dominated other forms of mental operations as to provide a cosmological paradigm, determining the notions of reality and truth.

Piaget's conception of cognition is clearly within the bourgeois, idealist tradition of Immanuel Kant, as Riegel has recently noted (1973, p. 363), Kant more than Descartes, the earlier dualist, because Piaget stresses the spontaneity of the subject in the cognitive act, claims thought is a form of praxis, and considers formal categories not innate ideas, but universal structures of experience. In the light of Lukács' critique of Kant, do Piaget's cognitive stages mark progressive assimilation of the structural principles of bourgeois industrialism? Do his tests capture a prototypical comprehension of alienation, reification, and exchange value?

If Lukács is correct, Kant's 'Copernican Revolution' needs an axial turn, for then the abstract mental forms not only structure reality but vice versa, and it follows that the thought processes which Piaget's tests record are developmental not only in an ontogenic sense, but in a socio-historical sense as well. Piaget has warned that the onto-genetic *sequence* of his stages does not correspond with their chronological appearance in the history of Western thought. This, of course, is not the point, but rather that abstract formalism became the dominant cognitive structure with the emergence of Western capitalism which first made possible a shift in the mode of production from agriculture to industry. This hypothesis challenges the argument that the abstract nature of Piagetian cognitive operations guarantees their psychological universality. At the same time, if this form of thinking reflects a specific socio-economic structure, then the argument of the cultural relativists needs revision as well. Indeed, from Lukács' frame of reference, the very concept of culture would appear to be a reification, as it refers to the historical perpetuity of objective determinants: 'culture' is resistant to change, whereas the Marxian notion of social structure is a dynamic one which can account for historical transformation. Although cultural factors may still explain why abstract formalism and industrialized production appeared in the West when they did, Western 'culture' can make no ontological claim to a monopoly over either. Indeed, neither can the capitalism that spawned them. The formal, abstract nature of thought and social reality seems to be equally characteristic of industrialization in Communist countries as neo-Marxists who 'rediscovered' Lukács in the 1960s have argued, and as the recently published research of the Soviet psychologist Luria (1971) has dramatically demonstrated.

SOCIO-ECONOMIC BIAS IN PIAGET'S THEORY

What happens when the familiar Piagetian landmarks toward cognitive maturity are viewed from this altered perspective?* How can they be said to reflect, not a particular culture (cf. Simpson, 1974), but a particular socio-economic structure?

In the first 18 months of life, the child's experience of the world is most immediate, most concrete, and during this stage Western children are not superior in psycho-motor development. On the contrary, they 'lag' significantly behind African infants of their age group (Geber, 1957; Werner, 1972), and within Western society there is not yet a class distinction in test performance (Golden and Birns, 1968). Furthermore, rural children perform better than urban children (Werner, 1972). (The effect of these variables is precisely the reverse in subsequent development of skills in formal abstraction.) Although some of Piaget's most interesting work has been done in this early stage when cognition is still tied to content, he presupposes that the most important thing is not so much what the child can do in this concrete world, as how quickly he can do without it. If the eclectic nature of his concern reflects a socio-economic bias, it is not surprising that he expresses the goal of the sensorimotor stage in strikingly Kantian terms; it is to develop those cognitive skills which 'will constitute the substructure of the subsequent, fully achieved ideas of permanent objects, space, time and causality' (Piaget, 1962, p. 122). For Piaget, the first great cognitive leap is the prototypical experience of alienation. It is the ability of the child to divorce subject from object, hence to grasp the building block of Kantian dualism (and of industrial production). The child can now separate the mental image or concept of an object from its actual empirical existence: he can 'bracket out' the empirical object, that is, he can accomplish what the neo-Kantian Husserl called *epoché*, and what the neo-Marxist Adorno (1970) criticized as a source of reified cognition, because now the object appears to be a product of thought rather than of society. With the attainment of object permanency, the idea of an object—in Piagetian theory it makes no difference whether that object is a piece of chain or the child's own mother—becomes a substitute for the thing itself, indeed, (just as in Husserl's phenomenology) is granted greater cognitive value than the material object, and the child is capable through symbolic play of leaving reality unchanged. This is the same idealist propensity which neo-Marxists criticize in all bourgeois philosophy: placing more value on the idea than reality, while it has been progressive in enabling the individual to imagine the totality of a complex society (as well as a society different from and better than the existing one), encourages a split between thinking and doing. The mind mistakes social contradictions for logical contradictions, labours over the latter, while leaving reality unchanged (Adorno, 1970). For Piaget, the culmination of learning is when the child can 'do' everything in his head, that is, when he can divorce theory from practice. As Berlyne (1965, p. 185) writes, the child ultimately ' . . . can be guided by the *form* of an argument or a situation and ignore its *content*. He need no longer confine his attention to what is real'. Piaget's insistence that 'the principle goal of education is to create men who are capable of doing new things, not simply repeating what other generations have done', and that its second goal 'is to form minds which can be critical, can verify, and do not accept everything they are offered' (cf. Duckworth, 1964, p. 175), would seem to contradict his emphasis on the purely formal operations of thought: innovation has to do with social as well as logical possibility, and if contradictions exist in reality, it is not enough to eliminate them in thought. Abstract, formal cognitive skills may indeed increase the child's ability to adapt to present society rather than to criticize or change it.

---

*This article cannot discuss all of the developmental processes with which Piaget's theory deals. We note only briefly that Piaget's conception of causality, like Kant's, is based on the bourgeois era's mechanistic model of cause and effect (already superseded, in physics at least, by Einstein's theory of relativity), as opposed, for example, to a theological view of causality, or to the view based on animism (which Piaget considers a 'low' developmental stage despite his findings that five-year-olds are less animistic and more mechanistic than six- or seven-year-olds).

As to the concept of spatial perspective, it should be noted that this was a fifteenth century invention first elaborated by the Florentine, Leone Battista Alberti, in 1435, and very much tied to the man-centred, secular cosmology which became dominant in the bourgeois era. Central to the logic of representing two dimensions in a three-dimensional space is the distinction between reality and appearance, and this has become a fundamental principle in the thinking of Western society, while in some traditional African languages, the verbal distinction does not even exist (Greenfield, 1966). African children have been found to score low in tests of perspective (Vernon, 1968; Munroe and Munroe, n.d.). However, they far excel Western children in a visual skill totally tied to content—eidetic imagery (Doob, 1974).

According to Piaget, logical thinking really first begins around age seven (in a Western child) in what he calls the stage of Concrete Operations. But again, what is remarkable about his tests for this stage is that they do not track concrete thinking at all, nor skills of 'concrete science' as Levi-Strauss (1973) has defined it, but progress toward formal abstraction. The actual contents of his conservation and classification tests are only arbitrary. It is their form which is important. They provide the excuse for testing the ability to identify an abstract quality that remains constant despite the diversity of appearance, and it parallels directly the ability to conceptualize commodities and labour in terms of abstract exchange value.

Whereas 'the bush child is more adept at assessing perceptual cues as indicators of object properties' (Furby, 1972, p. 247), the child in Western, industrialized society is quick to grasp logical structures that are indifferent to content. As several recent studies have shown (Adjei, 1974; Price Williams et al, 1974), non-Western children excel in Piaget's test for conservation of substance when their families are involved in the production of pottery, but it needs to be stressed that the Western child can perform the same conservation tasks even though his parents know nothing about pottery making not because he is more intelligent, but because abstraction structures his world,* including the occupations of his parents whose organizational or marketing skills can be applied to any content, and because productivity is gauged by the number of pieces produced per unit time and not by their social usefulness.†

The 'reification' of commodities refers to their appearance in the market as things cut off from the transforming activity of their production; they are simply 'given', unchanged and unchanging. Piaget's conservation tests have a similar structure: the trick is to see that despite the fact that adults have 'acted' on things, the right answer or the response that is valued is that nothing has happened: the important quality is the one that remains the same. The operational principle of the trick, 'reversibility', is that principle of abstract equivalency which cancels out all appearances of difference, which is also the secret of exchange. In contrast, concrete logic is cognitively inferior because its operations go in only one direction. The criterion of 'reversibility' thus condemns to inferiority any logic (e.g. dialectical logic) which bases itself on historical reality, for history is indeed irreversible.

In Piaget's classification tests, the goal is again equivalency—the abstraction of a common quality. Western children perform well on these tests (Dasen, 1972), while the Kpelle of Liberia, for example, still group things according to their 'function' (Cole et al, 1971), that is, their *use* value rather than exchange value. The findings of Maccoby and Modiano (1969) demonstrate that such abstraction is, in fact, a function of the child's socio-economic environment, and not of 'culture': their research in Mexico confirmed the hypothesis 'that equivalence reasoning characterizes the children of industrial workers and not peasant children, although both live within the same national culture' (1969, p. 23).

---

*By the same token, if the city child performs better than bush children of his age set in skills of Euclidean geometry, it may not be because his home is a 'carpentered world' of rectangle forms and square windows, but because he has learned to differentiate between form and content, and to see this distinction as significant. (Although the performances of bush children may indeed depend on their perceptual exposure to these forms as concrete objects [cf. Segall et al, 1963].)

†The factory time-clock was the logical culmination of an increasing rationalization of time which began with the bourgeois enlightenment when Deists viewed the universe as a clock with God the expert clock-maker. The abstract, formal time structure of industrial society is not limited to the factory. It has come to dominate all aspects of human existence, a development which prompted the protest of philosopher Henri Bergson at the turn of the century.

The more broadly the child can generalize, the more concrete content he can eliminate as he ascends the hierarchy of abstraction, the more 'advanced' will be his performance on Piaget's tests. (Such a classificatory structure is precisely the inverse of that which, as Levi-Strauss (1973) observes, has been most fully developed by traditional societies. The latter classify by differentiating rather than generalizing, with a degree of complexity which has repeatedly impressed Western ethnographers.) Adorno (1970) has argued that the bourgeois propensity for generalized abstraction reflects the social value of conformism and a fear of the non-identical view, or religion, or race, which leads to social oppression.

Piaget uses kinship relations to illustrate the formal principle of reciprocity in classification (although an organization chart might do as well: 'The worker's boss is also his boss's worker').* Kinship reciprocity assumes the symmetry and role division of the nuclear family. LeVine and Price-Williams (1974, p. 28) report that, when applied to the complex kinship structures of Hausa society (where the concrete content of social relations cannot be divorced from their logical arrangement): 'The assumptions that sibling relationships are conceptualized as symmetrical and that there is a nuclear family unit of unambiguous reference were exposed as ethnocentric'. Again, it can be argued that this cultural bias is rooted in the socio-economic structure, and that the form of kinship reciprocity is thus itself social content: the nuclear family with its symmetrical relations emerged as the dominant kinship structure with the development of industrialized economy in the West, while industrialization of African countries threatens no cultural tradition more than it does the extended family.

Goodnow (1969) has noted that children from non-technological 'cultures' have the greatest difficulty with Piagetian tasks involving 'mental shuffling' and Dasen (1972, p. 416) remarks that how these differences in competence 'are related to cultural characteristics is not clear at first glance'. If they are related to characteristics of the social structure, however, they no longer appear so mysterious. Piaget's tests thus interpreted record the ability to comprehend the principle of formal abstraction which governs the relations of production and exchange in industrial society and which under capitalism have been raised to the level of ideology, that is, assumed, uncritically, as 'second nature'. The stage of formal-logical operations which to Piaget represent the culmination of cognitive development is then the complete triumph of exchange value over use value.

It is not necessary to base this interpretation on speculation alone. For middle-class, Western children, achievement of Piaget's stages is in fact 'closely linked' (Kohlberg, 1969) to their comprehension of society's economic structure:

(1) Preconceptual (age 3—4). Money is not recognized as a symbol of value different from other objects and it is not understood that money is exchanged in purchase sale transactions . . .

(2) Intermediate (age 4—5). Children recognize that money transfer is required in stores, but do not recognize that the transfer is an exchange of equal economic value. The exchange of work as a job for salary is not understood, nor is the scarcity of money understood . . .

(3) Concrete operational (age 6—8). Children recognize money transactions as involving a logical relation of reversible, reciprocal, and equal exchange values. They understand that the storekeeper must pay money to others for his goods, they understand the work—salary exchange, and the scarcity or 'conservation' of money.

---

*Cf. the dialectical reciprocity in Hegel's analysis of the master and slave: the master becomes dependent on the slave's labour, and the slave, becoming conscious through his labour, gains independence (Reigel, 1973, p. 352).

These findings (cross-'cultural' comparative data would be illuminating) are cited by Kohlberg (1969, p. 452) in a different context, providing an introduction to his developmental theory of moral judgment, which is based on precisely the premise placed in question by this article, i.e. that abstract mental processes are by definition universal, free of particular social content. But unintentionally, the empirical research he cites provides an immanent criticism of his own position. Kohlberg claims that Piaget's own efforts to develop a theory of moral stages is too tied to 'Western' political and legal conventions to hold cross-culturally, that is, that they are 'really matters of content rather than cognitive form' (p. 375); but what he does not consider is whether form itself is content, whether the very notion that morality can divorce form from content, or from 'culturally universal' or 'natural', manifests the structure of a specific society at a specific stage of economic development. Instead, he claims that 'retardation' of moral development (which occurs both in non-Western cultures and in the lower classes) is attributable to 'the amount of social and cognitive stimulation provided by the culture (or subculture) in question'. He notes that lower-class teenagers see the law as an external force which must be obeyed, indicating that they are still only at Stage 1 of moral development, whereas upper-middle-class teenagers are more prone to make autonomous moral judgments relative to circumstances and to awareness that bad laws can be changed (Stage 5). Perhaps the moral rigidity of the lower-class child reflects the reality of authoritarian or arbitrary enforcement of law against his segment of society, whereas the upper middle class's greater flexibility of principle reflects its ability to bend the law in its interest, and to avoid its punishment even when caught—the exchange principle is indeed inherent in 'plea-bargaining'.

In comparison, Piaget's 'content'-filled principle of 'judgment by peers' might seem a preferable criterion, as it implicitly assumes social equality as the precondition for moral justice. Yet the word 'peer' itself contains the history of class society. An empathy, which for Kohlberg represents the moral form of cognitive 'reciprocity', depends on the ability to identify with another self, an ability that too often stops at the barriers of class and race. Social 'reciprocity', as Habermas (1973, 1974) has emphasized, is an ideal rather than a reality in late capitalistic societies.

Not surprisingly, just as Piaget used Kant's cognitive categories, Kohlberg stands on the Kantian imperative as the epitome of moral development: 'Moral principles are categorical imperatives, all other standards are hypothetical imperatives contingent on the individual's aims in the situation' (1969, p. 412). Horkheimer and Adorno (1972, have argued that Kant's content-less morality is a reflection of bourgeois asceticism, expressing a fear of sensuous matter and a consequent desire to dominate it. Here the mind—body dualism takes the form of intellectual repression of sexuality. And even if the ideal of bourgeois justice is indeed equality, its present reality finds expression in the abstract formalism of the life insurance company: 'Whoever dies is unimportant: it is a question of the ratio between accidents and the company's liabilities' (p. 84). But whether one supports or criticizes abstract moral standards is not the point, which is to demonstrate that formal abstraction is no guarantee of universality.

SOCIO-ECONOMIC BIAS AND THE TIME-LAG: SOME HYPOTHESES

It has been argued that Piaget's theory has a socio-economic rather than a cultural bias, that the structure of cognition with which he is concerned reflects the structure of an industrialized society with abstract, formal relations of production and exchange.

The potential for such cognition and its sequential development is no doubt latent in all human beings, but its actual development may reflect the demands of assimilating and accommodating to a particular social reality.

Whether third-world countries choose to foster this kind of reasoning is a decision concerning which the issue of 'cultural imperialism' need have no bearing: it is a question of national policy towards industrialization, not towards the West. They should be forewarned, however, on the basis of Western experience, of the dangers inherent in this mode of cognition when it becomes more than a tool for technical productivity and begins to dominate all thought, when abstract, formal logic, divorced from social and human considerations, becomes an end in itself and men and women become a tool of technology rather than vice versa.* Whether in this regard Communist countries provide a more desirable model for industrialization remains open to debate.

To argue that there is a parallel between social structure and cognitive structure is not yet to explain the connection. On this question, Fromm and Maccoby (1970) see the socialization process as providing a kind of built-in regulator which manages to adjust cognitive style to socio-economic reality. LeVine (1969), using a more elaborate Darwinian model in order to account for the dynamics of social transition, also talks in terms of cognitive adaptation. The analogy to natural evolution may make the selection process in cognitive survival appear more random than in fact is the case, obscuring some very unnatural, *social* determinants such as class and race (cf. Riegel, 1972). For it is well documented by Western studies that lower-class children lag in Piaget test performance, even though they live in industrialized societies (and despite compulsory schooling) (Almy, Chittenden and Miller, 1966; Peluffo, 1962, 1967; Vernon, 1969). It thus appears that socio-economic structure is not the only variable, that industrialization may be a necessary but not sufficient condition for the development of abstract cognitive skills.

A full discussion of this question goes beyond the scope of this article. However, some observations of others are suggestive. Several observers have independently concluded that social change results in an alteration of people's consciousness only when they actively participate in that change (see Luria, 1971, on the Soviet experience of agricultural collectivization, Freire, 1970, 1973, on third-world rural development), and lack of participation has been identified as a source of 'retarded' cognitive and moral development among lower classes in the West (see Kohlberg, 1969, on the US lower class, Habermas, 1973, on class and the reciprocity of social roles). What the lower classes in industrialized countries have in common with the face-to-face societies of third-world rural villagers is that their experience is limited to a realm of concrete immediacy. Meanwhile, the workings of the larger social whole take place literally 'over their heads'. But for those who participate consciously in the abstract, mediated levels of society, direct perception, even if always partial, at least exists, so that experience provides concrete touchstones, 'perceptual cues', if one will, for a cognitive grasp of the social whole—to cite Luria (1971, p. 27): 'Abstract operations begin to make sense in terms of people's activity'.

The objective factor of socio-economic structure together with the subjective factor of conscious participation in the abstract levels of the social whole would seem to account for the variables associated with the time-lag in Piaget test performance—West

---

*Cf. Maccoby and Modiano (1966, p. 216): 'At best the North American child develops an interest in theory, in the abstract equivalences and differences among objects. At worst he merely manipulates things in a formal and increasingly reductionist manner. In fact, a few of the older children completely lose the ability to analyse, because the concrete attributes of objects have become buried beneath formal and abstract notions'.

versus non-West, urban versus rural, upper versus lower class, degree of Western contact (Dasen, 1972). Such a theoretical frame might allow the following tentative hypotheses:

(1) Among certain groups, cognitive development in the skills of abstract thinking may be *a priori* impaired by these groups' exclusion from direct, conscious participation in the abstract levels of society. The child's imitation of parental models would function to perpetuate inequalities of cognitive development: whereas for the middle-class Western child or the children of the third-world urban elite, identification with parents and education in formal logic are mutually reinforcing experiences in socialization, they are conflicting in the case of the out-groups, where 'satellization' on parental models and the development of abstract cognitive competence lead in opposite directions.

(2) Differences in cognitive style both reflect and perpetuate class distinction within industrialized countries, and reflect and perpetuate the domination of urban elites in developing countries. To count on the socialization process as a self-regulating mechanism to adjust disparities between social and cognitive structures would seem to be overly optimistic.

(3) Development of abstract cognitive skills among groups who presently lag behind demands socio-economic and political reform as much as reform in educational curriculum.

With regard to research, the implications of viewing *Piaget's* stress on abstract formalism as expressing a socio-economic bias would suggest the importance of relating test results to the structure of the child's society and his place within it, as well as his cognitive grasp of that structure. It also suggests the need for developing theories of cognitive structures other than abstract formalism, where the content of thought determines its logic, as it does not only in the structure of myths, oral legends, and dreams, but also in the Hegelian-Marxist tradition of dialectical thought.

REFERENCES

Adjei, E. W. K. (1974) Piaget conservation testing of Ghanaian children, the effects of parental occupation. Unpublished dissertation, University of Strathclyde.

Adorno, T. W. (1970) Metakritik der Erkenntnistheorie. Gesammelte Schriften, **5.** Frankfurt/M: Suhrkamp.

Almy, M., Chittenden, E. and Miller, P. (1966) *Young Children's Thinking.* New York: Teachers College Press.

Berlyne, D. E. (1965) Recent developments in Piaget's work. In Ausubel and Anderson, *Readings in the Psychology of Cognition.* New York: Holt, Rinehart & Winston.

Berry, J. W. (1974) Radical cultural relativism and the concept of intelligence. In Berry, J. W. and Dasen, P. R. *Culture and Cognition, Readings in Cross-cultural Psychology.* London: Methuen.

Berry, J. W. and Dasen, P. R. (Eds.) (1974) *Culture and Cognition, Readings in Cross-cultural Psychology.* London: Methuen.

Bruner, J. S., Olver, R. and Greenfield, P. (1966) *Studies in Cognitive Growth.* New York: Wiley.

Buck-Morss, S. (1975) Socio-economic bias in Piaget's theory and its implications for cross-culture studies. *Human Development,* **18,** 34-49. Reprinted in this volume by kind permission of the author and the publisher, S. Karger AG, Basel, Switzerland.

Chomsky, N. (1968) *Language and Mind.* New York: Harcourt, Brace & World.

Cole, M., Gay, J., Glick, J. A. and Sharp, D. W. (1971) *The Cultural Context of Learning and Thinking.* New York: Basic Books.

Cole, M. and Scribner, S. (1974) *Culture and Thought, a Psychological Introduction.* New York: Wiley.

Dasen, P. R. (1972) Cross-cultural Piagetian research, a summary. *Journal of Cross Cultural Psychology,* **3,** 23-39.

Dasen, P. R. (1974) The influence of ecology, culture and European contact on cognitive development in Australian aborigines. In Berry, J. W. and Dasen, P. R. *Culture and Cognition, Readings in Cross-cultural Psychology.* London: Methuen.

Doob, L. W. (1974) Eidetic images among the Ibo. In Berry, J. W. and Dasen, P. R. (Eds.) *Culture and Cognition, Readings in Cross-cultural Psychology.* London: Methuen.

Duckworth, E. (1964) Piaget rediscovered. *Journal of Research and Science Teaching,* **2,** 170-178.

Evans, J. L. (1970) *Children in Africa, a Review of Psychological Research.* New York: Teachers College Press.

Freire, P. (1970) *Pedagogy of the Oppressed.* New York: Seabury Press.

Freire, P. (1973) *Education for Critical Consciousness.* New York: Seabury Press.

Fromm, E. (1936) Sozialpsychologischer Teil. In Horkheimer, M. (Ed.) *Studien über Autorität und Familie.* Paris: Alcan.

Fromm, E. (1941) *Escape from Freedom.* New York: Holt, Rinehart & Winston.

Fromm, E. and Maccoby, M. (1970) *Social Character in a Mexican Village, a Socio-psychoanalytic Study.* Englewood Cliffs: Prentice-Hall.

Furby, L. (1972) A theoretical analysis of cross-cultural research in cognitive development, Piaget's conservation tasks. *Journal of Cross Cultural Psychology,* **2,** 241-255.

Geber, M. (1957) Gesell tests on African children. *Pediatrics,* Springfield, **20,** 1055-1065.

Golden, M. and Birns, B. (1968) Social class and cognitive development in infancy. *Merrill Palmer Quarterly,* **14,** 139-149.

Goodnow, J. J. (1969) Cultural variations and cognitive skills. In Price-Williams, D. R. (Ed.) *Cross-cultural Studies.* New York: Penguin.

Greenfield, P. (1966) On culture and conservation. In Bruner, J. S., Olver, R. and Greenfield, P. (Eds.) *Studies in Cognitive Growth.* New York: Wiley.

Habermas, J. (1973) *Stichworte zur Theorie der Sozialisation, Kultur and Kritik.* Frankfurt/M: Suhrkamp.

Habermas, J. (1974) Können komplexe Gesellschaften eine vernünftige Identität ausbilden? In *Habermas und Henrich Zwei Reden aus Anlass des Hegel-Preises, Frankfurt am Main.* Frankfurt/M: Suhrkamp.

Horkheimer, M. and Adorno, T. W. (1972) *Dialectic of Enlightenment.* New York: Herder & Herder.

Kohlberg, L. (1969) Stage and sequence, the cognitive-developmental approach to socialization. In Goslin, (Ed.) *Handbook of Socialization Theory and Research.* Chicago: Rand McNally.

LeVine, R. A. (1969) Culture, personality, and socialization an evolutionary view. In Goslin, (Ed.) *Handbook of Socialization Theory and Research.* Chicago: Rand McNally.

LeVine, R. A. and Price-Williams, D. R. (1974) Children's kinship concepts: cognitive development and early experience among the Hausa. *Ethnology,* **13,** 25-44.

Levi-Strauss, C. (1973) *The Savage Mind.* Chicago: University of Chicago Press.

Lukács, G. (1971) *History and Class Consciousness.* Cambridge: MIT Press.

Luria, A. K. (1971) Towards the problem of the historical nature of psychological processes. *International Journal of Psychology,* **6,** 259-272.

Maccoby, M. and Modiano, N. (1966) On culture and equivalence. In Bruner, J. S., Olver, R. and Greenfield, P. (Eds.) *Studies in Cognitive Growth.* New York: Wiley.

Maccoby, M. and Modiano, N. (1969) Cognitive style in rural and urban Mexico. *Human Development,* **12,** 22-33.

Marx, K. (1967) Capital, a Critique of Political Economy, Volume 1. New York: International Publisher.

Munroe, R. and Munroe, R. L., Reading pictures, a cross-cultural perspective. Unpublished paper, Child Development Research Unit, University of Nairobi (n.d.).

Peluffo, N. (1962) Les notions de conservation et de causalité chez les infants provenant de différents milieux physiques et socioculturels. *Archives de Psychologie,* Genève, **38,** 275-291.

Peluffo, N. (1967) Culture and cognitive problems. *International Journal of Psychology,* **2,** 187-198.

Piaget, J. (1962) The stages of intellectual development of the child. *Bulletin Menninger Clinic,* **26,** 120-128.

Piaget, J. (1966) Need and significance of cross-cultural studies in genetic psychology. *International Journal of Psychology,* **1,** 3-13.

Price-Williams, D. R. (Ed.) (1969) *Cross-cultural Studies.* New York: Penguin.

Price-Williams, D. R., Gordon, W. and Ramirez, M., III (1974) Skill and conservation, a study of pottery-making children. In Berry, J. W. and Dasen, P. R. (Eds.) *Culture and Cognition, Readings in Cross-cultural Psychology.* London: Methuen.

Riegel, K. F. (1972) Influence of economic and political ideologies on the development of developmental psychology. *Psychological Bulletin,* **78,** 129-141.

Riegel, K. F. (1973) Dialectical operations, the final period of cognitive development. *Human Development,* **16,** 346-380.

Segall, M. H., Campell, D. T. and Herskovits, M. J. (1963) Cultural differences in the perception of geometric illusions. *Science,* N.Y. **139,** 769-771.

Simpson, E. L. (1974) Moral development research, a case study of scientific cultural bias. *Human Development,* **17,** 81-106.

Vernon, P. E. (1968) Measurements of learning. In Scrimshaw and Gordon, *Malnutrition, Learning and Behaviour.* Cambridge: MIT Press.

Vernon, P. E. (1969) *Intelligence and Cultural Environment.* London: Methuen.

Werner, E. E. (1972) Infants around the world. Cross-cultural studies of psycho-motor development from birth to two years. *Journal of Cross-cultural Psychology, 3,* 111-134.

Chapter 15

An Evaluation of Piaget's Theory from a Cross-cultural Perspective

PAUL A. S. GHUMAN

Piaget's article in the *International Journal of Psychology* in 1966 was a landmark in the history of cross-cultural psychology. In this paper he gave a cogent explanation of his theory, outlining the role of cultural factors in cognitive development and suggesting a number of research questions which could be fruitfully explored in cross-cultural studies. Since then, numerous scholars (see Modgil and Modgil, 1976) have been working all over the world to tease out the antecedent variables affecting cognitive growth. Numerous research articles have appeared in scholarly journals (for example: *International Journal of Psychology; Journal of Cross-Cultural Psychology*) and a number of books (or parts of books) have been written on Piagetian psychology from the cross-cultural perspective. A regular newsletter edited by Cibrowski et al is circulated to interested scholars throughout the world, and an entire journal (*Piaget for the Helping Professions*) is devoted to Piagetian researches. Thus, Piagetian psychology is in danger of becôming an institution and even an ideology: such a development might prove inimical to the pursuit of truth.

The purpose of this paper is to evaluate Piaget's theory from a cross-cultural perspective, and to offer suggestions for prospective cross-cultural investigations. However, before we embark on such a venture, it is important to remind the reader that excellent reviews of this nature have already been written by a number of scholars (Lloyd, 1972; Ashton, 1975; Carlson, 1976; Greenfield, 1976; Modgil and Modgil, 1976; Dasen, 1977, 1978). The approach of the present paper, however, is somewhat different: it is considered important to analyse the substantive issues within the theory and thus gain a clear understanding on one crucial point; namely what specific theoretical problems can be resolved or illuminated (and by implication those which cannot) by cross-cultural work alone.

Firstly, it is argued here that the key concepts of the system, and their role in the theory, have not been understood clearly even by the 'vintage' Piagetian scholars: as a consequence confusion and misinterpretation of the theory are widely spread (Piaget, 1972; 1971a; Inhelder, 1977). Secondly, it seems that a number of problems (issues) within the theory do not require empirical validation—they are truisms (Hamlyn, 1967). Thirdly, if it can be shown that the key concepts of the theory do not stand up to the empirical data from the Western-based research, they are hardly likely to be supported by the data from the cross-cultural studies. Finally, there is a serious issue relating to the objection that the Piagetian model is an ethnocentric one (Greenfield, op. cit.) and/or is ideologically based (Buck-Morss, 1975). If this were shown to be a valid objection, there would be little point in wasting efforts on cross-cultural studies. I will discuss these points at some length:

Piaget (1962, p. 8), in a foreword to Flavell's book, wrote:

> It seems clear to me that Professor Flavell is more interested in the experiments than in the theory, which sometimes gives me the impression—perhaps not of having been misunderstood, but, if you will—of having been understood on certain issues more from without than from within.

Of course, one would expect that better understanding might ensue after years of study and research. However, Flavell commented at a conference in 1971 (p. 190):

> Now he made some comments later on [referring to Beilin's paper] which I also found interesting. These concern his reinterpretation of Piaget's theory as essentially maturationist, a reinterpretation with which I am largely in accord although I didn't realize it until last year or so.

Piaget's reply was:

> My friend, Daniel Berulyne, wrote an article maintaining that I was a neo-behaviourist, and today Beilin has read a paper showing that I am a maturationist. In fact, I am neither . . . and Beilin's paper has proved very instructive in that it has shown how difficult it is for me to make myself understood. (Piaget, 1971a, p. 192)

These verbatim extracts are quoted at length to show how difficult it is for scholars to come to grips with the essentials of the theory. Recently, Meadows (1979, p. 36) reviewing several books on Piaget, comments:

> I could not say that I enjoyed either of these two books: McNally's because it repeats, though quite well, what many others have done before, and Piaget's (referring to the development of thought: Equilibration of cognitive structures) because of the apparent inability of his theory to accommodate any work done outside Geneva, except by ignoring it . . . The most common excuse from Geneva for this has been that English and American critics, such as Bruner and Bryant, have misunderstood the theory, and their disproofs are therefore invalid.

Echoes of this are to be found in a recent foreword written by Inhelder to Modgil's (1976) works, where she complained of not being fully understood by the scholars pursuing research in Piagetian theory. More specifically, Flavell (1971, p. 190) expressed his doubts about the clarity of the concept of equilibration; Dasen (1978) suggests that the domain consistency is not as central to the theory as is supposed by many scholars, and Flavell and Wohlwill (1969, p. 105) are also not very sure of its status within the system:

> This property of developmental stages is thus of limited significance as a source of empirically testable hypotheses; nonetheless the concept of *structures d'ensemble* remains of both theoretical and empirical consequence, in the sense that it provides a standard against which the progress of a child along the road to the establishment of the stage can be gauged.

Similarly, there is a confusion over the use of the term structures—has it got an empirical base (Piaget, 1971b) or is it a mere invention to explain a set of phenomena (Jahoda, 1976)?

It follows from our analysis that rigorous conceptual analysis of the central notions of the theory are badly needed. Several authors (Flavell and Wohlwill, 1969; Pinard and Laurendeau, 1969), including Piaget and Inhelder (op. cit.), have made significant contributions to this end; but confusion still surrounds the basic tenets of the theory. Experimental research based on this type of theory is likely to be open to varying interpretations, and hence likely to be inconclusive. For instance, it is difficult to falsify the hypothesis on the 'unity of stages', as it is extremely difficult to understand the precise meaning and interpretation of the concepts of stage and horizontal decalage. (Pinard and Laurendeau's discussion, op. cit., is extremely useful on this point and so is Piaget's 1971a.)

Related to this is the problem of verification of the invariant sequence of stages. From a philosophical viewpoint Hamlyn argues (1967, pp. 40—41):

> Is it, therefore, any surprise that what Piaget calls the stage of concrete operations must in general precede that of abstract operations? As Aristotle said, while in knowledge the general is prior in itself, the particular is prior relative to us. This is what Piaget's point comes down to . . . The possibility of creatures who come to knowledge of, say, the principles of physics before knowledge of their immediate surroundings is a science-fiction conception, but it corresponds to nothing human. Insofar as our concept of knowledge is really a concept of 'human' knowledge, it is doubtful whether the possibility which I have mentioned is even one which is intelligible to us.

Admittedly, such an interpretation of Piaget is an oversimplification of his theory, but there is a substantive point in the analysis that children would find it easier to grasp, and apply concrete knowledge before they can deal with abstract and propositional knowledge. Such a stance considerably weakens the importance of the Piagetian model in understanding children's intellectual development. Another line of attack is from an anthropological perspective that:

> Cultural differences in cognition reside more in the situations to which particular cognitive processes are applied than in the existence of a process in one cultural group and its absence in another. (Cole et al, 1971, p. 233)

The stronger version of this stance (see Kreber, 1948, who also believes in the psychic unity of man) would imply that cross-cultural and indeed intra-cultural work should concentrate on social and linguistic antecedents of intellectual development, rather than on ascertaining whether children in a given culture or indeed sub-culture possess cognitive structures as described by Piaget. Similarly, Bruner (1967) has argued that our ideas of cause and effect, of the continuity of space and time, of invariances in experiences are given in the innate nature of our three techniques for representing reality: action, imagery and symbolism. It becomes difficult, if not impossible, to falsify hypotheses from these axiomatic points of view. If evidence is not forthcoming to support a hypothesis, it can always be argued, especially in cross-cultural contexts, that the researcher did not set about finding a process or mechanism in a suitable manner (Cole et al, 1971; Cole and Bruner, 1972). It does not follow from the above that researchers should give up cross-cultural investigations, but should be very clear about the objectives of their researches and be aware of the basic theoretical principles of the model which they wish to test. In a recent paper, Sechrest (1976) has argued cogently and with empirical evidence to show that most of the cross-cultural research is poor in conception as well as in experimental rigour and so far has contributed little to the general body of psychological theory.

One of the implications of the foregoing discussion is that a psychological theory ought to be properly established, both conceptually and empirically, in its culture of origin before it can be used to explore behaviour across cultures. The reason for this is a simple one: if a theory cannot be fully supported from the data on a relatively homogeneous population sharing a common language, beliefs and values, and social skills, it is highly unlikely that it would find support in cultures with radically different value and belief systems. There is a serious challenge (from within culture) to the concept of unity of stages (Brown and Desforges, 1977), and the concept of egocentrism has been challenged by Donaldson in her recent book (1978), in which she persuasively argues that even younger children (five years) are capable of giving responses which show decentration, provided they understand the problems as well as the intentions of the investigators.

Related to this, of course, is the issue and charge of ethnocentrism. Simply stated, it implies that Piagetian psychology is impregnated with explicit as well as implicit value assumptions about the nature of man (including his cognitive functioning) from a Western point of view. Greenfield (op. cit.) has put forward a strong argument to demonstrate that Piaget's theory presupposes an end point of intellectual growth which is Western European in conception; namely that the development is conceived to be moving towards scientific thinking which is hypothetico-deductive in nature. Real problems arise when this system is used to study intellectual development across cultures: the type of intelligence prized and nurtured in another culture may vary radically from the notion of logico-mathematical intelligence.

An ideological bias is levelled against the theory by Buck-Morss (1975, p. 41) who argues that Piagetian stages reflect the social and economic structure of Western societies. She argues:

> According to Piaget, logical thinking really first begins around age seven (in a Western child) in what he calls the stage of concrete operations. But again, what is remarkable about his tests for this stage is that they do not track concrete thinking at all . . . but progress towards formal abstraction. The actual contents of his conservation and classification tests are only arbitrary. It is their form which is important. They provide the excuse for testing the ability to identify an abstract quality that remains constant despite the diversity of appearance, and it directly parallels the ability to conceptualize commodities and labour in terms of abstract exchange value.

At the other end of the spectrum lie scholars like Kaufman (1978, pp. 19—20) who argues forcefully that the bases of constructionist theory of Piaget are dialectical in nature and share a common epistemological foundation with the ideology of socialism. He goes on to suggest that it is the behaviourist psychology, with its emphasis on quantification, its single norm of measurement and its mechanistic view of man, which has an affinity with the monopoly capitalism. These extreme ideological interpretations of Piaget make interesting reading, but are not likely to establish the scientific merit of the theory—which should be judged on conceptual and empirical bases alone, and not from the viewpoints of the sociology of knowledge. Before we leave this topic, it is important here to mention that some scholars, pursuing the discipline of the sociology of knowledge (Schutz, 1968; Young, 1971), cast doubt on the very concept of rationality. Their stance can be summarized as follows: that all knowledge is socially determined and all truth is relative to particular legitimizing agencies; therefore not only knowledge but also rationality itself are merely conventions. Such an extreme position would make the pursuit of knowledge and understanding (especially across cultures) almost impossible, as the rules governing the truth validity of statements also become arbitrary. Thus the very concept of 'intelligible' becomes redundant. Such an approach to research would yield idiosyncratic and descriptive data which would be difficult to interpret. Schaeffer's evaluation of this perspective is worth quoting (1966, p. 19. Comments on Kuhn's *The Structure of Scientific Revolution*.):

> Independent and public controls are no more, communication has failed, the common universe of things is a delusion, reality itself is made by the scientist rather than discovered by him. In place of a community of rational men following objective procedures in the pursuit of truth, we have a set of isolated monads, within each of which belief forms without systematic constraints.

An emic approach to cross-cultural research, in its extreme form anyway, might have some affinity with the position taken by the modern radical sociologists (op. cit.). A very good discussion of this topic is to be found in Berry's article (1969) in which he argued that the problem of an emic versus an etic approach in cross-cultural comparability studies can be resolved. He suggests three steps: first, compare only those behaviours where functional equivalence of the behaviours can be shown to exist; second, start with an emic approach and then modify the concepts, etc., to the extent that they become an adequate description of the behaviours from within the system—

hopefully this would lead to a build-up of new categories valid for both systems; third, devise instruments, etc., to assess the newly conceived etic categories. However, according to Jahoda (1976, p. 12) the solution proposed is not a satisfactory one and he concludes:

> The general answer to the question in the title is therefore, in my view, negative. The pursuit of the emic—etic distinction appears to me a little like the alchemists' search for the philosopher's stone. As in that case, perhaps an entirely new way of transmuting emic into etic will be found in future, which we cannot imagine now.

(Of course, Piagetian scholars, with some exception, have used an etic approach in their cross-cultural work. Discussion of these follows later.)

Thus it emerges from our discussion that cross-cultural research is unlikely to resolve the basic issues in the theory, such as unity of stages (*structures d'ensemble*), sequential development of cognitive structures, and clarification of key concepts such as equilibration. However, such a research strategy can illuminate the importance of socio-cultural and linguistic factors to cognitive development by selecting societies with contrasting value systems, and can pinpoint the role of specific experience on the acquisition of cognitive operations. Furthermore, research across cultures can demonstrate in a dramatic way the significance of the Western style of living (within traditional contexts) to the development of logical thinking processes. The pragmatic value of the theory, however, has been considerable: it has generated fresh insights and understanding of the functioning of the child's mind; it has drawn the attention of cross-cultural workers to the processes of thinking and to the fact that clinical methods of interviewing children can yield a rich variety of data for theory-building. We shall discuss these aspects later.

It has been shown by various investigators (Greenfield, 1966; Dasen, 1974; Ghuman, 1975, 1978a) that cultural traditions and conventions of a given society can influence or even determine children's responses on the cognitive tasks of conservation. In Punjabi culture (Ghuman, op. cit.) children are brought up to regard their teachers as *gurus* (especially in rural areas) who have to be respected and admired at all times. As a result, children rarely question the expositions and expertise of the teachers and tend to rote learn the subject-matter. Thus styles of learning engendered by *guru—chale* (master—disciple) relationships are not conducive to active responding and the 'constructionist' way of thinking. On the conservation problem of area and length Punjabi children of 10 to 11 years of age when asked to justify their answers tended to change their responses, the reasoning being: 'If I was correct in the first instance I would not have been asked to explain reasons for my responses'. Such an attitude reflected their deference and respect for the person in authority (Ghuman, 1978b). This conclusion is reinforced by the fact that the children were on the lookout for facial cues to affirm or to deny their answers. It is interesting to note that success rates on these tests were quite low as compared with the success rate on the conservation of weight: length 6 per cent; area 27 per cent; weight 75 per cent. Dasen (1974, p. 234) reports a similar attitude of Australian Aboriginal children. He remarked:

> . . . the Aboriginal child is not used to expressing and maintaining his own opinion. Any counter-suggestion is likely to be taken as criticism, and the subject will change his answer.

Greenfield (1966) also mentions the prevalence of the belief amongst the illiterate Wolof children that the experimenter is capable of changing the quantity of water through magic. These researchers alert us to the very real problem of perceptions and interpretations given by children to the probing questions of the investigators. Children's responses, therefore, may not reflect their true competencies (abilities), but might demonstrate their ability to please the person in authority, especially in traditional cultures. Irvine's (1970, p. 29) conclusion seems to suggest, if a little too definitely, that values and attitudes held by the subjects are important considerations:

> Thus theories of intelligence are incomplete without reference to the centrality of affect and values in determining the directions that human abilities will follow in different societies.

Thus it is not unreasonable to suggest that the time-lag often found in the cognitive development of children from non-Western countries may be due to the complex interplay of the socio-cultural factors with the cognitive operations rather than low genetic potential.

Next we turn to the role of specific experience in the acquisition of cognitive skills. A number of investigators working with children from a variety of backgrounds have demonstrated a link between specific forms of experiences and cognitive tasks (Price-Williams, Gordon and Ramirez, 1967; Inhelder, 1971; Duraojaye, 1972; Dasen, 1974; Ghuman, 1975). Earlier in the text, I alluded to the fact that the Punjabi children from a farming background performed significantly better on the conservation of weight than they did on the conservation of area and length. The reason for this is as follows: children from the farming families learn to measure and weigh quantities and develop keen awareness of the fact that the shapes of the containers of rice, corn and butter, etc., do not alter the weight of the objects. As I was reminded by one of the boys who was asked to justify his conservation response:

> The weight remains the same no matter how the ball changes its shape. I have learnt this from my father—the weight of a thing is not altered by the shape of the container.

Inhelder (op. cit.) has reported similar findings with Algerian children, and Price-Williams et al's studies with the potters' children are well known in this field (1967). Likewise Dasen's (op. cit.) investigation has also shown quite clearly the influence of daily life activities on the development of cognitive operations. While working with Aboriginal children, he hypothesized that children living within the traditional context of their culture would perform significantly better on the spatial tests of ability and not as well on the conservation problems as would the Aboriginal children living near the modern city of Canberra. His hypothesis was confirmed.

These findings alert us to the possibility that lack of certain cognitive operations in children from other cultures may not be due to the low genetic potential, as academics like Eysenck seem to think (1971), but simply may be a result of inadequate experience or absence of experiences which are deemed necessary to energize and thereby actualize the latent cognitive structures. There is some evidence to support this viewpoint. Following Flavell and Wohlwill (op. cit.), Kroger (1978, p. 2) draws a distinction between competence and performance:

> Especially with somewhat older subjects, and in the cross-cultural context, it seems to make sense that subjects may have the competence (i.e. the operational structure) but not yet the performance (i.e. in this particular context) of a concept.

To test this hypothesis, she gave training sessions of ten minutes each to children from three different ethnic backgrounds: Indians, West Indians, and indigenous whites. All the children were post-tested on the Piagetian matrices and the Raven matrices. Results of the study are rather complex but the significant finding is that both the immigrant groups showed more improvement in their scores on the Piagetian matrices than the indigenous group, and there was some transfer effect on the Raven matrices test. Likewise Dasen et al (1978) have demonstrated the effect of training sessions on the acquisition of conservation skills and cognitive operations in the Western African context. Obviously much more research is needed to clarify this distinction between competence and performance, but a good start has been made in this direction.

Piaget (1974, p. 303) in his article suggested that:

In so far as cognitive processes can vary from one culture to another, it is obvious that one ought to consider this group of factors which is distinct from the former (i.e. biological). To start with, one could look at the various languages which are likely to have a more or less strong influence, if not on the operations themselves, at least on the detail of the conceptualizations (e.g. content of classifications, relations).

Several researchers have taken up this challenge (for example, Keats, Keats and Rafaei, 1976; Sevinc and Turner, 1976). Sinclair de Zwart (1968) found that children who could conserve used vector words (more and less) as compared with the children who could not conserve—they used scalar words (much and little). Ghuman and Girling (1974) confirmed this finding with a group of English children. Sevinc and Turner (op. cit.) set out to explore the effect of the linguistic factors (vectors versus scalars) on cognitive operations in two samples of Cypriot children who came from similar social backgrounds but had dissimilar linguistic backgrounds: (1) English and Greek; (2) English and Turkish. The results of the study are rather complex, but their important conclusion is that (pp. 246-247)

> the structure of development is not constant across languages . . . and that in a language such as Turkish, which allows an identical form to be used in both classification and comparison, we find an overlapping in the development of conservation and classification skills and no association between mastery of the vector form and performance on the conservation problems.

Keats, Keats and Rafaei (1976) studied the importance of language on the acquisition of the concept of weight with two groups of five-year-old Malaysian children. The first group consisted of bilinguals in English and Malay and the second group was composed of bilinguals in English and Chinese. Children were trained in one language and post-tested on their other language, and a delayed test of conservation of weight was also given. Their results support Piaget's contention that language plays only a minor part in the acquisition of cognitive structures, no matter in what language children are tested or trained.

Next we consider a group of studies with children from developing countries, who had had varying degrees of contact with Western European culture. Ghuman (1975, 1978a,b) investigated the development of concrete operations by selecting Punjabi children with varying degrees of contact with Western culture: (1) British Punjabis born and schooled in England; (2) Brahmins and other upper-class Punjabis; (3) Intermediate group of Kshatriya and Vaishya; and (4) Lowest group—Harijan Punjabis. There was also a control group of indigenous English children. As predicted, the performance of the British Punjabi and the English children was similar on a variety of cognitive tests (including Piagetian conservation tests) and significantly different from the other three groups save on the conservation of weight test. Brahmins and professionals were significantly better (these children came from Western-orientated homes and also went to private schools run along European lines) than the other two groups except on conservation of weight. The most interesting finding, however, was that the British Punjabis attended so-called Educational Priority Area schools, which were considered to be deficient in providing effective education; but even these subjects performed better on the Raven matrices, WISC blocks and the conservation of area test than the Punjabi professional group. Thus there is strong evidence that even the impoverished or weak Western style of education has enormous effect on the growth of mental abilities as conceived within the Western context!

Likewise Lloyd (1972) working in Nigeria found that the performance of children from the so-called elite homes, on a variety of Piagetian problems, was significantly superior to the performance of children from the other strata of society. However, the children from the upper-class families performed as well as the middle-class American children. A number of other scholars (Peluffo, 1967; Beard, 1968; Poole, 1968; and

Prince, 1968) have also found this connection between the Western type of education and performance on the Piagetian tasks. This conclusion is reinforced by the evidence emanating from some of the studies which used school as an independent variable (of course, much depends on the nature of schooling; see Modgil and Modgil, 1977, for a detailed discussion of this issue). Bruner, Oliver and Greenfield (1967) showed the effect of Western-type schooling on the conservation ability of the Wolof children and their performance on a sorting test. Likewise Cole et al (1971) relate superior performance of school-going Kepple subjects on a variety of cognitive tasks to the Western style of schooling.

The implications of the findings reviewed so far may be summarized as follows: firstly, though biological bases are necessary for the growth of cognitive structures (Piaget, 1971c), the environmental factors, such as socialization practices and cultural and educational factors, are equally important in the actualization of these structures; secondly, the time-lag found with the non-Western children is largely due to their differential experiences with the physical and social worlds; thirdly, albeit a truism, the subjects who are exposed to the Western-type of life-style perform better than the subjects who are rooted in the indigenous cultures; and finally, though we have not discussed researches relating to the basic theoretical issues, e.g. *structures d'ensemble*, the theory has run into similar kinds of difficulties as it did with the research data from the Western contexts (Heron and Dowell, 1974; Ashton, op. cit.; Dasen, op. cit.).

Piaget's model of intellectual development is a considerable advance over the psychometricians' model of intelligence which was frequently used across cultures (Lloyd, 1972). Piaget's model stresses the process rather than the product approach; its methodology is flexible and therefore more relevant to cross-cultural work; both genetic and environmental factors are considered equally necessary for intellectual development, and no attempt is made to quantify the contributions of these factors, as the interplay between the two variables is considered complex and amenable only to qualitative discourse. In addition, conceptual links between cognitive structures (in their logico-mathematical form) and mathematical and scientific concepts have now been identified and researched by a number of scholars, including Piaget (Piaget, 1971b; Peel, 1974; Lunzer, Dolan and Wilkinson, 1976).

Such a model has a considerable pragmatic value in generating new knowledge, hypotheses and hard data which can be extremely useful in curriculum-planning in the developing countries. I referred to the fact that Punjabi teachers use mechanistic methods of teaching and treat children as if they were receptacles to be filled with ready-made knowledge. This notion has been reinforced through the use of normative tests of intelligence—indigenous as well as Western European in conception.

Piagetian psychology has directed researchers' as well as educators' attention to the 'constructivist' (constructionalist) nature of knowledge. Of course, several other philosophers and educationists (Whitehead, 1949; Dewey, 1964; Pestalozzi and Froebel, etc.) have also stressed the importance of the child's participation in knowledge-getting processes; but Piaget's contribution is unique in that scholars have developed and built on the basic theoretical ideas and have spelt out in detail the changes required in the pedagogy. For instance, Peel's recent book (1974) contains a wealth of both theoretical and empirical ideas relating to adolescents' thinking and the way they make judgments. Resulting principles are related to the practice of teaching history, geography and other social sciences. In cross-cultural contexts, a book named *Concept Development in African Children* has been planned and a number of symposiums held to consider the implications of Piagetian theory for curriculum design in African countries. The present author is planning to write a book for Punjabi teachers based predominantly on Piaget's theory. These developments are as a direct result of Piaget's theories.

It is now apposite to mention one of the chief objections raised by some radical academics (e.g. Buck-Morss, op. cit.; Prieswerk, quoted in Modgil, 1976) regarding the application of Piagetian theory to curriculum design etc. in the developing countries. The gist of their argument is that because the theory is basically ethnocentric in conception, it imposes its inherent assumptions about the nature of man and society on the people of the Third World—thereby posing a moral problem. This is a serious challenge which must not go unanswered. I suggest that a vast majority of the people in the traditional countries wish to modernize their production and distribution systems and would very much like to see the application of new technologies to overcome the endemic shortage of food and to cure crippling and debilitating diseases. For instance, witness the large-scale emigration of people from the Indian sub-continent to the United Kingdom, and likewise the enormous influx of so-called guest workers from the developing countries to the capitalist countries of Western Europe. There is also an enormous demand by the third-world countries, including socialist China, for the new technologies of the West. Whether the developing countries wish to retain those elements of their own cultures which give them stability and roots is a different matter and is open for discussion and debate. Iran is a case in point: it has rejected the wholesale adoption of the Western way of life, but still wants to continue to use Western technology for industrial production. It seems that the stance of the radical thinkers is not based on any authentic empirical evidence, but possibly based on their idiosyncratic interpretation of the situation and on ideological bias—a mixture of romantic and Marxist views of man and society.

It follows, therefore, that Piagetian psychology with its emphasis on logico-mathematical modes of thinking can make a significant contribution towards the education of the younger generation of the Third World. Piaget (1972, p. 7) seemed to have laid more emphasis than hitherto on the socio-cultural and educational factors:

> However, the formation and completion of cognitive structures imply a whole series of exchanges and a stimulating environment; the formation of operations always requires a favourable environment for 'co-operation', that is for operations carried out in common (e.g. the role of discussion, mutual criticism or support, problems raised as the result of exchanges of information, heightened curiosity due to the cultural influence of a social group, etc.). Briefly, our first interpretation would mean that in principle all normal individuals are capable of reaching the level of formal structures on the conditions that the social environment and acquired experience provide the subject with the cognitive nourishment and intellectual stimulation necessary for such a construction.

Several authors to date have written on the problems involved in cross-cultural research and have suggested a variety of solutions. For instance, Cole (1977) seems to argue for an interdisciplinary approach consisting of perspectives from anthropology and cognitive psychology. Poortinga (1978) suggests a more rigorous experimental approach: special attention being paid to functional equivalence of constructs, attitudes of the subjects and the nature of the instruments used for data collection. Greenfield (op. cit.) urges researchers to follow the spirit of the Piagetian theory rather than its procedures: she suggests ethnographic analysis of the cultures concerned and that careful attention be paid to those cognitive skills which have had survival values for the people concerned. Price-Williams et al (1976) have followed such a lead and have studied the 'intelligence' of rural Hawaiian children through kinship terminology. For our part we would like to suggest that: (1) more attention should be paid to the communication aspect of experimental testing—it is so easy for children from other cultures to interpret the question in a different fashion; (2) if possible cross-cultural work should be carried out by a team consisting of psychologists (indigenous as well as European based), an anthropologist and a person who knows the children very closely—a teacher, or a community leader etc.; and (3) the researchers ought to be quite clear about the nature of the questions they wish to pursue through cross-cultural work. It has often been the case (see Scherect, 1976) that research across cultures is done for all sorts of trivial reasons, and that certain issues in the theory are not likely to be resolved through empirical research.

It would be fair to conclude that, on balance, Piagetian theory has not been supported in the hard sense of the verification procedures normally used by the physical scientists (for instance, Popper's canon of falsification, 1971). Nevertheless, the theory is considerably more complex and broadly based than, say, the psychometricians' theory, and has been an instrument in generating a rich source of data on childrens' thinking and concept formation. In addition, it has enlarged psychologists' understanding of the concept of intelligence and its development and has been a contributory factor in improving the pedagogical methods in primary schools. We let Piaget speak for himself (1971a, p. 213):

> Finally, my last comment, Engleman said that I have proved nothing. He is quite right. There are many ways of proving something: the first is to study one problem in as great detail as possible, using statistical methods, calculation of variations, and whatever else you may think feasible; the second is to keep moving from problem to problem, from field to field, seeking—and this is what counts—convergences and links between one field and another . . . When you pass from one field to another, either there is chaos or you find results which link up with observations already made, i.e. you find all sorts of convergences and analogies. I personally think it is far more satisfactory, as far as proof is concerned, to find these convergences and connections between fields than it is to work only one problem using increasingly accurate statistical methods.

REFERENCES

Ashton, P. T. (1975) Cross-cultural Piagetian research: an experimental perspective. *Harvard Education Review,* **5** (4), 475-505.

Beth, E. W. and Piaget, J. (1966) *Mathematical Epistemology and Psychology.* New York: D. Reidal.

Beard, R. M. (1968) An Investigation into Mathematical Concepts among Ghanaian Children. *Teacher Education,* May 1968, 9-14, and November 1968, 132-145.

Berry, J. W. (1969) On cross-cultural comparability. *International Journal of Psychology,* **4** (2), 119-128.

Brown, G. and Desforges, C. (1977) Piagetian psychology and education: time for revision. *British Journal of Educational Psychology,* **47,** 7-17.

Bruner, J. S. (1967) An overview. In Bruner, J. S., Olver, R. R. and Greenfield, P. M. (Eds.) *Studies in Cognitive Growth.* London: Wiley.

Bruner, J. S., Olver, R. R. and Greenfield, P. M. (1967) *Studies in Cognitive Growth.* London: John Wiley.

Buck-Morss, S. (1975) Socio-economic bias in Piaget's theory and its implications for cross-cultural studies. *Human Development,* **18,** 35-49.

Carlson, J. S. (1976) Cross-cultural Piagetian Studies: What can they tell us. In Riegel, K. and Meacham, J. (Eds.) *The Developing Individual in a Changing World,* Volume 1, pp. 334-345. The Hague: Mouton.

Cole, M. (1977) An ethnographic psychology of cognition. In Johnson-Laird, P. N. and Wason, P. C. (Eds.) *Thinking: Readings in Cognitive Science,* pp. 468-482. London: Cambridge University Press.

Cole, M. and Bruner, J. S. (1972) Preliminaries to a theory of cultural differences. In Gordon, I. J. (Ed.) *Early Childhood Education,* pp. 161-181. Chicago: The University of Chicago Press.

Cole, M. and Scribner, S. (1974) *Culture and Thought: A Psychological Introduction.* London: John Wiley.

Cole, M., Gay, J., Glick, A. J. and Sharp, W. D. (1971) *The Cultural Context of Learning and Thinking.* London: Methuen.

Dasen, P. R. (1974) The influence of ecology, culture and European contact on cognitive development in Australian Aboriginees. In Berry, J. W. and Dasen, P. R. (Eds.) *Culture and Cognition,* pp. 381-408. London: Methuen.

Dasen, P. R. (1977) *Piagetian Psychology: Cross-cultural Contributions.* Chapter I, pp. 1-23. New York: Gardner Press.

Dasen, P. R. (1978) *The cross-cultural relevance of developmental theories.* Piaget. Paper presented at the IVth IACCP Congress, Munich.

Dasen, P. R., Ngini, L. and Lavallee, M. (1978) *Cross-cultural training studies of concrete operations.* Paper presented at the IVth IACCP Congress, Munich.

Dewey, J. (1964) *Democracy and Education.* New York: Macmillan.

Donaldson, M. (1978) *Children's Minds.* London: Fontana/Collins.

Duraojaye, M. (1972) *Conservation in six cultures.* Paper presented at the 20th International Congress of Psychology, Tokyo, August, 1972.

Eysenck, H. J. (1971) *Race, Intelligence and Education.* London: Temple-Smith.

Flavell, J. H. (1967) *The Developmental Psychology of Jean Piaget.* London: D. Van Nostrand.

Flavell, J. H. (1971) Comments on Beilin's paper. In Green, D. R. et al. (Eds.) (1971) *Measurement and Piaget,* pp. 189-191. London: McGraw-Hill.

Flavell, J. H. and Wohlwill, J. F. (1969) Formal and functional aspects of cognitive development. In Elkind, D. and Flavell, J. H. (Eds.) *Studies in Cognitive Growth,* pp. 67-120. London: OUP.

Ghuman, P. A. S. (1975) *The Cultural Context of Thinking: A Comparative Study of Punjabi and English Boys.* Slough: NFER.

Ghuman, P. A. S. (1978a) *A comparative study of British and Punjabi teachers' attitude to children's learning and thinking.* Paper read at the International Conference on Cross-cultural Psychology, July 1978. To be published in the Proceedings.

Ghuman, P. A. S. (1978b) Nature of intellectual development of Punjabi children. *International Journal of Psychology,* **13-14,** 281-294.

Ghuman, P. A. S. and Girling, L. (1974) A study of children's cognitive operations in relation to their language. *Indian Journal of Psychology,* 49 (2), 127-138.

Greenfield, P. M. (1966) On culture and conservation. In Bruner, J. S. et al (Eds.) *Studies in Cognitive Growth,* pp. 225-257. London: Wiley.

Greenfield, P. M. (1976) Cross-cultural research and Piagetian theory: paradox and progress. In Riegel, K. and Meacham, J. (Eds.) *The Developing Individual in a Changing World,* Volume 1, pp. 322-333. The Hague: Mouton.

Hamlyn, D. W. (1967) The logic and psychological aspects of learning. In Peters, R. S. (Ed.) *The Concept of Education.* London: Routledge and Kegan Paul.

Heron, A. and Dowell, W. (1974) The questionable unity of the concrete operations stage. *International Journal of Psychology,* 9 (1), 1-9.

Inhelder, B. (1971) Developmental theory and diagnostic procedures. In Green, R. D. et al (Eds.) *Measurement and Piaget,* pp. 148-168. London: McGraw-Hill.

Inhelder, B. (1976) Foreword. In Modgil, S. and Modgil, C. *Piagetian Research: Compilation and Commentary.* Volume 8, pp. 7-8. Slough: NFER.

Irvine, S. H. (1970) Affect and construct—a cross-cultural check on theories of intelligence. *Journal of Social Psychology,* **80,** 23-30.

Jahoda, G. (1976) *In pursuit of the emic-etic distinction: can we ever capture it?* Paper presented at the Third IACCP Conference at Tilburg.

Kaufman, B. A. (1978) Piaget, Marx and the political ideology of schooling. *Journal of Curriculum Studies,* **10** (1), 19-45.

Keats, D. M., Keats, J. A. and Rafaei, W. (1976) Concept acquisition in Malaysian bilingual children. *Journal of Cross-Cultural Psychology,* **7** (1), 87-99.

Kroeber, A. R. (1948) *Anthropology.* New York: Harcourt, Brace.

Kroger, E. (1978) *Cognitive development in the acculturation of migrant children: the role of training in the assessment of learning ability.* Paper read at the IVth IAAP Congress, Munich.

Lloyd, B. (1972) *Perception and Cognition: A Cross-cultural Perspective.* London: Penguin.

Lunzer, E., Dolan, J. and Wilkinson, J. E. (1976) *The Effectiveness of Measures of Operativity, Language and Short-term Memory in the Prediction of Reading and Mathematical Understanding.*

Meadows, S. (1979) Book reviews: The development of thought: equilibration of cognitive structures by Piaget. *Bulletin of the British Psychological Society,* **32.**

Modgil, S. and Modgil, C. (1976) *Piagetian Research: Compilation and Commentary,* Volume 8. Slough: NFER.

Peel, E. A. (1959) *The Pupils' Thinking.* London: Oldbourne.

Peel, E. A. (1974) *The Nature of Adolescent Judgment.* London: Staple Press.

Peluffo, N. (1967) Culture and cognitive problems. *International Journal of Psychology,* **2,** 187-198.

Piaget, J. (1962) Foreword. In Flavell, J. H. (1967) *The Developmental Psychology of Jean Piaget,* pp. 7-9. London: Van Nostrand.

Piaget, J. (1971a) Closing remarks. In Green, D. R. et al (Eds.) *Measurement and Piaget,* pp. 120-213. London: McGraw-Hill.

Piaget, J. (1971b) The theory of stages in cognitive development. In Green, D. R. et al (Eds.) *Measurement and Piaget,* pp. 1-11. London: McGraw-Hill.

Piaget, J. (1971c) *Science of Education and the Psychology of the Child.* London: Longman.

Piaget, J. (1972) Intellectual evolution from adolescence to adulthood. *Human Development,* **15,** 1-12.

Pinard, A. and Laurendeau, M. (1969) Stage in Piaget's cognitive development theory: exegesis of a concept. In Elkind, D. and Flavell, J. H. (Eds.) *Studies in Cognitive Development.* London: OUP.

Poole, H. E. (1968) The effect of urbanization upon scientific concept attainment among Hausa children of North Nigeria. *British Journal of Educational Psychology,* **38** (1), 57-63.

Poortinga, Y. H. (1978) *Methodological Problems of Cross-cultural Psychological Research.* Research Report, Department of Psychology, Katholicke Hodgeschool, Tilburg.

Popper, K. R. (1971) *Objective Knowledge: An Evolutionary Approach.* Oxford: Clarendon Press.

Price-Williams, D., Gordon, W. and Ramirez, M. (1967) *Skill and Conservation: A Study of Pottery-making Children.* Special Report (III), Rice University, USA.

Prince, J. R. (1968) The effect of western education on science conceptualization in New Guinea. *British Journal of Educational Psychology,* **38,** 64-74.

Schutz, A. (1968) The problem of rationality in the social world. In Emmet, D. and Macintyre, A. (Eds.) *Sociological Theory and Philosophical Analysis.* London: Macmillan.

Scheffler, I. (1966) *Science and Subjectivity.* New York: Bobbs-Merrill.

Sechrect, L. (1976) *On the dearth of theory in cross-cultural psychology: there is a madness in our method.* Paper presented at the Third IACC Conference at Tilburg, 1976.

Sevinc, M. and Turner, C. (1976) Language and the latent structure of cognitive development. *International Journal of Psychology,* **11** (4), 231-250.

Sinclair de Zwart, H. (1968) Developmental psychologistics. In Elkind, D. and Flavell, H. (Eds.) *Studies in Cognitive Growth.* London: John Wiley.

Young, M. (Ed.) (1971) *Knowledge and Control.* London: Collier-Macmillan.

Whitehead, A. N. (1949) *The Aims of Education and Other Essays.* London: Ernest Benn.

Interchange

BUCK-MORSS REPLIES TO GHUMAN

Paul Ghuman has assumed a difficult task in synthesizing the issues raised by the cross-cultural application of Piaget's theory. His comments on my own article are understandably brief, and I would be unfair to claim that he has dismissed it too quickly. I do, however, question the grounds for his dismissal.

My contention was that abstract, formal operations reflect the structure of money exchange which, with the Industrial Revolution, came to mediate all social relations, those of production (in the form of wage—labour) as well as consumption (in the form of commodity exchange). Ghuman writes that this approach is 'not likely to establish the scientific merit' of Piaget's theory because it is a 'radical' and 'extreme ideological interpretation'. Yet just what distinguishes 'science' from 'ideology' he does not explain. Is my argument 'ideological' because it is Marxist? If this is Ghuman's position,* the situation is ironic, as Piaget's notion of science may have more in common with Marx than with Ghuman. Let me be specific. Piaget's contribution to cognitive psychology is his demonstration that scientific cognition is a developmental process that evolves through the child's practical interaction with the material world, and that cognition is not merely the passive reception of diverse sensory impressions, but an active ordering of those impressions in structural wholes. These premises are not opposed to a dialectical materialist position, if they are taken one step further the child's world is itself structured. That world is not the formless aggregate of phenomena suggested by such terms as 'style of life' or 'complex interplay of socio-cultural factors' (both used by Ghuman). What Theodor Adorno (op. cit.) wrote about the experience of the social scientist is thus also valid for the developing child:

> The social scientist's experience does not give him undifferentiated, chaotic material to be organized; rather, the material of his experience is the social order, more emphatically a 'system' than any ever conceived by philosophy.

In my article I credited Marx and Lukács with insight into the connection between the social structure and abstract cognitive structures. But they were not lone radicals or ideologues in arguing this position. At the turn of the century (among the generation of Piaget's own parents), social theorists of a wide variety of political beliefs considered the mediation by money of all social interactions to be the decisive characteristic of their era, and they linked this structure to the abstract, formal rationality of 'scientific'

---

*It would appear to be, at least at first. Later he says my approach is an example of the 'sociology of knowledge', which was a discipline founded by bourgeois theorists in a self-conscious attempt to use Marx's insights against his own intent, by translating Marx's dialectical, critical concepts into descriptive, 'value-free' ones. (See particularly Karl Mannheim, *Ideologie und Utopie*, 1929.)

285

cognition. In 1887, the German sociologist Ferdinand Tönnies made his still-famous distinction between modern society (*Gesellschaft*) and traditional, face-to-face village society (*Gemeinschaft*).

Gesellschaft was characterized as follows (Tönnies, op. cit., p. 71):

> In the form of paper money, the *Gesellschaft* reproduces its own idea . . . For the *Gesellschaft* is merely abstract reason in which every reasonable being takes part . . . Abstract reason in a special investigation is scientific reason, and endowed with it is the man who discerns objective relations, i.e. who thinks abstractly . . . [S]cientific concepts assume the same position in a scientific system as commodities do in the *Gesellschaft*. In the scientific system they come together in much the same way as commodities do on the market. A supreme scientific concept that no longer denotes something real, e.g. the concept of the atom or the concept of energy, is similar to the concept of money.

One can find a similar argument in Georg Simmel's major work, *Philosophie des Geldes* (1900):*

> The ability to construct . . . symbolic objects attains its greatest triumph in money. For money represents pure interaction in its purest form; it makes comprehensible the most abstract concept . . . Thus, money is the adequate expression of the relationship of man to the world . . . (English translation, p. 129)

Max Weber, the best-known sociologist of the period, examined the 'formal rationality' of the laws of money exchange which governed contemporary society in the form of wage—labour and capital accounting, and contrasted it with what he termed 'substantive rationality', which governed socialist planning, for example, the calculation of 'an optimum use of the available productive resources for the provision of consumers' goods for a given population' (op. cit., volume 1, p. 105).

These social theorists, in analysing the impact of industrial society on social relations and cognition, were commenting, not on what made Western *culture* unique, but on what, within that culture, made their own era unique. It follows that it is impossible to 'universalize' Piaget's tests by changing their format in an attempt to eliminate 'cultural bias', because the bias does not reside merely within the tests as a cultural form (although it may be here too), but within the structure of that society in which those tests were developed and to which they apply.

The socio-historical specificity of Piaget's theory does not mean it is 'unscientific'. (Instead it can be argued that the formal-abstract ideal of an ahistorical, trans-social, universal psychology is a cognitive prejudice which developed within a formal-abstract social structure.) Piaget's developmental stages may indeed be empirically verifiable in industrialized societies, and high test performance may in fact indicate superior ability to function pragmatically within them. This raises another question, however, one perhaps more important, and certainly more radical: Do such operations merely reflect the social structure and enable performance within it, or do they also allow that structure to be critically comprehended? To cite Adorno (op. cit.):

> What decides whether [the social scientists'] concepts are right or wrong is neither their generality nor, on the other hand, their approximation to 'pure' fact, but rather the adequacy with which they grasp the real laws of movement of society and thereby render stubborn facts transparent.

I have argued elsewhere (op. cit.) that another, very different set of critical cognitive operations, a series of stages that deals dialectically with problems of substantive rather than formal reason, may be necessary for this cognitive task.

---

*Simmel further argues that this relationship of man to the world is new historically: 'The extent to which money becomes absolute for the consciousness of value depends on the major transformation of economic interest from primitive production to industrial enterprise. Modern man and the ancient Greek have such different attitudes toward money largely because formerly it served only consumption whereas now it essentially serves production.' (Op. cit., p. 232.)

REFERENCES

Adorno, T. W. (1967) *Prisms,* p. 43. London: Neville Spearman. Tr. by Samuel and Shierry Weber.
Buck-Morss, S. (1979) Piaget, Adorno and the possibility of dialectical operations. In Silverman, H. (Ed.) *Piaget, Philosophy and the Human Sciences.* New York: Humanities Press.
Simmel, G. (1978) *The Philosophy of Money.* London: Routledge and Kegan Paul. Tr. by Tom Bottomore and David Frisby.
Tönnies, F. (1963) *Community and Society.* New York: Harper and Row. Tr. and ed. by Charles Loomis.
Weber, M. (1978) *Economy and Society.* (2 volumes) Guenther, R. and Wittich, C. (Eds.) London: University of California Press.

GHUMAN REPLIES TO BUCK-MORSS

Buck-Morss's major criticism of Piaget's theory seems to rest on the thesis that formal cognitive processes reflect a particular social structure, embodying the principle of exchange value, reification, and alienation, which govern production and exchange in the industrialized West. Therefore the time-lag often found amongst children from non-industrialized societies is a reflection of a social structure based on a particular mode of production and distribution, and that such a time-lag cannot be explained away by invoking cultural differences or deficits. Towards the end of the article, Buck-Morss recommends three hypotheses, presumably for empirical testing or for further analysis and evaluation.

Her analysis is underpinned by a thesis derived from Lukács' (1971) work *History and Class Consciousness.* Simply put, she argues that abstract formalism was the particular logical structure of Western capitalism.

It seems to me that the Piagetian system of theory-building by no means fits this paradigm for the following reasons. In the first place she states that:

> . . . abstract formalism [incidentally abstract seems to be redundant here] is a particular kind of abstraction. It is the ability to separate form from content, and the structuring of experience in accord with that distinction. Its model is the supra-empirical, purely formal language of mathematics.

This hard definition (stronger version) of the concept is not, by any means, shared or accepted by other academics. For instance, English and English (1958) describe it as:

> . . . the framework not necessarily *a priori* and philosophical—it generally attempts to base itself on observed facts. But it is a relatively rigid structure that determines and limits both theorizing and the direction in which facts are being sought. (Op. cit., p. 108)

In other words, the 'hypothetico-deductive method'. Other scholars, for instance Warren (1934), uses it in the context of aesthetics.

Now, according to the definition of formalism by English and English, Piaget, in my view, certainly belongs to a formalist tradition; but this interpretation is certainly a very much weaker interpretation (a softer version or, perhaps, even different) of formalism than that of Buck-Morss and/or Lukács.

In the second place, Piaget as early as 1954 was aware of this thorny problem. In his classic work, *Logic and Psychology,* he painstakingly analysed the relationship between logic on the one hand (described by Buck-Morss as the formal language to which mathematical propositions and axioms can be reduced) and psychology on the other. The following quote sums up his position:

On this issue . . . the fact that psychology is some centuries behind physics, we can argue that, like physics, it is an experimental science, but one concerned with the study of mental life, whilst its criterion of truth is also agreement with empirical facts. Logic based on the axiomatic method is, on the other hand, a formal science whose sole criterion of truth is deductive rigour. (Ibid., p. 25)

He reiterates his position in the book entitled *Mathematical Epistemology and Psychology* (Beth and Piaget, 1966). Similarly, he clarifies the genesis of structures as follows (op. cit., 1973, p. 62):

Now observation and experiment show as clearly as can be that logical structures are constructed, and that it takes a good dozen years before they are fully elaborated.

Piaget and his associates (see Beard, 1969; Elkind, 1970; for detailed references) have painstakingly collected massive amounts of data both on children's and adolescent's thinking to support their theories, and have also revised their theories in the light of new evidence (see Elkind and Flavell, 1969). However, if we accept the hypothetico-deductive version of formalism then certain aspects of Marx's work and that of Lukács would surely fall within the scope of this definition.*

Thirdly, the reference to capitalism and bourgeois industrialism are simplistic. It is by no means self-evident that the 'capitalism' with which Lukács was concerned was that of Marx or that with which we are concerned. The implication for her argument of this line of attack is clear. The simple linkage between the economic infrastructure and mental activity which she points out is really crude Marxism. Witness:

The stage of formal-logical operations which to Piaget represent the culmination of cognitive development is then the complete triumph of exchange value over use value.

Finally, Buck-Morss's interpretation of Lukács' thesis, in my opinion, is a vulgarized one: the essential point is that he (Lukács) is not to be read literally as Buck-Morss does, but within the context of Hegelian philosophy, which certainly does not point to a simple relationship between social being and social consciousness. In addition, according to an eminent scholar, McInness (1967),

Lukács has rejected Engel's and Lenin's conception of the Marxist dialectic as a set of laws applying to nature and he rejected too the notion that historical materialism deduces all social and moral life from the economic base. (Op. cit., p. 103)

Now a few minor points about the nature of evidence she presents, and the hypotheses suggested to support her meta-theoretical criticism.

It is disputable whether abstract formalism is the dominant paradigm in capitalist countries, there are others; for instance, empiricism and materialism (see Gellner, 1974). After all, mathematics and myth-making went on in ancient India amongst the Brahmins (Nehru, 1945; Rawlinson, 1954) and amongst the Egyptians, to name only two countries, when capitalism in its present form was non-existent (admittedly they did comprise the dominant modes of thinking in those countries).

The stance which the author takes in the article can lead to infinite regress; historical materialism must be applied to itself until it is seen as relative and provisional. Hence any criterion of validity of theories becomes arbitrary and relative. Surely such a stance would lead to chaos in the structuring of academic disciplines.

In the concluding part of the paper the author suggests three 'tentative hypotheses', which strictly speaking are not hypotheses at all; they are prescriptive and programmatic—nay, ideological—statements for the educationists and the psychologists. To illustrate this let us take the third hypothesis as an example, since, unlike the other two, it is expressed concisely:

---

*I am grateful to John Rowett, lecturer in the history department of the University College of Wales, ex-Research Fellow St John College, Oxford, and Dr Roy Gallop (education) for their suggestions and advice on this section.

Development of abstract cognitive skills among groups who presently lag behind demands socio-economic and political reform as much as reform in educational curriculum.

At the empirical level there is some evidence to refute the very first part of her second hypothesis, which was tested by Bernstein (1961), though in a modified form. Bernstein used social class as an independent variable and linguistic codes (restricted—elaborated), including forms of cognition, as a dependent variable. His researches have been severely criticized both from conceptual and empirical viewpoints by such academics as Lawton (1968), Coulthard (1969), and Labov (1970). As a result Bernstein (1971, 1973) has revised his theory considerably (some critics say he has even abandoned it altogether and moved on to new areas of research). There are genuine problems in operationalization of the concepts suggested by Buck-Morss:

(1) Social class (see Dharendorf, 1972, and Reid, 1977);
(2) Elite (Boyd, 1968);
(3) Reflect;

to name but a few, present enormous difficulties.

In sum, all the above-mentioned points, in my view, render the article a feeble attempt to undermine a relatively strongly supported constructionalist theory (despite its shortcomings) by invoking largely ideological arguments which do not really stand up to close scrutiny. On the positive side, however, Buck-Morss has attempted to broaden the framework (metatheoretical) within which debate on Piagetian theories can be fruitfully conducted.

REFERENCES

Beard, R. (1969) *An Outline of Piaget's Developmental Psychology*. London: Routledge and Kegan Paul.

Bernstein, B. (1961) Social class and linguistic development: A theory of social learning. In Halsey, A. H. (Ed.) *Education, Economy and Society*. London: Routledge and Kegan Paul.

Bernstein, B. (1971) *Class, Codes and Control, Vol. 1: Theoretical Studies Towards a Sociology of Language*. London: Routledge and Kegan Paul.

Bernstein, B. (1973) *Class Codes and Control, Vol. 2: Applied Studies Towards a Sociology of Language*. London: Routledge and Kegan Paul.

Beth, W. E. and Piaget, J. (1966) *Mathematical Epistemology and Psychology*. New York: Gordon and Breach.

Boyd, E. (1968) *Elites and their Education*. Slough: NFER.

Coulthard, M. (1969) A discussion of restricted and elaborated codes. In *Educational Review,* **22** (1), 38-50.

Dahrendorf, R. (1972) *Class and Class Conflict in Industrial Society*. London: Routledge and Kegan Paul.

Elkind, D. (1970) *Children and Adolescents*. London: OUP.

Elkind, D. and Flavell, H. (1969) (Eds.) *Studies in Cognitive Development: Essays in Honour of Jean Piaget*. London: OUP.

English, B. H. and English, C. A. (1958) *A Comprehensive Dictionary of Psychological and Psycho-analytical Terms: A Guide to Usage*. London: Longmans, Green.

Gellner, E. (1974) *Legitimation of Belief*. Cambridge: Cambridge University Press.

Labov, W. (1969) The logic of non-standard English. In Altais, J. A. (Ed.) *School of Languages and Linguistic Monograph*. Series No. 22. Georgetown: Georgetown Press.

Lawton, D. (1968) *Social Class, Language and Education*. London: Routledge and Kegan Paul.

Lukács, G. (1971) *History and Class Consciousness*. Cambridge: MIT Press.

McInness, N. (1967) Lukács, G. In *The Encyclopedia of Philosophy,* Edwards, P. (Ed.) London: Collier-Macmillan.

Nehru, J. (1945) *The Discovery of India*. London: Meridian Books.

Piaget, J. (1954) *Logic and Psychology*. Manchester: Manchester University Press.

Piaget, J. (1973) *Structuralism*. London: Routledge and Kegan Paul.

Rawlinson, G. H. (1954) *India: A Short Cultural History*. London: The Cresset Press.

Reid, I. (1977) *Social Class Differences in Britain: A Source Book*. London: Open Books.

Warren, H. G. (1934) *Dictionary of Psychology*. New York: Houghton and Mifflin.

Chapter 16

Piaget and Education: A Negative Evaluation

DEREK BOYLE

In 1964, the *Journal of Research in Science Teaching* (Ripple and Rockcastle, 1964) published the report of a symposium under the title: *Piaget Rediscovered*. Piaget himself contributed a paper on 'Development and Learning', the remainder of the symposium being devoted to two themes. The first was a discussion of how Piaget's theory contributes to education; the second concerned itself with reform of the curriculum. The main thrust of the argument of the curriculum reformers was that advances in education are more likely to come from pragmatic analysis of what is taught and how it is taught, than from an attempt to link educational practices to a theory of cognitive development, Piaget's or any other. It will be valuable to take this symposium as a starting point, and then see how the arguments have developed in the ensuing 15 years.

Let us first summarize Piaget's statement on that occasion. Piaget distinguishes *development* from *learning:* 'Development is a process which concerns the totality of the structures of knowledge . . . The development of knowledge is a spontaneous process, tied to the whole process of embryogenesis . . . In the case of the development of knowledge in children, embryogenesis ends only in adulthood . . . Embryogenesis concerns the development of the body, but it concerns as well the development of the nervous system and the development of mental functions'. On the other hand, we have learning: 'In general, learning is provoked by situations . . . It is provoked, in general, as opposed to spontaneous. In addition, it is a limited process—limited to a single problem, or to a single structure'. Piaget summarizes the difference in the following words. So I think that development explains learning, and this opinion is contrary to the widely held opinion that development is a sum of discrete learning experiences . . . development is the essential process and each element of learning occurs as a function of total development, rather than being an element which explains development.'

Development, of course, means development of operations. Inasmuch as Piaget's theory of cognitive development must be highly familiar to every reader of this text, it would be superfluous and tedious to recapitulate it here. The main feature, however, must be stressed, because it will be the subject of discussion later on. This feature is that operations derive ultimately from the internalization of actions upon physical objects, which implies that activity is necessary for effective cognitive development. The necessity for action has been questioned by recent commentators.

In view of the importance of this feature of Piaget's argument, we should be quite clear about what is envisaged. Piaget claims that the child learns from experience, by which he means *logical-mathematical experience*, which he distinguishes from *physical* experience. Whereas physical experience is drawn from objects (e.g. weighing two objects to discover which is heavier), in logical-mathematical experience 'the knowledge is not drawn from the objects, but it is drawn by the actions effected upon the objects' (e.g. a child discovers that however he counts a pile of pebbles the number is always the same). The child assimilates this logical-mathematical experience, thereby achieving cognitive equilibrium. Assimilation is not possible until the child has attained a given level of development. This brings us directly to a feature of Piaget's psychology that causes many of his readers great unease, namely the apparently circular nature of the argument, for it is by no means clear how equilibrium or the lack of it can eventuate in assimilation of experience, logical-mathematical or otherwise.

The other source of unease is Piaget's theory of stages, which was a major concern of the Piaget supporters in the symposium that we are discussing. A stage theory maintains that everyone goes through the same stages of intellectual development, although some go through them more rapidly than others, while some never get past the three-quarters mark. This seems plausible enough, for it would be biologically unparsimonious, to say the least, if development did not follow a general pattern. The difficulty lies in the attempt to be more specific about what precisely is meant by a stage. The reason for the difficulty is an ambiguity that is at the heart of the unease about Piaget's theory.

The ambiguity is introduced by the concept of *decalage*. If the child is at the stage of concrete operations, there are certain ways in which one expects him to think. He should be able to appreciate the conservation of volume and of weight; he should understand the reversibility of actions with respect to liquid and solid. If he has attained a certain level of cognitive structure, then he should be able to apply this level of structural thinking to all materials to which this structure can be applied. However, as is well known, this is not the case. Piaget and Inhelder (1969) acknowledge this when they write '. . . at the level of concrete operations logical forms are not yet independent of their content. They are a structurization of the particular content and there is no necessary generalization' (1969, p. 70). If the structurization is specific to the content, what is the warrant for talking about a 'stage'? Would it not beg fewer questions simply to describe as accurately as possible the various skills that any one child displays at a given age?

The justification for talking in terms of stages is that it simplifies our analysis and description of disparate skills by relating these analyses and descriptions to higher-order concepts. Many critics have objected that, far from simplifying this analysis, the concept of an intellectual structure which varies in its nature according to the material to which it is applied makes confusion worse confounded. Piaget acknowledges the difficulty and draws an analogy between *decalage* in his theory and friction in Newton's. However, friction is something that can be experienced and demonstrated, it can be given mathematical expression, and this expression can be used to make allowances for departure of observations from expectations. It is clear to no-one how this is equivalent to explaining heterogeneity of intellectual functioning when the theory predicts homogeneity.

One of the best-known commentators to discuss the problem of stages is Flavell (1971). He argues that a stage theory '*entails qualitative rather than quantitative changes in thinking*' (Flavell's italics). He elaborates this with an example: 'For instance, the best current evidence indicates that the typical, say, nine-year-old is given to making transitive inferences (e.g. if shown only that A<B and B<C, he is likely to conclude that A<C must also be the case), whereas the typical four-year-old is not'. Flavell argues that we must define a stage in terms of when certain types of thinking (e.g. reversibility) appear, rather than when earlier types (e.g. sensorimotor thinking) disappear. The reason why is that even mature adults can and do display immature thinking in certain circumstances. Nevertheless, Flavell holds with Piaget's conception of the *structure opératoire d'ensemble*. He claims that: 'Whenever one looks for examples of cognitive items one discerns psychologically real and measurable connections among the entities found'. Moreover: 'It is in the nature of cognitive items to become functionally interrelated in various ways as they develop, and therefore "cognitive structure" must have real referents in human cognitive developments.'

Flavell acknowledges that this analysis may appear to erode the concept of stage, but says that he finds it 'profitless to think in the terms ["denial", "rejection"] of such arguments' because he conceives his task as being 'not to contend with this concept and that theorist, but to seek a clearer picture of developmental reality, to try to understand how development actually proceeds'. However, the option of deferring judgment on Piaget's theory is not open to the educator seeking to base upon it a technology of pedagogy. If we cannot be sure precisely what is meant by stages we cannot devise procedures for helping children to progress through them, which in Piagetian terms would seem to be the true aim of education.

It is for this reason that the curriculum reformers who contributed to the 1964 symposium were not impressed by the claims of Piaget's theory to provide a basis for educational practice. The fact is that while most educators are agreed on certain principles to be applied in educational practice, for instance, that a degree of discovery is valuable for the child, there is no systematic theory to say how much, or when it should be introduced. This is as true of Piaget's theories as of traditional learning theories (Cronbach in Ripple and Rockcastle, 1964).

Many contributors to the symposium (e.g. Karplus, Duckworth, Nicholls, Mason, Kilpatrick) argued forcefully that curriculum improvements arise from studying the structure of the material to be taught, although investigators may be stimulated to undertake such study by Piaget's work. However, Kilpatrick quotes from the Introduction to *Goals for School Mathematics* (1963) as follows:

> Piaget is not a teacher but an observer. He has tried to find out what it is that children understand, at a given age, when they have been taught in conventional ways. The essence of our enterprise is to alter the data which have formed, so far, the basis of his research. If teaching furnishes experiences which few children now have, then in the future such observers as Piaget may observe quite different things.

It seems, however, that Piaget would probably not accept these arguments, as his conception of cognitive development is of a necessary and, indeed, inevitable progression towards a state of thinking that is the ultimate outcome of evolution. This argument is the central concern of Rotman (1977). Before we turn to this argument, which will be elaborated in the middle section of this chapter, we must look at a more recent symposium on Piaget and education. This symposium appeared in the *British Journal of Educational Psychology* for 1977 (Volume 47). One of the contributors was Smedslund, who has made many contributions to Piagetian research, and who was a contributor to the 1964 symposium. In the interim, Smedslund has to a degree changed his mind about Piaget's theory, and now expresses reservations, while still finding much of value in the Piagetian approach.

Smedslund tells us: 'My conversations and dealings with children never quite convinced me that their behaviour could be adequately described as reflecting the presence or absence of certain operatory structures. Partly, this was a matter of intuitive impression. I found that I could not deal with the children as if they had such operatory structures in the same natural and confident way that I dealt with them as being conscious, as perceiving, thinking and feeling, and utilizing the modes of everyday language.'

Taking a cue from Smedslund, I also feel justified in referring to intuition. I once spent a few fruitless years endeavouring to understand how infant-school children think about roads, in an attempt to draw up a code of conduct, based on Piagetian stages, to advise parents on the road skills to be expected from children of given ages. In retrospect the project seems to have been doomed to failure, but at the time it seemed feasible. Many hours were devoted to talking to children about model cars on model roads, real cars on real roads, the notions of speed, relative distance and movement, before the following conclusion was reached. As soon as children think at all about roads, they think about them in an adult way. The accidents in which they are involved as pedestrians have the same causes as those involving adult pedestrians (Boyle and Gilhooly, 1972; Boyle, 1973). This conclusion is not the sort of conclusion that can be proved. It is intuitive. However, no evidence was found to contradict this view, despite the most earnest search.

This underlines one of the great difficulties of Piagetian research. It is very difficult to find conclusive evidence that Piaget is wrong because it is almost impossible to say what form such evidence must take. Conversely, it is difficult to find evidence that Piaget is right, because, while individual pieces of evidence may confirm one or other of Piaget's propositions, no-one can say what sort of evidence can support the theory as a whole. This is almost certainly because Piaget's is not the sort of theory that can be said to be true.

There is a view held by many philosophers of science that theories cannot be said to be true or false, only more or less useful. However, if educators wish to base teaching practice on a theory, then there must be a sense in which they believe it to be true. Even if the educator limits his claims for the theory to its being useful rather than true, one can object that Piagetian notions are less useful than the traditional concepts of perception, thinking and feeling. Smedslund is concerned with 'utilizing the words of everyday language'. The phrase is ambiguous, as it can be interpreted as an injunction to the psychologist to describe the child's activities in straightforward terms rather than those used by Piaget, or it can mean that we should examine the words that children use, and try to discover what they mean.

The second interpretation is very important, because our data from investigations of children solving problems consist of the ways in which children use the symbolic system of words and numbers. Mastering this system is the major task of intellectual development, and it should not surprise us that everyone goes through the same stages in mastering it. The objection to theorizing lies in taking the step from observation of the relative inadequacy of the symbolic skill to postulation of the underlying mental mechanisms that a given level of adequacy reflects. Specification of these mechanisms requires evidence not derived from observation, but 'evidence' of a quite different sort. Piaget's evidence is the integrated set of ideas constituting his theory. He is saying, in effect, 'this theory encompasses the facts better than any other'. However, the 'facts' so encompassed are not the observables of the experimental situation, but the postulated mechanism itself.

I shall argue in the third section of this chapter that any theory should be about the observable facts themselves, which in this instance are, as we have seen, examples of the use of language. Before developing this argument, however, I want to draw attention to the one empirical recommendation of Piaget's theory which has implications for education, namely the stress on activity. It is the modern fashion to 'involve' the child in his own education, which means guiding him to 'find out through doing', even when this entails massive time-wasting that could be circumvented by the simple traditional expedient of answering the child's questions directly.

This emphasis on action derives from the tradition of Froebel and Montessori and their stress on sensorimotor involvement. We should remember, however, that they were in revolt against mechanical drilling of verbal lessons into children who often did not understand what the words meant. Even Pestalozzi required children to engage in long hours of bible study. Yet the adjuration that children be active comes very oddly from Piaget, whose methods of investigation consist almost exclusively of asking children questions and interpreting their answers. The one recommendation that one would expect to come from such a theory would be that one should learn to *talk* properly to children, so as to understand their questions and ensure that they understand one's replies.

There is one striking piece of evidence about the importance of verbal interchange between adults and children, and it is McCurdy's classic survey of the childhoods of men of genius (McCurdy, 1958). In every case these geniuses, when children, had spent much time in the company of adults, who gave them companionship and support, and who treated them on terms of equal footing. John Stuart Mill is probably the most striking example. His father taught him many things, including Greek, by verbal discussion at a very early age. All the children, however, *talked* a great deal with adults, from whom they learnt many things, and in interchange with whom they clarified their ideas. Not every child is a John Stuart Mill, and not every teacher a James Mill. Nor should we expect or want all children to learn Greek by the time they are three. However, the model of children learning about the world by discussing their ideas with adults seems to me a very good one on which to base a theory of education.

Perhaps it would be appropriate for me to make clear my view of the true purpose of education. It is, I believe, to open the gates of knowledge to all who wish to walk through. To refuse to answer a child's questions on the grounds that he must 'find out by doing' amounts to refusing to open the gates and telling the child to pick the lock himself.

Two other contributions to the 1977 symposium previously mentioned adduce evidence that supports the arguments that I have developed, though their authors would probably not be quite so firm in their conclusions. Brown and Desforges are critical of the concept of stage, and argue that greater understanding can be derived from a model based upon the integration of skills, while Anthony argues that Piaget's emphasis on the need for the child actively to manipulate objects is not supported by empirical research. Nor, as Anthony points out, does Piaget's commitment to this view appear to be shared by Piaget's close collaborators (Inhelder and Sinclair, 1969; Inhelder, Sinclair and Bovet, 1974). While some active handling can undoubtedly be beneficial, Anthony concludes that: 'The extreme Piagetian insistence on physical activity has been excessive'.

Let us now try to summarize this first part of this chapter. Many people claim to have found in Piaget's theory a sound basis for teaching practice. Others have not found this. Part at least of the reason for the disagreement probably lies in the fact that people are not entirely sure of what Piaget's theory is, or how the various recommendations (such as the stress on physical activity) fit in. They are by no means clear precisely what Piaget means by 'development', and what most teachers mean by 'learning' is probably different from what Piaget means. In the next section, therefore, I want to do two things. First, I want to outline the philosophical basis of Piaget's theory, which is usually overlooked by teachers, to show just how recondite it is, and how remote from the concerns of educators. Second, I shall discuss three works that claim to be about education based upon Piagetian principles, to illustrate my contention that they are full of special pleading that it is difficult for the impartial reader to distinguish from dishonesty.

In this middle section of the chapter I will argue that Piaget's theory cannot provide a solid basis for education, because it does not address itself to the essential questions with which education must deal, namely the intellectual and emotional development of the individual. Growth is not just a matter of developing new ways of looking at the world. It is essentially a process of sharing viewpoints with other people, which leads to the development of the personality as well as the intellect. Piaget writes as if problems of personality can be subsumed under those of the intellect; this attitude leaves out vast areas of child development. Moreover, he is not interested in the individual, but in a sort of group mind, which he calls the 'epistemic subject' (Beth and Piaget, 1966). Inasmuch as psychology is concerned primarily with the individual, this approach omits most of the one area of child psychology where Piaget could be expected to make a contribution, namely cognitive development.

Piaget's primary concern is, of course, 'genetic epistemology' about which he has this to say: 'Genetic epistemology attempts to explain knowledge and, in particular, scientific knowledge, on the basis of its history, its sociogenesis, and especially the psychological origins of the notions and operations upon which it is based'. Scientific knowledge, he maintains, is not static, but constantly changing. We can understand the nature of knowledge only by understanding the nature of thinking (Piaget, 1970).

Piaget claims that his view of epistemology has an advantage over the traditional view that epistemology is the study of knowledge, because the traditional view implies that knowledge is static. In fact the 'traditional' view does not imply this. Epistemology is generally understood to be a study of how we think about what we know. It makes a clear distinction between thought processes and the contents of our thought. Piaget's approach confuses the two to no clear advantage. Piaget further argues that epistemology seeks to explain scientific knowledge as it actually is. This is not a view of epistemology that would be recognized by many philosophers. Genetic epistemology, says Piaget, seeks to explain how the mind goes from one state of knowledge to another that is judged to be superior. Again there is a confusion between 'knowledge' and 'structure of the mind'. (Piaget's examples are: first, Louis de Broglie's changing views of indeterminism; second, views on categories of the Bourbaki group.)

It is this conception of the growth of knowledge as the mind's progression from inferior to superior states that is the main focus of the criticism by Rotman (op. cit.). Rotman, who is a mathematician, argues that Piaget misconceives the nature of mathematics, and in particular the role of proof in mathematical progress. He writes: 'The central error of Piaget's structuralism is the belief that it is possible to explain the origin and nature of mathematics independently of the non-structural justificatory questions of how mathematical assertions are validated' (p. 44). Behind this error Rotman sees two issues. 'The first is the nature of proof as Piaget sees it . . . The second is the problem of language. If, as we maintain, mathematics really consists of justifying assertions about structure, then only an impoverished view of language, and mathematical language in particular, could support the kind of analysis Piaget gives' (ibid.).

Rotman goes on to discuss the social aspects of mathematical progress. Piaget views mathematical progress as the growth of structures through progressive decentration and the co-ordination of individual viewpoints with the viewpoints of others. Rotman comments: 'But there is a certain puzzle here. Who or what co-ordinates these viewpoints? Clearly not the psychological subject, the individual mathematician, who by definition cannot be aware of the distortions due to his own centredness. Piaget agrees with this and his answer . . . is to invoke the epistemic subject . . . [progress in mathematics according to Piaget] occurs independently of language, and it is this, in the context of Piaget's notion of proof, that is puzzling. For the viewpoints of others are public entities, made meaningful to an individual subject through the inter-subjective agreements and conventions embodied in language,' (op. cit., pp. 153—154).

Rotman is undoubtedly correct in this analysis of Piaget's theory. Although Rotman is concerned with mathematics, the point is of much wider relevance, for the lack of treatment of linguistic interchange is a severe limitation on any theory of cognitive development. Much of our development takes place through linguistic interchange, whether with other children or with our teachers, parents and other adults. To base education on a theory that reduces social interaction to a negligible role is to base it upon a theory whose influence must be pernicious. Piaget's theory is, in essence, not concerned with how individual children grow and develop intellectually, either alone or in interaction with others; it is concerned with the development of his postulated neo-Aristotelian essence—the 'epistemic subject', of which the workings of any individual mind can afford only an illustration. This is an extremely bizarre, theoretical basis for the practice of education, which is inevitably concerned with the development of individual children.

There is a further objection to using Piaget's theory as the basis of education, and that is that it takes as its model the mature scientific mind, by which Piaget means the mathematical mind. But what of history, geography, the study of literature? Are these to be counted as of minor worth because they do not conform to the style of thinking characteristic of mathematical science? Are they to be regarded as exhibiting the workings of the mature intellect only to the extent that they approach the ideal form of mathematical thinking? Piaget sometimes writes as if he believes that this is indeed the case, but there would be very few to agree with him, and these few would be unlikely to count many teachers among their number.

If, as we have argued, Piaget's theory is concerned essentially with the growth of mathematical notions in a group mind, it is worth devoting a little time to understanding why this is. As Rotman among others points out, Piaget is concerned with the problems that also concerned Kant, namely how the mind knows the world. For Kant, mathematical knowledge was perfect, whereas knowledge obtained by discursive reasoning about contingent facts was not. It follows that one cannot prove mathematical theorems discursively. Piaget seeks to explain 'perfect' knowledge in terms of cognitive structures. These cannot arise through discourse (from which it would seem to follow that teaching must be ineffectual) so they must arise through the spontaneous organization of the intellect. Inasmuch as all intellects develop in the same way, all individuals at a given stage of intellectual development will have the same cognitive structures. (The circular nature of this argument appears for some reason to have escaped most commentators.)

Piaget is dedicated to a belief in historical inevitability, this inevitability being a reflection of the way in which the mind must develop. In support of this belief he develops a version of the recapitulation hypothesis and argues that, inasmuch as the history of thought from Neanderthal times is not open to inspection, genetic epistemology must study ontogenesis in children's thinking instead (Piaget, 1970). The proposition that the ontogenesis of thinking in children follows the same pattern as the development of thought from primitive men to modern scientists gives the appearance of being empirical, but it is not. There is no conceivable way in which the proposition could be tested. Piaget's view of development is that of August Comte in modern guise, and it is a metaphysical view. Metaphysical views are justified by the possibility that they make sense of numerous disparate data in the same way as scientific theories, such as, for example, the theory of evolution. In reality, there are few, if any, facts that Piaget's conflation of the individual and the group illuminates.

Piaget's whole theory rests upon confusion and conflation, whether of group and individual, or of knower and known. When Piaget argues that 'to know is to assimilate reality into systems of transformations that become progressively adequate' he confuses reality with ways of talking about it. When the child, by 'reflective abstraction' (e.g. on his manipulations of a group of pebbles) develops logical and mathematical notions, we can say that he 'knows' that the number stays the same. But what does 'knowing' mean here? If there is no distinction between subject and object, then 'knowing' means 'having arrived at a given stage of thinking'. Is there a sense in which we can say that the number remains constant independently of what the child does? No, because if everyone adhered to a convention whereby the number changed with the order of counting, then the number would not be constant. In fact, our convention is that the number remains constant, and conventions are expressed in language; therefore, mathematics must, as Rotman argues, be a form of language. Piaget is unable to accept the proposition that mathematics is a form of language, because he maintains that mathematical thinking reflects the world *as we know it*. Ideal mathematics would reflect the world *as it is*. Hence Piaget defines knowledge as 'a system of transformations that becomes progressively adequate' (Piaget, 1970), the operative word being 'adequate'.

Piaget's position on the question 'Is there a reality separate from the cognizer?' has been a source of worry to critics for many years. Inhelder (1964) reports a conversation that Piaget held with Soviet philosophers. (What follows is my own translation of the original, which differs somewhat from the version in the cited source.)

> The philosopher Kedrov opened the debate: 'for us the object exists before our knowledge of it. Are you of the same opinion?' I replied: 'As a psychologist, I think that the subject knows an object only in acting upon it and transforming it somewhat. Thus I do not know what the object is before our knowledge of it.' Rubinstein then proposed this conciliatory formula: 'The object is a part of the world, which could doubtless be divided up into objects in different ways. Do you agree, then, that the world exists before knowledge?' I replied: 'As a psychologist, I think that knowledge supposes an activity of the brain; now the brain is part of the organism—so, I agree.'

This reply satisfied the Russians that Piaget was not an idealist, i.e. someone who believes, with Berkeley, that the mind does more than reflect the objects in the external world. As Inhelder (op. cit.) points out: 'Piaget is quite willing to label himself a "relativist" because his interest is neither in the knower nor in the known, but in the *relation between knower and known*; it is this relationship, which changes in the course of development, that is the material of Piaget's genetic studies'.

It is the belief that Piaget's theory is concerned with the 'relation between knower and known' that is at the basis of attempts to use Piaget's theory as a guide to the development of the child's intellect. However, as we saw in the first part of this chapter when discussing the importance of activity, Inhelder does not always appear to be at one with Piaget. Here, as there, we must draw attention to divergence in interpretation. In the light of all that we have said about thinking and the objects of thought, we cannot agree that Piaget is concerned with the relation between knower and known, for there is a fundamental ambiguity in the way in which he talks about knowledge. Nothing in the conversation on which Inhelder is commenting justifies her interpretation of Piaget's point of view.

We repeat our contention that Piaget's attitude to knowledge and the knower is fundamentally ambiguous. A theory as ambiguous as Piaget's cannot provide a basis for sound pedagogy. It must follow that any educational text claiming to base its recommendations on Piaget's work is either mistaken in its interpretation of Piaget, or is guilty of making misleading claims. I believe the latter is the case. Some years ago I attempted to illustrate this argument by analysing the works of Furth and Wachs (1974), and Schwebel and Raph (1974) (Boyle, 1974). As I have in no way changed my mind since then, I shall summarize here what I wrote on that occasion, and supplement those observations with comments on a more recent contribution to this genre (Wadsworth, 1978).

The school described by Furth and Wachs is the Tyler Thinking School in Charleston, West Virginia. This 'School for Thinking' aims to create 'Thinking environments, happy places for children to live and learn . . created not only in our schools but also in our homes and places of work' (p. 4). The purpose of the environment is 'to implement Piaget's theory by providing the child with experiences best designed to develop his thinking'.

In line with Piaget's theory they distinguish *development* from *learning*. Whereas development refers to '*general* mechanisms of action and thinking', learning means 'the acquisition of specific skills and facts and the memorizing of *specific* information'. Basically, this appears to mean that acquisition of specific skills like geographical names and mathematical formulae would be useless unless the child had developed contexts in which these facts made sense, a point with which one would suppose that few teachers would disagree, so it is difficult to understand how this particular interpretation follows from Piaget's distinction. Furth and Wachs call 'learning' the result of teaching that does not basically alter the child's intelligence, and 'development' the result of teaching bringing about intellectual change. Throughout Piaget's writings one gains the impression that development must be spontaneous, yet here we hear about teaching that brings about this development. Furth and Wachs admit that in practice one cannot separate such teaching from the transmission of specific skills, yet they claim that separating them conceptually has value. To someone not committed to a belief that Piaget's theory can provide a basis for education this seems remarkably like a *post hoc* justification.

Another example illustrates the determination of the authors to force facts into the framework of a Piagetian interpretation. An eight-year-old living in Washington, DC, at a time when the mayor was named Washington, believed that the mayor of Philadelphia would be called Mr Philadelphia. Furth and Wachs assumed that the boy 'would have been capable of thinking at a more mature level if . . . motivated to do so' (p. 17). It seems quite unwarranted to describe this thinking as 'low level', resulting from inadequate motivation. The boy was drawing a hypothesis from the facts at his disposal, and he was wrong. Being right or wrong has nothing to do with motivation; improvement in the child's performance would be contingent upon an increase in factual knowledge, which would make the child realize that his first experience was of a coincidence.

In addition to forcing interpretations into a framework, Furth and Wachs are guilty of what can only be described as misrepresentation. They point out that there is a 'difference between knowing a word (word knowledge) and comprehending a situation (intelligence)' and maintain that 'the whole weight of the scholastic tradition leads the teacher to oppose this conclusion'. This is sheer nonsense. What tradition, scholastic or otherwise, leads teachers or others to oppose the conclusion that there is a difference between 'word knowledge' and 'intelligence'? (Of course, I am writing on the basis of my own experience of educational systems, which are those of the British Isles. Things may be different in the USA.)*

The book is full of such desperate attempts to justify the authors' educational practices by reference to Piaget's theory. The point is not whether the practices are good or bad in themselves, nor whether Piaget's theory is right or wrong. It is simply that it is never clear how one is derived from the other.

The book by Schwebel and Raph is a collection of chapters by different authors. One

*On this point see Murrow and Murrow, 1971.

is by Sinclair, and it deserves special attention because it illustrates how the work of the critic is made difficult by a peculiar use of words that marks so much of Piagetian writing. It is as follows.

> . . . Piaget and his collaborators did not conclude that any kind of learning procedure would be useless . . . [They] meant only that empirical methods, whereby the subject has to accept a link between events because this is imposed upon him, do not result in progress; progress results only when the subject himself discovers the link. This active discovery of links is what happens in development; it is therefore called spontaneous—maybe unfortunately—for development is always the result of interaction . . . Learning is dependent on development, not only in the sense that certain things can be learned only at certain levels of development, but also in the sense that in learning—that is, in situations specifically constructed so that the subject has active encounters with the environment— the same mechanisms as in development are at work.

The first part of this quotation is based on a false dichotomy that is forced upon Sinclair by the very theory that she is discussing, the dichotomy being between *imposition* of a link and *discovery* of that link. Most teachers would maintain that effective teaching consists of *explaining* links, but Piaget's theory implies that whatever is not discovery is imposition. Presumably if the teacher successfully explained a link this would count as having allowed the child to discover it! In other words, the theory is self-justifying and there is no way of testing it. Sinclair's reference to activity amounts to no more than saying that intellectual development occurs only when the child understands what he is doing, a proposition with which few people would disagree. The second part of the question shows that 'spontaneous' development is not 'spontaneous' at all, but dependent upon the environment provided by the teacher. The advice to teachers to provide environments in which children can discover things for themselves does not seem specifically Piagetian.

In fact, Piaget, himself recognizes that the stress on activity is not new. Writing on the genesis of the 'new methods' (Piaget, 1971) he acknowledges that the stress on activity is in the tradition of Rousseau, Pestalozzi, Froebel and Montessori, and even of Socrates. He conceives his own unique contribution as being the objective establishment of the truth of the principle that activity is vital.

Wadsworth (op. cit.) is both a Piagetian scholar and a teacher who has attempted to apply Piaget's theory to the practice of education, calling on the theory 'only to the extent necessary to provide a rationale for the teaching practices and principles presented'. Chapters are devoted to most of the topics dealt with in the primary school. Wadsworth emphasizes that 'in most respects Piagetian theory is a conservative approach to educating children', but claims that 'Piagetian methods are a more efficient set of methods than traditional methods for acquiring skills and knowledge'.

What, then, are these methods? It is, in fact, remarkably difficult to learn from Wadsworth's text precisely what is Piagetian about these methods. For instance: 'Reading about and talking about things are not neglected, though they are not emphasized to the exclusion of everything else, as in traditional classrooms'. Where are these 'traditional' classrooms that exclude everything but reading and talking? What 'tradition' is this? Wadsworth's characterization of non-Piagetian classrooms as being exclusively verbal is entirely false to any primary school classroom that I can ever remember encountering since I first went to school more than 40 years ago.

Once again I must stress that I am writing from experience of British, and specifically English, schools, which have for generations been influenced by Froebel and Montessori. American education may have followed a different pattern, and if Piaget has been responsible for introducing a more relaxed atmosphere into rigid classrooms, as Furth and Wachs, Schwebel and Raph, and Wadsworth all claim, then for this he must be given credit. If he has done more than this, the evidence to prove it is hard to come by.

We have argued that Piaget's metaphysical system has not been demonstrated to constitute a sound basis for educational theory and practice. Indeed, we have argued that it is not of a nature to do this, because it is not concerned with the primary factors in child development, which are linguistic and social. In the final section of this chapter I shall discuss the nature of children's language on the basis of some observations of my own.

I have previously indicated that I believe that successful education is the outcome of a particular kind of experience, viz. social interaction. Piaget conceives of development as the result of progressive decentrations, whereby the child comes to understand that his point of view is not that of others. This appears to describe the sort of experience that we have in mind, but it does not. Piaget's reference is the individual child's point of view and how it changes under the force of contradictions resulting from encounters with the environment, this environment including other children and adults. The child does not change his point of view as a result of sharing his experiences with other people, for his experiences are exclusively his own. This leads, as we have seen, to the paradox that the individual's egocentricity debars him from taking part in true social thinking: this paradox is resolved by postulation of the 'epistemic subject'.

Now there is a perfectly good sense in which one's experiences are one's own and cannot be shared with other people; but there is an equally good sense in which we *can* share experiences with others. We share experiences through the use of a common language. It is through discussion with others that we not only alter our points of view but also come to experience reality differently. Indeed, with respect to *social* reality, the best information we have to tell us whether or not our experience is correct is to be found in the language that we hear other people speak. It would seem appropriate, therefore, that an account of language should form part of any study of cognitive development but, as we have seen, one of Rotman's major criticisms of Piaget is that he has no theory of language. If, as I have suggested, Piaget is relatively uninterested in social interaction, then, of course, he does not need a theory of language.

It is consistent with Piaget's approach that he studies children individually. Indeed, most people working in this area do so. However, I am interested in how children influence each other, so I have made a number of investigations under controlled conditions on groups of children from three to ten years of age. Here I shall limit myself to describing my observations of three five-year-olds, Catherine, Helen and Kirsten, who were playmates and well known to me, being the children of my neighbours and frequent visitors to my house and garden. They were therefore relaxed in the company of each other and me. In addition, they were enthusiastic about making a television programme with me, being aware of the programmes that I had previously made with other children, so we sat around a table in the studio of the Aberdeen University Television Service where this session and others with older children were recorded.*

The observations confirmed what every teacher of young children knows, viz. that children learn from each other and often learn the wrong solution to a problem if the dominant member of a group has the wrong notion of the state of things. Banal as this may seem, the point is worth making in this context because so much of what Piaget says appears to imply that this will not happen. What is more important is the focus of my investigation, which was on the language the children used. Piaget's subjects all appear to speak grammatically correct, if rudimentary French. The subjects of other investigators seem to speak almost perfect English. My three little girls, although their

---

*The videotape, entitled *Children Solving Problems*, may be hired from the Television Service, University of Aberdeen, Aberdeen, AB9 2UB, Scotland.

fathers were university lecturers (one indeed a psychologist!) spoke what appeared, on close inspection, to be a foreign language. I shall give examples of what I mean, and then discuss why this should be so.

We started by discussing lies.

[E]	Do you know what a lie is?
[All in chorus, emphatically]	No!
[E]	Does anyone ever say you mustn't tell lies?
[All]	Yes!
[E]	Then do you know what a lie is?
[All]	Yes!

The discussion continued as follows.

[E]	Supposing I said 'two and two are five' is that a lie?
[All]	No.
[E]	Why is that not a lie?
[Catherine]	Because it's only four really.

We broadened the discussion to embrace questions of morality and guilt. I told them two stories, one about June who rushed into a room, knocking over a tray and smashing a large number of cups and saucers, the other about Jane, who climbed on to a chair to get a jelly that her mother told her not to touch and in the process smashed one cup. (I modified this and the next example from a series of films made some years ago for the BBC by Joan Bliss.) The question was which girl had been naughtier. Most five-year-olds argue that June was naughtier, because she smashed more cups, but whereas Helen and Kirsten took this view, Catherine argued that June's action was an accident. The interest of this inquiry, however, comes next, when I started to present two more stories, this time about lies told by June and Jane respectively.

[E]	I want to tell you two more stories about Jane and June.
[Helen]	But different ones?
[E]	They're different stories.
[Helen]	But there was one about one of the girls—and then another one. Was that the same story?

We proceeded to an experiment on conservation. I spread out six 10p pieces and six 1p pieces, lining them up in the familiar way.

[E]	See those silver coins there and copper coins here: are there as many copper coins as there are silver ones?
[Catherine]	Yes.
[Helen]	No.
(Kirsten was puzzled, and said nothing.)	
[E]	You say 'No' Helen?
[Helen]	Because there's the same number.
[E]	The same number?
[Catherine]	Five here and six here.

As the experiment proceeded, it was clear that Catherine believed that the numbers of coins stayed the same, but Helen was convinced that they changed when one group (either the copper or the silver, for we did it both ways) was pushed together. Towards the end of the experiment, Catherine was agreeing with Helen, and so was Kirsten (who, incidentally, seemed to have no firm views of her own). I asked: 'How has it become more copper? Count them and tell me.' (They did, and found that the number was six in each case.)

[E]	So, is there more silver or more copper?
[All]	More copper.
[E]	But they both came to six, didn't they?
[All]	Yes.
[E]	But there's still more copper?
[Helen and Kirsten]	Yes.
[Catherine]	They're equal.

Before I put the coins away, the girls spontaneously totalled the money, starting with the 10p pieces. The counting began like this.

[In unison]	Ten, twenty, thirty, forty, fifty, sixty.
[E]	What about the copper ones?
[In unison]	Seventy, eighty, ninety, twenty, twenty-one, twenty-two.

Is it surprising that, with so little command of the verbal and numerical systems in terms of which adults communicate, children give apparently irrational answers to questions about difficult matters like class inclusion? I did one experiment with five green rubber balls and five red rubber balls, and found that Helen would hardly let me formulate the question. Having put five red balls in one box while Catherine (in time with me) put five green balls in another (Helen and Kirsten observing and counting), I asked if there was the same number of balls in each box. Catherine was not sure, so they all counted them and agreed that the number was the same. Then I transferred all the balls to a third box and began to put my question, when Helen interrupted, as follows:

[E]	There are green rubber balls . . .
[Helen]	And red rubber balls.
[E]	. . . and red rubber balls. But are there more red rubber balls . . .
[Helen, clearly misunderstanding what I was about to ask]	No, equal.
[E]	Are there more rubber balls or more red balls?
[Catherine]	Neither.
[E]	Are there more green balls or more rubber balls?
[Catherine]	Neither.
[E]	How many rubber balls are there?
[Helen]	Five.
[Catherine]	Ten.
[E]	There are ten. So are there more rubber balls or more green ones?
[Helen and Catherine]	More rubber.
[E]	Are there more rubber ones or more red ones?
[Helen and Catherine]	More red.
[E]	Do you agree with that Kirsten?
[Kirsten, uncertainly]	Red ones.

Quite clearly in situations like this, the answer one gets depends upon the way in which one phrases the question. If a perfectly rational, highly educated adult were asked Piagetian-type questions in a language with which he was not perfectly familiar, he would, I suggest, give answers not unlike those given by Catherine, Helen and Kirsten.*

Every child has to learn how to use the language spoken around him; until he masters it fully, he is like a foreigner in his own land. The way in which he achieves mastery has been the subject of much debate in recent years, with Chomsky's (1959) criticism of Skinner's (1957) analysis of verbal behaviour being the starting point of many investigations. Few psychologists would now accept the behaviourist account of language development in terms of differential reinforcement of random utterances (a Darwinian model of the survival of the fittest response) but would prefer Chomsky's (1972) view of language as representing active striving on the child's part to give verbal expression to his cognitive grasp of events. Macnamara (1972) has taken this line further by arguing that children first make sense of situations involving human interaction and then use language to express this sense. In the typical Piagetian situation it is difficult to make much sense of the material, so it is not surprising that the language used by children in these settings does not always appear to make much sense. This does not necessarily mean that they are thinking irrationally, but it does mean that we cannot confidently make inferences from what children *say* to what they *think*. The arguments here are well known, and the reader who wishes to learn more of the details is referred to the discussion by Donaldson (1978).

Observations of children's language inevitably suggest a parallel with studies of perception. Whereas today psychologists debate whether language is best explained in terms of nativism or empiricism, about twenty years ago a similar debate raged about perceiving. Then the question was: 'To what extent can it be said that we learn to perceive?' That question has never been answered: psychologists have simply stopped asking it. Fashions change, in psychology as in everything else, and we are now asking about the extent to which we can be said to learn to talk articulately. However, many of the lessons that were learnt in the debate about perception have important implications for the understanding of language development. Understanding language development in turn has important implications for education.

I propose to examine some of the old arguments about perceptual development to illustrate the parallels with linguistic development. In particular, I want to draw attention to the views of a rather neglected European master, Albert Michotte. Michotte is best known in English-speaking countries for his book *The Perception of Causality* (Michotte, 1963), a rather unconvincing attempt to deal with what is essentially a philosophical problem by psychological analysis based upon rather feeble experimental methods (see Boyle, 1972); but he is better known in Continental Europe as a perceptual theorist who frequently and convincingly took a stand in opposition to Piaget. Essentially, Michotte held a view of perception that was in direct line of descent from Leibnitz's theory of 'pre-established harmony'.

As T. R. Miles, Michotte's translator and commentator, put it (Michotte, 1963, p. 405):

What he [Michotte] is saying is that for most of the time vision is reliable. Visual cues give a good indication of the sort of results that we might expect from examining the dial of a measuring

---

*Normally, there would be more balls of one colour than of the other, for instance 10 red and five green. Had I in that case asked 'are there more red balls or more rubber balls', the answer 'more red' could be interpreted as showing that the child had misunderstood me to ask 'are there more red balls or more green balls?' Since, however, the numbers of red and green were equal in this case, numerical difference could not have influenced the answer. We may be sure that the answer was the result only of linguistic confusion.

instrument, and they thus enable the organism to take appropriate action. For example, something which according to physical measurement is a cube normally *looks* like a cube . . . and in general the visual cues from any solid object are usually a reliable guide as to what results would be obtained if one measured its size.

I shall argue that in Michotte's distinction between vision and reality there is a parallel with a distinction between language and thinking. When we are adults we can usually, but not always, say what we mean. When we are children we cannot, because our language does not bear a sufficiently close relationship to our thinking. To the extent that children agree with each other or with adults, it is on the level of language. If there is a divorce between language and thinking, and my evidence suggests there often is in childhood, the agreement will be more apparent than real. That is to say, they will be *saying* the same things, but meaning *different* things. If I am correct in this assumption, it follows that a vital task of educational psychology must be a thorough analysis of the language used by children with a view to discovering precisely how it is related to their thinking.

Of course, as every reader will be aware, there have already been a number of analyses of language in relation to thinking. Piaget's own work on child language (first published in English in 1926, revised in 1959) developed the thesis that the language used by children expresses their intellectual structures, a view to which my own is clearly opposed. Piaget's work introduced the term 'egocentric' to describe the utterances of young children, a term that unfortunately misled many commentators, as Piaget acknowledged in his 1959 revision. One psychologist so misled was Vygotsky (1962), who maintained that the language used by the child could affect his actions. This view that thinking is in some way secondary to language has been extensively developed by Vygotsky's student, Luria (1961). A third view is associated with the name of Jerome Bruner (Bruner, 1964; Bruner et al, 1966). This view maintains that language is used by children to bring order into their experiences. My own view is that all these views are to some extent right and to some extent wrong. The differences in the empirical findings of different investigators can readily be accounted for on my hypothesis of an overall 'loose fit' between language and thinking. Obviously, the fit is going to be tighter in some places than in others, and if different investigators examine different regions of tightness they will arrive at different conclusions as to what is being fitted. I want to explore the consequences of my 'loose-fit' model and their implications for education.

One obvious implication is that we should pay far more attention to what children actually say, both in the classroom and in the experimental situations in which we study them. Even the anti-Piagetian investigators often limit themselves to telling us how many children, under what conditions, 'solved' a problem: but unless they tell us precisely what the children said, we can be misled. For instance, in one of my demonstrations with three-year-olds, videotaped for teaching purposes,* I poured liquid from two identical vessels into vessels of different shapes in the familiar manner, and put each in front of a doll. I was using green food colouring dye so that the levels would show up clearly on the television screen. I asked Jane, a forthcoming and articulate child, if the dolls originally had the same amount to drink. She agreed that they had. After I had poured the liquid into the vessels of different shapes, I asked if the dolls still had the same amount to drink. Jane said yes. I asked 'How do you know it's still the same?' and she replied 'Because they've both got green'. No doubt everyone who has worked in this area has obtained similar replies, but it is rarely that

---

Young Children's Understanding of the World, obtainable from the Aberdeen University Television Service.

we read the detailed protocols. What we generally learn is not what was actually observed (i.e. what the investigator heard the child say) but whether or not the child's (unreported) response met the criterion of pass or fail.

I believe that we misunderstand children more often and more drastically than we suppose, which implies that they correspondingly fail to understand us. In the field of education it is supremely important that teachers and children fail to understand each other as little as possible. In view of the vast amount of educational failure, the widespread semi-literacy of our society, not to mention the low level of numerical competence, one must suppose that failures of communication in schools are on a monumental scale. Could the wider application of Piagetian methods reduce the scale of this problem?

It must be clear from all that I have said above that my answer to this question is an unambiguous 'No'. For what would these methods entail. McClinton and Meier (1978) tell us: 'Many schools claim a Piaget-based curriculum. Since Piaget did not endorse specific educational practices, these schools vary considerably. In some schools, skills studied by Piaget, such as classification, measurement and matching, are taught. In other schools, these skills are benignly neglected on the assumption that children eventually learn them on their own' (p. 341). However, they go on to list the focus of 'most Piagetian schools', as follows (ibid.):

(1) Mental traits important for learning, such as independence, curiosity, and confidence.
(2) Interaction among children and opportunities for children to resolve their own conflicts.
(3) Co-operative and egalitarian attitudes.
(4) Co-ordination of physical actions.
(5) Respect for a child's ideas, even if they are 'wrong'.
(6) Mild challenges to egocentric thought.
(7) Play as a method of learning.
(8) Learning by doing rather than by seeing or hearing.

With the best will in the world I cannot see how these practices derive from Piaget's theory, which is concerned essentially with the development of intellectual structures in the epistemic subject, only incidentally with how real children develop, and hardly at all with learning, which Piaget and his disciples constantly denigrate. Even if we brought to our aid all the armamentarium of special pleading to which we have previously drawn attention, there would still be enormous hiati between, on the one hand, the theory and these recommendations and, on the other, the application of these methods and any certainty that children would grow up literate and numerate.

But there's the rub. Do we *want* children to grow up literate and numerate? It often seems that progressive educators are inclined to slight these traditional skills, arguing that instruction in the use of our symbolic system in some way restricts children's intellectual and affective growth. This ignores the considerable body of evidence to the effect that providing children with such instrumental competence is one of the surest ways to encourage healthy personality development (Baumrind, 1972).

The almost religious fervour of the Piagetian education lobby, their misleading arguments, their air of self-righteousness, allied to their apparent disregard for the need to cite convincing evidence for their case (a characteristic that they share with their master) should tell us that we are dealing with a dogma. This dogma, which has potentially disastrous consequences for education, is that, in child education, actions come first, words a very poor second. Why is it that so many educators have lost faith in the spoken word? No-one would argue that teaching should be exclusively verbal, but surely we are not to abandon altogether the practice of teaching through talking.

After surveying the available evidence, I come to the conclusion that Piaget's theory has had no discernible influence on educational practice, at least as we know it in Britain. The one practical recommendation is that we encourage children to discover things through manipulative activity rather than by talk and discussion: this recommendation (a very lame conclusion to emerge from the vast Piagetian literature) would, if widely applied, be intellectually stultifying to our brightest children.

It is not just in the area of educational practice that the refusal to accept the essentially verbal nature of human intellectual functioning has had unfortunate consequences. The almost arrogant refusal to listen to what children actually say, allied to a predilection for fitting their responses into a predetermined theoretical framework, has given rise to a distorted view of cognitive development that is only now beginning to be challenged. It is good that these challenges are being made. It is good for psychology in general; it is good in particular for the study of intellectual development. Above all, it is good for the children whose education might otherwise be blighted by a mistaken model of the mind.

SUMMARY

In this chapter it is argued that there is confusion among educational theorists about the relationship of Piaget's theory to educational practice. This confusion arises from the fact that the nature of Piaget's theory is not always clearly understood. Even if it were, it would not constitute a sound theoretical basis for pedagogy, because it is concerned essentially with the growth of logical-mathematical structures in an abstract epistemic subject, whereas education is concerned with interactions between individuals. A theoretical basis for education must treat questions of social interaction, in particular, the psychology of language.

REFERENCES

Anthony, W. S. (1977) Activity in the learning of Piagetian operational thinking. *British Journal of Educational Psychology,* **47,** 18-24.

Baumrind, D. (1972) Socialization and instrumental competence in young children. In Hartup, W. W. (Ed.) *The Young Child: Reviews of Research,* **2,** Washington, D.C., National Association for the Education of Young Children.

Beth, E. W. and Piaget, J. (1966) *Mathematical Epistemology and Psychology.* Dordrecht: Reidel.

Bliss, Joan. *Children Thinking.* (A series of four films) London, BBC TV Enterprises.

Boyle, D. G. (1972) Michotte's ideas. *Bulletin of The British Psychological Society,* **25,** 89-91.

Boyle, D. G. (1973) Teaching road safety to infant-school children. *Education in the North,* **10,** 46-62.

Boyle, D. G. (1974) Has psychology anything to offer the teacher? *Scottish Educational Studies,* **6,** 49-62.

Boyle, D. G. and Gilhooly, Mary (1972) *Conceptual problems in teaching young children road safety.* (Unpublished) report submitted to the Transport and Road Research Laboratory of the Department of the Environment, Crowthorne, Berkshire.

Brown, G. and Desforges, C. (1977) Piagetian psychology and education: time for revision. *British Journal of Educational Psychology,* **47,** 7-17.

Bruner, J. S. (1964) The course of cognitive growth. *American Psychologist,* **19,** 1-15.

Bruner, J. S., Olver, R. R. and Greenfield, P. M. et al (1966) *Studies in Cognitive Growth.* London: Wiley.

Chomsky, N. (1959) Review of Skinner's Verbal Behaviour. In *Language,* **35,** 26-58.

Chomsky, N. (1972) *Language and Mind.* New York: Harcourt Brace Jovanovich.

Cronbach, L. J. (1964) *Learning Research and Curriculum Development.* (See Ripple and Rockcastle, pp. 204-207.)

Donaldson, M. (1978) *Children's Minds.* Glasgow: Collins.

Duckworth, E. (1964) The elementary science study. (See Ripple and Rockcastle, pp. 241-243.)

Flavell, J. H. (1971) Stage-related properties of cognitive development. *Cognitive Psychology,* **2**, 421-453.

Furth, H. G. and Wachs, H. (1974) *Thinking Goes to School: Piaget's Theory in Practice.* New York: OUP.

Inhelder, B. (1964) Piaget's genetic approach to cognition. In Cohen, J. (Ed.) *Readings in Psychology.* London: Allen.

Inhelder, B. and Sinclair, H. (1969) Learning cognitive structures. In Mussen, P., Langer, J. and Covington, J. (Eds.) *Trends and Issues in Developmental Psychology.* New York: Holt, Rinehart and Winston.

Inhelder, B., Sinclair, H. and Bovet, M. (1974) *Learning and the Development of Cognition.* London: Routledge and Kegan Paul.

Karplus, R. (1964) The science curriculum improvement study—report to the Piaget conference. (See Ripple and Rockcastle, pp. 236-240.)

Kilpatrick, J. (1964) Cognitive theory and the school mathematics study. (See Ripple and Rockcastle, pp. 247-251.)

Luria, A. R. (1961) *The Role of Speech in the Regulation of Normal and Abnormal Behaviour.* Oxford: Pergamon Press.

Macnamara, J. (1972) Cognitive basis of language learning in infants. *Psychological Review,* **79**, 1-13.

McClinton, B. S. and Meier, B. G. (1978) *Beginnings: Psychology of Early Childhood.* St Louis: Mosby.

McCurdy, H. C. (1958) The childhood pattern of genius. *Smithsonian Report for 1958*, pp. 527-542. Smithsonian Publication No. 4373.

Mason, H. L. (1964) Concepts in biology. (See Ripple and Rockcastle, pp. 244-246.)

Michotte, A. (1963) *The Perception of Causality.* London: Methuen. (Original Belgian edition 1946, revised 1954.)

Murrow, C. and Murrow, L. (1971) *Children Come First.* London: McGraw-Hill.

Nicholls, B. (1964) Additional comments on Duckworth's paper. (See Ripple and Rockcastle, p. 243.)

Piaget, J. (1959) *The Language and Thought of the Child.* London: Routledge and Kegan Paul.

Piaget, J. (1970) *Genetic Epistemology.* (The Woodbridge Lectures at Columbia University in 1968.) Columbia: Columbia University Press.

Piaget, J. (1971) *Science of Education and Science of the Child.* London: Longman.

Piaget, J. and Inhelder, B. (1969) Intellectual operations and their development. In Fraisse, P. and Piaget, J. (Eds.) *Experimental Psychology: Its Scope and Method.* London: Routledge and Kegan Paul.

Ripple, R. E. and Rockcastle, V. N. (Eds.) (1964) Piaget Rediscovered: A Report of the Conference on Cognitive Studies and Curriculum Development. *Journal of Research in Science Teaching,* **2**.

Rotman, B. (1977) *Jean Piaget: Psychologist of the Real.* Hassocks: Harvester Press.

Schwebel, M. and Raph, J. (Eds.) (1974) *Piaget in the Classroom.* London: Routledge and Kegan Paul.

Skinner, B. F. (1957) *Verbal Behaviour.* New York: Appleton-Century-Crofts.

Smedslund, J. (1977) Piaget's psychology in practice. *British Journal of Educational Psychology,* **47**, 1-6.

Vygotsky, L. S. (1962) *Thought and Language.* Cambridge, Massachusetts: MIT Press.

Wadsworth, B. (1978) *Piaget for the Classroom Teacher.* London: Longman.

Chapter 17

Some Educational Implications of Piaget's Theory

JOAN TAMBURRINI

'If I had to reduce all of educational psychology to just one principle, I would say this: The most important single factor influencing learning is what the learner already knows. Ascertain this and teach him accordingly.' (Ausubel, 1968)

INTRODUCTION

Educational theory is value bound. This should be sufficiently obvious not to require stating, but the naturalistic fallacy is alive and well: one can still find educational practices advocated on no other grounds than pet psychological theories and evidence. An examination of the importance of Piaget's theory, as of any psychological account of learning or development, requires not only the usual appraisal for such qualities as conceptual adequacy and consistency and the force of supporting and confirming evidence, but also consideration of ethical issues. Ausubel's statement above is a value statement as well as a factual one. It prescribes what teachers ought to do. Conversely, the direct translation of psychological findings into practice in schools may sometimes be rejected on the grounds that the outcome and/or the methodology conflicts with what is justifiable as good educational practice or objectives.

It is possible, however, for a psychological theory to measure up to value consider-ations in education but prove to be impracticable. Constraints stemming from the quality of teacher training, teacher/pupil ratio, the material provision available and imposed curricular content and organization may affect the viability of highly desirable practices. A communication barrier between the academic and the practitioner in education is likely to be the outcome should the former fail to take account of practical considerations.

In this chapter, two of the most controversial issues with respect to Piagetian theory will be examined: the nature of the relationship between learning and development; and the performance/competence issue. The educational implications will then be discussed in the light of ethical and practical considerations.

LEARNING AND DEVELOPMENT

Encapsulated in Piaget's distinction between learning and development is his conception of knowledge as a construction of reality. The two major differences between the processes, he claims, are that cognitive development is spontaneous whereas learning is provoked, and that learning is relatively particularistic in contrast to development which is concerned more with generalities:

> First I would like to make clear the differences between two problems: the problem of development in general, and the problem of learning. I think these problems are very different, although some people do not make this distinction.
>
> The development of knowledge is a spontaneous process . . . a process which concerns the totality of the structures of knowledge.
>
> Learning presents the opposite case. In general, learning is provoked by situations—provoked by a teacher with respect to some didactic point, or by an external situation. It is provoked, in general, as opposed to spontaneous. In addition, it is a limited process—limited to a single problem, or a single structure. (Piaget, 1964)

Piaget's emphasis on the spontaneity of development has led to misconceptions concerning the theory and hence its educational implications. The theoretical misconception is that development is a purely maturational process. Piaget's insistence that development is a spontaneous process has to be seen within his constructivist account of knowledge which he opposes to an empiricist account. An individual is said to construct reality through his actions on objects and events rather than receiving it as a copy. Thus didacticism, whether through verbal or visual presentations, will not of itself produce knowledge in a child. What is presented by a teacher will be assimilated to a child's schemas and, hence, modified or distorted if those schemas are insufficiently mature or inappropriate. The emphasis is on 'match', and social interaction, which includes teaching, is one factor affecting development, but the superordinate factor is 'equilibration' which implies that successful interactions are those that bring about new accommodations.

The mistaken assumption that Piaget's theory of development is a maturationist one has resulted in the equally mistaken assumption that a teacher can have little impact on development, and that an appropriate teaching style is one in which the teacher provides appropriate materials with which pupils may interact but, thereafter, adopts a passive, non-intervening style. Such an emasculation of their role is unattractive to many teachers and the issue of the relationship between learning and development, and hence teaching and development, is of major concern to them.

It is an issue that has been the subject of a massive amount of investigation in studies usually known as 'training research', that is, research which attempts to bring about the acquisition of a Piagetian concept in children as a result of specific training procedures (c.f. Modgil and Modgil, 1976). The type of training used has varied according to the investigator's particular theoretical stance. The techniques used include, among others: cognitive conflict (e.g. Brainerd and Allen, 1971); focusing subjects' attention on relevant cues (e.g. Bryant and Trabasso, 1971; Frank, 1966); language training (e.g. Sigel, Roeper, and Hooper, 1966; Sinclair, 1976); and a hierarchically or sequentially arranged instructional programme (e.g. Parker, Rieff, and Sperr, 1971).

There is not the space in this chapter to go into details of the successes and failures of these training techniques, but the overall results suggest that all methods achieved a measure of success, some more than others. However, three problems have emerged in drawing firm conclusions from many of these studies. First, it has not always been clear at which sub-stage the subjects were before training. In some cases subjects were categorized on the basis of a pretest as, say, nonconservers but no finer discrimination was made among transitional and earlier pre-operational levels. Second, subjects with whom the training seemed to be successful were not always tested on content sufficiently different from that used in the training sessions when attempts were made to discover the extent to which the acquisition was generalized. Third, subjects were often given only one post-test, whereas a second post-test after an appropriate lapse of time would have given some indication of the stability of any acquisition. These three issues are crucial to the consideration of the educational significance of training research. Generalizability and stability of concepts should be educational objectives, and teachers need to know whether the prior level of a child is a factor contributing to the likely success of teaching strategies.

One of the most rigorous series of studies of learning and cognitive development is that carried out by Inhelder, Sinclair and Bovet (1974). The investigators met the objections to some of the previous training research studies listed above. They made pretest discriminations among four sub-levels reached by subjects with respect to the concept being studied. They administered two post-tests, the second after a suitable lapse of time. They post-tested on material different from that involved in the training sessions.

The studies used different types of training methods, but the investigators do not analyse or compare their relative success. What the training methods had in common, however, was that the child's activity was encouraged and 'the procedures provided the subjects with a series of situations which favoured their apprehension of the experimental facts and which led to numerous comparisons and conflicts between the subjects' predictions and ideas and the actual outcome of certain manipulations'.

In terms of the educational significance of these training studies to be discussed later, it is important to note that the cognitive conflicts induced in this way were of two kinds. One kind involved a conflict between a subject's schema reflected in a particular prediction and what actually occurred. The other kind involved a conflict between schemas, as, for example, when a subject who conserves number but not length is confronted with the problem of making a road of equal length to a model and the matches given to him to use for the task are of a different length from those used in the model: there is a conflict between the subject's schemas when, on the basis of numerical equality, he predicts equality of length.

Each of the training techniques had some success and for many subjects development was clearly accelerated and concepts were attained in a relatively short time. However, the extent of a subject's progress was dependent upon his initial level. Subjects at sub-level 4, the most mature of the intermediate levels, made more progress more often than subjects at the earlier sub-levels. Thus, in the main, the hierarchical order of the subjects remained the same in the two post-tests as it was in the pretest, and in some cases the gaps between the subjects' levels were greater after the training than before.

Of particular educational significance are the results concerning generalizability and stability of the acquisitions. Once a subject had shown a clear understanding in the first post-test of either conservation or class inclusion, the acquisition seemed to be stable as measured on the second post-test. However, many subjects who progressed from an earlier to a later intermediate level between pretest and the first post-test regressed between the first and second post-tests. Inhelder and her associates write: 'It seems that regressions occur when the subject only momentarily establishes certain co-ordinations suggested by a specific situation: his reasoning seems strictly local, cannot be generalized to other situations and is probably not accompanied by the feeling of logical necessity that is another characteristic of a truly operatory construct'. Perhaps even more remarkable was the discovery that some subjects progressed between the first and second post-tests suggesting 'the intervention of organizational processes'.

In sum, the results demonstrated quite clearly that appropriate teaching techniques could bring about cognitive development in terms of acquisitions that were both stable and generalized. This is quite contrary to a maturationist conception of development. However, it must be emphasized that this occurred for the most part when the training procedures involved situations to which a subject's level of development made it possible for him to accommodate. Thus the results are also contrary to an empiricist account of learning. In the words of the investigators:

> The contribution of the environment must be stressed, since there appears to be a revival of the nativist view of cognitive development and since the psychogenetic, as opposed to an empiricist position, is often confused with that of the maturationist.

PERFORMANCE AND COMPETENCE

Over the past decade or so, a number of studies have yielded results suggesting that a subject's performance on a Piagetian-type of task is much more likely than we have hitherto supposed to depend on various situational factors. At the sensorimotor stage of development differences have been found with respect to the concept of object permanence. For example, Bower (1974), Kessen, Haith and Salatapek (1970), and Cornell (1978), have found that infants as young or younger than those who do not search for an object that has disappeared from view in the standard Piagetian tests do so in other specific situations. In relation to concrete operational thinking various studies have purported to show that young children's capabilities are greater than the results of standard Piagetian tests would lead one to suppose. Studies by Borke (1971, 1973, 1975) and Hughes (1978) have reputedly shown that children much younger than seven or eight years of age are able to think non-egocentrically. Bryant and Trabasso (1971) have claimed that under certain conditions children can solve transitive inference problems at an age when they would fail on the orthodox Piagetian test. Donaldson (1978) has reported a study showing that in a modification of one of Piaget's tests children conserved numerical quantity at a younger age than is usual in the standard version of the test. By contrast, Wason and Johnson-Laird (1972) have reported studies which show that adult subjects of well above average intelligence who, it is therefore presumed, would succeed on one of Piaget's tests for formal operational thought failed to solve problems which, though they differed in content from the standard Piagetian tests, required the same structures of thought that Piaget calls 'formal operations'.

Cornell (op. cit.) has drawn a distinction between explanations of Piaget's tests of the concept of object permanence in infants in terms of competence and performance. Piaget's account is a competence explanation and assumes that the behaviour of the infant on a standard Piagetian task is a measure of his knowledge about the permanence of objects. The competence theory, Cornell claims, underestimates the capacities of young infants as evidenced by their search behaviour in the studies cited above. By contrast, a performance explanation, he suggests, is that 'either the child is unable to perform certain aspects of the task or the researcher is incompetent in posing tests of the concept to the child'. This is, in effect, two performance explanations, not one, and the difference between them is of major importance not only to Piagetian theory but also to its educational significance. The first 'performance' explanation, that there are aspects of the task that the child cannot yet perform, requires considerable elaboration. It leaves open the question of what these aspects are and hence of how critical they are to Piaget's theoretical constructs. If they are critical, it would be possible to assert that the Piagetian tests tap an overall competence that the other tasks do not. The second 'performance' explanation querying the validity of Piagetian tests is again meaningless without some elaboration of the kinds of competences for which the investigator has failed to generate adequate tests.

Thus Cornell implies that performance explanations could satisfactorily replace competence explanations in Piaget's account of the permanence of object concept. While this might be possible without serious dilution of the theory in so far as it concerns the sensorimotor stage of development, there would be serious difficulties with respect to the subsequent stages of development with which this chapter, since it deals with educational implications of the theory, is concerned.

Cognitive development at the concrete operational and formal operational levels is defined by Piaget in terms of the development of cognitive structures, and Piaget's tests are intended to determine whether a child possesses such structures. Piaget has formalized his account of these structures by introducing the notion of 'groupings' to refer to the organization of classes and relations at the concrete operational stage and of 'groups' to describe the synthesizing of 'groupings' in formal operational thought. In sum, these structures involve systems of relationships. As Halford (1978) points out, it is characteristic of systems that their elements are defined by their distribution or arrangement within the system rather than by properties inherent to them as elements. 'This means that the system can remain invariant despite drastic changes in the elements'. What this entails psychologically is that a concept characterized as a cognitive structure or system is more or less independent of problem content and thus has considerable generality. Of formal operations, Piaget (1953) writes that it includes the acquisition of 'the logic of propositions, which is both a formal structure holding independently of content and a general structure co-ordinating the various logical operations into a single system'. With respect to concrete operations, however, the notion of independence of content is modified by the notion of *horizontal decalages.*

Piaget has used the notion of horizontal decalages, or time-lags, primarily to refer to differences in the age of acquisition of the various conservations. The most frequently quoted example is that conservation of weight is preceded by conservation of substance and followed by conservation of volume. This is hardly surprising since conservation of volume presupposes conservation of weight which, in turn, presupposes conservation of substance: there seems to be a logical necessity in the hierarchy. By contrast, it is less easy to account for the decalage that has been found to exist between children's responses on two different tests for the conservation of numerical quantity. One test involves the subjects in putting beads into a container one by one as the experimenter puts beads into another container. Another test involves a visual display of two aligned rows of equal numbers of objects which are then unaligned. It is not uncommon to find young children giving a conservation response in the first test but not in the second.

An even wider decalage has been found by Szeminska (1965). Her investigation was of stages of development with respect to classification using shapes and colours as criterial attributes. She found a range of successful concrete operational responses from the age of five to six years, when the material to be classified involved three sizes and four colours, to the age of 13 or 14 years, when the material to be categorized involved 'irregular forms or images evoking many functional schemas'. Her studies indicate that differences in content, in type of activity and in the situations in which the material is learned are the salient factors underlying these horizontal decalages.

The evidence to be discussed later which suggests that children's performance on certain modified versions of Piagetian tasks is sometimes superior to that on the standard tests may be interpreted in terms of horizontal decalages. However, it is problematical whether such an extended notion of decalages can be accommodated within Piagetian theory without bringing into question the concept that there are stages of thought each of which is characterized by a particular organizational structure defined as being generalized, and thus relatively independent of content. As Pinard and Laurendeau (1969) point out: 'if it were true that heterogeneity of objects alone brings about asynchronisms that are both too numerous and too striking, the typical behaviours at the level concerned could entirely lose their identity and the lines of demarcation between levels would be completely blurred'.

Thus, if it could be shown that situational factors differentially affect subjects' performance on a variety of tasks each involving the same concept, then it might be argued that one should abandon the notion of competence and, instead, regard each task including the standard Piagetian test as assessing performance only on the specific task. In that case no assumptions should be made that a subject could generalize a concept to materials or situations other than those of the specific task. As has been argued, this would mean that along with the notion of competence the crucial concept that cognitive development involves the development of mental structures would also have to be abandoned.

However, an alternative resolution to the problem of situational factors affecting performance that retains the notion of competence is possible, on the basis of a distinction between the two kinds of competence proposed by Flavell and Wohlwill (1969). One kind of competence is concerned with the processing of input and output. Certain horizontal decalages, or differences in performance according to differences in situational factors among various tasks, might be accounted for in terms of this kind of competence. The other kind of competence is with regard to 'rules, structures or mental operations embodied in the task' and would be the kind with which standard Piagetian tests are concerned.

If these two notions of competence are to resolve satisfactorily the problem presented by the findings that situational factors affect performance on Piagetian-type tasks, two requirements must be met.

The first requirement is that there should be evidence of a positive relationship between the extent to which a particular concept is generalized and the level of a subject's performance on the Piagetian test of that concept; subjects at an optimum stage level should generalize more than those at lower sub-stages. It has been shown in the section on learning and development that as far as concrete operations are concerned positive evidence exists in this respect.

The second and related requirement is that the first kind of competence should emerge before the second kind, for, by definition, the first kind of competence is situation specific, whereas the second kind is relatively independent of content. The examination of the evidence which follows will show that in the light of this second requirement the status of Piagetian tests as content-independent tests of competence with respect to 'rules, structures and mental operations' differs between concrete operational and formal operational tests.

The Evidence: Concrete Operations

As indicated earlier, there have been several claims that young children's capacities with respect to concrete operational thought are greater than Piaget's tests have led us to believe. The investigators who have made these claims have generated tasks which reputedly test the same concept as the corresponding standard Piagetian tests. An examination of these claims must establish whether, in fact, they do, for there are some whose content is so conceptually different from that of the standard Piagetian tests that they lead one to query whether they are assessing the same thing.

For example, Borke's earlier studies (1971, 1973) of egocentricity in young children must be queried on these grounds. She presented subjects aged three to six years of age with short stories involving situations in which the outcome would be likely to produce happiness, fear, sadness or anger. The subjects were then required to select from a range of drawings of faces representing these four emotions the one that best represented the emotion involved in the story. The studies indicated that children as young as three years of age can identify accurately these basic emotional responses in other people. Borke claims that these results do not support Piaget's account of egocentricity. This claim, however, confuses the popular meaning and associations of the term 'egocentric' with its highly specific and theory-bound meaning when used by Piaget. It is illustrated by Borke's use of the word 'empathy' synonymously with the absence of egocentricity in Piaget's sense. Empathy may involve no more than an assimilatory process as when a person identifies in another those feelings he himself has experienced or is experiencing. But as Chandler and Greenspan (1972) point out, 'egocentricity' in Piaget's terms involves the inability to accommodate to another person's point of view when it is different from one's own. Chandler and Greenspan devised a task requiring such a shift in perspective. The first part of their task resembled Borke's in that subjects were asked to identify the emotional reaction of someone after being shown a story in cartoon form. However, subjects were then asked to describe the perspective of a person who arrived late and whose knowledge of the story situation was thus limited. Their results supported Piaget's findings that non-egocentric responses develop in middle childhood.

Borke's later series of studies (1975) are, however, more central to the performance/competence issue. These studies used tasks which deviated from the 'mountains' test of egocentricity of Piaget and Inhelder (1956), in terms of both input and output. The input differed by employing stimulus materials more familiar to the children, including a wide variety of miniature people and animals in natural settings, as well as a display replicating Piaget's and Inhelder's three mountains. The output differed in that subjects were required to demonstrate awareness of another person's perspective by rotating a three-dimensional model instead of selecting a photograph as in the standard Piagetian test. Subjects demonstrated an accurate awareness of another person's perspective over 80 per cent of the time with the scenes using more familiar materials. For the mountains scene the three-year-old subjects gave 42 per cent correct responses and the four-year-old subjects 67 per cent correct responses. This contrasts with the standard Piagetian test in which non-egocentric responses in subjects under the age of seven years are rare. Thus, it would appear that the most powerful variable determining the level of the children's performance was when the input consisted of familiar materials, and that the variation from the standard Piagetian test in terms of output, viz. asking subjects to rotate a three-dimensional model instead of asking them to select a photograph, increased the overall level of performance but to a lesser extent. The latter finding accords with Sigel's (1968) findings that a group of young socio-economically underprivileged children performed on a categorization task at a higher level with three-dimensional models than they did with two-dimensional representations of the same objects.

The use of familiar materials is one way of producing a task which in Donaldson's (1978) terms makes more 'human sense' to young children than the standard Piagetian tests. Donaldson reports a number of studies testing Piagetian concepts in such meaningful contexts. Hughes, for example, devised a test for egocentricity using two intersecting 'walls' to form a cross and three small dolls representing a little boy and two policemen. The policemen are placed so that they can see some areas, while others are hidden from them by the walls. The child is required to place the doll so that he is hidden from the view of the policemen. The subjects were thirty children aged 3½ to five years. There was a 90 per cent correct response rate overall on this test, with the youngest children achieving a success rate of 88 per cent. Hughes repeated the test using more complex arrangements of walls with five or six sections and with three policemen. The youngest children achieved a 60 per cent correct response rate, while the four-year-old children still succeeded at the 90 per cent level.

Donaldson comments that this is a task which 'makes human sense' to the children because they know from experience what it is to try to hide and that misdemeanours lead to the need to hide. In sum, the motives and intentions of the characters are comprehensible to them. The task also differs in input from the 'mountains' test in another way: the intersecting walls in the display produce a symmetrical configuration and thus, as Hughes acknowledges, do not require the children to deal with left—right reversals in co-ordinating perspectives as does the 'mountains' test.

Donaldson regards the child's ability to make sense of people's intentions as one of the important situational factors contributing to young children's success on modified versions of Piagetian tests as compared with their performance on the standard ones. Children's capabilities are at their optimum, she claims, when a task involves intentions similar to ones they have had themselves or that they have come to impute to people in their everyday transactions with them. One of the most dramatic of the studies reported by Donaldson deviates from the standard Piagetian test only with respect to the apparent intention of the experimenter. The task, devised by McGarrigle, was a version of the conservation of number test in which the transformation of the elements in the display was ostensibly accidental, rather than the result of an intentional act by the experimenter. This was achieved by the introduction of a teddy bear ('naughty Teddy') who disarranged the stimulus material. More children between the ages of four and six years conserved in this situation than is usual in the standard test.

Some studies have deviated in terms of input from the standard Piagetian tests by using the strategy of drawing subjects' attention in some way to pertinent features of the stimulus material. This is the strategy adopted, for example, by Hughes (1978) in another study of egocentricity. Three dolls of different colours were used instead of three mountains. A child sitting at a table would see the full face of the doll nearest him and the profiles of the other two dolls. The experimenter sat at the table oriented at 120 degrees to the child so that he, too, saw the full face of the doll nearest him and the profiles of the other two. The child was required to indicate his ability to decentre and co-ordinate perspectives by identifying from three pictures that which represented the view seen by the experimenter. The subjects, forty pre-school children aged between four years and four years ten months, were divided into two groups, A and B. Before they were tested group B received preliminary questions designed to help them focus on relevant attributes. Thus they were asked, with no pictures present and for each position of the base, 'Which face do you see?' and 'Which face do I see?' Three preliminary questions were similarly asked for each of the pictures. Group A received no preliminary questions. It was found that 13 of the 20 children in group B succeeded in selecting the correct picture in the test compared with only one child in group A.

Bryant and Trabasso (1971) also used a strategy involving giving children pertinent cues with respect to transitive inference. Bryant and Trabasso argue that the standard Piagetian transitivity problem is a successive one and therefore involves memory: in order to infer the relationship between A and C from the fact that A>B and B>C, the child must remember the AB and BC comparisons. Bryant and Trabasso therefore devised an experiment with children of four, five and six years of age, which involved training them to remember the four initial direct comparisons, A>B, B>C, C>D and D>E where A, B, C, D, E were five rods whose lengths and colours were different. The rods fitted into holes of different depths in a block so that it was possible to make the rods protrude equally from it. It was thus possible to show a child two rods of different colours and ask him which was longer without him being able to see. When the subjects had been trained in this way, the child's ability to infer the relationships, particularly of B to D, was tested. The results showed that all three age levels were able to make transitive inferences. Bryant claims, 'children as young as four years can combine separate perceptual experiences inferentially, provided that they can remember the information which has to be combined'.

A criticism of the Bryant and Trabasso study has come from Furth (1977) derived from Piaget's distinction between figurative and operative aspects of knowledge, where figurative aspects are those which are perceptible, whereas operative aspects are those which are non-perceptible and involve an understanding of relationships. To test this claim, Furth presented two tasks to children of five and eleven years of age. The first was modelled on the Bryant and Trabasso procedure and the second superficially resembled it, but did not allow operative transitivity and required a comparison which was logically nonsensical. Of the five-year-old children 23 out of 30 made a logically nonsensical inference in the second task, whereas only two out of 30 of the eleven-year-old children gave an illogical 'transitive' reply. The remainder said, 'I don't know. This does not make sense'. Furth concludes that different psychological processes accounted for the difference in performance of the two age groups on the second task: 'we can say that figurative knowledge was similar in both age groups . . . but they differed in operative knowledge, that is, the understanding of logical inference'.

Furth's criticism is of considerable theoretical importance. The distinction between figurative and operative knowledge is central to Piaget's theory. However, Furth's experimental evidence should be treated with caution. The Bryant and Trabasso study is one among many that are based on the notion that under certain favourable conditions young children's capabilities will be at their greatest. The corollary of this would be that under unfavourable conditions children will perform at their least successful, and Furth's strategy of giving children a nonsensical problem must surely rank among the least favourable of conditions that can be devised.

However, Furth's criticism of the Bryant and Trabasso study, and the defects in Borke's earlier studies highlight the need to submit studies purporting to show that young children think at a concrete operational level earlier than Piaget's tests suggest to a close examination in terms of conceptual rigour. When this is done, there remains, nonetheless, sufficient evidence to support the claim. In sum, it would seem that there are conditions under which a young child may perform at a more successful level than he does in a standard Piagetian test, and that these include tasks:

(1) Where the input involves materials familiar to the child.
(2) Where the input involves motives and intentions of the participants that match a child's experiences and expectations.
(3) Where the input includes drawing subjects' attention to relevant, significant features of a task.
(4) Where the child is required to represent his understanding in a way that is easier for him than in the standard Piagetian tests.

It would seem, then, that the requirements discussed earlier for resolving the problem of differences between subjects' performance under these kinds of conditions and under those of the standard tests can be formulated in terms of the two kinds of competence explicated by Flavell and Wohlwill. Competence in terms of processing input and output explains subjects' earlier successes in the modified tasks. In addition, it develops with respect to increased complexities in input and output until it culminates in a competence that involves cognitive structures. It is stable and more generalized, and is reflected in successful performance on standard Piagetian tests.

The Evidence: Formal Operations

There is no reference to horizontal decalages at the formal operational level although there is at the concrete operational level. In fact, Piaget regards formal operational generalizability as a logical necessity.

> At the concrete operatory level a structure cannot be generalized to different heterogeneous contents but remains attached to a system of objects or the properties of these objects (thus the concept of weight only becomes logically structured after the development of the concept of matter, and the concept of physical volume after weight): a formal structure seems in contrast generalizable as it deals with hypotheses. (Piaget, 1972)

However, in spite of this logical independence of formal operations of the reality content to which they are applied, Piaget accepts that in actuality 'subjects vary in terms of the areas of functioning to which they apply formal operations according to their aptitudes and their professional interests' (Piaget, ibid.).

There is now a substantial body of evidence to suggest that subjects respond successfully in the Piagetian tests for formal operational thought involving physical science experiments at an earlier age than in certain other tasks differing in content but requiring the same formal operational structures.

Hallam (1967) devised problems to test subjects' ability to think at a formal operational level with respect to historical content. The subjects were 100 pupils from the first five years of a secondary school. The results indicated that formal operational thinking in relation to this material did not begin on average until 16 years of age. Jurd (1978) studied the development of thinking with regard to the curriculum subject history using subjects covering the age range from 11 to 18 years. To examine formal operational thinking in this area tests were devised that were concerned with the kinds of concepts which are important in history but which also have a parallel in Piaget's and Inhelder's tests using physical science concepts. These included the concept of 'the situation being as it was' and the notion of the balance of forces in history. Jurd claims that the concept of 'the situation being as it was' is akin to the schema of 'all other things being equal' that Piaget and Inhelder (1958) suggest are evidenced in the development of proof of a hypothesis at the formal operational stage, and that the notion of the balance of forces in history is analogous to the concept of the balance of forces in their experiment with the hydraulic press. Jurd's results provide substantial evidence for a sequence of development in relation to historical material which can be categorized satisfactorily in terms of the stages of concrete operations and formal operations as delineated by Piaget and Inhelder. However, like Hallam, he found that formal operational thought with respect to historical material does not emerge on average until mid-adolescence.

Rhys (1972) studied formal operational thought with respect to geographical material. The subjects covered a range from 9 to 16 years of age and the material used included maps, photographs and verbal matter. A variety of questions was posed including some which required the subjects to contrast British farming practices with those in another country. The most mature answers required hypothetico-deductive reasoning and were not given by subjects below a mental age of approximately 15½ years.

Wason and Johnson-Laird (1972) have devised a number of tasks requiring subjects to evaluate the truth/falsity of conditional sentences. These are tasks which, to be performed correctly, require the use of propositional logic. Wason and Johnson-Laird concluded from their results that many of their subjects, adults of high intelligence, were not capable of this type of formal operational reasoning. However, Lunzer, Harrison and Davey (1972) found that subjects' performance in these kinds of tasks can be improved considerably if the material is presented in a more familiar form than in the studies by Wason and Johnson-Laird and if the subjects are provided with relevant experience. Lunzer and his associates suggest that subjects who have reached the level of formal operational reasoning can be induced to apply propositional logic correctly given the right circumstances. This claim is supported by studies by Seggie (1978) using concept-learning tasks with stimulus material involving four geometric figures, which could be white or shaded, and the presentation of sixteen combinations of stimuli. The studies were designed to examine search procedure, a method that allows the subject to find for himself which attributes are relevant and which are irrelevant prior to concept learning, and that utilizes the logical relations between each of the stimuli and the classification. Seggie concludes that, '. . . the performance of the subjects was such as to lend support for Lunzer's weaker form of the [formal operations] model. Subjects did not spontaneously apply the ideal strategy and they did not spontaneously hypothesize the existence of particular logical relations and then test for their existence. They had, on the whole, to be led to the application of the logical relations which they were dealing with'.

Thus there is considerable evidence to suggest that formal operational thought is contextually bound. The performance/competence issue cannot be resolved in the same way as has been suggested above for concrete operational thought. It was argued that in order to conceive the standard Piagetian test as assessing the kind of competence that is independent of content, and competence on other Piagetian-type tasks as of another kind that is content bound and that involves processing of input and output, it is a necessary requirement that the latter is seen to emerge before the former. In the case of formal operational thought this position seems to be reversed, and formal operational responses are produced on standard Piagetian tests at an earlier age than they are on the other tasks with different content reported above. The age at which, on average, formal operational thinking with respect to particular content appears probably depends on both the complexity and familiarity of the material.

Lunzer has argued from his studies that familiarity of material is of considerable importance. Hallam has suggested that the relatively late acquisition of formal operational thought with respect to historical material may be due to the fact that the subject is dealing with verbal material describing experiences remote from his own.

The influence of familiarity of material would lead one to expect differences within a subject area as well as differences between subject areas. With respect to historical material, for example, Jurd, commenting on the work of Miller, Kessell and Flavell (1970), writes: 'Whereas thinking about other people as social objects is comparatively easy and 80 per cent of the fourth grade can think about people talking to each other, only 50 per cent of the sixth grade can "think about X thinking" . . . It seems that the more remote X's experience is from that of the child, the more difficult to understand his purposes in bringing about an event. It would thus be difficult for an early adolescent to understand a political leader's motives'. The extent of familiarity with particular content is not, however, simply a question of its degree of remoteness in space and time. In subjects like history and geography, where the sources of experience are more secondary than primary, much will depend on pupils' exposure to material at an earlier stage in their education.

In sum, although different stages of development can be identified, the process of development in adolescence is gradual, with a comparatively late age for the emergence of formal operational thinking depending on whether the material is verbal/symbolic or concrete, on the complexity of relations involved, and on the relevance of a pupil's experience. This means that no assumptions should be made that a pupil's performance at the formal operational level on a standard Piagetian test is evidence of an overall competence which will be found in relation to other content.

SOME EDUCATIONAL IMPLICATIONS

This chapter began with the recommendation by Ausubel that a teacher should take account of what the learner already knows. The evidence discussed above concerning the performance/competence issue at the pre-operational/concrete operational levels would suggest that this recommendation can be put into practice if the primary school curriculum involves the pupils in self-chosen activities with familiar materials. In these contexts their capabilities are likely to be at their greatest. It might even be argued that Piagetian theory is, therefore, irrelevant to teachers of pupils at these age levels. However, there are serious flaws in this latter conclusion.

Children may sometimes arrive at conclusions concerning specific problems they have generated in the context of self-chosen activities that do not hold good as generalizations. The following example illustrates this problem. A five-year-old child chose to build a tree-like structure from constructional materials. His intention was to build a structure which would not overbalance, and his strategy was to build a symmetrical structure, a viable strategy with these particular materials, as a symmetrical structure would be one whose weight was evenly distributed. The teacher's questions elicited from the child that he had concluded that symmetry was a necessary and sufficient condition not only to achieve balance with a structure made from these particular materials but for balance in general. This is, of course, a false conclusion, and if possible the child should be helped to an understanding that distribution of weight is the critical factor and that asymmetrical things may balance. The problem for the teacher is whether the child can be brought to this understanding at the generalized level of competence or only with respect to this specific situation. In actuality, the child's continuing exploration of the material fortuitously led to a new problem for him when a new structure was built which was symmetrical but did not balance, and he was led to discover the reason was that the peg of one piece of the constructional material was not pushed far enough into the hole of the adjoining piece. Eventually, the child built a structure that balanced but was asymmetrical. Whether he could have been brought to generalize this new level of understanding beyond this specific situation to achieve conservation of weight is a matter of conjecture, but the studies of Inhelder, Sinclair and Bovet, discussed in the section on Learning and Development, would suggest that the success of any attempt by the teacher to bring him to this level of understanding would depend on his present sub-level which thus needs to be diagnosed.

This example is meant to illustrate that it would be false to assume that all the conclusions a child will reach in contexts involving self-chosen materials and problems will necessarily be correct. However, it is not meant to suggest that such contexts should not provide the basis of primary education. In fact, the child did eventually achieve a remarkably high level of understanding for his age in relation to the specific problem he explored. This was not the case in the following contrasting example of a six-year-old child pursuing an activity initiated and structured by the teacher. The child was required to experiment with balance using scales and a variety of natural materials such as nails, nuts, beans, pegs, small toys and dog biscuits. At the teacher's direction the child recorded her findings in the form, '1 dog biscuit weighs the same as 4 nails, 3 nuts weigh the same as 2 pegs', and so on. A visitor asked the child which weighed the most, a dog biscuit or a toy car, and was told 'the toy car'. Asked how she knew, the child answered, 'because 10 beans weigh the same as a toy car, but only 4 nails weigh the same as a dog biscuit', thus revealing her assumption that it was numerical quantity that is critical.

Both of these examples illustrate the need for a teacher to have considerable knowledge of Piagetian theory if he is to elicit a pupil's conclusions and level of understanding and then to decide on whether there are strategies that might extend the child's understanding or rectify his misunderstanding.

In coming to conclusions about the educational implications of the findings that children's capabilities are likely to be at their greatest in contexts that are most related to their experiences in terms of both intentions and materials, it is important to distinguish between pedagogical strategies and educational aims. It has been argued that these findings would support a pedagogical strategy that exploits this kind of context as a starting point in an episode of learning. However, there are strong grounds for rejecting the notion that the acquisition of contextually bound competences should be the sole aim of education as far as cognitive development and conceptual learning are concerned. Education should be concerned with getting pupils to generalize principles beyond specific, familiar content and to come to understand increasingly the procedural rules within the various domains of knowledge. Donaldson has drawn a distinction between 'embedded' and 'disembedded' thought. Embedded thought deals with 'people and things in the context of fairly immediate goals and intentions and familiar patterns of events'. By contrast, disembedded thought operates outside 'the supportive context of meaningful events'. Disembedded thought must inevitably entail competences that are generalizable and stable, the competences that, it has been argued, are assessed by Piagetian tests, in contrast to situation-specific competences. It follows that to produce a shift from 'embedded' to 'disembedded' thinking in a particular pupil in relation to a specific concept, at the critical time a teacher needs considerable diagnostic skill that must inevitably entail an understanding of Piagetian theory and tests.

Although the evidence on formal operational thinking suggests that, in contrast to pre-operational/concrete operational thinking, pupils achieve operatory level on Piagetian tests for the most part before they do in some other educationally important contexts, the same conclusion must be drawn that teachers require a thorough understanding of Piaget's theory. This would seem to be so for two reasons. First, a teacher needs to be able to examine particular content and problems within his own subject field to ascertain where formal operational thinking is required. Second, he needs to be able to examine pupils' responses in terms of stages of thought. The following example may illustrate the complexities involved in these requirements.

A teacher produced for a class of thirteen-year-old pupils the task of determining how best to develop an imaginary underdeveloped country. They were given a map on which were marked relevant geographical features. The task required not only that all the features were taken into account, but also an understanding of their relative importance, for the particular problem could not be solved by exploiting all the natural resources and the existing population distribution equally. In other words, it was a formal operational task of a relatively complex kind.

The pupils' performance on this task was poor and clearly not what the teacher expected. Their difficulties may have arisen for one or both of two reasons. Some of the pupils clearly did not have the necessary understanding of the relevance and relative importance to the problem of the various geographical features. Many of them, however, seemed incapable of the formal operational reasoning required at this complex level. This example is meant to illustrate the need for teachers at the secondary stage of education to examine curricular content in terms of: (1) the extent to which particular content requires concrete operatory or formal operatory thinking; and then in the case of formal operatory content (2) the extent to which the material is verbal/ symbolic or concrete; (3) the number of elements, factors or variables involved in the problem; and (4) the relationship between these elements, whether, that is, they are of equal or unequal significance. Curricula may then be organized in terms of expected psychological sequences and hierarchies, as well as any intrinsic to a discipline.

Though the planning of sequenced material on this basis is important, the effectiveness of its outcome is paramount. However carefully planned the curriculum material has been, there are likely to be some pupils whose particular experiences lead them to assimilate it to inappropriate schemas, and some who have simply not reached the cognitive level required to deal with it. Thus an important part of a teacher's educational dialogues with pupils should be concerned with eliciting information in these respects.

These diagnoses should not be thought of in psychometric terms, that is, as tests that can be given at infrequent intervals to pupils as a whole. The research reviewed above indicated that formal operational thinking is contextually bound and that differences in levels of functioning are of intra-individual as well as inter-individual kinds. The assessment of teaching/learning outcomes thus needs to be contextually based and concerned with individual pupils' responses.

At both the primary and secondary levels of education teachers who have assessed pupils' cognitive levels also need to understand how to bring about, if possible, the competence required for particular curricular content. In the section on learning and development, it was shown that Piaget's theory is not a maturationist one, and thus that it is wrong to conclude that teaching can have little effect on cognitive development. Training research, in particular the studies cited above by Inhelder, Sinclair and Bovet, would suggest that there are successful strategies teachers might adopt to bring about the acquisition of more mature levels of cognitive functioning in their pupils. It is important, however, that a distinction is made between facilitation and acceleration as educational aims with respect to cognitive development.

Conceptually, the difference between facilitation and acceleration is largely a matter of emphasis. Acceleration must, by definition, refer to a concept not yet acquired. It makes no sense to talk of accelerating a competence a pupil already possesses. The connotations of facilitation, however, are less future directed. It is as possible to talk of facilitating a pupil's present development, for example, by making it possible for him to consolidate and systematize present knowledge and to assimilate a wider range of materials and exemplars to a present schema, as it is to talk about facilitating the development of a competence not yet acquired. In any case, the concept of facilitation, even when applied in a future-directed way, entails some attention to the kinds of strategies that are most likely to be effective, for facilitation, by definition, means to adopt methods that favour a process.

Though this conceptual difference may seem trivial, the way it may be reflected in educational practice is important. When acceleration is the objective and the focus of a teacher's attention is on the particular concept to be acquired, a pupil's present level of development and his particular experience and interests may be given insufficient attention. By contrast, when facilitation is the objective, a teacher's attention is more likely to be given also to the level, experience and interests of the learner.

The work of Inhelder, Sinclair and Bovet would suggest that a pupil's level of cognitive functioning is a critical factor in determining the success of teaching strategies in relation to a particular concept, where success is defined as generalization and stability of an acquisition. The strategies may be of different kinds, as are the strategies of training research in general and of the studies of Inhelder and her associates in particular. However, the conclusion to be drawn from these latter studies is that it is important for the child to be actively engaged. The child's activity need not necessarily be physical manipulation, though the younger the child, the more important it is. Mental activity can take place when a child observes a teacher's actions and, conversely, a child may engage in physical activity without his thinking being engaged. One important way in which a teacher may engage a pupil's mental activity is by arranging outcomes and by eliciting the pupil's ideas so that dissonances are made explicit. A dissonance may be between an outcome and a pupil's prediction, or, most importantly, between two different interpretations of a phenomenon arising from two distinct schemas. Making these kinds of dissonances explicit requires astute questioning which can only be expected if a teacher knows the kinds of schemas a child is likely to possess and hence how he is likely to predict or explain an outcome. When their ideas are made explicit in this way, pupils may be helped to develop the ability to reflect on their own ideas and the propensity to do so. These are very necessary requisites of formal operational thought.

SUMMARY AND SOME PRACTICAL CONSIDERATIONS

The theory and evidence with respect to two important issues in Piagetian theory, the learning and development and the performance/competence issues, have been examined. It has been argued that the significance of these findings is different for education in the early, middle and adolescent to young adult years.

It is in early childhood education that the evidence in relation to the performance/competence issue is of special importance. This evidence is perhaps not as dramatic as has sometimes been claimed, for in some cases there is an inadequate conceptualization which makes it dubious whether Piagetian concepts have in fact been the objects of study. There remains, nonetheless, some less refutable evidence that situational factors do affect the level of young children's cognitive functioning and that where the content is familiar and intentions are understood, their capabilities are at their greatest. This evidence provides support for the kinds of practices in primary education which arrange matters so that pupils generate problems and pursue interests in contexts and with materials that are related to their experiences.

It has been argued, however, that Piagetian tests of concrete operations assess a competence that is relatively stable and generalized, in contrast with these specific situations where competence is contextually bound. This former kind of competence is a prerequisite for pupils' increasing understanding of the central concepts and procedural rules in various domains of knowledge. At the end of the early childhood years and in the middle years it is thus important that a teacher is able to diagnose pupils' cognitive levels as explicated by Piaget and his associates. These diagnostic skills are also necessary if a teacher is to be successful in the strategies he adopts to facilitate the development of concrete operational thought. This is not to say that the curriculum should not continue to take into account pupils' experience and interests, but rather that the embedded thinking that takes place in these contexts should be extended to become increasingly disembedded.

The performance/competence issue cannot be resolved in the same way with respect to formal operational thought. The evidence strongly suggests that it is contextually bound and that where there are a number of variables or factors complexly interrelated, and/or where the material is verbal/symbolic, formal operational thinking is a relatively late acquisition. Thus, at the secondary level of education, teachers need to have considerable understanding of Piagetian theory in order to diagnose pupils' levels and to assess the kind of thinking necessary for various concepts and problems within a particular subject discipline.

At all levels of education these diagnostic and teaching skills require not only firm understanding of Piagetian theory and curricular content, but also considerable organizational ability. Diagnostic questions are likely to reveal a wide range of individual differences among pupils and the studies of Inhelder, Sinclair and Bovet suggest that if strategies aimed at facilitating cognitive development are successful, not only does the same hierarchy of individual differences exist, but the gaps between pupils may be widened rather than narrowed.

It would be unrealistic to suppose these organizational abilities and levels of theoretical understanding are not extremely demanding of teachers. It would be unrealistic, too, to suppose that such understanding and competence can be acquired in more than a rudimentary way at the level of initial teacher education. It is important, however, that a beginning is made at this stage, or otherwise teachers may later have to unlearn some assumptions they have made. It is, however, in in-service education and training of teachers that theoretical understanding needs to be extended and deepened. While one short exposure to theory at the level of initial teacher education is inadequate, another isolated period of in-service exposure is, though better than nothing, insufficient. In the words of the Report on Primary Education in England (1978):

> Initial training must be followed *throughout a teacher's career* by a supporting pattern of in-service education and training.

REFERENCES

Applebee, A. (1978) *The Child's Concept of Story: Ages Two to Seventeen*. Chicago: University of Chicago Press.

Ausubel, D. P. (1968) *Educational Psychology: A Cognitive View*. London: Holt, Rinehart and Winston.

Borke, H. (1971) Interpersonal perceptions of young children: egocentrism or empathy? *Developmental Psychology*, 5, 263-269.

Borke, H. (1973) The development of empathy in Chinese and American children between the ages of three and six years of age. A cross-cultural study. *Developmental Psychology*, 9, 102-108.

Borke, H. (1975) Piaget's mountains revisited: changes in the egocentric landscape. *Developmental Psychology*, 11, 240-243.

Bower, T. G. R. (1974) *Development in Infancy*. San Francisco: Freeman.

Brainerd, C. J. and Allen, T. W. (1971) Training and generalization of density conservation: effects of feedback and consecutive similar stimuli. *Child Development*, 42, 693-704.

Bryant, P. E. and Trabasso, T. (1971) Transitive inferences and memory in young children. *Nature*, 237, 456-458.

Chandler, M. J. and Greenspan, S. (1972) Ersatz egocentrism: a reply to H. Borke. *Developmental Psychology*, 7, 104-106.

Cornell, E. H. (1978) A reinterpretation of object permanence studies. In Siegel, L. S. and Brainerd, C. J. (Eds.) *Alternatives to Piaget: Critical Essays on the Theory*. London: Academic Press.

Donaldson, M. (1978) *Children's Minds*. London: Fontana.

Flavell, J. H. and Wohlwill, J. F. (1969) Formal and functional aspects of cognitive development. In Elkind, D. and Flavell, J. H. (Eds.) *Studies in Cognitive Development*. London: Oxford University Press.

Frank, F. (1966) Perception and language in conservation. In Bruner, J. S., Olver, R. R., Greenfield, P. M., et al (Eds.) *Studies in Cognitive Growth*. New York: Wiley.

Furth, H. (1977) The operative and figurative aspects of knowledge in Piaget's theory. In Geber, B. A. (Ed.) (1977) *Piaget and Knowing: Studies in Genetic Epistemology*. London: Routledge and Kegan Paul.

Halford, G. S. (1978) Towards a working model of Piaget's stages. In Keats, J. A., Collis, K. F., and Halford, G. S. (Eds.) *Cognitive Development: Research Based on a Neo-Piagetian Approach*. New York: Wiley.

Hallam, R. N. (1967) Logical thinking in history. *Educational Review,* **119,** 182-202.

H.M. Inspector of Schools (1978) *Primary Education in England.* London: HMSO.

Hughes, M. (1978) Selecting pictures of another's view. *British Journal of Educational Psychology,* **48** (2), 210-219.

Inhelder, B., Sinclair, H. and Bovet, M. (1974) *Learning and the Development of Cognition.* London: Routledge and Kegan Paul.

Jurd, M. F. (1978) An empirical study of operational thinking in history-type material. In Keats, J. A., Collis, K. F. and Halford, G. S. (Eds.) *Cognitive Development: Research Based on a Neo-Piagetian Approach.* New York: Wiley.

Kessen, W., Haith, M. M. and Salapatek, P. H. (1970) Human infancy: a bibliography and guide. In Mussen, P. (Ed.) *Carmichael's Manual of Child Psychology.* Volume 1. New York: Wiley.

Lunzer, E. A., Harrison, C. and Davey, M. (1972) The four-card problem and the generality of formal reasoning. *Quarterly Journal of Experimental Psychology,* **24,** 326-339.

Miller, P. H., Kessel, F. S. and Flavell, J. H. (1970) Thinking about people thinking about people thinking about . . . a study of social cognitive development. *Child Development,* **41,** 613-623.

Modgil, S., and Modgil, C. (1976) Piagetian Research. *Compilation and Commentary.* Windsor: NFER.

Parker, R. K., Rieff, M. L. and Sperr, S. J. (1971) Teaching multiple classification to young children. *Child Development,* **42,** 1779-1789.

Piaget, J. (1953) *Logic and Psychology.* Manchester: University of Manchester Press.

Piaget, J. (1964) Development and learning. In Ripple, R. and Rockcastle, U. (Eds.) (1970) *Piaget Rediscovered.* Ithaca, New York: Cornell University Press.

Piaget, J. (1972) Intellectual evolution from adolescence to adulthood. *Human Development,* **15,** 1-12.

Piaget, J. and Inhelder, B. (1956) *The Child's Conception of Space.* London: Routledge and Kegan Paul.

Piaget, J. and Inhelder, B. (1958) *The Growth of Logical Thinking from Childhood to Adolescence.* New York: Basic Books.

Pinard, A. and Laurendeau, M. (1969) 'Stage' in Piaget's cognitive developmental theory: exegesis of a concept. In Elkind, D. and Flavell, J. H. (Eds.) *Studies in Cognitive Development.* London: Oxford University Press.

Rhys, W. T. (1972) Geography and the adolescent. *Education Review,* **24** (3), 183-196.

Seggie, J. L. (1978) Concept learning and the formal operational model. In Keats, J. A., Collis, K. F. and Halford, G. S. (Eds.) *Cognitive Development: Research Based on a Neo-Piagetian Approach.* New York: Wiley.

Sigel, I. E. (1968) The distancing hypothesis: a causal hypothesis for the acquisition of representational thought. In Jones, M. R. (Ed.) (1970) *Miami Symposium on the Prediction of Behavior: Effect of Early Experiences.* Florida: University of Miami Press.

Sigel, I. E., Roeper, A. and Hooper, F. H. (1966) A training procedure for the acquisition of Piaget's conservation of quantity: a pilot study and its replication. *British Journal of Educational Psychology,* **36,** 301-311.

Sinclair, H. (1976) Developmental psycholinguistics. In Inhelder, B. and Chipman, H. H. (Eds.) *Piaget and his School.* New York: Springer-Verlag.

Szeminska, A. (1965) The evolution of thought: some applications of research findings to educational practice. *Monographs for the Society for Research in Child Development,* **30** (2), 47-57.

Wason, P. C. and Johnson-Laird, P. N. (1972) *Psychology of Reasoning: Structure and Content.* Cambridge, Massachusetts: Harvard University Press.

Interchange

BOYLE REPLIES TO TAMBURRINI

Tamburrini opens with a quotation from Ausubel, with which it would be hard to disagree. Clearly one would be wasting one's time trying to extend non-existent knowledge. However, the debate is about the meaning, in this context, of the verb 'to know'.

If we observed a child correctly performing a task, we could be misled into thinking that he knew what he was doing. To check on this we should have to ask him to perform a task that *we* knew to be structurally similar, to see if *he* perceived the structural similarities. If performance on the second task revealed that he did not, then we should know that he had not understood fully the initial task. We should say that he did not really know what he was doing. In Tamburrini's terms, we should describe him as of limited *competence*, even though his initial *performance* was adequate. This is a valuable distinction because we can generalize from this one example to say that one cannot predict success on task B from successful performance of task A, unless one has first diagnosed the child's competence.

Later I shall suggest a limitation to the usefulness of this distinction, but here I want to address myself to the central point at issue, namely the relevance of this to Piaget's theory. Repeatedly Dr Tamburrini claims, as do so many others, that a thorough knowledge of Piaget's theory is needed if one is successfully to diagnose competence from performance. On this point I am quite unconvinced. I have argued in my own chapter that the elaborate pseudo-logico-mathematical edifice that Piaget has erected over the years is not the sort of theory that helps us to help children. The most that can be said of it is that it provides *one* way of describing competence. The whole point of assessing competence in an educational context is that it will help the teacher to assist the child in achieving a better performance. The evidence that Piaget's theory is better at this than simpler diagnoses expressed in everyday language is hard to come by. If it is argued that successful teachers show, by their success, that they do understand the child in Piagetian terms, this is akin to M. Jourdain's talking prose without knowing it.

I indicated above that, while the competence/performance distinction is useful, its usefulness is limited. I shall illustrate this by a brief discussion of Tamburrini's example of the class of thirteen-year-olds determining the hypothetical development of an imaginary underdeveloped country. At 13 one would expect these pre-adolescents to have reached the level of formal operations, and presumably the task would not have been attempted had they not previously shown this level of competence. Nonetheless they failed the task. This indicates that while one cannot predict performance from knowledge of performance, one cannot always predict it from knowledge of competence either. It also suggests very strongly that the teacher must teach the pupils how to use their intellect. Presumably this is what is meant by 'facilitation'.

Throughout the 'Piaget for education' canon one meets cases of special pleading and extended use of terms, and one comes across them again among Tamburrini's examples. The most striking is the desperate attempt by Jurd (1978) to draw parallels between, on the one hand, 'the situation being as it was' (in history) and 'the notion of balance of forces in history'; and, on the other, the schema of 'all other things being equal' and 'balances of forces . . . with [a] hydraulic press', as studied by Piaget and Inhelder (1958). Ours is an age in which words are constantly devalued by use in misappropriate contexts, but this is the most blatant I have ever encountered in academic research.

The example does have a virtue, however, in confirming the conclusion that I drew from the example of reasoning about economic geography, namely that one cannot conclude from the fact that pupils are at the age of formal operations (which they are from about 11 years) that they will reason correctly about sophisticated economic and historical concepts (which they cannot do before about 16 years).

I cannot entirely absolve Tamburrini herself from the charge of using terms in an extended sense. Her chapter concludes with a reference to the necessity for the child to be 'actively engaged'. Again, I cannot imagine that anyone would disagree with the necessity for the child to be more than merely passive, but the characteristic feature of Piaget's argument has been the stress on physical manipulation. Here we are told that a child needs to have his thinking engaged even when he is involved in physical activity, and that 'mental activity can take place when a child observes a teacher's actions'. In short, I cannot see that this amounts to more than saying that, in order to learn, you have to use your mind. Sound traditional advice, no doubt, but we do not need Piaget to tell us that.

TAMBURRINI REPLIES TO BOYLE

It is impossible in a reply of this length to deal with all the specific details of the claims made by Boyle in his chapter. I shall, therefore, examine his more general claims and those specific aspects with which he supports them. I hope that the selection I have made in so doing is not so biased as to do an injustice to his case.

It is, perhaps, somewhat banal, but nonetheless necessary to an examination of Boyle's case, to state that science does not deal in absolute truths. One criterion of a 'good' theory (there are other criteria which cannot be dealt with here) is its generative power: it should lead to the generation of testable hypotheses yielding empirical data which, in turn, lead to elaborations and modifications of the theory. Scientific theories deal in relative, not absolute, truths. Perhaps, as Boyle suggests, they should be appraised in terms of utility rather than truth or falsity. But, whether in terms of usefulness or relative truth/falsity, any appraisal should take account of experimental evidence. The recent burgeoning of research evidence requiring modifications of Piaget's theory is to be welcomed and reflects its generative power. In my chapter, I have examined some of the more recent experimental evidence relating to Piagetian theory and I have attempted to show how it modifies the theory in relation, for example, to the concept of 'stage'. Some of the more esoteric constructs within the theory have recently been the subject of investigation. For example, Bower's (1974) investigations into the use of schematic conflict to bring about cognitive gains in infants have given some support to the 'equilibrium' construct. Other constructs may, in the future, prove to be equally generative, while others may need to be discarded.

Educationists who receive Piagetian theory as dogma clearly fail to appreciate this basic fact concerning the nature of scientific theory. I am in total agreement with Boyle that such 'religious fervour' is potentially damaging to education, but uncritical acceptance or misinterpretations of the theory by educationists are insufficient grounds for rejecting it as having no importance for education. If all theories likely to be misinterpreted were rejected, education would be in the unfortunate position of being based either on unchanging traditional practices or on curricular experimentation for which, since it was free of theory, it would be difficult to evaluate successes and failures.

If an uncritical and dogmatic acceptance of Piaget's theory is unacceptable, its rejection without an adequate appraisal of relevant experimental evidence is equally unacceptable. Boyle has been guilty in three instances of the latter. His references to the experimental literature are both thin and biased: he ignores the details of relevant supporting evidence, while quoting other evidence which, he claims, refutes aspects of the theory.

The first instance concerns his argument against Piaget's claim regarding the centrality of action in cognitive development. In support of this argument he quotes Anthony (1977), who refers to training research to support his claim, that verbal and visual demonstrations may lead to the acquisition of Piagetian concepts. As I have argued in my chapter, the implications of the results of some of the training research is ambiguous because there have been inadequate diagnoses of the pre-training levels of the subjects and, hence, of the differences in this respect between subjects who acquired the concept as a result of training and those who did not. In the studies of Inhelder, Sinclair and Bovet (1974), training tended to be most successful with subjects at the most mature pre-operational sub-stage. Moreover, the investigators' techniques invariably involved the subjects in activity: 'the experimental situations were constructed to encourage the child's activity and to elicit the co-ordination and differentiation of thought patterns that are characteristic of the different levels of development' (Inhelder, Sinclair and Bovet, p. 243). It is puzzling that Boyle refers in parentheses to the studies of Inhelder, Sinclair and Bovet to support his and Anthony's argument when, in fact, their evidence suggests that Anthony's claim is a gross over-simplification of the effects of visual and verbal demonstrations on the acquisition of Piagetian concepts, and in no way refutes the importance of action in cognitive development.

The second instance concerns Boyle's claims on the development of language and its role in cognitive development. His references to this area are made to support his claim that successful education involves social interactions in which experiences are shared through the use of a common language. I have no disagreement with this claim, and I find Piaget's treatment of this area relatively slight though I do not agree with Boyle (after Rotman) that 'he has no theory of language'. But to accept that language plays a crucial role in education is to beg a number of questions. How can we be sure that in our interactions with children we are sharing a common language, that what the children understand the words to mean is what we intend them to mean? To what extent is language necessary and sufficient to cognitive development? Does the relationship of language to cognition differ according to the stage of cognitive development? There is evidence to suggest that although language is not a sufficient condition for cognitive development, it plays a more critical role in the development of formal operational thinking than it does at earlier stages. In sum, the relationship between language and thought is a highly complex issue of which Boyle's acknowledgment of a 'loose fit' is an over-simplification.

Boyle's references to empirical studies in the area of language development, apart from his anecdotal illustrations, are to Macnamara (1972) and Donaldson's (1978) commentary. Macnamara's particular contribution to the psychology of language development is that he gives more weight than previous investigators to human interaction and adult intentions. Macnamara's position is not a mere extension of Chomsky's, as Boyle implies. As Donaldson says, his paper 'stands Chomsky's argument about the language acquisition device upon its head'. Macnamara's thesis is more a support for a third position known as the 'cognition hypothesis'. This hypothesis states that non-verbal understanding precedes and to some extent determines the language acquired, and is, strangely in the light of Boyle's argument, very close to Piaget's account of the relationship between language and cognition. Other studies reported, for example, by Cromer (1974), which support the 'cognition hypothesis', have involved older children than those who were the subjects of Macnamara's work. None of these is referred to in Boyle's paper.

Boyle draws on Macnamara's work and Donaldson's discussion of it to point out that 'we cannot confidently make inferences from what children say to what they think'. This is part of Donaldson's argument that in some specific situations young children's capabilities are greater than they might appear to be in a standard Piagetian test, and that their performance in the latter is sometimes the result of their failure to understand adult intentions or reflects their different interpretations of the language used. There is considerable evidence to support this claim as I have argued in my chapter, but, as Donaldson herself suggests, education is concerned with disembedded thinking, where intentions are not as clear as they are in the everyday contexts of embedded thinking and where the language used is not always the language of everyday transactions. If 'we cannot confidently make inferences from what children say to what they think', how then can we know what they think and understand in these contexts of disembedded thought? Some diagnostic instruments that do not rely too heavily on language are necessary. At this point in time Piagetian tests are the best we have. Piaget's testing has been called 'clinical' because, as in the psychoanalytic analyst/ client dyad, it is meant to take a child's first verbal response as only a starting point from which to probe further until the experimenter is satisfied that he has appraised accurately the child's level of understanding. Nonetheless, a justified criticism of Piaget's earlier work is that the testing relied too heavily on children's verbal responses. His later work has used children's manipulations of materials as well as their verbal responses.

The third issue on which Boyle ignores experimental evidence is a central one to his case. He claims that Piaget's theory 'takes as its model the mature scientific mind, by which Piaget means the mathematical mind'. He goes on to ask, 'But what of history, geography, the study of literature?' It is not clear what Boyle means here. There are two possibilities. One is that the stages of thinking described by Piaget have no relevance to subjects like history, geography and literature. The other is that these disciplines are concerned with psychological processes not investigated by Piaget, such as the ability to feel compassion for characters in history and literature. If his claim is the first of these, it is unsupported by the experimental literature. Shayer (1979) has pointed out that there is sometimes a confusion between the 'meta-theory' which encodes the characteristics of thinking in terms of symbolic logic, and the behavioural descriptions of the stages, and that difficulties with the meta-theory have erroneously been thought to invalidate the behavioural descriptions. I have quoted sources in my chapter where evidence has been produced that children's abilities to deal with material in history and geography reflects stages analogous to the behavioural descriptions of Piaget and his associates. Applebee (1978) has found similar stages with respect to children's appreciation of literature.

The arts and the humanities should, of course, entail a concern for the development of capacities like compassion and aesthetic appreciation not just reason, but reason is still an essential aspect. Moral education provides a clear example. One cannot conceive of a person being morally educated who feels no compassion, but he must also be able to understand moral principles. Kohlberg has shown that his stages of moral understanding resemble Piaget's stages of thinking insofar as the Piagetian stages are necessary, though not sufficient, conditions to the corresponding stages in moral understanding.

We should not try to make out of Piagetian theory a Procrustean bed for which all our concerns in education are stretched to the point of distortion. But to dismiss it as being of no concern to education is to ignore a large body of experimental evidence relating to cognitive development, which is, if not the only concern of education, among its major ones.

REFERENCES

Anthony, W. S. (1977) Activity in the learning of Piagetian operational thinking. *British Journal of Educational Psychology,* **47**, 18-24.

Applebee, A. (1978) *The Child's Concept of Story: Ages Two to Seventeen.* Chicago: University of Chicago Press.

Bower, T. G. R. (1974) *Development in Infancy.* San Francisco: Freeman.

Cromer, R. F. (1974) The development of language and cognition: the cognition hypothesis. In Foss, B. (Ed.) *New Perspectives in Child Development.* Harmondsworth: Penguin.

Macnamara, J. (1972) Cognitive basis of language learning in infants. *Psychological Review,* **79**, 1-13.

Shayer, M. (1979) Has Piaget's construct of formal operational thinking any utility? *British Journal of Educational Psychology,* **49** (3), 265-276.

Chapter 18

Psychological and Epistemological Alternatives to Piagetian Developmental Psychology with Support from Empirical Studies in Science Education

JOSEPH D. NOVAK

INTRODUCTION

For more than half a century, Jean Piaget and his colleagues have been studying cognitive development in children. During most of this period, stimulus—response psychology was dominant in North America and Piaget's important work was a 'breath of fresh air' for those of us who saw little relevance between the lever-pressing of a rat or cat and the acquisition of an understanding of important ideas in science or mathematics. Piaget's work, with its careful analysis of how individual children performed on selected tasks, was also a blessed relief from the statistical barrage of education researchers in the 1960s and early 1970s who substituted complex analysis of scores on batteries of dubious tests to construct predictions for hypothetical population parameters. What I will try to show in this chapter is how new developments in psychology and epistemology, and research studies such as those conducted by our group at Cornell University, may contribute a new alternative to the evolutionary path of conceptual invention in educational studies so well advanced by Piaget's work. I will present emerging ideas on epistemology, especially those of my colleague D. Bob Gowin, and some of our empirical findings that point in favour of David Ausubel's (1963, 1968, 1978) theory for cognitive learning.

EPISTEMOLOGY AND GOWIN'S 'V'

Creative scientists are aware that concepts and theories guide both what they choose to observe and also the kinds of records and transformations of records that they make.

To observe the frequency of white-, pink-, or red-flowered sweetpeas and to construct ratios of these phenotypes resulting from planned cross-pollination made sense once Mendel had invented his concepts of hereditary factors, dominance, and independent assortment. It took Mendel's creative genius to *choose* to observe the ratios of different sweetpea progeny resulting from planned crossings. It also took creative genius to *ignore* some observations which Mendel undoubtedly made. Independent assortment of factors occurs only when each factor considered is on a separate chromosome, and it would have been extraordinarily good luck if the only seven factors Mendel happened to observe were all located on seven different chromosomes (sweetpeas only possess seven chromosomes) and dozens of other traits were probably noted by Mendel. So, we see that our concepts and theories not only guide what we observe, but also guide what we choose not to observe, in other words, observations we choose to ignore.

James Conant was one of the first to stress the importance of concepts in guiding the work of scientists. His 'case study' approach to science education for the nonspecialist also emphasized the changing nature of concepts over time; his ideas are presented in his concise book, *On Understanding Science* (1947). The most articulate spokesman for the way that concepts guide (or constrain) our observations was a protégé of Conant, Thomas Kuhn. In his book, *The Structure of Scientific Revolutions*, Kuhn emphasized the theme that we are both illuminated by and imprisoned by the *paradigms* we hold, and which guide our inquiry. Later critics of Kuhn pointed out that a more realistic picture of science does not place focus on the rigid adherence to a paradigm or its eventual 'overthrow' leading to a new revolution in thinking; scientists may hold or use competing paradigms for decades and all of these paradigms may undergo gradual modification. Toulmin (1972) precisely characterized the evolutionary character of concepts with gradual changes taking place over time and some new concepts emerging from a kind of hybridization of older concepts. Today, we observe, in the leading writers on the history and philosophy of science, a general concensus that occasional invention and gradual modification of concepts are central elements in the epistemology of science.

One of the constantly troublesome areas of science teaching is to conceptualize the nature and role of laboratory instruction in science classes. Struggling with this issue in seminars for college science-teachers, Professor D. Bob Gowin invented a simple heuristic device, the 'Epistemological V' (see Figure 18.1), to show the interplay of key elements in laboratory experience. On the right-hand side of the V, the methodological side, we have: (1) the events or objects under study; (2) the records made of events or objects; (3) transformations of records or events (including tabular, graphic, or statistical transformation); (4) knowledge claims that derive in part from the data and transformations; and (5) value claims which address the question 'so what?' On the left-hand side of the V, the conceptual—theoretical side, we have: (1) events or objects *selected* for analysis; (2) concepts (regularities in events or objects coded by some signs or symbols); (3) principles—two or more concepts that prescribe some regularity (e.g. force = mass x acceleration, or living things are made of cells); (4) conceptual systems (e.g. kinetics in physics or metabolism in biology); (5) theories (e.g. kinetic-molecular theory or theory of evolution); and (6) philosophies (e.g. a capricious universe *vs* an orderly, predictable universe). The right side and the left side of Gowin's V are not independent; in scientific research, there is a constant interplay between these two domains. The nature of the interplay is controlled in part by the 'key question(s)' we address, as well as by the elements on the two sides of the V. As I will note later, one of the most important problems in public understanding of science is at the 'top' of the left side of Gowin's V—most citizens really do not believe that nature is rationally predictable and hence horoscopes, and so forth, are more carefully studied than data on oil reserves or barometric and temperature isobars.

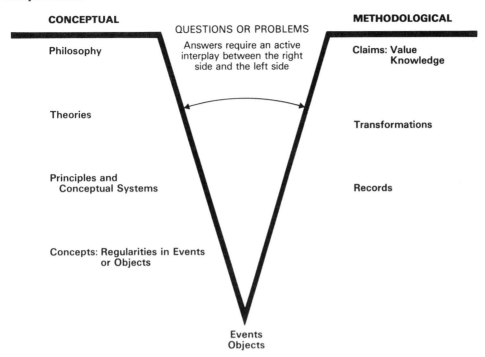

CONCEPTUAL — QUESTIONS OR PROBLEMS — **METHODOLOGICAL**

Philosophy

Answers require an active interplay between the right side and the left side

Claims: Value
Knowledge

Theories

Transformations

Principles and
Conceptual Systems

Records

Concepts: Regularities in Events
or Objects

Events
Objects

Figure 18.1 Gowin's (1978) Epistemological V. This device can be used as an heuristic for viewing the nature of science for the science of education.

Let us turn now to consider how Gowin's Epistemological V can be used to clarify our understanding of the role of theory in interpretation of human cognitive development. Figure 18.2 includes a representation of some key conceptual—theoretical ideas in Piaget's developmental theory and some records, transformations, and claims that derive from the observation of a selected set of events. The key question chosen here is one that relates to some of Piaget's classic studies (Inhelder and Piaget, 1958).

Piaget's contributions are prodigious in a manner analogous to Mendel, Darwin, or Newton, in that he *invented* concepts and a theory to explain observed differences in children's responses to carefully selected tasks. He also contributed to methods for recording data (the 'clinical interview') and for transforming data (construction of response categories). His commitment to a philosophy of rational inquiry as a basis for the study of cognitive development is evident in his book, *Psychology and Epistemology* (1972). In this book, Piaget points out that theories are constructed tentatively and that:

> Scientific epistemology can only be the result of a collective work over a long period opposing from the very outset possible diversities. Nothing in advance, for example, proves that the idealism of reality necessary to the mathematician is linked in a direct and simple manner to the basic realism of the biologist for whom any simplification of data runs the risk of distorting the essential traits. The notion of growth of knowledge at once implies many hypotheses and requires the collaboration of many researchers, whose very opposition of intellectual attitude cannot help but be fruitful. (P. 99)

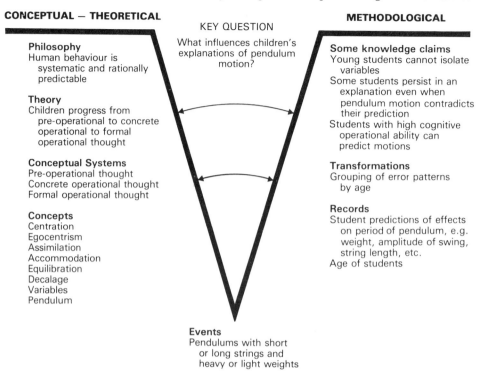

CONCEPTUAL — THEORETICAL

KEY QUESTION
What influences children's
explanations of pendulum
motion?

Philosophy
Human behaviour is
  systematic and rationally
  predictable

Theory
Children progress from
  pre-operational to concrete
  operational to formal
  operational thought

Conceptual Systems
Pre-operational thought
Concrete operational thought
Formal operational thought

Concepts
Centration
Egocentrism
Assimilation
Accommodation
Equilibration
Decalage
Variables
Pendulum

METHODOLOGICAL

Some knowledge claims
Young students cannot isolate
  variables
Some students persist in an
  explanation even when
  pendulum motion contradicts
  their prediction
Students with high cognitive
  operational ability can
  predict motions

Transformations
Grouping of error patterns
  by age

Records
Student predictions of effects
  on period of pendulum, e.g.
  weight, amplitude of swing,
  string length, etc.
Age of students

Events
Pendulums with short
  or long strings and
  heavy or light weights

Figure 18.2   Piaget's 'pendulum problem' described in the format of Gowin's Epistemological V. (Inhelder and Piaget, 1958)

It is this necessity for systematic application of an alternative theory that is the central thesis of this chapter. We believe Gowin's Epistemological V is a helpful schematic to illustrate theoretical and methodological alternatives.

One of the reasons why Piaget's work was largely ignored by American educators in the 1940s and 1950s was that 'objective' testing became the dominant mode of assessing cognitive performance. Furthermore, rapidly developing computer technology and statistical tools for data transformation led to the misguided belief that esoteric data-processing would somehow extract powerful, truthful knowledge claims from student performance that was not apparent in the raw data (i.e. the student answers to 'objective' test items). American educators became data-transformation enthusiasts, ignoring almost completely the conceptual-theoretical vacuum that accompanied their data-gathering and data-transformation preoccupation. By 1964, some disenchantment with data-processing began to set in and American educators 'rediscovered' Piaget's work (Ripple and Rockcastle, 1964). Too prone to climb aboard the latest bandwagon, many American educators in the late 1960s and 1970s have tried to explain every success and every failure in school learning as predictable from Piaget's theory. Neither the early eschewing nor the more recent uncritical acceptance of Piaget's concepts has done credit to the powerful theoretical model and data-gathering strategy (the clinical interview) that he has promulgated. We would hope that the publication of the present volume will be received as a more balanced and perhaps more useful view of the place of Piaget's work.

AN ALTERNATIVE VIEW OF COGNITIVE DEVELOPMENT

For the past fifteen years, the work of our research group has been guided by the cognitive learning theory of David Ausubel (1963, 1968, 1978). We embraced Ausubel's theory primarily because it afforded a framework to explain some of our earlier research that was not explained by our previous adherence to a cybernetic model* (see Novak, 1977a, ch. 8). Our earlier studies dealt mainly with questions of variation in the problem-solving abilities of students and hence were more easily related to early cybernetic *learning* models (cf. Ashby, 1960) than to the *developmental* psychology of Piaget. Contrary to the allegations of some of my colleagues, our research group was not then, nor are we now, opposed to Piaget's theory. We simply do not see great relevance of his theory to many of the key issues involved in success or failure of high-school and college students in meaningful learning and problem-solving. As our research programme turned increasingly to the central role that concepts play in problem-solving and to the nature of concept learning in specific areas of science, Ausubel's theory became more useful, and also led in part to some modifications of his theory (see Ausubel, Novak and Hanesian, 1978). From our perspective, the kind of questions studied by researchers adhering to a Piagetian research paradigm produced data that are better explained through Ausubel's cognitive learning theory (see Novak, 1978). Thus, what is intended here is to show that Ausubel's learning theory is more relevant and has more interpretative power for a variety of important science and mathematics education questions than Piaget's developmental psychology.

In order to study concept learning in young children, we embarked upon a programme to develop audio-tutorial science lessons for use by primary-grade children. Audio-tutorial (Postlethwait et al, 1964, 1972) instruction involves the use of tape-recorded audio guidance to students while they are manipulating and observing science materials. Figure 18.3 shows a first-grade child engaged in an audio-tutorial lesson on energy transformations. Some sixty lessons were developed to teach basic science concepts with lesson development guided by Ausubel's learning theory (Novak, 1972). To assess concept development, we tried various forms of student evaluation using paper-and-pencil picture tests. However, we found that these tests failed to reveal adequately the children's concept development as indicated by later interviews with children in which they were asked why they had marked test items as they did. We found that children were frequently responding to spurious cues on the paper-and-pencil tests, or arbitrarily marking answers. Further probing suggested that students usually knew more about the phenomenon under study than was indicated by their subsequent oral explanations of written test responses. We decided to abandon paper-and-pencil testing and use instead a modified form of Piagetian clinical interview (see Pines et al, 1978).

Although our recent strategies for data-gathering subsequent to audio-tutorial instruction have been similar to that developed by Piaget, we have proceeded in our research under a different theoretical framework, namely, our research has been guided by Ausubel's cognitive learning theory. Our research, therefore, rests upon a different epistemological foundation, and results in significantly different claims.

---

*Cybernetic learning models have had an extraordinary rebirth and popularity in recent years in North America as most psychologists abandon behaviourist models of learning and turn to new variations of computer 'information-processing' models such as those of Newell and Simon (1972) and Lindsey and Norman (1977).

Figure 18.4 shows the epistemological structure of our work as viewed by Gowin's V. Although some of our research and some studies undertaken by Piaget and his co-workers observe similar events, i.e. students performing on interview tasks, we have designed different kinds of tasks and have used different kinds of data transformations.

Figure 18.3 A second-grade child working with apparatus demonstrating energy transformations in an audio-tutorial science lesson.

At the 1979 meetings of the National Association for Research in Science Teaching, the programme theme stressed the importance of paradigms to guide research in science teaching. In the paper that I presented there (Novak, in press), I tried to illustrate how the nature of the paradigms we select guides our inquiry and also restricts the nature of the observations and interpretations we can legitimately make. Our paradigms are what Kuhn (1962) has called our 'conceptual goggles'. They are both the windows and the blinkers through which we see events and objects in the world. If we are guided strictly by a Piagetian paradigm, it is unlikely that we would instruct eight-year-old children in earth, space and gravity concepts and that we would seek their answers to tasks that demand what Piaget would describe as formal operational thought. And yet, the tasks presented to children that lead to the characterization of their earth concepts as sophisticated scientific models (see below) require precisely the hypothetical-deductive, propositional thinking Piaget (Inhelder and Piaget, 1958) described as characterizing formal operational thought.

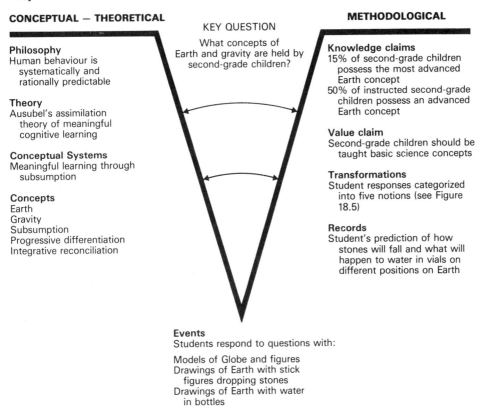

CONCEPTUAL — THEORETICAL

Philosophy
Human behaviour is
systematically and
rationally predictable

Theory
Ausubel's assimilation
theory of meaningful
cognitive learning

Conceptual Systems
Meaningful learning through
subsumption

Concepts
Earth
Gravity
Subsumption
Progressive differentiation
Integrative reconciliation

KEY QUESTION
What concepts of
Earth and gravity are held by
second-grade children?

METHODOLOGICAL

Knowledge claims
15% of second-grade children
possess the most advanced
Earth concept
50% of instructed second-grade
children possess an advanced
Earth concept

Value claim
Second-grade children should be
taught basic science concepts

Transformations
Student responses categorized
into five notions (see Figure
18.5)

Records
Student's prediction of how
stones will fall and what will
happen to water in vials on
different positions on Earth

Events
Students respond to questions with:

Models of Globe and figures
Drawings of Earth with stick
figures dropping stones
Drawings of Earth with water
in bottles

Figure 18.4 Sample research study from our audio-tutorial science programme as viewed on Gowin's V, based on research of Nussbaum (1971).

EMPIRICAL STUDIES OF CONCEPT DEVELOPMENT

Working in the context of our audio-tutorial elementary science project, Nussbaum designed five lessons to present concepts of earth and gravity to second-grade (approximately age eight) children. Nussbaum devised a series of interview tasks that involved the use of model figures on a globe and drawings of bottles (with water) and stick figures on a circle. He found important qualitative differences in the 'earth notions' held by the children and characterized five different levels of conceptualization as shown in Figure 18.5. Although instructed, students tended to demonstrate more sophisticated earth notions than non-instructed students. The most important findings reported in Nussbaum's work (Nussbaum and Novak, 1976) are the great qualitative differences in earth notions held by these eight-year-old subjects.

A recent replication study of Nussbaum's work by Mali and Howe (1979) serves both to confirm the general classification scheme developed by Nussbaum (see Figure 18.5) and to relate these results to performance on Piagetian tasks. However, Mali and Howe found that the performance of *twelve*-year-old Nepali youth closely approximated that of *eight*-year-old American youth. In other words, without the benefit of science-oriented home and school experience (perhaps, especially television), the kind of

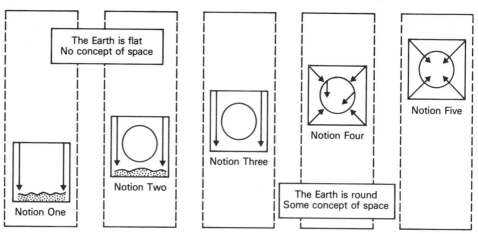

Figure 18.5 A schematic mapping of children's notions of an earth concept. The arrows point in the direction that is believed by the child to be 'downward'.

thinking required to demonstrate notion four- or five-level earth concepts does not appear until some four years later. Figure 18.6 shows a comparison of student performance by American and Nepali children.

The evidence found by Mali and Howe is pertinent in several respects. First, the subjects were selected from two different regions of Nepal. The Katmandu Valley subjects were from a more urban setting, including the capital city of Katmandu, with

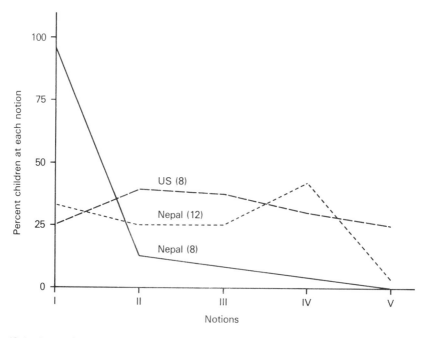

Figure 18.6 Comparison of eight- and twelve-year-old Nepali children's earth concepts with those for eight-year-old US students. (Mali and Howe, 1979)

considerable industrial development. The Pokhara Valley subjects were from a more rural region that has primarily an agrarian economy. Television and other modern Western sources of information were not available in either region. The more industrial and mercantile economy of the Katmandu region undoubtedly did contribute to a generally greater contact of students with scientific and technological developments as compared with the children in the Pokhara Valley region. This is reflected in the somewhat more advanced earth notions held by Katmandu children as indicated in Table 18.1, especially by twelve-year-old children. The 'depressed' development of earth concepts by Nepali as compared with American children is consistent with

Table 18.1 *Response frequencies for each notion by age and region (from: Development of earth and gravity notions[a] among Nepali children; Mali and Howe, 1979)*

Age	Region	n	Notions				
			I	II	III	IV	V
8	Katmandu	41	36	2	1	1	0
	Pokhara	44	39	4	0	1	0
10	Katmandu	52	18	18	9	6	1
	Pokhara	47	23	12	10	2	0
12	Katmandu	36	6	7	5	15	2
	Pokhara	34	13	6	5	8	2

[a]See Figure 18.5 for the illustrations of these notions.

Vygotsky's (1962) view that 'scientific' concepts are subject to environmental influence. This would also account for the differential effect on older Katmandu children as compared with Pokhara children (Table 18.2). These data point in favour of a theoretical framework that has as its central concepts the role of experience in influencing *progressive differentiation* and *integrative reconciliation* of relevant concepts and the consequence for differential performance on tasks of the sort utilized in the 'earth notions' assessment. Progressive differentiation and integrative reconciliation are key concepts in Ausubel's learning theory and are discussed elsewhere (Novak, 1978; Ausubel et al, 1978).

Table 18.2 *Correlation coefficients (Spearman) for Piagetian tasks and selected variables at three ages (Mali and Howe, 1980)*

	Cons.	Ser.	Class	Earth
Age 8				
Grade	0.09	0.14	0.32[a]	0.42[a]
Years Schooling	0.03	0.00	0.21	0.23
Age 10				
Grade	0.19	0.05	0.17	0.34[a]
Years Schooling	0.12	−0.14	0.04	0.29[a]
Age 12				
Grade	0.12	0.10	0.19	0.37[a]
Years Schooling	0.04	−0.05	0.07	0.27[a]

[a]$p \leq 0.01$

Second, Mali and Howe also administered a group of Piagetian tasks and found some significant variations among Katmandu and Pokhara youth. These data are shown in Figure 18.7. Most of the differences are not statistically significant, but Mali and Howe report (1980) significant differences ($p < 0.01$) favouring eight-year-old Pokhara children on conservation of area tasks and favouring ten- and twelve-year-old Katmandu children on a classification task. The data are shown in Table 18.3. Mali and Howe (1980) account for these results in the more common trade and barter experience in homes of the Pokhara children as compared with Katmandu children, whereas the latter have generally better schools that use lessons involving classification-type activities. For both Nepali groups, the Piagetian tasks performance was below

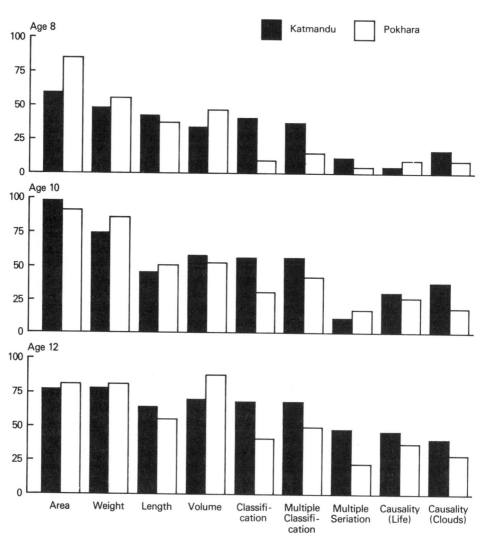

Figure 18.7 Percentage of Katmandu and Pokhara children performing successfully on nine Piagetian tasks. (Mali and Howe, 1980)

Table 18.3 *Chi-square by region and stage for children achieving and not achieving the highest stages at ages 8, 10 and 12 (Mali and Howe, 1980)*

Tasks	Age 8	Age 10	Age 12
Conservation of Length	0.12	0.25	1.37
Conservation of Volume	0.44	0.20	3.05 (0.10) (P)
Conservation of Area	8.78 (0.01) (P)	1.52	0.34
Conservation of Weight	0.76	2.02	0.00
Classification	3.67 (0.10) (K)	7.05 (0.01) (K)	9.12 (0.01) (K)
Multiple Classification	6.36 (0.02) (K)	3.17 (0.06) (K)	3.09 (0.06) (K)
Multiple Seriation	1.26	0.04	5.53 (0.02) (K)
Causality (Life)	1.74	0.02	0.73
Causality (Movement of Clouds)	0.70	3.70 (0.06) (K)	1.25

Note: (K) = Katmandu children achieving higher   *p* in parentheses
    (P) = Pokhara children achieving higher
    df = 1

that characteristic of Western students on most tasks and probably reflects a general influence of culture on cognitive development of the sort measured by either Piagetian or earth notion tasks. The comparative data are shown in Table 18.4.

Third, Mali and Howe (1979) investigated the effects of schooling and age on task performance. The data are shown in Table 18.2. Except for eight-year-old children, there are no significant ($p < 0.01$) correlations between grade or years of schooling and performance on Piagetian tasks, whereas both of these variables correlate significantly with performance on earth notion tasks. Since many Nepali youth may repeat some grades one or more times, the significant correlation coefficients for grade, but not years of schooling, for eight-year-old students probably reflects the important contribution of successful school learning for classification and earth notion tasks as noted earlier. These data also point in favour of a theory that focuses on specific concept differentiation rather than one which stresses predominantly sequential development of stages of cognitive operations. Ausubel (1968, 1978) stresses in the epigraph to his book and throughout his theory that the most important factor influencing learning is the adequacy of specifically relevant concepts held by the learner.

Table 18.4 *Comparison of Nepalese and European children on age of attainment of tasks (Mali and Howe, 1979)*

Tasks	Age range for European children for attaining Stage 3	Percentage of Nepalese children at Stage 3 at the upper limit of the age range
Conservation of Length	7—9	62
Conservation of Weight	9—10	83
Conservation of Area	7—8	72
Conservation of Volume	10—12	80
Classification	7—8	21
Multiple Classification	7—8	26
Causality (Life)	9—10	32
Causality (Clouds)	11—12	42
Multiple Seriation	7—8	5

Table 18.5 *Outline of demonstrations and questions used in Interview 1*

Demonstration	Questions	Task No.
Place ice-cube in cup.	What do you think will happen to this ice if we leave it here for a while?	
Present covered jar containing 1/4 of an onion.	What's in this jar? Anything else? Is there any air in it? How do you know there is [isn't] air in it?	
Remove top from jar.	Can you smell the onion? How come you can smell the onion even though it's down at the bottom of the jar and your nose is up here? Where does the smell come from? What is the smell made of? Can you see the smell? Why [Why not]?	(1)
Present covered jar containing onion and filled with water.	What's in this jar? Could you smell this onion if I took the top off the jar? Would the smell be as strong as it was in the other jar?	
Remove top from jar.	Can you smell the onion? Why can't you smell the onion in this jar like the one in other jar?	(2)
Present a small piece of sugar and a cup of water.	Do you know what this is? What? Could it be broken into smaller pieces? How small? Could it be broken into molecules? What are molecules? Where are they found? Can you see them? Why not? What things are made of just molecules or molecules and something else?	(6)
Have child put sugar in water and stir.	What would happen to the sugar if you put it in the water and stirred it up? Try it. What's happening? How does that work? If I stirred this up very well could I make it so that we couldn't see the sugar anymore? Where would the sugar be? (Where is the sugar now?) Why can't we see it?	(3)
Present 3 bottles filled with plaster, water, and air.	What is in these bottles? How do you know that there's air in this one? Are all of the bottles full?	(4)
Present bag of marbles.	Could these marbles fit in any of the bottles? Which one(s)? Why won't they go in the plaster? What makes the plaster so hard? Why will [won't] they go in the water? Why will they go in air so easily? Are there molecules in any of these bottles? Which? How do you know? Which one has the most molecules, or do they all have about the same amount?	(7)
Present crayon and worksheet.	Would you draw a picture to show what the molecules would be like if we could see them? Be sure to show any differences that you think there are in the molecules of the solid, the water, and the air.	(5)
Present cup containing partially melted ice-cube.	What's been happening to this ice? What makes it do that? Are water and ice made of the same stuff? What's different about them? Are there molecules in water? In ice? Do you think the molecules would be the same in ice and in water? How would they be different? Would anything happen to the molecules in ice when it melts into water? What? Would anything happen to the molecules in water when it freezes into ice? What?	(8)

In conjunction with our continuing programme of studies on science concept learning in combination with audio-tutorial science lessons, Whitman (1975) administered interviews dealing with several tasks involving content related to our science lessons and five Piagetian (Piaget, Inhelder and Szeminska, 1960; Piaget and Inhelder, 1962) tasks dealing with conservation (1 = continuous substance; 2 = discontinuous substance; 3 = length; 4 = area; 5 = volume). The structure of the interview on the science tasks is shown in Table 18.5, with eight problem tasks noted. The interviews were administered to second-grade children. Whitman devised a rating scale for the science tasks (shown in Table 18.6) and for the Piagetian tasks (shown in Table 18.7). Transcripts for each child's interview were analysed and ratings were assigned as noted in the tables. A summary of ratings on each science task and each Piagetian task is shown in Table 18.8.

Table 18.6 *Categories used in rating responses on Tasks 1—4 and Tasks 6—8 of Interview 1*

Category	Description
Tasks 1—4	
0	*No response*—failure to respond or to state that no explanation can be given.
1	*Precausal*—information given in response is not causally related to the phenomenon in question.
2	*Observational description*—response refers to observable objects and processes only.
3	*Experience-based description*—response is directly based on previous experiences.
4	*Ineffective use of an abstract concept term*—response contains abstract terms but gives no indication that their meaning is understood.
5	*Effective use of a mechanism (non-abstract model)*—response explains the phenomenon by reference to unobservable processes but uses no abstract terms or concepts.
6	*Effective use of a semi-abstract model*—response explains the phenomenon through use of abstract terms but underlying concept has dominant concrete components.
7	*Effective use of an abstract model*—response explains the phenomenon in abstract terms; underlying concept is not distinctly concrete based.
Tasks 6—8	
1	*No response*—statement is made that no explanation can be offered; or explanation ignores references to molecules in question.
2	*Superficial response*—response acknowledges mention of molecules but is superficial, with no understanding evident.
3	*Concrete response*—response deals with molecules in a concrete or restricted manner.
4	*Effective use of concept*—response shows use of an effective molecule concept having distinct concrete features.
5	*Abstract concept*—response shows use of a basically abstract molecule concept.

Correlation coefficients were computed for each science task and each Piagetian task. Table 18.9 shows the correlation coefficient matrix for students in the study. We see that ratings on the science tasks were significantly correlated for all but two cases (tasks 3/2 and 3/4). Similarly, there were significant correlations for all but one comparison of Piagetian ratings (conservation of volume *vs* conservation of area, $r = 0.27$). However, we see that only two out of 35 correlation coefficients between science ratings and Piagetian ratings are significantly correlated, and the coefficients are low. It is evident that the science tasks are influenced by variables that share common variance (up to 68 per cent in some cases) and that Piagetian tasks also show a certain degree of internal consistency. However, the science tasks did not account for the same sources of variance in cognitive variables as did the Piagetian tasks (only 10 per cent shared variance at best).

The data in Table 18.9 show several important pieces of evidence. First, we see that correlation coefficients (calculated for repeated measures, since the same subjects were given all tests) between science tasks are all positive and generally significant, and the same is true for correlation coefficients between Piagetian tasks. Thus, the data indicate that a certain level of reliability in task assessment must be present, and this is

Table 18.7 *Categories used in rating responses on Interview 2 Piagetian tasks (Whitman, 1975)*

Rating Category	Description
0	Absolute nonconservation and guesses.
1	Uncertain nonconservation—change from initial conservation response to a non-conservation response; change from one incorrect assessment to another.
2	Vascillating conservation—change from a nonconservation response to a conservation one.
3	Conservation with no explanation, with totally inadequate explanation, or with expressed uncertainty.
4	Definite conservation—conservation response with adequate explanation.

Table 18.8 *Percentage of second-grade children obtaining each rating on science tasks and five Piagetian tasks (n = 65)*

Rating/Task No.	Science Tasks							Piagetian Tasks				
	1	2	3	4	6	7	8	1	2	3	4	5
0	3	0	0	0	—	—	—	10	15	29	41	60
1	7	1	3	3	24	24	34	6	3	7	9	7
2	31	19	15	1	15	19	29	4	3	9	9	1
3	20	43	22	79	35	26	16	7	7	10	6	21
4	6	0	7	0	19	19	13	72	72	44	35	10
5	13	28	43	12	7	12	7	—	—	—	—	—
6	4	4	6	0	—	—	—	—	—	—	—	—
7	15	4	4	4	—	—	—	—	—	—	—	—

in line with most cognitive researchers' views that Piagetian-like clinical interviews, when properly administered, do provide a reliable assessment of cognitive performance. Second, the relatively high correlations between similar science tasks ($r = 0.84$ between probes regarding 'molecules' in tasks numbers 6 and 7) and between certain Piagetian tasks ($r = 0.85$ between tasks 1 and 2 dealing with continuous and discontinuous substance), signals that we are probing areas of cognitive structure that show relatively parallel development. In contrast, science tasks 3 and 4 (dissolving and structure of solids, respectively) show a nonsignificant correlation ($r = 0.16$) and Piagetian tasks 4 and 5 (area estimation and volume estimation, respectively) show low correlation ($r = 0.27$). In the latter case, the low correlation was most likely due to poor performance with only 34 per cent and 10 per cent of the subjects showing conservation on area and volume tasks, respectively. Thus, we see that the conceptual framework 'tapped' by a given task is likely to show parallel development when concepts necessary for task solution are closely relevant, but less likely to show parallel development when substantially different areas of cognitive structure are 'tapped'.

Table 18.9 *Correlation coefficient matrix for science tasks and Piagetian tasks (computed from Whitman, 1975)*

		Science Tasks							Piagetian Tasks				
		1	2	3	4	6	7	8	1	2	3	4	5
Science Tasks	1												
	2	0.57[a]											
	3	0.46[a]	0.21										
	4	0.39[a]	0.33[a]	0.16									
	6	0.6[a]	0.54[a]	0.33[a]	0.45[a]								
	7	0.54[a]	0.55[a]	0.34[a]	0.40[a]	0.84[a]							
	8	0.45[a]	0.48[a]	0.32[a]	0.51[a]	0.81[a]	0.69[a]						
Piagetian Tasks	1	0.13	0.25	0.12	0.17	0.20	0.16	0.25					
	2	0.11	0.31[a]	0.09	0.21	0.33[a]	0.3	0.29	0.85[a]				
	3	−0.19	0.03	−0.02	0.06	0.04	−0.02	0.11	0.46[a]	0.46[a]			
	4	0.05	0.03	0.02	0.24	0.16	0.06	0.21	0.45[a]	0.42[a]	0.53[a]		
	5	0.02	0.17	0.02	−0.04	0.23	0.12	0.21	0.31[a]	0.37[a]	0.42[a]	0.27	

[a] 0.30 is significant at the one per cent level; n = 65

These data support conclusions presented in an earlier paper (Novak, 1978) in which it was proposed that Ausubel's (1978) idea that *progressive differentiation* of specifically relevant concepts is a more significant aspect of performance on cognitive development assessments than general stages of cognitive operations as advanced by Piaget and his colleagues.

In 1971 we commenced a long-term study of concept development with an initial sample of 191 children. These children were provided with audio-tutorial science instruction in grades one and two. After a sequence of six to ten lessons were completed, clinical interviews were administered to each student; tasks and questions that were appropriate to the subject matter of the preceding set of lessons were used. By grade three, children in the study had received some thirty audio-tutorial lessons and up to five clinical interviews that were tape-recorded. The audio-tutorial lessons were set up in classrooms with a new lesson presented after one or two weeks. Almost all children experienced each lesson at least once, with some children repeating a lesson two to three times. Although there was a relatively long duration of science lesson exposure, the total minutes of audio-tutorial instructional time for any one child in grades one and two was seldom more than 600 minutes. In spite of this relatively limited exposure to audio-tutorial lessons, Hibbard (1971), Friedman (1977) and Rowell (1978) showed significant gains in achievement when audio-tutorial instructed students were compared wtih students in comparable classes not receiving these lessons.

Very little formal science is taught in grades one and two in Ithaca, New York, or in any other American schools. However, both instructed and non-instructed subjects showed wide variability in their knowledge of basic science concepts, with some ten to twenty-five per cent of the groups studied showing relatively sophisticated, adult-like concepts, such as earth notion five in Nussbaum's study. Clearly, students are acquiring much knowledge about their natural environment in their homes, or through other contacts. Television viewing may be a significant contributing source of science concept learning. Our hypothesis has been that if Ausubelian theory is valid, students who demonstrate significantly better concepts in early grades (whatever the source of their knowledge) should also demonstrate superior knowledge in later years. As we continue our follow-up studies on children instructed during 1971—1973, our data are supportive of this view.

A sample of eighteen students given audio-tutorial science lessons in grades one and two were re-interviewed in the fall semester of grade eight, some six to seven years after instruction and after a one-semester descriptive course in biology in grade seven. The interview dealt with the concept, 'Particulate nature of matter'. The five notions examined regarding this concept are shown in Table 18.10. Also shown are the misconceptions observed and the observed performance for each subject on each of the five notions.

Pooling data for all five notions, it was observed that in 64.2 per cent of the cases, subjects either retained correct notions or improved their concepts; in 27.6 per cent of the cases, subjects retained misconceptions or failed to demonstrate knowledge of the notions; and in only 7.7 per cent of the cases, subjects lost ground or remained poor. These data are summarized in Table 18.11.

There is considerable information packed into Table 18.10 in terms of what the data mean for understanding the cognitive development of these eighteen subjects. For each of the five scientific notions tested (A through E), we note that the most common tendency is for misconceptions to become 'corrected' (see Table 18.11). For example, in Table 18.10, subject number one, notion A, moved from the misconception that molecules are little pieces of air to a more generic view that molecules are small, nonvisible units of matter. We see in this case some *progressive differentiation* of cognitive structure that Ausubel et al (1978, p. 127) indicate results in 'refinement of meanings and enhanced potential for providing anchorage for further meaningful learning'. Instead of the restricted concept that molecules are parts of air, the molecule concept has differentiated to include the idea that the basic structure of any substance is composed of tiny units called molecules. However, subject number one still retains some misconception (notion B), in that the smell of an onion is seen as a small chunk of

Table 18.10 *Performance of 18 children on five basic science notions in interviews administered in grades two and eight*

Subject	Notion A Grade 2	8	Notion B Grade 2	8	Notion C Grade 2	8	Notion D Grade 2	8	Notion E Grade 2	8
1	M^1	E	E	M^4	M^7	E	O	E	O	E
2	E	E	M^4	E	M^8	E	O	E	M^8	E
3	M^2	M^2	E	M^4	E	M^8	E	E	M^{12}	E
4	E	M^2	E	O	M^8	E	E	M^{10}	E	E
5	M^a	E	M^4	E	M^8	M^8	M^8	M^{10}	M^8	M^{11}
6	M^3	E	M^4	E	$M^{7,8}$	E	M^8	E	M^7	M^{12}
7	$M^{1,2}$	E	O	M^4	M^8	E	O	E	M^{13}	M^{13}
8	E	E	E	E	M^7	E	O	O	M^{13}	E
9	$M^{2,3}$	M^3	O	M^4	M^7	E	M^7	O	M^7	M^{13}
10	E	E	$M^{4,5}$	E	M^7	E	O	E	M^{13}	E
11	E	E	E	E	M^8	E	E	E	E	M^{11}
12	M^1	E	M^a	O	M^7	E	O	E	M^{13}	M^{12}
13	E	E	M^4	E	E	E	E	E	M^{13}	E
14	M^1	M^3	M^5	M^4	M^7	E	$M^{7,10}$	M^{10}	M^{13}	M^{12}
15	E	E	$M^{4,5}$	M^4	M^7	E	M^7	O	M^{13}	E
16	M^a	M^2	O	$M^{4,6}$	M^a	E	O	E	M^{13}	E
17	E	E	O	O	M^9	E	O	O	E	E
18	O	E	$M^{5,6}$	E	E	E	M^{10}	O	M^{12}	E

KEY
E = Evidence of correct knowledge of notion.
M = Misconception.
O = No evidence.

NOTIONS
A = Molecules are nonvisible units (particles, structures).
B = A smell is made up of molecules.
C = Everything is made of molecules.
D = Different things are made of different kinds of molecules.
E = In a solid, molecules are bonded together more than in a liquid.
   (In liquid, more than in a gas.) Per unit volume, more molecules in solid than a gas.

MISCONCEPTIONS (and/or incomplete conceptions)
M^a = Fragmentary evidence. Rater must make inferences.
M^1 = Molecules are little pieces of air.
M^2 = Molecules can be seen with microscope or eye.
M^3 = Molecules are small cells, dust, germs, strings, rectangles, squares, etc.
M^4 = Smell is made up of onion parts such as cells, chemicals, germs, chunks.
M^5 = Smell is made of air.
M^6 = Smell is carried by air.
M^7 = Everything is not made of molecules (some things have no molecules).
M^8 = Things are made of molecules and 'other stuff'.
M^9 = Molecules are on things.
M^{10} = Everything has the same kind of molecules in it.
M^{11} = Molecules in liquid are more loosely packed than in air or solids.
M^{12} = Molecules are packed the same in everything.
M^{13} = Air has more molecules than solids or liquids.

onion rather than a component atomic-molecular element. Subject number two had a similar misconception in grade two, but *integratively reconciled* the concept of particulate nature of smells with the concept of the specificity of molecules distinctive for each substance by grade eight (as evidenced in changes in performance for notions B, C, D, and E). It is reasonable to suggest that in every case shown in Table 18.11, we see a manifestation from grade two to grade eight of either (1) acquisition of a new relevant concept, (2) progressive differentiations (elaborations) of an existing concept *or* misconception, and/or (3) integrative reconciliation of new and existing concepts leading to progressive differentiation of a concept, 'correction' of a misconception, or both.

Table 18.11 *Summary of changes in understanding of five basic science notions from grade two to grade eight*

Kind of Change	Grade 2	Grade 8	Number of Cases[a]	%
No Change	E	E	16	17.7
	O	O	3	3.3
	M	M	15	16.6
Worse	E	O	1	1.1
	E	M	6	6.6
Improvements	M	E	34	37.7
	O	E	8	8.8
Other	O	M	3	3.3
	M	O	4	4.4

[a]There are 90 possible cases since there are 18 subjects and five notions per subject being considered.
KEY
E = Evidence for correct knowledge of notion.
M = Misconception.
O = No evidence.

The data are generally supportive of Ausubel's contention that concepts which are meaningfully learned are retained for impressive periods of time. His idea of *progressive differentiation* of concepts was supported, in that explanations of the five notions offered by eighth-grade subjects were generally more precise, more elaborate, and stated with perhaps greater confidence. Although we have found that audio-tutorial science can also result in progressive differentiation of *misconceptions* (Pines, 1977), we have also observed that misconceptions can become corrected when new relevant concepts are acquired and new *integrative reconciliations* between concepts result. This process of integrative reconciliation probably accounts for the fact that some 38 per cent of misconceptions observed in grade two were replaced by correct notions by grade eight.

The data shown above are significant in several important ways. First, they show that nonspontaneous science concepts can be acquired by some 20 per cent of young children (age 7 to $8\frac{1}{2}$ years), confirming earlier research by Hibbard (1971), Friedman (1977), and Rowell (1978). Second, they show that even when misconceptions are acquired in early years (some 58 per cent of cases), these are generally 'reconciled' with elapsed time for the majority of the subjects. The latter is very important to curriculum planning, since these data suggest that there is relatively little danger in introducing basic science concepts in early grades—concepts that may develop 'misconceptions' at first—since the long-term effect may still provide a positive contribution to cognitive growth when later integrative reconciliation of concepts occurs. Third, they show that general cognitive development, as suggested by performance on Piagetian tasks, is only weakly correlated at best with cognitive development as measured by tasks relevant to specific science concept learning.

CONCLUSIONS

When viewed all together, we interpret our own research and the research of others to support the following conclusions:

(1) Wide cultural variation in concept development, and performance on interviews to assess attainment of these concepts, can be expected when there are significant differences in educational opportunity for development of these concepts.
(2) Piagetian tasks, being somewhat less culture dependent than tasks requiring knowledge of scientific concepts, are less prone to variation due to cultural differences, but are still influenced by educational experience.
(3) Correlations between performance on tasks that are highly culturally dependent (tasks measuring attainment of scientific concepts) will be greater than correlations between such tasks and Piagetian tasks.
(4) A theoretical model for cognitive learning that places emphasis upon the role of specifically relevant concepts and specifically relevant learning experiences as the major sources of variation in concept development is favoured over a theoretical model that places major emphasis upon stages of development of cognitive operations.
(5) The curriculum implications, while they do not mean that any child can learn any subject matter at any stage of development (Bruner, 1960, p. 33), point in favour of the potential for substantive influence on cognitive development through carefully devised, *meaningful* learning experiences (Ausubel, 1968, 1978).
(6) An epistemological model as suggested by Gowin (1978) can be useful in advancing our understanding of the role of theory and concepts in guiding selection of educational events to be observed, data recorded, data transformation, and useful knowledge claims.

Far more research and interpretation is needed, of course, before the six 'claims' cited above can be promulgated with unmitigated confidence. As is usually the case in any scientific enterprise, further research is likely both to modify and to extend the list of claims cited at this time, and to lead to further evolution of the theory and concepts that guide our inquiry.

REFERENCES

Ashby, William R. (1960) *Design for a Brain.* 2nd Edition. New York: Wiley.
Ausubel, D. P. (1963) *The Psychology of Meaningful Verbal Learning.* New York: Grune and Stratton.
Ausubel, D. P. (1968) *Educational Psychology: A Cognitive View.* New York: Holt, Rinehart and Winston.
Ausubel, D. P., Novak, J. D., Hanesian, H. (1978) *Educational Psychology: A Cognitive View.* 2nd Edition. New York: Holt, Rinehart and Winston.
Bruner, J. (1960) *The Process of Education.* New York: Vintage.
Conant, J. B. (1947) *On Understanding Science.* New Haven: Yale University Press.
Friedman, G. S. (1977) *Meaningful learning and the development of causal thought.* Ph.D. thesis, Cornell University.

Gowin, D. B. (1978) *The Domain of Education.* Unpublished manuscript, Cornell University.

Hibbard, K. M. (1971) *An approach to the development of instruction in science at the first-grade level: The concept of a particulate model for matter.* Ph.D. thesis, Cornell University.

Inhelder, B. and Piaget, J. (1958) *The Growth of Logical Thinking from Childhood to Adolescence.* New York: Basic Books.

Kuhn, T. S. (1962) *The Structure of Scientific Revolutions. International Encyclopedia of Unified Science.* 2nd Edition, enlarged Volumes 1 and 2. Foundations of the Unity of Science, Vol. 2, No. 2. Chicago: University of Chicago Press.

Lindsay, P. H. and Norman, D. A. (1977) *Human Information-Processing: An Introduction to Psychology.* New York: Academic Press.

Mali, B. and Howe, A. (1979) Development of earth and gravity concept among Nepali children. *Science Education,* **63** (5), 685-691.

Mali, G. B. and Howe, A. (1980). A study on cognitive development of Nepalese children. *Science Education,* **64** (2), 213-221.

Newell, A. and Simon, H. A. (1972) *Human Problem-Solving.* Englewood Cliffs, N.J.: Prentice Hall.

Novak, J. D. (1972) The use of audio-tutorial methods in elementary school instruction. In Postlethwait, S. N., Novak, J. D. and Murray, H. *The Audio-Tutorial Approach to Learning.* Minneapolis: Burgess.

Novak, J. D. (1977a) *A Theory of Education.* Ithaca: Cornell University Press.

Novak, J. D. (1978) An alternative to Piagetian psychology for science and mathematics education. *Studies in Science Education,* **5,** 1-30.

Novak, J. D. (1979) The reception learning paradigm. *Journal of Research in Science Teaching,* **16** (6), 481-488.

Nussbaum, J. (1971) An approach to teaching and assessment: The earth concept at the second-grade level. Unpublished Ph.D. thesis, Cornell University.

Nussbaum, J. and Novak, J. D. (1976) An assessment of children's concepts of earth utilizing structured interviews. *Science Education,* **60** (4).

Piaget, J. (1972) *Psychology and Epistemology.* New York: Viking.

Piaget, J. and Inhelder, B. (1962) *Le Developpement des Quantités Physiques Chez l'Enfant.* Neuchatel (Suisse): Delachaux et Niestle.

Piaget, J., Inhelder, B. and Szeminska, A. (1960) *The Child's Conception of Geometry.* New York: Basic Books.

Pines, A. L. (1977) *Scientific concept learning in children: The effect of prior knowledge on resulting cognitive structure subsequent to A-T instruction.* Ph.D. thesis, Cornell University.

Pines, A. L., Novak, J. D., Posner, G. J. and VanKirk, J. (1978) *The Clinical Interview: A Method for Evaluating Cognitive Structure.* Research Report, Cornell University.

Postlethwait, S. N., Novak, J. and Murray, H. T. Jr. (1st Edition 1972) *The Audio-Tutorial Approach to Learning.* 3rd Edition. Minneapolis: Burgess.

Ripple, R. E. and Rockcastle, V. N. (Eds.) (1964) *Piaget Rediscovered.* Report of a conference. Ithaca, New York.

Rowell, R. M. (1978) *Concept mapping: Evaluation of children's science concepts following audio-tutorial instruction.* Ph.D. thesis, Cornell University.

Toulmin, S. (1972) *Human Understanding, Vol. 1: The Collective Use and Evolution of Concepts.* Princeton: Princeton University Press.

Vygotsky, L. S. (1962) *Thought and Language* (Trans. and Ed.) Hanfmann, E. and Vakar, G. Cambridge: MIT Press.

Whitman, J. C. (1975) *An approach to the evaluation of selected spontaneous and scientific concepts and misconceptions of second-grade children.* M.S. thesis, Cornell University.

Chapter 19

Piaget and Science Education: A Stage of Decision*

ROSALIND DRIVER

INTRODUCTION

This chapter attempts to review the main areas where Piaget's work has made a significant contribution to science education in order to indicate problem issues and outline fruitful areas for future development.

Few people in the field of science education would dispute the influence that the work of Jean Piaget and his collaborators has had on the curriculum and teaching in primary and more recently secondary school science. In the curriculum development period of the 1950s and 1960s, science educators were looking for a useful framework to use in developing science materials: a framework which would give some guidance from a psychological point of view on fundamental issues such as what to teach, when to teach it and how. Many saw in Piaget's writings a coherent basis on which to build.

As a result, his work has been used explicitly as a basis and rationale for several science programmes: The Science Curriculum Improvement Study (SCIS) in America, Science 5/13 in England and the Australian Science Education Project (ASEP); and undoubtedly it has influenced many others.

Of course, Piaget is not an educator. It is not until recently that he himself has written about the application of his work to education (Piaget, 1970a). Nor does he consider himself primarily a psychologist. His major underlying concern, one which his early works demonstrate and to which he has recently returned, is that of genetic epistemology. It should not be surprising, however, that science educators have found and continue to find his work of immense interest and value.

He and his collaborators have systematically collected data on the performance of

---

*This manuscript was received in September 1979.

children and adolescents on several hundred tasks. The majority of these involve the manipulation of physical materials and yield information on how children develop their understanding of the physical world: how they structure their ideas about such factors as time, space, matter and motion. The results of these investigations by themselves would provide the science educator with rich and useful insights into the ideas children may bring to formal school learning, and what to expect in their development.

However, there is, of course, a more significant aspect of Piaget's work which is of interest: that is the underlying mental operations which these tasks are designed to elucidate.

The large number of studies undertaken by Piaget and his collaborators in Geneva between 1930 and 1950 formed a basis for his elaboration of the development of underlying structures or operations of thought. The operations of interest in the school years being those identified as characteristic of the thinking of five- to eleven-year-olds, the logical groupings concerned with seriation and classification, and the infralogical groupings concerned with space and time. The operations he identified as developing during adolescence differ essentially from the earlier ones in that they are not now performed on concrete objects or representations of them, but on the operations themselves. As is well known, Piaget suggests that operations of this kind, i.e. second order operations, enable a child to think hypothetico-deductively, to see reality as a subset of possibilities. He has represented such operations by a mathematical model or metatheory involving the complete combinational system and the operations of the INRC group.

These sets of concrete and formal operations are held to characterize two major stages in children's thinking. The underlying assumptions behind the stage theory being that as children develop, the operations characteristic of that stage become better articulated and integrated and form a 'structured whole' (Pinard and Laurendeau, 1969). As will be outlined later, there is currently some debate about this aspect of the theory, specifically whether it is children or operations which should properly be ascribed to a stage.

If such a model can be shown to represent the development of children's thinking skills, then it can be seen why it should be of interest to science educators. The operations Piaget identifies are ways of thinking which underlie much of scientific thinking: classification, ordering and the use of hypothetico-deductive thought. Conversely, if children have not developed such operations, this, too, will have implications for their achievement in school science classes.

EQUILIBRATION AND THE PROCESS OBJECTIVES OF SCIENCE EDUCATION

Underlying his theory of the development of operations, and prior to it, is his view about the nature of learning, which contrasts with the views of classical psychology.

> For classical psychology, intelligence was to be conceived of either as a faculty given once and for all, and susceptible of knowing reality, or as a system of associations mechanically acquired under the pressure exerted by things. Hence, we have seen the importance attributed by older educational theories to receptivity and the furnishing of memory. (Piaget, 1970a, p. 157)

The contrasting views of Piaget are well known. He distinguishes between learning and development, that is, development of the operations referred to earlier. In an important paper (Piaget, 1964) he suggests four factors that influence the development of operations: *maturation*, *experience* of the effects of the physical environment, *social transmission* including linguistic transmission and education, and, lastly, what he calls *equilibration*.

This concept of equilibration derives from Piaget's biological ideas of man as an adaptive organism.

> . . . this adaptation is a state of balance . . . between two inseparable mechanisms: assimilation and accommodation. We say, for example, that an organism is well adapted when it can simultaneously preserve its structure by assimilating into it nourishment drawn from the external environment and also accommodate that structure to the various particularities of that environment: biological adaptation is thus a state of balance between an assimilation of the environment to the organism and an accommodation of the organism to the environment. Similarly, it is possible to say that thought is well adapted to a particular reality when it has been successful in assimilating that reality into its own framework while also accommodating that framework to the new circumstances presented by the reality. Intellectual adaptation is thus a process of achieving a state of balance between the assimilation of experience into the deductive structures and the accommodation of those structures to the data of experience. (Ibid., pp. 153—154)

It is clear that such a view implies an active approach to learning:

> . . . adaptation presupposes an interaction between subject and object, such that the first can incorporate the second into itself while also taking account of its particularities; and the more differentiated and the more complementary that assimilation and that accommodation are, the more thorough the adaptation. (Ibid., p. 154)

Man is therefore seen from his earliest days as an active, goal-seeking problem-solving organism. This view perhaps underlies the prime influence that Piaget's work has had on education as a whole and science education in particular. It has given support and credibility to the idea that the child learns naturally, through interaction with its environment. This view underlies much of the developments in primary science in this country, and elsewhere.

Of course, Piaget is by no means unique in his ideas. Many educators including Rousseau, Froebel and Dewey have espoused this view. The special contribution that Piaget has made to 'modern methods' in education is to move beyond the statement of principles or polemics to outline in some detail the nature of the developments which children undergo; thus laying a foundation for practical educational programmes based to a greater extent on empirical findings.

When we look at the recommendations that Piaget himself makes for science education, we see the major emphasis he would place on science as a process, an active engagement in enquiry:

> . . . the repetition of past experiments is still a long way from being the best way of exciting the spirit of invention, and even of training students in the necessity for checking or verification . . . if the aim of intellectual training is to form the intelligence rather than to stock the memory and to produce intellectual explorers rather than mere erudition, then traditional education is manifestly guilty of a grave deficiency. (Ibid., p. 51)

As he indicates in his writings, the operations children develop between the ages of 11 and 16 provide them with the necessary tools of thought for undertaking such an investigatory approach.

Several science curriculum projects have specified process objectives for their courses based on Piagetian operations. The Science Curriculum Improvement Study (SCIS, 1974) has as a main objective to develop formal thinking structures. Karplus (1977) has outlined a three-phase learning cycle involving exploration, concept introduction and concept application which purports to encourage such development. The Australian Science Education Project (ASEP) also includes process objectives:

A child makes sense of his environment through the organization of his experiences into some stabilized, internalized structure which, once it has been built up, enables the student to process more effectively and more quickly information received. If the new experience does not fit the child's established mental structure, then the structure must be modified or new ones built. We believed that the exploration of the environment using the processes of science would assist in the establishing of the necessary structures. (ASEP Handbook, p. 5)

Piaget's ideas about equilibration are clearly reflected here. Science 5/13 is also a project that outlines its process objectives around a Piagetian stage framework.

Such courses are therefore using Piaget's operations as specific curriculum objectives. They have become the 'what' in 'what to teach'. Many attempts to evaluate the effectiveness of such programmes, especially the SCIS programme, in accelerating development have been undertaken. Linn and Thier (1975) report particularly encouraging results of the effect of SCIS materials in developing pupils' ability to control variables.

Nussbaum (1979) also reports positive results in using the relativity unit in developing pupils' spatial reasoning. He does report, however, that it is the pupils who are at a transition stage already who are most likely to improve as a result of instruction.

So far we have considered the concept of equilibration in terms of the educational support it has given to 'natural learning' or 'enquiry teaching' methods. Much educational research and practice accepts the equilibration model as a premise. But what empirical evidence is there for the equilibration model itself? There have been few critical experiments reported which compare Piaget's equilibration or cognitive conflict theory with that of classical learning theory. One notable exception is an experiment on learning in infants reported by Bower (1974), which does give support to the Piagetian model.

The idea of provoking cognitive conflict to encourage learning has its appeal. Palmer (1965) outlines the implications of the cognitive conflict model for science education. Smedslund (1961) reports how children have acquired conservation of substance and weight through practice in a conflict situation. Murray (1972) reports the use of conflict through social interaction as promoting the development of conservation concepts. He grouped one nonconserver with two conservers and required the group to come to a consensus on a conservation task. Bredderman (1973) compared training with external reinforcement with conflict training on the development of pupils' abilities to control variables. His results indicated no significant difference between the groups. A recent experiment reported by Johnson and Howe (1978) compares conflict training involving one-to-one contact with an adult, with conflict training between peers on an area conservation task. The results indicate that peer interaction gives the most beneficial results. These studies do give some support to Piaget's claim that social interaction affects development. They also indicate what may be fruitful approaches in teaching methods, giving some guidance on the question not simply of 'what' and 'when' to teach, but 'how' to teach it.

EPISTEMOLOGY AND CONCEPTUAL DEVELOPMENT IN SCIENCE

Developing skills in the process of scientific enquiry is not the only stated aim of many science courses. The development of an understanding of scientific principles and ideas gains more importance with older pupils. Piaget does not place these two goals in simple opposition. For him, the development of major scientific concepts comes as a consequence of the development of operativity. The two are closely related.

We can comprehend his position if we consider that his main concern is for epistemology. Piaget is a genetic epistemologist, and as such his concern is for the 'epistemic man' and the development of knowledge, specifically that of the physical world. It was this interest that motivated his early work in the 1920s and lately he has returned to give it particular attention. His book, *Biology and Knowledge* (1971), outlines his ideas concerning man the knower, his environment and the central importance of the logical operations in the development and communication of knowledge. Briefly, Piaget puts forward the theory that our knowledge develops through an active interplay of experience and the developing structures which process and order our perceptions. In addition, similar structures or operations have developed throughout the human species through interaction with common elements in the environment; because of these shared structures knowledge can be communicated.

In fact, Piaget clearly sees these cognitive structures and their development as a continuation of the evolutionary process of adaptation:

> these cognitive mechanisms are an extension of the organic regulations from which they are derived, and these mechanisms constitute organs of such regulation in their interaction with the external world. (Piaget, 1971, p. 346)

We are left in little doubt about Piaget's main focus of interest in this passage from his book, *Genetic Epistemology* (1970b, p. 13):

> The fundamental hypothesis of genetic epistemology is that there is a parallelism between the progress made in the logical and rational organization of knowledge and the corresponding formative logical processes. Of course, the most fruitful field of study would be reconstituting human history— the history of human thinking in prehistoric man. Since this field of biogenesis is not available to us, we shall do as biologists do and turn to ontogenesis.

With the considerable insight into the development of operational thought behind him, Piaget returned in the 1960s to reconsider the problem of causality. In an extended series of tasks he attempts to trace out the development of children's understanding of a range of physical concepts (mostly on dynamics but including aspects of heat, light and the structure of matter) in an attempt to understand the development of the subject matter itself (Piaget, 1974).

The underlying claim in these studies is that the development of causal or conceptual explanations by individuals reflects a dialectic between the developing logico-mathematical operations of the knower, which structure observations and events in certain ways, and the experiences that are assimilated. An example is given of the operation of additive composition being fundamental to the development of children's construction of the idea of atomicity. For example, children from the age of eight or nine infer that matter is conserved, and that dissolving involves an initial visible substance disintegrating into little pieces ending in an invisible form, and that these parts can be brought back again adding up to the initial whole. (More details about these studies can be found in a review by Driver and Easley, 1978.)

Underlying this work is a very optimistic assumption. Piaget suggests that his studies on causality show that pupils are capable of developing an understanding of physical principles without instruction, through interaction with physical systems, and even that formal instruction obstructs learning (Piaget, 1973). Here I would not dispute that children do impose meanings on events of their own accord and that they construct implicit theories as ways of handling novel or familiar situations. What I would dispute is that by experience alone children will come to develop the conceptual framework of accepted science (Driver, 1979). Children can be given experiences and practical materials to manipulate, but they may then impose meanings on them which are at variance with the accepted scientific view.

Two pupils in a science class had been heating blocks of different metals using an electrical heating coil. They had plotted graphs of the temperature of each block against time and noticed that the thermometer readings went up at different rates. When asked how they interpreted this one of them said:

> that different . . . um . . . that different materials and that see how heat could travel through them . . . heat went through the iron more easier than it did through the aluminium.

Here an activity that was designed to develop the idea of variation in thermal capacity was interpreted instead in terms of thermal conductivity.

Piaget himself has indicated the importance of social transmission in development. The arguments he has put forward for it are in terms of enabling pupils to discuss ideas to help them decentre by listening to other points of view. A further function of social transmission, and one which is significantly different from that presented by Piaget, is the transmission by the teacher, or through the written materials provided, of the agreed conventions of the scientific community. When Galileo was conducting his investigations into falling bodies, his first formulations of accelerated motion were in terms of changing speed over a given distance. It took him considerable time before he found his data was much more elegantly handled if he adopted what we now accept as a conventional way of computing acceleration.

Those who found Piaget's work useful as a basis for science teaching would not dispute this position either. Atkin and Karplus (1962) make a useful distinction between discovery and invention in teaching, and the approach is used as a basis of the learning cycle recommended as a foundation for using SCIS materials.

THE STAGE THEORY AND MATCHING THE CURRICULUM TO THE LEARNER

As was outlined earlier, this aspect of Piaget's theory specifies the operations that children develop as a result of the action of four factors: maturation, experience, social transmission and equilibration. It also specifies the general order in which operations develop. Lastly, it suggests that rather than taking the form of a gradual build-up of operations in a child's repertoire, development occurs in stages; the operations characteristic of each stage become integrated and consolidated so they have an internal coherence before significant development takes place in the operations characteristic of the next stage.

Currently, there is considerable debate among science educators about aspects of the theory. The most fundamental criticisms come from those who adopt a traditional, learning-theory approach which does not hypothesize the existence of internal structures of operations guiding behaviour, but instead interprets behaviour as a response to external reinforcements. If reinforcement patterns change then behaviour changes. More complex behaviours or skills can be built up by careful programmes integrating prior-learned behaviours.

The distinction between these two positions is not merely an academic one. They do have significantly different implications for educational practice in terms of the selection and ordering of teaching experiences. In a much quoted passage Ausubel writes:

> If I had to reduce all educational psychology to just one principle, I would say this: The most important single factor influencing learning is what the learner already knows. Ascertain this and teach him accordingly! (Ausubel, 1968, vi)

It is probable that either developmentalists or classical learning theorists would agree with this statement, but the meaning they would each ascribe to it would be significantly different. If learning a new idea depends primarily on what has been acquired previously, then any idea can be taught to a child of any age provided a carefully sequenced teaching programme of necessary subordinate ideas is used. Developmental theory, on the other hand, would also take into account what the learner already knows, but in this case it would be in terms of the cognitive operations he has available to him. If there is a great mismatch between the logical demands of what is to be taught and the operations available to the child, little permanent learning may take place.

Experiments have been undertaken on various occasions to put the two theories to the test (e.g. Anderson, 1968). So far results obtained by traditional learning techniques have not been as dramatic as might have been expected, thus lending support to the developmental position.

Important replication studies of many of Piaget's tasks have shown his results to be repeatable (Elkind, 1961; Smedslund, 1961), such studies are too numerous to cite individually: they have been surveyed by Lovell (1961a). The studies do indicate, however, that the ages at which specific operations appear may differ from Piaget's results. It is also recognized that the time of their appearance may vary from child to child and depend on the context in which the task is set.

Although empirical studies tend to confirm Piaget's results, there is some dispute over their interpretation. The logical metatheory Piaget constructed to give coherence to his stage descriptions has been critically reviewed and found wanting (Parsons, 1960; Bynum, Thomas and Weitz, 1972). Alternative models to Piaget's structuralist model have been suggested to account for the development of operations based on cybernetic principles (McLaughlin, 1963; Pascual Leone, 1969; Case, 1974). Such studies are not questioning the existence of the operations Piaget has identified, but are offering a different interpretation of them.

Another aspect of the stage theory that is a current focus of research is the question of the internal coherence of the stages. This is a matter of some practical concern in science education. If attempts are made to match the logical demands of a curriculum to the operational capabilities of the learner, it is important to know how generalizable any assessment of a pupil's stage of thinking will be. If a pupil is tested to see whether he can control variables using, for example, the pendulum task, will this mean he will be able to control variables in other situations? Or, more generally, will an assessment of his stage of thinking based on the pendulum task generalize to problems involving other formal level operations such as proportionality?

The question of the homogeneity of the stage of concrete operations has been reviewed by Lunzer (1965), who confirms the unitary nature of concrete operations. A review by Ennis (1975) presents a more sceptical interpretation. Studies on the coherence of the operations involved in formal thinking have been undertaken by several people. One of the earliest replication studies was undertaken by Lovell (1961b). He used ten of Piaget's tasks described in the *Growth of Logical Thinking* (Inhelder and Piaget, 1958). His results suggested general internal coherence within the stage.

More recently, factor analytic studies have been undertaken by Lawson and Renner (1974), Lawson and Norland (1976), and Shayer (1978a), which give support to the underlying unity of the formal operational schemes. Lawson, Karplus and Adi (1978) also report a factor analytic study using tasks involving proportions, probability, correlations and propositional logic. Their results indicate the possibility of a developmental link between the first three types of task but not the fourth.

Other investigators report less homogeneity within formal level tasks (Berzonsky, 1968). Further critical studies are reviewed by Brown and Desforges (1977). Lunzer

(1976) indicates his scepticism in the existence of all underlying processes in formal operations, and suggests instead types of development in reasoning beyond the concrete level. One point he makes that is supported by the recent study by Lawson, Karplus and Adi, is that propositional logic has little to do with the development of higher forms of thought during adolescence.

One factor which has been shown clearly to affect the level of pupils responses to a task is the content or context in which it is set. Wason and Johnson-Laird (1972) report an important series of experiments on adult thinking. They gave subjects tasks with similar logical structures but set in different contexts. They conclude that: 'Content is crucial, and this suggests that any general theory of human reasoning must include an important semantic component' (ibid., p. 245). According to their study the way the content affects the subject's responses is also interesting:

> The experiment confirmed our view that the individual tends naturally to think in a causal fashion and that if this tendency is set into opposition with the logical requirements of an inference, it is extremely difficult for the correct deductions to be drawn. (Ibid., p. 74)

Useful reviews of other studies indicating the relative importance of content over form are reported in Wason (1977) and Donaldson (1978). These findings obviously have important implications for science education which we will return to later.

In this brief review of research related to the stage theory the following issues have emerged:

(1) The developmental, or stage, theory differs from that of traditional learning theory in the implications that can be drawn for educational programmes.
(2) Although Piaget's metatheory, which accounts for the existence of the operations he identifies in the concrete and the formal stages, is questionable, the actual results appear to be replicable.
(3) Studies on the coherence of operations within a stage indicate some conflicting results.
(4) The content of a task is at least as important as its logical structure in determining a subject's success at solving it.
(5) The results of research on the coherence of stages has implications for science education on what might be called the *matching model*.

Two curriculum projects already mentioned, Science 5/13 and ASEP, organize the material to be presented to pupils according to the underlying cognitive demands it makes. Both schemes have prepared materials appropriate for pupils at these stages of development. Suggestions are given to teachers in the guides on how to diagnose the level of thinking a pupil is capable of and hence how to select material which is matched so as to stimulate development but not to be completely beyond the capabilities of the pupil. The emphasis in both approaches is to place the teacher in the role of diagnostician. Such programmes suggest that pupil learning depends on developmental level but it has been left to later studies to indicate this empirically.

A study by Lawson and Renner (1975) identified the degree of possible mismatch between the demands of secondary science courses and the developmental level of the learners. Sayre and Ball (1975) assessed the level of thinking of 14- to 18-year-old pupils using interviews and showed the scores obtained on the tasks correlated with grades obtained in science courses. Both studies drew attention to the low number of students who operate on the tests at a formal level. This matching model has been considered in greater detail with secondary-school pupils in a sequence of work by Shayer.

In a series of papers, Shayer analysed the cognitive demands of a range of secondary science courses in terms of Piagetian levels (Shayer, 1970, 1972, 1974). He and his team have devised group forms of some of Piaget's tasks and have undertaken a major survey of the level of operation of British school-children (Shayer, Kuchemann and Wylam, 1976). The purpose behind the work is to enable a better match to be made between the logical demands of the curriculum and the cognitive capabilities of the students. It is argued that learning best occurs where the match is appropriate. Shayer reports results of an empirical study in which pupil performance on tasks assessed to be at a late concrete level is predicted from their performance on group-administered Piagetian tasks. The correlation coefficient reported is 0.77 indicating that about 60 per cent of the variance in the attainment scores is predictable on the basis of the Piagetian tests (Shayer, 1978b). The study is of value in showing the current problem in our secondary schools of the mismatch between the courses we offer and the capabilities of the pupils. In addition, it does give some support to the matching model. However, there are reasons for being cautious before allowing such studies to have a prescriptive influence on the school science curriculum. The first concerns the reliability of the analysis of the cognitive demand of the curriculum materials themselves. The level to which any topic of lesson can be ascribed does depend on the teacher's interpretation of the materials and the approach used, in other words, it is a pedagogical, as opposed to a curricular, matter. A prescribed topic may be treated in a way that possibly demands formal operations as outlined in a teacher's guide. However, in practice the teacher uses an approach which only requires concrete reasoning.

Earlier in the paper, it was indicated that the content as well as the form of a task affects the pupil's response. Pupils will perform at different levels depending on the content or topic under consideration. Various studies report different levels of correlation between levels of performance on different formal level tasks by the same pupils (reported results vary between 0.3 and 0.7). Even taking the highest reported level, any prediction based on a diagnostic test that a teacher may make about a pupil's level of operativity in a given situation would only be a weak guide.

Group diagnostic tests of the level of operativity of learners may have some part to play in guiding teachers in a broad way to select material and approaches that are appropriate. There is a danger that the results will be interpreted in too narrow and prescriptive a way. Instead of being an aid to the teacher, guiding his expectations and helping him to be sensitive to the differences between individuals, it will interfere with teachers' own professional judgments.

Although there is reason to be cautious about the application of a general matching model, information on the articulation of logical operations within the learning of specific concepts may be a more profitable line of enquiry.

Raven (1974) gives evidence that training in the logical operations can enhance learning of concepts such as force, speed and work. Wheeler and Kass (1977) report that there is a significant relationship between students' ability to apply general proportional reasoning and their achievement in the four areas of chemistry that depend on it. Boulanger (1976) reports a small but significant effect between instruction in proportional reasoning in relation to the concept of speed and parallel development of proportional reasoning in a more general set of tasks.

This section has attempted to outline the contribution that the stage theory has made and can continue to make to science education. Although knowledge of the development of general logical operations is an important consideration in planning and ordering a science teaching programme it is not the only consideration. Information about the way children's causal thinking develops is also an important consideration and one we will now give attention to.

CHILDREN'S CAUSAL THINKING

If, as Wason's studies suggest, causal thinking acts as a control on the logical operations employed, then it should be of interest to science educators to consider the development of pupils' causal thinking in its own right.

Here I am not suggesting as is fashionable in the current literature a pro- or anti-Piagetian position. This I think is misleading. There is evidence for the age dependence of a range of logical operations that are important in science. What is suggested here is that another dimension, and one just as important, needs to be considered and that is the development of pupils' sets of beliefs about natural phenomena in the world around them.

These two concerns are not mutually exclusive but may be viewed as orthogonal axes when considering children's conceptual developments (see Figure 19.1). From the earliest age children have constructed implicit theories or beliefs about natural phenomena and the way they work. As some studies show, these implicit theories or conceptual frameworks influence the way pupils tackle problems, the variables they consider significant and the factors they observe and pay attention to (Driver, 1973; Karmiloff-Smith and Inhelder, 1976; Kuhn and Brannock, 1977).

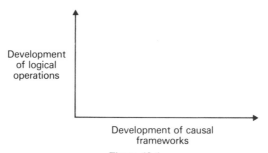

Figure 19.1

Piaget's early causality studies (Piaget, 1929, 1930) are a source of information for some beliefs children have about the natural world. In his recent research on causality, already mentioned, Piaget and his collaborators study the development of a range of children's ideas. It is unfortunate that in interpreting the extensive number of tasks undertaken in this study, Piaget was looking for evidence for the articulation of children's causal thinking with their operational development. In this way much information concerning the development of the causal or conceptual frameworks themselves has not been reported.

Other researchers are using Piaget's method of clinical interviewing to investigate pupils' conceptual frameworks in a range of areas. In these studies pupils are probed to assess their underlying conceptualizations, the interview data from children of a range of ages are then subjected to analysis not to determine the underlying logical operations that are embodied in the thinking, but to categorize different and developing sets of beliefs or conceptual frameworks used by the pupils in responding to the tasks.

Studies of this kind have been reported by Delacôte and his team on the topics of heat (Tiberghien and Delacôte, 1976a), light (Guesne, 1976) and electricity (Tiberghien and Delacôte, 1976b). Nussbaum and Novak (1976) report on the development of children's concept of the earth in space. Erickson (1979) reports on what he calls conceptual inventories concerning children's conceptions of heat and temperature. Viennot (1974) has studied the reasoning of university students about dynamics problems and has identified Aristotelian thinking even at that level.

All these studies indicate that pupils may have conceptual frameworks developed from their own experience which can differ fundamentally from those presented to them in science lessons.

Some studies indicate the importance of allowing pupils to disprove already existing ideas as well as confirming accepted ones (Cole and Raven, 1969). Rowell and Dawson (1977) report that despite designing a sequence of instruction to refute pupils' misconceptions about floating and sinking, some still persisted.

Changing conceptual frameworks is not easy for pupils and takes time. In fact, learning the accepted conceptualizations in school may place pupils in a parallel position to scientists who have to undergo a paradigm shift in their thinking. We are optimistic or unrealistic if we think we can programme it to happen at the time in the order and at the rate at which our teaching takes place.

Just as educators are currently concerned about the possible mismatch between the logical demands of school science and the logical capabilities of pupils, so similar consideration may need to be given to the problem of mismatch in conceptual frameworks. As mentioned before, the most important single factor influencing learning may be what the learner already knows. However, we may need to ascertain this not to build on it but to challenge it.

As a final comment on the contribution of Piaget's work to science education, I would like to mention his methodology.

The very method by which Piaget has worked, i.e. the clinical interview, is itself a contribution to research methods and, indeed, to education. The clinical interview enables the elucidation of the subject's way of thinking without prior knowledge of what that might be. It makes the important assumption that another person may think about and structure a problem differently from that conceived initially by the researcher and enables this structure to be elaborated. Training in this method of listening and talking to children can make a useful contribution to teacher education. Several of the science courses developed over the last twenty years place some emphasis on the teacher as a diagnostician. If this is to be effective, teachers need to learn to listen to and to probe children's ideas without asking leading questions, so they can understand better the child's way of thinking about a problem or reveal underlying difficulties from the child's point of view.

Learning to do this effectively is not easy. Piaget himself comments

> It is hard not to talk too much when questioning a child, especially for a pedagogue! It is so hard not to be suggestive! And above all, it is so hard to find the middle course between systematization due to preconceived ideas (on the part of the interviewer) and any directing hypothesis. (Piaget, 1929, p. 9)

There is some concern about the mismatch between science courses in secondary schools and pupils' ability to comprehend them. One of the most important ways of avoiding this is to have teachers who are able to listen and to reflect on pupils' learning, as well as structure and present their own teaching materials.

REFERENCES

Anderson, R. C. (1968) *An Analysis of a Class of Problem-Solving Behavior.* Report to US Dept of Health, Education and Welfare, Office of Education, Bureau of Research.

Ausubel, D. P. (1968) *Educational Psychology: A Cognitive View.* New York: Holt, Rinehart and Winston.

ASEP A Guide to ASEP: The ASEP Handbook.

Atkin, J. M. and Karplus, R. (1962) Discovery or invention? *Science Teacher,* **29**, 45-51.

Berzonsky, A. (1968) Interdependence of Inhelder and Piaget's model of logical thinking. *Developmental Psychology,* **4** (3), 469-476.

Boulanger, F. D. (1976) The effects of training in the proportional reasoning associated with the concept of speed. *Journal of Research in Science Teaching,* **13** (2), 145-154.

Bower, T. G. R. (1974) *Development in Infancy.* San Francisco: Freeman.

Bredderman, T. A. (1973) The effects of training on the development of the ability to control variables. *Journal of Research in Science Teaching,* **10** (3), 189-200.

Brown, G. and Desforges, C. (1977) Piagetian psychology and education: time for revision. *British Journal of Educational Psychology,* **47,** 7-17.

Bynum, T., Thomas, J. and Weitz, L. (1972) Truth functional logic in formal operational thinking: Inhelder and Piaget's evidence. *Developmental Psychology,* **7** (2), 129-132.

Case, R. (1974) Structures and strictures: some functional limitations on the course of cognitive growth. *Cognitive Psychology,* **6,** 544-573.

Cole, H. and Raven, R. (1969) Principle learning as a function of instruction on excluding irrelevant variables. *Journal of Research in Science Teaching,* **6,** 234-241.

Donaldson, M. (1978) *Children's Minds.* London: Fontana, Collins.

Driver, R. (1973) The representation of conceptual frameworks in young adolescent science students. Ph.D. thesis, University of Illinois, Urbana, Illinois.

Driver, R. (1979) *The role of science in general education: A critical review of some claims.* Paper delivered at London Institute of Education Seminar, January, 1979.

Driver, R. and Easley, J. (1978) Pupils and paradigms: A review of literature related to concept development in adolescent science students. *Studies in Science Education,* **5,** 61-84.

Elkind, E. (1961) The development of quantitative thinking: a systematic replication of Piaget's studies. *Journal of Genetic Psychology,* **98,** 37-46.

Ennever, L. and Harlen, W. (1972) *With Objectives in Mind Guide to Science 5/13.* London: Macdonald Educational.

Ennis, B. (1975) Children's ability to handle Piaget's propositional logic: A conceptual critique. *Review of Educational Research,* **45** (1), 1-41.

Erickson, G. L. (1979) Children's conceptions of heat and temperature. *Science Education,* **63** (2), 221-230.

Guesne, E. (1976) Lumière et vision des objets: un exemple de représentations des phénomènes physique pré existant à l'enseignement. Proceedings of GIREP.

Inhelder, B. and Piaget, J. (1958) *The Growth of Logical Thinking from Childhood to Adolescence.* New York: Basic Books.

Johnson, J. K. and Howe, A. C. (1978) The use of cognitive conflict to promote conservation acquisition. *Journal of Research in Science Teaching,* **15** (4), 239-247.

Karmiloff-Smith and Inhelder, B. (1976) If you want to get ahead, get a theory. *Cognition,* **3,** 195-213.

Karplus, R. (1977) *Workshop on Science Teaching and the Development of Reasoning.* Berkeley, California: Laurence Hall of Science.

Kuhn, D. and Brannock, J. (1977) Development of the isolation of variables scheme in experimental and 'natural experiment' contexts. *Developmental Psychology,* **13** (1), 9-14.

Lawson, A. E. and Nordland, I. (1976) The factor structure of some Piagetian tasks. *Journal of Research in Science Teaching,* **13,** 461-466.

Lawson, A. E. and Renner, J. W. (1974) A quantitative analysis of responses to Piagetian tasks and its implications for curriculum. *Science Education,* **58** (4), 545-559.

Lawson, A. E. and Renner, J. W. (1975) Relationships of science subject matter and developmental levels of learners. *Journal of Research in Science Teaching,* **12,** 347-358.

Lawson, A., Karplus, R. and Adi, H. (1978) The acquisition of propositional logic and formal operational schemata during the school years. *Journal of Research in Science Teaching,* **15** (6), 465-478.

Linn, M. C. and Thier, H. (1975) The effect of experiential science on development of logical thinking in children. *Journal of Research in Science Teaching,* **12,** 49-62.

Lovell, K. (1961a) *The Growth of Basic Mathematical and Scientific Concepts in Children.* London: University of London Press.

Lovell, K. (1961b) A follow-up of Inhelder and Piaget's 'The Growth of Logical Thinking'. *British Journal of Psychology,* **52,** 143-153.

Lunzer, E. A. (1965) Problems of formal reasoning in test situations. In Mussen, P. H. (Ed.) *European Research in Cognitive Development.* Mon. Soc. Res. Child. Dev., **30** (2), 19-46.

Lunzer, E. A. (1976) *Formal reasoning: a re-appraisal.* Paper presented at the meeting of Jean Piaget Society.

McLaughlin, G. H. (1963) Psycho-logic: a possible alternative to Piaget's formulation. *British Journal Educational Psychology,* **33,** 61-67.

Murray, F. (1972) Acquisition of conservation through social interaction. *Developmental Psychology,* **6** (1), 1-6.

Nussbaum, J. (1979) The effect of the SCIS 'Relativity' unit on the childs conception of space. *Journal of Research in Science Teaching,* **16** (1), 45-51.

Nussbaum, J. and Novak, J. (1976) An assessment of children's concepts of the earth utilizing structural interviews. *Science Education,* **60** (4), 535-550.

Palmer, E. L. (1965) Accelerating the child's cognitive attainments through the inducement of cognitive conflict. An interpretation of the Piagetian position. *Journal of Research in Science Teaching,* **3**, 318-325.

Parsons, C. (1960) Inhelder and Piaget's 'The Growth of Logical Thinking'. II: A Logician's viewpoint. *British Journal of Psychology,* **51**, 75-84.

Pascual-Leone, J. (1969) Cognitive development and cognitive style: A general psychological integration. Unpublished doctoral dissertation, University of Geneva.

Piaget, J. (1929) *The Child's Conception of the World.* New York: Harcourt, Brace.

Piaget, J. (1930) *The Child's Conception of Physical Causality.* London: Routledge and Kegan Paul.

Piaget, J. (1964) Cognitive development in children: Development and learning. *Journal of Research in Science Teaching,* **2**, 176-186.

Piaget, J. (1970a) *The Science of Education and the Psychology of the Child.* New York: Orion Press.

Piaget, J. (1970b) *Genetic Epistemology.* Columbia: Columbia University Press.

Piaget, J. (1971) *Biology and Knowledge.* Edinburgh: Edinburgh University Press.

Piaget, J. (1973) Comments on mathematical education. In Howson, A. G. (Ed.) *Developments in Mathematical Education.* London: Cambridge University Press.

Piaget, J. (1974) *Understanding Causality.* New York: W. W. Norton.

Pinard, A. and Laurendeau, M. (1969) 'Stage' in Piaget's cognitive developmental theory: Exegesis of a concept. In Elkind, D. and Flavell, J. H. (Eds.) *Studies on Cognitive Development: Essays in honor of Jean Piaget.* New York: OUP.

Raven, R. J. (1974) Programming Piaget's logical operations for science inquiry and concept attainment. *Journal of Research in Science Teaching,* **II** (3), 251-261.

Rowell, J. A. and Dawson, C. J. (1977) Teaching about floating and sinking: An attempt to link cognitive psychology with classroom practice. *Science Education,* **61** (2), 245-253.

Sayer, S. and Ball, D. (1975) Piagetian cognitive development and achievement in science. *Journal of Research in Science Teaching,* **12**, 165-174.

SCIS Teacher's Handbook. (1974) Berkeley, California: Lawrence Hall of Science.

SCIS Science Curriculum Improvement Study. University of California. New York: Rand McNally.

Shayer, M. (1970) How to assess science courses. *Education in Chemistry,* **7** (5), 182-186.

Shayer, M. (1972) Conceptual demands in the Nuffield O-level physics course. *School Science Review,* **54,** 26.

Shayer, M. (1974) Conceptual demands in the Nuffield O-level biology course. *School Science Review,* **56,** 381-388.

Shayer, M. (1978a) *Is Piaget's construct of formal operational thinking valid?* Paper given at British Educational Research Association Conference. Leeds, September, 1978.

Shayer, M. (1978b) The analysis of science curricula for Piagetian level of demand. *Studies in Science Education,* **5,** 115-130.

Shayer, M., Kuchemann, D. E. and Wylam, H. (1976) The distribution of Piagetian stages of thinking in British middle- and secondary-school children. *British Journal of Educational Psychology,* **46,** 164-173.

Smedslund, J. (1961) The acquisition of conservation of substance and weight in children. V Practice in conflict situation without external reinforcement. *Scandinavian Journal of Psychology,* **2,** 156-160.

Tiberghien, A. and Delacôte, G. (1976a) Conception de la chaleur chez les enfants de 10 à 12 ans. *Proceedings of GIREP.*

Tiberghien, A. and Delacôte, G. (1976b) Manipulations et représentations de circuits électrique simples par des enfants de 7 à 12 ans. *Review Francaise de Pedagogie,* **34.**

Viennot, L. (1974) Sens physique et raisonnement formel en dynamique elementaire. *Encart Pedagogique,* **II,** 35-46.

Wason, P. C. (1977) The theory of formal operations—A critique. In Geber, B. A. (Ed.) *Piaget and Knowing.* London: Routledge and Kegan Paul.

Wason, P. C. and Johnson-Laird, P. N. (1972) *Psychology of Reasoning.* London: B. T. Batsford.

Wheeler, A. E. and Kass, H. (1977) *Proportional reasoning in introductory high-school chemistry.* Paper presented to the fiftieth Annual Meeting of the National Association for Research in Science Teaching, Ohio.

Interchange

NOVAK REPLIES TO DRIVER

Those readers who look to this volume for sharply contrasting views on the value of Piaget's work will be disappointed with the chapters on science prepared by Driver and myself. It is my impression that our two chapters represent close to consensus on the promise and limitations of the 'Piagetian paradigm' for science education. However, although Driver recognizes some key aspects of Ausubel's cognitive learning theory, it would be improper to suggest that she shares my enthusiasm for his work as an alternative paradigm.

It may be useful to summarize some of the key areas where Driver and I are in agreement. In a general way, we both share respect and enthusiasm for the careful, voluminous research output of the Geneva school led by Piaget, and especially for his contributions to the development and use of the clinical interview as a data-gathering methodology. We are also both critical of unwarranted extrapolations from Piagetian work to rigid prescriptions for science instructional practice or grade placement of science subject matter. We also agree on some relatively specific issues.

Driver observes that 'there is currently some debate . . . whether it is children or operations which should be ascribed to a stage'. In an earlier paper (Novak, 1978), I questioned whether the stage concept is useful even for groups of students, and our research indicates that children of any school age might exhibit thinking at any level of cognitive operation. Moreover, our more recent research suggests that any one student may exhibit all three levels of cognitive operations sometimes within a single interview session. Even since my chapter was drafted, we have moved closer to the view that stages of cognitive operations are poor characterizations of any child's cognitive functioning. In recent weeks we have been re-analysing some of our previous interviews of children and we now lean towards the view that every child from age six onwards (the ages we have interviewed) can be interpreted always to operate *formally*. Our technique has been to 'place the interview on Gowin's V' and ask: given the claims the student makes (during the interview) in response to questions and the events or objects presented 'at the bottom of the V', what inferences can we make regarding the concepts, principles or theory that the child holds? Now if we accept our inferences regarding the child's concepts, we see that the claims made by the child satisfy the general requirements for formal operational thinking *and* remain consistent through subsequent interviews with the same child and with similar content. We are beginning to say that viewed from a given *child's* conceptual perspective, almost all children respond formal operationally. If we impose a certain bias in the questions we ask and the responses we are seeking to carefully selected tasks, we create student responses that result in a more pejorative classification of the child's cognitive functioning. Aristotle (and university students in a study cited by Driver) was not concrete operational because his cognitive operations were limited, but rather because the framework of explanatory concepts available to him did not permit him to demonstrate formal operational thought as judged by our present perspectives. The emerging view of our research group is that to the extent that a student possesses the currently available framework of explanatory concepts relevant to a given task, we may *judge* them pre-operational, concrete, transitional or formal operational thinkers.

Driver cites Piaget's work that 'puts forward the theory that our knowledge develops through an active interplay of experience and the developing structures which process and order our perceptions'. The crucial difference between the Ausubelian view and the Piagetian view is the extent to which this active interplay should be guided to develop specifically relevant explanatory concepts, or whether, as Driver observes, 'pupils are capable of developing an understanding of physical principles without instruction, through interaction with physical systems, and even that formal instruction obstructs learning'. Driver and I agree when she states 'What I would dispute is that by experience alone children will come to develop the conceptual framework of accepted science'. If Aristotle thought 'Aristotelian', surely the average students in our classes will do no better without deliberate, explicit transmission of key ideas in our cultural heritage. And Driver's example of Galileo's shift in thinking shows again how new concepts shift the way we observe events and the claims we subsequently make. What is at issue is *how* this cultural heritage should be transmitted, and it is to this end that we need the powerful guidance of a *learning* theory such as that of Ausubel. Educators were on solid epistemological ground, as well as backed by empirical evidence, when they began to discard behaviourism as an explanatory model for school learning. In urging a concern for something other than structuring sequences of behavioural reinforcements, Piaget and Ausubel have been in the same camp.

The three conclusions reached by Driver from her review of Piagetian studies are all consistent with my own views. I also agree with her conclusion that 'any prediction based on a diagnostic test that a teacher may make about a pupil's level of operativity in a given situation [of Piagetian operational level] would be only a weak guide [for content selection]'. While I agree with her view that development of causal frameworks and development of logical operations are not on the same continuum, I am not sure that it is useful to show a continuum for logical operations, except in narrow disciplinary specialties. Driver's observation that 'Piaget was looking for evidence for articulation of children's causal thinking with their operational development' makes the point I have tried to show schematically in Figure 18.2.

Our research group has been using Ausubel's cognitive learning theory to guide our work for some fifteen years. I believe that other scholars who choose to give the Ausubelian paradigm a fair trial will see both the power and limitations of Piaget's work, and the greater power and parsimony of Ausubel's theory.

DRIVER REPLIES TO NOVAK

It appears that there are two main areas of agreement between Professor Novak and myself. First, we both recognize the important contribution Piaget has made in the use and development of the clinical interview as a data-gathering strategy. Second, it is clear that we both value studies in which this technique is used to investigate the development of specific science and mathematics concepts in pupils. Clearly, we differ in the importance we place on the information gained from Piagetian tasks in guiding curriculum-planning and teaching.

First, I shall comment on Novak's position with respect to Piagetian theory. Then I shall comment on the potential of the Ausubelian framework he offers as an alternative view.

It is not clear in Novak's paper whether he is rebutting the very existence of a developmental sequence for the acquisition of logical skills, or whether he is merely questioning its usefulness to science and mathematics educators. There is evidence of some inconsistency here. He indicates that, if guided strictly by a Piagetian paradigm, one would not teach eight-year-old children such concepts as earth, space and gravity, as he purports they demand formal operational thought. The argument in support of this claim is not clear. The 'earth' tasks outlined in Nussbaum's study have much more in common with the Piagetian tasks on frames of reference, and as such demand concrete level thinking. It is not very surprising, therefore, that Nussbaum's results indicate that some eight-year-old children are capable of understanding these ideas. This is not well-chosen evidence to use to challenge the stage theory.

At another point, however, Novak indicates he is not opposing Piaget's stage theory: 'We simply do not see great relevance of his theory to many of the key issues involved in success or failure of high-school and college students in meaningful learning and problem-solving'. Some clarification of his stance is necessary.

Despite his excursion into the debate over the validity of the Piagetian stage theory, in fact, Novak is addressing a different problem from Piaget. As he indicates in his final summary, he argues for 'a theoretical model for cognitive learning that places emphasis upon the role of specifically relevant concepts . . . as the major sources of variation in concept development over a . . . model that places emphasis upon "stages" of development of "cognitive operations" '.

The data he presents on pupils' responses to questions on specific science concepts are interesting and I would argue potentially important for science educators. However, I question the utility of the Ausubelian framework which he elevates inappropriately to the level of theory. Let us look at the claims of this 'theory'. First, there is the claim that concept development takes place through *differentiation* and *integrative reconciliation* of relevant concepts. It is far from clear how these constructs offer specific insights into the data presented in the paper (specifically the data collected in Nepal). A second claim is made: '. . . if Ausubelian theory is valid, students who demonstrate significantly better concepts in early grades (whatever their source of knowledge) should also demonstrate superior knowledge in later years'. Although Novak's data is in keeping with this view, this is hardly surprising.

Many alternative explanations are possible, including—dare we mention it?—a general intelligence factor, so that this is far from strong evidence. These ideas of Ausubel do not constitute a theory. They do not enable predictions to be made, nor are they amenable to critical testing.

As it stands, there is much of interest in Novak's paper in terms of information on pupils' conceptual development in specific areas. However, the Ausubelian framework into which he attempts to assimilate it is unnecessary and adds nothing to his case.

Finally, one of the more significant points made by Novak, and supported by the data collected by Whitman, is that scores on Piagetian tasks do not correlate highly with scores on science tasks, indicating that studies of the development of specific concepts would be of greater value to educators than Piagetian tasks. This, of course, is one of the main points of debate at the moment. Other relevant studies were surveyed in my paper, and I will not repeat the arguments here.

In conclusion, the Piagetian theory and its associated tasks are addressing a different problem to that focused on by Novak. The task of outlining pupils' conceptual development in specific science or mathematics areas is therefore not in opposition to Piagetian theory. On the contrary, it could complement it in enabling a clearer, if more complex, picture of pupils' learning in science and mathematics to be produced.

Chapter 20

Piaget's Theory and the Learning Disabled: A Critical Analysis*

FRANK FINCHAM

The sudden emergence of learning disabilities as an area of special education has been paralleled by the recent burgeoning of interest in Piaget's theory. In fact, Flavell's (1963) classic text, which introduced Piaget to the English-speaking world, appeared in the very same year that Kirk coined the term 'learning disability'. Although temporally synchronous the two areas have developed independently. Recent introductory tests on learning disabilities (e.g. Lerner, 1976; Myers and Hammill, 1976; Farnham-Diggory, 1978) make few, and mainly incidental, references to Piaget, while not one of ten major contributors to the field acknowledges Piaget in describing their professional development (cf. Kauffman and Hallahan, 1976). Similarly, Piaget has not studied learning-disabled (LD) children nor do words such as reading or writing, tasks on which learning disabilities are mostly manifest, appear in the indices of his works. Finally, there have been very few attempts even to investigate the performance of LD children within a Piagetian framework (Reid, 1978). It is the purpose of the present chapter to consider whether this studied neglect reflects real difficulties in combining these two fields or is merely an historical accident.

PRELIMINARY PRECAUTIONS

A common error in evaluating a theory *qua* theory is to ignore its frame of reference and to criticize it for what it has not covered or attempted to explain. This is often unjust when considering its focus of convenience but when, as in the present context, an attempt is made to extend its range of convenience, this is not only permissible but

*I am grateful to Professor Peter Bryant and Dr Kathy Sylva of Oxford University for commenting on the draft chapter.

essential. Piaget's theory is, as he has always pointed out (for summary statements see Piaget, 1970a; Piaget and Inhelder, 1969), one of genetic epistemology, which seeks to resolve certain philosophical questions. It is not strictly speaking a psychological theory and even less a theory of education, let alone special education. Insofar as the theory is illuminating in these latter areas it is so only indirectly, and any hypothesis derived from it must be empirically and not merely deductively verified (Piaget, 1974). The indirectness of the connection between Piaget's theory and learning disabilities raises not only the problem of deciding whether it can contribute to the latter but also what constitutes an acceptable derivation from the theory. Finally, and most fundamentally, it presupposes, like any application, clarity within the theory and at least some modicum of empirical support.

It is therefore suggested that any attempt to use the theory in the field of learning disabilities necessitates knowledge of related applications which are closer to the theory (e.g. education) together with a thorough grasp of the theory and its status *vis-à-vis* basic research. The present review attempts to expand on and consolidate this viewpoint being especially mindful of Inhelder's (1976) observation that the extension of Piaget's theory is not always accompanied by an understanding of its basic principles. It is thus uncharacteristic of work on the learning disabled as it deals fairly extensively with the first links (viz. the theory itself and basic research) of the application chain, in the firm belief that the strength of later links depends on the status of earlier ones.

Faced with the scope and difficulty of Piaget's writings, it is all too easy to focus on the niceties of application and even worse to consider only certain aspects of the theory. This leads to the kind of fragmentation which Piaget (quoted in Evans, 1973, p. 40) considers the most common abuse of his work. It will be argued that any attempt to explore the value of Piaget's theory for learning disabilities involves a consideration of his views on learning, which takes one to the heart of his work—the theory of intelligence. By considering this in some detail and, as far as is practically possible, in relation to other aspects of his work, it is hoped to avoid this criticism. Indeed, it is the wholeness of Piaget's diverse writings which suggests that his theory might have a contribution to make to learning disabilities, itself an interdisciplinary field. In order to understand the relationship, or rather the lack thereof, between these two areas, it is necessary to ask two seemingly terminological questions. First, what constitutes a 'learning disability'? Secondly, what does 'learning' mean in Piaget's theory?

LEARNING DISABILITIES: BLOOMING, BUZZING AND DEFINITELY CONFUSED

There is no easy answer to the first question. The field of learning disabilities was not born to a unified framework of thinking, which is to some extent inevitable as it lies at the interface between medicine, education, psychology, language and several other professions (Lerner, 1976). This is reflected in the terminological confusion surrounding the description of these children, who despite intact sensory and emotional functioning as well as average to above intelligence, display difficulties in learning. Territorial imperatives have been jealously guarded and over forty terms have been used to refer to the LD child (Cruickshank and Paul, 1972), each reflecting the author's personal predictions, background training and professional interests. Generic to almost all approaches, however, are three characteristics: a disparity between potential and actual achievement, a basic disorder of the learning process and exclusion criteria such as subnormal intelligence, etc. (Myers and Hammill, 1976). Notwithstanding, there is little consensus regarding the precise nature of learning disabilities (Clements, 1966, lists over 100 symptoms associated with learning disabilities, which are still quoted in contemporary texts) and in the United States only two of the 42 states reported in Mercer, Forgnone and Sabatino's (1976) recent study have attempted to quantify the criteria for identifying LD children.

The false belief that a concept has specificity, when, as is apparent in the present case, it has not, is possibly one of the gravest dangers in special education. Recognition of this danger led Wepman et al (1975), in response to the United States Secretary for Health, Education and Welfare's reappraisal of present classification systems, to insist that the term be reserved for children demonstrating a deficiency in some academic area owing to a perceptual or perceptual—motor handicap. This would not include all presently specified LD children, as there are as yet unresolved conceptual problems in specifying whether factors such as poor attention, short-term memory deficits and so on have a perceptual basis. Nevertheless, such factors do inhibit learning. With essentially the same aim in mind, Hallahan and Kauffman (1976) adopt the opposite strategy and propose a broader conception which would force recognition of heterogeneity. They argue that the emotionally disturbed, educable mentally retarded and learning disabled should be treated as a single exceptional group, as the traditional differences between them are held to be quantitative rather than qualitative, while neither aetiology nor teaching methods distinguish these children. More radically, it has been argued that a further widening of the concept, which would herald the death of learning disabilities as a distinct area in special education, is implied by and a logical extension of, the spirit in which Kirk founded the field (Fincham, 1978a). In the present context, it is necessary at least to distinguish between a broad approach encompassing learning handicaps in general (e.g. Hallahan and Kauffman, 1976) and more traditional, narrow definitions which exclude the mentally retarded, sensory impaired, emotionally disturbed, etc. To avoid confusion, the term 'learning disability' is restricted to the latter. Although this chapter focuses primarily on learning disabilities, some consideration is given to learning handicaps, as it was the former's early severance of its ties with other fields of exceptionality that is partly responsible for the above-mentioned confusion.

Another major contributing factor is the essentially applied programmatically oriented nature of the field (Hallahan and Cruickshank, 1973, p. 271; Keogh, 1977). Whether justified or not the claim that a learning disability can 'have more devastating effects on children than most childhood diseases' (Tarnopol, 1971, p. 1) has given rise to tremendous practical demands which run far ahead of the field's conceptual development. In truth there has been little real clarification of fundamental constructs or basic theory-building so that the field remains a 'complex, confused conglomerate of ideas and professional personnel' (Cruickshank, 1972, p. 5). Faced with a practical problem, pragmatic solutions have been sought without much effective attention to Dewey's aphorism that the most practical of all things is theory.

At one level, the problem initially posed in this chapter has been answered. The question now arises as to whether the lacuna of Piaget-inspired work in LD literature is justified. It could well be that because even philosophically sophisticated commentators have found it 'difficult to sort out the strictly empirical from the theoretical framework, let alone the philosophical presuppositions' (Hamlyn, 1978, p. 43) the LD specialist has shunned Piaget's theory. The pressurized practitioner, pushed for time, might consider it quite sensible to ask: is learning Piaget a handicap? Nonetheless, Grossman (1978) has recently appealed for our openness to any theory, regardless of its status, which might prove useful to the field. But the slightly desperate note in this plea, while understandable, should not lead one to clutch blindly at straws.

It is absolutely essential to maintain a highly critical attitude given that the field of learning disabilities has 'been particularly vulnerable to the hasty application of untested theories and to domination by a line of strong personalities . . . [rather] than to the accumulation of knowledge' (Senf, 1976, p. 251).

Before finally turning to Piaget, it is worth noting that the 'accumulation of knowledge' regarding LD children is no easy task. A major problem emerging from the definition debate is sample classification which often means that the independent or predictor variable is defined at a level inappropriate to the dependent measure which class membership is meant to predict. In addition, the 'urgency problem' has resulted in a lack of methodological sophistication which together with an emphasis on standardized tests led Hallahan (1975, p. 53) to conclude that our knowledge concerning the psychology of learning disabled as compared to that of normal children is still rather crude. Can cognizance of Piaget's theory remedy this deficit? In answering this question, it seems necessary to examine whether, and in what way, Piaget deals with learning.

LEARNING IN PIAGET'S THEORY

Piaget's *volte face* regarding learning research, which he long dismissed as 'the American question', might tempt one to assume that the question of learning has only recently received attention in his work. While it is true that empirical research on this question only began to emerge from Geneva in the sixties, the issue of learning is at the heart of Piaget's theory. Perhaps this is best illustrated by drawing attention to the continuity in Piaget's writings as many of the key concepts in his theory of child development are to be found in his earlier biological research. It is this early work which constitutes the building blocks for his views on learning in children.

Essentially, Piaget sees a parallel between phylogenetic and ontogenetic change. In respect to the former, his study of *Limnaea Stagnalis*, a fresh water mollusc, led him to believe that innate knowledge cannot be accounted for by Lamarckism (the acquisition of characteristics under environmental pressure) or Darwinism (the chance mutation of hereditary structures). He observed that when this mollusc was moved from still to disturbed waters certain morphological changes, resulting from the movement it makes during its growth to resist the water's agitation, were hereditarily stable. Piaget argues the only explanation possible is that the environment effected a reflex mechanism which resulted in morphological change (Piaget, 1967, p. 118; 1971, section 19). It is precisely this kind of solution that Piaget uses to account for the first ontogenetic changes in intelligence. More specifically, the assimilation of different objects to hereditary structures (primitive reflexes) leads to their differentiation and organization as general action patterns which, when co-ordinated, give rise to knowing structures that are not innately given. Similarly, with the advent of the semiotic function 'logico-mathematical structures fill the same sort of role at the representation level as do hereditary frameworks at the initial learning stages' (Piaget, 1971, p. 335). In short, the organism always provides a framework for the acquisition of knowledge which simultaneously influences and is influenced by what is learned.

From this simplified sketch, it is clear that action-related structures are central to Piaget's thinking. It is precisely because of the role accorded to action and the consequent emphasis on the organism's construction of knowledge that Piaget is similarly able to reject both nativist and empiricist viewpoints in considering the evolution of knowledge during ontogeny. But it is also for this very same reason that Piaget in setting out to study the growth of intelligence squarely faces the question 'What is learning?'

Piaget's answer draws heavily on the distinctions between different types of knowledge. He considers two sorts besides that which is linked with hereditary mechanisms and hence distinguishes two different forms of learning (1969, p. 236; 1970a; 1973; 1977). First, there is knowledge derived from the object, which results from 'simple abstraction' of its physical properties. It corresponds to phenotypic accommodation in biology. On the other hand, 'reflective abstraction' leads to logico-mathematical structures, a form of knowledge which constitutes the base on which Piaget's epistemological perspective rests. This knowledge stems from the actions of the organism *vis-à-vis* the object, that is, transformations. It is based on the co-ordination of actions (not individual actions which yield knowledge of the first kind) and is analogous to regulatory systems in biology.* Piaget refers to acquisition of the first kind of knowledge as learning in the 'strict sense' and links it to the content of schemes. The form of a scheme is tied to equilibration, which together with its content constitutes learning in the 'broad sense'. Hence,

> What is learned in the strict sense is the totality of differentiations due to accommodation as the source of new schemes *vis-à-vis* the increasing diversity of contents. But what is not learned in the strict sense is the assimilative activity with its consequence of an equilibration between assimilation and accommodation . . . The interactions between assimilation and accommodation imply therefore two factors, learning in the strict sense and equilibration. These two factors underlying the functional process in its totality can be called learning in the broad sense and are practically identical with development. (Piaget, 1969, p. 236)

Having drawn the necessary distinctions, it is now possible to summarize Piaget's views on learning which are expressed in a number of his own (e.g. 1969; 1970a, section 13—17; 1970b; 1971) and several of his colleagues' (e.g. Inhelder et al, 1966; Inhelder, Sinclair and Bovet, 1974; Sinclair, 1974) writings. Essentially, Piaget considers an adequate notion of learning as one which explains not how knowledge is acquired by repetition or discovery (learning in the strict sense) but how it is invented (learning in the broad sense). However, he restricts the word 'learning' to learning in the strict sense and hence claims that 'learning is not more than a sector of cognitive development which is facilitated or accelerated by experience' (1970a, p. 714). Consequently, the Piagetian theory of learning is really synonymous with its theory of development. The subordination of learning to development is also apparent in the other major Piagetian principle which, unlike the previous one, governs the process rather than the content of learning. All learning must reflect spontaneous development and hence an accelerated acquisition of Piagetian stage concepts would 'only occur if the training resembled the kinds of situations in which progress takes place outside an experimental set-up' (Inhelder, Sinclair and Bovet, 1974, p. 24).

Having considered both the concept of 'learning disability' and 'learning' in Piaget's theory, it remains to evaluate the utility of his theory for the practitioner confronted with a LD child. It has been argued that this involves, *inter alia*, analysing how adequate Piaget's above claims are as a model of normal functioning. This issue is dealt with before turning to the possible applications of his model in the field of learning disabilities.

---

*The biological emphasis is perhaps most clear in this form of experience as the relations between subject and object are directly comparable to those between organism and environment in phylogenetic development (Piaget, 1977, p. 10).

PIAGET'S VIEWS ON LEARNING: A CRITIQUE

The Content of Learning

Clearly development cannot be defined independently of learning as 'every acquisition that presents an aspect of equilibration involves at the same time a more or less direct element of learning' (Piaget, 1969, p. 238). Thus whether an ontogenetic behavioural change is attributed to learning or development depends on the viewpoint from which the question is asked. This means that the structures which define Piaget's stages, being themselves inferred from behaviour on Piagetian tasks, cannot be used to explain any behavioural change (learning) on these tests. It is for this reason that any attempt to solve the problem by 'independently' assessing stage and learning using different Piagetian tasks fails (e.g. Younniss, 1971). Any definitive test of the learning— development hypothesis is therefore not possible as there is no access to the stage structures except via the very behaviours they are supposed to explain. Consequently, Brainerd has concluded that 'until the circularity problem is cleared up, stage versus learning will remain a pseudo-issue' (1977, p. 937).

From the practitioner's viewpoint this means that when confronted with a child diagnosed as deficient in operational thinking one has no means of evaluating the efficacy of any treatment in terms of one's supposed goal, viz. the teaching of operatory thought structures. All that is possible is to observe the relationship between behaviours on specific tasks at different points in time. On this level, Piaget's theory predicts that the stage of functioning reached by the child should constrain what can be learned. More precisely, two closely allied claims are made, both of which have obvious implications for remediation. First, children who have some notion of the concept to be learned (transitional children), will learn more easily than those who do not have any idea of the concept. Second, 'teaching children concepts they have not acquired in their spontaneous development . . . is completely useless' (Piaget, 1970b, p. 30). While these hypotheses are at least falsifiable, their verification cannot substantiate the theory and hence make its application in special education any more credible.

Prima facie, the above substantive claims appear to be straightforward, empirical issues. However, they are not devoid of conceptual difficulties. One problem stems from Piaget's view on how learning occurs. Given that training techniques must contain no direct intervention, either in the form of explicit instruction or even corrective feedback (what seems to be a rather artificial situation with little ecological validity), it is not surprising that more advanced children with respect to the to-be-learned concept gained more from these exercises (Inhelder, Sinclair and Bovet, 1974, p. 268). Intuitively, it is difficult to imagine how a child with absolutely no notion of the concept could benefit from such experience. But this is hardly an insurmountable problem, for if other training techniques produced similar results, it would confirm Piaget's position on this point (at the same time posing problems for his views on the process of learning). But this would not necessarily point to the unique value of Piaget's theory because there is nothing in Piaget's predictions that distinguishes his system from the claims of learning theories (Brainerd, 1978, p. 98). Virtually no learning theorist would deny that it is easier to transfer a concept than learn it *ab initio* or that it is easier to show learning in those who partly understand a concept.

Notwithstanding these difficulties of interpretation, the empirical data available simply does not provide unambiguous support for Piaget's claims (see comprehensive reviews by Modgil and Modgil, 1976; Brainerd, 1977, 1978, 1979). For instance, there is evidence showing that pre-operational children who possess no notion of conservation whatsoever (including number) can be taught to conserve (e.g. Gelman, 1969; Murray, 1972; Botvin and Murray, 1975). Moreover, even the Genevan data (Inhelder, Sinclair and Bovet, 1974), when re-analysed so as to remove the contaminating effect of test reliability, does not support Piaget's claims regarding the relationship between pre- and post-test performance (Brainerd, 1977).* But previous research (eight non-Genevan studies are also re-analysed) is also plagued by the problem of ceiling effects and hence Brainerd (1979) has recently gathered data which show less equivocally the lack of any connection between development and learning. In conclusion, it should be noted that despite the plethora of research in this area, it is largely concerned with the acquisition of concrete operational concepts, especially conservation, and thus even if favourable, does not necessarily substantiate Piaget's views when other developmental levels are considered.

The Process of Learning

Piaget's position regarding the process of learning seems equally problematic. Genevan researchers would most likely accept as incorrect any attempt to argue that because some arbitrary technique produces an age-related behaviour change, it necessarily reflects a developmental process. Yet the converse position advocated by Piaget, that spontaneous development, or the simulation thereof, is the only possible means to produce such a change, seems equally unjustified. It just does not seem to derive logically from the theory. This conclusion is reinforced by the fact that the Genevans do not provide any rationale for their stance and simply assert it as a self-evident truth (e.g. Inhelder, Sinclair and Bovet, 1974, p. 24). To insist that there is only one route for an ontogenetic acquisition seems to invoke a model of man which is very different from the emphasis placed on adaption derived from a biological approach. Like Skinnerian man in its dependence on direct reinforcement, *l'homme Piagetian* would have been extinct long ago.

What characterizes spontaneous development? Undoubtedly, the major feature is active construction of knowledge. Consequently, Piaget recommends that even when a child has difficulty with a problem, the teacher's role is not to correct him directly but to give 'counter-examples' (1977a, p. 731). Indeed, he asserts that anything less is actually harmful as 'each time one prematurely teaches a child something he could have discovered for himself, that child is kept from inventing it and consequently from understanding it completely' (1970a, p. 715). In evaluating these powerful statements, it behoves one to be clear about what is meant by action, a precaution not always taken by educators (cf. Piaget in Evans, 1973) and which is purported to be the biggest stumbling block in applying the theory to education (Gallagher, 1978). Indeed, the ease with which Piaget's name is used to justify perceptual—motor remedial programmes in general is rather disturbing as almost without exception they derive from epistemological positions very different from his own.

In respect to action the Genevans speak with two tongues. On the one hand Piaget emphatically states that actions 'refer to the manipulation of objects' (1974, p. ix) and hence 'it is necessary that learners have at their disposal concrete material experiences' (ibid., p. x). Although there are other points to be made about Piaget's view of action, such as the suitability of the materials for the child's cognitive level etc., these need not be elaborated in the present context (for a concise statement of his views see Piaget,

---

*This reanalysis requires two qualifications. First, it was conducted on the first post-test data only and, second, it assumed that on average half the test items were passed by transitional children as the exact scores for these subjects were not specified in the original report. It is possible that these factors may be responsible for the results obtained but this seems unlikely as they concur with several other studies.

1977, and Gallagher, 1978). On the other hand, his colleagues, perhaps finding this position difficult to defend in view of their own research, still claim that '. . . the more active a subject is, the more successful his learning is likely to be'. However, they add the proviso that '. . . being cognitively active does not mean that the child merely manipulates a given type of material; he can be mentally active without physical manipulation, just as he can be mentally passive while actually manipulating objects' (Inhelder, Sinclair and Bovet, 1974, p. 25). Within this view, one can explain any observation. For instance, if active manipulation fails to produce learning, then it can easily be held that the child was mentally passive and vice versa. The definition is obviously tautologous and renders the position untestable.

In turning to Piaget's stronger stance, it is apposite to note that his claim is double edged. Not only do children learn by physical manipulation but the 'observed activities of others, including those of the teacher, are not formative of new organizations in the child' (Piaget, 1974, p. x). In short, the child's manipulation of objects is a necessary condition for learning. It is not difficult to find empirical evidence that contradicts this assertion. In fact, it is another instance where data from Geneva can be used to discredit one of Piaget's claims. As noted by Antony (1977), Inhelder, Sinclair and Bovet (1974, ch. 3) describe one experiment which stands out from the rest in that the child did not physically manipulate the objects during training (he did equate two sets of objects by one-to-one correspondence which was, however, incidental and preliminary to training) but was presented with different types of situations by the experimenter. The experimenter asked appropriate questions at different points during the exercise but throughout the child merely observed an adult producing transformations and did not act on the objects himself.* The results indicated that the five intermediate (transitional) children acquired a stable operatory structure while only two of the remaining nine subjects made no progress on the first post-test. All children had improved by the second post-test (after 6 to 8 weeks), although two, one of which had made no progress on the earlier test, did not participate in this phase of the study. In defence of Piaget's position, one could dispute these results by pointing to the lack of a control group in this experiment, a feature characteristic of several of their studies which is particularly worrying in view of the fact that when used controls have been observed to show some spontaneous progress during the course of the experiment (e.g. Chap. 6, 7).

Happily, there exists a great deal more evidence on this issue although non-Genevan in origin. Unfortunately, however, there have been no direct comparisons of active versus non-active training and hence it is difficult to evaluate the relative efficacy of the two approaches with any confidence. Despite the difficulties involved, Brainerd (1978, pp. 89—93) has attempted to do just this. He points out that not only does one have to assume that the results of the six Genevan experiments are replicable, stable findings, but in the only conservation experiment where nonconservers were included, self-discovery was not efficacious. In contrast, numerous 'tutorial training' studies have shown rather more substantial learning in both conservers and nonconservers (see also Modgil and Modgil, 1976; Brainerd, 1977). Finally, it is noteworthy that several researchers claim to have shown the acquisition of Piagetian concepts by the use of modelling (c.f. review by Zimmerman and Rosenthal, 1974). In sum, there is no clear

---

*Indeed, it would have been a difficult, if not impossible, experiment to administer were this not so. Moreover, as Inhelder et al points out, in at least three of the presentations it would have been extremely hard 'to carry out the specific concrete action which reconstitutes the original situation' (1974, p. 97), a fact that casts doubt on the extent to which the training reflects spontaneous development if the latter is held to occur only via actual physical manipulations (Piaget, 1970a, p. 704). This again emphasizes Piaget's and his colleagues' differing views on action.

empirical evidence to support Piaget's assertion that learning occurs *only*, or even more efficaciously via physical manipulations, a notion which in any event appears counter-intuitive.

Piaget's views regarding both the content and process of learning appear to be problematic in terms of conceptual clarity and empirical support. This undermines any attempt to argue for their direct application in the field of learning disabilities. But the status of Piaget's views on learning and their application to the learning disabled might not arise if it can be shown that in Piagetian terms these children are not 'learning disabled'.

PIAGET AND LEARNING DISABILITIES

It has become apparent that Piaget's 'theory of learning' is really an account of development. Even though experimental knowledge (learning) is held to be just as important as logico-mathematical knowledge (development) it is, in effect, a false equality for while learning is determined by development, the converse is not true (Piaget, 1971, p. 334). It thus remains to decide whether learning disabilities are best conceptualized in terms of developmental dysfunctions. More particularly, there is the empirical question as to whether it is possible to display a learning disability without a concomitant cognitive-developmental problem. If this is indeed the case, then not only is Piaget's theory unhelpful in remedying the deficit, but his claim of cognitive or developmental determinism seems inappropriate, or at best untenable, in its present generalized form.

In turning to this question, it is apposite to consider first Genevan research, not only because it provides evidence in support of the present argument, which is probably closest to Piaget's thinking, but also for several other reasons. First, it is historically important as it pioneered the application of Piaget's theory in the area of exceptionality. As Piaget puts it, it 'succeeded in getting the operational hypothesis out from behind the boundaries of pure theory construction into the field of effective reality' (1968), p. 12). Second, this work has not found its way into the LD literature where much of what is known about the cognitive functioning of LD children has been extrapolated *en bloc* from earlier work done with the brain-injured (see research reviews by Hallahan, 1975; Torgesen, 1975; Parucka, 1976). This is possibly due to the field's isolation in the area of exceptionality where this tendency is not as marked. Finally, it highlights further fundamental difficulties in Piaget's theory.

Initially, Genevan research in psychopathology (in its widest sense) focused on the extent to which Piaget's developmental stage hierarchy was preserved in exceptional groups (Schmid-Kitsikis, 1973; Reid, 1978). For instance, Inhelder (1968) demonstrated that the mentally retarded are characterized by delays and fixations in operative activity due to lack of closure in their thought structures which results in a false equilibrium (i.e. passive and perseverative stability). Similarly, more recent work has shown the same stage sequence in dysphasics, dyspraxics and several other exceptional groups (e.g. Inhelder, 1966; Schmid-Kitsikis, 1972, 1973). Such data is seen as evidence which testifies to the utility of Piaget's theory in dealing with exceptional children (see e.g. Inhelder, 1966, p. 302). However, the force of this 'evidence' is somewhat diminished when it is noted that Piaget's stage theory is based on axiomatic analysis as well as the study of intellectual development. In other words, the order in which Piaget's stages occur is logically guaranteed, since notions from a later stage always presuppose knowledge of those at an earlier stage (cf. Flavell and Wohlwill, 1969;

Flavell, 1972). It is therefore simply not possible to conceive of any other sequence. Admittedly the point remains that these groups' responses are not so bizarre or unintelligible that they cannot be portrayed in terms of operational structures.

Inhelder (1968) painstakingly emphasizes though that it is not intended merely to identify certain kinds of pathology with fixations at particular levels, as this would only replace the IQ with developmental stages. Rather it is to see behaviour as determined by a constructive process which must, according to Piagetian theory, be related to the general cognitive structures available to the person (1968, p. 306). But the very notion of generalized cognitive structures, viz. stages, is itself problematic and warrants consideration in evaluating the above point.

If, for Piaget, learning comprises 'the extension to new content matter of structures already formed or in the process of formation' (1969, p. 238) then obviously structures emerge in relation to different objects at different times. Piaget describes this phenomenon as horizontal decalage and accounts for it in terms of the resistance of the situation.* A question thus arises concerning the structural unity of operations or *structure d'ensemble* of Piagetian stages. To what extent can decalage exist before it threatens the concept of *structure d'ensemble*? Recently, Wason (1977) has shown that even at the level of formal operations, where the content of thought is supposedly at last subordinated to its form, the nature of the task material profoundly influences the level of the operational structure utilized. Indeed, Brown and Desforges (1977), after reviewing similar empirical evidence relating to much of the life-span, conclude that the extent of decalage exceeds that of *structure d'ensemble* and hence reject Piaget's stage descriptions. Lawton and Hooper (1978) even go as far as to draw an analogy with the quest for the Holy Grail.

In the present context this would mean that a Piagetian practitioner is left without an explanation for the learning handicap with which he is faced. Inhelder in her initial work on the retarded acknowledged this difficulty in noting that, 'The impossibility of generating the operatory structure *a priori* to any intuitive content is often disconcerting when an attempt is being made to establish general stages of reasoning' (1968, p. 302). But she continues by claiming that in mental diagnosis the situation is far clearer owing to the homogeneity of the thought processes in her retarded subjects. As she explored only three areas of functioning, it is perhaps not surprising that Woodward (1963) challenged this claim by showing that retardates function differently in different substantive areas. In fact, Schmid-Kitsikis (1972, pp. 56-57) who admits to homogeneity only 'in a very general sense', points out that inconsistencies in pathology are indeed frequent. This may be particularly important in considering LD children. In one of the few studies that explicitly aims to determine the cognitive abilities of LD children, Myklebust, Bannochie and Killen (1971) found, on the basis of a wide range of cognitive tasks, that the mental abilities of this group are structured differently from those of normal achievers. Using Piagetian-type tests Fincham (1979) confirmed this conclusion in finding that success on one decentration task is not predictive of that on another. Consequently, it may not prove possible to assess LD children adequately in terms of cognitive stages, but it still remains to examine just how they achieve on Piagetian concept tasks.

Although the Genevans have not studied LD children *per se*, some of the groups they have worked with certainly would be classified as 'learning disabled' (either in its broad or narrow sense) elsewhere. For those accepting a broader definition aspect of Inhelder's (1968) results may be important. Some children (less than 10 per cent) whom

---

*Besides the limited explanatory power of this construct, Smedslund (1977) notes that it forces one, *a priori*, into accepting the ontological reality of Piagetian cognitive structures and into assuming that persons function abstractly, notions which he finds alienating in practice as a clinician and 'without sufficient scientific foundation' (p. 3).

Inhelder refers to as slow learners appear to be borderline retardates (EMR) as they showed progress during the experimental interview. Nonetheless, they, too, were delayed in terms of operative thinking which suggests that Piaget's 'stage' theory can be used to characterize all levels of mental retardation. In fact, it is in this area that most research on exceptional children has been conducted (see the review by Klein and Safford, 1977) and where the theory has had its most forceful impact.* Results pertaining to a narrower conception of learning disability are markedly dissimilar. Schmid-Kitsikis (1972, 1973) and Inhelder (1966, 1968) report work on dyspraxic, dysphasic and dyslexic groups which shows that they are not slow in acquiring operative thought.

Consider, for instance, Schmid-Kitsikis' research on dyspraxics. These children of normal intelligence (measured by IQ) but with serious motoric difficulties were tested on a logico-arithmetic task, seriation of sticks and class inclusion. They passed the latter test but failed the former ones, tasks which differed in terms of the degree of manipulation required by the child. As it was observed that the children were often able to announce the solution to the seriation task but not actually carry it out, several modifications were made to its presentation. Under these new conditions the test was passed revealing that these dyspraxic children did not suffer from a deficit in their logical thinking (they attain the same levels as children of their own age) but rather they could not actualize their thinking. The care exercised to assess the child's true competence rather than some performance variable seems characteristic of Genevan research on psychopathology (see e.g. Inhelder, 1968, Ch. 4). It is both commendable and instructive. In the field of learning disabilities it emphasizes the importance of the competence—performance distinction which has been ignored until only recently (Hallahan, 1975; Torgesen, 1975; Reid, 1978). The number of null hypotheses rejected as a result of this oversight is indeed alarming as it may even have altered our conception of the LD child. But its major impact lies in its implications for Piaget's theory as a whole and justifies a major digression.

It is incorrigible that the Genevans have not considered seriously this distinction in relation to normal children but instead assume that performance on Piaget's tasks reflects the child's cognitive competence. Indeed, Bryant (1977, p. 60) notes that it was not until 1970 that any attempt was made to check whether a young child could remember the information given in the premises of a transitive inference problem before drawing conclusions about his logical abilities (or rather inabilities) on the basis of his performance. Instituting such simple controls (and rectifying difficulties relating to the use of only three stimuli), it was found that even four-year-olds make transitive inferences (Bryant and Trabasso, 1971). He claims that there has not been one demonstrated instance of where children have not been able to make such inferences given that they can remember the essential information (1977, p. 62). However, it does appear that young children only make transitive inferences when they recognize the fallibility of non-logical strategies (McGarrigle and Donaldson, 1974; Bryant and Hopytynska, 1976).

Although the issue of transitive inferences in development is by no means settled (cf. Thayer and Collyer, 1978), the essential point remains. Simply, cognizance of the competence—performance problem may radically affect one's account of cognitive development. Indeed, it is this awareness that unifies several challenges to Piaget's theory (e.g. Bryant, 1974; Anderson and Cuneo, 1978; Siegel and Brainerd, 1978). These strike at the very pith of Piaget's theory and question his explanations for the phenomena he has discovered which are themselves not disputed. It is one thing to

---

*For a comprehensive bibliography of Piagetian-inspired research on exceptional children conducted from 1963 to 1973 see Warner and Williams (1975).

assert that the child is incapable of making certain logical moves but quite another to suggest that either he does not implement these moves owing to some non-logical performance factor or because he merely does not recognize the situation as one which calls for them. Obviously, this affects not only our very conception of the child which has been held to be Piaget's major contribution to education, but also has concrete and far-reaching pedagogical implications. Teaching a concept *ab initio* is not the same as a remedial approach which teaches the child when to use a concept he already has. Awareness of this developing crisis creates a dilemma for the practitioner and blunts any enthusiasm for a straightforward implementation of the theory in remediation. While this is a problem regarding learning handicaps in general, it may not be important with respect to the learning disabled as Genevan research suggests that this group does not necessarily manifest disturbances in logical thinking.

Non-Genevan results tend to support this viewpoint although, as noted earlier, there has not been much Piagetian-inspired research in this area. Learning-disabled children have been found to perform at the same level as their normal achieving peers (Fincham and Meltzer, 1977; Meltzer, 1978; Fincham, 1979) on several concrete operational tasks (seriation, conservation of number, length, mass and liquid). Although Brekke reports a deficit in weight conservation among the learning disabled (Brekke et al, 1976) and motorically impaired (Brekke, Johnson and Williams, 1975), the difference in results is more apparent than real as these groups were also much lower in intelligence. With IQ statistically controlled, the significantly poorer performance of these groups disappeared. In similar vein, Klees and Lebrun (1972) note that the dyslexics they studied showed delays in the acquisition of seriation, liquid conservation and classification. It is unfortunate that, in the absence of a control group, this assertion is made on the basis of a comparison with Piaget's results obtained sixteen years earlier, and, more especially, in view of the sensitivity of Piagetian tasks to variations in administration and scoring (cf. Cowan, 1978, p. 308; Schmid-Kitsikis, 1972, p. 60). However, their more credible intra-group comparison showed that all the children with severe perceptual handicaps had difficulties with these tasks but none of the perceptually intact children did.

This finding is important as it can be related to the question posed at the beginning of this section regarding learning disabilities and cognitive-developmental problems. A related but more restricted approach to this issue is to utilize Piaget's distinction between understanding the transformation of states (operative thought) and the ability to represent the figural aspects of reality or the states themselves (figurative thought) expressed in perception imitation and mental images. Essentially, Piaget adopts the same solution with regard to operative and figurative thought as to the learning-development question. For example, in relation to perceptual activity he claims it 'only functions when integrated with, and directed by, action as a whole, which means by sensorimotor or even, from a certain level of development, by representational intelligence' (see also Inhelder, 1966, p. 308; Piaget, 1969, p. 353). As Piaget (1970a, p. 717) himself points out, the 'learning' principles he discusses in relation to development apply only to the operative aspects of thought. One might thus formulate a further question analogous to that first posed and ask whether there are learning disabilities which result from figurative thought disorders only.

Klees and Lebrun (1972) argue that the operative difficulties they observed in their dyslexics were due to disturbed figurative functioning, which *prima facie* supports a unitarist view of the perception—cognition relationship. However, Piaget (1977, p. 18) admits that descriptors (figurative thought) are necessary for comprehension and can hence assimilate such results without modifying his theory. Similarly, evidence which shows that normal operative development can be accompanied by figurative thought disorders (e.g. Inhelder, 1966; Schmid-Kitsikis, 1972, 1973; Meltzer, 1978) is seen as equally consistent with Piaget's 'interactionist' viewpoint. But the latter evidence also suggests that the figurative processes (descriptors) are not a necessary condition for operational thought. The status of such data *vis-à-vis* the theory seems to depend on what aspects of the interaction one focuses on and furthermore on how these are interpreted.

Notwithstanding Piaget's extensive attempts to clarify the similarities and differences between figurative and operative thought (e.g. 1969, Ch. 6 and 7), their relationship remains problematic and has been a stimulus to further psychopathological research in Geneva (Schmid-Kitsikis, 1973, p. 697). Indeed, one might well ask if Piaget's position of 'operative determinism' has been demonstrated at all. Although work from diverse sources is quoted in support of this viewpoint, perhaps the most vaunted is Sinclair's (e.g. Inhelder, Sinclair and Bovet, 1974) research on language. But even this evidence is far from compelling. Having found a strong relationship between the ability to conserve and the use of certain linguistic terms (relational, differentiated and co-ordinated descriptives), Sinclair claims to have shown that verbal training does not affect operative functioning. The fact that 36 per cent (7) of the nonconservers became transitional while 10 per cent (3) acquired conservation is seen almost as incidental. In the absence of control subjects their progress is simply dismissed as inadequate pretesting and so on. The progress of 18 subjects (78 per cent of the sample) on a seriation task is equally problematic. But even if these difficulties are ignored, such evidence does not necessarily support Piaget's determinist position. It only shows that language need not necessarily affect the development of concrete operational thought but does not mean that operative functioning therefore determines linguistic acquisitions. This remains to be demonstrated and cannot be assumed a priori. It is difficult to conceive that this is indeed the case, for how then does the Piagetian child so limited in his cognitive abilities acquire language which reflects logical rules way beyond his capacity?

Consideration of the above issue is not merely an academic exercise as it is fundamental to the theory's application. For example, the attention given to perception, language and memory in special education has recently been severely criticized in view of Piaget's emphasis on operative thought (Reid, 1978). This preoccupation with operativity seems to reflect an extension of the tendency shown by Piagetian-inspired educators in normal education to throw out the proverbial baby with the bath water (e.g. Sinclair, 1974; Furth, 1977). It suggests that confronted with, say, language disabled children, the most common form of learning disability (McGrady, 1968), this problem should be seen as an epiphenomenon of operative immaturity. But even if our conception of education is radically altered in order to profit from Piaget's theory (Sinclair, 1974, p. 42), at present it is by no means certain that promoting operative thinking will set such problems right. Would it not be more realistic to allow that direct linguistic training is required?

It seems possible that many learning disabilities might merely reflect an inability to represent reality or simply abstract knowledge about the world (learning in the strict sense). Alternatively, Koppell (1979) argues that learning disabilities can be accounted for in terms of an attentional deficit, a diminished capacity to process information, and specific processing deficits. Such factors may not, however, be unrelated to Piagetian cognitive competence, as a recent study showed that while concrete operational, normal and LD children differed in ability on arbitrary memory tasks, they performed equally well on Piagetian memory tests. But the relationship between information-processing abilities and Piaget's theory is not at all clear and has been labelled 'the major research and theoretical problem of the decade' (Murray, 1977, p. 56). Until this problem is resolved it is by no means self-evident that Piaget's work assists in understanding the ability (or lack thereof) to acquire specific skills or information which, however repugnant as an educational goal, seems destined to remain part of the educative process by virtue of its necessity for survival. No matter how attractive the goals of education are from a Piagetian perspective, the application of Piaget's stage theory irrespective of the content to be acquired seems questionable.

Focus on Reading

The problem of applying Piaget's theory to basic academic skills becomes clear in considering a concrete task such as reading. Piaget himself doubts whether the concept of readiness, which is clearly embodied in his ideas on learning, can be applied to reading (1970b, p. 30). Indeed, the problems involved in interpreting the practical implications of his theory in such a field seem to be reflected by the fact that despite the overwhelming multiplicity of reading theories only recently has a Piagetian model (Furth, 1978) been proposed. (Most of the work to date has been almost exclusively correlational. See Murray, 1978a, and Waller, 1977, for reviews of relevant research.) But the very title of the paper 'Reading as thinking' betrays the reductionistic nature of the model. Reading is seen as a spontaneous by-product of high-level thinking owing to the asymmetrical relation between language and thought, which once again is merely asserted rather than demonstrated by research. Both Murray (1978a) and Barron (1979) have expressed severe doubts about the model for this very reason. There are, in addition, several more specific problems with this application.

While not wishing to become enmeshed in the complex issue of what constitutes reading, it is worth noting that even though a case can be made for the functioning of operational intelligence in various aspects of reading tasks (e.g. Waller, 1977; De Young and Waller, 1979) it requires a great leap of faith to accept that these operative activities (e.g. classifications) affect the reading process itself (e.g. decoding) rather than the child's understanding of this process which is a different matter altogether. But this assumption is crucial as the principal implication of Piaget's theory for reading is that operations constitute prerequisites or necessary conditions for reading (Waller, 1977). Such an assumption remains dubious in view of Murray's observation that pre-operational children do, in fact, learn to read. However, his assertion that these intellectual abilities are sufficient conditions for reading (Murray, 1978a, b) is similarly repudiated by the fact that there are many cognitively mature adults who do not learn to read (Sticht, 1978). Just what Piaget means for reading depends on which view you follow.

Perhaps this is a problem deriving from educators' misapplication of Piaget (cf. his own views on readiness above) rather than the theory itself, which demonstrates a problem mentioned earlier in this chapter. Such difficulties, however, seem inevitable in such a field because there is no appeal to Piaget's authority as he does not seem to have a position on reading. On one occasion where Piaget does specifically mention reading, his claim that children learn to spell by reading (1970b, p. 30) is contradicted by empirical fact. There do appear to be children who can spell words but not read them, as well as vice versa (Bryant and Bradley, 1979), suggesting that the acquisition of reading and spelling may reflect fundamentally different processes. Nor is this problem necessarily restricted to reading, for Piaget says 'I am not a pedagogue myself, and I don't have any advice to give educators' (quoted from Evans, 1973, p. 51). From Piaget's statements on education (e.g. Piaget, 1970b; Piaget, 1977a) it is clear that what the right hand takes the left hand gives. Essentially, these really are essays from the left hand as they represent vague and general statements which do not clearly delineate the relationship of the theory to educational practice. Despite the several realizations of this relationship, which are limited to pre-school education, not one has proved to be more efficacious than traditional approaches (cf. Lawton and Hooper, 1978).

The point of considering reading in some detail is manifold. Not only does it illustrate concretely many of the earlier objections made on a more theoretical level, but it also represents a task central to learning disabilities, which often present as, or are at least accompanied by, reading disorders. Moreover, it is representative of the complex skills with which the remedial teacher must work and indicates the looseness of the connections between Piaget's work and such academic tasks. Indeed, it seems justifiable to ask whether, given the lack of clarity as to how, or even if, the theory can contribute to understanding such skills, it is perhaps not premature to expect that it can contribute to their remediation? Perhaps the soundest advice comes from Murray (1978b, p. 189) who with respect to reading recommends that application of the theory should wait for a more explicit determination of its relationship to this skilled process. It is suggested that until this is done not only for reading but with regard to other academic tasks, the remedial teacher can hardly hope to obtain substantive guidance from Piaget's theory.

In conclusion, it appears that the weight of the evidence argues against any obvious use of Piaget's theory in the field of learning disabilities. First, Piaget's position on learning does not seem relevant for remediating learning disabilities as often there does not appear to be a difficulty with reflective abstraction but rather empirical knowledge. Where learning handicaps do represent a developmental delay, this in itself is not a satisfying explanation as it does not specify why this occurs nor what transition mechanisms are faulty. It is the general uncertainty regarding transition mechanisms which has, in part, inspired recent Genevan research on both learning and psychopathology (Schmid-Kitsikis, 1973; Inhelder, Sinclair and Bovet, 1974), an issue which nonetheless is far from being resolved. Second, even if difficulties in learning or school failure are accompanied by operative thought problems it is by no means established that remediating this deficit will affect any figurative disorder which may also be associated with the handicap. Similarly, if the relationship between these two aspects of thought was clear at the level of more basic research, preliminary evidence suggests that LD children might exhibit a dissociation between them. Again concern for the regulatory processes governing the relationship between these two elements has stimulated Genevan research on psychopathology, which now focuses on self-regulatory processes rather than the static, structural emphasis previously characteristic of their work (Schmid-Kitsikis, 1973). Finally, it was argued in considering a concrete academic task such as reading, that there is no clear referent for the remedial teacher as the relevance of Piaget's theory for such tasks is at best unclear.

Lest it appear otherwise, it must be stated clearly that given the present corpus of knowledge in this area, these remain, like many aspects of Piaget's work, tentative hypotheses rather than definitive conclusions. Nor is it intended to suggest that Piaget has absolutely no contribution to make to the field of learning disabilities, a consideration which is now addressed.

SOME IMPORTANT IMPLICATIONS

Piaget's use of the *methode-clinique* is undoubtedly one of the major factors that made possible his contribution to knowledge. Not only did it reveal many new facts but it also drew attention to the distinction between the product and processes of thought.

His continued emphasis on understanding how children think is especially instructive for a field where performance on standardized tests has become so important. Much is known about the various deficits related to learning disabilities, but there is little evidence in terms of the relevant psychological processes that give rise to them. This may seem rather surprising in view of the fact that Heinz Werner (1937), a co-founder of the field, long ago noted the utility of describing abilities with respect to processes rather than test scores. Cognizance of Piaget's method thus has two major implications. First, because it stresses how a child functions rather than the level at which he performs, it has implications for differential diagnosis which when conceived in these terms leads more directly to remediation. Indeed, the fundamental notion of clinical teaching (cf. Johnson and Myklebust, 1967) is most cogently actualized under these circumstances. Second, it draws attention to the field's severance of its ties with the past and other areas of exceptionality out of which it grew, and asserts the value of restoring these historical links. The lacunae in LD research resulting from this historical development are slowly becoming apparent and the importance of concepts such as motivation, which has been emphasized in mental retardation for some time, are now being recognized (cf. Hallahan and Heins, 1976).

In addition to Piaget's method, several of his fundamental concepts also seem to have a potentially fruitful application. Possibly the most important is equilibration. The idea of an internal mechanism of self-regulation co-ordinating changes in maturation, physical and social experience seems valuable. It gives rise to a view of the child that is incompatible with the way in which the learning disabled are often treated. Rather than seeing the child as a series of abilities, or more accurately disabilities, diagnosed along the lines of different professions or disciplines, it emphasizes the dynamic manner in which these different facets are interrelated. Looked at from this cybernetic viewpoint the compensations and adjustments made in the whole system for specific deficits become apparent. Thus Inhelder (1966), for example, tries to show how the development of operativity is used to compensate for figurative thought impairments. Moreover, the active equilibrium proposed by Piaget serves to remind us of the continually changing nature of the system and points to the danger of remediation based on a single, one-shot diagnosis.

Closely allied to the idea of self-regulation and its consequent compensations is another feature of the system as a whole—organization. As an organized totality man is not merely the bearer of certain facts or S-R links but has reflected on and actively organized his experience. This active reflection or construction, with its attendant emphasis on the interaction between subject and object, seems particularly valuable. It acts as a caution to the exigencies of practitioners who see learning disabilities as due to either some environmental contingency (e.g. bad teaching) or within-child disorder (e.g. minimal brain dysfunction). The inordinate amount of effort expended in evaluating the locus of a learning disability in this sterile manner might be spent more profitably on specifying the child—environment mismatch which provides a differentiated picture of the child's problem. Also, despite Piaget's interest in the epistemic subject, it points to the individual way in which knowledge is constructed and hence the inadmissability of rigidly standardized diagnostic and remedial procedures.

It is important to note that use of Piagetian constructs such as those mentioned above does not necessarily commit one to Piaget's theory. For instance, in accepting a process approach to learning disabilities it is as well to be aware that his is only one possible system. This point is not always clear when Piaget's work is contrasted with some other viewpoint, usually an extreme form of empiricism. Essentially, it is suggested that the value of Piaget's writings does not lie in the substantive nature (content) of his theory. Rather it is the constructs that constitute what may loosely be called his metatheory which are seen as the most important aspects of his work for the field of learning disabilities. They question many of the accepted practices in this area and raise new problems. In Piaget's own terms this would constitute a satisfying contribution, for he says 'my role has been above all to raise problems' (quoted in Evans, 1973, p. 33). But the LD literature is fraught with problems. The hope is that the distinctions he has made (e.g. between figurative and operative thought) and the questions he has asked from an interdisciplinary perspective (e.g. the relationship between these two aspects of thought) might provide a useful framework for clarifying the nature of learning disabilities and hence facilitating the discovery of practical answers to this urgent problem. This in itself would be a phenomenal contribution considering the philosophical nature of the task Piaget initially set out to accomplish.

SUMMARY AND CONCLUSIONS

It is difficult to evaluate Piaget's actual or even potential contribution to a field in which child development or psychology plays a role. For better or for worse developmental research has become virtually synonymous with his name, while many of his ideas are being incorporated into the very framework of psychology. Thus, like Freud before him, he probably has or will in the near future influence many people's thinking without their explicitly acknowledging or even being aware of his role in their development. These observations together with the scope of Piaget's theory suggest that it would be naïve to claim that the present chapter represents a comprehensive and hence non-controversial assessment. It is unashamedly selective but nonetheless attempts to deal as broadly as possible with some of the salient issues which arise when considering the relevance of Piaget's theory to learning disabilities.

Starting from the observation that there appears to be no overt connection between the two areas, it became apparent that this was partly due to the historical fact that learning disabilities as a field are underdeveloped in terms of theory. This by itself recommended examination of Piaget's potential contribution. But close inspection of the most crucial notion, viz. learning, reveals several problems for Piaget's theory *qua* theory in terms of experimental evidence. At a conceptual level there are elements of circularity in the theory (e.g. development 'explains' learning) while certain distinctions are either ignored or rejected. For instance, Piaget does not distinguish between rote learning and aspects of receptive learning which are more meaningful. The fact remains that children do acquire a great deal by observation, possibly even the logico-mathematical knowledge of which Piaget speaks. Whatever the process governing its acquisition, a theory of learning which deals almost exclusively with this one type of knowledge is restricted unless, as Piaget holds, it determines other forms of learning. Empirical evidence shows that the veridicality of Piaget's position has yet to be demonstrated.

Clearly, though, not all the necessary evidence for a final evaluation is yet available as certain implications of Piaget's theory have not received much attention. This is partly because it is only in relatively recent times that Piaget, with the help of his colleagues, has attempted to explicate more fully the regulatory mechanisms of development, viz. equilibration. It is not intended to suggest that this notion is in any way new, for it has always been an intrinsic part of the theory, but this fact alone makes it difficult to understand why it has received comparatively little attention (notwithstanding Piaget's probabilistic model, e.g. 1967, 1970a), and remained on the level of vague generalizations (c.f. Brown and Desforges, 1977, p. 13). In focusing on structures, ironically Piaget neglected the operations which govern their transformation. The instability of this 'pre-operational' solution seems to have stimulated the recent Genevan emphasis on equilibration. The move away from an 'epistemic subject' (structural analysis) to a 'psychological subject' (thought in action) is significant as it is ignorance of this new development that is held to retard the proper application of Piaget's theory to education (c.f. De Vries, 1978; Gallagher, 1978). Notwithstanding attempts to apply the latter dynamic aspects of the theory which Inhelder long ago emphasized in her work on the retarded, she warns that it is too early to form far-reaching conclusions from this current work (Inhelder, 1978).

Examination of research on exceptional populations also highlights some of the general problems with the theory. Besides the irrepressible question regarding general stages of development, recognition of the competence—performance issue has spawned a series of recent challenges to Piaget's theory. Casting aside these numerous doubts and assuming that Piaget is correct, the relevance of this work in the present context is still open to question, as the available research suggests that LD children do not on the whole manifest operative thought disorders. In all fairness, it must be added that this evidence is problematic owing to the definition problem. When learning disabilities are conceived more broadly to include the mentally retarded the data favour Piaget. It does appear that mental retardation can be characterized in terms of delayed development in reasoning. Yet the 'minor revolution' created by Piaget in this area (Klein and Safford, 1977, p. 205) generates hope that remains to be fulfilled. It is still not known why the delays occur nor how a process tending toward equilibrium, viz. regulation, can remain unstable for such protracted time periods.

Piaget's theory thus appears to be applicable to the field of learning disabilities insofar as it is held to include children with lower IQs but has yet to prove its worth in respect to the learning disabled as traditionally conceived (i.e. with the exclusion clauses operative). But even if children in the latter category can be described in Piagetian terms, the theory is of limited utility. This is because, assuming also that Piaget's views on learning are correct, it informs the practitioner confronted with a learning disability of only one necessary condition which may be a source of the child's problem. However, if it is found that the child's operative thought processes are intact, the theory offers little in the way of further guidance. Cast in slightly different and more specific terms, there may be a figurative thought disorder even though the supporting conditions of operative thinking are intact. While it is not intended to decry the value of this limited contribution, it must be emphasized that there are at present too many ifs and buts to justify the *volte face* in special education required for its realization.

There are, moreover, additional problems that arise from any attempted application of Piaget's ideas. In the present context, the theory is too narrow, for despite the inseparable tie which Piaget sees between emotions and intelligence, he, in effect, deals almost exclusively with mental development. His references to affect are scattered and even when drawn together provide an incomplete and empirically unsubstantiated picture (cf. Antony, 1976). This is an important factor in considering learning disabilities, as social and emotional problems are associated with the disorder both as primary causes and secondary symptoms (cf. Hallahan and Kauffman, 1976; Shelton, 1977). In addition, there is evidence indicating that these problems may not be associated with Piagetian-type social judgment abilities such as role-taking or moral judgment (Fincham, 1977, 1979), but rather with variables less obviously related to Piaget's work, viz. popularity, helpfulness, feelings of lack of control, rejection and so on (c.f. Bryan, 1978; Fincham, 1978b; Fincham and Barling, 1978). The devastating effects of these emotional problems necessitate that they be treated in their own right and hence require that the cognitive—affective link in Piaget's theory be solidly filled if it is to be of practical use. But even within the restricted realm of intelligence, the limited nature of the tasks Piaget uses, *inter alia*, results in the theory being so narrow as to be 'relatively useless for practical purposes' (Smedslund, 1977, p. 5). While acknowledging his debt to Piaget, Smedslund is forced to conclude, on the basis of clinical and experimental experience, that the utility of practising within a Piagetian framework is questionable, for despite Piaget's 'brilliant and penetrating insights, they must be incorporated into a view of psychology which can be lived and practised rather than merely written and talked about in academic settings' (ibid., p. 6).

Paradoxically, the theory is also too broad despite its narrowness. Often it appears that Piaget is more concerned with refuting opposing viewpoints than in precisely delineating his own theory. The claims he makes are in most instances too general and cannot be sustained. This is indeed unfortunate as the positions he attacks are so extreme that it is difficult to recognize them as representing anyone's viewpoint (e.g. Hoptopf, 1977, p. 167). It is perhaps because he has strayed too far into generality that applications of his theory in education 'which can be lived' are so difficult to distinguish from other approaches. For instance, Murray (1978a) argues that in educational practice operant and Piagetian models do not result in different pedagogies and insofar as teachers' behaviours are different, these may reflect restrictive interpretations of the models as much as any true difference between them. In similar vein, Lawton and Hooper (1978) note that Piagetian programmes have a great deal in common with open-classroom models and traditional approaches in nursery school which are themselves subject to evaluation. It seems that when applied to education Piaget's theory can be interpreted in different ways which do not distinguish it in practice from widely disparate approaches. These problems of application serve to emphasize the indeterminate nature of any attempted connection between learning disabilities as a field of special education and what essentially remains an epistemological theory.

In conclusion, it must be reiterated that any final judgment regarding the value of Piaget's theory for learning disabilities is premature. Obviously, not all the relevant evidence is available but several aspects of the theory require clarification. However, it is not intended to suggest that the theory should be ignored in research on LD children. On the contrary, this would not only help to clarify the relationship between the two areas but is likely to assist in showing where and how the theory should be modified. This would not perturb a man like Piaget who has always considered himself as the chief revisionist of his theory. Indeed, the conclusion reached in this chapter might well satisfy him, for when asked whether he considered there were any pitfalls facing psychology, Piaget replied:

> The danger to psychologists lies in practical applications. Too often psychologists make practical applications before they know what they are applying. We must always keep a place for fundamental research and beware of practical applications when we do not know the foundation of our theories. (Piaget, 1970b, p. 32)

REFERENCES

Anderson, N. H. and Cuneo, D. O. (1978) The height and width rule in children's judgments of quantity. *Journal of Experimental Psychology: General,* **107,** 335-378.

Anthony, E. J. (1976) Emotions and intelligence. In Varma, V. P. and Williams, P. (Ed.) *Psychology and Education.* London: Hodder and Stoughton.

Antony, W. S. (1977) Activity in the learning of Piagetian operational thinking. *British Journal of Educational Psychology,* **47,** 18-24.

Barron, R. W. (1979) Review of the acquisition of reading. *Journal of Child Psychology and Psychiatry.*

Botvin, G. J. and Murray, F. B. (1975) The efficacy of peer modelling and social conflict in the acquisition of conservation. *Child Development,* **46,** 796-799.

Brainerd, C. J. (1977) Cognitive development and concept learning: an interpretative review. *Psychological Bulletin,* **84,** 919-939.

Brainerd, C. J. (1978) Learning research and Piagetian theory. In Siegel, L. S. and Brainerd, C. J. (Eds.) *Alternatives to Piaget: Critical Essays on the Theory.* New York: Academic Press.

Brainerd, C. J. (1979) Concept learning and development. In Klausmeier, H. J. (Ed.) *Cognitive Development from an Information-processing and a Piagetian View: Results of a Longitudinal Study.* Cambridge, Mass: Gallanger.

Brekke, B., Johnson, L. and Williams, J. D. (1975) Conservation of weight with the motorically handicapped. *Journal of Special Education,* **9,** 389-393.

Brekke, B., Williams, J. D., Johnson, L. D. and Johnson, M. (1976) Conservation of weight with the learning disabled. *Journal of Teaching and Learning,* **2,** 25-33.

Brown, G. and Desforges, C. (1977) Piagetian psychology and education: time for revision. *British Journal of Educational Psychology,* **47,** 7-17.

Bryan, T. H. (1978) Social relationships and verbal interactions of learning disabled children. *Journal of Learning Disabilities,* **11,** 58-66.

Bryant, P. E. (1974) *Perception and Understanding in Young Children.* New York: Basic Books.

Bryant, P. E. (1977) Logical inferences and development. In Geber, B. A. (Ed.) *Piaget and Knowing.* London: Routledge and Kegan Paul.

Bryant, P. E. and Bradley, L. (1980) Why children sometimes write words which they do not read. In Frith, U. (Ed.) *Cognitive Processes in Reading and Spelling.* London: Academic Press.

Bryant, P. E. and Kopytynska, H. (1976) Spontaneous measurement by young children. *Nature,* **260,** 773.

Bryant, P. E. and Trabasso, T. (1971) Transitive inferences and memory in young children. *Nature,* **232,** 456-458.

Clements, S. D. (1966) *Minimal brain dysfunction in children.* NINDB Monograph No. 3 Public Health Service Bulletin No. 1415. Washington D.C.: Department of Health, Education and Welfare.

Cowan, P. A. (1978) *Piaget with Feeling.* London: Holt, Rinehart and Winston.

Cruickshank, W. M. (1972) Some issues facing the field of learning disabilities. *Journal of Learning Disabilities,* **5,** 380-388.

Cruickshank, W. M. and Paul, J. L. (1972) The psychological characteristics of brain-injured children. In Cruickshank, W. M. (Ed.) *Psychology of Exceptional Children and Youth.* Englewood Cliffs, N.J.: Prentice-Hall.

De Vries, R. (1978) Early education and Piagetian theory. In Gallagher, J. and Easley, J. A. (Eds.) *Knowledge and Development.* Volume 2. London: Plenum Press.

De Young, T. and Waller, T. G. (1979) Piagetian operative competence and learning to read. Manuscript submitted for publication.

Evans, R. I. (1973) *Jean Piaget: the Man and His Ideas.* New York: Dutton.

Farnham-Diggory, S. (1978) *Learning Disabilities.* London: Open Books.

Fincham, F. D. (1977) A comparison of moral judgment in learning-disabled and normal achieving boys. *Journal of Psychology,* **96,** 153-160.

Fincham, F. D. (1978a) Pig and pepper: adventures in the field of learning disabilities. *Symposium,* **8,** 23-25.

Fincham, F. D. (1978b) Recipient characteristics and sharing behaviour in the learning disabled. *Journal of Genetic Psychology,* **133,** 143-144.

Fincham, F. D. (1979) Conservation and cognitive role-taking ability in learning-disabled boys. *Journal of Learning Disabilities,* **12,** 25-31.

Fincham, F. D. and Barling, J. (1978) Locus of control and generosity in learning-disabled, normal achieving and gifted children. *Child Development,* **49,** 530-533.

Fincham, F. D. and Meltzer, L. J. (1977) Learning disabilities and arithmetic achievement. *Journal of Learning Disabilities,* **10,** 508-510.

Flavell, J. H. (1963) *The Developmental Psychology of Jean Piaget.* Princetown, N.J.: Van Nostrand.

Flavell, J. H. (1972) An analysis of cognitive-developmental sequences. *Genetic Psychology Monographs,* **86,** 279-350.

Flavell, J. H. and Wohlwill, J. F. (1969) Formal and functional aspects of cognitive development. In Elkind, D. and Flavell, J. H. (Eds.) *Studies in Cognitive Development.* New York: Oxford University Press.

Furth, H. G. (1974) Two aspects of experience in ontogeny: development and learning. In Reese, H. W. (Ed.) *Advances in Child Development and Behaviour,* Volume 9. London: Academic Press.

Furth, H. G. (1977) Intellectual health in school. In Margary, J. F., Poulsen, M. K., Levinson, P. J. and Taylor, P. A. (Eds.) *Piagetian Theory and The Helping Professions,* Volume 6. Los Angeles: University of California.

Furth, H. G. (1978) Reading as thinking: a developmental perspective. In Murray, F. B. and Pikulski, J. J. (Eds.) *The Acquisition of Reading.* Baltimore: University Park Press.

Gallagher, J. (1978) Reflexive abstraction and education. In Gallagher, J. and Easley, J. S. (Eds.) *Knowledge and Development*, Volume II. London: Plenum Press.

Gelman, R. (1969) Conservation acquisition: a problem of learning to attend to relevant attributes. *Journal of Experimental Child Psychology, 7*, 167-187.

Grossman, R. P. (1978) Learning disabilities and the problem of scientific definitions. *Journal of Learning Disabilities, 11*, 120-123.

Hallahan, D. P. (1975) Comparative research studies on the psychological characteristics of learning-disabled children. In Cruickshank, W. M. and Hallahan, D. P. (Eds.) *Perceptual and Learning Disabilities in Children, 1*. New York: Syracuse University Press.

Hallahan, D. P. and Cruickshank, W. M. (1973) *Psycho-educational Foundations of Learning Disabilities.* Englewood Cliffs, N.J.: Prentice-Hall.

Hallahan, D. P. and Heins, E. D. (1976) Issues in learning disabilities. In Kauffman, J. M. and Hallahan, D. P. (Eds.) *Teaching Children With Learning Disabilities: Personal Perspectives.* Columbus, Ohio: Charles E. Merril.

Hallahan, D. P. and Kauffman, J. M. (1976) *Introduction to Learning Disabilities: a Psycho-Behavioural Approach.* Englewood Cliffs, N.J.: Prentice-Hall.

Hamlyn, D. W. (1978) *Experience and Growth of Understanding.* London: Routledge and Kegan Paul.

Hoptopf, W. H. (1977) An examination of Piaget's theory of perception. In Geber, B. A. (Ed.) *Piaget and Knowing.* London: Routledge and Kegan Paul.

Inhelder, B. (1966) Cognitive development and its contribution to the diagnosis of some phenomena of mental deficiency. *Merrill-Palmer Quarterly, 12*, 299-319.

Inhelder, B. (1968) *The Diagnosis of Reasoning in the Mentally Retarded.* New York: John Day.

Inhelder, B. (1976) Foreword. In Modgil, S. and Modgil, C. (Eds.) *Piagetian Research,* Volume 5. Slough: NFER.

Inhelder, B. (1978) New currents in genetic epistemology and developmental psychology. In Bruner, J. S. and Garton, A. (Eds.) *Human Growth and Development.* Oxford: Clarendon Press.

Inhelder, B., Sinclair, H. and Bovet, M. (1974) *Learning and the Development of Cognition.* London: Routledge and Kegan Paul.

Inhelder, B., Bovet, M., Sinclair, H. and Smock, C. D. (1966) On cognitive development. *American Psychologist, 21*, 160-164.

Johnson, D. J. and Myklebust, H. (1967) *Learning Disabilities: Educational Principles and Practices.* New York: Grune and Stratton.

Kauffman, J. M. and Hallahan, D. P. (1976) *Teaching Children with Learning Disabilities: Personal Perspectives.* Columbus, Ohio: Charles E. Merril.

Keogh, B. (1977) Working together: a new direction. *Journal of Learning Disabilities, 10*, 13-17.

Klees, M. and Lebrun, A. (1972) Analysis of the figurative and operative processes of thought of 40 dyslexic children. *Journal of Learning Disabilities, 5*, 389-396.

Klein, N. K. and Safford, P. L. (1977) Application of Piaget's theory to the study of thinking of the mentally retarded: a review of research. *Journal of Special Education, 11*, 201-216.

Koppell, S. (1979) Testing the attentional deficit notion. *Journal of Learning Disabilities, 12*, 43-48.

Lawton, J. T. and Hooper, F. H. (1978) Piagetian theory and early childhood education: a critical analysis. In Siegel, L. S. and Brainerd, C. J. (Eds.) *Alternatives to Piaget.* New York: Academic Press.

Lerner, J. W. (1976) *Children With Learning Disabilities.* London: Houghton Mifflin.

McGarrigle, J. and Donaldson, M. (1974) Conservation accidents. *Cognition, 3*, 341-350.

McGrady, H. J. (1968) Language pathology and learning disabilities. In Myklebust, H. R. (Ed.) *Progress in Learning Disabilities,* Volume I. New York: Grune and Stratton.

Meltzer, L. J. (1978) Abstract reasoning in a specific group of perceptually impaired children: namely the learning disabled. *Journal of Genetic Psychology, 132*, 185-192.

Mercer, C., Forgnone, L. and Sabatino, D. (1976) Definitions of learning disabilities used in the United States. *Journal of Learning Disabilities, 6*, 376-386.

Modgil, S. and Modgil, C. (1976) *Piagetian Research: Compilation and Commentary,* Volume 7. Windsor: NFER.

Murray, F. B. (1972) Acquisition of conservation through social interaction. *Developmental Psychology, 6*, 1-6.

Murray, F. B. (1977) Some cautions on the implications of Piaget's theory for education of the handicapped. In Margary, J. F., Poulson, M. K., Levinson, P. J. and Taylor, P. A. (Eds.) *Piagetian Theory and the Helping Professions,* Volume 6. Los Angeles: University of California.

Murray, F. B. (1978a) Critique: development of intellect and reading. In Murray, F. B. and Pikulski, J. J. (Eds.) *The Acquisition of Reading.* Baltimore: University Park Press.

Murray, F. B. (1978b) Human behavior and reading instruction. In Gallagher, J. and Easley, J. A. (Eds.) *Knowledge and Development,* Volume 2. London: Plenum Press.

Myers, P. E. and Hammill, D. D. (1976) *Methods for Learning Disorders.* New York: John Wiley.

Myklebust, H. R., Bannochie, M. N. and Killen, J. R. (1971) Learning disabilities and cognitive processes. In Myklebust, H. R. (Ed.) *Progress in Learning Disabilities,* Volume II. New York: Grune and Stratton.

Parucka, M. R. (1976) A review of the research on concept formation and the child with learning disabilities. In Anderson, R. P. and Halcomb, C. G. (Eds.) *Learning disability/minimal brain dysfunction syndrome.* Springfield, Ill.: Charles C. Thomas.

Piaget, J. (1967) *Six Psychological Studies.* London: University of London Press.

Piaget, J. (1968) Preface to second edition. In Inhelder, B. (Ed.) *The Diagnosis of Reasoning in the Mentally Retarded.* New York: John Day.

Piaget, J. (1969) *The Mechanisms of Perception.* London: Routledge and Kegan Paul.

Piaget, J. (1970a) Piaget's theory. In Mussen, P. H. (Ed.) *Carmichael's Manual of Child Psychology.* New York: Wiley.

Piaget, J. (1970b) A conversation with Jean Piaget. *Psychology Today,* **3,** 25-32.

Piaget, J. (1971) *Biology and Knowledge.* Edinburgh: Edinburgh University Press.

Piaget, J. (1973) Genetic epistemology. In Evans, R. I. (Ed.) *Jean Piaget: The Man and His Ideas.* New York: Dutton.

Piaget, J. (1974) Foreword. In Schwebel, M. and Raph, J. (Eds.) *Piaget in The Classroom.* London: Routledge and Kegan Paul.

Piaget, J. (1977) The role of action in the development of thinking. In Overton, W. F. and Gallagher, J. (Eds.) *Knowledge and Development,* Volume 1. London: Plenum Press.

Piaget, J. (1977a) Comments on mathematical education. In Gruber, H. E. and Vonèche, J. J. (Eds.) *The Essential Piaget.* London: Routledge and Kegan Paul.

Piaget, J. and Inhelder, B. (1969) *The Psychology of the Child.* London: Routledge and Kegan Paul.

Reid, D. K. (1978) Genevan theory and the education of exceptional children. In Gallagher, J. and Easley, J. A. (Eds.) *Knowledge and Development,* Volume 2. London: Plenum Press.

Schmid-Kitsikis, E. (1972) Exploratory studies in cognitive development. In Monks, F. J., Hartup, W. W. and de Wit, J. (Eds.) *Determinants of Behavioural Development.* London: Academic Press.

Schmid-Kitsikis, E. (1973) Piagetian theory and its approach to psychopathology. *American Journal of Mental Deficiency,* **77,** 694-705.

Senf, G. (1976) Future research needs in learning disabilities. In Anderson, R. P. and Halcomb, L. G. (Eds.) *Learning Disability/Minimal Brain Dysfunction Syndrome.* Springfield, Ill.: Charles C. Thomas.

Shelton, M. N. (1977) Affective education and the learning-disabled student. *Journal of Learning Disabilities,* **10,** 618-624.

Siegel, L. S. and Brainerd, C. J. (Eds.) (1978) *Alternatives to Piaget: Critical Essays on the Theory* New York: Academic Press.

Sinclair, H. (1974) Recent Piagetian research in learning studies. In Schwebel, M. and Raph, J. (Eds.) *Piaget in the Classroom.* London: Routledge and Kegan Paul.

Smedslund, J. (1977) Piaget's psychology in practice. *British Journal of Educational Psychology,* **47,** 1-6.

Sticht, I. (1978) The acquisition of literacy by children and adults. In Murray, F. B. and Pikulski, J. J. (Eds.) *The Acquisition of Reading.* Baltimore: Baltimore University Park Press.

Tarnapol, L. (1971) *Learning Disorders in Children: Diagnosis, Medication, Education.* Boston: Little. Brown.

Thayer, E. S. and Collyer, C. E. (1978) The development of transitive inference: a review of recent approaches. *Psychological Bulletin,* **85,** 1327-1343.

Torgesen, J. (1975) Problems and prospects in the study of learning inabilities. In Hetherington, E. M. (Ed.) *Review of Child Development Research,* Volume 5. Chicago: University of Chicago Press.

Trepanier, M. L. (1978) The performance of learning-disabled and normal children on Piagetian memory tasks. Ph.D. thesis submitted to University of Rochester, New York.

Waller, T. G. (1977) Think first, read later. In Murray, F. B. (Ed.) *Development of the Reading Process.* Newark, Dela: International Reading Association Monograph.

Warner, B. J. and Williams, R. (1975) Piaget's theory and exceptional children: a bibliography, 1963-1973. *Perceptual and Motor Skills,* **41,** 255-261.

Wason, P. C. (1977) The theory of formal operations—a critique. In Geber, B. A. (Ed.) *Piaget and Knowing.* London: Routledge and Kegan Paul.

Wepman, J. M., Cruickshank, W. M., Deutsch, C. P., Morency, A. and Strother, C. R. (1975) Learning disabilities. In Hobbs, N. (Ed.) *Issues in the Classification of Children,* Volume 1. San Francisco: Jossey-Bass.

Werner, H. (1937) Process and achievement—a basic problem of education and developmental psychology. *Harvard Educational Review,* **7,** 353-368.

Woodward, M. (1963) The application of Piaget's theory to research in mental deficiency. In Ellis, N. R. (Ed.) *Handbook of Mental Deficiency.* New York: McGraw-Hill.

Younniss, J. (1971) Classificatory schemes in relation to class inclusion before and after training. *Human Development,* **14,** 171-183.

Zimmerman, B. J. and Rosenthal, T. L. (1974) Observation learning of rule-governed behavior by children. *Psychological Bulletin,* **81,** 29-42.

Chapter 21

Contributions of Piagetian Theory and Research to an Understanding of Children with Learning Problems

THOMAS McFARLAND AND FREDERICK GRANT

INTRODUCTION

Purpose

A theory is no more the child than a map is the territory. Nor does a map represent all of the territory any more than current theory describes or explains all of the child. However, as we either broaden our universe of knowledge or narrow our universe of ignorance about the child, we find analogy useful.

Let us begin then by considering our present understanding of the development of the child as an incomplete mosaic map. Flavell (1963, p. 412) asserts:

> Piaget has staked out a lot of virgin territory in the area of cognitive growth. As is often the case with new explorations, the cartography was not always accurate. But at least there are stakes there now, and we cannot and should not ignore them.

With Piaget as our Mercator of child development, we shall extend our mapping analogy and attempt to chart some of the many issues of children with learning problems.

We intend to make explicit how our interpretation of Piagetian theory and research contributes to our understanding of children with learning problems. Just as the cartographer must strive to outline and identify virgin territory amidst obstacles and mazes, the helping professions need to define, categorize, classify, and label children with learning problems in spite of the many difficulties and ambiguities. We ask what aspects of Piagetian theory contribute to our definition and understanding of children with learning problems? Later, we plan to explore both the 'why' and 'how' of definitions related to learning and individual differences. We assert that the concept of learning to be useful for the helping professions must be defined, and we follow immediately with the question: What are the implications for defining learning within the construct of development? We observe as we continue our questioning that the holistic and interdisciplinary approach to Piagetian theory with its conceptual framework offers us a point of departure where we may raise questions of learning and development. Just as every question presupposes some answer, we presuppose that Piaget's work is the place to begin.

We visualize development—a synoptic construct—as an inverted cone. When we keep in mind that children at whatever stage of growth are constructing their own cones of development, then we have our beginning. Our analogy becomes even more appropriate when we recognize the difficulty encountered in mapping a cone, realizing that surface structures are observable but that deep structures are not. In mapping, a description of the surface features includes concepts of enclosure, proximity, order and continuity. Similarly, a description of the development of the child involves content analysis of surface features, such as an exploration of patterns, clusterings and hierarchical sequences. In addition, we believe the Piagetian system is a profitable framework for the description and analysis of deep structures of the child's cognitive development. We accept Piaget's contribution as suitable for the understanding and measurement of differences in children.

After an exploration of definitions and descriptions, we will move toward the future directions of theory-building. Piaget and Inhelder (1963) in *The Child's Conception of Space* indicate that topological relations are the foundation and genesis of the studies of specific geometries. In *Science of Education and the Psychology of the Child,* Piaget (1971) stressed the importance of adequate understanding of the development of the child as a prerequisite for related studies in education. Although theorists and researchers of individual differences have developed specific explanations and predictions, we hold that these may prove inadequate without a more comprehensive mapping of the surface and deep structures. Further, we will consider the possibility of applying Piagetian theory not only to children with special needs, but also to their teachers.

To clarify without analogy, our intention is to discuss the relationship of Piagetian theory and research to the field of special education. As we bring Piagetian theory and research together with theory-building and research of special education, we find both differences and similarities. Since the total area of interface is far too extensive to evaluate in this paper, we have selected the stage-dependent contributions of Piagetian theory and research as our focus. Our illustrations will be chosen from applications in linguistics and curriculum development.

When discussing controversial issues of explanation and modification, we have listed only primary sources and reviews of literature through which the controversy may be pursued. Although we admit to being influenced by the sources favourable to Piaget— most notably Flavell (1963, 1977)—we have attempted to include critical discussions such as Brainerd (1978), and Siegel and Brainerd (1978). Our strategy is to synthesize viewpoints and information from both developmental psychology and special education.

We have illustrated graphically the holistic aspects of Piagetian theory in Figure 21.1.

Our interpretation of Piaget's theory subsumes intelligence, defined as adaptive behaviour, under the more inclusive construct of development. Through the model we indicate three aspects of intelligence: content, function and structure. Content and structure are viewed as variant, while function remains invariant. The model also represents the interrelationship between and among the content: observable behaviours, structure, the inferred schemata of the intellect; and function, the process by

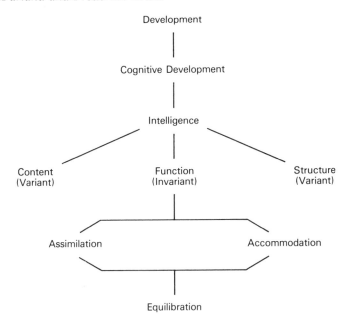

Figure 21.1 Model of interpretation.

which structure undergoes transformation. Further, the model serves as a reference point to stages of development which, in turn, we represent by a second model, the inverted cone (see Figure 21.2). Stages, it should be noted, are tied to the variant structures and content of intelligence as well as to the mode of invariant functioning in the equilibrating process of assimilation and accommodation. In addition, these models exhibit the overarching concept and significance of the equilibration process, and reveal not only the interrelated but the synergistic aspects of intelligence as well.

Although using models has some inherent dangers, their application can have heuristic value for active students and help them grasp readily Piaget's theoretical process. The model illustrates graphically the power of Piaget's theory, for with few constructs considerable description and explanation of phenomena, i.e. intelligence as adaptive behaviour, is possible. The tests of adequacy and economy in theory-building are definitely approached if not met in Piaget's system.

Theory

Let us first look at the relationships between the models and theoretical concerns of Piagetian developmental psychologists and special education professionals. Piagetian theory exemplifies the organismic-developmental model (Nesselroad and Reese, 1973). This structural—theoretical model has methodological implications for the description, explanation, and modification of children. Theory construction and problem selection are determined in part by the model. The organismic-developmental model is one of the two models that have great impact on developmental psychology. The mechanistic

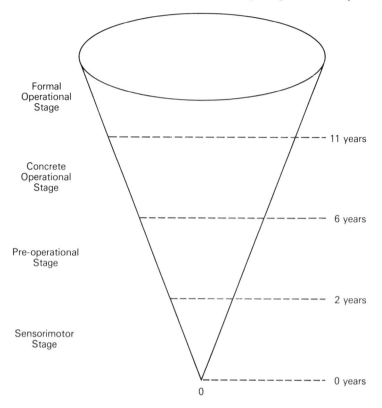

Formal
Operational
Stage

- - - - - - - - - - - - - - - -/- - - 11 years

Concrete
Operational
Stage

- - - - - - - - - - - - - - -/- - - - - 6 years

Pre-operational
Stage

- - - - - - - - -/- - - - - - - - - 2 years

Sensorimotor
Stage

-/- - - - - - - - - - - - 0 years

0

Figure 21.2   Cone of development. Note: we view development as an inverted cone of ever-expanding structures influenced and shaped by four factors: maturation, physical experience, social interaction and equilibration.

model has an impact on developmental psychology, but an even greater influence on special education. Empiricist tradition and various neo-behaviouristic theoretical systems are consistent with this mechanistic model.

Model differences may or may not be resolved through a synthesis of models. Recent writings of Inhelder (1972) on information-processing point out directions for synthesis. Rapprochement between models has been a goal evident in the work of Berlyne (1965). However, organismic and mechanistic structural—theoretical models may be incompatible for some purposes.

Theory-builders choose different areas of focus. Piagetian theory has focused on the description and explanation of universal aspects of cognitive development in children. His theory is both comprehensive and holistic. Piaget has chosen not to focus on individual differences. By the nature of their responsibility, special education professionals are required to construct theories on how children differ, what explains this difference, and how to facilitate, modify, or accelerate development. Some Genevan developmental psychologists have shifted the focus of Piagetian theory to special populations.

Theory construction about normal development and variance may be complementary. Inhelder (1968, p. 329) describes the advantages of normal and pathological comparisons:

While pathological phenomenon of thought profits from analysis in a developmental perspective, the analysis of pathological aspects enriches and helps refine operational theory itself.

Although the initial Inhelder (1968) research with special populations started with a pragmatic interest in diagnosis and assessment, Inhelder asserts that the research has given unexpected support to Piagetian theory. Many disciplines including medicine have utilized the study of deviance to clarify issues and problems in normal development. Conversely, a description and understanding of normal development is a prerequisite for a complete understanding of deviance.

According to Baltes, Reese and Nesselroade (1977, p. 4):

Developmental psychology deals with the description, explanation, and modification (optimization) of intra-individual change in behaviour across the life-span, and with inter-individual differences (and similarities) in intra-individual change.

This definition encompasses the concerns of the special educator. Interdisciplinary research within the comprehensive framework of Piagetian theory has provided insight into each of these concepts. According to Beth Stephens, an interdisciplinary special educator and Piagetian researcher:

The search for a mapping of the pathways of early development leads to the work of Jean Piaget . . . While he has worked to outline the stages of cognitive development, special educators have sought to incorporate his findings into intervention programmes. (P. 237)

Piaget has provided impetus for theory-building through his efforts in the context of discovery. Special educators and developmental psychologists have adopted some of his ideas and clarified others in the context of confirmation and justification.

Research

A review of research into children with learning problems creates ambiguity concerning the contribution of either Piagetian theory or research. A cursory review from the perspective of a special educator in the United States reveals limited interest in either the theory or the research. Books of the profession and textbooks of special education teacher-training have few significant references to Piaget. Few references each year have been indexed under the subject of Piaget in *Exceptional Child Education Resources*, the primary abstract journal of the field of special education.

However, an indepth review from an interdisciplinary perspective indicates some notable exceptions within the field of special education and numerous studies with special populations from other disciplines. Smith (1974), Robinson and Robinson (1976), Lerner (1978), and Wyne and O'Connor (1979) are authors of special education textbooks that have referred to Piaget's contributions. *The Journal of Mental Deficiency* has published research and a monograph. Reviews of research which include developmental psychology indicate research with special populations is increasing (Modgil and Modgil, 1976).

Although research with special populations has had little present impact on the special educational professional, potential implications require careful evaluation. *The Diagnosis of Reasoning in the Mentally Retarded* by Barbel Inhelder (1968) has provided the impetus for Genevan research with special populations.

Since an historical overview and analysis of research with special populations is provided by Reid (1978), we will only consider research which falls within the context of our paper. *The Proceedings of Sixth Interdisciplinary Conference on Piagetian Theory and Its Implication for the Helping Professions* (Magary et al, 1977) also provides a bibliography and relevant presentations on the handicapped child.

DEFINITION

Purposes and Problems

Samuel Johnson determined that definitions were hazardous; Erasmus pronounced them dangerous, and Disraeli declared his hatred for them, yet in spite of history's caution scientists and philosophers alike fall into semantical snares and traps, for disciplines demand definitions. Special education is no different; it too asks: 'Who are the children with learning problems and how shall they be defined?'

Borrowing from the medical field, it can be noted that the 'why' of definition has at least four purposes: (1) to establish an aetiology; (2) to make a prognosis; (3) to make a diagnosis; and (4) to offer some treatment. The third and fourth purposes are more clearly a focus of education than either the first or second.

Definition permits classification or categorization and can be justified on the basis of purpose. On the other hand, the 'how' of definition may take more than an Alexandrian sword to cut the definitional knot. However, there is, in traditional classification, some sense of direction for special education, namely, the construct of adaptive behaviour with its four degrees of mild, moderate, severe and profound.

Categories and Classifications

The helping professions continue to categorize, classify and label children with learning problems. Two categories of special education related to children with learning problems are mental retardation and learning disabilities. Mild, moderate and severe classifications of children are each relevant to learning. To receive special education services, children must be labelled and classified. According to Hobbs (1975):

> Increased precision in describing children and increased capacity for handling data make obsolete the familiar and limiting categories of exceptionality. Improvements in classification procedures must be sought not as an end in itself but as a means to deeper understanding and to improved programming for children. (Pp. 281-282)

This recommendation appears in *The Futures of Children—Categories, Labels, and their Consequences*, a report from the Project on the Classification of Exceptional Children. This landmark interdisciplinary study in the United States indicates that new approaches to defining children with learning problems must replace inadequate categorizations and arbitrary classifications. In particular, an approach is needed which attempts to resolve the difficulty of defining the concept of learning itself, but defining individual differences more than compounds the problem. We are encouraged by Reid's penetrating observations that differences may be variations in the rate of development or growth of children, or the route they take in that growth or development (Reid, 1978).

Development and Learning

Increased ability to describe children requires that learning be defined broadly within the construct of development. Piaget (1962) defines learning holistically within the context of development:

> Development is the essential process and each element of learning occurs as a function of total development rather than being an element which explains development.

Children with learning problems then become children with problems in development. Piaget's distinction between learning and development derives from the organismic-developmental model. Piaget's theory contrasts with 'learning theories' in that in Piagetian theory learning does not play a central role. Development is necessary if the child is to acquire structures instead of new information of responses. This distinction between development and learning is controversial (Brainerd, 1978). Although operational definitions of development and learning may be necessary for research within this controversial area, development as commonly denoted in the growth model is sufficient for a consideration of usefulness for pragmatic purposes.

Holistic and Interdisciplinary

Cognitive development is a concern for both Piagetian theorists and special educators. Cognition has traditionally been defined to include thinking, intelligence, knowledge, problem-solving, consciousness, conceptualization, and symbolizing. Contemporary developmental psychologists have added perception, imagery, memory, attention, and learning to the traditional components (Flavell, 1977). Piagetian theory utilizes a comprehensive approach which divides cognition into two aspects—figurative and operative. Perception, imitation, and mental imagery are the categories of the figurative aspect. Operative aspects are described in cognitive stages or periods.

Flavell (1963) makes a useful distinction between Piaget's theory *about* perception and his theory *of* perception. Piaget describes what perception is, how it develops, and how it relates to cognition in his theory *about* perception. In contrast, his theory *of* perception is a precise descriptive model of how the perceptual apparatus functions. The same distinction may generally apply to other components such as language. The ability to consider components both within the concept of cognition and yet separately as an area of theory-building represents a useful and comprehensive framework for interdisciplinary research.

Cognitive developmental approaches provide opportunities for both interaction of disciplines and specific research within a discipline. Each helping profession has tended to categorize children from their own perspective without adequate incorporation of other perspectives. Piagetian theory and research has provided the focus for conferences on multi-handicapping conditions. The annual conference on Piagetian theory and its implications for the helping professions has considered the psychological, social, and biological complexity of children from an interdisciplinary perspective. A multitude of research has been and will be presented as generated from Piagetian theory. The usefulness of a theory and its definitions may be evaluated by the research it generates.

DESCRIPTION

Content Analysis

In his early works, Piaget analyses the content of the child's thoughts about the reality of the world and physical causality. By content, Piaget refers to 'raw uninterpreted behavioural data themselves' (Flavell, 1963). Piaget utilizes a discovery approach called the clinical method, which psychiatrists use as a means of diagnosis. He found this method a compromise between 'pure observation' and tests. This approach as utilized in his early research depended entirely on verbal responses. The revised clinical method involves concrete objects. Piaget set qualitative criteria for the evaluation of these responses. Like Freudian psychoanalysis and interpretation, Piaget noted that 'precise rules for the diagnosis' could not be stated, and that this research skill required 'at least a year of daily practice' (Piaget, 1929).

In contrast, but not inconsistent with Piaget's original research, content analysis approaches from other disciplines are based on quantitative procedures which encourage the use of computers. According to Kerlinger (1973, p. 525):

> Content analysis is a method of studying and analysing communication in a systematic, objective, and quantitative manner to measure variables.

This method of observation and analysis has been used in linguistics to study phonemes, morphemes and other surface structures. It is utilized most often in the computer content analysis of writing with the smallest major unit of analysis being the word. Quantification of any observable behaviour makes content analysis potentially useful to areas besides communication.

The analysis of curriculum content has become an important trend in special education. The content analysis approach is distinguished from other strategy approaches which focus on either the 'analysis of the student' or the 'analysis of environmental conditions' (Lerner, 1978). A specific class of content analysis useful in special education is skills development. Skills development, as the name suggests, involves both the systematic determination of the developmental sequence through which learning and instruction should proceed and the direct teaching of skills in that sequence. The skills-developmental approach has often been referred to in the special education literature as task analysis (Salvia and Ysseldyke, 1978). Task analysis is a process for identifying instructional objectives in a developmental sequence (Gagné, 1977). The purpose of task analysis is to divide the curricular learning path into smaller steps by beginning with goals and subdividing into specific objectives in a teaching sequence. Each instructional objective may then become the target of a lesson and be further subdivided. Direct teaching includes instructional techniques and procedures which maximize the establishment of new skills and behaviours. Direct teaching has been contrasted with the ability-training approach which identifies cognitive-process weaknesses for remediation (Salvia and Ysseldyke, 1978).

Assessment procedures for measuring the child's skills are important by-products from the study of the skills development of the child. Diagnostic aspects of assessment involving decisions of readiness have been studied through skills development. Assessment is the measurement of the child's skills and individual differences viewed in relationship to the optimal path of development and learning. New techniques in data reduction should make description of the child's development and differences more useful and accurate in the near future. Factor analysis, cluster analysis, and multi-dimensional scaling are all techniques which should prove invaluable in the description and surface understanding of the child. Patterns, or sequential hierarchies, can be validated through assessment and analysis utilizing these techniques. As previously indicated, the topological relations of proximity, order, enclosure and continuity can be mapped. This information on surface development can then be utilized as the foundation for research in a variety of disciplines. Just as Piaget questioned children to determine the content of their thought at the beginning of his research efforts, we need to begin our research at this point.

Our own research has combined the functional-skills research and the Piagetian system to investigate the relationship between the child's learning of coin equivalence and the conception of number (McFarland and Grant, 1980). The skills-development patterns of one hundred children previously classified as mild mentally retarded were examined through assessment procedures, cluster analysis and multidimensional scaling procedure to clarify the learning problems of these children.

Task analysis has been utilized to develop an initial learning hierarchy limited to coin learning up to a maximum of one dollar. A learning hierarchy is defined by a succession of behaviours which constitute a hypothesized optimal learning sequence. As indicated, the procedures of construction involve identifying terminal objectives and then stating subordinate objectives based on hypothesized dependencies in linear order. In this hierarchical sequence, the expectation is that the acquisition of simpler steps in the developmental sequence will make the attainment of more advanced and complex behaviours highly likely, while failure would make acquisition less probable. Skill tests are needed to measure each behavioural objective in the learning hierarchy if the sequence is to be validated. The elements of the task analysis model are objectives of learning and instruction, which are defined in terms of what the learner can do. These objectives describe the scope of the content, while the learning hierarchy designates the sequence.

A scalogram analysis (Torgerson, 1958) and complete link cluster analysis (Johnson, 1967) has been used to validate empirically the learning hierarchies during formative evaluation. Scalogram analysis provides a procedure for rearranging behavioural objectives, such that passing a test item based on each objective in the sequence will predict passage of all objectives lower in the sequence and failing an item predicts failure of all subsequent items. Cluster analysis provides a multidimensional procedure for rearranging objectives or other items to summarize order and relationships (Hubert and Baker, 1976). A matrix of association and clusters of items have been determined. Cluster analysis was chosen as a useful method of both content and structural analysis. Our primary goal has been to synthesize these useful research approaches to map the surface features of these children—to try to understand and determine the concepts and skills of children with learning problems.

Structural Analysis

Piaget defines structural changes from the perspective of an organismic-developmental psychologist. His research focuses on changes in patterns of elements or organization over time. Structures, which he calls schemas or schemata, are inferred. Piaget (1970) relates structures to three key ideas: wholeness, transformation and self-regulation. Although Piaget's definition of structure is not precise, it is more exacting than the definition of other developmental psychologists (Bart, 1975).

The construct of structures is one of the unresolved issues in the study of stages or periods. *Structures d'ensemble*—unified structures of the whole—are major criteria for defining a stage. Stages constitute an important and controversial Piagetian developmental pattern. This pattern involves a group of similar or related cognitive entities which emerge concurrently during a certain period. Stage criteria have been discussed frequently by Piaget (1967, 1970), his proponents (Flavell, 1963, 1977), and his critics (Brainerd, 1978).

Sequence can be both related to and contrasted with stage. The construct of stage implies a hierarchical sequence. In contrast to stage, sequence involves temporarily ordered cognitive entities which develop in a regular pattern. Both Piagetian theory and statistical-measurement theory discuss issues and problems related to the determination of hierarchical sequences and stages. Piagetian theory includes discussions of both within-stage sequences and stages, and across-stage transitions.

The investigation of patterns—stages and sequences—of children's development and learning is an important present and future contribution of Piagetian research. This research contributes to the explanation of why children differ.

Piaget describes a comprehensive, detailed, and documented system of cognitive development. Structural analysis is presented within the framework of the sensori-motor, concrete operational, and formal operational periods and a sequence of stages constituting each period. In his early works, Piaget investigated the language, thought, moral judgment and reasoning of the child utilizing the clinical method. In his later works, he has systematically explored the child's conception and understanding of quantity, logic, number, time, movement, velocity, space, geometry, chance and perception (Flavell, 1963). He utilizes specific tasks for each area. Recent studies have focused on the child's 'grasp of consciousness—action and concept' (Piaget, 1976).

Piaget's stage-dependent contribution has catalysed developmental research. Original research, replication studies and analysis have been generated in each of these modes of knowledge and experiences. Piaget, his collaborators and his replicators have developed a multitude of tasks, methodologies and formats for exploring and measuring the stage development of the child. A large proportion of this exploration involves the usefulness of specific cognitive entities such as conservation.

Conservation is the cognitive entity utilized in the description of the child's development in the concrete operational period. This construct has been most intensively researched and evaluated. The utilization of a construct such as conservation involves both conceptual and practical problems of relevance to children with learning problems. The construct of conservation was formulated by Piaget who also developed the methodology for its assessment. Conservation is central to a Piagetian understanding of the concepts of number, ordinal, cardinal, transversity, reversibility and groupings. Conservation serves as the indicator of the concrete operational period, index of number development and signal of the onset of logical reasoning (Flavell, 1963). Piaget and Inhelder (1958, p. 32) define conservation:

> The term 'conservation' is used in a sense specific to the authors' meaning—a particular empirical factor (weight, volume, etc.) remains an invariant in the child's mind throughout observed changes of state. Piaget describes successive qualitative changes of state preceding, during transition, and following conservation for factors such as quantity, weight, and volume. Although the timing of each factor varies, the dominant characteristics of the concrete period come from conservation experimentation.

According to descriptive research, the child with a lower mental age lacks the cognitive ability to do other than guess or make simple perceptual estimates. The child with a higher mental age utilizes quantitative judgment and understands that groups are invariant during irrelevant transformations. However, according to Piagetian methodology, questioning strategies must be utilized to determine whether the child is operating from a qualitative, 'guestimate-minded approach or a quantitative', measurement-minded approach (Flavell, 1977).

Although many organismic-developmental psychologists and many special education professionals find the construct of structure, stage and conservation useful, controversy revolves around the definitions of each. The lack of definitional consensus hinders the potential usefulness of these constructs. Clarification is needed. Operational definitions and statistical measurement techniques will need to be developed if the construct is to be programmatically useful as the construct of sequence.

Theory construction and research in language illustrate a potential clarification for cognitive theory and research. Piaget has contributed to theory about language and theory of language. This contribution is compatible with structuralist theorists utilizing an organismic-developmental model. Chomsky advanced a theory of language in *Syntactic Structures* (1964) and *Aspects of Syntax* (1965). This theory postulates that:

Knowledge of a language involves the ability to assign deep and surface structures to an infinite range of sentences, to relate these structures appropriately, and to assign a semantic interpretation and phonetic interpretation to the paired deep and surface structure . . . then a person who knows a specific language has control of a grammar that generates (that is, characterizes) the infinite set of potential deep structures, maps them onto associated surface structures, and determines the semantic and phonetic interpretations of these abstract objects. (Chomsky, 1968, Note 1)

Phonological components that reside in the surface structure may be studied as a foundation for the study of semantic components that reside in the deep structure. Linguistics explore sentences in our language which may appear simple on the surface, but manifest deep conceptual structures by intricate principles of syntax. Although correspondences between surface and deep structures may be complex, the study of this correspondence is fruitful.

Just as Chomsky's theory demonstrates the complexity of language, Piaget's theory of cognitive development demonstrates the complexity of the child. Both language and the child are marvels to behold—language in its ubiquity of the human condition and the child from its moment of conception to its senescence.

Although Chomsky and his followers distinguish between language competence and language performance, their attempts to formalize what we know when we know a language is just beginning. Further, their attempt to make explicit the interrelationships between and among the phonological, syntactical, and semantical components of language leaves gaps as wide and as glaring as split infinitives. Even the chasm between deep and surface structure seems to widen with each new insight, while the adequacy of the theory leaves much unexplained.

Chomsky, in his theory, speaks of language universals, transformations, deep and surface structure. Piaget's theory has similar concepts that may be applicable to understanding the child:

This much recalled, the most important conclusion to be distilled from our series of investigations is that the study of structure cannot be exclusive and that it does not suppress . . . . Quite the contrary, it tends to integrate them, and does so in the way in which all integration in scientific thought comes about, by making for reciprocity and interaction . . . Thus, to recall just one example, after linguistics had earlier inspired all sorts of fruitful but somewhat one-sided ideas, there came the unexpected inversions of Chomsky to broaden those overly narrow views. (Piaget, 1970, p. 137)

Any naïve visitor to another country or culture will observe how similar the behaviour of children is—perhaps something universal in their behaviour pattern that the child changes over time. These transformations, deep and surface structures, exist in all children. Structural analysis from an approach similar to that of Chomsky will contribute to both our understanding of universals and differences.

Chomsky (1965) also reminds us in our theory-building that our theory may be descriptively adequate and yet leave much unexpressed. We also can raise questions of explanatory adequacy without being descriptively adequate, perhaps with a theory of cognitive development as with a theory of language, the questions of explanation are the ones we really want to get at.

In curriculum development, structural analysis involves an analysis of the student rather than the curriculum content. Piagetian theory is representative of the sequential-stage-of-development approach (Lerner, 1978). Diagnosis and remediation consists of determining the stage and helping the student to complete growth of a period. Growth is assumed to be dependent on earlier stages and to be sequential. Curriculum development or the child's learning path should be consistent with the child's stage and inferred structures.

The comparative studies of the child's conception of number and coin learning is interesting in that both included a complex blend of informally learned and formally taught concepts and skills involving logical-mathematical entities and natural-social phenomena. Many children with learning problems fail to learn and develop these skills and concepts through the natural process of incidental experience and maturation.

Although our study was primarily surface descriptive, pattern descriptions may lead to an understanding of causes if explanations and patterns are consistent. The usefulness of the construct of conservation of number was examined in relationship to diagnosis and prediction. Besides the determination of interesting acquisition patterns, we further hope to investigate stage as a predictor of readiness. Provoked correspondence, spontaneous correspondence, and discontinuous quantity tasks were given to determine their relationship to coin summation and selection items. After determining that statistically significant relationships and unique patterns of development existed prior to intervention, twenty children were introduced to coin learning utilizing a variation of Piaget's active method approach. Then their patterns were reassessed.

Although our study involved primarily an exploratory investigation of children with learning problems, we were particularly impressed by the usefulness of several descriptive aspects. First, we considered the multidimensional scaling and cluster analysis results to be extremely interesting. Descriptions of children incorporated both tasks related to Piagetian theory and functional skills of concern to special educators. Second, the complexity of stage as a predictor became clear. The issues of Piagetian methodology, criterion of stages, and horizontal decalage generated many problems. However, this does not preclude the possibility of better prediction when the description of development is improved and these issues are resolved.

In describing Genevan research which uses structural analysis with special populations, Reid (1978) notes that this method of inquiry approaches 'the indepth nature of the analysis of regulations'. She correctly points out that factor analysis and other structural analysis techniques observe only the results of functioning itself to verify operational findings.

Functional Analysis

A recent trend in Genevan research with special populations has been the analysis of regulations. According to Reid (1978) in her review of these studies:*

> The analysis of regulation seems more appropriate to explanation since its data are the dynamic, rather than the static, properties of thought.

The dynamic properties of thought hold true for all ages and children—an invariant function. Equilibration is the constructivist aspect of Piagetian theory which is both unique and the most controversial. Although it is obviously beyond the scope of this paper to discuss whether this factor and the other three factors cited by Piaget explain either development or individual differences, these factors, i.e. maturation, physical experience, social interaction and equilibration, have the greatest potential for future implications.

Many studies involving children with learning problems have been completed with focus on active method—empirical and reflexive abstraction—disequilibrium, social interaction, or other issues related to acceleration and modification. Unfortunately, most studies have failed to utilize careful surface descriptions of children. A theory of instruction must be generated from a theory of development that includes both descriptive and explanatory aspects. Obviously, both training studies and active versus

---

*This chapter which parallels the purposes of our chapter is recommended reading. We will strive not to duplicate her effort.

receptive method studies will be relevant to special education as well as general education. Although these stage-independent aspects may be the most useful contributions of Piagetian theory and research in the future, stage-dependent contributions have greater implications for the present.

Directions

If Piagetian theory and research contributes to an understanding of children with problems in development and learning, it may also contribute to an understanding of their helpers. Teacher educators, helpers of helpers, should emulate Piaget. The organismic-developmental model provides the assumption that professionals are growing individuals. In the context of discovery, the helping professionals may be observed and questioned. (Insight may be obtained into their actions and consciousness.) The surface description of helping professionals such as special educators should provide the foundation for the explanation, prediction and modification of their actions. Like the understanding of the development of the child, the understanding of each helping profession is an incomplete mosaic map. Individuals in the helping professions are struggling with problem-solving and theory-building related to individual differences in children. A content analysis of their actions in the classroom can be provided by a variety of presently available systems such as Flanders' System of Interactions Analysis. A surface description of the actions will provide information for an exploration of deep structures.

Many professionals who deal with children on the basis of surface behaviours prefer to think about their own structures from a deep structure perspective. This may explain the lack of popularity of teacher observation systems in conjunction with an emphasis on behavioural approaches to children.

We have utilized a case-method approach to study the deep structure understandings of professionals. During pre-service courses, in-service workshops, and conferences, we have investigated the understandings and theory-building of both elementary and special education teachers. Unfortunately, we have not developed these cases or our questioning strategies to the experimentally useful level of the Piagetian task, nor do we have the gift of insight of Jean Piaget. We hope that other gifted observers might study this phase of life-span developmental psychology. If the helping professional is to deal with individual differences in behaviour across life-span, they should have the ability to describe, explain and modify not only the behaviour of children but also their teachers.

Piaget has not only mapped the pathways of early development, but also the formaoperational pathways of advanced development. Could his method of charting the formaoperational period be used in teacher observation? What would a protocol of the teacher in the classroom look like?

A new area of Piagetian research might provide interesting insight. Piaget's observation and questioning of children reveal that their actions may precede their consciousness by many years. How many teachers are cognizant of their actions or realize what theory-base they utilize? Applying Piaget's approach to action and cognizance to the classroom teacher is both exciting and useful.

SUMMARY

In Summary, we focus on the understanding of individual differences in children. Content analysis of the child's surface structures has been stressed as the foundation for structural analysis, which in turn leads to functional analysis. We believe the Piagetian system has contributed extensively to our understanding of the child's cognitive development.

The issue of explanation has been primary to Piaget's theory and may become the major aspect of contribution in the future. Decisions regarding change and modification will be greatly influenced by the results of the explanatory theory-building and research. We have limited our discussion of this area not because it may not be crucial, but simply because this area needs further clarification.

Each helping profession possesses significant problems related to the description, explanation and modification of children with learning problems. Each profession with its many theorists and researchers focuses on those problems, but as professionals within specific disciplines, we have become aware of overlapping issues, continuing ambiguities and unanswered questions. We are hopeful that unifying efforts may resolve some of those ambiguities and offer us some solutions to our questions. We hold the opinion that the present and future areas of research generated from Piaget's theory will offer us this interdisciplinary effort. We are encouraged by the ferment from the many and diverse disciplines relying on Piaget's work.

REFERENCES

Baltes, P. B., Reese, H. W. and Nesselroad, J. R. (1977) *Life-Span Developmental Psychology: Introduction to Research Methods.* Monterey, California: Wadsworth Publishing.

Bart, W. M. (1975) *The Process of Cognitive Structure Complexification.* (Research Report, No. 49.) Minneapolis: University of Minnesota. Research, Development, and Demonstration Center in Education of Handicapped Children.

Bart, W. M. and Airasian, P. W. (1974) Determination of the ordering among seven Piagetian tasks by an ordering—theoretical method. *Journal of Educational Psychology, 66,* 277-284.

Berlyne, D. E. (1965) *Structure and Direction In Thinking.* New York: Wiley.

Brainerd, C. J. (1978) *Piagetian Theory of Intelligence.* Englewood Cliffs, N.J.: Prentice-Hall.

Chomsky, N. (1964) *Syntactic Structures.* The Hague: Mouton.

Chomsky, N. (1965) *Aspects of the Theory of Syntax.* Cambridge, Massachusetts: The MIT Press.

Chomsky, N. (1968) *Language and Mind.* New York: Harcourt, Brace and World.

Flavell, J. (1963) *The Developmental Psychology of Jean Piaget.* Princeton, N.J.: D. Van Nostrand.

Flavell, J. (1977) *Cognitive Development,* Englewood Cliffs, N.J.: Prentice-Hall.

Gagné, R. M. (1977) *The Conditions of Learning.* New York: Holt, Rinehart and Winston.

Ginsburg, H. and Opper, S. (1979) *Piaget's Theory of Intellectual Development.* Englewood Cliffs, N.J.: Prentice-Hall.

Grant, F. A. (1978) Reading: from function to schemata—a theory of reading based on linguistics and Piaget's theory of cognitive development. *Piagetian Theory and Its Implications for the Helping Professions. Proceedings Seventh Interdisciplinary Conference.* Volume 11 (Eds.) Lubin, G. L. et al.

Hobbs, N. (1975) *The Futures of Children*—Categories labels, and their consequences. San Francisco: Jossey-Bass.

Hubert, L. J. and Baker, F. B. (1976) Data analysis by single-link and complete-link hierarchical clustering. *Journal of Educational Statistics, 1,* 87-111.

Inhelder, B. (1968) *The Diagnosis of Reasoning in the Mentally Retarded.* New York: John Day.

Inhelder, B. (1972) Information-processing tendencies in recent experiments in cognitive learning-empirical studies. In Farnham-Diggory, S. (Ed.) *Informational Processing in Children.* New York: Academic Press.

Inhelder, B. and Piaget, J. (1958) *Growth of Logical Thinking from Childhood to Adolescence.* New York: Basic Books.

Inhelder, B., Chipman, H. H. and Zwingmann, C. (1976) *Piaget and His School: A Reader in Developmental Psychology.* New York: Springer-Verlag.

Johnson, S. C. (1967) Hierarchical clustering and schemes. *Psychometrika, 32,* 3.

Kerlinger, F. N. (1973) *Foundations of Behavioral Research.* New York: Holt, Rinehart and Winston.

Lane, M. *Introduction to Structuralism.* New York: Basic Books.

Lerner, J. W. (1978) Instructional strategies: A classification schema. In Mann, L., Goodman, L. and Wiederholt, J. L. (Eds.) *Teaching the Learning-disabled Adolescent.* Boston: Houghton Mifflin.

Magary, J. R. et al (1977) Piagetian Theory and Its Implications For the Helping Professions—Emphasis: The Handicapped Child. *Proceedings of Sixth Interdisciplinary Conference.*

McFarland, T. D. and Grant, F. A. (1980) A relationship between the educable mentally retarded child's learning of coin equivalence and the concept of number. *Proceedings of Ninth Interdisciplinary Conference.*

Modgil, S. and Modgil, C. (1976) *Piagetian Research: Compilation and Commentary.* Atlantic Highland, New Jersey: Humanities Press.

Nesselroad, J. R. and Reese, H. W. (1973) *Life-span Developmental Psychology: Methodological Issues.* New York: Academic Press.

Piaget, J. (1929) *The Child's Conception of the World.* New York: Littlefield, Adams.

Piaget, J. (1955) *The Language and Thought of the Child.* New York: Meridian Books.

Piaget, J. (1962) Development and learning. *Journal of Research in Science Teaching.*

Piaget, J. (1967) *Biology and Knowledge: An Essay on the Relations Between Organic Regulations and Cognitive Processes.* Chicago: The University of Chicago Press.

Piaget, J. (1968) *Structuralism.* New York: Harper and Row.

Piaget, J. (1969) *The Mechanisms of Perception.* New York: Basic Books.

Piaget, J. (1971) *Science of Education and the Psychology of the Child.* New York: Viking Press.

Piaget, J. (1973) *Main Trends in Inter-disciplinary Research.* New York: Harper and Row.

Piaget, J. (1973) *The Child and Reality—Problems of Genetic Psychology.* New York: Grossman Publishers.

Piaget, J. (1973) *To Understand Is to Invent.* New York: The Viking Press.

Piaget, J. (1976) *The Grasp of Consciousness—Action and Concept in the Young Child.* Cambridge, Mass.: Harvard University Press.

Piaget, J. and Inhelder, B. (1963) *The Child's Conception of Space.* Atlantic Highland, New Jersey: Humanities Press.

Piaget, J. and Inhelder, B. (1969) *The Psychology of the Child.* New York: Basic Books.

Piaget, J. and Inhelder, B. (1973) *Memory and Intelligence.* New York: Basic Books.

Reid, D. K. (1978) Genevan theory and the education of exceptional children. In Gallagher, J. M. and Easley, J. A. (Eds.) *Knowledge and Development*, Volume 2, *Piaget and Education.* New York: Plenum Press.

Reynolds, M. C. and Birch, J. W. (1977) *Teaching Exceptional Children in All America's Schools.* Reston, Virginia: The Council for Exceptional Children.

Robinson, N. M. and Robinson, H. B. (1976) *The Mentally Retarded Child: A Psychological Approach.* New York: McGraw-Hill.

Salvia, J. and Ysseldyke, J. E. (1978) *Assessment in Special and Remedial Education.* Boston: Houghton Mifflin Company.

Sapir, S. A. and Nitzburg, A. C. (1973) *Children with Learning Problems: Readings in a Developmental-Interaction Approach.* New York: Brunner/Malel.

Siegel, L. S. and Brainerd, C. J. (1978) *Alternatives to Piaget: Critical Essays on the Theory.* New York: Academic Press.

Smith, R. M. (1974) *Clinical Teaching—Methods of Instruction for the Retarded.* New York: McGraw-Hill.

Stephens, B. (1977) A Piagetian approach to curriculum development for the severely and profoundly handicapped. *Educational Programming for the Severely and Profoundly Handicapped.* Reston, Virginia: The Council for Exceptional Children.

Torgerson, W. S. (1958) *Theory and Methods of Scaling.* New York: Wiley.

Warner, B. J. and Williams, R. (1975) Piaget's theory and exceptional children: A bibliography, 1963-1975. *Perceptual and Motor Skills*, **41**, 255-261.

Wyne, M. D. and O'Connor, P. D. (1979) *Exceptional Children—A Developmental View.* Lexington, Massachusetts: D. C. Heath.

Interchange

FINCHAM REPLIES TO McFARLAND AND GRANT

Imagine Piaget were literally on trial with McFarland and Grant as prosecutors and myself constituting the defence. You, the reader, are a juror. The charge is read 'Jean Piaget without obtaining registration as a bona fide LD specialist has conducted work which contributes to the understanding of LD children'. Judge Modgil instructs you to attend only to the facts of the case as these constitute the basis on which your verdict must rest. The court proceeds.

Prosecution (P): The defendant provides a cartography of normal development. Theories of normal development and variance may be complementary.

Defence (D): It is true that theories of 'normal' and pathological development often enrich each other. Indeed, one presupposes the other. But the issue in question is whether Piaget's theory in particular, assists in understanding learning disabilities. In this respect, the prosecution merely quotes Inhelder's conclusion that the study of pathology 'helps refine operational theory', an innocuous and, in the present context, irrelevant argument. Similarly, Stephen's opinion is cited as testimony to the value of Piagetian work for special education. Such opinion, however, must be weighted against the fairly extensive evidence I have led attesting to the questionable veridicability of Piaget's 'map' and hence its use in charting alien territory. This evidence has not been refuted nor even questioned by the prosecution. Unlike them, I have tried to determine which parts of the original land were correctly surveyed as durable constructions cannot be built on shifting sands.

P: An interdisciplinary perspective indicates an increasing amount of Piagetian-inspired research with special populations.

D: Both parties seem to agree that on the basis of LD research Piaget's contribution to knowledge in this area is at best ambiguous. Can the prosecution therefore justifiably argue that the use of Piagetian ideas in relation to other exceptional groups (which may bear no relation to the LD!) substantiates the present charge? In any event, it is the result of such research not its mere existence that is crucial. Furthermore, such findings as do exist require interpretation. The mere cataloguing of where this research is to be found is hardly admissible evidence and does nothing to detract from my earlier analysis of extant findings.

P: Piaget's work assists in the definition of LD children.

D: Johnson, Erasmus and Disraelia notwithstanding, the issue here is not the question of definition *per se* but whether the defendant's pen *is* mightier than the 'Alexandrian sword' when it comes to the 'definitional knot'. The prosecution case rests on two points. First, they quote Piaget's learning/development distinction and although they do not mention learning disabilities, it is implicitly assumed that this somehow resolves or assists in the definition problem. How? Moreover, there is nothing in their general portrayal of Piaget's views which differentiates his work from earlier attempts to make this distinction (e.g. Dewey). By contrast, I have considered what is uniquely Piaget's and tried to show explicitly the limited utility of his ideas *vis-à-vis* LD children as well as pure research. Second, the holistic and interdisciplinary nature of Piaget's theory is held to bear on definition. Again one asks precisely how? And again there is a deafening silence. Surely the mere fact that it has these characteristics is not testimony to its suitability just because learning disabilities affect the whole child and hence various professions? Is it really being suggested that providing 'the focus for conferences on multi-handicapping conditions' is a criterion for evaluating theories?

P: Piaget's theory is useful in description.

D: This is the most confusing aspect of the prosecution case. Under the heading of description is included the three Piagetian components of intelligence: content, structure, and function. Are these therefore all seen as descriptors with the same epistemological status? Consider the statement, 'Conservation is the cognitive entity utilized in the description of the child's development in the concrete operational period'. *Inter alia*, this view poses the problem that if Piagetian structures merely describe development then it cannot also be argued that development explains learning. Furthermore, the prosecution's reification of Piagetian structures explains why their exposition stops after 'definition' and 'description'. Initially, they claimed that Piaget's theory provides insight into the definition or description, explanation and modification of intra-individual change and inter-individual differences. They proposed to explore all three aspects but by including Piagetian structures as descriptors rather than explanators understandably stop after the first. It is misleading to suggest or imply that the functional invariants and Piagetian structures have any status other than that of hypothetical constructs.

But what are the prosecutor's substantive claims *vis-à-vis* description? As regards content, none (at least with relevance to the issue at hand). After a perfunctory reference to Piaget, they continue by extolling the virtues of quantitative techniques in content analysis. Although it has no bearing on the case, it is perhaps worth correcting any false impressions created by these remarks. It is not uncommon for social scientists to overlook the fact that statistical analyses are means and not ends—they yield results as strong or weak as the data analysed, which are themselves collected on the basis of theoretical and conceptual analysis. Indeed, for several of the multivariate techniques mentioned (e.g. multidimensional scaling) an adequate solution has to be decided on and invariably rests on theoretical rather than purely statistical considerations. Why these techniques should be introduced in evaluating Piaget's theory remains a mystery. One suspects that their consideration is based as much on the fact that the authors used them in their study as on anything else. Unfortunately, no reference is given to the research and from their cryptic description it is not possible to work out what was done let alone whether the statistical techniques were appropriately applied.

In relation to structure and functional analysis Piaget's work does receive somewhat greater attention. Again, however, it is little more than a simplified sketch of the defendant's position. Reference to research is vague and merely asserts general conclusions (e.g. 'According to descriptive research, the child with a lower mental age lacks the cognitive ability to do other than guess or make simple perceptual estimates'. My own rather more detailed evidence attempts to refute such critical statements. None of the points I raised is even considered in the prosecution case.

Finally, it should be noted that much of the prosecution's evidence is limited to the defendant's metatheory. As argued earlier, this in no way commits one to Piaget's substantive theory for presumably anyone using such constructs (e.g. structure, etc.) may also contribute to the LD field.

P: 'If Piagetian theory and research contributes to an understanding of children with problems in development and learning, it may also contribute to an understanding of their helpers'.

D: This is an interesting and potentially fruitful suggestion. Unfortunately, it is not developed and perhaps advisedly left to 'other gifted observers'. En passant, it is worth noting (1) a new-found hesitation as to whether Piaget really does promote understanding of the LD child (2) that whereas learning problems were earlier reduced to those of development they are acknowledged above to be co-existent with one another.

P: Summary (see McFarland and Grants' reply to my chapter).

D: In summary, may I remind the jury that the charge must be determined on its own merits. Incidentally, providing a cartography of child development in one's attempt to resolve epistemological questions is not misdemeanour. If uncritical cartologists wish to accept such a map without evaluating its internal consistency or relationship to the landscape, that is their responsibility. Merely quoting LD practitioners' references to or preferences for Piagetian theory does not establish his contribution.

It is also worth remembering that the charge must be decided on the facts. I submit that the prosecution's case is almost devoid of facts and rests instead on a series of vague and unsubstantiated generalizations. They lead no conceptual or empirical evidence and instead merely cite Reid (1978). But this paper reviews Piagetian theory and special education as a whole and hence does not deal with learning disabilities in much detail. Moreover, the research reviewed is, as the author admits, highly selective rather than exhaustive. Not surprisingly many of the LD studies covered in my earlier evidence are not cited by Reid. Nor, incidentally, does she mention the problems I point out with regard to the Genevan research. Indeed, there is nothing in the prosecution case which answers the various issues raised. Rather, there is substantial agreement with my claims as the major Piagetian constructs alluded to are acknowledged as controversial or unclear (e.g. the development/learning distinction is 'controversial'; Piagetian methodology, stage criteria and horizontal decalage generate 'Problems'; equilibration is 'unique and the most controversial'. How can the authors thus argue for the utility of these constructs with regard to LD children? I suggest that had they tried to illustrate concretely and substantiate their general claims, they would have become far more aware of their inconsistency. I submit that there is no case to answer.

Judge: On the basis of the evidence, can you convict Piaget, beyond all reasonable doubt, for contributing, or even potentially contributing to the field of learning disabilities? Consider your verdict.

McFARLAND AND GRANT REPLY TO FINCHAM

The issue

On the surface—*prima facie*—it may appear that the writings of Fincham and ourselves are addressed to the same central issue—the contribution of Piagetian theory and research to an understanding of children with learning problems. However, careful examination reveals that the focuses of our papers are different. We have focused our paper on the practitioner and the question of usefulness. Fincham has focused on the researcher and the question of the 'truth' of the theory. Because of this difference in thrust and emphasis, it is difficult to reply to the 'heart' of his paper. In fact, we are able to agree with many aspects of his paper. Unfortunately, we do not agree with his assumption that usefulness cannot be considered prior to the resolution of basic research questions.

Let us illustrate by referring to the presently dominant theory in special education— Skinner's operant conditioning principles. Gallagher (1979) points out that a great amount of time has elapsed between Skinner's basic research of the 1930s and 1940s and the acceptance of research ideas as applied to children with learning problems in the 1960s and 1970s. Note, however, that as alluded to in Fincham's comment on 'Skinnerian man', such a basic concept as reinforcement has not been resolved in spite of the now existing 'commonsense' acceptance of its usefulness. In his paper, Fincham agrees that Piagetian theory 'has or will in the near future', influence many people's thinking without their explicitly acknowledging it. This contribution may be similar to the utilization of Freudian concepts, such as aggression and identity, by social learning theorists or the application of treatment in medicine prior to the understanding of the reason for its effectiveness.

We believe that concepts from Piagetian theory will prove useful regardless of basic research findings. We do not mean to imply that basic research and the careful review of Fincham is unimportant. To the contrary, we feel that what is presently known from this research can contribute to operational definitions of constructs and offer guidance against abuses in Piaget's name. Like a skilled debater, Fincham has argued the opposing position of a debate when selected to do so, in spite of many aspects of the paper which note useful concepts, and in spite of several articles which indicate his affinity with the pro-Piagetian position. We would now like to review some useful concepts recognizing the support and review of Fincham. We suggest that his review like that of Reid (1978) provides an excellent summary of basic research issues relevant to the area of special education and concepts of Piaget.

The concepts

The definition of who are children with learning problems may be clarified through both general and specific concepts of Piagetian theory. We agree totally with Fincham regarding the 'blooming, buzzing and definitely confused' status of definitions in learning disabilities. That is why we have chosen the 'broad' category of children with learning problems similar to Hallahan and Kauffman (1976). Fincham has selected the narrow definition for his focus.

We have stressed the need for a comprehensive approach to categorization and classification which is both holistic and interdisciplinary. Piaget's figurative and operative distinctions allow for an exploration of several constructs relevant to the definitional process. Just as attempts to understand the processes of children should not simply be set aside as phrenology, neither should an exploration of cognitive development be called 'grasping at straws'. Fincham seems to be using reductionism as he moves his argument from the usefulness of cognition to operativity to specific conservation tasks.

The controversy over development and learning as described by Fincham may be relevant to basic research, but in pragmatic terms the argument of 'the chicken' and 'the egg' may be useful. Practical problems of research circularity may be solved in applied research by developing operational definitions. A developmental perspective is clearly needed in special education, for the field has become overdependent on behavioural approaches. Further, a change in model from mechanistic to organismic-developmental could provide a growth of knowledge. When combined in an information-processing model, valuable concepts may emerge.

Mapping the surface and deep structures of children with learning problems is the 'stage-dependent' area of Piagetian theory and research which we indicated to be most useful at present. Fincham (1979) indicates that conservation tasks may provide useful information which contribute to 'criteria used to identify LD children' and the 'structure of their intellect'. Fincham's present paper notes that the *methodes clinique* is undoubtedly one of the major factors which made possible his contribution to knowledge. Although we indicate the limited investigation of content by Piaget and the problems with defining stage and structure, this mapping of the child's skills and understanding still seems to be a necessary pursuit. Although we have focused on content and structure, Fincham, like Reid (1978), has preferred to indicate his support for functional contributions such as the 'fundamental concepts' of equilibration, organization and construction. Fincham notes in his 'some important implications' section that the constructs or metatheory seem to be the contribution of Piaget. We are in agreement with this statement from the applied perspective of professionals in a field with immediate needs.

The direction of future Piagetian research should consider both basic research and applied research needs. We have indicated our opinion regarding related research in curriculum development, linguistics and teacher education. Obviously, these areas contribute to an understanding of reading disabilities. Many other constructs can be identified that will interface with reading and other learning problems. Field experiments should be implemented to determine their usefulness. If like a certain psycho-linguistic processes model, they do not demonstrate effective results, then they should be revised or discarded. Methodological applications like active learning and concrete materials in a variety of forms should be tested. Answers to the usefulness question will be derived by practitioners while the basic research answers are forthcoming.

REFERENCES

Fincham, F. D. (1979) Conservation and cognitive role-taking ability in learning-disabled boys. *Journal of Learning Disabilities,* **12,** 25-31.

Gallagher, J. J. (1979) Rights of the next generation of children. *Exceptional Children,* **46,** 98-107.

Grossman, R. P. (1978) Learning disabilities and the problem of scientific definitions. *Journal of Learning Disabilities,* **11,** 120-123.

Hallahan, D. P. and Kauffman, J. M. (1976) *Introduction to Learning Disabilities: a Psycho-Behavioral Approach.* Englewood Cliffs, N.J.: Prentice-Hall.

Reid, D. K. (1978) Genevan theory and the education of exceptional children. In Gallagher, J. and Easley, J. A. (Eds.) *Knowledge and Development,* Volume 2. London: Plenum Press.

Piaget, J. et al (1980b) *Les Formes Élémentaires de la Dialectique.* Paris: Gallimard.

Piaget, J. et al (1981) *Recherches sur le Possible et le Nécessaire.* (Vol. I: Le Développement des Possibles.) Paris: Presses Universitaires de France.

Piaget, J. et al (In press) *Recherches sur les possible et le nécessaire.* (Vol. II: Le Développement du Nécessaire.) Paris: Presses Universitaires de France.

Chapter 23

Tabulated Summary

SOHAN AND CELIA MODGIL

PHILOSOPHY

Negative Orientation	Positive Response to Negative Orientation	Positive Orientation	Negative Response to Positive Orientation
Quantity of work does not establish claim to serious philosophical attention—three related defects: material convoluted; often badly argued; evades central points at issue.	A thinker should be understood within his own framework of thought. Hunting for inconsistencies does not lead to a better understanding of work: some criticisms too simplistic; others reflect radical misunderstandings of Piaget's position.	Piaget often criticized for not taking sufficient notice of social factors in account of development of knowledge. This criticism overlooks the sociological roots of Piaget's genetic epistemology—close to giving sociology of knowledge.	May's paper does not exonerate Piaget from charge that is cited for he focuses on much narrower issue—the development of social knowledge in the child.
Piaget's theory of mind is Kantian.	Phillips is talking about a different kind of cognitive structure than that posited by Piaget. Piaget refers to general structures involved in any problem-solving.	Development of affective experience, logical, moral and legal thought are dependent on relations with others—social co-operation plays important role in development of reason.	Paper primarily a favourably oriented, non-critical exposition of Piaget's position on these matters and expositor is at pains to tell what Piaget *really* is getting at and to put his work in the context of other sociological writing (which Piaget neglected to do).
Good grounds for argument that there is only trivial difference between Piaget and views of many contemporary philosophers with respect to the structure of cognitive structures.	Piaget does not believe that cognitive structures are found ready-made in the child's mind.	Behaviour has both a psychological and a sociological aspect. Relations between individuals continually modify our consciousness. Concept of a social system as a nexus of relationships has considerable similarities to idealistic system of internal relations—perhaps 'relativistic structuralism' has most affinities with this.	Piaget does not discuss social factors in relation to cognitive development in any detail and neither does Mays.
Contemporary literature in philosophy of science contains abundance of advice on matter of change but overall thrust is that experience alone cannot dictate that a change be made—contemporary thought reveals Piaget's discussion of process of change of cognitive structures to be deficient.	Piaget does take account of social factors in the development of reason and objective knowledge. Influence of Baldwin greater than alleged Kantian influence.		Appears Piaget's sociological writings are a mixture of empirical generalization (without clarity of what constitutes relevant evidence), a dose of *a priori* and topped with the attempt to formalize in quasi-mathematical terms.

No grounds to support Piaget's assumption that there is only one particular configuration of a cognitive structure that will set it in equilibrium. No escaping conclusions that notions like isomorphism and equilibration (and the related assimilation, accommodation and homeostasis) cannot do the work Piaget requires of them. There is a growing body of critical literature.

Piaget's attempt to biologize and psychologize Kant are a rejected fundamental misunderstanding, in Piaget's work, both of twentieth-century philosophical empiricism and epistemology.

(Phillips)

Touchstone of modern empiricism— ordinary discourse—will not give logical justification of philosophical concepts.

For Piaget, genesis and validity deal with two different approaches to the problem of knowledge. Piaget would argue that an account of the development of concepts needs a discussion of their validity.

Phillips has difficulty in under-standing Piaget's work because of misunderstanding of how the term *epistémologie* is used in French philosophy.

(Mays)

Piaget specifies social relation of self to others in terms of notion of inter-individual exchange. Posits social exchange values which have qualitative character as opposed to quantitative nature of economic exchange.

There exists scale of values—a comparison or ordering of previously obtained satisfactions. Actions of another evaluated in terms of personal scale of values, each such action tending to elicit a return action. Incorporates conception of sympathy.

Also group values derived from valuations of individuals constituting social group.

Also obligated by moral values in dealings with others.

Exchange theory applied to legal transactions—relationship between morality and law-equality between individuals' basic value in society.

Also regards development of thought and rational argument due to social factors.

(Mays)

Mays gives no reason to believe Piaget's sociological theory success-fully reinforces other aspects of his life's work, nor does discussion remove doubts as to Piaget's capabilities as a philosopher. The discussion does not show Piaget's work on sociology is acceptable *qua* sociology.

(Phillips)

PSYCHOLOGY

Negative Orientation	Positive Response to Negative Orientation	Positive Orientation	Negative Response to Positive Orientation
Concept of stage does not receive clear theoretical justification or empirical support.	Concept of stage does not serve central function in Piaget's theory, descriptive concept accounting for change dually composed of invariance and transformation. Ideal order of development confirmed by replicatory research.	Piagetian psychology is not the answer to all problems in developmental theory and practice, although psychologists do not focus on most appropriate difficulties in the theory.	Treat learning as passive, mechanistic process. Learning involves response-produced changes in organism's perception of and reaction to environment and not static process.
Many methodological problems: investigators typically ignore social psychological processes involved in child—experimenter interaction.	Piaget's purpose not social psychology of cognitive development or psycho-linguistics.	Important to stress the biological foundations of the theory and to reinstate the basic tenets of genetic epistemology—five points are noteworthy: animal adaptation and human intelligence; biology and knowledge; the close relation between ontogeny and phylogeny; insistence on developmental mechanisms; and focus on commonalities and not differences.	Training is not 'drill training' and does generalize.
Measurement of Piagetian operations is completed by the role of language, perception, attention and memory which have been ignored in the Piagetian system. Tasks are multidimensional in nature: language difficulties influence conservation failure—non-verbal and less verbal tasks appropriate and better; perception and memory influence cognition, much variation in response depending on nature of stimulus materials, memory factors need controlling; child may need help to focus attention by filtering out irrelevant information.	Not a child psychologist but genetic epistemologist using children for his purposes not for their sake. Nevertheless, has shown himself conservation easier with smaller numbers than larger ones; also conservation and perception presented interesting partial isomorphisms. Decalages are marks that dissociation between form and content not yet complete.

Training has received treatment in Vonèche and Bovet chapter. | Various methodologies stem from various epistemologies and different methodologies accomplish very different tasks in science. Should not be confused with one another, and there should not be any sort of worshipping for any specific method regardless of aims of the | Learning psychologists interested in process, not only outcome, also long-term effects of training.

If learning can occur easily through observation or experimentation then pre-operational child has little meaning. Ease with which learning can occur casts doubt on structuralist position.

Different operational definitions of same concept; Piagetian version is not the only one. |

Piagetians disregarded possible significance of specific experiences and training in the acquisition of concepts.

Illustration of these problems can be taken from several areas of investigation: infant object concept development; class-inclusion paradigm; studies of animism; long-term memory improvement and formal operational structure.

Piagetian theory has provided a useful framework but is incorrect in many aspects.

(Siegel and Hodkin)

Piaget cannot be wrong at same time for not paying enough attention to senses *and* for putting too much emphasis on sensorimotor co-ordinations.

In case of class inclusion, Piaget's point is not for child to respond to saliency but produce it spontaneously.

Animism is not central in Piaget's thinking—not easy to completely deny animism in children.

No good reason to postulate relation between operational improvement and memory improvement; operational improvement can alleviate memory load.

Formal operational debate illustrates plasticity of concept attainment as measured by psychologists of different persuasions.

(Vonèche and Bovet)

epistemology for which it is instrumental: Piagetians interested in discovering what child thinks about a given question and not why child could achieve more and better performances; Piagetian learning research paradigm differs from S—R paradigm. It does not compare levels of performance before and after training primarily, but focuses on what has been transformed in course of training. The before/after paradigm overlooks processes by which learning occurs in favour of score. Such approach fuses performance and competence instead of feedback of performance upon competence.

What seems misunderstood in learning research about operatory concepts is necessity of an equilibration between two co-ordinated dynamic factors: internal regulatory forces and external argumentative powers. Latter only amenable to direct pressure from environment, former depends on integration of different levels of cognitive development within individual.

Welcome polemical methodological discussions to clarify approach. Field more scientific, scholastic crossfires and personal paradigms substituted by general consensus.

(Vonèche and Bovet)

Child—experimenter interaction must be viewed from social psychological perspective.

Piagetian approach useful but not considered alternate approaches—need to incorporate other data into theoretical model.

(Siegel and Hodkin)

LOGIC

Negative Orientation	Positive Response to Negative Orientation	Positive Orientation	Negative Response to Positive Orientation
Piaget's work dominates literature on children's logical capacities but provides no guidance for those interested in logic. Normative dimension of Piaget's claim (that is, Piaget's logic) is mistaken. It prohibits certain inferences one is entitled to make because it invites over-generalization and because of other odd results. Since Piaget uses this logic to judge adequacy and describe children's thinking, these inadequacies are a significant flaw. Descriptive dimension (the claim about what children and adolescents can and cannot do) appears defective. Evidence can be provided to falsify most obvious interpretation of claim. In the event of Piaget not intending such interpretation, many people take the claim in that interpretation, making recommendations based upon it.	(Tomlinson-Keasey already aware of argument when presenting her perspective, as Ennis's paper is a reprint of previously published work. It is felt, therefore, that Ennis's viewpoint has already received response.)	Few theorists have attempted to account for whole of logical development. Piaget has been very successful—he has altered course of developmental psychology and revitalized other areas of investigation. In examination of three critical theoretical components: *Structural component* necessary to differentiate two forms of structuralism, (variously labelled), referred to here as 'structuralism' and 'elementarism'. *Structuralism* necessitates specification of activities and functions under study, specifies functional invariants, describes variety of logical skills present during phases of development, skills scrutinized for underlying organization (*structure d'ensemble*). However, to try to reduce holistic construct to its component parts is to change nature of structure from entity that explains to one explained by component parts.	Unfortunate that Tomlinson-Keasey limits herself to two alternative paradigmatic approaches to viewing Piaget's structuralism, as there are strong arguments against elementarism. It is regretted that elementarism is only other category given besides structuralism and that Ennis's approach is classified as elementarist. Features of a third approach are: insistence that there be indication of kind of empirical evidence counting for and kind of evidence counting against a theory; refusal to attempt reduction of theoretical concepts to observational terms. Tomlinson-Keasey not appreciated requirement being made that there be indication of what would count as evidence for theory, e.g. Gou protocol. Piaget owes an account of what sort of things would count for and against theory and how identified.

When searching for a satisfactory interpretation of the claim considering four possible criteria for judging whether someone is working within Piaget's combinatorial system, no matter what the interpretation, it is concluded that claim is either false, or untestable, or not about deductive logic.

Open to others to unearth new interpretations and to consider truth and application of claim. Danger lies in justifying claim using one interpretation and applying and predicting using another interpretation.

(Ennis)

Elementarism views structuralist approach as circular and untestable. Structuralists armchair-theorize and over-generalize. Elementarist structure not primary or guiding role, since structure can be reduced to basic concepts. Component parts are important aspects, criticized as reductionist, atheoretical, empirical.

Resolution of structural issue requires more agreement among investigators from different theoretical perspectives on relationship between behavioural assessments and structures they elucidate.

Functional Component consists of all processes that spur child to interact with environment and translate interaction into progressively more consistent and stable thought-patterns.

Functional components received attention. Results generally supported view that self-regulation and active involvement contribute to cognitive process; information-processing studies contributed to a more detailed picture of functioning and to better understanding of processes child goes through in evaluating information; more progress likely to be evident in functional assessment as clash in structuralist paradigms less important in functional variables.

Follower of third approach does not insist on reductive-behavioural definition of a theoretical term. Rather on an indication of meaning of theoretical term by specification of kinds of evidence counting for and against theory containing term. Without such specification, predictions cannot be made from such a theory (for if they could, then satisfaction of predictions would count as evidence for theory and failure of predictions would count as evidence against) and theory is not empirically meaningful.

(Ennis)

Negative Orientation	Positive Response to Negative Orientation	Positive Orientation	Negative Response to Positive Orientation
		Stage Component: worn issue—question of existence of stages reappears because of link between stages and structures. Years of research on thought processes labelled concrete provided detailed picture skills and operations acquired while children learning to order and classify world. Stage of formal thought not similarly described.	
		As more information acquired, stage issue will recede in importance and investigators will chart structural changes in logical reasoning without needing defence of rigid discontinuous stage view of development.	
		The theoretical edifice constructed from three components has elegance and general service—ability unmatched in history of developmental psychology. Still need for revisions and changes and more specific understanding of relationships between and within components. Progress is hindered by clash of paradigms. Some tolerance could produce powerful explanation of development.	
		(Tomlinson-Keasey)	

LANGUAGE

Are Piaget's theories of knowing endangered by his relative lack of concern with language? He adopts an epistemological position and then considers what it implies about language.	Emphasizes child's spontaneous search for knowledge and verbal questions in works cited, both in sketching outline of theory of development of logical implication and causal explanation and in account of experimental method.	Raising of profound issues and triggering of passionate controversies: roots of thinking are in activity, not in language. However, functional aspects, representation and communication might influence thought: the representational function being explained by social interaction. Speaking and understanding speech are actions and partake in the mechanisms and structures of other actions. Functional identity between inter- and intra-individual operations as regards the structures of social interaction (of which language is a particular case).	Distinction between structure and function very helpful.
Emphasizes the receptive aspect of interpersonal verbal exchange rather than the active use of language—the child as questioner. Centres upon notion that knowledge transmitted verbally is knowledge passively received, *not* complementary notion that knowledge verbally requested is knowledge actively sought.	Regret that Piaget did not devote more study to interpersonal verbal exchange.		Draws attention to places where Piaget gives recognition to aspects of language acquisition which he does not usually stress.
	Piaget's study was epistemological, not construction of tests but data from verbal and non-verbal tasks obtained cross-culturally confirm the epistemological notions. If transformed into statistical tests, not reliable indicator of cognitive level.	(Sinclair)	Have no quarrel with Sinclair's interpretation of Piaget's views.
Trusts child's receptive language in research methodology, but is suspicious of 'pre-operational' stage expressive language. Two sides to attitude: during development of structure language can give a misleading estimate of understanding level but when understanding demonstrated, verbal expression of it is a later development which is a reliable indicator of conscious understanding.	Interesting that children do better under certain conditions. This raises different issues but no challenge to theory.		(Elliot and Donaldson)
	Bring to light aspects not discussed by Piaget, but not in contradiction with *the* theory.		
(Sinclair)	(Sinclair)		

Negative Orientation	Positive Response to Negative Orientation	Positive Orientation	Negative Response to Positive Orientation
Data concerning cognitive development of pre-operational subjects to be reinterpreted in accordance with new evidence indicating insufficient account of the extent language embedded in context. Errors in conservation tasks have source in misinterpretation of questions or instructions. Although likely children encounter difficulties postulated by Piaget, concepts need new study—essential to have highly interactive model of way pre-school child approaches experimental test. Difficult to conclude with Piaget that while both systems are developing, language follows behind cognition. (Elliot and Donaldson)			

MORAL DEVELOPMENT

	Theory unfinished, incoherent, contradictory, but central ideas can be confirmed with conviction of their relative validity.	Wright's approach generated striking insights. Going beyond Piaget, he has made underlying assumptions explicit.
	Restatement involves reducing Piaget's morality of duty as not truly moral, but he offers a uniquely valuable way of conceiving the nature and origins of moral obligation.	However, Wright is conflating two issues separated by Piaget: mono-graph concerns the transmission of morality from one generation to the next—the social and developmental mechanisms of this process concern interaction with others. However, his definition of morality is implicit in his methodology—justice and fairness; Wright is focusing on a different definition of morality than Piaget—how the individual becomes a moral being.
	The essential basis of Piaget's developmental theory, in moral as in logical fields, is that cognitive representation is a reflection upon already existing actions. The relationship between practical and theoretical morality conceived differently than by, e.g. Kohlberg—the child experiences a sense of obligation to others and acts increasingly co-operatively in the social context. As a consequence of the conscious realization of these events develops a morality based upon mutual respect.	Taking Piaget's conception of the development of mutual respect a stage further, implications for the development of the moral motive is a fundamental departure from Piaget's position.

(Weinreich-Haste) |
| Wholeness of original monograph obscured. Piaget less interested in the actual moral development of the child and more interested in the social—psychological question: the mechanisms operating between individual and society in the transmission of morality. Developmental social psychology impoverished by its failure to attend to Piaget's social psychological insights, although incomplete.

Asserts importance of parent and peer behaviour but does not test it.

Failed to take up questions about social cognition which his moral research generated.

Neither the definition of morality nor ways Piaget used it were adequate: priority of the rule; negotiation not considered in context of retributive justice; omits analyses of positive aspects of morality—sharing; not recognized significance of concept of fairness in data; intentionality is only partly a moral question; there are wider implications for causality; focuses much on conventional moral behaviour. | Comprehensive and useful review. Critique is cogent and convincing. In the main there is agreement.

Need to stress importance of distinction Piaget draws between practical and theoretical morality.

Conflict between unilateral and mutual respect not sufficiently stressed. Development is less a transition from one to the other than the increasing salience of mutual respect and the decreasing salience of unilateral—more subtle.

To Piaget's credit that concept of relationship is at heart of theory—a concept not discussed by Weinreich-Haste or adequately dealt with by philosophers, psychologists, socio-logists, or social-psychologists.

Weinreich-Haste does not do justice to the elements in Piaget's thinking that can be taken as starting points for further elaboration of a novel kind.

(Wright) | |

Negative Orientation	Positive Response to Negative Orientation	Positive Orientation	Negative Response to Positive Orientation
In developmental sequence: he ignored the subtleties of the second phase—the significance of change from unity to diversity; says little about reciprocity and relationship between peers—distinction can be made between developmental change in rhetorical moral statements and conceptual comprehension; insufficient development of 'stage' of equity; irrelevance or inappropriateness of the concept of respect.		Obligation arises from social interaction therefrom contingent upon mutual and reciprocal affection. Respect, obligation is the equilibrating factor having a developmental and social function.	
Selman, Damon and Kohlberg provide theoretical advance; other research confirms the interlocking relationship between moral thinking and social reasoning.		Basic interpretation of development more complex than usually stated. Unilateral and mutual respect are modes of relating and both can be present at different times with modes intermediate between extremes; Piaget does not recognize that there cannot be a heteronomous morality.	
Subsequent writings have not tackled Piaget's social psychological thesis adequately.		Parent—child relationships characterized by reciprocal affection, generating moral obligation through mutual respect, facilitate at the cognitive level: conscious cognitive decentring; objectivity of thought and logical structures; socialization of the intellect; personality development; theoretical morality.	
(Weinreich-Haste)		(Wright)	

PSYCHOMETRIC

Piaget had no interest in psycho-metrizing his work.	Elliott's reply to Hofmann has been incorporated in Elliott's chapter.	Although writing primarily from a negative stand-point, Hofmann makes a number of important points which should be taken into account by constructors of developmental tests—the contents of Elliott's paper are not incompatible with these points.	Elliott and Hofmann agree on a number of points yet are at odds on several points.
When operationalizing Piaget by utilizing a psychometric approach, structural invalidity exists if results of an assessment of individual do not show a substantial relationship to results of second assessment assumed to be logically equivalent.			Both assume that a well-constructed instrument should minimize the effects of composite confusion, i.e. the number of ways to obtain a given score.
Spirit of essay is of being critical of present state of theory regarding Piaget and psychometrics with realization that such critical discussion will lead to methodological research resulting in a stronger, pragmatic approach to Piagetian assessment.		Elliott is writing primarily from stand-point of relating Piagetian and neo-Piagetian tasks to measurement theory and in particular to latent trait theory.	Both support the importance of the distinction between assessment and measurement. Hofmann assumes that no social science instrument is a measurement instrument; Elliott assumes by using the Rasch model a measurement procedure results.
		There are difficulties in applying psychometrics to developmental tasks and the paper is therefore not wholly positive.	Hofmann would argue that with any statistical sampling continuity there would not only be task-difficulty variation but there would also be a hierarchical ordering of the tasks which would generally hold for all respondents.
Eleven sources of structural invalidity can be noted in Piagetian assessment procedures—the first eight can be discussed within three modes of assessment: stimulus presentation; performance response and verbal/non-verbal response.		However, it is possible to reconcile the requirements of psychometric and developmental theory in certain cases.	
These sources of structural invalidity are a function of not knowing where an assessment procedure is located within the faceted task structure.		Many tests in psychology and education come into the assessment category rather than the measurement category of observation. The majority of Piagetian tests are probably in the former category due to the problem of assessment across stages and the problem of horizontal decalage.	Elliott's conservation results seem neither to conform with Piagetian expectations nor appear to occur as a function of any of the discussed sources of structural invalidity.

Negative Orientation	Positive Response to Negative Orientation	Positive Orientation	Negative Response to Positive Orientation
Additional three sources of invalidity noted as occurring within content of task content variation.		However, from research in relation to the British Ability Scales it was reasonable to conclude that the items in the Formal Operational Thinking Scale form an internally consistent, homogeneous, unidimensional set; that quantitative individual differences in scores on the scale represent quantitative differences in ability to reason about hypothetical propositions; and that the results indicate that the attempt to fit a psychometric model with strong assumptions to a Piagetian test seems to have been successful.	One property of the Guttman scaling model is that a reproducibility can be obtained for a collection of tasks, for the tasks separately and also for each respondent.
Task understanding also included in debate dealing with judgment and explanation criteria leading to structural invalidity.			It appears to Hofmann that the Rasch model does not consider respondent characteristics. Piagetian theory does not appear to be sensitive to learning disorders that might be disruptive to developmental sequences.
Essay should be viewed as first attempt to impose general psychometric structure on Piagetian theory. Piaget has chosen to ignore such a structure without weakening his theoretical position, but has made it difficult for others to operationalize his theory psychometrically.		Conservation items which looked as if they might form a unidimensional set showed a high level of fluctuation and items were not measuring a common dimension.	Hofmann's suspicion is that differences in interpretations of Piaget are tempered by the psychometric models to which they adhere. However, any differences in thinking are believed to become reconciled through personal discussion.
(Hofmann)		It is concluded that it is possible in certain cases to produce tests as measurement tools which reconcile the requirements of psychometric and developmental theory.	(Hofmann)
		(Elliott)	

CROSS-CULTURAL

Psychological universalist position implies cultural superiority of the West. Lukács' critique of Kant suggests Piaget's cognitive stages mark progressive assimilation of structural principles of bourgeois industrialism. Piaget's theory has a socio-economic rather than a cultural bias. Structure of cognition reflects the structure of industrialized society with abstract, formal relations of production and exchange. Third-world countries should be forewarned of dangers when this mode of cognition begins to dominate all thought, divorced from social and human considerations. Lack of participation in the abstract levels of the social whole further identified as a source of 'retarded' cognitive and moral development among lower classes in West. Important to relate test results to structure of child's society and his place within it. (Buck-Morss)	Disputes Buck-Morss's definition of abstract formalism. Piaget analysed relationship between logic and psychology in cited references. If hypothetico-version of formalism accepted then aspects of Marx's work and Lukács' would fall in the scope of definition. Simple linkage between economic infra-structure and mental activity is 'crude Marxism'. Interpretation of Lukács' theory is a 'vulgarized' one. Disputable whether abstract formalism is dominant paradigm in capitalist countries. Feeble attempt to undermine a relatively strongly supported con-structionalist theory by involving largely ideological arguments which do not stand up to close scrutiny. However, framework broadened within which debate can be conducted. (Ghuman)	Cross-cultural research unlikely to resolve basic issues in theory. Implications of findings can be summarized: environmental factors (socialization, cultural and edu-cational) are important in actuali-zation of structures; time-lag found in non-Western children due to differential experiences with physical and social worlds. Piaget's model considerable advance over psychometric model of intelli-gence used across cultures. Model has considerable pragmatic value in generating new knowledge, hypotheses and hard data useful in curriculum planning in developing countries. In response to objections raised by radical academics, vast majority of people in traditional countries want new technologies in order to overcome endemic shortage of food and disease. Stance of radical thinkers is based on idiosyncratic interpretation of the situation and on ideological bias. Piagetian psychology can make a significant contribution towards education of third-world younger generation. (Ghuman)	Question dismissal of Buck-Morss's article. Impossible to universalize Piaget's tests by changing format in attempt to eliminate 'cultural bias'. Bias does not reside merely within tests as a cultural form, but within structure of that society in which tests were developed and to which they apply. Do Piagetian operations merely reflect the social structure and enable performance within it or do they also allow that structure to be critically comprehended? A different set of critical cognitive operations, a series of stages that deals dialectically with problems of substantive rather than formal reason may be necessary for this cognitive task. (Buck-Morss)

EDUCATION

Negative Orientation	Positive Response to Negative Orientation	Positive Orientation	Negative Response to Positive Orientation
Many claim to have found in Piaget's theory a sound basis for teaching practice. Others have not found this. Part of the reason for disagreement lies in the fact that people not entirely sure what Piaget's theory is or how various recommendations fit in. Not clear what Piaget means by 'development', what most teachers mean by 'learning' different from Piaget. Piaget's theory cannot provide solid basis for education. Does not address itself to questions with which education must deal—intellectual and emotional development of individual. Takes as its model, mature scientific (mathematical) mind. Attitude to knowledge and knower is ambiguous and cannot provide a basis for sound pedagogy.	Recent burgeoning of research evidence requiring modifications of Piaget's theory is to be welcomed and reflects its generative power. In agreement that educationists receiving Piagetian theory as dogma potentially damaging to education. Misinterpretations, however, insufficient grounds for rejecting theory's importance for education. Boyle guilty of inadequate appraisal of relevant experimental evidence in three instances: argument against Piaget's claim regarding the centrality of action in cognitive development; claims on the development of language and its role in cognitive development; claims that Piaget's theory 'takes as its model the mature scientific mind', and lacks means of application to arts and humanities.	Necessary to examine two important issues in Piagetian theory: learning and development and performance/competence. Significance of these findings is different for education in early, middle and adolescent years. Performance—competence issue of special importance in early childhood education. Although some evidence questionable, there remains less refutable evidence that situational factors affect level of cognitive functioning and where content familiar and intentions understood, capabilities greatest. Support for primary practices allowing pupil generation of problems and pursuit of interests in contexts and with materials related to experiences.	Unconvinced that a thorough knowledge of Piaget is needed if competence from performance is to be successfully diagnosed. Whole point of assessing competence in educational context is to help teacher to assist child in achieving better performance. Evidence that Piaget's theory is better at this than simpler diagnoses is lacking. Usefulness of performance—competence distinction limited. While performance cannot be predicted from knowledge of performance, it cannot be predicted from knowledge of competence either. Perhaps teacher must teach pupils to use intellect.

435

A theoretical basis for education must treat questions of social interaction, in particular psychology of language. Education concerned with interactions between individuals not growth of logical-mathematical structures in abstract 'epistemic subject'.

Piaget's theory no discernible influence on educational practice. One practical recommendation, manipulative activity (a lame recommendation from a vast literature)—if widely applied would stultify our brightest children.

(Boyle)

We should not try to make out of Piagetian theory a Procrustean bed on which all our concerns in education are stretched to point of distortion, but to discuss it as being of no concern to education is to ignore a large body of experimental evidence relating to cognitive development which is, if not the only concern of education, among its major ones.

(Tamburrini)

Piagetian tests of concrete operations assess a relatively stable and generalized competence. This is a prerequisite for understanding of central concepts and procedural rules in various knowledge domains. Important in middle years for teacher to be able to diagnose pupils' cognitive levels as explicated by Piaget. Diagnostic skills necessary for adoption of strategies to facilitate development of concrete thought—'embedded' thinking should be extended to become increasingly 'disembedded'.

Performance—competence issue not resolved for formal operational thought. Evidence strongly suggests contextually bound. Where number of variables complexly interrelated and/or material verbal/symbolic, it is a late acquisition. Teachers at secondary level need to have considerable understanding of Piagetian theory to diagnose levels and assess thinking necessary for various concepts and problems within a subject discipline.

Diagnostic and teaching skills need firm understanding of Piagetian theory and curricular content and organizational ability. Wide range of individual differences are revealed.

(Tamburrini)

Tamburrini reinforces, through her examples, the exaggerated extension of Piagetian notions by 'Piagetian educationalists'.

Emphasis on activity says nothing more than in order to learn you have to use your mind. We do not need Piaget to tell us that.

(Boyle)

Negative Orientation	Positive Response to Negative Orientation	Positive Orientation	Negative Response to Positive Orientation
		SCIENCE EDUCATION	
Not opposed to Piaget's theory, simply does not see great relevance of theory to many of key issues involved in success or failure of students in meaningful learning and problem-solving.

Ausubel's learning theory more relevant and has more interpretative power for variety of important science and mathematics education questions than Piaget's developmental psychology.

Research shows that 20 per cent of eight-year-old children consistently demonstrate formal thinking with regard to earth and gravity concepts and other basic science concepts. Replication with Nepali children shows similar patterns of concept development but four years later than for American or Israeli children. Long-term studies of concept-learning show that concepts acquired in early grades are retained and/or elaborated and functional when children reach grade eight. Most misconceptions evidenced in early grades are lost or altered suggesting a generally positive impact of early instruction on basic science concept development. | Both recognize important contribution made by Piaget in use and development of clinical interview, and both value studies in which technique is used to investigate development of science concepts.

Differ in importance placed on information gained from Piagetian tasks in guiding curriculum planning and teaching.

Not clear whether Novak rebutting existence of developmental sequence or merely questioning its usefulness to science and mathematics educators.

Data presented on pupils' responses to questions on specific science concepts interesting and potentially important for science educators, however, question utility of Ausubelian framework which is elevated to level of theory. Far from clear how constructs of differentiation and integrative reconciliation offer specific insights into data presented in paper. Hardly surprising students who demonstrate significantly better concepts in early grades also demonstrate superior knowledge in later years. Ideas of | Piagetian investigations by themselves provide the science educator with rich and useful insights into ideas children bring to school learning and what to expect in development. However, underlying mental operations elucidated by tasks constitute a more significant aspect.

Several science curriculum projects have specified process objectives for their courses based on Piagetian operations, using Piaget's operations as specific curriculum objectives.

Would not dispute that children impose meanings on events of their own accord and they conduct implicit theories as ways of handling novel or familiar situations, dispute, however, that by experience alone children come to develop conceptual framework of accepted science.

Piaget indicated importance of social transmission, discussing ideas, helping them to decentre by listening to other points of view. Does not mention transmission by teacher, written materials or agreed conventions of scientific community. | Two contributions represent close to consensus on promise and limitations of Piagetian paradigm for science education.

Both share respect for voluminous output of Genevan School.

Both critical of unwarranted extrapolation from Piagetian work to rigid prescriptions for science instructional practice.

With respect to Driver's observation that there is currently some debate whether it is children or operations to be ascribed to a stage, it is Novak's emerging view that to the extent that student possesses currently available framework of explanatory concepts relevant to given task, he can be judged pre-operational, concrete, transitional, or a formal operational thinker.

Driver cites Piaget's emphasis on active interplay of experience and developing structures. Crucial difference between Ausubelian view and Piagetian is the extent the active interplay should be guided to develop specifically relevant explanatory concepts. |

A theoretical model for cognitive learning placing emphasis upon role of specifically relevant concepts and specifically relevant learning experiences as major sources of variation in concept development is favoured over a theoretical model that places major emphasis upon 'stages' of development of 'cognitive operations'.

Curriculum implications, while they do not mean that any child can learn any subject matter at any stage of development, do point in favour of the potential for substantive influence on cognitive development through carefully devised, meaningful learning experiences.

(Novak)

Ausubel do not enable predictions to be made nor are they amenable to critical testing. Ausubelian framework into which Novak attempts to assimilate his interesting data is unnecessary and adds nothing to his case.

Piagetian theory is addressing a different problem to that focused on by Novak. It is not in opposition and could complement Piaget's theory.

(Driver)

Experiments undertaken to put developmentalist and classical learning theories to test show results of traditional learning techniques to have not been as dramatic as expected, thus lending support to developmental position.

Although empirical studies confirm Piaget's results, there is some dispute over interpretation.

Studies on the coherence of operations within a stage indicate conflicting results but have implications for science education—the matching model.

Reason to be cautious about application of general matching model. Information on articulation of logical operations within the learning of specific concepts may be more profitable.

Piaget's early causality studies are source of information on beliefs children have about natural world. Some studies indicate importance of allowing pupils to disprove already existing ideas as well as confirming accepted ones. Changing conceptual frameworks takes time.

Piaget's clinical method is itself a contribution to research methods and education. Teachers need to learn to listen and probe children's ideas without asking leading questions to understand child's thinking better.

(Driver)

Conclusions reached by Driver from review of Piagetian studies consistent with Novak's views.

Other scholars will see both the power and limitations in Piaget's work and greater power and parsimony of Ausubel's theory.

(Novak)

Negative Orientation	Positive Response to Negative Orientation	Positive Orientation	Negative Response to Positive Orientation
		SPECIAL EDUCATION	
Texts on learning disabilities make few references to Piaget. Piaget did not study learning-disabled children. Are there difficulties in combining the two fields?	Different focus: Fincham on researcher and truth of theory; McFarland and Grant on the practitioner and question of usefulness.	Piaget's theory powerful for description and explanation. Provides impetus for theory-building.	Argument for value of Piagetian work for special education not convincing—counter material not refuted or questioned.
		Generated interdisciplinary research.	Mere cataloguing of where Piagetian-inspired research with special populations from an interdisciplinary perspective occurred is hardly admissible evidence. Such findings as do exist require interpretation.
Piaget's theory is not a psychological theory, less a theory of education and certainly not of special education. Therefore necessary to decide what constitutes acceptable derivation from theory and empirical support. Extension of theory not always accompanied by understanding of basic principles.	Agree with many aspects but not assumption that usefulness cannot be considered prior to resolution of basic research questions. Concepts from Piagetian theory useful regardless of research findings.	Task analysis has been utilized for objectives of learning and instruction, describing scope of content together with the Piagetian system for designating the sequence.	
	Agree with confused status of definitions in learning disabilities, therefore chose 'broad' category unlike Fincham.	Functional analysis has been attempted with focus on active method, empirical and reflexive abstraction, disequilibrium, social interaction, or other issues related to acceleration and modification.	Are content, structure and function all seen as descriptors with the same epistemological status, misleading to suggest or imply that functional invariants and Piagetian structures have any status other than hypothetical constructs.
Learning is subordinate to development. Views both content and process of learning problematic in terms of conceptual clarity and empirical support. Undermines attempt to argue for direct application of Piagetian views in field of learning disabled.	Exploration of cognitive development should not be called 'grasping at straws'.	Teacher educators should emulate Piaget. The developmental model provides the assumption that professionals are growing individuals: a content analysis of actions in classroom can be provided by a variety of Interactions Analysis Systems (case method approach).	Content analysis has no bearing on case. It is inadequately dealt with.
	Controversy over development and learning may be relevant to basic research, but in pragmatic terms argument of 'chicken and egg' may be useful.		In relation to structure and functional analysis, Piaget's work receives greater attention.

Treatment of learning does not appear useful when applied to the learning disabled, as research suggests that children show adequate operative thinking and are not 'learning disabled' in Piagetian terms. It is not self-evident that Piaget's work assists in understanding the ability (or lack thereof) to acquire specific skills or information which however repugnant as an educational goal seems destined to remain part of the educative process. Application of stage theory irrespective of content acquired questionable. Value of Piaget's work for teaching complex academic skills (e.g. reading) in which learning disabilities are most manifest is questioned.	Developmental model is needed in special education. Change from mechanistic to organismic—developmental combined in an information-processing model. Agree on contribution of Piagetian constructs from applied perspective of professionals. (McFarland and Grant)	However, it is little more than a simplified sketch of position. Reference to research is vague and merely asserts general conclusions. That Piagetian theory can contribute to understanding of helpers is an interesting and potentially fruitful suggestion; however, it is not developed.
Important implications: stresses how child functions; equilibration concept emphasizes internal mechanism of self-regulation, a view of child incompatible with way learning disabled often treated; individual active construction of knowledge points to inadmissibility of rigidly standardized diagnostic and remedial procedures. However, until Piaget's theory of learning clarified it remains of limited value to field of learning disabilities. (Fincham)	Use of formal operational model for teacher observation. (McFarland and Grant)	Argument is devoid of facts and rests on a series of vague and unsubstantiated generalizations. Reviews Piagetian theory and special education as whole but does not deal with learning disabilities in much detail. Nothing which answers various issues is raised as there is no case to answer. (Fincham)

Index